Group Policy Category	Features	Where is it in this book?
Folder Redirection	These settings can anchor specific special folders, such as My Documents, to network shares.	Chapter 9
Disk Quotas	You can set up Group Policy to automatically protect your servers from users who gobble up all your disk space.	Chapter 9
Encrypted Data Recovery Agents (EFS Recovery Policy)	Use this Group Policy to dictate the recovery policy for different computers.	Chapter 6
Internet Explorer Maintenance	All sorts of user and computer settings for Internet Explorer can be set here.	Chapter 6
IP Security Policies	Use Group Policy to set local IPSEC filtering.	Chapter 6
Software Restriction Policies	This allows administrators to prevent users from running certain programs on Windows XP or Windows 2003.	Chapter 6
Quality of Service (QoS) Policies	These allow packets on the network to have higher priorities, say, for video conferencing.	QoS is briefly touched on in "What's New in Windows 2003 and Windows XP Group Policy" on the book's website.
802.11 Policies	Allows administrators to set Windows XP and Windows 2003 machines' 802.11 wireless policies.	Chapter 6

Group Policy, Profiles, and IntelliMirror for Windows® 2003, Windows® XP, and Windows® 2000

Jeremy Moskowitz

Mark Minasi
Windows® Administrator
Library

SYBEX®

San Francisco
London

Associate Publisher: Joel Fugazzotto

Acquisitions Editor: Ellen Dendy

Developmental Editor: Tom Cirtin

Production Editor: Elizabeth Campbell

Technical Editor: David Shackelford

Copyeditor: Pat Coleman

Compositor and Graphic Illustrator: Happenstance Type-O-Rama

Proofreaders: Laurie O'Connell, Nancy Riddiough

Indexer: Lynnzee Elze

Book Designer: Bill Gibson, Judy Fung

Cover Designer: Ingalls + Associates

Library of Congress Card Number: 2003115666

ISBN: 0-7821-4238-2

To my parents and grandparents.

Acknowledgments

Working to bring this book to you was one of the most rewarding experiences in my life. I would be lying if I took credit for all the juicy bits inside. I have a small army of people to thank.

At the top of the list of thanks is the chief lieutenant of this army, Mark Williams within the Group Policy team at Microsoft. His raw dedication to make this book the best it can be is simply astounding. Mark took on the hard job of filtering my huge number of questions and finding answers to them throughout the various product teams within Microsoft. He located reviewers for each and every chapter—sometimes as many as four reviewers for a single chapter! In a nutshell: this book would not have been the same without him, and I'm incredibly grateful.

Additionally, I want to thank Michael Dennis, Lead Program Manager for Group Policy at Microsoft, for so thoroughly endorsing my efforts and granting Mark the required time to assist me. To the other members of the Group Policy team, Steve Whitford and BJ Whalen, I thank you for helping me guide the book in the direction it took.

Additional thanks to the battalion of technical reviewers at Microsoft: Mike Treit, Nick Finco, Anitha Bagyam, Judith Herman, Mike Danseglio, Chris Corio, Wei Wang, Craig dos Santos, John Lambert, Scott Cousen, Anshul Rawat, David Steere, Dan Boldo, Brian Aust, Navjot Virk, Vishal Ghote, Rajeev Nagar, Keith Hageman, Wes Miller, and many more people. These amazing people didn't review these chapters because they had to; they did it because they wanted to. Each one has a clear dedication to their craft, and I'm thrilled that they took the time out of their work lives to help this book be its best.

Special thanks goes to Todd Myrick and Jerry Cruz as my two "beta readers" for the heavy-hitting Group Policy material. Their help was invaluable, and I'm very thankful to have had their expertise and input on the material they reviewed!

Special thanks goes to the dedicated folks behind the book. First, my "official" technical editor, David Shackelford, whose insights and comments were instrumental in making this book what it is today. To the Sybex magicians: Pat Coleman for smoothing out my raw text; Tom Cirtin for calming me down whenever I got panicky; and Elizabeth Campbell for allowing me to really be me in this project. Tom, Elizabeth, and Pat worked tirelessly to make this project a success, and I'm very grateful for their dedication to its success.

Thanks to Jill Knapp and Jeff Knapp for loaning me your modems. You're way more than just modems to me.

Thank you, Mark Minasi, for allowing me to write about the subject I love most. Thanks to Bill Boswell for writing Chapter 7 (it's awesome). Moreover, thanks for simply always being there for me to bounce an idea off (and thanks for your phone line simulator I borrowed for eight months). Mark and Bill: without your guidance—both technical and otherwise—I simply wouldn't be the guy I am today.

I want to give special thanks to current and previous contributors to this book. Derek Melber (MCSE) was a contributing author and technical editor of the first edition. Catherine Moya (MCT, MCSE) was a technical editor of the first edition. Conan Kezema's (MCSE, MCT, CCA) material appears in "New Policy Settings for Windows 2003 and Windows XP" and "Security Options Comparison." on the book's website.

Jeremy's photo on the back cover appears courtesy of Windows & .NET Magazine.

Foreword

I first met Jeremy when he approached the Microsoft Group Policy team with a handful of questions for the first edition of this book. All of us were very busy getting Windows® XP ready to ship and Windows Server™ 2003 into beta; we couldn't answer Jeremy's questions right away. But with his own deadlines looming, Jeremy was persistent. He wanted answers to the toughest Group Policy questions, so he could deliver them to you.

At Microsoft, we have a lot of downloadable documentation on Group Policy, Profiles, and IntelliMirror®. What Jeremy provides with this book is a "one-stop-shop" for practical, how-it-works information, including real-world examples of implementing and troubleshooting Group Policy, Profiles, and IntelliMirror. Indeed, his digging and prodding into the Group Policy internals means that there is information in his book that you simply cannot find anywhere else. Jeremy has always provided an independent eye into how Group Policy works. Best of all, his writing style will keep you engaged throughout the entire book.

The Goal of the Group Policy team is to give you the power you need to control your desktops and servers in the most efficient way possible. This vision began in Windows 2000 with an interface designed around how we built the underlying infrastructure. But it didn't make it easy for administrators to use the power of Group Policy. Customers kept telling us that the way they used Group Policy just didn't reflect the way the interface worked. We listened hard, and then we developed the Group Policy Management Console (GPMC), which is available for free to anyone with a Windows 2000 or Windows Server 2003 license. This is the single most important development in the evolution of Group Policy management. In keeping with this customer-driven approach, you can be involved in the continued evolution of Group Policy by sending your feedback and suggestions to GPWish@Microsoft.com. We look forward to hearing what you want next!

Jeremy's book uncovers the basics of Group Policy and GPMC and then reveals the hidden nuggets that truly unleash the power of Group Policy. He describes the many underlying and overt changes since Windows 2000 that make this book a valuable successor to his previous work. The practical, (often prescriptive) technical information just keeps rolling in—chapter after chapter.

Many teams within Microsoft have provided input to Jeremy's book: from our folks on the Group Policy team (Chapters 1, 2, 3, 4, 7, and Appendix B), to the Security team (Chapter 6), to the various constituent components of IntelliMirror (Chapters 8, 9, and 10), and RIS and Shadow Copies (Chapter 11). Jeremy kept feeding us the tough nuts to crack so that he could make it accessible to you in this book.

At Microsoft, we've enjoyed working with Jeremy, and reviewing each chapter to make this the best book possible. It's our hope that you enjoy the power and control Group Policy provides. It's also our hope that you enjoy the additional power and control you'll get after reading Jeremy's very practical book on Group Policy, Profiles, and IntelliMirror.

—Michael Dennis
  Lead Program Manager, Group Policy, Microsoft

Contents at a Glance

Table of Contents

**Chapter 10   IntelliMirror, Part 2: Software Deployment
via Group Policy   431**

Introduction

If you've got an Active Directory, you need Group Policy. Group Policy has one goal: to make your administrative life easier. Instead of running around from machine to machine tweaking a setting here or installing some software there, you'll have ultimate control from on high.

Turns out that you're not alone in wanting more power for your desktops and servers. Managing user desktops (via Group Policy) was the top-ranked benefit of migrating to Active Directory, according to 1000 members who responded to a poll with TechTarget.com. You can find the study at searchwin2000.techtarget.com/originalContent/0,289142,sid1_gci901356,00.html.

Like Zeus himself, controlling the many aspects of the mortal world below, you will have the ability, via Group Policy, to dictate specific settings about how you want your users and computers to operate. You'll be able to shape your network's destiny. You'll have the power. But you need to know exactly how to tap in to this power and exactly what can be powered—and what can only *appear* to be powered.

In this introduction, I'll describe just what Group Policy is all about and give you an idea of its tremendous power.

To get the most out of this book, you'll likely want a Windows 2003 Server machine with at least one Windows XP client (running at least SP1) and possibly a Windows 2000 Professional machine (running at least SP4.) If you don't have a copy of Windows 2003 Server, you can download a free evaluation copy from Microsoft (www.microsoft.com/windowsserver2003/evaluation/trial/evalkit.mspx) or have them send you a CD. (You only pay for shipping.)

Group Policy Defined

If we take a step back and try to analyze the term *Group Policy*, it's easy to become confused. When I first heard the term, I thought it was an NT 4 System Policy that applied to groups. But, thankfully, the results are much more exciting. Microsoft's perspective is that the name "Group Policy" is derived from the fact that you are "grouping together policy settings." Group Policy is, in essence, rules that are applied and enforced at multiple levels of Active Directory. All policies you design are adhered to. This provides great power and efficiency when manipulating client systems.

When going though the examples in this book, you will play the parts of the end user, the OU administrator, and the enterprise administrator. Your mission is to create and define Group Policy using Active Directory and witness it being automatically enforced. What you say goes! With Group Policy, you can set policies that dictate that users quit messing with their machines. You can dictate what software will be deployed. You can determine how much disk space a user can use. You can do pretty much whatever you want—it is really up to you. With Group Policy, you hold all the power. That's the good news. The bad news is that this magical power only works on Windows 2000 or later machines. That includes Windows 2000, Windows XP, and Windows 2003 Server. That's right; there is no way—no matter what anyone tells you—to create the magic that is known as Group Policy in a way that affects Windows 95, Windows 98, or Windows NT workstations or servers.

The application of Group Policy does not concern itself with the mode of the domain. Windows 2000 or Windows 2003 domains need not be in any special functional mode. Windows 2000 domains can be in Mixed or Native mode. Windows 2003 domains can be in domain mode: Mixed, Interim, or Functional.

If the range of control scares you—don't be afraid! It just means more power to hold over your environment. You'll quickly learn how to wisely use this newfound power to reign over your subjects, er, users.

Group Policy versus Group Policy Objects

Before we go headlong into Group Policy theory, let's get some terminology and vocabulary distinctions out of the way:

- The term *Group Policy* is the concept that, from upon high, you can do all this "stuff" to your client machines.

- A *policy setting* is just one individual setting that you can use to do some actual control.

- A *Group Policy Object (GPO)* is the "nuts-and-bolts" on Active Directory Domain Controllers that contains anywhere from one to a zillion individual policy settings.

It's my goal that after you work through this book, you'll be able to jump up on your desk one day and declare: "Hey! Group Policy isn't applying to our client machines! Perhaps a policy setting is misconfigured. Or, maybe one of our Group Policy Objects has gone belly up! I'd better read what's going on in Chapter 3, 'Group Policy Processing Behavior.'"

This terminology can be a little confusing—considering that each term encompasses the word *policy*. In this text, however, I've tried especially hard to use the correct nomenclature for what I'm trying to describe.

Where Group Policy Applies

Group Policy can be applied to many machines at once, or it can be applied only to a specific machine. For the most part in this book, I'll focus on using Group Policy within either a Windows 2000 or Windows 2003 Active Directory environment where it affects the most machines.

A percentage of the settings explored and discussed in this book are available to member or stand-alone Windows 2000 Server, Windows 2000 Professional, and Windows XP Professional machines—which can either participate or not participate in an Active Directory environment. However, the Folder Redirection settings (discussed in Chapter 9) and the Software Distribution settings (discussed in Chapter 10) are not available to stand-alone machines (that is, computers that are not participating in an Active Directory domain). I will pay particular attention to non–Active Directory environments. However, most of the book deals with the more common case; that is, we'll explore the implications of deploying Group Policy in an Active Directory environment.

Most of the book shows screens of Windows XP clients within Windows 2003 domains. However, most of the book is still applicable for Windows 2000 domains with Windows 2000 and Windows XP clients. Where appropriate, I've noted the differences between the operating systems.

Final Thoughts

Group Policy is a big concept with some big power. This book is intended to help you get a handle on this new power to gain control over your environment and to make your day-to-day administration easier. This book is filled with practical, hands-on examples of Group Policy usage and troubleshooting. It is my hope that you enjoy this book and learn from my experiences so you can successfully deploy Group Policy and IntelliMirror to better control your network. I'm honored to have you aboard for the ride, and I hope you get as much out of Group Policy as I enjoy writing and speaking about it in my seminars.

As you read this book, it's natural to have questions about Group Policy or IntelliMirror. Until recently there was no "one stop shop" place to get your questions answered. To form a community around Group Policy, I have started a free service that can be found at www.GPOanswers.com. I encourage you to visit the website and post your questions to the forum or peruse the other resources that will be constantly renewed and available for download. For instance, in addition to the forum, you'll find additional scripts (beyond Chapter 7) and ADM templates to download (beyond Chapter 5), tips and tricks, and more!

If you want to meet me in person, my website has a calendar of all my upcoming appearances at various conferences, events, and classes. I'd love to hear how this book met your needs or helped you out.

Group Policy Essentials

In this chapter, you'll get your feet wet with the concept that is Group Policy. You'll start to understand conceptually what Group Policy is and how it's created, applied, and modified, and you'll go through some practical examples to get at the basics.

The best news is that the essentials of Group Policy are the same in Windows 2000, Windows 2003, and Windows XP. If you have a mature Windows 2000 Active Directory or a fresh (and soon-to-be-mature) Windows 2003 Active Directory, the essentials are the same for both. Indeed, if you have a mature Windows 2000 Active Directory and think you have a handle on Group Policy essentials, I still encourage you to read and work through the examples in this chapter. With the changes in store, I'm sure you'll find some goodies waiting for you.

If you've done any work at all with Group Policy and Windows 2000 Active Directory, you're likely familiar with the "usual" Group Policy interface. The best news of all, though, is that there's a new (free) tool in town, called the GPMC, or Group Policy Management Console. It's goal is to give us an updated, refreshing way to view and manage Group Policy; indeed, this tool enables us to view and manage Group Policy the way it was meant to be viewed and managed. The new GPMC interface provides a one-stop shop for managing nearly all aspects of Group Policy in your Active Directory.

To use the new GPMC tool, it doesn't matter if your entire Active Directory (or individual domains) are Windows 2000 or Windows 2003—it just matters that you have Active Directory.

And did I mention it's free?

Stay tuned, dear reader. We'll get to that exciting new and free stuff right away in this first chapter. I don't want to keep you in suspense for too long.

Getting Started with Group Policy

In the Introduction, you learned about the 13 major categories of Group Policy (and where to locate them in this book):

- Administrative Templates (Registry Settings)
- Security Settings (in the Windows Settings folder)
- Scripts (under Windows Settings)
- Remote Installation Services (User node only under Windows Settings)

- Software Installation (Application Management)
- Folder Redirection
- Disk Quotas
- Encrypted Data Recovery Agents (EFS Recovery Policy)
- Internet Explorer Maintenance
- IP Security Policies
- Software Restriction
- Quality of Service (QoS) Policies
- 802.11 Policies

In this section, you'll learn how to gain access to the interface, which will let you start configuring these categories.

Group Policy is a twofold idea. First, without an Active Directory, there's one and only one Group Policy available, and that lives on the local Windows XP or Windows 2000 workstation. Officially, this is called a *Local Policy*, but it still resides under the umbrella of the concept of Group Policy. Later, once Active Directory is available, the nonlocal (or, as they're sometimes called, *Domain-Based* or *Active Directory–Based*) Group Policy Objects come into play, as you'll see later. Let's get started and explore both options.

Understanding Local Group Policy

Before we officially dive in to what is specifically contained inside this magic of Group Policy or how Group Policy is applied when Active Directory is involved, you might be curious to see exactly what your interaction with the Local Group Policy might look like.

You can begin to edit Group Policy in multiple ways. One way is to load the MMC (Microsoft Management Console) snap-in by hand. You can do so logged on to any workstation or member server (but not a Domain Controller) as a local administrator.

For the examples in this book, we'll do most of the workstation work on one workstation, XPPro1, and most of the Active Directory and server work on one Windows 2003 Domain Controller, WINDC01, in a domain called Corp.com. Feel free to follow along if you like. Because Group Policy can be so all-encompassing, it is highly recommended that you try these examples in a test lab environment first, before making these changes for real in your production environment.

To load the Group Policy Object Editor by hand, follow these steps:

1. Choose Start ➢ Run to open the Run dialog box, and in the Open box, type **MMC**. A "naked" MMC appears.

2. From the File menu, choose Add/Remove Snap-in to open the Add/Remove Snap-in dialog box.

3. Click Add.

4. Locate and select the Group Policy Snap-in and click Add to open up the potential list of snap-ins.

5. At the "Select Group Policy Object" screen, keep the default "Local Computer Policy" and click Finish.

6. At the Add Standalone Snap-in dialog box, click Close.

7. At the Add/Remove Snap-in dialog box, click OK.

You should see something similar to Figure 1.1.

To see how a Local Group Policy applies, drill down through the User Configuration folder, Administrative Templates folder ➢ Windows Components folder ➢ Windows Messenger folder and select **Do Not Allow Windows Messenger To Be Run**.

You are now exploring the Local Group Policy of this Windows XP workstation. Local Group Policy is unique to each specific machine.

You can think of Local Group Policy as a way to perform decentralized Group Policy administration. A bit later, when we explore Group Policy with Active Directory, we'll saunter into centralized Group Policy administration.

FIGURE 1.1   Edit your first Local Group Policy by drilling down into the User Configuration settings.

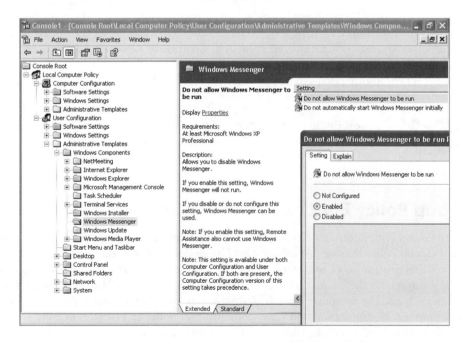

Local Group Policy affects everyone who logs on to this machine—including normal users and administrators. Be careful when making settings here; you can temporarily lock yourself out of some useful functions. For instance, frequently administrators want to remove Run from the Start menu. Then, the first time they themselves want to go to a command prompt, they can't choose Start ⮞ Run. It's just gone!

To fix, you have to click the MMC.exe icon in Explorer and manually load the Group Policy Snap-in.

As we stated in the Introduction, most of the settings we'll explore in this book are available to workstations or servers that aren't joined to an Active Directory domain. However, the Folder Redirection settings (discussed in Chapter 9), the Software Distribution settings (discussed in Chapter 10), and Remote Installation Services (discussed in Chapter 11) are not available to stand-alone machines without Active Directory present.

You can also start the Local Group Policy Object Editor by choosing Start ⮞ Run to open the Run dialog box and then typing **gpedit.msc** in the Open box. You can point toward other computers by using the syntax gpedit.msc /gpcomputer: "*targetmachine*" or gpedit.msc /gpcomputer:"*targetmachine.domain.com*"; the machine name must be in quotes.

You can think of Local Group Policy as way to perform decentralized Group Policy. That is, you need to run around, more or less, from machine to machine to set the Local Group Policy.

The other strategy is a centralized approach. Centralized Group Policy application works only in conjunction with Active Directory.

We'll return to other ways to fire up the Group Policy Object Editor—so stay tuned.

Local Group Policy is stored in the c:\windows\system32\grouppolicy directory. The structure found here mirrors what you'll see later in Chapter 4 when we inspect the ins and outs of how Group Policy applies from Active Directory.

Group Policy Entities and Policy Settings

Every Group Policy contains two halves: a User half and a Computer half. This goes for the Local Group Policy that we just saw and for Group Policy objects that are created when we use Active Directory, as you'll see later in this chapter. These two halves are properly called *nodes,* though sometimes they're just referred to as either the user half and the computer half or the user branch and the computer branch. A sample Group Policy Object Editor screen with both the Computer Configuration and User Configuration nodes can be seen in Figure 1.1.

The first level under both the User and the Computer nodes contains Software Settings, Windows Settings, and Administrative Templates. If we dive down into the Administrative Templates of the Computer node, underneath we discover additional levels of Windows Components, System,

Network, and Printers. Likewise, if we dive down into the Administrative Templates of the User node, we see some of the same folders plus some additional ones, such as Shared Folders, Desktop, and Start Menu And Taskbar.

In both the User and Computer half, you'll see that policy settings are hierarchical, like a directory structure. Similar policy settings are grouped together for easy location. That's the idea anyway; though, admittedly, sometimes locating the specific policy you want can prove to be a challenge.

When manipulating policy settings, you can choose to set either Computer policy settings or User policy settings (or both!). We'll see examples of this shortly. (See the section "Using the Only Show Configured Policy Settings Option" in Chapter 3 for tricks on how to minimize the effort of finding the policy setting you want.)

 Most policy settings are not found in both nodes. However, there are a few. In that case, if the computer policy setting is different from the user policy setting, the computer policy setting overrides the user policy setting.

Active Directory–Based Group Policy

To use Group Policy in a meaningful way, you need an Active Directory environment. An Active Directory environment needn't be anything particularly fancy; indeed, it could consist of a single Windows 2000 or Windows 2003 Domain Controller and perhaps just one Windows 2000 or Windows XP workstation joined to the domain.

But Active Directory can also grow extensively from that original solitary server. You can think of an Active Directory network as having four constituent and distinct levels:

- the local computer
- the site
- the domain
- the organizational unit (OU)

The rules of Active Directory state that every server and workstation must be a member of one (and only one) domain and be located in one (and only one) site.

In Windows NT, additional domains were often created to partition administrative responsibility or to rein in needless chatter between Domain Controllers. With Active Directory, administrative responsibility can be delegated using OUs.

Additionally, the problem with needless domain bandwidth chatter has been brought under control with the addition of Active Directory sites, which are concentrations of IP (Internet Protocol) subnets with fast connectivity. There is no longer any need to correlate domains with network bandwidth—that's what sites are for!

Group Policy and Active Directory

When Group Policy is created at the local level, everyone who uses that machine is affected by those wishes. But once you step up and use Active Directory, you can have nearly limitless

Group Policy Objects (GPOs)—with the ability to selectively decide which Users and Computers will get which wishes. A GPO stores these wishes, which are, more technically, known as policy settings or, colloquially, just policies.

 Actually, you can have only 999 GPOs applied to a user or a computer.

When we create a GPO that can be used in Active Directory, we actually create some brand-new entries within Active Directory, and we automatically create some brand-new files on our Domain Controllers, both of which are known as GPOs.

You can think of Active Directory as having three major levels:

- Site
- Domain
- OU

Additionally, since OUs can be nested within each other, Active Directory has a nearly limitless capacity for where we can tuck stuff away.

In fact, it's best to think of this design as a three-tier hierarchy: site, domain, and each nested OU. When wishes, er, policy settings, are set at a higher level in Active Directory, they automatically flow down throughout the remaining levels.

In our example in the Introduction, we likened Group Policy to kings, nobles, and serfs. Now, start to shift your thinking toward site, domain, and OU. So, to be precise:

- If a GPO is set at the site level, the policy settings contained within affect those accounts within the geography of the site. Sure, their user accounts will be in a domain (and/or possibly in an OU), but the account is affected only by the policy settings here because the account is in a specific site.

- If a GPO is set at the domain level, it affects those folks within the domain and all OUs and all other OUs beneath it.

- If a GPO is set at the OU level, it affects those folks within the OU and all other OUs beneath it (usually just called child OUs.)

By default, when a policy is set at one level, the levels below *inherit* the settings from the levels above it. You can have "cumulative" wishes that keep piling on.

You might wonder what happens if two policy settings conflict. Perhaps one policy is set at the domain level, and another policy is set at the OU level, which reverses the edict in the domain. Policy settings further down the food chain take precedence. If a policy setting conflicts at the domain and OU levels, the OU level "wins." Likewise, domain-level settings override any policy settings that conflict with previously set site-specific policy settings.

However, one giant caveat should be mentioned at this point. If the Local Group Policy has been set on a specific workstation, everyone logging on to that workstation is affected by that policy setting. Then, the policy settings within Active Directory (the site, domain, and OU) apply. So, sometimes people refer to the *four* levels of Group Policy: local workstation, site, domain, and OU. Nonetheless, GPOs set within Active Directory always "trump" the Local Group Policy should there be any conflict.

Very rarely, the same policy setting exists in both the User node and the Computer node in the Group Policy Object Editor. If there is a conflict in such a case, the Computer node setting wins.

If this behavior is undesired for lower levels, all the settings from higher levels can be blocked with a "Block Inheritance" attribute. Additionally, if a higher-level administrator wants to guarantee that a setting is inherited down the food chain, they can apply the "Enforced" attribute via the GPMC attribute (or "No Override" attribute in the old-school parlance) (Chapter 3 explores both Block Inheritance and Enforced attributes in detail.)

   Don't sweat it if your head is spinning a little bit now from the Group Policy application theory. I'll go through specific hands-on examples to illustrate each of these behaviors so that you understand exactly how this works.

Linking Group Policy Objects

Another technical concept that needs a bit of description here is the "linking" of GPOs. When a GPO is created at the site, domain, or OU level, via the GUI (which we'll do in a moment), the system automatically associates that GPO with the level in which it was created. That association is called *linking*.

Linking is an important concept for several reasons. First, it's generally a good idea to understand what's going on under the hood. However, more practically, the new Group Policy Management Console, or GPMC, as we'll explore in just a bit, displays GPOs from their linked perspective.

You can think of all the GPOs you create in Active Directory as children within a big swimming pool. Each child has a tether attached around their waist, and an adult guardian is holding the other end of the rope. Indeed, there could be multiple tethers around a child's waist, with multiple adults tethered to one child. A sad state indeed would be a child who has no tether but is just swimming around in the pool unsecured. The "swimming pool" in this analogy is a specific Active Directory container named Policies (which we'll examine closely in Chapter 4). All GPOs are born and "live" in that specific domain. Indeed, they're replicated to all Domain Controllers. The adult guardian in this analogy represents a *level* in Active Directory—any site, domain, or OU.

In our swimming pool example, multiple adults can be tethered to a specific child. With Active Directory, multiple levels can be linked to a specific GPO. Thus, any level in Active Directory can leverage multiple GPOs, which are standing by in the domain ready to be used.

Remember, though, unless a GPO is specifically linked to a site, a domain, or an OU, it does not take effect. It's just floating around in the swimming pool of the domain waiting for someone to make use of it.

I'll keep reiterating and refining the concept of linking throughout these first four chapters. And, in Chapter 3, I'll discuss why you might want to "unlink" a policy.

This concept of linking to GPOs created in Active Directory can be a bit confusing. It will become clearer a bit later as we explore the processes of creating new GPOs and linking to existing ones. Stay tuned. It's right around the corner.

An Example of Group Policy Application

At this point, it's best not to jump directly into adding, deleting, or modifying our own GPOs. Right now, it's better to understand how Group Policy works "on paper." This is especially true if you're new to the concept of Group Policy, but perhaps also if Group Policy has been deployed by other administrators in your Active Directory.

By walking through a fictitious organization that has deployed GPOs at multiple levels, you'll be able to better understand how and why policy settings are applied by the deployment of GPOs. Let's start by taking a look at Figure 1.2, the organization for our fictitious example company, Corp.com.

FIGURE 1.2   This fictitious Corp.com is relatively simple. Your environment may be more complex.

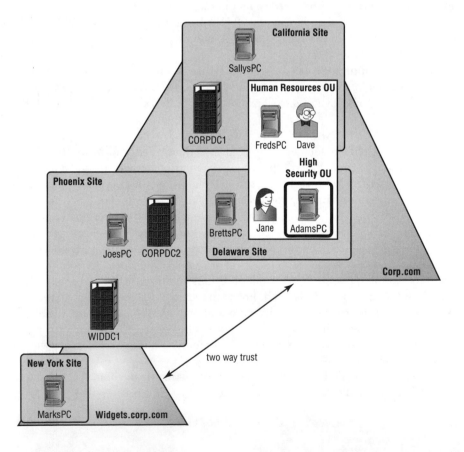

This picture could easily tell 1000 words. For the sake of brevity, I've kept it down to around 200. In this example, the domain Corp.com has two Domain Controllers. One DC, named CORPDC1, is physically located in the California site. Corp.com's other Domain Controller, CORPDC2, is physically located in the Phoenix site. Using Active Directory Sites and Services, a schedule can be put in place to regulate communication between CORPDC1 located in California and CORPDC2 located in Phoenix. That way the administrator controls the chatter between the two Corp.com Domain Controllers, and it is not at the whim of the operating system.

Inside the Corp.com domain are two OUs: **Human Resources,** and (inside **Human Resources**) another OU called **High Security.** FredsPC is located inside the **Human Resources** OU, as are Dave's user account and Jane's user account. There is one PC, called AdamsPC, inside the **High Security** OU. There is also JoesPC, which is a member of the Corp.com domain. It physically resides at the Phoenix site and isn't a member of any OU.

Another domain, called Widgets.corp.com, has an automatic transitive two-way trust to Corp.com. There is only one Domain Controller in the Widgets.corp.com domain, named WIDDC1, and it physically resides at the Phoenix site. Last, there is MarksPC, a member of the Widgets.corp.com domain, which physically resides in the New York site and isn't in any OU.

Understanding where your users and machines are is half the battle. The other half is understanding which policy settings are expected to appear when they start logging on to Active Directory.

Examining the Resultant Set of Policy

As stated earlier, the effect of Group Policy is cumulative as GPOs are successively applied—starting at the local computer, the site, the domain, and each nested OU. The end result of what affects a specific user or computer—after all Group Policy at all levels has been applied—is called the *Resultant Set of Policy*, or *RSoP*. This is sometimes referred to as the *RSoP Calculation*.

Throughout your lifetime working with Group Policy, you will be asked to troubleshoot the RSoP of client machines.

 Much of our dealings with Group Policy will be trying to understand and troubleshoot the RSoP of a particular configuration. Getting a good understanding early of how to perform manual RSoP Calculations on paper will be a useful troubleshooting skill. In Chapter 3 and Chapter 4, we'll also explore additional RSoP skills—with tools and additional manual troubleshooting.

Before we jump in to try to discover what the RSoP might be for any specific machine, it's often helpful to break out each of the strata—local computer, site, domain, and OU—and examine, at each level, what happens to the entities contained in them. I'll then bring it all together to see how a specific computer or user reacts to the accumulation of GPOs. For these examples, assume that no local policy is set on any of the computers: The goal is to get a better feeling of how Group Policy flows, not necessarily what the specific end-state will be.

At the Site Level

Based on what we know from Figure 1.2, the GPOs in effect at the site level are as follows:

Site	Computers Affected
California	SallysPC, CORPDC1, and FredsPC
Phoenix	CORPDC2, JoesPC, and WIDDC1
New York	MarksPC.
Delaware	AdamsPC and BrettsPC.

Users are affected by site GPOs only when they log on to computers that are at a specific site. In Figure 1.2, we have users Dave in California (on a California PC) and Jane in Delaware (on a Delaware PC).

At the Domain Level

Here's what we have working at the domain level:

Domain	Computers/Users Affected
Corp.com Computers	SallysPC, FredsPC, AdamsPC, BrettsPC, JoesPC, CORPDC1, and CORPDC2
Corp.com Users	Dave and Jane
Widgets.corp.com Computers	WIDDC1 and MarksPC

At the OU Level

At the organizational unit level, we have the following:

Organizational Unit	Computers/Users Affected
Human Resources OU Computers	FredsPC is in the Human Resources OU; therefore it is affected when the Human Resources OU gets GPOs applied. Additionally, the High Security OU is contained inside the Human Resources OU. Therefore, AdamsPC, which is in the High Security OU, is also affected whenever the Human Resources OU is affected.
Human Resources OU Users	The accounts of Dave and Jane are affected when the Human Resources OU has GPOs applied.

Bringing It All Together

Now that you've broken out all the levels and seen what is being applied to them, you can start to calculate what the devil is happening on any specific user and computer combination. Looking at Figure 1.2 and analyzing what's happening at each level makes adding things together between the local, site, domain, and organizational unit GPOs a lot easier.

Here are some examples of RSoP for specific Users and Computers in our fictitious environment:

FredsPC	FredsPC inherits the RSoP of the GPOs from the California site, then the Corp.com domain, and then, last, the Human Resources OU.
MarksPC	MarksPC first accepts the GPOs from the New York site and then the Widgets.corp.com domain. MarksPC is not in any OU; therefore, no organizational unit GPOs apply to his computer.
AdamsPC	AdamsPC is subject to the GPOs at the Delaware site, the Corp.Com domain, the Human Resources OU, and the High Security OU.
Dave using AdamsPC	AdamsPC is subject to the computer policies in the GPOs for the Delaware site, the Corp.com domain, the Human Resources OU, and finally the High Security OU. When Dave travels from California to Delaware to use Adam's workstation, his user GPOs are dictated from the Delaware site, the Corp.com domain, and the Human Resources OU.

> At no time are any domain GPOs from the Corp.com parent domain automatically inherited by the Widget.corp.com child domain. Inheritance for GPOs only flows downward to OUs within a single domain—not between any two domains—parent to child or otherwise.

If you want one GPO to affect the users in more than one domain, you have three choices:

- Precisely re-create the GPOs in each domain with their own GPO.
- Copy the GPO from one domain to another domain (using the GPMC, as explained in the Appendix).
- Do a generally recognized no-no called *cross-domain policy linking*. (I'll describe this no-no in detail in Chapter 3.)

Also, don't assume that linking a GPO at a site level necessarily guarantees the results to more than one domain. In this example, as in real life, there is not necessarily a 1:1 correlation between sites and domains.

Group Policy, Active Directory, and the GPMC

Windows 2000 administrators already somewhat familiar with Group Policy will tell you that finding what you need and understanding what's going on under the hood can sometimes be confusing. The interface used to create, modify, and manipulate Group Policy in Windows 2000 has led to numerous missteps and head scratching when people try to figure out why something isn't going the way it should.

Occasionally, Microsoft has recognized that the first iteration of a product release has missed the mark a little in the way the product works, acts, or interfaces. They often request additional customer feedback, embrace it, regroup, and return a "2.0 version" of the product.

To make optimal use of Group Policy in an Active Directory environment, the Group Policy team at Microsoft introduced a free, downloadable "2.0 version" for managing Group Policy in Active Directory. It's called the Group Policy Management Console, or GPMC, as mentioned earlier. The GPMC isn't part of the Windows 2000, Windows 2003, or Windows XP operating systems; you need to fetch it and install it.

Kickin' It Old-School

Out of the box, Windows 2000 and Windows 2003 domains use the old-style GPMC interface. If you've never seen the old-style interface, you can do so right now before we leave it in the dust for the new GPMC in the next section.

FIGURE 1.3   Right-click the domain name and choose Properties.

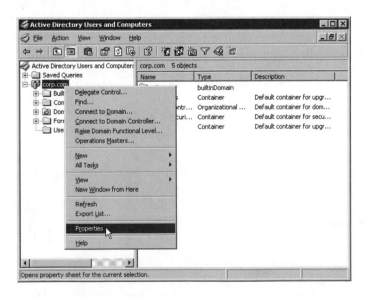

To see the old-style interface and create your first GPO at the domain level, follow these steps:

1. Log on to the Domain Controller WINDC01 as Domain Administrator.

2. Choose Start ➢ Programs ➢ Administrative Tools and select Active Directory Users And Computers.

3. Right-click the domain name and choose Properties from the shortcut menu, as shown in Figure 1.3, to open the Properties dialog box for the domain.

4. Click the Group Policy tab.

 There is a "Default Domain Policy" GPO but you won't modify it at this time. (I'll talk about it in Chapter 6.) As I'll discuss, it is not recommended that you modify the "Default Domain Policy" GPO for regular settings.

5. Click the New button to spawn the creation of your first GPO.

6. For this first example, type **My First GPO**, as shown in Figure 1.4.

7. Highlight the policy, and click Edit to open the Group Policy Object Editor.

At this point, things should look familiar, just like the Local Group Policy Object Editor, with the user and computer nodes. For example, if you drill down into the Administrative Templates folder in the User Configuration folder, you can make a wish at the domain level, and all your computers will obey.

For now, don't actually make any changes; just close the Group Policy Object Editor and read on.

FIGURE 1.4   You've just created your first GPO in Active Directory.

Why Abandon Old School?

In Figure 1.4, we were able to create our first GPO (even though we didn't actually place any policy settings in there). The interface seems reasonable enough to take care of such simple tasks. And, heck, this interface is already part of the operating system, so, why move away from it?

The old-school way of viewing and managing Group Policy just isn't scalable over the long haul. This interface doesn't show us any relationship between the GPO we just created and the domain it's in. As you'll see in this chapter, the new interface demonstrates a much clearer relationship between the GPOs you create, the links it takes to use them, and the domains where the GPOs actually "live."

The old-style interface also provides no easy way to figure out what's going on inside the GPOs you create. To determine what changes are made inside a GPO, you need to reopen each GPO and poke around. I've seen countless administrators open each and every GPO in their domain and manually document their settings on paper for backup and recovery purposes.

Indeed, backup and recovery is a really, really big deal, and the old-school mechanism (via NTBACKUP) provided no realistic way to back up and recover GPOs without copious amounts of surgery.

With that in mind, I encourage all of you—those from the original Windows 2000 old school and those who haven't even yet been to school—to step up and try the new way of doing things, the GPMC.

Throughout this chapter and the book, I'll give you pointers about what to do if you're still stuck on working with the old-school way of doing things. However, there's little reason to stay old school when the new way has so much to offer. Did I mention that the GPMC is free? (Yes, Jeremy, about 10 times already.)

It's my hope that those of you already familiar with Group Policy will use the examples in this chapter to get comfy with the new GPMC interface. Also, if you're totally new to the concept of Group Policy, I hope you'll keep your eyes forward and don't look back to the old-school way.

Microsoft has made it quite clear that their direction for all future Group Policy efforts, including white papers, TechNet articles, paid phone support, free newsgroup support, Microsoft Official Curriculum, and even future MCSE/MCSA (Microsoft Certified Systems Engineer/ Microsoft Certified Systems Administrator) exams, will be geared with a heavy eye toward the use of the GPMC.

Basically, the GPMC is here to stay; we need to get up to speed with it and embrace it. The good news is that it's quite pleasant to work with and it's powerful to boot. The best news is that it only takes one Windows XP machine to load the GPMC, and it can be used with both Windows 2000 Active Directory and Windows 2003 Active Directory domains.

So enough yakkin' already about the virtues of the GPMC. Let's get going already!

GPMC Overview

The GPMC is a tool you download from Microsoft for free, which can then be loaded on Windows XP or Windows 2003 client machines. Once loaded, the GPMC provides a one-stop shop for managing nearly all aspects of Group Policy in your Active Directory. Again, it doesn't matter if your Active Directory or domains are Windows 2000 or Windows 2003; it just matters that you have Active Directory.

Even though you cannot load the GPMC on a Windows 2000 Domain Controller or a Windows 2000 Professional machine, it's still capable of controlling Windows 2000 domains. Again, the idea is to simply load the GPMC on just one Windows XP machine in your Windows 2000 domain, and you'll be in good company managing your Windows 2000 Active Directory.

The GPMC's name says it all. It's the Group Policy Management Console. Indeed, this will be the MMC snap-in that you use to manage the underlying Group Policy mechanism. The GPMC just helps us tap into those features already built into Active Directory. I'll highlight the mechanism of how Group Policy works throughout the next three chapters.

One major design goal of the GPMC is to get a Group Policy–centric view of the lay of the land. Compared with the old interface, the GPMC does a much better job of aligning the user interface of Group Policy with what's going on under the hood.

The GPMC also provides a programmatic way to manage your GPOs. In fact, the GPMC scripting interface allows just about any GPO operation (other than to dive in and create or modify actual policy settings). We'll explore scripting with the GPMC in Chapter 7. So, if you're interested in scripting, you'll need to have the GPMC bits loaded on the XP systems you want to script.

You'll load the GPMC on the same machines that you use to manage your current Group Policy universe. Some people walk up to their Domain Controllers, log on to the console, and manage their Group Policy infrastructure there. Others use a management workstation and manage their Group Policy infrastructure from their own Windows XP workstations. In either case, to use the GPMC, you'll need to load the GPMC installation software (and the prerequisites) on the machines on which you want this sexy new view to appear. GPMC will only load on Windows XP/SP1 (or greater) and Windows 2003 machines (Domain Controllers and member servers) as discussed in the next section.

I'll talk more about the use and best practices of a Windows XP management workstation in Chapter 5.

Installing the GPMC

As I mentioned, the GPMC isn't part of the standard Windows 2003 or Windows XP package out of the box. You can, however, download it for free from www.microsoft.com/grouppolicy. Click the link for the Group Policy Management Console to locate the download.

The Original GPMC versus the GPMC with SP1

By the time you read this, the GPMC will be at least up to its first service pack and will likely be named GPMC with SP1. And it's all good. Not just because of the minor bug fixes, but because of the licensing agreement the GPMC with SP1 provides.

The original GPMC license stipulated that the GPMC was to be loaded only on machines with at least one license of Windows 2003 server on record. However, with GPMC with SP1, that licensing restriction has been lifted. GPMC with SP1 can be used to manage domains without any Windows 2003 servers and without any Windows 2003 Client Access Licenses (CALs).

Therefore, for shops with only Windows 2000, the only requirement is that you have but one Windows XP machine (with at least Service Pack 1) with which to load the GPMC and manage your Active Directory and Group Policy. Oh, and, of course, that one Windows XP client needs a CAL. And that's it.

Once it's downloaded, the GPMC is called GPMC.MSI. You can install this on either Windows 2003 or Windows XP with at least SP1, but nothing else. That is, you cannot load the GPMC on Windows 2000 servers or workstations; but, as I noted before, the GPMC can manage Windows 2000 domains with Windows 2000 and Windows XP clients as well as Windows 2003 domains with Windows 2000 or Windows XP clients.

If you will use the GPMC to manage Windows 2003 domains, all the functionality of the tool is present. If you will use the GPMC to manage Windows 2000 domains, some functionality will not be present. Windows 2003 Active Directory contains several new Group Policy features that Windows 2000 domains cannot use. I'll explicitly explain those features that are not accessible within Windows 2000 domains as they come up. These features are largely explored in Chapter 3.

Additionally, if you have any remaining Windows 2000 Domain Controllers, you should have at least SP2 and preferably SP3 applied to them. This is because most Windows 2003 tools, including the GPMC, use LDAP (Lightweight Directory Access Protocol) signing for all communication. For more information, see the Microsoft Knowledge Base article 325465, "Windows 2000 Domain Controllers Require SP3 or Later When Using Windows Server 2003 Administration Tools."

Installing the Prerequisites and GPMC Manually

Installing the GPMC does require certain prerequisites, which must be loaded in the order listed here.

Loading the GPMC on Windows XP

If you intend to load the GPMC on a Windows XP machine to manage Group Policy in your domain, follow these steps:

1. The Windows XP Service Pack 1 is required. If you are unsure whether SP1 (or later) is installed, run the WINVER command, which will tell you whether a service pack is installed. So, if your Windows XP system doesn't have at least SP1 installed, you should install it.

2. Windows XP requires the .NET Framework to run properly. If it's not installed, you'll need to download and install it. At last check, the .NET Framework download was at http:/ /msdn.microsoft.com/downloads/list/netdevframework.asp. If it's not there, search the Microsoft site for ".NET Framework."

   After downloading .NET Framework, double-click the install to get it going on your target Windows XP/SP1 (or greater) machine. It isn't a very exciting or noteworthy installation.

3. To install the GPMC, double-click the GPMC.MSI file you downloaded. If you're running Windows XP with SP1, the GPMC installation routine will report that a hotfix (also known as a QFE) is required and then proceed to automatically install the hotfix on the fly. This hotfix (Q326469) will be incorporated into Windows XP's SP2.

Loading the GPMC on a Windows 2003 Domain Controller

If you intend to load the GPMC on a Windows 2003 Domain Controller or a member server, there are just a couple of things to do:

1. Although there aren't any Windows 2003 prerequisites, it's a good idea to install the latest version of the .NET Framework and the latest version of the Windows 2003.

2. To install the GPMC, double-click the GPMC.MSI file you downloaded.

Installing the Prerequisites and GPMC via Group Policy Software Distribution

In Chapter 10, you'll learn how to automate your software distribution with Group Policy. Here, however, is a quick reference for how to perform automated installations of the GPMC and its prerequisites. Again, recall that you can load the GPMC only on Windows XP and Windows 2003 machines.

The .NET Framework 1.1 or later must be installed on all target Windows XP machines intended to use the GPMC. And there's no penalty for loading it on Windows 2003 target machines. Download the Redistributable Package (from the Microsoft link described above), expand its contents, and assign the NETFX.MSI to the Windows XP (and/or Windows 2003) machines on which you intend to load the GPMC.

You'll find an expanded discussion on how to deploy the .NET Framework via Group Policy Software Distribution (and also Microsoft SMS) at http://msdn.microsoft.com/vstudio/using/deploying/default.aspx?pull=/library/en-us/dnnetdep/html/redistdeploy.asp.

You can also assign the GPMC.MSI file itself to either Windows XP or Windows 2003 machines—either member servers or Domain Controllers.

Here is a sample GPO depicting how this might look when deploying to Windows XP (assuming it's already at least SP1) or Windows 2003 servers.

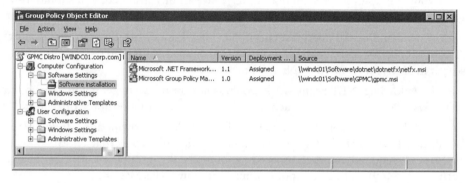

Cleaning Up Old GPOs

The first time you run the GPMC, you may be prompted to "clean up" older GPOs the first time you touch one. You should do so. Under the hood, the GPMC is adjusting some key security descriptors in Active Directory.

The precise error message you'll get is "the permissions for this GPO in the SYSVOL folder are inconsistent with those in Active Directory. It is recommended that these permissions be consistent. To change the SYSVOL permissions to those in Active Directory, click OK."

By allowing this, you can do some fancy footwork later, as you'll see in the section "Advanced Security and Delegation with the GPMC" in Chapter 2. You will only see this message if your Windows 2000 PDC-Emulator domain was upgraded from anything prior to SP4.

The Results of Loading the GPMC

After the GPMC is loaded on the machine from which you will manage Group Policy (the management workstation), you'll see that the way you view things has changed. If you take a look in Active Directory Users And Computers (or Active Directory Sites And Services) and try to manage a GPO, you'll see a curious link on the existing Group Policy tab (as seen in Figure 1.5).

Additionally, you'll see a Group Policy Management icon in the Administrative Tools folder in the Start Menu folder.

Creating a One-Stop Shop MMC

As you'll see, the GPMC is a fairly comprehensive Group Policy management tool. But the problem is that right now, the GPMC and the Active Directory Users And Computers snap-ins are not integrated beyond what you see in Figure 1.5.

Often, you'll want to change a Group Policy on an OU and then move computers to that OU. Unfortunately, you can't do so from the GPMC; you must to return to Active Directory Users And Computers to finish the task. This can get frustrating quickly. The GPMC does allow you to right-click at the domain-level to choose to launch the Active Directory Users And Computers console when you want, but I prefer a one-stop shop view of my Active Directory management. It's a matter of taste.

To that end, my preference is to create a custom MMC by running MMC from the Run dialog box and then add in both Active Directory Users And Computer and Group Policy Management snap-ins as shown here.

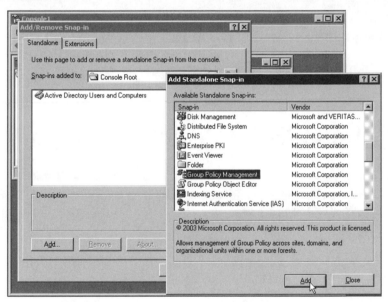

Now, you'll really have a near-unified view of most of what you need at your fingertips. Both Active Directory Users And Computers and the GPMC can create and delete OUs. Both tools also allow administrators to delegate permissions to others to manage Group Policy, but that's where the two tools' functionality overlap ends.

The GPMC won't show you the actual users and computer objects inside the OU; so deleting an OU from within the GPMC is dicey at best, because you can't be sure of what's inside!

You can choose to add other snaps-ins too, of course, including Active Directory Sites And Services or anything else you think is useful. The illustrations in the rest of this book will show both snap-ins loaded in this configuration.

FIGURE 1.5   The Group Policy tab now refers you to the GPMC and provides a link.

You can launch the GPMC from either the new link in Active Directory Users And Computers (or Active Directory Sites And Services) or directly from new icon in the Start Menu. However, clicking Open in the existing tools has a slight advantage of telling the GPMC to "snap to" the location in Active Directory on which you are currently focused.

Using the GPMC in Active Directory

For the examples in this book, I'll refer to our sample Domain Controller, WINDC01, which is part of my example Corp.com domain. For these examples, you can choose to rename the Default-First-Site-Name site or not—your choice.

Since many of us are still warming up to Group Policy, and even more people are warming up to the GPMC, I'll start with some basics to ensure that things are running smoothly. For most of the examples in this book, you'll be able to get with just the one Domain Controller and one or two workstations that participate in the domain, for verifying that your changes took place.

Again, I encourage you to not try these examples on your production network, in order to avoid a CLM (*Career-Limiting Move*).

Active Directory Users and Computers versus GPMC

The main job of Active Directory Users And Computers is to give you an "Active Directory object centric" view. Active Directory Users And Computers lets you deal with users, computers, groups, contacts, the operations masters (FSMOs), and delegation of control over user accounts as well as change the domain mode and define advanced security and auditing inside Active Directory. When you drill down inside Active Directory Users And Computers into an OU, you see the computers, groups, contacts, and so on contained within the OU.

But the GPMC has one main job: to provide you with a "Group Policy centric" view of all you control. All the OUs that you see in Active Directory Users And Computers are visible in the GPMC; however, the GPMC does not show you users, computers, contacts, and such. When you drill down into an OU inside the GPMC, you see but one thing—the GPOs that affect the objects inside the OU.

In Figure 1.6, you can see the Active Directory Users And Computers view as well as the GPMC view—rolled up into one MMC that we created earlier. The Active Directory Users And Computers view of **Temporary Office Help** and the GPMC view of the same OU is radically different.

FIGURE 1.6   GPMC shows the same OUs as Active Directory Users and Computers. However, the GPMC shows GPO relationships, not users, computers, or other objects.

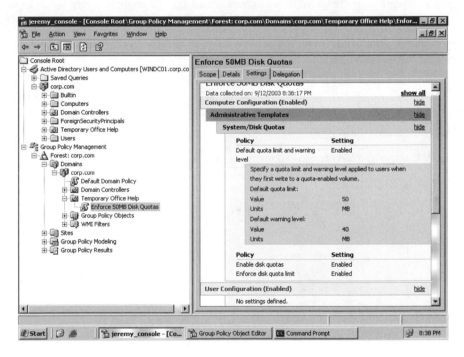

When focused at a site, a domain, or an OU within the GPMC, you see only the GPOs that affect that level in Active Directory. You don't see the same "stuff" that Active Directory Users And Computers sees, such as users, computers, groups, or contacts.

The basic overlap in the two tools is the ability to create and delete OUs. If you add or delete an OU in either tool, you need to refresh the other tool by pressing F5 to see the update. For instance, in Figure 1.6, you can see that my Active Directory has several OUs, including one named **Temporary Office Help**.

Deleting an OU from inside the GPMC is generally a bad idea. Since you cannot see the Active Directory objects inside the OU (such as users and computers), you don't really know how many objects you're about to delete. So be careful!

If I delete the **Temporary Office Help** OU in Active Directory Users And Computers, the change is not reflected in the GPMC window until it's refreshed. And vice versa.

Adjusting the View within the GPMC

The GPMC lets you view as much or as little of your Active Directory as you like. By default, you view only your own forest and domain. You can optionally add in the ability to see the sites in your forest, as well as the ability to see other domains in your forest or domains in other forests, although these views might not be the best for seeing what you have control over.

Viewing Sites in the GPMC   When you create GPOs, you won't often create GPOs that affect sites. The designers of the GPMC seem to agree; it's a bit of a chore to apply GPOs to sites. To do so, you need to link an existing GPO to a site. You'll see how to do this a bit later in this chapter.

However, you first need to expose the site objects in Active Directory. To do so, right-click the Sites object in GPMC, choose "Show Sites" from the shortcut menu, and then click the check box next to each site you want to expose.

In our first example, we'll use the site level of Active Directory to deploy our first Group Policy Object. At this point, go ahead and enable the Default-First-Site so that you can have it ready for use in our own experiments.

FIGURE 1.7   You need to expose the Active Directory sites before you can link GPOs to them.

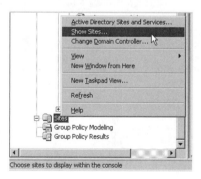

Viewing Other Domains in the GPMC   To see other domains in your forest, drill down to the Forest folder in Group Policy Management, right-click Domains, choose Show Domains, and select the other available domains in your forest. Each domain will now appear at the same hierarchical level in the GPMC.

Viewing Other Forests in the GPMC   To see other forests, right-click the root (Group Policy Management), and choose "Add Forest" from the shortcut menu. You'll need to type the name of the Windows 2003 forest you want to add. If you want to add or subtract domains within that new forest, follow the instructions in the preceding paragraph.

> You can add forests with which you do not have a two-way cross-forest trust. However, GPMC defaults will not display these domains as a safety mechanism. To turn off the safety, choose View menu ➤ Options to open the Options dialog box. In the General tab, clear "Enable Trust Detection" and click OK.

Now that we've adjusted our view to see the domains and forests we want, let's examine how to manipulate our GPOs and GPO links.

The GPMC-centric view

As we stated earlier, one of the fundamental concepts of Group Policy is that the GPOs themselves live in the "swimming pool" that is the domain. Then, when a level in Active Directory needs to use that GPO, there is simply a link to the GPO.

Here's what our swimming pool will eventually look like when we're done with the examples in this chapter.

FIGURE 1.8   Imagine your upcoming GPOs as just hanging out in the swimming pool of the domain.

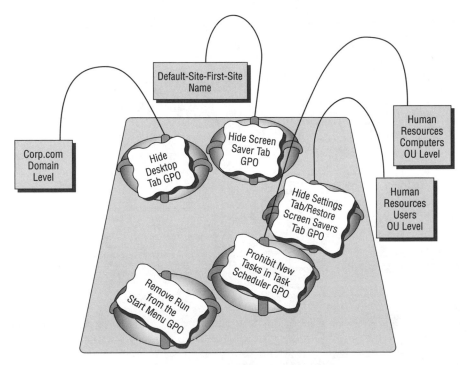

The Corp.com GPO Swimming Pool

Our swimming pool will be full of GPOs, with various levels in Active Directory "linked" to those GPOs. To that end, you can drill down, right now, to see the representation of the swimming pool. It's there, waiting for you. Click Group Policy Management ➤ Forest ➤ Domains ➤ corp.com ➤ Group Policy Objects to see all the GPOs that exist in the domain. (See Figure 1.9.)

If you're just getting started, it's not likely you'll have more than the "Default Domain Controllers Policy" GPO and "Default Domain Policy" GPO. That's OK. You'll start getting more GPOs soon enough. Oh, and for now, please don't modify the default GPOs. They're a bit special and are covered in great detail in Chapter 6.

All GPOs in the domain are represented in the Group Policy Objects folder. As you can see, when the **Temporary Office Help** OU is shown within the GPMC, a relationship exists between the OU and the "Enforce 50MB Disk Quotas" GPO. That relationship is the tether to the GPO in the swimming pool—the GPO link back to Enforce 50MB Disk Quotas. You can see this linked relationship because the "Enforce 50MB Disk Quotas" icon inside **Temporary Office Help** has a little arrow icon, signifying the link back to the actual GPO in the domain.

FIGURE 1.9   The Group Policy Objects folder highlighted here is the representation of the swimming pool of the domain that contains your actual GPOs.

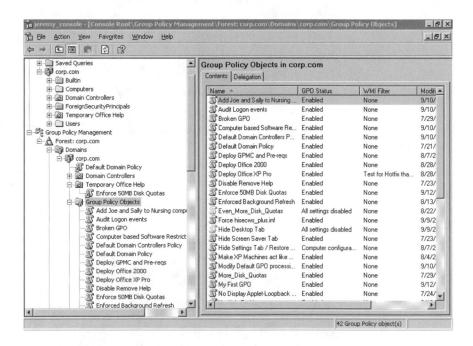

Our Own Group Policy Examples

While you're plunking around inside the Group Policy Object Editor, you'll see lots of policy settings that are geared toward Windows 2000, Windows XP, and/or Windows 2003. Some are geared only for Windows XP, and others are geared only for Windows 2003. If you happen to apply a policy to a system that isn't listed, the policy is simply ignored. For instance, policy settings described as working for Windows XP will not typically work on Windows 2000 machines.

Now that you've got a grip on honing your view within the GPMC, let's take it for a quick spin around the block with some examples!

For this series of examples, we're going after the users who keep fiddling with their display applets in Windows XP (and Windows 2000). In the Display Properties dialog box (right-click the Desktop and choose Properties from the shortcut menu) are several tabs, including Screensaver, Appearance, and Settings, as shown in Figure 1.10.

FIGURE 1.10   In Windows XP, all the tabs in the Display Properties dialog box are available by default.

For our first use of Group Policy, we're going to produce four "edicts." (For dramatic effect, you should stand on your desk and loudly proclaim these edicts with a thick British accent):

- At the site level, there will be no more Screen Saver tabs.
- At the domain level, there will be no more Desktop tabs.

- At the **Human Resources Users** OU level, there will be no more Settings tabs. And, while we're at it, let's bring back those Screen Saver tabs!

- At the **Human Resources Computers** OU, we'll prohibit the use of the Task Scheduler.

Following along with these concrete examples will reinforce the concepts presented earlier. Additionally, they are used throughout the remainder of this chapter and the book.

Understanding GPMC's Link Warning

As you work through the examples, you'll do a lot of clicking around. When you click a GPO link the first time, you'll get this message:

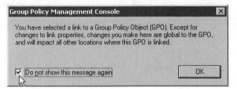

This message is trying to convey an important sentiment. That is, multiple levels in Active Directory may be linked back and using the exact same GPO. The idea is that multiple levels of Active Directory could be using the exact same Group Policy Object contained inside the Group Policy Objects container—but just linked back to it.

What if you modify the policy settings by right-clicking a policy link and choosing Edit from the shortcut menu? All instances in Active Directory that link to that GPO embrace the new settings. If this is a fear, you might want to create another GPO and then link it to the level in Active Directory you want. More properties are affected by this warning, and we'll explore them in Chapter 3.

If you've squelched this message by selecting "Do not show this message again", you can get it back. In the GPMC in the menus, choose View ➢ Options and select the General tab and select "Show Confirmation Dialog To Distinguish Between GPOs And GPO Links" and click OK.

More about Linking and the Group Policy Objects Container

The GPMC is a fairly flexible tool. Indeed, it permits the administrator to perform many tasks in different ways. One thing you'll do quite a lot in your travels with the GPMC is to actually create your own Group Policy Objects. Again, GPOs live in a container within

Active Directory and are represented within the Group Policy Objects container (the swimming pool) inside the domain (seen in Figure 1.9, earlier in this chapter.) Any levels of Active Directory—site, domain, or OU—simply link back to the GPOs hanging out in the Group Policy Objects container.

To apply Group Policy to a level in Active Directory (site, domain, or OU) using the GPMC, you have two options:

- Create the GPOs in the Group Policy Objects container first. Then, while focused at the level you want to command in Active Directory (site, domain, or OU), manually add a link to the GPO that is in the Group Policy Objects container.

- While focused at the level you want to command in Active Directory (domain or OU), create the GPOs in the Group Policy Objects container and automatically create the link. This link is created at the level you're currently focused at *back* to the GPO in the Group Policy Objects container.

Which is the correct way to go? Both are perfectly acceptable, because both are really doing the same thing.

In both cases the GPO itself does not "live" at the level in Active Directory at which you're focused. Rather, the GPO itself "lives" in the Group Policy Objects container. The link back to the GPO inside the Group Policy Objects container is what makes the relationship between the GPO inside the Group Policy Objects container swimming pool and the level in Active Directory you want to command.

FIGURE 1.11   You create your first GPO in the Group Policy Object container by right-clicking and choosing New.

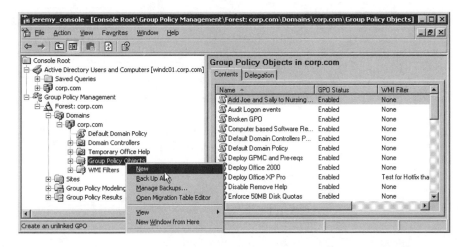

To get the hang of this, let's work through some examples. First, let's create our first GPO in the Group Policy Objects folder. Follow these steps:

1. Launch the GPMC.

2. Traverse down by clicking Group Policy Management ➢ Forest ➢ Domains ➢ corp.com ➢ Group Policy Objects.

3. Right-click the Group Policy Objects folder and choose New from the shortcut menu to open the New GPO dialog box as seen in Figure 1.11.

4. Let's name our first edict, er, GPO, something descriptive, such as "Hide Screen Saver Tab."

5. Once the name is entered, you'll see the new GPO listed in the swimming pool. Right-click the GPO, and choose Edit to open the Group Policy Object Editor as seen in Figure 1.12.

6. To hide the Screen Saver tab, drill down by clicking User Configuration ➢ Administrative Templates ➢ Control Panel ➢ Display. Double-click the **Hide Screen Saver Tab** policy setting to open the **Hide Screen Saver Tab** Properties screen, as shown in Figure 1.13. Clear the Not Configured setting, click the Enabled setting, and click OK.

7. Close the Group Policy Object Editor.

FIGURE 1.12　You can right-click the GPO in the Group Policy Objects container and choose Edit from the shortcut menu to open the Group Policy Object Editor.

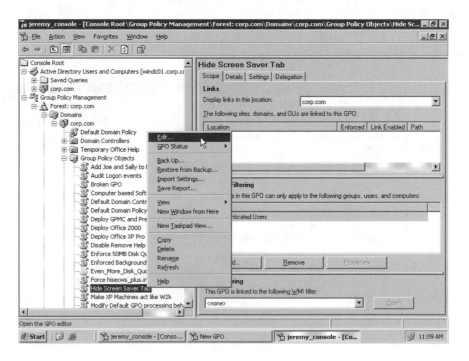

FIGURE 1.13   Double-click the policy setting and enable it.

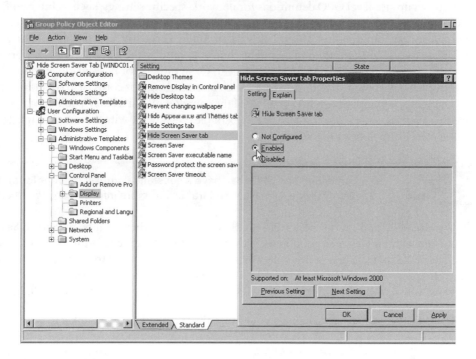

Understanding Our Actions

Now that we have this "Hide Screen Saver Tab" edict floating around in the Group Policy Objects container—in the representation of the swimming pool of the domain—what have we done? Not a whole lot, actually, other than create some bits inside Active Directory and upon the Domain Controllers. By creating new GPOs in the Group Policy Objects folder, we haven't inherently forced our desires on any level in Active Directory—site, domain, or OU.

To actually make a level in Active Directory accept our will, we need to link this new Group Policy Object to an existing level. Only then will our will be accepted and embraced. Let's do that now.

Applying Group Policy Object to the Site Level

The least-often-used level of Group Policy application is at the site. This is because it's got the broadest stroke but the bluntest application. Additionally, since Active Directory states that only members of the Enterprise Administrators (EAs) can modify sites and site links, it's equally true that only EAs (by default) can add and manipulate GPOs at the site level.

When a tree or a forest contains more than one domain, only the EAs and the Domain Administrators (DAs) of the root domain can create and modify sites and site links. When multiple domains exist, DAs in domains other than the root domain cannot create sites or site links (or site-level GPOs).

However, site GPOs might come in handy on an occasion or two. For instance, you might want to set up site-level GPO definitions for network-specific settings, such as Internet Explorer proxy settings or IP security policy for sensitive locations. Setting up site-based settings is useful if you have one building (set up explicitly as an Active Directory site) that has a particular or unique network configuration. You might choose to modify the Internet Explorer proxy settings if this building have a unique proxy server. Or in the case of IP security, perhaps this facility has particularly sensitive information, such as confidential records or payroll information.

Therefore, if you're not an EA (or a DA of the root domain), it's likely you'll never get to practice this exercise outside the test lab. In this example, we'll work with a basic example to get the feel of the Group Policy Object Editor.

Implementing site GPOs can have a substantial impact on your logon times and WAN (Wide Area Network) traffic. For more information, see Chapter 3.

We already stood on our desks and loudly declared that there will be no Screen Saver tabs at our one default site. The good news is that we've already done two-thirds of what we need to do to make that site accept our will: we exposed the sites we want to manage, and we created the "Hide Screen Saver Tab" GPO in the Group Policy Objects container.

Now, all we need do is to tether the GPO we created to the site with a GPO link.

FIGURE 1.14   Once you have your first GPO designed, you can link it to your site.

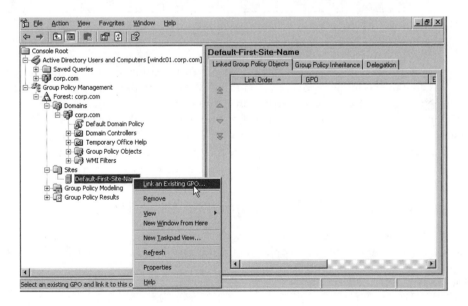

To remove the Screen Saver tab using the Group Policy Object Editor at the site Level, follow these steps:

1. Inside the GPMC snap in, drill down by clicking the Group Policy Management folder, the Forest folder, and the Sites folder.

2. Find the site to which you want to deliver the policy. If you have only one site, it is likely called Default-First-Site-Name.

3. Right-click the site, and choose "Link an Existing GPO", as shown in Figure 1.14.

Now you can select the "Hide Screen Saver Tab" GPO from a list of GPOs in the Group Policy Objects container in the domain. Once you have chosen the GPO, it will be linked to the site. You can also view it in the "Linked Group Policy Objects" tab in the right pane.

Did you notice that there was no Are You Sure You Really Want To Do This? warning or anything similar? The GPMC trusts that you set up the GPO correctly. If you create GPOs with incorrect settings and/or link them to the wrong level in Active Directory, you can make boo-boos on a grand scale. Again—this is why you want to try any setting you want to deploy in a test lab environment first.

Verifying Your Changes at the Site Level

Now, log onto any workstation or server that falls within the boundaries of the site to which you applied the site-wide GPO. You can choose any user you have defined—even the Administrator of the domain.

If you are logged onto a Windows XP Professional machine, you can open up the Display applet in Control Panel and note that the Screen Saver tab is missing, as shown in Figure 1.15 below.

Don't panic if you do not see the changes reflected the first time you log on. See the sections "Group Policy processing behavior" and "Forcing Background Processing" in Chapter 3 to find out how to encourage changes to occur. To see the Screen Saver tab disappear on Windows XP machines right now, log off and log back on. The policy should take effect.

This demonstration should prove how powerful Group Policy is, not only because everyone at the site is affected, but more specifically because administrators are not immune to Group Policy effects. Administrators are not immune because they are automatically members in the Authenticated Users security group. (You can modify this behavior with the techniques explored in Chapter 3.)

Applying Group Policy Objects to the Domain Level

At the domain level, we want an edict that says the Desktop tab should be removed from the Display Properties dialog box. Active Directory domains allow only members of the Domain Administrators group the ability to create Group Policy over the domain. Therefore, if you're not a DA (or a member of the EA group), it's likely that you'll never get to practice this exercise outside the test lab.

FIGURE 1.15   The Screen Saver tab in Windows XP is missing because the site policy is affecting the user.

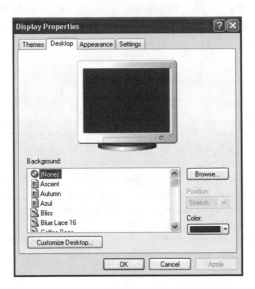

To apply the edict, follow these steps:

1. In the GPMC, drill down by clicking Group Policy Management ≻ Forest ≻ Corp.com.

2. Right-click the domain name to see the available options, as shown in Figure 1.16.

FIGURE 1.16   At the domain level, you can create the GPO in the Group Policy Objects container and then immediately link to the GPO from here.

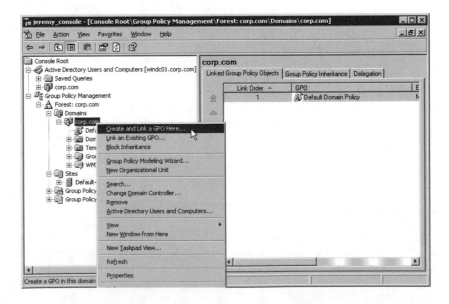

Create and Link a GPO Here versus Link an Existing GPO

In the previous example we forced the site level to embrace our Hide Screen Savers Tab edict. First, we created the GPO in the Group Policy Objects folder, and then in another step we linked the GPO to the site level. However, at the domain level (and, as you're about to see, the OU level), we can take care of both steps at once via the Create And Link A GPO Here command.

This tells the GPMC to create a new GPO in the Group Policy Objects folder and then automatically link the new GPO back to this focused level of Active Directory. This is a time-saving step so we don't have to dive down into the Group Policy Objects folder first and then create the link back to the Active Directory level.

So why is this "Create and Link a GPO Here" option possible only at the domain and OU level, but not the site level? Because Group Policy Objects linked to sites can often cause excessive bandwidth troubles using the old-school way of doing things. With that in mind, the GPMC interface makes sure that when you work with GPOs that affect sites, you're consciously choosing from which domain the GPO is being linked.

I'll talk more about this concept and how it's rectified with the GPMC way of doing things at the top of Chapter 3.

Don't panic when you see all the possible options. We'll hit them all in due time; right now we're interested in the first two: "Create and Link a GPO Here" and "Link an Existing GPO."

Since you're focused at the domain level, you are prompted for the name of a new Group Policy Object when you right-click click to "Create and Link a GPO Here." For this one, type a descriptive name, such as "Hide Desktop Tab." Your new "Hide Desktop Tab" GPO is created in the Group Policy Objects container, and, automatically, a link is created at the domain level from the GPO to the domain.

 You can be sure that the GPO was created by simply drilling down through Group Policy Management, Forest, Domains, Corp.com, and Group Policy Objects and looking for your new Hide Desktop Tab GPO.

Right-click either the link to "Hide Desktop Tab" (or the GPO itself) and choose Edit to open the Group Policy Object Editor. To hide the Desktop tab, drill down through User Configuration, Administrative Templates, Control Panel, and Display, and double-click Hide Desktop Tab. Change the setting from Not Configured to Enabled, and click OK. Close the Group Policy Object Editor to return to the GPMC.

Verifying Your Changes at the Domain Level

Now, log on as any user in the domain. You can log on to any computer in the domain or as any user you have defined—even the administrator of the domain. Open the Display Properties dialog box. You'll see that the Desktop tab is now also missing, as in Figure 1.17.

FIGURE 1.17   The Desktop tab is now also missing because the user is affected by the domain-level policy.

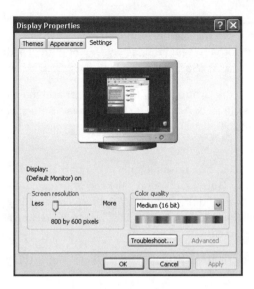

Once again, administrators are not immune to Group Policy effects. You can change this behavior as you'll see in Chapter 3.

Applying Group Policy Objects to the OU Level

OUs are wonderful tools for delegating away unpleasant administrative duties, such as password resets or modifying group memberships. But that's only half their purpose. The other half is to be able to apply Group Policy.

You'll likely find yourself making most of Group Policy additions and changes at the OU level, because that's where you have the most flexibility and the OU is the most-refined instrument to affect users. Once OU administrators become comfortable in their surroundings, they want to harness the power of Group Policy.

Preparing to Delegate Control

To create a GPO at the OU level, you must first create the OU and a plan to delegate. For the examples in this book, we'll create three OUs that look like this:

- **Human Resources**
  - **Human Resources Users**
  - **Human Resources Computers**

Having separate OUs for your users and computers is a good idea—for both delegation of rights and also GPO design. Microsoft considers this best practice.

In the **Human Resources Users** OU in our Corp.com domain, we'll create and leverage an Active Directory security group to do our dirty work. We'll name this group HR-OU-Admins and put our first HR-OU-Admins inside that group. We'll then delegate the appropriate rights necessary for them to use the power of GPOs.

To create the **Human Resources Users** OU, follow these steps:

1. Log on to the Domain Controller WINDC01 as Domain Administrator.

2. In Active Directory Users And Computers, right-click the domain name and choose New ➢ Organizational Unit, which will allow you to enter in a new OU name. Enter **Human Resources** as the name.

3. Inside the **Human Resources** OU, create two more OUs—**Human Resources Computers** and **Human Resources Users,** as shown in Figure 1.18.

FIGURE 1.18   When you complete all these steps, your **Human Resources** OU should have Frank Rizzo and the HR-OU-Admins as well as the **Human Resources Users** OU and **Human Resources Computers** OU.

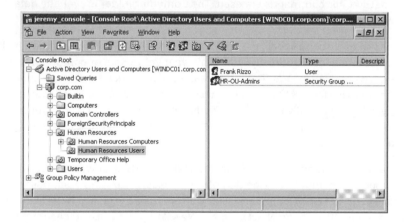

 Alternatively, you can create the OU in the GPMC. Just right-click the domain and choose "New Organizational Unit" from the shortcut menu.

To create the HR-OU-Admins group, follow these steps:

1. In Active Directory Users And Computers, right-click the new **Human Resources Users** OU and choose New ➢ Group.

2. Create the new group HR-OU-Admins as a new Global Security group.

To create the first user to go inside HR-OU-Admins, follow these steps:

1. In Active Directory Users And Computers, right-click the **Human Resources Users** OU and choose New ➢ User.

2. Name the user Frank Rizzo, with an account name of **frizzo,** and click Next.

3. If you've established a Windows 2003 domain, you must now enter a complex password for a user.

4. Finish and close the wizard.

Easily Manage New Users and Computers

The Computers folder and Users folder in Active Directory Users and Computers are not OUs. They are generic containers. You'll notice that they are not present in the GPMC view of Active Directory. This is because you cannot dictate Group Policy upon them.

These folders have two purposes:

- If an NT 4 domain is upgraded, the user and computer accounts will wind up in these folders. (Administrators are then supposed to move the accounts into OUs.)

- It's the default location where older tools create new users and computers. These older tools are in the Windows NT 4 User Manager (which still works in a Windows 2000 or Windows 2003 domain). This is also the default location for when the net use, net user, net group, and netdom add commands are used. The Computer folder is even the default location for any new client workstation or server that joins the domain.

If you execute one of these commands, the objects you create will wind up in either the Users folder or the Computers folder. But really, you don't want your users or computers to be in these folders—you want them in OUs. That's where the action is because you can apply Group Policy to OUs, not to these folders! Yeah, sure, these users and computers are affected by site and domain level GPOs. But really the action is at the OU level, and you want your computer and user objects to be placed in OUs as fast as possible—not sitting around in these generic Computers and Users folders.

To that end, Windows 2003 domains (in full functional level) have two tools to redirect the default location of new users and computers to the OUs of your choice. For example, suppose you want all new computers to go to a **NewComputers** OU and all new users to go to a **NewUsers** OU. And you want to link several GPOs to the **NewUsers** and **NewComputers** OUs to ensure that new accounts immediately have some baseline level of security, restriction, or protection. Without a little magic, new user accounts created using older tools won't automatically be placed there.

In Windows 2003 Active Directory, Microsoft has provided REDIRUSR and REDIRCMP commands that takes a distinguished name, like:

```
REDIRCMP ou=newcomputers,dc=corp,dc=com and/or
REDIRUSR ou=newusers, dc=corp, dc=com
```

Now if you link GPOs to these OUs, your new accounts will get the Group Policy Objects dictating settings to them at an OU level. This will come in handy when users and computers aren't specifically created in their final destination OUs.

To learn more about these tools, see the Microsoft Knowledge Base article 324929.

To add Frank Rizzo to the HR-OU-Admins group, follow these steps:

1. Double-click the HR-OU-Admins group.

2. Click the Members tab.

3. Add Frank Rizzo.

When it's all complete, your OU structure with your first user and group should look like Figure 1.18.

Delegating Control for Group Policy Management

Now that you've created the **Human Resources** OU, which contains the **Human Resources Users** OU and the **Human Resources Computers** OU and the HR-OU-Admins security group, and put the actual **HR-OU-Admins** into the group, you're ready to delegate control. You can delegate control to use Group Policy in two ways: using Active Directory Users And Computers, and using the GPMC.

> For this first example, we'll kick it old school and use the Active Directory Users And Computers way. Then, in Chapter 3, I'll demonstrate how to delegate control using the GPMC.

To delegate control for Group Policy management, follow these steps:

1. In Active Directory Users And Computers, right-click the top-level **Human Resources** OU you created, and choose Delegate Control from the shortcut menu to start the "Delegation of Control Wizard."

2. Click Next to get past the Wizard introduction screen.

3. You'll be asked to select users and/or groups. Click Add, add the HR-OU-Admins group, and click Next to open the "Tasks to Delegate" screen, as shown in Figure 1.19.

FIGURE 1.19   Select the "Manage Group Policy Links" task.

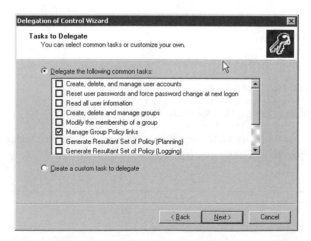

4. Click "Manage Group Policy links", and then click Next.

> You might want to click some or all the other check boxes as well, but for this example, only "Manage Group Policy links" is required. Try to avoid selecting "Generate Resultant Set of Policy (Planning)" and "Generate Resultant Set of Policy (Logging)" at this time. You'll see where they come in handy in Chapter 3.

5. At the wizard review screen, click Finish.

> The Manage Group Policy Links task assigns the user or group "Read" and "Write" access over the gPLink and gPOptions properties for that level. To see or modify these permissions by hand, open Active Directory Users And Computers, choose View ➢ Advanced Features, If later you want to remove a delegated permission, it's a little challenging. You can locate the permission that you set by right-clicking the delegated object (such as OU), then click on the Properties tab, click the Security tab, choose Advanced, and dig around until you come across the permission you want to remove. Finally, delete the corresponding access control entry (ACE).

Adding a User to the Server Operators Group

Under normal conditions, nobody but Domain Administrators, Enterprise Administrators, or Server Operators can walk up to Domain Controllers and log on. For testing purposes only, though, we're going to add our user, Frank, to the Server Operators group so he can easily work on our WINDC01 Domain Controller.

To add a user to the Server Operators group, follow these steps:

1. In Active Directory Users And Computers, double-click Frank Rizzo's account under the **Human Resources Users** OU.

2. Click the Member Of tab and click Add.

3. Select the Server Operators group and click OK.

4. Click OK to close the Properties dialog box for Frank Rizzo.

Normally, you wouldn't give your delegated OU administrators Server Operators access. You're doing it solely for the sake of this example to allow Frank to log on locally to your Domain Controllers.

Testing Your Delegation of Group Policy Management

Log off as Administrator on WINDC01 and log back on as Frank Rizzo. Now follow these steps to test your delegation:

1. Choose Start ➢ Programs ➢ Administrative Tools ➢ Group Policy Management to open the GPMC.

> If the Administrative Tools folder is not present, you'll need to choose Start ➢ Run to open the Run dialog box, and then type mmc in the Open box to load a "naked" MMC. Then load the Group Policy Management snap-in.

2. Drill down through Group Policy Management, Domains, Corp.com, and Group Policy Objects. If you right-click Group Policy Objects in an attempt to create a new GPO, you'll see the shortcut menu shown in Figure 1.20.

FIGURE 1.20   Frank cannot create new GPOs in the Group Policy Objects container.

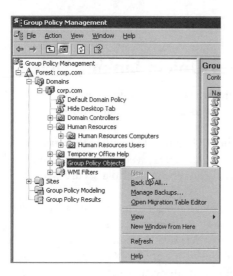

As you can see, Frank is unable to create new GPOs in the swimming pool of the domain. Since Frank has been delegated some control over the **Human Resources** OU (which also contains the other OUs), let's see what he can do. If you right-click the **Human Resources** OU in the GPMC, you'll see the shortcut menu shown in Figure 1.21.

Because Frank is unable to create GPOs in the swimming pool of the domain (the Group Policy Objects container), he is also unable by definition to create and link a GPO here. Although Frank (and more specifically, the HR-OU-Admins) has been delegated the ability to "Manage Group Policy links", he cannot *create* new GPOs. Frank (and the other potential HR-OU-Admins) has only the ability to *link* an existing GPO.

FIGURE 1.21   Frank's delegated rights allow him to link to existing GPOs, but not to create new GPOs.

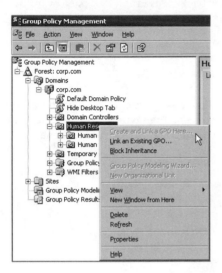

Understanding Group Policy Object Linking Delegation

When we were logged on as the Domain Administrator, we could create GPOs in the Group Policy Objects container, and we could create and link a GPO here at the domain or OU levels. But Frank cannot.

Here's the idea about delegating the ability to link to GPOs: someone with a lot of brains in the organization does all the work in creating a complex, well-thought-out and well-tested GPO. Maybe this GPO distributes software, or maybe it sets up a secure workstation policy. You get the idea.

Then, others in the organization, like Frank, are delegated just the ability to *link* to that GPO and use it at their level. This solves the problem of delegating perhaps too much control. Certainly some administrators are ready to create their own users and groups, but other administrators may not be quite ready to jump into the cold waters of Group Policy Object creation. Thus, you can design the GPOs for other administrators; they can just link to the ones you (or others) create.

When you (or someone with the right to link GPOs) selects "Link an Existing GPO", as seen in Figure 1.21 you can choose a GPO that's already been created—and hanging out in the domain swimming pool—the Group Policy Objects container.

In this example, the HR-OU-Admins members, such as Frank, can leverage any currently created GPO to affect the users and computers in their OU—even if they didn't create it themselves. In this example, Frank has linked to an existing GPO called "Word 2000 Settings". Turns out that some other administrator in the domain created this GPO, but Frank wants to use it. So, because Frank has "Manage Group Policy Links" rights on the **Human Resources** OU (and OUs underneath it), he is allowed to link to it.

But, as you can see in Figure 1.22, he cannot edit the GPOs. Under the hood, Active Directory doesn't permit Frank to edit GPOs he didn't create (and therefore doesn't own).

FIGURE 1.22   The GPMC will not allow you to edit an existing GPO if you do not own it (or do not have explicit permission to edit it).

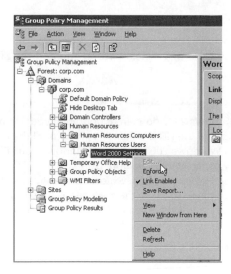

 In Chapter 3, I'll show you how to grant specific rights to allow more than just the original creator (and now owner) of the object to edit specific GPOs.

Giving the ability to just link to existing GPOs is a good idea in theory, but often OU administrators are simply given full authority to create their own GPOs (as you'll see later.) For this example, don't worry about linking to any GPOs. Simply cancel out of the Select GPO screen, close the GPMC, and log off from the server as Frank Rizzo.

Granting OU Admins Access to Create New Group Policy Objects

By using the Delegation of Control Wizard to delegate the Manage Group Policy Links attribute, you've performed half of what is needed to grant the appropriate authority to Frank (and any additional future HR-OU-Admins) to create GPOs in the Group Policy Objects container and link them to the **Human Resources** OU, the **Human Resources Users** OU, or the **Human Resources Computers** OU. (Though we really won't want to link many GPOs directly to the **Human Resources** OU.)

You can grant the HR-OU-Admins the ability to create GPOs in the Group Policy Objects container in two ways. For now, I'll show you the old-school way; in Chapter 3, I'll show you the GPMC way.

One of Active Directory's built-in security groups, "Group Policy Creator Owners", holds the key to the other half of our puzzle. You'll need to add those users or groups whom you want to have the ability to create GPOs to a built-in group, cleverly named Group Policy Creator Owners. To do so, follow these steps:

1. Log back on as Domain Administrator.

2. Fire up Active Directory Users And Computers.

3. By default the Group Policy Creator Owners group is located in the Users folder in the domain. Double-click the "Group Policy Creator Owners" group and add the HR-OU-Admins group and/or Frank Rizzo.

> If you just created a new Windows 2003 domain or upgraded your domain from NT 4, you will not be able to add the HR-OU-Admins group until the domain mode has been switched to Windows 2000 Native or Windows 2003 Functional level. Switch the domain by using Active Directory Domains and Trusts. Switching the domain mode is a one-way operation, which shuts out older Domain Controllers. If you are not prepared to make the switch to Native mode, you'll only be able to add individual members, such as Frank Rizzo—and not a group.

4. Log off as Domain Administrator from WINDC01.

> In Chapter 3, you'll see an alternate way to allow users to create GPOs.

Creating and Linking Group Policy Objects at the OU Level

At the site level, we hide the Screen Saver tab in the Display Properties dialog box. At the domain level, we chose to hide the Desktop tab in the Display Properties dialog box. At the OU level, we have two jobs to do:

- Hide the Settings tab in the Display Properties dialog box.
- Restore the Screen Saver tab that was taken away at the site level.

To create a GPO at the OU level, follow these steps:

1. Log off as Administrator on WINDC01 and log back on as Frank Rizzo.

2. Choose Start ➢ Programs ➢ Administrative Tools ➢ Group Policy Management to open the GPMC.

> If the Administrative Tools are not present on the machine you are using, choose Start ➢ Run to open the Run dialog box, and in the Open box, type mmc to load a "naked" MMC. Then load the Group Policy Management snap-in.

3. Drill down until you reach the **Human Resources Users** OU, right-click it, and choose "Create and Link a GPO Here" from the shortcut menu to open the "New GPO" dialog box.

4. In the "New GPO" dialog box, type in the name of your new GPO, say "Hide Settings Tab/ Restore Screen Saver Tab." This will create a GPO in the Group Policy Objects container and link it to the **Human Resources Users** OU.

5. Right-click the Group Policy link and choose Edit from the shortcut menu to open the Group Policy Object Editor.

6. To hide the Settings tab, drill down through User Configuration ➤ Administrative Templates ➤ Control Panel ➤ Display and double-click the **Hide Settings Tab** policy setting. Change the setting from "Not Configured" to "Enabled", and click OK.

7. To restore the Screen Saver tab, double-click the **Hide Screen Saver Tab** policy setting. Change the setting from "Not Configured" to "Disabled", and click OK.

8. Close the Group Policy Object Editor to return to the GPMC.

By disabling the Hide Screen Saver Tab policy setting, you're reversing the Enable setting set at a higher level. See the sidebar "A Note about the Three Possible Settings: Not Configured, Enabled, and Disabled" later in this chapter.

Verifying Your Changes at the OU Level

On your test Windows XP machine in the domain, log back on as Frank. Right-click the Desktop and choose Display from the shortcut menu to open the Display Properties dialog box. Note that the Settings tab is missing, but that the Screen Saver tab is back, as shown in Figure 1.23.

FIGURE 1.23   The Settings tab is missing along with the Desktop tab, but the Screen Saver tab has returned.

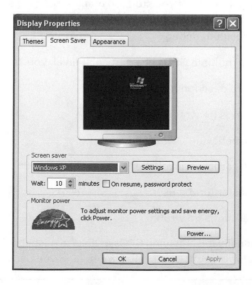

This test proves, once again, that even OU administrators are not automatically immune from policy settings. Chapter 3 explains how to change this behavior.

Group Policy Strategy

At times, you'll want to lock down additional functions for a collection of users or computers. For example, you might want to specify that no users in the **Human Resources Users** OU can use Control Panel.

At the **Human Resources Users** OU level, you've already set up a GPO that contained a policy setting to hide the Settings tab in the Display Properties dialog box. You now have a decision to make. You can create a new GPO that affects the **Human Resources Users** OU, give it a descriptive name, say "No One Can Use Control Panel", and then drill down through User Configuration ➢ Administrative Templates ➢ Windows Components ➢ Control Panel and enable the policy setting named **Prohibit Access to Control Panel**.

Or you could simply modify your existing GPO, named "Hide Settings Tab/Restore Screen Saver Tab" so that it contains additional policy settings. You can then rename your GPO to something that makes sense and encompasses the qualities of all the policy changes, say, "Our **Human Resources Users**' Desktop Settings."

Here's the quandary: The former method (one policy setting per GPO) is certainly more descriptive and definitely easier to debug should things go awry. If you have only one policy set inside the GPO, you have a better handle on what each one is affecting. If something goes wrong, you can dive right into the GPO, track down the policy setting, and make the necessary changes, or disable the ornery GPO (as discussed later).

The second method (multiple policy settings per GPO) is teeny-weeny bit faster for your computers and users at boot or logon time, because each additional GPO takes some minute fraction of additional processing time. But if you stuff too many settings in an individual GPO, the time to debug should things go wrong goes up exponentially. Group Policy has so many nooks and crannies that can be difficult to debug.

So, in a nutshell, if you have multiple GPOs at a particular level, you can do the following:

- Name each of them more descriptively.

- Debug them easily if things go wrong.

- Disable individually misbehaving GPOs.

If you have fewer GPOs at a particular level, the following is the case:

- Logging on is slightly faster for the user.

- Debugging is difficult if things go wrong.

- You can disable individually misbehaving GPOs or links to misbehaving GPOs. (But if they contain many settings, you might be disabling more than you desire.)

So, how do you form a GPO strategy? There is no right or wrong answer; you need to decide what's best for you. Several options, however, can help you decide.

One middle-of-the-road strategy is to start with multiple GPOs and one lone policy setting in each. Once you are comfortable that they are individually working as expected, you can create another new GPO that contains the sum of the settings from, in this example, **Hide Settings Tab** and **Prohibit Access to Control Panel** and then delete (or disable) the old individual GPO.

You might also choose to create GPOs such that they affect only the User half or the Computer half. You can then disable the unused portion of the GPO (either the Computer half or the User half). This allows for policy settings affecting one node to be grouped together for ease of naming and debugging and allows for flexible troubleshooting. This is Microsoft's recommendation.

Creating a New Group Policy Object in an OU

For the sake of learning and working through the rest of the examples in this section, you'll create another GPO and link it to the **Human Resources Computers** OU. This GPO will remove the ability to create new scheduled tasks using the Task Scheduler for all the Windows 2000 and Windows XP machines in the **Human Resources Computers** OU.

> The same setting exists under the User node, but we'll experiment with the Computer node policy.

First, you'll need to create the new GPO and modify the settings. You'll then need to move some client machines into the **Human Resources Computers** OU in order to see your changes take effect.

To disable the ability to use the Task Scheduler for the **Human Resources Computers** OU, follow these steps:

1. Log off as Administrator on WINDC01, and log back on as Frank Rizzo, the **Human Resources** OU administrator.

2. Choose Start ➢ Programs ➢ Administrative Tools ➢ Group Policy Management to start the GPMC.

> If the Administrative Tools are not present, choose Start ➢ Run to open the Run dialog box, and in the Open box, type mmc to load a "naked" MMC. Then load the GPMC.

3. Drill down until you reach the **Human Resources Computers** OU, right-click it, and choose "Create and Link a GPO Here" from the shortcut menu.

4. Name the GPO something descriptive, such as "Prohibit New Tasks in Task Scheduler."

5. Right-click the GPO, and choose Edit to open the Group Policy Object Editor.

6. We want to affect our Windows XP computers, so we need to use the Computers node. To disable the Task Scheduler, drill down through Computer Configuration ➢ Administrative Templates ➢ Windows Components ➢ Task Scheduler, and double-click **Prohibit New Task Creation**. Change the setting from Not Configured to Enabled, and click OK, as shown in Figure 1.24.

7. Close the Group Policy Object Editor to return the GPMC.

 Be aware of occasional strange Microsoft verbiage when you need to enable a policy to disable a setting. In Windows 2003, most policy settings have been renamed to Prohibit <*whatever*> to reflect the change from confusion to clarity.

FIGURE 1.24   By enabling this policy setting, you're disabling the Task Scheduler.

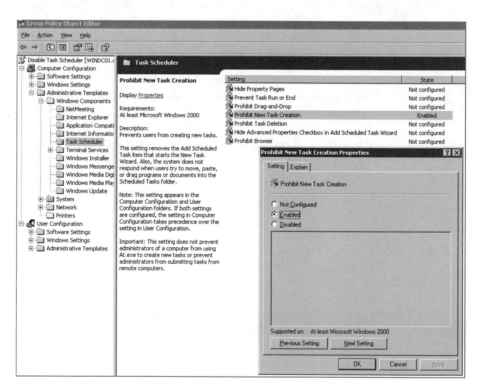

Moving Computers into the Human Resources Computers OU

Since you just created a policy that will affect computers, you'll need to place a workstation or two inside the **Human Resources Computers** OU to see the results of your labor. You'll need to be logged on as Administrator to WINDC01 to do this.

Quite often computers and users are relegated to separate OUs. That way, certain GPOs can be applied to certain computers but not others. For instance, isolating laptops, desktops, and servers is a common practice.

In this example, we're going to use the Find command in Active Directory Users And Computers to find a workstation named XPPro1 and move it into the **Human Resources Computers** OU. To find and move computers into a specific OU, follow these steps:

1. In Active Directory Users And Computers, right-click the domain, and choose Find from the shortcut menu, as shown in Figure 1.25, to open the Find Users, Contacts, and Groups dialog box.

2. From the Find drop-down menu, select Computers. In the Name field, type **XPPro1** to find the computer account of the same name. Once you've found it, right-click the account and choose Move from the shortcut menu. Move the account to the **Human Resources Computers** OU.

Repeat these steps for all other computers that you want to move to the **Human Resources Computers** OU.

FIGURE 1.25 Use the Find command to find computers in the domain so you can move them.

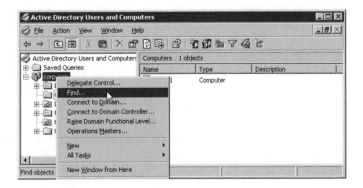

After you move the computer accounts into the **Human Resources Computers** OU, reboot your client machines. As you'll see in Chapter 3, the computer does not recognize the change right away when computer accounts are moved between OUs.

As you can see in this example (and in the real world), a best practice is to separate users and computers into their own OUs and then link GPOs to those OUs. Indeed, underneath a parent OU structure, such as the **Human Resources** OU, you might have more OUs, (i.e., **Human Resources Laptops** OU, **Human Resources Servers** OU, etc.). This will give you the most flexibility in design between delegating control where it's needed and the balance of GPO design within OUs. Just remember that in order for GPOs to affect either a user or computer, that user or computer must be within the scope of the GPO—site, domain, or OU.

Verifying Your Cumulative Changes

At this point, you've set up three levels of Group Policy that accomplishes multiple actions:

- At the site level, the "Hide Screen Saver Tab" GPO is in force for users.
- At the domain level, the "Hide Desktop Tab" GPO is in force for users.
- In the **Human Resources Users** OU, the "Hide Settings Tab / Restore Screen Saver Tab" GPO is in force for users.
- In the **Human Resources Computers** OU the "Prohibit New Tasks in Task Scheduler" GPO is in force for computers.

At this point, take a minute to flip back to Figure 1.8 (the swimming pool graphic) to see where we're going here. To see the accumulation of your policy settings inside your GPOs, you'll need to log on as a user who is affected by the **Human Resources Users** OU and at a computer that is affected by the **Human Resources Computers** OU. Therefore, log on as Frank Rizzo on XPPro1.

Right-click the Desktop and choose Display from the shortcut menu to open the Display Properties dialog box. Note that the Settings tab is still missing from the previous exercise (and the Screen Saver tab is restored). In Control Panel, select Classic View, and double-click Scheduled Tasks. Now missing is the ability to create new tasks. (Although you can choose File ➤ New ➤ Schedule Task, you won't to able to create a new task once this policy setting is in force.)

This test proves that even OU administrators are not automatically immune from GPOs and the policy settings within. Under the hood, they are in the Authenticated Users security group. See Chapter 3 for information on how to modify this behavior.

Again, don't panic if you don't see the changes reflected right away. See Chapter 3, for more text on how to encourage changes to occur.

A Note about the Three Possible Settings: Not Configured, Enabled, and Disabled

As you saw in Figure 1.24 earlier in this chapter, nearly all policy settings can be set as Not Configured, Enabled, or Disabled. These three settings have very different consequences, so it's important to understand how each works.

Not Configured   The best way to think about Not Configured is to imagine that it really says "Don't do anything" or even "Pass through." Why is this? Because if a policy setting is not configured, the policy is set at a higher level than simply "pass through" those configured settings to this level.

Enabled   When a specific policy setting is enabled, the policy will take effect. In the case of the Hide Screen Saver Tab policy, the effect is obvious. However, lots of policy settings, once enabled, have myriad possibilities *inside* the specific policy setting! (For a gander at one such policy setting use the Group Policy Object Editor and drill down to User Configuration ➢ Administrative Templates ➢ Windows Components ➢ Internet Explorer ➢ Toolbars and select the policy setting named **Configure Toolbar Buttons**.) So, as we can see, enabled really means "Turn this policy setting on." It will then either do what it says, or there will be more options inside the policy setting that can be configured.

Disabled   This setting leads a threefold life.

- Disabled usually means that if the same policy setting is enabled at a higher level, reverse its operation. For example, we chose to enable the **Hide Screen Saver Tab** policy setting at the site level. If at a lower level (say, the domain or OU level), we chose to Disable this policy setting, the Screen Saver tab will pop back at the level at which we disabled this policy.

- Additionally, Disabled often forces the user to accept the administrator's will. That is, if a policy setting is disabled, some default behavior of the policy setting is enforced, and the user cannot change it. To see an example policy setting like this, use the Group Policy Object Editor and drill down through User Configuration ➢ Administrative Templates ➢ Control Panel and select the policy setting named **Force Classic Control Panel Style**. Once this policy setting is disabled, the policy forces Windows XP users to use the Control Panel in the new task-based style. The point here is that the Disabled setting is a bit tricky to work with. You'll want to be sure that when you disable a policy setting, you're doing precisely what you intend.

- Disabled sometimes has a special and, typically, rare use. That is, something might already be hard-coded into the Registry to be "turned on" or work one way, and the only way to turn it off is to select Disabled. One such policy setting is the **Shutdown Event Tracker**. You Disable the policy setting, which turns it off, because on Windows 2003 it's already hard-coded on. In Windows XP, it's already hard-coded off.

So, think of Not Configured as having neither Allow nor Deny being set. Enabled will turn it on, and possibly have more functions. Disabled has multiple uses, and be sure to test, test, test to really make sure that once you've manipulated a policy setting, it's doing precisely what you had in mind.

Things That Aren't Group Policy but *Look* Like Group Policy

Windows Server 2003 is a big place. There are a lot of nooks and crannies, and occasionally things start to look similar, even though they're unrelated. Indeed two sections inside Windows 2000 and Windows 2003 sometimes look like they might have some tie-ins to Group Policy. Actually, they're totally separate.

Terminal Services

Both Windows 2000 Server and Windows Server 2003 come with a built-in Terminal Services service. To configure the service in Windows 2000, you have only one option—use the Terminal Services Configuration utility.

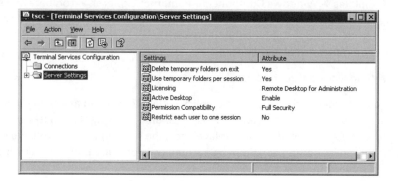

Don't let the little binary 1/0 icons fool you into thinking this window is Group Policy related. It is not. However, Windows 2003 does have multiple policy settings, and once they are set, the outcome is reflected in this window. (See Chapter 3 for information about how to locate the applicable policy settings.)

Routing and Remote Access

Routing and Remote Access (RRAS) allows users to connect to Windows 2003 servers over dial-in or VPN (virtual private network) connections, among other functions. To specify who can and cannot get through the gates, Windows Server 2003 has a facility to create rules to allow or deny access. Those rules happen to be called "Policies," as shown in Figure 1.26.

Don't let the little "scroll" icons fool you into thinking these are somehow related to Group Policy. They're not.

FIGURE 1.26   RRAS policies are not associated with Windows 2003 Group Policy.

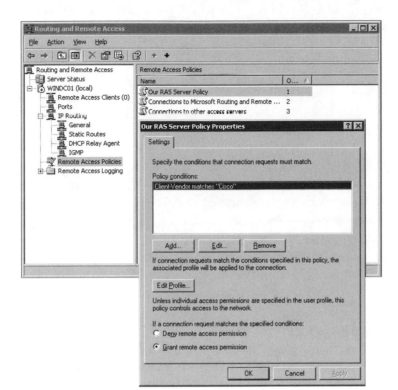

Final Thoughts

The concepts here are valid whether your Active Directory domains are Windows 2000 or Windows 2003. The point is that to make the most use of Group Policy, you'll need an Active Directory. But the best news is that the GPMC (once loaded on a Windows XP or Windows 2003 machine) can control either Windows 2000 or Windows 2003 domains.

The more you use and implement GPOs in your environment, the better you'll become at the basic use while at the same time avoiding pitfalls when it comes to using them. The following tips are scattered throughout the chapter, but are repeated and emphasized here for quick reference, to help you along your Group Policy journey:

GPOs don't "live" at the site, domain, or OU level.   GPOs "live" in Active Directory and are represented in the swimming pool of the domain called the Group Policy Objects container. To use a GPO, you need to link a GPO to a level in Active Directory that you want to affect: a site, a domain, or an OU.

GPOs apply to Active Directory sites, domains, and OUs. Active Directory is a hierarchy, and Group Policy takes advantage of that hierarchy. There is one local GPO that can be set, which affects everyone who uses that machine. Then, Active Directory Group Policy Objects apply—site, domain, and then OU. Active Directory GPOs "trump" any local policy settings if set within the Local Group Policy.

Avoid using the site level to implement GPOs. Users can roam from site to site. When they do, they can be confused by the settings changing around them. Use GPOs linked to the site only to set up special site-wide security settings, such as IPSec or the Internet Explorer Proxy. Use the domain or OU levels when creating GPOs whenever possible.

Implement common settings high in the hierarchy when possible. The higher up in the hierarchy GPOs are implemented, the more users they affect. You want common settings to be set once, affecting everyone, instead of having to create additional GPOs performing the same functions at other lower levels, which will just clutter your view of Active Directory with the multiple copies of the same policy setting.

Implement unique settings low in the hierarchy. If a specific collection of users is unique, try to round them up into an OU and then apply Group Policy to them. This is much better than applying the settings high in the hierarchy and using Group Policy filtering later.

Use more GPOs at any level to make things easier. When creating a new Group Policy, isolate it by creating a new GPO. This will enable easy revocation using the Disable command should something go awry and not affect your other GPOs.

Round up multiple policy settings into one GPO. Start your Group Policy journey by having only one or two settings per GPO. Then use the Disable feature to disable the smaller GPOs and concatenate them into one large GPO once you're absolutely sure the settings are working as advertised. However, this isn't required; it's just an idea to clean things up over time. It will usually not make processing GPOs noticeably "faster."

2

Managing Group Policy with the GPMC

In the last chapter, you got to know how and when Group Policy works. We used Active Directory Users And Computers to create and manage users and computers, but we used the GPMC to manage Group Policy. We got a little workout with the GPMC when creating new GPOs and linking them to various levels in Active Directory.

And, for just a moment, we went back to the old-school way to delegate control to Frank and the HR-OU-Admins group to link existing GPOs to their **Human Resources** OU structure.

In this chapter, I'll cover the remainder of daily tasks you can perform using the GPMC. As a reminder, the GPMC is for all implementations of Active Directory. That is, you can use the GPMC to manage Windows 2000 and/or Windows 2003 domains. You just need the GPMC loaded on a Windows XP machine (with SP1) or a Windows 2003 computer.

I'll tackle most of the remaining features the GPMC has to offer in this chapter, but loading the GPMC brings two other goodies to the table. We'll tackle those goodies in Chapter 7, "Scripting GPMC Operations," and for additional information, see the Appendix.

So, with that in mind, let's get to know the GPMC a bit better.

Common Procedures with the GPMC

In the last chapter, we created and linked some GPOs, which we can see in the Group Policy Objects container, to see how, at each level, we were affecting our users. In this section, we'll continue by working with some of the more advanced options for applying, manipulating, and using Group Policy.

Clicking either a GPO itself, or a link, lets you get more information about what they do. For now, feel free to click around, but I suggest that you don't change anything until we get to the specific examples.

Various tabs are available to you once you click the GPO itself or a link. Let's take a look at them now.

The Scope Tab   Clicking a GPO, or a GPO link, opens the Scope tab. The Scope tab gives you an at-a-glance view of where and when the GPO will apply. We'll examine the Scope tab in the sections "Deleting and Unlinking Group Policy Objects" and "Filtering Group Policy Objects" in this chapter, and "WMI Filters" in Chapter 10. For now, you can see that the "Hide Settings Tab/Restore Screen Saver Tab" GPO is linked to the **Human Resources** OU. But you already knew that.

The Details Tab   The Details tab contains information describing who created the GPO (the owner) as well as the status (Enabled, Disabled, or Partially Disabled) as well as some nuts-and-bolts information about its underlying representation in Active Directory (the GUID.) We'll examine the Details tab in the sections "Disabling 'Half' (or Both Halves) of the Group Policy Object" and "Understanding GPMC's Link Warning" in this chapter and in Chapter 4.

Should you change the GPO status here, say, by disabling the User Configuration of the policy, you'll be affecting all other levels in Active Directory that might be using this GPO by linking to it. See the section "Understanding the GPMC's 'Link' Warning" section as well as the sidebar "On GPO Links and GPOs Themselves" a bit later in the chapter.

The Settings Tab   The Settings tab gives you an at-a-glance view of what's been set inside the GPO. In our example, you can see the Enabled and Disabled status of the two policy settings we manipulated. You can click Hide (or Show) to contract and expand all the configured policy settings:

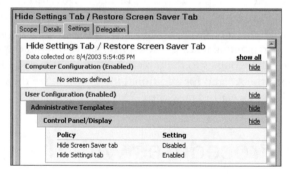

- Clicking Hide at any level tightens that level. You can expose more information by clicking the inverse of Hide when available, which is Show.

- Clicking the actual policy setting name, for example, **Hide Settings tab** displays the help text for the policy setting. This can be useful if someone set up an oddball policy setting, and you want to know what it's supposed to do.

- If you want to change a setting, you can right-click the settings area and select Edit. The familiar Group Policy Object Editor will appear. Note, however, that the Group Policy Object Editor will not "snap to" the policy setting you want to edit. The editor always starts off at the root.

If you chose to load the GPMC on a Windows 2003 machine, you may run into an initial problem when clicking the Settings tab. That is, certain aspects of the GPMC, such as the Settings tab, tap into Internet Explorer. Since Windows 2003 is hardened on a Windows 2003 machine, you will have limited access to the whole picture. If you're presented with a warning box, simply add the `security_mmc.exe` as a trusted website. This should make your problems go away. You can also turn off IE Security in Windows 2003 in Add/Remove Programs. (This isn't recommended.)

You can also edit the settings by clicking the GPO or any GPO link for that object and choosing Edit. However, you *always* affect all containers (sites, domains, or OUs) to which the GPO is linked. It's one and the same object, regardless of the way you edit it. See the sidebar "On GPO Links and GPOs Themselves" a bit later in the chapter to get the full gist of this.

The Delegation Tab   The Delegation tab lets you set the security for who can do what with GPOs, their links, and their properties. You'll find the Delegation tab in a lot of places, and at each location it enables you to do something different:

- Clicking a GPO link or clicking a GPO in the Group Policy Objects container
- Clicking a site
- Clicking a domain
- Clicking an OU
- Clicking the "WMI Filters" node.
- Clicking a WMI filter itself

I'll discuss what each instance of this tab does a bit later in the "Advanced Security and Delegation with the GPMC" section.

WMI stands for Windows Management Instrumentation, and is discussed in Chapter 10.

Minimizing the View with Policy Setting Filtering

Imagine you were just given the task to prevent all your Windows XP desktops from using the Internet Connection Firewall component. Where do you start to look for that policy setting?

Sometimes, you just don't know where to start clicking inside the Group Policy Object Editor. You could be in the editor for a variety of reasons. Perhaps you want to locate a new policy setting to enable. With more than 700 possible settings in Windows 2003, finding the policy setting you want can sometimes be a challenge.

If you type **hh spolsconcepts.chm** at a command prompt, you'll have documentation about the security-related policy settings. In the Appendix we'll explore GP.CHM (from the Windows 2000 reskit) which will expose even more policy settings.

To that end, the updated Group Policy Object Editor has a new way to filter the view. The good news is that this feature is very powerful. The bad news is that this feature works only while browsing the Administrative Templates branch.

While in the Group Policy Object Editor, to examine the filtering option, choose either User Configuration ➢ Administrative Templates or Computer Configuration ➢ Administrative Templates. Then, choose View ➢ Filtering to display what's in Figure 2.1, which is described in the following sections.

FIGURE 2.1 The Windows 2003 Group Policy Object Editor allows for filtering of the Administrative Template branch.

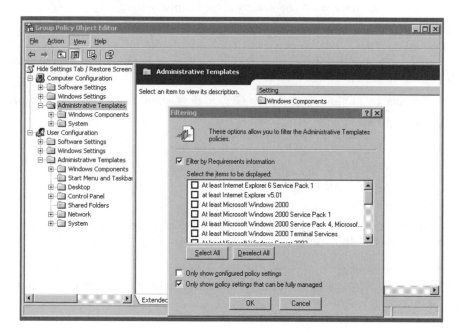

 The Filter settings are independent on each of the User and Computer nodes.

The "Only show configured policy settings" Setting

If you want to modify an existing policy setting, you needn't click every branch in one of the Administrative Templates folder in order to hunt-and-peck. Once the "Only show configured policy settings" option, as seen in Figure 2.1 is selected, you will only see policy settings that have been enabled or disabled within either the User Configuration ➢ Administrative Templates or Computer Configuration ➢ Administrative Templates.

By default, the "Only show configured policy settings" check box is not checked, and therefore you can see policy settings that are enabled, disabled, and not configured. The "Only show configured policy settings" check box is independent for both the Computer and User node settings. Additionally, when you close the editor, the check box is always cleared.

Policy Setting Filtering Based on Operating System and Service Pack

As you learned in the Introduction, policy settings are specific to the operating system. For instance, a Windows XP policy setting such as **Turn off creation of System Restore Checkpoints** makes no sense to a Windows 2000 machine. This is because Windows 2000 doesn't have the System Restore feature.

There are times when you want to search for policy settings specific to the computers you want to target. Simply click the "Filter by Requirements information" check box as seen in Figure 2.1, and then proceed to check the items on which you want to filter.

You have a huge variety of policy types to choose from, including operating system, service pack, and even unique items such as Internet Explorer level and Windows Media Player.

If the description of the filter is too long to read, simply hover the mouse over the description (don't click) to display the entire description in a floating Tool-Tip style window.

Using the "Only show policy settings that can be fully managed" Option

As we'll explore in Chapter 5, you can actually use old-style "legacy" NT 4 ADM templates inside the Windows 2003 Group Policy Object Editor. Normally, they are "bad" because they don't modify the "correct" portion of the Registry. In general, this is highly undesirable because most NT 4 templates don't act like Windows 2003 Group Policy. NT 4–style ADM preferences usually permanently "tattoo" the target machine until the settings are explicitly removed. For more on the distinction between policies and preferences with respect to Windows 2003 settings, see the "Policies vs. Preferences" section in Chapter 5, "Windows ADM Templates."

This check box is checked by default, as seen in Figure 2.1. This gives a gentle persuasion to avoid the importation of old NT 4 ADM templates.

You can wisely keep this check box permanently checked by using the "Enforce Show Policies Only" policy setting as described Chapter 3, in the "Using Group Policy to Affect Group Policy" section.

Raising or Lowering the Precedence of Multiple Group Policy Objects

You already know the "flow" of Group Policy is inherited from the site level, the domain level, and then from each nested OU level. But, additionally, *within* each level, say at the

Temporary Office Help OU, multiple GPOs are processed in a ranking precedence order. Lower-ranking GPOs are processed first, and then the higher GPOs are processed.

In Figure 2.2, you can see that some administrator has linked two GPOs to the **Temporary Office Help** OU. One GPO is named "Enforce 50MB Disk Quotas", and another is named "Enforce 40MB Disk Quotas."

FIGURE 2.2   You can link multiple GPOs at the same level.

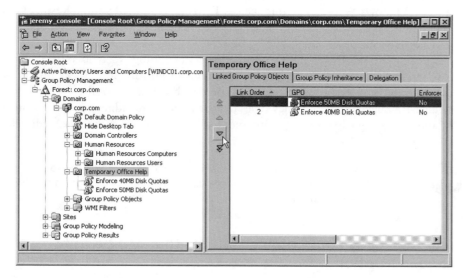

If the policy settings inside these GPOs both adjust the disk quota settings, which one will "win"? Client computers will process these two GPOs from lowest-link order to highest-link order. Therefore, the "Enforce 40MB Disk Quotas" GPO (with link order 2) is processed before "Enforce 50MB Disk Quotas" (link order 1). Hence, the GPO with the policy settings to dictate 50MB disk quotas will "win."

So, if two (or more) GPOs within the same level contain values for the same policy setting (or policy settings), the GPOs will be processed from lowest-link order to highest-link order. Each consecutively processed GPO overlays (and perhaps overwrites) overlapping policy settings. This could happen where one GPO had a specific policy setting enabled and another GPO at the same level had the same policy setting disabled.

Changing the order of the processing of multiple GPOs at a specific level is an easy task. For instance, suppose you want to change the order of the processing such that the "Enforce 40MB Disk Quotas" GPO is processed after the "Enforce 50MB Disk Quotas" GPO. Simply click the policy setting you want to process last, and click the down arrow icon. Similarly, if you have additional GPOs that you want to process first, click the GPO and click the up arrow icon. The multiple arrow icons will put the highlighted GPO either first or last in the link order—depending on the icon you click.

Again—the last applied GPO "wins." So the GPO with a link order of 1 is always applied last and, hence, has the "final" say at that level. This is always true unless the "Enforced" flag is used (as discussed later).

Understanding GPMC's Link Warning

In the previous chapter, I pointed out that the first time you click a GPO link, you get the message shown in Figure 2.3.

FIGURE 2.3   You get this message any time you click the icon for a link.

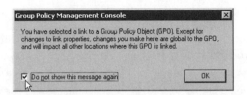

This message is trying to convey an important sentiment: no man is an island, and neither is a Group Policy Object. Just because you created a GPO and it's seen swimming in the Group Policy Objects container doesn't mean you're the only one that's using it.

As we work through examples in this chapter, we'll manipulate various characteristics of GPOs and links to GPOs. If we manipulate any characteristics of a GPO we're about to play with, such as the following:

- The underlying policy settings themselves
- The security filtering (on the Scope tab)
- The WMI filtering (on the Scope tab)
- The GPO status (on the Details) tab
- The delegation (on the Delegation tab)

all other levels in Active Directory that also link to this GPO will be affected by our changes.

This is sometimes a tough concept to remember, so it's good to see it here again. You can choose to squelch the tip if you like. Just don't forget its advice.

> The difference between the GPO itself and the links you can create can be confusing. Be sure to check out the sidebar "On GPO Links and GPOs Themselves" a bit later.

You can see principle in action if you like by locating the "Prohibit new Tasks in Task Scheduler" GPO. In either the link upon the **Human Resources Computers** OU or the object itself with "GPOs," go to the Details tab and change the GPO status to some other setting. Then, go to the link or the actual GPO, and see that your changes are reflected. You can even create a new OU, link the GPO, and see that the change is still there. This is because you're manipulating the actual GPO, not the link. If you choose to squelch the message, you can get it back by choosing View ➤ Options ➤ General and selecting "Show confirmation dialog to distinguish between GPOs and GPO links."

Stopping Group Policy Objects from Applying

After you create your hierarchy of Group Policy that applies to your users and computers, you might occasionally want to temporarily halt the processing of a GPO—usually because some user is complaining that something is wrong. You can prevent a specific GPO from processing at a level in Active Directory via several methods, as explained in the following sections.

Disabling the "Link Enabled" Status

Remember that all GPOs are contained in the Group Policy Objects container. To use them at a level in Active Directory (site, domain, or OU), you link back to the GPO. So, the quickest way to prevent a GPO's contents from applying is to remove its "Link Enabled" status. If you right-click a GPO link at a level, you can immediately see its "Link Enabled" status, as shown in Figure 2.4.

FIGURE 2.4   You can choose to enable or disable a GPO link.

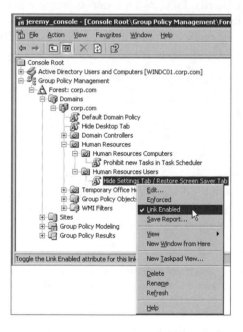

To prevent this GPO from applying to the **Human Resources Users** OU, simply click "Link Enabled" to remove the check mark. This will leave the link within the OU back to the GPO, but disable the link, rendering it innocuous. The icon to the left of the name of the GPO will change to a scroll with the link arrow dimmed. You'll see a zoomed-in picture of this later in the "GPMC At-a-Glance Icon View" section.

Disabling "Half" (or both halves) of the Group Policy Object

The second way to disable a specific GPO is by disabling just one half of a Group Policy Object. You can disable either the user half or the computer half. Disable both halves, and the entire GPO is disabled.

You might be wondering why you might want to disable only half of a GPO. On the one hand, disabling a GPO (or half of a GPO) actually makes startup and logon times a teeny-weeny bit faster for the computer or user, because each GPO you add to the system adds a smidgen of extra processing—either for the user or the computer. Once you disable the unused portion of the GPO, you've shaved that processing time off the startup or logon time. Microsoft calls this "modifying Group Policy for performance."

Don't go bananas disabling your unused half of GPO just to save a few cycles of processing time. Trust me, it's just not worth the headaches figuring out later where you did and did not disable a half of a policy.

So, disabling half of the GPO makes troubleshooting and usage quite a bit harder, as you might just plumb forget you've disabled half the GPO. Then, down the road, when you modify the disabled half of the policy for some future setting, it won't take effect on your clients! You'll end up pulling your hair out wondering why, once things *should* change, they just don't!

Why Totally Disable a Group Policy Object?

One good reason to disable a specific GPO is if you want to manually "join" several GPOs together into one larger GPO. In the previous example, we might want to make sure each policy is working as expected. Then, once we're comfortable with the reaction, we can re-create the policy settings from multiple GPOs into another new GPO and disable the old individual GPOs. If there are signs of trouble with the new policy, you can always just disable (or delete) the large GPO and reenable the individual GPOs to get right back to where you started.

You might also want to immediately disable a new GPO even before you start to edit it. Imagine that you've chosen "Create and link a new GPO here" for, say, an OU. Then, imagine you have lots of policy settings you want to make in this new GPO. Remember that each setting is immediately written inside the Group Policy Object Editor, and computers are continually requesting changes when their background refresh interval triggers. The affected users or computers might hit their background refresh cycle and start accepting the changes before you've finished writing all your changes to the GPO! Therefore, if you disable the GPO before you edit and re-enable the GPO after you edit, you can ensure that your users are getting all the newly changed settings at once.

This tip works best only when creating new GPOs; if you disable the GPO *after* creation, there's an equally likely chance that critical settings will be removed while the GPO is disabled when clients request a Background Refresh. We'll discuss the ins and outs of Background Refresh in Chapter 3.

To disable an unused half of a GPO, follow these steps:

1. Select the GPO you want to modify. In this case, select "Prohibit new Tasks in Task Scheduler," and select the Details tab in the right pane of the GPMC.

2. Since the policy settings within the "Prohibit new Tasks in Task Scheduler" GPO modify only the Computer node, it is safe to disable the User node. Select the "User configuration settings disabled" drop-down box, as shown in Figure 2.5.

3. You will be prompted to confirm the status change. Choose to do so.

FIGURE 2.5   You can disable half the GPO to make Group Policy process a weeee bit faster.

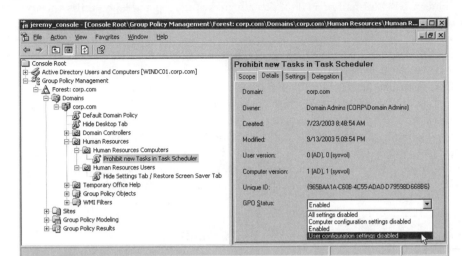

Here are some additional items to remember regarding disabling portions of a GPO:

- It is possible to disable the entire GPO (both halves) by selecting the GPO, clicking the Options button, and selecting the "All Settings Disabled" option. If you select "All Settings Disabled," the scroll icon next to the name of the GPO "dims" a bit to show that there is no way it can affect any targets. You'll see a zoomed-in picture of this later in the "GPMC At-a-Glance Icon View" section.

- As I stated in the "Understanding the GPMCs Link Warning" section, changing the "GPO Status" entry (found on the Details tab) will affect all GPOs linked to any level, anywhere in Active Directory!! You cannot just change the GPO status for the instance of this link— this affects all links to this GPO! The only good news here is that only the person who created the GPO itself can manipulate this setting. To get the full thrust of this, be sure to read the "On GPO Links and GPOs Themselves" sidebar a bit later in this chapter.

- The GPMC does not have any indication, other than this "GPO status", that the link has been fully or half disabled. However, the old-school interface in Windows 2003 will alert you to a GPO that is "half disabled." You'll see a yellow triangle warning icon next to the name of the GPO.

Deleting and Unlinking Group Policy Objects

As you just saw, you can prevent a GPO from processing at a level by merely removing its "Link Enabled" status. However, you can also choose to remove the link entirely. For instance, you might want to return the normal behavior of the Task Scheduler to the affected client computers. You have two options:

- Delete the link to the GPO
- Delete the GPO itself

Deleting the Link to the Group Policy Object

When you right-click the GPO link of "Prohibit new Tasks in Task Scheduler" in the **Human Resources Computers** OU, you can choose Delete. When you do, the GPMC will confirm your request and remind you of an important fact, as shown in Figure 2.6.

FIGURE 2.6 You can delete a link (as opposed to deleting the GPO itself).

Recall that the GPO itself doesn't "live" at a level in Active Directory; it really lives in a special container in Active Directory (and can be seen via the Group Policy Objects Container in the GPMC). We're just working with a link to the real GPO. And, in Chapter 4, you'll see where this folder relates directly within Active Directory itself.

When you choose to delete a GPO link, you are simply choosing to stop using it at the level it was created, but keep the GPO itself alive in the representation of the swimming pool the Group Policy Objects container. This leaves other administrators at other levels to continue to link to that GPO if they want.

Truly Deleting the Group Policy Object Itself

You can choose to delete the GPO altogether—lock, stock, and barrel. The only way to delete the GPO itself is to drill down through Group Policy Management ➢ Domains ➢ Corp.com and locate the Group Policy Objects container and delete it. It's like plucking a child directly from the swimming pool. Before you do, you'll get a warning message as shown in Figure 2.7.

FIGURE 2.7 Here, you're actually deleting the GPO itself.

This will actually remove the bits on the Domain Controller and obliterate it from the system. No other administrators can then link to this GPO.

 Once it's gone, it's gone (unless you have a backup).

If you delete the GPO altogether, there's only one problem. There is no indication sent to the folks who are linking to this GPO that you've just deleted it. The idea is simple: you might be done with the "Prohibit new Tasks in Task Scheduler" GPO and don't need it anymore to link to *your*

locations in Active Directory. But what about other administrators? In this case, while I was out to lunch, Freddie, the administrator for the **Temporary Office Help** OU, has already chosen to link the "Prohibit new Tasks in Task Scheduler" GPO to his OU, as shown in Figure 2.8.

FIGURE 2.8   The "Prohibit Tasks in Task Scheduler" GPO (lowest circle) is linked at both the Temporary Office Help OU (Middle circle) and this Human Resources Computers OU (topmost circle).

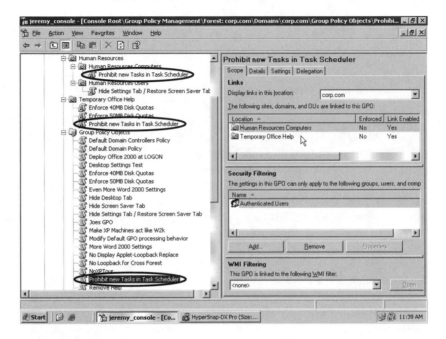

What if I had deleted the "Prohibit new Tasks in Task Scheduler" GPO? I'm pretty sure I would have received an angry phone call from Freddie. Or, maybe not—if Freddie didn't know who created (and owned) the GPO.

Since we only have a handful of OUs, this link back to the GPO was easy to find. However, once you start getting lots of OUs, locating additional links back to a GPO will become much harder. Thankfully, the GPMC shows you if anyone else is linked to a GPO you're about to delete. I call this ability "Look before you leap." You can just look in the Scope tab under the Links heading as indicated in Figure 2.8 by the mouse pointer. There you can see that both the **Temporary Office Help** OU and the **Human Resources Computers** OU are utilizing the GPO named "Prohibit new Tasks in Task Scheduler."

If you're confident that you can still continue, you can delete the GPO contained within the Group Policy Objects container. However, for now, let's leave this GPO in place for use in future examples in the book.

WARNING   The Scope tab shows you the links to the GPOs from your own domain. It is possible for other domains to choose to use your GPOs and link to them. When you delete a GPO forever, you're deleting the ability for other domains to use that GPO as well. So, before you really delete the GPO forever, click "Display links in this location" to select other domains to see where else the GPO is linked.

For now, don't delete the GPO. We'll use it again in later chapters. If you want to play with deleting a GPO, create a new one and delete it.

Block Inheritance

As you've already seen, the normal course of Group Policy inheritance applies all policies settings within GPOs in a cumulative fashion from the site to the domain and then to each nested OU. A setting at any level automatically affects all levels beneath it. But perhaps this is not always the behavior you want. For instance, we know that an edict from the Domain Administrator states there will be no Desktop tab in the Display Properties dialog box.

This edict is fine for most of the OU administrators and their subjects who are affected. But Frank Rizzo, the administrator for the **Human Resources** OU structure, believes that the folks contained within his little fiefdom can handle the responsibility of the Desktop tab and the Screen Saver tab, and he wants to bring them back to his users. (But he's not ready to give back the Settings tab.)

In this case, Frank Rizzo can prevent GPOs (and the policy settings within them) defined at higher levels (domain and site) from affecting his users, as shown in Figure 2.9. If Frank chooses to select "Block Inheritance," Frank is choosing to block the flow of *all* GPOs (with all their policy settings) from *all* higher levels.

FIGURE 2.9   Use the "Block Inheritance" feature to prevent all GPOs (and the policy settings within them) from all higher levels from affecting your users and computers.

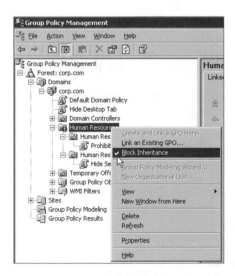

When Frank does this, the **Human Resources** OU icon changes to include a blue exclamation point (!) as seen in Figure 2.9. Once the check is present and the GPOs are reprocessed on the client, only those settings that Frank dictates within his **Human Resources** OU structure will be applied.

If you want to see the effect of "Block Inheritance," ensure the check is seen as shown in Figure 2.9. Then, log on as any user affected by the **Human Resources** OU—say, Frank Rizzo.

You'll notice that the Desktop tab has reappeared in the Display Properties dialog box, but that the Settings tab is still absent because that GPO is explicitly defined at the **Human Resources Users** OU level, which contains Frank's user account.

The Enforced Function

Frank Rizzo and his Human Resources folks are happy that the Screen Saver and Desktop tabs have made a triumphant return. There's only one problem: the Domain Administrator has found out about this transgression and wants to ensure that the Desktop tab is permanently revoked.

Because the normal flow of inheritance is site, domain, and then OU, policy settings inside GPOs linked to the domain can trump the "Block Inheritance" definition of the **Human Resources** OU (or any OU). Likewise policy settings inside GPOs linked to the site can trump domain policies. To trump a lower level's "Block Inheritance," a higher-level administrator will use the "Enforced" function.

 Enforced was previously known as "No Override" in old-school parlance.

The idea behind the Enforced function is simple: it guarantees that policies and settings within a specific GPO at a higher level are always inherited by lower levels. It doesn't matter if the lower administrator has blocked inheritance or has a GPO that tries to disable or modify the same policy setting or settings.

In this example, you'll log on as the Domain Administrator and set an edict to force the removal of the Desktop tab from Display settings.

To use Enforced to force the settings within a specific Group Policy Object setting, right-click the "Hide Desktop Tab" GPO link and select Enforced, as shown in Figure 2.10.

FIGURE 2.10   Use the Enforced check box to guarantee settings contained within a specific GPO affect all users downward via inheritance.

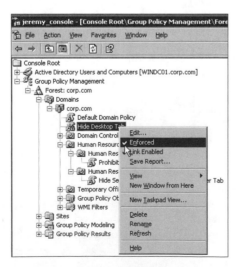

Notice that the GPO link now has a little "lock" icon, demonstrating it cannot be trumped. You can see this in the "Hide Desktop Tab" GPO link icon in Figure 2.10. You'll see a zoomed-in picture of this later in the "GPMC At-a-Glance Icon View" section.

To test your Enforced edict, log on as a user affected by the **Human Resources** OU—Frank Rizzo. In the Display Properties dialog box, the Desktop tab should be absent because it is being forced from the Enforced edict at the domain level even though "Block Inheritance" is used at the OU level.

On Group Policy Object Links and Group Policy Objects Themselves

The GPMC is a cool tool, but, in my opinion, it actually shows you a bit *too* much. Sometimes, it can be confusing what can be performed on the GPO's link and what can be performed on the GPO itself. Remember that GPOs themselves are displayed in the GPMC via the Group Policy Objects container. The links back to them are shown at the site, domain, and OU levels. So here's a list of what you can "do" to a GPO link and what you can "do" to a GPO *itself*.

You can only do three things on a GPO link that applies to a site, a domain, or an OU:

- Link Enable (that is, enable or disable the settings to apply at this level).

- Enforce the link (and force the policy settings).

- Delete the link.

Everything else is always done on the *actual* GPO itself:

- Change the policy settings inside the GPO (found on the Settings tab).

- Apply security filters, rights (such as the "Apply Group Policy" privilege and delegation (such as the "Edit this GPO" privilege) discussed in the "Advanced Security and Delegation with the GPMC" section.

- Enable/disable the computer and/or user half of the GPO via the GPO status (found on the Details tab).

- Place a WMI filter upon the GPO (discussed in Chapter 10).

If this seems clear as mud, consider this scenario:

- Fred and Ginger are the two Domain Administrators. By definition, they are members of the "Group Policy Creator Owners group" and, hence, can create GPOs.

- Imagine that Fred designs the "Desktop Settings" GPO, which contains policy settings that affect both users and computers. Perhaps one user policy setting is **Remove Run off Start Menu**. Perhaps one computer policy setting is **Enforce disk quota limit**. And Fred sets the quota limit to 50MB.

- Fred links the "Desktop Settings" GPO to the **Dancers** OU as well as the **Audition Halls** OU.

- Ginger gets a phone call from the folks in the **Audition Halls** OU. The users in the **Audition Halls** OU report that the 50MB disk quotas are too restrictive. "Can they just turn off the computer-side settings for us Audition Halls folks?" one of them cries.

- Ginger goes to the "Desktop Settings" GPO link (which is linked to the **Audition Halls** OU), clicks the Details tab, and disables the computer settings using the "GPO Status" setting drop-down box.

- Fred then gets a phone call that the **Dancers** OU no longer has disk quotas being applied.

Why did this happen?

Because the Group Policy engine has certain controls on the GPO *itself* and has other controls on the Group Policy *link*. Because Fred and Ginger are both Domain Administrators, they jointly have ownership of the ability to change the GPO and the GPO link.

Whenever Ginger modifies any characteristic in the previous bulleted list, she's changing it "globally" for any place in Active Directory that might be using it. That's what the warning in Figure 2.3, earlier in this chapter, is all about.

If you'll allow me to get on my soap box for the next 10 seconds…the level of finite control over what Ginger can and cannot do to the GPO itself is fairly limited. In the future, I'd love to see the Group Policy engine extended so that we can delegate more aspects of control about the GPO link, not just about the GPO itself.

In any event, delegating what we can control over the GPO itself is precisely what the next section is about, specifically the "Granting User Permissions on a GPO" section.

Advanced Security and Delegation with the GPMC

Mere mortals' access to Group Policy can be and, indeed, should be controlled. Users' access to all things Group Policy related is judged in many forms. However, the first question you'll want to answer and understand well is basic: To whom should Group Policy be applied, and to whom should it not be applied?

Once we can answer that, we can move on to some more advanced topics:

- What kind of access can I grant to mere mortals to manipulate the GPO itself? That is, can a user read or modify the GPO's settings or security?

- How can I grant a mere mortal access to create GPOs in the domain?

- Can a user perform special Group Policy–related stuff, such as the creation and management of WMI filters or access to RSoP tools?

You can answer all these questions by determining what security is placed on Active Directory and specific GPOs. Let's tackle these questions one at a time to locate all the places users' access touches our Group Policy infrastructure and where that access can be managed.

Filtering Group Policy Objects

The normal day-to-day Human Resources workers inside the **Human Resources** OU structure are fine with the facts of life:

- The Enterprise Administrator says that no one at the site will have the Screen Saver tab.

- The Domain Administrator says that no one will have the Desktop tab. He is forcing this edict with the "Enforced" option.

- Frank Rizzo, the **Human Resources** OU Manager, says that for the **Human Resources Users** OU he will remove the Settings tab, but restore the Screen Saver tab. For the **Human Resources Computers** OU, he'll be removing the Scheduled Tasks icon. Additionally, at the top-level **Human Resources** OU, he will enable the "Block Inheritance" setting to give back the Screen Saver tab removed by the Enterprise Administrator at the site level. But Frank is forced to live with the fact that he won't be able to return to his people the Desktop tab that the Domain Administrator has taken away.

But Frank and other members of the HR-OU-Admins Security group are getting frustrated that they cannot access the Settings tab. And they're also getting frustrated that they can't schedule tasks on the machines they use every day. Sure, it was Frank's own idea to make these two policy settings—one that affects the users he's in charge of, and one that affects the computers he's in charge of. The problem is, however, it also affects Frank (and the other members of the HR-OU-Admins team) when they're working, and you can see where that can be annoying.

Frank needs a way to "filter" the "Scope of Management" (*SOM*) of the "Hide Settings Tab/Restore Screen Saver Tab" as well as the "Prohibit new Tasks in Task Scheduler" GPOs. By scope or SOM, I mean "how far and wide" the GPOs we set up will be embraced.

> Occasionally you will see references to SOM in your travels with Group Policy. An SOM is simply a quick-and-dirty way to express where and when a GPO might apply. An SOM can be nearly any combination of things: linking a GPO to the domain, linking a GPO to an OU, and linking a GPO to a site. However, if you start to filter GPOs within the domain, that's also an SOM. In essence, an SOM indicates when and where a GPO applies to a level in Active Directory.

In our case, the idea is twofold:

- Frank and his team are excluded from the "Hide Settings Tab/Restore Screen Saver Tab" GPO edict.

- The specific computers that Frank and his team use are excluded from the "Prohibit new Tasks in Task Scheduler" GPO edict.

Recall from Chapter 1 that, despite the wording of the term *Group Policy*, Group Policy does not directly affect Security groups. You cannot just wrap up a bunch of similar users or computers in a Security group and thrust a GPO upon them. There's nowhere to "link" to. You need to round up the individual user or computer accounts into an OU first and then link the desired GPO on that OU.

Here's the truly strange part: even though you can't round up users in Security groups and apply GPOs to them, it's the Security group that we'll leverage (in most cases) in order to enable us to filter Group Policy application!

In order for users to get GPOs to apply to them, they need two under-the-hood access rights to the GPO itself:

- Read
- Apply Group Policy

These permissions must be set on the GPO in question. By default, all Authenticated Users are granted the "Read" and "Apply Group Policy" rights to all new GPOs. Therefore, anyone who has a GPO geared for them will process it.

How Is a Computer an Authenticated User?

I was shocked to learn that a computer falls under the category of an Authenticated User. It's true: the computer account has the Authenticated User's SID in its access token. I was skeptical, but Über-Guru Bill Boswell (and author of Chapter 7) proved it to me. And you can prove it to yourself by following these steps:

1. Use the at command and specify a time at least one minute ahead of the current time to open a system-level console:

   ```
   at <one minute in the future> /interactive cmd
   ```

2. Use WHOAMI to verify that the cmd has run as System. Now use WHOAMI /ALL to verify that you have the Authenticated Users group in the access token.

Note that the System does not have domain credentials. When it touches another machine, it uses the Kerberos ticket issued to the local computer. You can take advantage of this for this experiment.

1. Set the NTFS permissions on a folder in a shared volume on another machine to deny access to Authenticated Users but allow access by Everyone.

2. Map a drive from the system console to the share point and try to access the contents of the protected folder. You'll be denied access.

Because Deny for Authenticated Users comes before Allow for Everyone, you've proved that the computer account has the Authenticated Users group in its access token.

The following two thing might not be immediately obvious:

- Administrators are not magically exempt from applying Group Policy; they are members inside Authenticated Users. You can change this behavior with the techniques described in the very next section.

- Computers need love too. And for computers to apply their side of the Group Policy Object, they need the same rights: "Read" and "Apply Group Policy." Since computers are technically Authenticated Users, the computer has all it needs to process GPOs meant for it.

With this fundamental concept in mind, let's look at several ways to filter who gets specific GPOs.

If you want to filter GPOs for either specific users or specific computers, you have three distinct approaches. For our three examples (which will all do the exact same thing), we want the "Hide Settings Tab/Restore Screen Saver Tab" GPO to "pass over" our heroes in the HR-OU-Admins security group, but apply to everyone else who should get them. We also want the "Prohibit new Tasks in Task Scheduler" GPO to pass over the specific computers our heroes use at their desks.

Group Policy Object Filtering Approach #1: Leverage the "Security Filtering" Section of the Scope Tab in GPMC

In the first approach, you'll round up only the users, computers, or Security groups who should get the GPO applied to them. To make things easier, we'll create two Active Directory Security groups—one for our users who will get the GPO, and one for computers who will get the GPO. Good names might be People Who Get Hide Settings Tab-Restore Screen Saver Tab GPO and Computers That Get The Prohibit New Tasks In Task Scheduler GPO. You do this in Active Directory Users And Computers as seen in Figure 2.11.

FIGURE 2.11   Create a new Active Directory Security group for whom you want the GPO to apply.

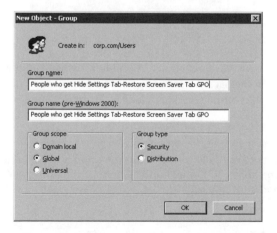

Next, add all user accounts you want to get the GPO into the first Security group. Then, add all computer accounts you want to get the GPO into the second Security group. Because we don't want these GPO to apply to Frank or Frank's computer (XPPRO1), don't add Frank to the first group (which contains users) and don't add XPPRO1 to the second group (which contains computers).

Next, click the link to the "Hide Settings Tab / Restore Screen Saver Tab" GPO found in Group Policy Management ➤ Forest ➤ Corp.com ➤ **Human Resources** OU ➤ **Human Resources Users** OU. In the Security Filtering section, you can see that Authenticated Users is listed. This means that any users inside the **Human Resources Users** OU will certainly get this GPO applied.

However, now we're about to turn the tables. We're going to click the "Remove" button to remove the Authenticated Users in the Security Filtering section; then we're going to add the People Who Get Hide Settings Tab-Restore Screen Saver Tab GPO Security group, as shown in Figure 2.12.

FIGURE 2.12   When you remove "Authenticated Users," no one will get the effects of the GPO. Add only the users or groups you want the GPO to affect.

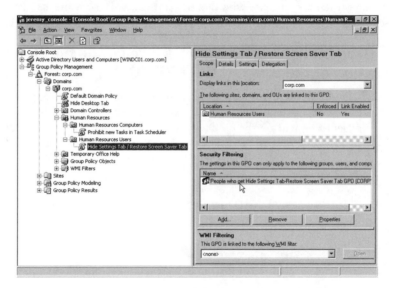

Next, click the "Prohibit new Tasks in Task Scheduler" GPO link (which is under the **Human Resources Computers** OU). In the Security Filtering section of the Scope tab, you'll remove Authenticated Users and add the Computers That Get The Prohibit New Tasks In Task Scheduler GPO Security group.

In both cases, what we're really doing under the hood is giving these new Security groups the ability to "Read" and "Apply Group Policy." You'll see this under-the-hood stuff in a minute.

Testing Your First Filters

To see if this is working, log on to your Windows XP machine as Frank (Frizzo). Even though the GPO applies to the **Human Resources Users** OU, the GPO will pass over him and anyone else not explicitly put into that Security group since Frank is not a member of the People Who Get Hide Settings Tab-Restore Screen Saver Tab GPO Security group.

For another test, add a new user account or two to the **Human Resources Users** OU (via Active Directory Users And Computers.) Then, log on as one of these new users (in the OU) and verify that they, indeed, do not get the GPO. This is because the GPO is only set to apply to members of the security group. Then, add the user to the Security group, and log on again. The GPO will then apply to your test users (inside the Security group) as well. In fact, you can add users to the Security group by simply clicking the Properties button in the Security Filtering section. Doing so opens the Security Group Membership dialog in which you can add or delete users or computers.

Repeat your tests by adding XPPRO1 into the Security group named Computers That Get The Prohibit New Tasks In Task Scheduler GPO. When the computer is in the group, it will apply the GPO. Now, try removing XPPRO1 and see what happens. When the computer is out of the group, the GPO will pass over the computer.

 You might have to reboot the machine or run GPUPDATE /FORCE to immediately see computer-side results.

What's Going on Under the Hood for Filtering

As I implied, when you add Security groups to get the GPOs in the "Security Filtering" section, you're really doing a bit of magic under the hood. Again, that magic is simply granting two security permissions: "Read" and "Apply Group Policy" to the users or Security groups that you want to apply the GPOs in the OU.

To see which security permissions are really set under the hood for a particular GPO (or GPO link, because it's the same information), click the Delegation tab and select the Advanced button as shown in Figure 2.13.

FIGURE 2.13 Selecting "Advanced" in the Delegation tab for the GPO (or GPO link) shows the under-the-hood security settings for the GPO.

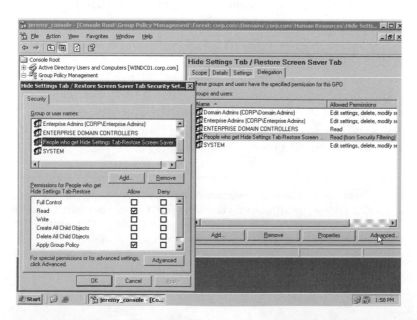

When you do, you can see the actual permission on the GPO itself. You can easily locate the Security group named People Who Get Hide Settings Tab-Restore Screen Saver Tab GPO and see that they have both the "Read" and "Apply Group Policy" access rights set to "Allow." This is why they will process this GPO.

Filtering Approach #2: Identify Who You Do Not Want to Get the Policy

The other approach, typically used in environments that do not use the GPMC, is to leave the default definition in for the GPO such that the "Authenticated Users" group is granted the "Read" and "Apply Group Policy." Then, figure out who you *do not* want to get the policy applied to them, and use the "Deny" attribute over the "Apply Group Policy" right.

When Windows security is evaluated, the designated users or computers will not be able to process the GPO due to the "Deny" attribute; hence, the GPO passes over them.

See the "Positive or Negative" sidebar later in this chapter before doing this in your real environment.

For our examples, we want the "Hide Settings Tab/Restore Screen Saver Tab" GPO to pass over our heroes in the HR-OU-Admins Security group, but apply to everyone else by default. We also want the "Prohibit new Tasks in Task Scheduler" GPO to pass over the specific computers our heroes use at their desks.

To use this second technique, we'll use the "Deny" permission to ensure that the HR-OU-Admins Security group cannot apply (and hence process) the "Hide Settings Tab/Restore Screen Saver Tab" GPO. We'll also additionally prevent Frank's computer, XPPro1, from processing the "Prohibit new Tasks in Task Scheduler" GPO.

Again, you'll do this on the GPO (or the GPO link, because it's the same information), click the Delegation tab, and then click the Advanced button. Follow these steps:

1. Locate the "People who get Hide Settings Tab-Restore Screen Saver Tab GPO" Security group and remove it.

2. Locate the "Authenticated Users" group, select the "Read" permission, select Allow, select "Apply Group Policy" permission, and select Allow.

3. If you used Frank's account to originally create this GPO, he is specifically listed in the security list. You want to remove Frank and add the HR-OU-Admins group. Click Frank, and then click Remove. Click Add, and add the HR-OU-Admins group.

4. Make sure the "Apply Group Policy" check box is set to "Deny" for the HR-OU-Admins group, as shown in Figure 2.14.

Do not set the Deny check box for the "Read" or "Write" attributes from the HR-OU-Admins (the group you're currently a member of when logged in as Frank). If you do, you'll essentially lock yourself out, and you'll have to ask the Domain Administrator to grant you access again.

FIGURE 2.14 Use the "Deny" bit to prevent Group Policy from applying.

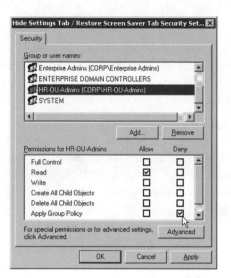

5. Click OK to close the Group Policy Settings dialog box. In the warning box that tells you to be careful about Deny permissions, click Yes.

6. Click OK to close the OU Properties dialog box.

To test your first filter again, log on to XPPro1 as Frank Rizzo. Note that the Settings tab has returned to him because he is part of the HR-OU-Admins group. The "Hide Settings Tab/ Restore Screen Saver Tab" GPO has passed over him because he is unable to process the GPO.

To bypass "Prohibit new Tasks in Task Scheduler" GPO on XPPro1, you'll perform a similar function. That is, you'll modify the security on the GPO to pass over the computers our heroes use by denying those specific computer accounts the ability to "Apply Group Policy." You can then test your second filter by logging on as anyone to XPPro1. You should be able to create new tasks in the Task Scheduler.

> If you want to filter many machines, you can just as easily create a Security group for the computers and deny the "Apply Group Policy" right to the entire group. It's just like you did for the HR-OU-Admins group, but, instead, think of putting computers in their own Security group.

Turns out, however, there's a major problem by using the aforementioned method. That is, if you performed the previous exercise and used the "Deny" attribute to pass over the HR-OU-Admins group using the Security on the GPO, you've got a small problem. Sure, it worked! That's the good news. The bad news is that GPMC isn't smart enough to interpret quite what you did back on the "Scope Tab" in the "Security Filtering" section as shown in Figure 2.15.

Positive or Negative?

Now that you can see the two ways to filter users from processing GPOs, which should you use? Approach 1 (adding only those you want to get the GPO) or Approach 2 (denying only those you don't want to get the GPO)? The data reflected within the GPMC's Scope tab clearly wants you to take the first approach. However, many Active Directory implementations I know take the second approach (and, in fact, it was my advice to do so in the first edition of this book.)

Now, you and your team need to make a choice for your approach. As you saw, when you create new GPOs, you can choose to filter via the Scope tab or the Advanced Delegation. So which do you choose? If you're going to be religious about using the first approach, you can then be reasonably confident that only the users, groups, and computers listed in the Security Filtering section of the Scope tab will, in fact, be the only users, groups, and computers who will get the GPO. You can then reduce your need to dive into the Security Editor as seen in Figures 2.13 and 2.14, earlier in this chapter.

However, if you (or other administrators) occasionally choose to use the "Deny" attribute upon users, computers, and groups from getting the GPO, you'll need to additionally inspect the Advanced Security Editor dialog in the Delegation tab as in Figures 2.13 and 2.14 earlier in this chapter.

The GPMC clearly encourages you to use Approach #1 for filtering. If you have older GPOs in your Active Directory that already use Approach #2 for filtering, consider changing it so that GPMC's Scope tab will actually reflect who will get the GPO.

FIGURE 2.15 The Security Filtering section on the Scope tab will not show you any use of "Deny" bits under the hood.

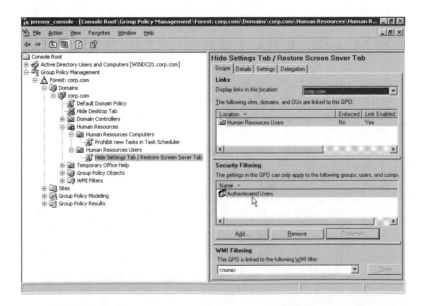

Yes, it's technically true what the Security Filtering section says: Authenticated Users will apply this GPO. However, it doesn't tell us the other important fact: that the HR-OU-Admins group will not process this GPO, because they were denied the ability to "Apply Group Policy."

The only way to get the full, true story of who will actually get the GPO applied to them is to look back within the GPO (or GPO link, because it's the same information), select the Delegation tab, and click the Advanced button to see who has "Read" and "Apply" Group Policy; then also see who is denied access to process the GPO via the "Deny" attributes.

The moral of the story? Always consult the Advanced tab to get the true story as to the security on the GPO.

Granting User Permissions upon an Existing Group Policy Object

You already know the three criteria for someone to be able to edit or modify an existing GPO:

- They are a member of the Domain Admins group.

- They are a member of the Enterprise Admins group.

- They created the GPO themselves and hence are the owner. (We saw this in Figure 1.22 in Chapter 1 when Frank couldn't edit the GPOs he didn't create.)

But sometimes, you also want to add rights to a user upon a GPO so that they can modify it. As we foreshadowed, the Delegation tab for a GPO (or GPO link, which reflects the same information) has a second purpose: to help you grant permissions to groups or users over the security properties of that GPO. If you click Add on the Delegation tab, you can grant any mere mortal user or group (even in other domains) the ability to manipulate this GPO, as seen in Figure 2.16.

FIGURE 2.16   The Delegation tab helps you set permissions on a GPO.

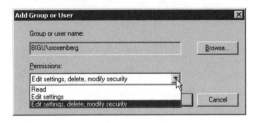

Once the permissions settings have been applied, the user has that level of rights over the GPO, as seen in Table 2.1.

TABLE 2.1   GPMC vs. Genuine Active Directory permissions

Permissions Option	Actual Under-the-Hood Permissions
"Read"	Sets the Allow permission for "Read" on the GPO.
"Edit settings"	Sets the Allow permission for "Read," "Write," "Create Child Objects," and "Delete Child Objects."
"Edit settings, delete, modify security"	Sets the Allow permission for "Read," "Write," "Create Child Objects," "Delete Child Objects," "Delete," "Modify Permissions," and "Modify Owner." This is near-equivalent to full control on the GPO, but note that "Apply Group Policy" access permission is not set. (This can be useful to set for administrators so they can manipulate the GPO but not have it apply to themselves.)
"Read (from Security Filtering)"	This isn't a permission located in the ACL Editor (see Fig 2.14); rather this is only visible if the user has "Read" and "Apply Group Policy" permissions on the GPO. This is a reflection of what is on the Scope tab.
Custom	Any other combinations of rights, including the use of the Deny permission. Custom rights are only added via the ACL editor but can be removed here. They can be removed using the Remove button as in the Delegation tab.

Granting Group Policy Object Creation Rights in the Domain

As you learned in Chapter 1, a user cannot create new GPOs unless that user is a member of the Group Policy Creator Owners group. Dropping a user into this group is one of two ways you can grant this right.

However, the GPMC introduces another way to grant users the ability to have Group Policy Creator Owner–style access. Traverse to the Group Policy Objects container as seen in Figure 2.17, and click the Delegation tab. You can now click Add and select any user, including any user in your domain, say a user named Joe User, or users across forests, such as Sol Rosenberg, who is in a domain called bigu.edu. As you can see in Figure 2.17, both users have been added.

This can be handy if you have trusted administrators in other domains that you want to have create GPOs in your domain. You might want to round them up into a group (instead of just listing them individually as Sol is listed here), but that's your option.

FIGURE 2.17   You can choose to delegate to users in your domain, in other domains, or in domains in other forests.

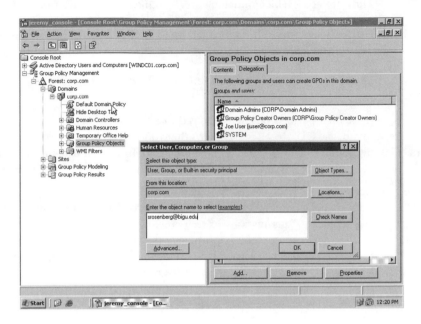

Special Group Policy Operation Delegations

You can delegate three special permissions at the domain and OU levels, and you can set one of those three special permissions at the site level. Clicking the level, such as an OU, and then clicking the Delegation tab for that level shows the available permissions as seen in Figure 2.18.

FIGURE 2.18   These operations are equivalent to the Active Directory Users And Computers "Delegation Wizard."

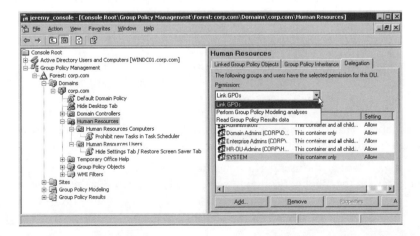

The interface is a bit confusing here. Specifically, you must first select the permission from the drop-down box. This lists the current users who can have permissions to use the right. You can then click the "Add," "Remove," or "Advanced" button to make your changes.

There are three Permissions that may be selected from the dropdown box, as seen in Figure 2.18. They are:

Linking GPOs   Of the three permissions here, this is the only permission that can be configured at all levels: site, domain, and OU. Recall in Chapter 1 that you ran the Active Directory Users And Computers "Delegation of Control Wizard" (see Figure 1.19). Instead of using Active Directory Users And Computers to perform that task, the GPMC can do the same job—right here.

Perform Group Policy Modeling Analyses   This right performs the same function as if we had used the Active Directory Users And Computers "Delegation of Control Wizard" to grant the "Generate Resultant Set of Policy (Planning)" permissions, as seen previously in Figure 1.18. The next section describes how to get more data about what's happening at the client. You'll see how to use this power in the "What-If Calculations with Group Policy Modeling" section later in this chapter. Group Policy Modeling lets you simulate what-if scenarios regarding users and computers.

By default, only Domain Admins have the right to perform this task. Domain Admins can grant other users or groups the ability to perform this function, such as the Help Desk, HR-OU-Admins, or your own desktop-administrator teams. You can choose to grant people the ability to perform Group Policy Modeling analyses on this specific container or this specific container and child containers. When you assign this right, the user performing the Group Policy Modeling analysis must have the delegated right upon the container containing the what-if user and also the container containing the what-if computer. If you don't grant rights in both containers, only half the analysis is displayed.

This right is available only if the domain schema has been updated for Windows 2003. Additionally, Group Policy Modeling analyses function only when at least one Windows 2003 Domain Controller is available in the domain.

Read Group Policy Results Data   This right performs the same function as if we used the Active Directory Users And Computers "Delegation of Control Wizard" to grant the "Generate Resultant Set of Policy (Logging)" permission, as seen previously in Figure 1.18. You'll see how to use this power in the "What's-Going-On Calculations with Group Policy Results" section later in this chapter. However, if you want to grant this power to others, you can. Again, a typical use is to grant this right to the Help Desk or other administrative authority.

When you assign this right, the user performing the Group Policy Results analysis must have the delegated right upon the container containing the target computer. Or this right can be applied at a parent container, and the rights will flow down via inheritance. The user must also have this right delegated upon any container containing any users who have logged on to the machine you want to analyze. If you don't grant rights in both containers, no analysis is displayed.

This right is available only if the domain schema has been updated for Windows 2003.

Who Can Create and Use WMI Filters?

Okay, okay, okay. I know the subject of WMI filters has come up before about 3000 times already, and every time I refer you, the poor reader, to Chapter 10. Once you've read what they are and how to create them in Chapter 10, please come back here and read how to manage them.

Two types of people are involved in the management of WMI filters:

- Those who can create them
- Those who can use them

Delegating Who Can Create WMI Filters

By default, only the Domain Administrator can create WMI filters. However, you might have some WMI whiz-kid in your company (and it's a good chance this isn't the same person as the Domain Administrator.) With that in mind, the Domain Administrator can grant that special someone the ability to create WMI filters. To do this, drill down to the domain ➢ WMI Filters node, and then select Delegation in the pane on the right. You can now grant one of two rights, as shown in Figure 2.19.

FIGURE 2.19   These are controls over the creation of WMI filters.

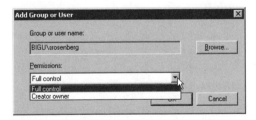

In Figure 2.19, we can see the two rights that appear in the drop-down box:

- Once a user has "Creator Owner" rights here, they can create and modify their own WMI filters, but they cannot modify others' WMI filters.
- A user with "Full Control" rights here can create and modify their own WMI filters or anyone else's.

> These rights are available only if the domain schema has been updated for Windows 2003.

Delegating Who Can Use WMI Filters

Once WMI filters are created (again, see Chapter 10), you'll likely want to assign who can apply them to specific GPOs. To do this, drill down to the specific WMI filter, as shown in Figure 2.20. Then click Add, and you'll see that two rights are available for the user you want.

FIGURE 2.20   These are controls over the WMI filters themselves.

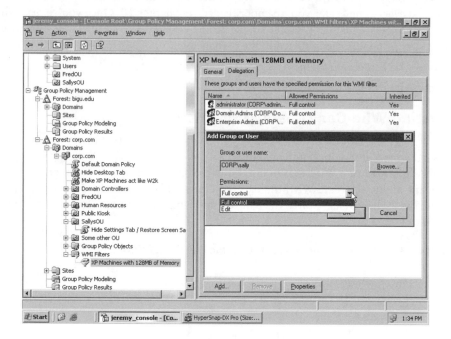

In Figure 2.20, we can see the two rights that appear in the drop-down box:

- Once a user has "Edit" rights here, they can edit and tailor the filter, as we do in Chapter 10.
- A user with "Full Control" rights here can edit the filter as well as delete it and modify the security (that is, specify who else can get "Edit" or "Full Control" rights here).

> These rights are available only if the domain schema has been updated for Windows 2003.

Performing RSoP Calculations with the GPMC

In Chapter 1, we charted out a fictitious organization's GPO structure on paper. We looked and saw when various GPOs were going to apply to various user and computers. Charting out the RSoP (Resultant Set of Policies) for users and computers on paper is a handy skill for basic understanding of GPO organization and flow; but in the real world, you'll need a tool that can help you actually figure out what's going on at your client desktops.

The GPMC has a handy feature to show us all the GPOs that are going to apply for the users and computers at a specific level in Active Directory. In Figure 2.21, when you click the **Human Resources Users** OU and then click the "Group Policy Inheritance" tab, you can see a list of all the GPOs that should apply to the **Human Resource Users** OU.

FIGURE 2.21   The Group Policy Inheritance tab shows you which GPOs should apply.

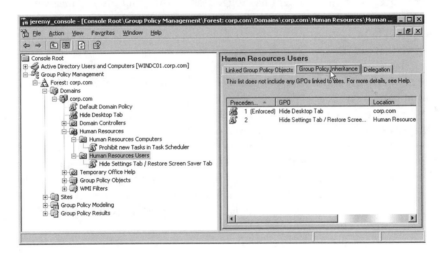

The site level is not shown in this Group Policy Inheritance tab. Because computers, particularly laptops, can travel from site to site, it is impossible to know for sure what site to represent here.

As I said, this tab in Figure 2.21 should really tell you what's going to happen. The operative word here is *should*. That's because a lot can go wrong between your wishes and what actually happens on the client systems. For instance, you already saw how to filter GPOs using Security groups, which would certainly change the experience of one user versus another on the very same machine. And in Chapter 10, you'll learn about WMI filters, which limit when GPOs are applied even more.

The point of all this RSoP stuff is help us know the score about what's going on at machines that could be many hundreds of millimeters, meters, or kilometers away. When users freak out about getting settings they don't expect or when they freak out about lacking settings they expect, the point is to know which setting is causing the stir and which GPO is to blame for the errant setting.

We know one thing's for sure: users do freak out a lot if anything changes; and it's our job to douse water on the problem (but not the user or computer). So the point of performing an RSoP calculation is to help you know what is going on and why it's going on that way. The GPMC can help with that.

What's-Going-On Calculations with Group Policy Results

If someone calls you to report that an unexpected GPO is applying, you can find out what's going on via the GPMC. You can find out what's going on if the machine in question is a Windows XP, Windows 2003, and presumably later client. Sorry, Windows 2000 computers are left in the dust.

Windows 2000 computers are not left in the dust for the what-if calculations with Group Policy Modeling in the next section.

Once the user with the problem has logged on to the machine in question, you can tap into the WMI provider built in to both Windows XP and Windows 2003. Without going too propeller-head here, the upshot of this magic is that the GPMC (and the GPRESULT command as you'll see in Chapter 4) can "pretend" to be any particular user that has ever logged on locally. It's then a simple matter to display the sexy results within the GPMC.

The magic happens when the computer asking "What's going on?" (in this case, the computer running the GPMC) asks the target client computer. The target client computer responds with a result of what has happened—which GPOs were applied to the computer side and to the user side (provided the user has ever, at least once, logged on).

Let me expand on this important point: this Group Policy Results magic only works if the target user has ever logged on to the target machine. They only need to have ever logged on once, and they don't need to be logged on while you run the test. But if the target user has never logged on to the target machine, the Group Policy Results will not allow you to select that user.

You can run your what's-going-on calculations inside the GPMC by right-clicking the Group Policy Results node at the bottom of the GPMC's hierarchy as shown in Figure 2.22. When you do, you can select the user and the computer and see their interaction.

FIGURE 2.22   The Group Policy Results Wizard performs What's-going-on calculations.

You need to remember the following before trying to run the Group Policy Results Wizard to figure out what's going on:

- The computer must be Windows XP, Windows 2003, or later. Windows 2000 machines are left out of the fun here.

- The computer you want to pretend to log on to must be actually turned on and on the network. If this is not the case, you'll get an error regarding this fact. It will state that it cannot contact the WMI service via RPC.

- The Windows Management Instrumentation service must be started.

- The user you want to find out about must have logged on to the target computer *at least once* to be eligible to perform a Group Policy Results calculation.

The output generated from the GPMC version when performing Group Policy Results RSoP calculations is quite powerful, as shown in Figure 2.23.

FIGURE 2.23   The Group Policy Results report shows lots of useful information.

Similar to the Settings tab, you can expand and contract the report by clicking Show and Side. Inside, you can clearly see which GPOs have been applied and any major errors along the way. At a glance you can see which GPOs have Applied and which were Denied (passed over) for whatever reason, such as filtering or that one-half of the GPO was empty.

The WMI filters category (shown in Figure 2.23) will not display data unless the target machine is running Windows 2003 or Windows XP with SP2.

If you click the Settings tab here, you get an extra bonus. That is, if there are conflicts along the scope of the GPO, you can see which other GPOs "won" in the contest for the ultimate Group Policy smackdown! Indeed, you can see this in Figure 2.24. Note, however, the GPMC doesn't show you which GPOs "lost" when there is a conflict. This can sometimes mean more troubleshooting to determine other GPOs with conflicting settings. In Chapter 4, you'll learn how to locate "losing" GPOs.

FIGURE 2.24   If specific settings conflict, you can quickly determine which GPO "wins."

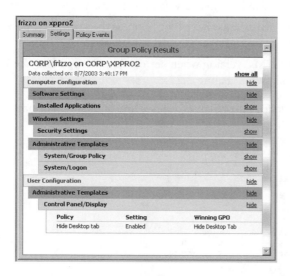

FIGURE 2.25   The Policy Events tab shows you events specific to this target computer.

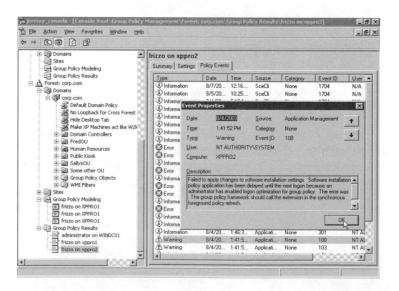

Additionally useful here is the Policy Events tab, which will dive into the target machine's Event Viewer and pull out the events related to GPOs, as shown in Figure 2.25. Just double-click the event to open it. Talk about handy!

In the actual description of this specific event code, the text states that "an administrator has enabled logon optimization." This is really talking about Windows XP's "fast boot" and is enabled by default. You'll learn more about Windows XP and fast boot in Chapter 3.

The GPMC will also save the query so you can reuse it later if you want to retest your assumptions. For example, you might want to retry this after you've corrected your Software Installation failure, added a new GPO to the mix, or moved a machine from one OU to another.

If you move a computer from one OU to another, you might not get the correct results right away, because the computer may not immediately recognize that it has been moved. If you move a computer from one OU to another, you might want to reboot the machine to get accurate results right away. This is further discussed in Chapter 3.

What-If Calculations with Group Policy Modeling

Finding out what's going on is useful if someone calls you in a panic. However, you might also want to plan for the future. For instance, would you be able to easily determine what would happen to the users inside the **Human Resources Users** OU if a somewhat indiscriminately named GPO called "Desktop Settings" was linked to it? Maybe or maybe not. (With a horribly named GPO like that, likely not.)

Or, what might happen if Frank Rizzo took a trip to another site? Which GPOs would apply to him then? Or which GPOs would apply if the HR-OU-Admins were granted (or revoked) different security rights? The Oracle, er, the Group Policy Modeling Wizard found in the GPMC can answer a million of these questions. It's job is to answer "What happens if?"

This function is available only if the domain schema has been updated for Windows 2003 and you have at least one Windows 2003 Domain Controller available. This is because a Windows 2003 Domain Controller runs a process that must be running for the calculation to occur.

The best news about What-If calculations is that Windows 2000 computers aren't left out of the picture. The most accurate answers are achieved with Windows XP and Windows 2003 machines as clients because, again, they tap directly into the computer's soul with the WMI providers for GPOs. Windows 2000 doesn't have this provider, so a "best guess" is used in calculation.

Windows XP–specific features and WMI filters are ignored when Windows 2000 clients are used with modeling calculations.

The only catch to this magic is that when you want to run What-If modeling calculations, the processing of the calculations must actually occur on a Windows 2003 Domain Controller. Even if you have the GPMC loaded on a Windows XP client, you'll still have to make contact with a Windows 2003 Domain Controller to assist in the calculations.

This is the biggest warning icon the publisher gives me, but it isn't big enough for this message. If your Windows 2003 domain has been upgraded from Windows 2000, and you want to perform Group Policy Modeling between domains, it is likely it will not work without some manual attention. There are ACL permission problems on GPOs upon performing a domain upgrade. To fix the problem in a flash you run the `GrantPermissionOnAllGPOs.wsf` script that is included with the GPMC. Specifically, you run `cscript GrantPermissionOnAllGPOs.wsf "Enterprise Domain Controllers"` This will "touch" all GPOs in SYSVOL, which will force replication to all Domain Controllers and, hence, may cause a lot of network traffic. This could be an issue with large or many GPOs.

You can kick off a modeling session by right-clicking the domain or any OU (as well as the "Group Policy Modeling" node and selecting "Group Policy Modeling Wizard" When you do, you'll be presented with the Group Policy Modeling Wizard Welcome screen.

You then choose which Windows 2003 Domain Controller will have the honor of performing the calculation for you. It doesn't matter which Windows 2003 Domain Controller you choose— even those in other domains. Just pick one. Just note that it does need to be a Windows 2003 Domain Controller and not anything less.

You'll then get to play Zeus and determine what would happen if you plucked a user and/ or computer out of a current situation and modified the circumstances. In the wizard screens, you get to choose the following:

- Which user and/or computer you want to start to play with

- Whether to pretend to apply slow-link processing (if not already present on the target)

- Whether to pretend to apply loopback processing (if not already present on the target)

- The site in which you want to pretend the object is starting

- Where to move the user (if the user account moves at all)

- Where to move the computer (if it moves at all)

- Whether to pretend to change the user's Security group membership

- Whether to pretend to change the computer's Security group membership

- Whether to pretend to apply WMI filters for users of computers (if not already present on the target)

You will likely get inaccurate results if you try to do something that isn't really possible. For instance, you can force the wizard into seeing what happens if Frank Rizzo's account is moved to another domain. But, since there isn't a way to actually move Frank's account, the displayed results will be cockeyed. You'll learn more about some of the new concepts, such as slow-link processing and loopback processing in Chapter 3. You'll learn more about WMI filters in Chapter 10.

The output in Figure 2.26 shows what would happen if Frank Rizzo were to be removed from the **Human Resources Users** OU (and plopped into the root of the domain).

FIGURE 2.26   You can simulate moving a computer and/or a user to other locations, among other scenarios.

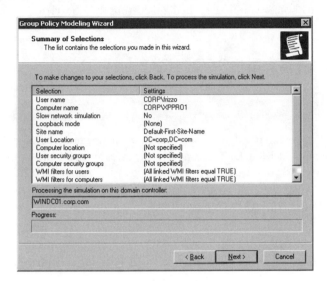

What to Expect from the Group Policy Modeling Wizard

When you first use the Group Policy Modeling Wizard, you may surprised to see that it has "Loopback," "WMI Filters," and "Slow Links" options. At first I was curious about why these were options in the wizard—if the wizard's whole job is to figure out what will be at the end of the simulation.

In a nutshell, the Group Policy Modeling Wizard allows you to simulate these additional items as if they all were *actually* going to be true. This way, you wouldn't have to create an OU and/ or a GPO with the specific policy settings (Loopback, and so on) *just* to turn it on. This makes sense: if you enable these options on the real OU, you change the live environment.

The point of the Group Policy Modeling Wizard is to let you just simulate what if you did this on the target. When using the wizard and selecting Loopback, Slow Links, or WMI Filters, don't expect it to tell you that any of these things are true in the target. The simulation will be correct if the target does have these properties, or you can additionally simulate what would happen if these properties came into the mix.

When the calculations are complete, you'll get a results dialog that looks quite similar to Figures 2.23 and 2.24. There, you can see how results will be displayed in both a Summary and Settings tabs. As a reminder, the Summary tab shows you which GPOs applied; the Settings tab shows you which policies inside the GPOs will "win" if there's a conflict. Present only in Group Policy Modeling output (not shown) is another item, called the Query tab, which can remind you of the choices you made when generating the query.

Backing Up and Restoring Group Policy Objects

Inadvertently deleting a single GPO can wreak havoc on your domain. Imagine what happens when a bunch of GPOs are inadvertently deleted. Let's just say that the users are suddenly happy because they can do stuff they couldn't, and you're not happy because now they're happy. Ironic, isn't it?

An administrator inadvertently deleting a portion of a SYSVOL container of one Domain Controller will quickly damage your GPOs, and you'll need a way to restore.

The Backup and Restore functions for GPOs only work within the same domain. However, you'll see in the Appendix how the GPMC can be used to "Copy" and "Import" a GPO to get the same effect between domains.

In our cases, if the policy settings inside the "Hide Settings Tab / Restore Screen Saver Tab" GPO were wiped out, the name of the GPO can surely help us put it back together. But the name alone might not be an accurate representation of what's really going on inside the GPO.

Then, there are still other questions: To what was this GPO linked? What was the security on the GPO? And other GPOs in your domain might configure some complex stuff such as IPSEC, Internet Explorer Maintenance settings, or Folder Redirection.

All said and done, you don't want to get stuck with a deleted or damaged GPO without a backup. Thankfully, the GPMC makes easy work of the once-laborious task of backing up and restoring GPOs.

These techniques are valid for both Windows 2000 and Windows 2003 domains, as I stated in the Introduction. So, back up those GPOs today with the GPMC regardless of your domain structure!

Backing Up Group Policy Objects

When you back up a GPO within the GPMC, you also back up a lot of important data:

- The settings inside the GPO
- The permissions upon that GPO (that is, the stuff inside the Delegation tab)

- The link to the WMI filter—however, the actual filter itself is not preserved. (Again, I'll talk about WMI filters in Chapter 10.) The WMI filter itself is contained within Active Directory. You must back it up separately. You can see one way to do this in the "Backing Up and Restoring WMI Filters" section later in this chapter.

As you'll learn in Chapter 4, there are two parts of GPOs: the GPT (Group Policy Template) from Active Directory and the GPC (Group Policy Container) from within the SYSVOL. When a backup is performed, the GPT and GPC are wrapped up and placed as a set of files that can be stored or transported.

What's additionally neat is that contained within the backup is a report of the settings inside that GPO you just backed up. So, if someone backs up a GPO named "Desktop Settings" (again, a horrible name), you can at least see the report of just what is inside the GPO before you restore it to your domain.

To back up a GPO, you need "Read" access to that GPO, as shown earlier in an example back at Figure 2.16. You can start by locating the GPO node in the GPMC and right-clicking it. Select either "Back up All" or "Manage Backups." For this first time, select "Back up All."

You then select the location for the backup (hopefully some place secure) and click Backup. You'll then see each GPO being backed up to the target location as shown in Figure 2.27. When you're finished, you can rest easy (or at least easier) that your GPOs are safe.

You can inspect the directories the backup produced if you like. You'll see a directory for each GPO, the XML file representing the GPT, and an XML report showing the settings. In the next section, you'll learn how to view the report (easily) by utilizing the "View settings" button (as shown in Figure 2.28).

FIGURE 2.27   You can back up all your GPOs at once, if desired.

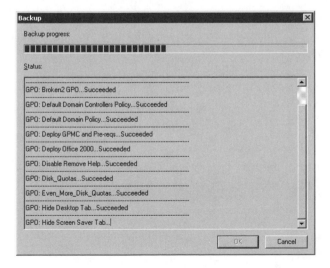

In Chapter 4, we'll learn more about the underlying "nuts and bolts" of GPOs. Specifically, you'll learn that the underlying name of a GPO relies on a unique GUID name being assigned to the GPO. What isn't immediately obvious here is that the directory names produced by the backup (which take the form of GUIDs) are *not* the same GUIDs that are actually used for the underlying identification of the GPO. These are additional, unique, random GUID directory names generated just for backup. This seemingly bizarre contradiction becomes useful, when you read the next paragraph.

The backup is quick, painless, and rather reasonably sized. The best part about the backup facility is that it's flexible. When you choose to run your next backup, you can keep your backups in the same directory you just choose, and you'll keep a history of the GPOs, should anything change. It's the underlying random and unique GUID names for the directories that allow you to keep plowing more GPO backups right into the same backup directory—there's no fear of overlap. Or you can keep the backups in their own directory; it's your choice.

If you dare, go ahead and delete the "Hide Settings Tab / Restore Screen Saver Tab" GPO. You'll restore it in the next section (I hope).

Now that you've backed up the whole caboodle, it should also be noted that you can back up just a solitary GPO. Right-click the *actual* GPO (which is located only in the Group Policy Objects container) and choose Backup. In Chapter 7, you'll find a script that enables you to script and automate your backups.

Restoring Group Policy Objects

The restore process is just as easy. It works for GPOs that were backed up in the same domain. Note that it's also possible to back up and restore between domains, but this is called a GPO Migration (see the Appendix).

When you restore a GPO, the file object you created in the backup process is "unrolled" and placed upon Active Directory. As you would expect, the following key elements are preserved:

- The settings inside the GPO
- The friendly name (which comes back from the dead)
- The GUID (which comes back from the dead)
- The security and permissions on that object (which come back from the dead)
- The link to WMI filters (which comes back from the dead)

Whomping a GPO doesn't delete the WMI filter itself. The filter is stored in a separate place in Active Directory.

The GPO does not have to be deleted to do a restore. For instance, if someone changed the settings and you want to simply restore the GPO to get an older version of the policy settings, you can certainly restore over an existing GPO to put a previously known "good" version back in play.

Restoring GPOs requires the following security rights:

- If you want to restore on top of a GPO that already exists, you need Edit, Delete, and Modify rights, as seen back in Figure 2.16.

- If you want to restore a deleted GPO, you need to be a member of the Group Policy Creator Owners security group.

Warning: Your Links Aren't Backed Up

Assuming you went ahead in the last example and deleted the "Hide Settings Tab / Restore Screen Saver Tab" GPO and are now ready to restore it, there is something you need to know before proceeding. That is, one critical item is missing: the Group Policy links to the GPO are *not* restored in this operation. The links are not backed up, and the links are not restored. You'll need a way to know where your GPOs are linked before the GPO is deleted.

This way, when the GPO is actually deleted, you can manually relink the GPOs back to the sites, domains, and/or OUs to which the policy should be linked! Without the knowledge of where your GPO needs to be relinked, you're restore isn't even remotely complete!

I have two suggestions to help collect this knowledge:

- Whip out a piece of paper and make notes about where your GPOs are linked.

- In Chapter 7, locate the "Documenting GPO Links and WMI Filter Links" section. The information there will save your bacon!! Set it up with a Scheduled Task to run, say, every six hours, to make notes about where your GPOs are linked.

Now, when you perform the restore, you'll have the GPO back in the swimming pool and additional documentation in hand as to where the GPO was linked. Just manually replace the links based on your documentation, and you're done! You'll save the day. I guarantee it!

You can start a restore by right-clicking the Group Policy Objects container and choosing "Manage Backups." You'll be able to select a location from which to locate your GPO backups; you might have multiple locations.

If you've chosen to keep backing up the GPOs into the same backup directory, you can select the "Show only the latest version of each GPO" option, which shows you only the last backed-up version. If you've forgotten what is contained in a backup, simply click the backup name and choose "View settings." You can see these options in Figure 2.28.

FIGURE 2.28   You can see all backups or just the latest versions.

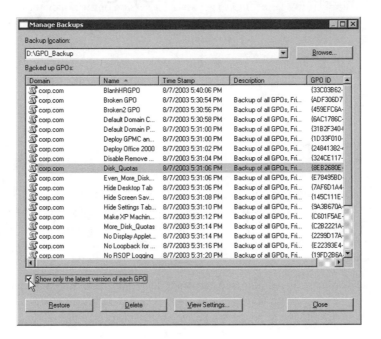

When ready, click the GPO to restore, and then click Restore. It's really that easy.

> You can also right-click the GPO itself (found only in the Group Policy Objects container) and choose "Restore from Backup," which in fact performs the same function. (See Chapter 7 for a script that will enable you to script and automate your restores.)

Backing Up and Restoring WMI Filters

As you read about WMI filters in Chapter 10 and learn what a pain in the tush they are to create, you'll be thankful that there's a mechanism that can back up and restore them. They are not backed up or restored in the process we just used. Rather, you must individually back up each WMI filter. Simply right-click the filter, and choose Export. To restore, right-click WMI Filters node and choose Import. Sometimes restoring a WMI filter adds excess and invalid characters to the query. Simply re-edit the query and clean up the characters, and you're back in business.

In the previous section, you saw that GPO links are not restored when the GPO is restored. The same is true for WMI filters: the WMI Filter links are not restored when the WMI filter is restored. Again, for information on how to automatically document this information, see Chapter 7.

Searching for Group Policy Objects with the GPMC

As your Active Directory grows, so will your use of GPOs. However, sometimes remembering the one GPO that you used to do some magic a while ago can be difficult. To that end, the GPMC has some basic searching functionality.

With the search feature, you can search for GPOs with any (and all) of the following characteristics:

- Display name (that is, friendly name)
- GUID
- Permissions on the GPO itself
- A link, if it exists (used in conjunction with the name, and so on)
- WMI filters used
- Specific client-side-extensions if they were used for either the user or computer side

To search for a GPO that matches the characteristics you're after, right-click the domain and choose Search. In the Search Item dialog box, enter your criteria in the condition fields. The Value field will change based on the Search Item field. In Figure 2.29 I'm searching corp.com for all GPOs with the word *Hide* in the name.

FIGURE 2.29   You can locate GPOs with lots of characteristics.

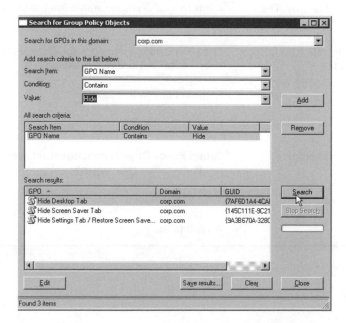

The one thing this search engine cannot do is to poke through the each and every GPO to see where you enabled some policy setting.

GPMC At-a-Glance Icon View

Because the GPMC contains so many icon types, it can be confusing to know specifically what an icon represents. That's what Table 2.2 is all about.

TABLE 2.2   GPMC icon list

Icon	Description	What the Icon Means
	Scroll.	A GPO itself. You'll only see this in the Group Policy Objects container.
	Scroll with arrow.	A link to an actual GPO.
	Scroll with arrow. Just the arrow is dimmed.	GPO link that has Link Status disabled.
	Scroll with arrow. The whole icon is dimmed.	A link to a GPO whose status (on the Details tab) has been set to "All settings disabled."
	Scroll. Whole icon is dimmed.	The GPO whose status (on the Details tab) has been set to "All settings disabled."
	Scroll with arrow; gray lock.	Enforced link to this level.
	Blue exclamation point.	Block inheritance at this level.
	Folder with scroll.	Group Policy Objects container that actually holds the GPOs themselves.
	Folder with filter.	WMI Filters node.
	Filter.	A WMI filter.

The GPMC At-a-Glance Compatibility Table

You learned a lot in this chapter. Sometimes it can be confusing to know just when a feature is compatible with your setup in the office or the test lab. Hopefully, Table 2.3 will clear things up.

TABLE 2.3   Group Policy Functionality compatibility table

Function	Requirement	Where Discussed
Create and link GPOs and apply them to client systems	Any Active Directory domain plus Windows 2000, Windows XP, and/or Windows 2003 clients.	Chapter 1
Load the GPMC console	Any Active Directory domain plus Windows XP/ SP1 or Windows 2003 to load GPMC.	Chapters 1 and 2
Back up and restore GPOs	Any Active Directory domain plus GPMC console.	Chapter 2
Transfer (migrate) GPOs between same forest	Any Active Directory domain plus GPMC console.	Appendix
Run Group Policy Results reports	Any Active Directory domain plus GPMC console. Targets must be Windows or Windows 2003. Target user must have logged on to target machine at least once.	Chapter 2
Run Group Policy Modeling reports	Any Active Directory domain plus GPMC console. Must have one Windows Server 2003 Domain Controller available to run the calculations. Targets may be Windows 2000, but increased accuracy achieved for Windows XP or Windows 2003.	Chapter 2
WMI filters	Windows 2003 domain or Windows 2000 with an updated Windows 2003 schema via the ADPREP / Domainprep command. Additionally, Windows XP or Windows 2003 clients required. Windows 2000 clients ignore WMI filters.	Chapter 10
Delegate Group Policy Results ability	Windows 2003 forest, or Windows 2000 updated schema via ADPREP /forestprep. Use Active Directory Users And Computers or GPMC to delegate rights.	Chapter 2
Delegate Group Policy Modeling ability	Windows 2003 forest or Windows 2000 updated schema via ADPREP /forestprep. Use Active Directory Users And Computers or GPMC to delegate rights.	Chapter 2

Final Thoughts

While using the GPMC throughout this chapter, you ran queries and created several reports. What you possibly didn't know is that all that time you were creating HTML reports that you can use to document your environment.

Back when you were first exploring a GPO's settings (see the graphic in the "Common Procedures with the GPMC" section earlier in the chapter) and when you were creating RSoP reports (that is, Figures 2.23 and 2.24 and what would result after Figure 2.26), you were really generating HTML reports. Any time you create those reports, you can right-click over anywhere in the report and choose "Save Report." Since these are standard HTML, you basically have an incredibly easy way to document just about every aspect of your Group Policy universe.

Backing up and restoring with the GPMC is simply awesome. Yet some manual labor is still required to be totally protected. As you'll recall, when you restore a deleted GPO, you can't restore the links to the locations in Active Directory that were using that GPO. Consequently, good documentation about where each GPO is linked will always be your ace in the hole (provided you have good backups).

I stopped short in this chapter of demonstrating two of the GPMC's major additional functions. That is, the GPMC provides a scriptable interface many of our day to day GPO functions—including backups, creation, and management. You'll see that in Chapter 7. Additionally, you can use the GPMC to migrate GPOs from one domain to another. I'll tackle that in the Appendix.

The GPMC isn't quite part of the Windows 2003 operating system, but I expect that someday it might be. I'm hoping the GPMC stays standalone and continues through incremental improvements. Then, once finally mature, the GPMC and Active Directory Users And Computers can merge into one unified tool, perhaps to be named the "Active Directory Management Console" to help me manage both my GPOs and my Active Directory objects, such as user accounts.

If Microsoft does come up with a tool, and names it that, I want royalties for the idea. Just $1 per Windows Client Access License they sell, and I'll be set for life.

Here are some parting tips for daily Group Policy Object management with the GPMC:

Check out these Microsoft documentation links.   Microsoft GPMC documentation is available at `http://go.microsoft.com/fwlink/?LinkId=14320`. Additionally, Microsoft has some other RSoP documentation available at `www.microsoft.com/technet/prodtechnol/windowsserver2003/proddocs/entserver/rspintro.asp`.

Use "Block Inheritance" and "Enforced" sparingly.   The less you use these features, the easier it will be to debug the application of settings. Figuring out at which level in the hierarchy one administrator has "Blocked Inheritance" and another has declared "Enforced" can eat up days of fun at the office. The GPMC makes it easier to see what's going on, but still, minimize your use of these two attributes

Remember what can only be applied at the link.   Three and only three attributes are set on a GPO link: Link Enable (Enable or Disable the settings to apply at this level), Enforce the link (and force the policy settings), and Delete the link

Remember what can be applied only on the actual GPO itself.   The following attributes must be set on the GPO itself: the policies and settings inside the GPO (found on the Settings tab),

Security filters, and rights (as in the "Apply Group Policy" permission), and delegation (as in the "Edit this GPO" permission), Enabling/Disabling half (or both halves) of the GPO via the GPO Status (found on the Details tab), and WMI filtering (discussed in Chapter 10).

Remember Group Policy is notoriously tough to debug.   Once you start linking GPOs at multiple levels, throwing a "Block Inheritance," an "Enforced," and a filter or two, you're up to your eyeballs in troubleshooting. The best thing you can do is document the heck out of your GPOs. The GPMC helps you determine what a GPO does in the Settings tab, but your documentation will be your sanity check when trying to figure things out.

Use Microsoft's spreadsheet.   Microsoft has an Excel spreadsheet of all the administrative templates for Windows 2000, Windows XP, and Windows 2003. My suggestion is to leverage this file every single time you create a new GPO and keep it in a common place for all administrators to reference to see what anyone else did inside a GPO. Be religious about it, and keep these files updated within your company. To locate the spreadsheet, go to www.microsoft.com/technet. Search for "Group Policy Settings Reference (Administrative Templates)." The file you're after is PolicySettings.xls. At last check, you could find the Group Policy Settings Reference Spreadsheet at http://go.microsoft.com/fwlink/?LinkId=15165.

3

Group Policy Processing Behavior

After you create or modify a GPO in the domain, the policy "wishes" are not immediately dropped on the target machines. In fact, they're not dropped on the target machines at all; they're requested by the client computer at various times throughout the day. GPOs are processed at specific times, based on various conditions.

Indeed, it's likely that you have Windows 2000, Windows XP, and, now, Windows 2003 machines in your environment. Each operating system that receives Group Policy instructions processes Group Policy at different times in different ways. With three operating systems, the expected behaviors can really get confusing quickly.

Additionally, other factors determine when and how a GPO applies. When users dial in over slow links, things can be—and usually are—different. And you can instruct the Group Policy engine (on specific or all computers) to forgo its out-of-the-box processing behaviors for a customized (and often more secure) way to process.

Also, if you are using Windows 2003's new Cross-Forest Trusts, Group Policy will process differently, depending on each operating system (and service pack) you use; understanding what is going on is paramount.

Often, people throw up their hands when the Group Policy engine doesn't seem to process the GPOs they dictate in an expected manner. Group Policies don't just process when they want to; rather, they adhere to a strict set of processing rules. This chapter's goal is to answer the question, When does Group Policy apply? Understanding the processing rules will help you better understand when Group Policy processes GPOs the way it does. Then, in the next chapter, you'll get a grip on why Group Policy applies. Between these two chapters, your goal is to become a better Group Policy troubleshooter.

Group Policy Processing Principles

If you're phasing out Windows 2000 in favor of Windows XP, it's likely to be a long time before all your Windows 2000 machines are totally out the door. With that in mind, we'll take a look at how Windows 2000, Windows 2003, and Windows XP process Group Policy. Indeed, to better understand how Windows XP processes its policy, I highly recommend that you understand how Windows 2000 does its thing first—to understand how and why Windows XP's processing is different.

To better understand how GPO processing works, we're going to walk through what happens to two users:

- Wally, who only uses a Windows 2000 Professional machine
- Xavier, who only uses a Windows XP Professional machine

By using Wally and Xavier as our two sample users (on our two sample computers), we can see precisely when Group Policy applies to them—when they're using Windows 2000 and Windows XP machines.

Before we go even one step further, let me debunk a popular myth about Group Policy processing. That is, Group Policy is never pushed from the server and forced upon the clients. Rather, the process is quite the opposite. Group Policy occurs when the Group Policy engine on a Windows client requests Group Policy. This happens at various times, but at no time can you magically declare from on high: "All clients?! Go forth and accept my latest GPOs!" It doesn't work like that. Clients request GPOs according to the rules listed in this chapter.

In Chapter 7, I'll show you a technique that emulates the same effect as if you were performing a push to all your clients.

In a nutshell, Group Policy is potentially triggered to apply at four times. Here's a rundown of those times; I'll discuss them in grueling detail in the next sections.

Initial Policy Processing   For Windows 2000 and Windows 2003 machines, processing occurs when the computer starts up or when the user logs on. By default, there is no initial policy processing for Windows XP machines.

Background Refresh Policy Processing (Member Servers)   For Windows 2000, Windows 2003, and Windows XP member machines, processing occur some time after the user logs on (usually 90 minutes or so). A bit later, you'll see how Windows XP is unique and leverages the background policy processing mechanism to a distinct advantage.

Background Refresh Policy Processing (Domain Controllers)   Windows 2000 and Windows 2003 Domain Controllers need love too, and to that end, they receive a background refresh every 5 minutes (after replication has occurred).

Security Policy Processing   For all operating systems, only the security settings within all GPOs are reprocessed and applied every 16 hours regardless of whether they have changed. This safety mechanism prevents unscrupulous local workstation administrators from doing too much harm.

You can change the default behavior of certain nonsecurity policy settings so that they are enforced in a manner similar to the way that security settings are automatically enforced. But you have to explicitly turn this feature on, and you have to do so correctly. In the "Security Policy Processing" section, I describe how to do this and give you several examples of why you would want to do so.

Special Case: Moving a User or Computer Object   Although all the previous items demonstrate a trigger of when Group Policy applies, one case isn't trigger specific; however, it's important to understand a special case of Group Policy processing behavior. When you move a user or a computer from one OU to another, background processing may not immediately understand that something was moved. Some time later, it should detect the change, and background processing should start normally again.

Don't Get Lost   There are definitely nuances in the processing mechanism among the various operating systems. The good news, if your head starts to swim a bit, is that you can dog-ear this page, and highlight this little area for quick reference:

- Windows 2000 Professional, Windows 2000 member servers, and Windows 2003 member servers all act the same way.

- Windows 2000 Domain Controllers and Windows 2003 Domain Controllers act the same way.

- Windows XP is a bit peculiar and does some things its own way, but you can make it act like it's Windows 2000 cousin.

Initial Policy Processing

Recall that each GPO has two halves, a computer half and a user half. This is important to remember when trying to understand when GPOs are processed. Windows 2000 and Windows 2003 are capable of what is called *initial policy processing*. Windows XP is also capable of initial policy processing, but it doesn't work quite the same as its Windows 2000 counterpart.

Windows 2000 Initial Policy Processing

Wally walks into his office and turns on his Windows 2000 Professional machine. The computer half of the policy is always processed at the target machines upon startup (or reboot). When a Windows 2000 or Windows 2003 machine starts up, it states that it is processing security policy. At that time, the workstation logs on to the network by contacting a Domain Controller. The Domain Controller (with DNS information) then tells the workstation which site it belongs to, which domain it belongs to, and which OU it is in. The system then processes the computer half of Group Policy in that order. When the processing is finished, the "Press Ctrl+Alt+Delete to begin" prompt is revealed, and Wally can log on by pressing Ctrl+Alt+Delete and giving his username and password.

After Wally is validated to Active Directory, the user half of the GPO is processed in the same precise order: site, domain, and then each nested OU.

Wally's Windows 2000 desktop is manipulated by the policy settings inside any GPOs. Wally's desktop is displayed only when all the user-side GPOs are processed.

If you look at how all this all goes, you'll see it's a lock-step mechanism: the computer starts up and then processes GPOs in the natural order: site, domain, and each nested OU. The user then logs on, and Group Policy is processed, again in the natural order: site, domain, and each nested OU. This style of GPO processing is called *synchronous processing*. That is, in order to proceed to the next step in either the startup or logon processes, the previous step must be completed. For example, the GPOs at the OU level of the user are never processed before the GPOs at the site level. Likewise, the GPOs at the domain level for the Windows 2000 (and Windows Server 2003) are never processed before the site GPOs that affect a computer.

Therefore, the default for Windows 2000 (and Windows Server 2003) for both the computer startup and user logon is that each GPO is processed synchronously. This same process occurs every time a user booting a Windows 2000 (or Windows Server 2003) machine turns on the machine and then logs on.

Windows XP Initial Policy Processing

Xavier walks into his office and turns on his Windows XP Professional machine. For a moment, let's assume this is the first time that this Windows XP Professional machine has started up since joining the domain. Perhaps it just landed on Xavier's desk after a new desktop rollout of Windows XP. If this is the case, the Windows XP Professional machine will act just like Windows 2000 (and Windows 2003). It will look to see which site, domain, and OUs the computer account is in and then applies GPOs synchronously.

Likewise, let's assume this is the first time Xavier is logging on to this Windows XP machine with his domain account. Again, imagine that this machine just arrived after a desktop rollout. In this case, again, Windows XP will act like Windows 2000 (and Windows 2003) and synchronously process GPOs based on the site, domain, and OU Xavier is logging on from.

So far, so good. However, Windows XP performs this initial synchronous processing only in this special case described here. That is, either the computer has never started in the domain before, or the user has never logged on to this particular Windows XP machine before. To understand Windows XP's normal default processing mode, take a deep breath and read on.

Background Refresh Policy Processing

Once Wally is logged on to Windows 2000 (or Windows 2003) and Xavier is logged on to Windows XP, things are great—for everyone. As the administrator, we're happy because both Wally and Xavier are receiving our wishes. They're happy because, well, they're just happy, that's all.

But, now, we decide to add a new GPO or to modify a policy setting inside an existing GPO. What if something is modified in the Group Policy Object Editor that should affect a user or a computer? Aren't both Wally and Xavier are already logged on—happy as clams? Well, when this happens, the new changes (and only the new changes) are indeed reflected on the user or computer that should receive them. But this delivery doesn't happen immediately; rather the changes are delivered according to the *background refresh interval* (sometimes known as the *background processing interval*).

The background refresh interval dictates how often changed GPOs in Active Directory are pulled by the client computer. As I implied earlier, there are different background intervals for the different operating systems' roles (that is, member vs. Domain Controller).

When the background refresh interval comes to pass, GPOs are processed *asynchronously*. That is, if a GPO that affects a user's OU (or other Active Directory level) is changed, the changes are pulled to the local computer when the clock strikes the processing time. It doesn't matter if the change happens at any level in Active Directory: OU, domain, or site. When changes are available to users or computers after the user or computer is already logged on, the changes are processed asynchronously . Whichever GPOs at any level have changed, those changes are reflected on the client.

Standard *application mechanism* still applies; and the precedence order is still reflected: site, domain, OU. In other words, even though a new GPO linked to a site is ready, it isn't necessarily going to trump a GPO linked to the OU.

When does this happen? According to the background refresh interval for the operating system (discussed next).

Background Refresh Intervals for Windows 2000/2003 Members

It stands to reason that when we change an existing GPO (or create a new GPO) we would want our users and computers to get the latest and greatest set of instructions and wishes. With that in mind, let's continue with our example. Remember that Wally is on his Windows 2000 machine and Xavier is on his Windows XP machine.

By default, the background refresh interval for Windows 2000 workstations and Windows 2000 and Windows 2003 member servers is 90 minutes, with a 0–30 minute positive random differential added to the mix to ensure that no gaggle of PCs will refresh at any one time and clog your network asking for mass GPO downloads. Therefore, once a change has been made to a GPO, it could take as little as 90 minutes or as long as 120 minutes for each user or workstation that is already logged on to the network to see that change.

Microsoft documentation isn't consistent in this description. Often, Microsoft documentation will say the offset is 30 minutes (which could be interpreted as positive or negative 30 minutes). Indeed, in the previous edition of this book, I incorrectly reported that "fact." However, since then, I have verified with Microsoft that the refresh interval is (and has always been) 90 minutes plus (not minus) 0–30 minutes.

Again, this is known as the background refresh interval. Additionally, the background refresh interval for the computer half of Group Policy and the user half of Group Policy are on their own independent schedules. That is, the computer or user half might be refreshed before the other half; they're not necessarily refreshed at the exact moment because they're on their own individual timetables. This makes sense: the computer and user didn't each get Group Policy at the precise moment in time in the first place, did they?

You can change the background refresh interval for the computer half and/or the user half using Group Policy, as described later in this chapter in the section cleverly entitled "Using Group Policy to Affect Group Policy."

You can manually prevent an individual computer from asking for the background refresh by hacking HKEY_LOCAL_MACHINE\SOFTWARE\Microsoft\Windows\CurrentVersion\policies\system, adding a DWORD key named DisableBkGndGroupPolicy and giving it a value of 1. You can set individual policy settings to prevent specific areas of Group Policy from being refreshed in the background, such as Internet Explorer Maintenance and Administrative Templates. See the "Using Group Policy to Affect Group Policy" section later in the chapter.

How Does the Group Policy Engine Know What's New or Changed?

The Group Policy engine on Windows 2000 and Windows XP can keep track of what's new or changed via a control mechanism called version numbers. Each GPO has a version number for each half of the GPO, and this is stored in Active Directory. If the version number in Active Directory doesn't change, nothing is downloaded. Since nothing has changed, the Group Policy engine thinks it has all the latest-greatest stuff—so why bother to redownload it (which takes time) and reprocess it (which takes more time)?

By default, when a background refresh interval arrives, a time-saving mechanism, "checking the GPO version numbers," is employed to minimize the time needed to get the latest-greatest GPOs. You'll learn more about GPO version numbers in Chapter 4.

To reiterate, when the background refresh interval arrives, only the new or changed GPOs are downloaded and processed.

Background Refresh Intervals for Windows 2000/2003 Domain Controllers

Even though neither Wally nor Xavier is logging on to Domain Controllers, other people might. And because Domain Controllers are a bit special, the processing for Windows 2000 Domain Controllers (and Windows 2003 Domain Controllers) is handled in a special way.

Because Group Policy contains sensitive security settings (for example, Password and Account Policy, Kerberos Policy, Audit Policy), any policy geared for a Domain Controller is refreshed within five minutes. This adds a tighter level of security to Domain Controllers. For more information on precisely how the default GPOs work, see Chapter 6.

You can change the background interval for Domain Controllers using Group Policy (as described later in the "Using Group Policy to Affect Group Policy" section). However, you really shouldn't mess with the default values here. They work pretty well.

 You'll learn more about affecting Domain Controllers' security in Chapter 6.

Background Refresh Exemptions

Wally has been logged on to his Windows 2000 machine 4 hours, and Xavier has been logged on to his Windows XP machine for the same amount of time. Clearly, the background refresh interval has come and gone—somewhere between two and three times.

If any GPOs had been created or any existing GPOs had changed while Wally and Xavier were logged on, both their user accounts and their computer accounts would have embraced the newest policy settings. However, four policy categories are exceptions and are never processed in the background while users are logged on:

Folder Redirection (explored in detail in Chapter 9)   Folder Redirection's goal is to anchor specific directories, such as the My Documents folder, to certain network shared folders. This policy is never refreshed during a background refresh. The logic behind this is that if an administrator changes this location while the user is using it (and the system responds), the user's data could be at risk for corruption. If the administrator changes Folder Redirection via Group Policy, this change affects only the user at next logon.

Software Installation (explored in detail in Chapter 10)   Software Installation is also exempt from background refresh. You can use Group Policy to deploy software packages, large and small, to your users or to your computers. You can also use Group Policy to revoke already-distributed software packages. Software is neither installed nor revoked to users or computers when the background interval comes to pass. You wouldn't want users to lose applications right in the middle of use and, hence lose or corrupt data. These functions occur only at startup for the computer or at logon for the user.

Logon, Logoff, Startup, and Shutdown Scripts (explored in detail in Chapter 6)   These are not run when the background processing interval comes around. They are only run at the appointed time (at logon, logoff, startup, or shutdown).

Disk Quotas (explored in detail in Chapter 9)   These are not run when the background processing interval comes around. They are only run at computer startup.

Windows XP and Background Processing

As I stated in the introduction to this section, Windows XP is the black sheep of the family. Let's see how this works.

Now that Xavier has now logged on to his Windows XP Professional machine for the first time, his session will continue to process GPOs in the background as I just described: every 90 minutes or so if any new GPOs appear or any existing GPOs have changed. Xavier now goes home for the night. He logs off the domain and shuts down his machine. When he comes in the next morning, he will not process GPOs the same way that Wally will on his Windows 2000 machine.

When Xavier logs on the second time (and all consecutive times) to his Windows XP machine, initial policy processing will no longer be performed as described in the "Initial Policy Processing" section earlier in this chapter. From this point forward, at startup or logon, Windows XP will not process GPOs synchronously like Windows 2000; rather, GPOs will be processed only in the background.

If you're scratching your head at this point as to why Windows 2000 and Windows XP are different, here's the short answer. When Windows XP Professional was in development, all the stops were pulled to make the "XPerience" as fast as possible. Both boot times and logon times are indeed now faster than ever, but the tradeoff does come at a price.

By default, Windows XP Professional processes GPOs asynchronously—both at computer startup and at user logon. Upon startup, the computer doesn't wait for the network interface to initialize before starting to process computer GPOs. Windows XP uses the last-known downloaded GPOs (held in cache) as its baseline, even if GPOs have changed in Active Directory while the Windows XP machine was turned off.

While the network card is still warming up and finding the network and the first Domain Controller, the previously cached computer GPOs are already being processed! Then, the "Press Ctrl+Alt+Delete to begin" prompt is presented to the user. While this prompt is presented, Windows XP downloads any new computer GPOs. These new computer GPOs are not applied until a bit later.

Assuming the user is now logged on, the desktop and Start menu appear. Again, the system will not synchronously download the latest site, domain, and OU Group Policy Objects and apply them before displaying the desktop. Rather, the system simply processes any cached user GPOs from the last-known GPOs applied in the cache. New GPOs are downloaded, but processing is deferred.

Once the computer has started, the user is logged on, and any cached computer and user GPOs are applied, newly downloaded GPOs (and the policy settings inside) are then processed asynchronously in the background. This net result is a bit of a compromise. The user feels that there is a faster boot time (when processing GPOs with computer policy settings) as well as faster logon time (when processing GPOs with user policy settings). The most important policy settings, such as updated Security settings and Administrative Templates (Registry updates), are applied soon after logon—and no one is the wiser. Microsoft calls this Windows XP Group Policy processing behavior *Fast Boot* (sometimes called Windows XP "Logon Optimization".) Yes, it does speed things up a bit, but at a cost.

Windows XP Fast-Boot Results

Windows XP Fast Boot affects two major components—Group Policy processing and user-account attribute processing. The (sometimes strange) results occur only for Xavier, on his Windows XP Professional machine when he has previously already logged on to it. Wally, on his Windows 2000 machine, is spared the following weird behavior.

WINDOWS XP FAST BOOT GROUP POLICY PROCESSING DETAILS

The immediate downside to Windows XP's Fast Boot approach is that, potentially, a user at a Windows XP Professional desktop could be totally logged on but not quite have all the GPOs processed. Then, once they are working for a little while—pop! A setting takes effect out of the blue. This is because not all GPOs were processed before the user was presented with the desktop and Start menu. Your network would have to be pretty slow for this scenario to occur, but it's certainly possible.

The next major downside takes a bit more to wrap your head around. Some Group Policy (and Profile) features can potentially take Windows XP Professional several additional logons or reboots to actually get the changes you want on them. This strange behavior becomes understandable when we take a step back and think about how certain policy categories are processed on Windows 2000. Specifically, we need to direct our attention to Software Distribution and Folder Redirection policy. I mentioned that on Windows 2000 these two types of policy categories must be processed in the foreground (or synchronously) to prevent data corruption.

But we have a paradox: If Windows XP Professional processes GPOs asynchronously, how are the Software Distribution and Folder Redirection polices handled if they must be handled synchronously?

Windows XP Professional fakes it and tags the machine when a Software Package is targeted for a Windows XP Professional client. The next time the user logs on, the Group Policy engine sees that the machine is tagged for Software Distribution and switches, just for this one time, back into synchronous mode. The net result: Windows XP Professional typically requires two logons (or reboots) for a user or computer to get a software distribution package. Again, note that Windows 2000 Professional machines only require one logon (for user settings) or one reboot (for computer settings).

Folder Redirection, as you'll see in Chapter 9, is a wonderful tool. It has two modes: Basic Folder Redirection (which applies to everyone in the OU) and Advanced Folder Redirection (which checks which security groups the user is in). Windows XP machines won't get the effects of Basic Folder Redirection for two logons! And Windows XP machines won't get the effects of Advanced Folder Redirection for a whopping three logons. The first logon tags the system for a Folder Redirection change; the second logon figures out the user's security group membership; and the third logon actually performs the new Folder Redirection—synchronously for just that one logon.

> Again, remember that Fast Boot is automatically disabled the first time any Windows XP machine is started as a member of the domain. It is also disabled the first time any new user logs on to a Windows XP Professional client. In these situations, Windows XP assumes (correctly) that no GPO information is cached and therefore must go out to Active Directory to get the latest GPOs. The net effect is that if settings for either (or both) Folder Redirection policy and Software Distribution policy already exist, the user will not require additional logons or reboots the first time they log on to a Windows XP machine or when the computer is started for the first time after joining the domain.

WINDOWS XP FAST BOOT USER-ACCOUNT ATTRIBUTE PROCESSING DETAILS

Group Policy is only one of two areas affected by Windows XP's Fast Boot. Some Microsoft documentation claims that other parts of the user's information could require several logons or reboots in order to take effect.

The idea is that certain attributes are cached and assumed to be accurate at logon. If, after a background download the information is actually changed, it would only be on the next logon that the change will take effect.

Microsoft says Windows XP takes two logons or reboots to process the following attributes:

- Roaming profile path (discussed in Chapter 8)
- The home directory
- Old-style logon scripts

Now, to be 100% honest, I have not observed this behavior. In my testing, the above attributes take exactly one logoff or reboot to process—regardless if Fast Boot is enabled or not.

Yet, Microsoft maintains that under certain circumstances (with Fast Boot enabled) the above will hold true. So, if the user is using Windows XP, and any of these properties is changed in Active Directory, it *could* take two logons for these changes to actually take effect.

Turning off Windows XP Fast Boot

If you want your Windows XP Professional users to log on a teeny-weeny bit faster, by all means, leave the default of Fast Boot on. If you're doing some no-nos in Group Policy, (namely setting up cross-domain Group Policy links or processing a lot of site-based GPOs), leaving Fast Boot on will, in fact, serve its purpose and likely make each and every logon a bit faster.

My recommendation, however, is to get all your machines—Windows XP and Windows 2000 Professional—to act the same. That is, I suggest that you force your Windows XP Professional machines to act like Windows 2000 Professional machines and perform synchronous policy processing. To do this, you need to set a Group Policy that contains a setting to revert Windows XP machines to the old behavior. It might be a smidge bit slower to log on, but no slower than your Windows 2000 machines already experience.

This will make your Windows XP machines perform initial policy processing at startup and logon—just like your Windows 2000 machines. That is, the computer will start up, locate all GPOs, and then process them—before displaying the "Press Ctrl+Alt+Delete to begin" prompt. Once the user is logged on, all GPOs are processed before the desktop is displayed.

Troubleshooting Group Policy is now a heck of a lot more predictable because you're not trying to guess when Software Distribution, Folder Redirection, or even the errant Administrative Template setting is going to be processed. Since your Windows 2000 machines already act this way (and you can't make Windows 2000 Fast Boot like Windows XP), it probably would be a good enterprise supportability practice to have all machines in your environment act as similarly as possible—even if they are different operating systems.

To revert Windows XP Professional to the Windows 2000 synchronous behavior, for Initial Policy Processing, create and link a GPO (preferably at the domain level) to simply enable the policy setting named **Always wait for the network at computer startup and logon**. This policy can be found in the Computer Configuration ➤ Administrative Templates ➤ System ➤ Logon branch of Group Policy.

Remember, to force Windows XP machines to receive this computer policy (or any computer policy), the computer account must be within the site, domain, or OU at which you set the policy. If you set this policy at the domain level, you're guaranteed that all Windows XP machines in your domain will get the policy.

 By performing this at the domain level, all your machines—Windows XP, Windows 2000, and Windows 2003—will receive the message. But remember that policy settings meant for Windows XP won't apply on Windows 2000 machines. And it's a moot point for Windows 2003 machines anyway, as you'll see in the next section.

Forcing Background Policy Processing

You get a phone call from the person who handles the firewalls and proxy servers at your company. He tells you that he's added an additional proxy server for your users to use when going out to the Internet. Excitedly, you add a new GPO that affects Wally's and Xavier's user objects so they can use the new proxy server via Internet Explorer Maintenance Settings. But you're impatient.

You know that when you make this setting, it's going to take between 90 and 120 minutes to kick in. And you don't want to tell Wally or Xavier to log off and log back on to get the policy—they wouldn't like that much.

In cases like these, you might want to bypass the normal wait time before background policy processing kicks in. The good news is that you can run a simple command that tells the client to skip the normal background processing interval and request an update of new or changed

GPOs from the server right now. Again, only new GPOs or GPOs that have changed in some way on the server will actually come down and be reflected on your client machines.

Initiating a Manual Background Refresh for Windows 2000

The command-line tool used to encourage your Windows 2000 machines to kick off a manual background refresh is SECEDIT. SECEDIT can request the refresh of GPOs (and the settings therein) from the User Configuration node, the Computer Configuration node, or both, but you'll need to run the command once for each half.

As I've mentioned, there is no way from up on high to say, "Go forth and refresh, all ye users or computers affected by this recent change in policy!" To utilize SECEDIT, you must physically be present at the Windows 2000 machine and execute the command. Otherwise, you must simply wait for the background refresh interval to kick in.

You can independently change the background refresh interval of both the user and computer. See the "Using Group Policy to Affect Group Policy" section later in this chapter.

But, because you're impatient, you want to see Wally on his Windows 2000 machine start using that new proxy server setting that you plunked into that GPO right away. So you physically trot out to his machine, log on with administrator-level authority, and enter the following commands to manually refresh the GPOs.

For Windows 2000, follow these steps to request a refresh of GPOs from the User Configuration node:

1. Choose Start ➢ Run to open the Run dialog box, and in the Open box, enter **cmd** to open the command-line window.

2. At the prompt, type **secedit /refreshpolicy user_policy**.

For Windows 2000, follow these steps to request a refresh of GPOs from the Computer Configuration node:

1. Choose Start ➢ Run to open the Run dialog box, and in the Open box, enter **cmd** to open the command-line window.

2. At the prompt, type **secedit /refreshpolicy machine_policy**.

See Chapter 6 for additional uses of the SECEDIT command.

You might want to create a batch file called s.bat or even gpupdate.bat, which run secedit to initiate machine and user policy settings to apply. Then, if you place this batch file on all your workstations, you can perform both in one stroke!

Initiating a Manual Background Refresh for Windows XP and Windows 2003

You now want to initiate a manual refresh for Xavier on his Windows XP machine. Windows XP and Windows 2003 refresh GPOs using a different command called GPUpdate. GPUpdate is similar to SECEDIT in that it can refresh either the user or computer half of a GPO or both. The syntax is GPUpdate /Target:Computer, /Target:User, or just GPUpdate by itself to trigger both.

Running GPUpdate while Xavier is logged on to his Windows XP machine immediately gives him the new settings in the GPO you just set. This is, of course, provided the Domain Controller that Xavier and his Windows XP machine are using has the replicated GPO information.

Additionally, GPUpdate can figure out if newly changed items require a logoff or reboot to be active. Since Windows XP's default behavior is to enable Fast Boot, Software Distribution and Folder Redirection settings are processed only at future logon times. Therefore, specifying GPUpdate with a /Logoff switch will figure out if a policy has changed in Active Directory such that a logoff is required and automatically log you off. If the updated GPO does not require a logoff, the GPO settings are applied, and the currently logged-on user remains logged on.

Similarly, with Windows XP's Fast Boot enabled, GPOs that have Software Distribution settings will require a reboot before the software will be available. Therefore, specifying GPUpdate with a /Reboot switch will figure out if a policy has something that requires a reboot and automatically reboot the computer. If the updated GPO does not require a reboot, the GPO settings are applied, and the user remains logged on.

The /Logoff and /Reboot switches are optional.

For information about how to turn off Windows XP's Fast Boot" and make it act like Windows 2000, see the "Turning Off Windows XP Fast Boot" section earlier in this chapter.

Security Background Refresh Processing

Even before Microsoft had the big, internal security hurrah, some modicum of security was built into the Group Policy engine. As I've stated, Windows 2000, Windows 2003, and Windows XP clients process GPOs when the background refresh interval comes to pass—but only those GPOs that were new or changed since the last time the client requested them.

Wally is on a Windows 2000 machine, and he's been logged on for 4 hours. Likewise, Xavier has been logged on to his Windows XP machine for 4 hours. Imagine for a second that there was a GPO in Active Directory named "Remove Run menu from Start menu" and its function was to do just that. The client would certainly do so according to the initial policy processing rules and/or the background refresh processing rules.

Assuming that the underlying GPO doesn't get any policy settings modified, or any new policy settings or that the GPO itself doesn't get removed, the client already knows to accept this edict. The client just accepts that things haven't changed and, hence, keeps on truckin'. Only a change inside the GPO will trigger the client to realize that new instructions are available, and the client will execute that new edict during its background policy processing.

Now, let's assume that we anoint Wally and Xavier as local administrators of their Windows 2000 and Windows XP machines. Since Wally and Xavier are now local administrators, they have total control to go around the Group Policy engine processes and make their own changes. These changes could nullify a policy you've previously set with a GPO and allow them to access and change features on the system that shouldn't be changed. In this case, there are certainly going to be situations in which the GPO on the domain controllers don't change, but certain parts of the workstation should remain locked down anyway.

Let's examine two potential exploits of the Group Policy engine.

Group Policy Exploit Example #1: Going Around an Administrative Template   Consider the Task Scheduler example we looked at in the previous chapters. We created a GPO named "Prohibit new Tasks in Task Scheduler" and put the enabled the policy setting named **Prohibit New Task Creation** within it. We linked the GPO to the **Human Resources Computers** OU. Our edit affected all users on our computers (including our administrators) such that the "Add scheduled Task" ability was not accessible in the Task Scheduler within Control Panel. Imagine, then, that someone with local administrative privileges (such as Wally) on the workstation changes the portion of the Registry that is affected, as shown in Figure 3.1.

After the local administrator changes the setting, then "Add Scheduled Task" ability is immediately displayed. (Again, only local administrators can make this change. Mere mortals do not have access to this portion of the Registry.) We're now at risk; a local administrator did the dirty work, and now all users on this workstation are officially going around our policy. Ninety minutes or so later, the background refresh interval strikes, and the client computer requests the background refresh from the GPOs in Active Directory. You might think that this should once again lock down the "Add Scheduled Tasks" ability. But it doesn't. This ability won't get relocked down upon a reboot, either. Why? Because the Windows client thinks everything is status quo. Because nothing has changed in the underlying GPO in Active Directory that is telling the client its instruction set.

In this example, the Group Policy processing engine on the client thinks it has already asked for (and received) the latest version of the policy; the Group Policy processing engine doesn't know about the nefarious Registry change the local workstation administrator performed behind its back. Windows 2000, Windows XP, and Windows 2003 clients are not protected from this sort of attack by default. However, the protection can be made stronger. (See the "Mandatory Reapplication for Non-Security Policy" section later in this chapter.) Okay, this exploit is fairly harmless, but it could be more or less damaging depending on precisely which policy settings we are forcing on our clients (as seen in this next example).

Group Policy Exploit Example #2: Going Around a Security Policy Setting   Via Group Policy, we use the material in Chapter 6 to create a security template (and corresponding security policy) that locks down the \windows\ repair directory with specific file ACLs. For this example, imagine we set the \windows\ repair directory so that only the Domain Administrators have access. Then, behind our backs, Xavier, now a local administrator, changes these file ACLs to allow everyone full control to these sensitive files. Uh-oh, now we could have a real problem on our hands.

Windows 2000 and Windows XP each offer protection to handle clean-up for exploits of these types. Let's see how that works.

In the first example, we went around the **Prohibit New Task Creation** policy setting by forcefully modifying the Registry. The Scheduled Tasks section of control panel isn't considered a security setting. So, by default there is no protection for Exploit #1 (note the emphasis on "by default"). But, before you start panicking, let's examine Exploit #2, which attempts to go around a security policy we set.

FIGURE 3.1 A simple deletion of the Registry entry will nullify our policy setting.

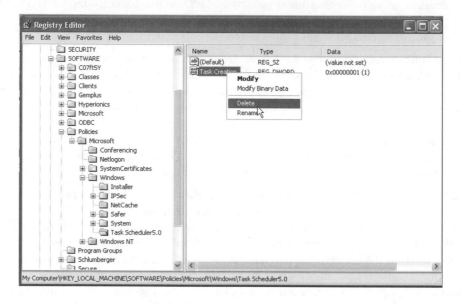

Background Security Refresh Processing for Windows 2000, Windows 2003, and Windows XP

The Group Policy engine tries to clean up after examples such as Exploit #2 by asking for a special background refresh—just for the security policy settings. This is called the *background security refresh*. Every 16 hours (with a 30-minute offset), a client asks Active Directory for all the security-related GPOs that apply for it (not just the ones that have changed). This ensures that if a security setting has changed on the client (behind Active Directory's back), it's automatically patched up within 16 hours.

You can manually change this security refresh interval in two ways. First, you can editing the local workstation's Registry at `HKEY_LOCAL_MACHINE\SOFTWARE\Microsoft\Windows NT\CurrentVersion\Winlogon\GPExtensions\{827D319E-6EAC-11D2-A4EA-00C04F79F83A}\MaxNoGPOListChangesInterval` and add a `REG_DWORD` signifying the number of minutes to pull down the entire security policy (by default, every 16 hours). You can also use the Security Policy Processing policy, which is described in the "Using Group Policy to Affect Group Policy" section, later in this chapter. For more information, see the Microsoft Knowledge Base article 277543.

To reiterate, background security refresh helps secure stuff only every 16 hours and only if the setting is security related. So, within a maximum of 16 hours, the `\windows\ repair` directory would have the intended permissions re-thrust upon it. Okay, great. But in Exploit #1, our evil administrator went around the **Prohibit New Task Creation** policy setting. And the background security refresh would *not* have re-enforced our intended will upon the system. The Task Scheduler is not considered a security policy setting. How do we secure those exploits, I hear you cry? Read on, I reply. (Hey, that rhymed.)

Mandatory Reapplication for Non-Security Policy

Your network is humming along. You've established the GPOs in your organization, and you've let them sit unchanged for several months. Wally logs on. Wally logs off. So does Xavier. They each reboot their machines a bunch. But imagine for a moment that the GPOs in Active Directory haven't changed in months.

When your users or computers perform initial Group Policy processing or background policy processing, a whole lot of nothing happens. If GPOs haven't changed in months, there's nothing for the clients to do. Since the engine has already processed the latest version of what's in Active Directory, what more could it possibly need?

True, every 16 hours the security-related policy settings are guaranteed to be refreshed by the background security refresh as. But what about Exploit #1 in which Wally (who was anointed as a local workstation administrator) went around the **Prohibit New Task Creation** policy setting by hacking his local Registry?

Well, the New Task Creation settings aren't a security policy. But it still could be thought of as a security hole you need to fill. With a little magic, you can enforce the nonsecurity sections of Group Policy to automatically close their own security holes. You can make the nonsecurity sections of Group Policy enforce their settings, even if the GPOs on the servers haven't changed. This will fix exploits that aren't specifically security related. You'll learn how to do this a bit later in the "Affecting the Computer Settings of Group Policy" section.

The general idea is that once the nonsecurity sections of Group Policy are told to mandatorily reapply, they will do so whenever an initial policy processing or background refresh processing happens.

You can choose to mandatorily reapply the following areas of Group Policy, along with the initial processing and background refresh:

- Registry (Administrative Templates)
- Internet Explorer Maintenance
- IP Security
- EFS Recovery Policy
- Wireless Policy
- Disk Quota

As you'll see in the "Affecting the Computer Settings of Group Policy" section, you can use the GUI to select other areas of Group Policy to enforce along with the background refresh. But, in three specific cases, selecting to do so will not actually do anything to change how they are processed by default: Software Distribution, Folder Redirection, and Scripts.

To recap, if the GPO in Active Directory has *actually* changed, you don't have to worry about whether it will be automatically applied or not. Rather, mandatory reapplication is an extra safety measure that you can place upon your client systems so your will is always download and re-embraced not just if an existing GPO has changed or a new GPO has appeared. And, you can specify specific Group Policy sections that you wish to do this for.

> As you'll see in Chapter 4, a bit more is going on between the client and the server. Underneath the hood, the client keeps track of the GPO version number. If the version number changes in Active Directory, the GPO is flagged as being required for download; it is then redownloaded and applied. If the version number stays the same in Active Directory, the Group Policy isn't redownloaded or applied. Stay tuned for more on GPO version numbers in Chapter 4.

Manually Forcing Clients to Process GPOs (Revisited)

In the "Forcing Background Refresh Processing" section, I talked a bit about what happens if you set up a new GPO (or change an existing one) and get impatient. That is, you want to force your client systems to embrace your new settings.

As I've said, there's no way from on high to shout to your client computers and proclaim: "Accept my latest GPOs, ye mere mortals and puny systems!"

If you want to kick off policy processing at a client, you need to trot on over to it to kick it in the shins. You use SECEDIT on Windows 2000 machines and GPUpdate on Windows XP and Windows 2003 machines. But the actions of these two similar tools are not quite the same, and that's what this section is about.

Windows 2000 *SECEDIT* with the */enforce* Switch

Recall that you must run the Windows 2000 SECEDIT command-line tool on the client that you want to refresh. SECEDIT has an additional switch, /enforce, that ensures that all security-related settings are processed by the Windows 2000 workstation—regardless of whether the underlying GPO has changed in Active Directory. Instead of waiting 16 hours, you can rush the hands of time and force the background security refresh processing to strike.

Again, only security-related policy that affects the user or computer will be requested from Active Directory to the Windows 2000 workstation. The commands are either:

```
secedit /refreshpolicy machine_policy /enforce
```

or

```
secedit /refreshpolicy user_policy /enforce
```

Windows XP and Windows 2003 *GPUpdate* with the */force* Switch

Recall that you must run the Windows 2003 and Windows XP command-line tool GPUpdate on the client that you want to refresh. The /force switch looks similar to the /enforce switch for the Windows 2000 command-line tool SECEDIT, but it's not the same—it's better.

GPUpdate /force ensures that all settings in all GPOs are processed by the Windows XP (or Windows 2003) workstation—regardless of whether the underlying GPO has changed in Active Directory. It doesn't just pull down the security-related policy—no siree, Bob. GPUpdate /force pulls down *all* aspects of Group Policy regardless of whether the underlying GPO has changed. In this manner, it's leaps and bounds more powerful than its Windows 2000 counterpart.

The command is typically specified as:

```
Gpupdate /force
```

Other options are available in conjunction with /force, such as the ability to logoff the user or reboot the machine should a foreground policy be required (in the case of, say, Software Distribution).

Special Case: Moving a User or a Computer Object

When you move a user or a computer within Active Directory, Group Policy may not immediately apply as you think it should. For instance, if you move a computer from **Human Resources Computers** OU to another OU, that computer may still pull GPOs from the **Human Resources Computers** OU for a while longer. This is because the Group Policy engine may get confused about where the accounts it's supposed to work with are currently residing.

The Group Policy engine syncs with Active Directory every so often to determine if a user or a computer has been moved. This happens, at most, about every 30 minutes or so. Once resynced, background processing continues as it normally would. Only this time the user and computer GPOs are pulled from the new destination. If you move a user or a computer, remember that Group Policy processing continues to pull from the old location until it realizes the switch.

Altogether, the maximum wait time after a move to get GPOs pulled from a new location is as follows:

- 30 minutes (the maximum Active Directory synchronization time) *and*

- 90 minutes (the maximum Group Policy default background refresh rate) *and*

- 30 minutes (the maximum Group Policy default background refresh rate offset)

So that's maximum of 150 minutes.

It could and usually does happen faster than that, but it can't take any longer. This behavior is important to understand if you move an entire OU (perhaps with many computers) underneath another OU!

 WARNING   But wait! There might be more wait time in store. If your Active Directory design has many Domain Controllers in sites with site links, the notification of the change also depends on the Active Directory site topology (intrasite and intersite replication wait times)!

Policy Application via Remote Access or Slow Links

You will certainly have situations in which clients use Windows 2000 and Windows XP to make inbound remote access connections to your Active Directory. Both client systems, by default, will detect the speed of the connection and make a snap judgment about whether to process Group Policy. If the machine uses TCP/IP to connect to RAS (Remote Access Service), it is considered "fast enough" to process Group Policy if the connection is 500 kilobits or greater. If the connection is deemed fast enough, portions of Group Policy are applied.

Surprisingly, even if the connection is not deemed fast enough, several sections of Group Policy are still applied. Both the security settings, software restriction policy (Windows XP only), and Administrative Templates are guaranteed to be downloaded during logon over an RAS connection—no matter the speed. And there's nothing you can do about it. Additionally, EFS (Encrypting File System) Recovery Policy and IPSec policy is always downloaded over slow links.

 WARNING The Group Policy interface suggests that downloading of EFS Recovery Policy and IPSec policy can be switched on or off over slow links. This is not true. (See the note in the "Using Group Policy to Affect Group Policy" section later in this chapter.)

If the user connects using RAS before logging on to the workstation (using the "Logon Using Dial-Up Connection" check box as seen in Figure 3.2), the security and Administrative Templates policy settings of the Computer node of the GPO are downloaded and applied to the computer once the user is authenticated. Then, the security and Administrative Templates policy settings of the User node of the GPO are applied to the user.

FIGURE 3.2 If you select "Log on using dial-up connection," you first process GPOs in the foreground (when Fast Boot is disabled).

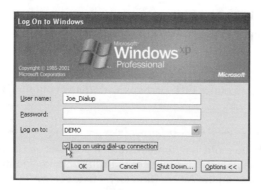

If the user connects using RAS after logging on to the workstation (using the "Network and Dial-up Connections" icons), after he has logged on locally to the machine, the security policy settings and the Administrative Templates policy settings for the user and computer are not applied right away; rather they are applied during the next normal background refresh cycle (every 90 minutes by default).

Other sections of Group Policy are handled as follows during a slow connection:

Internet Explorer Maintenance Settings   These are not downloaded by default over slow links. (You can change this condition using the information in the "Using Group Policy to Affect Group Policy" section later in this chapter.)

Folder Redirection Settings   These are not downloaded by default over slow links. (You can change this condition using the information in the "Using Group Policy to Affect Group Policy" section later in this chapter.)

Scripts (Logon, Logoff, Startup, and Shutdown)   These are not downloaded by default over slow links. (You can change this condition using the information in the "Using Group Policy to Affect Group Policy" section later in this chapter.) Also see the sidebar "Processing and Running Scripts over Slow Links" later in this chapter.

Disk Quota Settings   These are not downloaded by default over slow links. (You can change this condition using the information in the "Using Group Policy to Affect Group Policy" section later in this chapter.) The currently cached disk quota settings are still enforced.

Software Installation and Maintenance   These are not downloaded by default over slow links. More specifically, the offers of newly available software are not shown to users. Users do have the ability to choose whether to pull down the latest versions of applications at their whim, as detailed in Chapter 10. You can torture your dial-in users by changing the behavior of how offers are handled and permit the icons of new software to be displayed. They will hate you after you do this, but that is for you and them to work out. See the corresponding setting described later in this chapter in the "Using Group Policy to Affect Group Policy" section.

Software Restriction Policy (Windows XP Only)   These are guaranteed to download over slow links. You cannot turn off this ability.

802.11 Wireless Policy   These are not downloaded by default over slow links. (You can change this condition using the information in the "Using Group Policy to Affect Group Policy" section later in this chapter.) The currently cached 802.11 policy settings are still enforced.

Administrative Templates   These are guaranteed to download over slow links. You cannot turn off this ability.

EFS Recovery Policy   These are guaranteed to download over slow links. You cannot turn off this ability. The interface has an option that makes it appear as if you could turn off this ability, but you can't.

IPSec Policy   These are guaranteed to download over slow links. You cannot turn off this ability. The interface has an option that makes it appear as if you could turn off this ability, but you can't.

What is considered fast enough for all these policy categories can be changed from 500Kb to whatever speed you desire (independently for the computer half and the user half), as detailed in the "Using Group Policy to Affect Group Policy" section later in this chapter.

Processing and Running Scripts Over Slow Links

If your users try to run scripts while using slow links, they (and you) might notice some interesting behavior. First, computer startup scripts will not run over slow links. This just isn't supported by the Group Policy engine. However, one enterprising customer of mine had a service written to explicitly do this after the user was logged on. That said, logon scripts are currently still fair game. However, many factors play into whether the scripts will run.

When a user is dialed in over a slow link, the scripts policy itself will not process. That is, it will not receive information about new or updated scripts. The actual *running* of the scripts is a different matter altogether and is irrespective of whether the use has a slow connection. Therefore, if you applied the script policy while on a high-speed connection (for example, a home office LAN) and then a user should log on over a dial-up connection, scripts will indeed run; the script policy has already been download and set for takeoff. Indeed, your script policy might tell the client to execute the script from the server, which may or may not be available.

But until your users come back to the headquarters, they won't get updates to that script policy if any has occurred. For instance, if the script policy states to run the script from an alternate server location, this information won't be downloaded until they come back into headquarters.

Windows 2000 and Windows XP have slightly different behavior for the actual running of the scripts. Windows 2000 requires that the SYSVOL (NETLOGON share) be accessible for the scripts to even attempt to run. If the machine cannot see SYSVOL, no scripts will run.

Windows XP and Windows 2003 have addressed this problem, but it's thorny. If the machine is 100% offline (and, hence, SYSVOL isn't available), the scripts will indeed run. But if the system determines it's on a fast connection and SYSVOL is unavailable, scripts won't run.

Using Group Policy to Affect Group Policy

At times you might want to change the behavior of Group Policy. Amazingly, you actually use Group Policy settings to change the behavior of Group Policy! Several Group Policy settings appear under both the User and Computer nodes; however, you must set the policy settings in each section independently.

Affecting the User Settings of Group Policy

The Group Policy settings that affect the User node appear under User Configuration ➤ Administrative Templates ➤ System ➤ Group Policy. Remember that user accounts must be subject to the site, domain, or OU where these GPOs are linked in order to be affected. Most of these policy settings are valid for Windows 2000, Windows XP machines, and Windows 2003 servers, although some are explicitly designed and will operate only on Windows XP Professional and Windows 2003 servers.

Here's a list of the policy settings that affect the user side of Group Policy:

Group Policy Refresh Interval for Users

This setting changes the default User node background refresh rate of 90 minutes with a 0–30 minute positive randomizer to almost any number of refresh and randomizer minutes you choose. Choose a smaller number for the background refresh to speed up Group Policy happen faster on your machines, or choose a larger number to quell the traffic that a Group Policy refresh takes across your network. There is a similar refresh interval for computers, which is on an alternate clock with its own settings. A setting of 0 is equal to 7 seconds. Set to 0 only in the test lab.

Group Policy Slow Link Detection

You can change the default definition of *fast connectivity* from 500Kbps to any speed you like. Recall that certain aspects of Group Policy are not applied to machines that are determined to be coming in over slow links. This setting specifies what constitutes a slow link for the User node. There is an identically named policy setting located under the Computer node (explored later in this chapter) also needs to be set to define what is slow for the Computer node. Preferably set these to the same number.

Group Policy Domain Controller Selection

GPOs are written to the PDC emulator by default. When users (generally Domain Administrators or OU administrators) are affected by this setting, they are allowed to create new GPOs on Domain Controllers other than the PDC emulator. (See Chapter 4 for more information on this setting and how and why to use it.)

Create New Group Policy Object Links Disabled by Default

When users (generally Domain Administrators or OU administrators) are affected by this setting, the GPOs they create will be disabled by default. This ensures that users and computers are not hitting their refresh intervals and downloading half-finished GPOs that you are in the process of creating. Enable the GPOs when finished, and they will download during their next background refresh cycle.

Default Name for GPOs

If a user has been assigned the rights to create GPOs via membership in the Group Policy Creator Owners group and has also been assigned the rights to link GPOs to OUs within Active Directory, the default name created for GPOs is "New Group Policy Object." You might want all GPOs created at the domain level to have one name, perhaps "AppliesToDomain-GPO", and all GPOs created at the **Human Resources** OU level (and all child levels) to have another name, maybe "AppliestoHR-GPO." Again, in order for this policy to work, the user's account with the rights to create GPOs must be affected by the policy.

This policy setting is only valid when applied to Windows XP workstations and Windows 2003 servers.

Enforce Show Policies Only

When users (generally Domain Administrators or OU Administrators) are affected by this setting, the "Only show policy settings that can be fully managed" setting (explored in Chapter 4) is forced to be enabled. This prevents the importation of old-style NT 4 ADM templates, which have the unfortunate side effect of "tattooing" the Registry until they are explicitly removed. (See Chapter 4 for more information on using NT 4–style ADM templates with Windows 2003.)

Turn Off Automatic Update of ADM Files

ADM template files are updated by service packs. The default behavior is to check the launching point, that is, the \windows\INF folder, to see if the ADM template has yet been updated. This check for an update occurs, by default, every time you double-click the Administrative Templates section of any GPO as if you were going to modify it. However, if you enable this setting, you're saying to ignore the normal update process and simply keep on using the ADM template you initially used. In other words, you're telling the system you'd prefer to keep the initial ADM template regardless of whether a newer one is available. (See Chapter 5 for critical information on updating ADM templates when service packs are available for Windows XP or Windows 2003.)

Disallow Interactive Users from Generating Resultant Set of Policy Data

Users affected by this setting cannot use the "Group Policy Modeling" or "Group Policy Results" tasks in the GPMC. Enabling this setting locks down a possible entry point into the system. That is, it prevents unauthorized users from determining the current security settings on the box and developing attack strategies.

This policy setting is valid only when applied to Windows XP workstations and Windows 2003 servers.

Affecting the Computer Settings of Group Policy

The Group Policy settings that affect the Computer node appear under Computer Configuration ➢ Administrative Templates ➢ System ➢ Group Policy. Once computers are affected by these policy settings, they change the processing behavior of Group Policy. Remember that the computer accounts must be subject to the site, domain, or OU where these GPOs are linked in order to be affected.

Turn Off Background Refresh of Group Policy

When this setting is enabled, the affected computer downloads the latest GPOs for both the user and the computer, according to the background refresh interval—but it doesn't apply them. The GPOs are applied when the user logs off but before the next user logs on. This is helpful in situations in which you want to guarantee that a user's experience stays the same throughout the session.

Group Policy Refresh Interval for Computers

This setting changes the default Computer node background refresh rate of 90 minutes with a 30-minute randomizer to almost any number of refresh and randomizer minutes you choose. Choose a smaller number for the background refresh to speed up Group Policy on your machines, or choose a larger number to quell the traffic a Group Policy refresh takes across your network. A similar refresh interval for the Users node is on a completely separate and unrelated timing rate and randomizer. A setting of 0 equals 7 seconds. Set to 0 only in the test lab.

Group Policy Refresh Interval for Domain Controllers

Recall that Domain Controllers are updated regarding Group Policy changes within 5 minutes. You can close or widen that gap as you see fit. The closer the gap, the more network chatter. Widen the gap, and the security settings will be inconsistent until the interval is hit. A setting of 0 equals 7 seconds. Set to 0 only in the test lab.

User Group Policy Loopback Processing Mode

We'll explore this setting with an example in the next section.

Allow Cross-Forest User Policy and Roaming User Profiles

This policy is valid only in cross-forest trust scenarios. I'll describe how these work and how this policy works later in this chapter.

 This policy setting is valid only when applied to Windows XP workstations and Windows 2003 servers.

Group Policy Slow Link Detection

You can change the default definition of *fast connectivity* from 500Kbps to any speed you like. Recall that certain aspects of Group Policy are not applied to those machines that are deemed to be coming in over slow links. Independently, an identically named policy setting exists under the User node (explored earlier) also needs to be set to define what is slow for the User node. Preferably, set these to the same number.

Turn Off Resultant Set of Policy Logging

As you'll see in Chapter 4, users on Windows XP machines can launch the Resultant Set of Policy (RSoP) snap-in. Enabling this policy doesn't prevent its launch but, for all intents and purposes, disables its use. This policy disables the use for the currently logged-on user (known as the interactive user) as well as anyone trying to get the results using the remote features of the RSoP snap in.

 This policy setting is valid only when applied to Windows XP workstations and Windows 2003 servers.

Remove Users Ability to Invoke Machine Policy Refresh

By default, mere-mortal users can perform their own background refreshes using GPUpdate, as described in the Initiating a Manual Background Refresh for Windows XP and Windows 2003" section. However, you might not want users to perform their own GPUpdate. I can think of only one reason to disable this setting: to prevent users from sucking up bandwidth on Domain Controllers by continually running GPUpdate. Other than that, I can't imagine why you would want to prevent them from being able to get the latest GPO settings if they were so inclined. Perhaps one user is performing a denial of service (DoS) attack on your Domain Controllers by continually requesting Group Policy—but even that's a stretch.

Even if this policy is enabled, local administrators can still force a GPUpdate. But, again, GPUpdate only works when run locally on the machine needing the update.

This policy setting is valid only when applied to Windows XP workstations and Windows 2003 servers.

Disallow Interactive Users from Generating Resultant Set of Policy Data

This policy is similar to the "Turn off Resultant Set of Policy logging" setting, but affects only the user on the console. Enabling this setting might be useful if you don't want the interactive user to have the ability to generate RSoP data, but still allow administrators to get the RSoP remotely. Again, RSoP and its related functions are explored in Chapter 4.

This policy setting is valid only when applied to Windows XP workstations and Windows 2003 servers.

Registry Policy Processing

This setting affects how your policy settings in the Administrative Templates subtrees react (and, generally, any other policy that affects the Registry). Once this policy setting is enabled, you have two other options:

Do Not Apply During Periodic Background Processing   Typically, Administrative Templates settings are refreshed every 90 minutes or so. However, if you enable this setting, you're telling the client not ever to refresh the computer side Administrative Templates in the GPOs are meant for it after the logon. You might choose to prevent background refresh for Administrative Templates for two reasons:

- When the background refresh occurs, the screen may flicker for a second as the system reapplies the changed GPOs (with their policy settings) and instructs Explorer.exe to refresh the desktop. This could be a slight distraction for the user every 90 minutes or so.

- You might choose to disable background processing so that users' experiences with the desktop and applications stay consistent for the entire length of their logon. Having settings suddenly change while the user is logged on could be confusing, but my advice is to leave this setting alone unless you're seriously impacted by the background processing affecting your users' experience.

Process Even If the Group Policy Objects Have Not Changed   If this setting is selected, the system will update and reapply the policy settings in this category even if the underlying GPO has not changed when the background refresh interval occurs. Recall that this type of processing is meant to clean up should an administrator have nefariously gone around our backs and modified a local setting.

 You cannot turn off Registry policy processing over slow links. They are always downloaded and applied.

Internet Explorer Maintenance Policy Processing

Once enabled, this policy setting has three potential options:

Allow Processing Across a Slow Network Connection   Check this check box to allow Internet Explorer Maintenance settings to download when logging on over slow links. Enabling this could cause your users to experience a longer logon time, but adhere to your latest Internet Explorer wishes.

Do Not Apply During Periodic Background Processing   If this option is selected, the latest Internet Explorer settings in Active Directory GPOs will not be downloaded or applied during the background refresh.

Process Even If the Group Policy Objects Have Not Changed   If this option is selected, it updates and reapplies the policy settings in this category even if the underlying GPO has not changed. Recall that this type of processing is meant to clean up should a user or an administrator have nefariously gone around our backs and modified a local setting.

Software Installation Policy Processing

Once enabled, this policy setting has two potential options:

Allow Processing Across a Slow Network Connection   As I stated, by default, software deployment offers are not displayed to users connecting over slow links. This is a good thing; allowing users to click the newly available icons to begin the download and installation of new software over a 56K dial-up line can be tortuous. Use this setting to change this behavior.

 If you have already distributed software via Group Policy, and an offer has been accepted by a client computer (but perhaps not all pieces of the application have been loaded), setting this selection will likely not help, and your users may experience a long delay in running their application over a slow link. For more information on how to best distribute software to clients who use slow links, see Chapter 10.

Process Even If the Group Policy Objects Have Not Changed   For Software Installation and Maintenance, I cannot find any difference if this option is selected or not, though Microsoft has implied it might correct some actions should the software become damaged. Since software deployment offers are only displayed upon logon or reboot (otherwise known as foreground policy processing), in my testing, this setting seems not to have any outward effect.

 Users can still opt to download software over slow links, even if the "Allow Processing Across a Slow Network Connection" is selected. See the Software Installation settings described in detail in Chapter 10.

Folder Redirection Policy Processing

Once enabled, this policy setting has two potential options:

Allow Processing Across a Slow Network Connection   Recall that the Folder Redirection policy is changed only at logon time. Chances are, you wouldn't want dialed-in users to experience that new change. Rather, you would want to wait until they are on your LAN. If you want to torture your users and allow them to accept the changed policy anyway, use this setting to change this behavior.

Process Even If the Group Policy Objects Have Not Changed   I cannot find any difference if this setting is selected or not, though Microsoft has implied it might correct some folder-redirections woes should the user name get renamed.

 Folder Redirection settings are discussed in detail in Chapter 9.

Scripts Policy Processing

Once enabled, this policy setting has three potential options:

Allow Processing Across a Slow Network Connection   Recall that, by default, new or changed startup, shutdown, logon, and logoff scripts are not downloaded over slow networks. Change this to allow the download over slow links. The actual running of the scripts is a different process, as discussed earlier in the "Processing and Running Scripts Over Slow Links" sidebar.

Do Not Apply During Periodic Background Processing   This option will allow the newest script instructions to be downloaded. See the sidebar "Processing and Running Scripts Over Slow Links" earlier in the chapter.

Process Even If the GPOs Have Not Changed   This option will allow the newest script instructions to be downloaded. See the sidebar "Processing and Running Scripts Over Slow Links."

Security Policy Processing

Once enabled, this policy setting has two potential options:

Do Not Apply During Periodic Background Processing   Recall that the security settings are refreshed on the machines every 16 hours, whether they need it or not. Checking this option will turn off the check every 16 hours. It is recommended to leave this as is. However, you might want to consider enabling this setting for servers with high numbers of transactions that require all the processing power they can muster.

Process Even If the GPOs Have Not Changed   If this option is selected, nothing changes. After 16 hours, this policy category is always refreshed.

IP Security Policy Processing

Once enabled, this policy setting has three potential options:

Allow Processing Across a Slow Network Connection   When selected, this setting does nothing. IP Security settings are always downloaded, regardless of whether the computer is connected over a slow network. So, you might be asking yourself, what happens when you select this check box, which is shown in Figure 3.3? Answer: nothing—it's a bug in the interface. To repeat: IP Security is always processed, regardless of the link speed.

FIGURE 3.3   The "Allow processing across a slow network connection" setting is not used in Windows 2000, Windows XP, or Windows 2003 for IP Security or EFS settings.

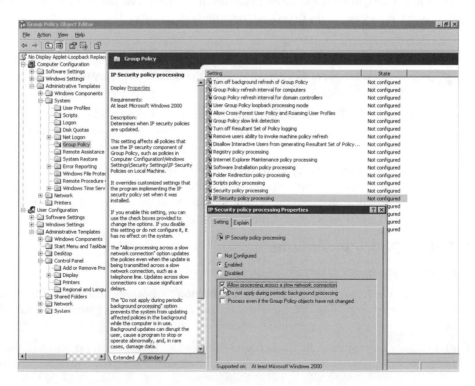

IP Security policies act slightly different from other policy setting categories. IP Security policy settings are not additive. For IP Security, the last applied policy wins.

Do Not Apply During Periodic Background Processing   If this option is selected, the latest IP Security settings in Active Directory GPOs will not be downloaded or applied during the background refresh.

Process Even If the Group Policy Objects Have Not Changed   If this option is selected, it updates and reapplies the policy settings in this category even if the underlying GPO has not changed. Recall that this type of processing is meant to clean up should a user or an administrator have nefariously gone around our backs and modified a local setting.

EFS Recovery Policy Processing

Once enabled, this policy setting has three potential options:

Allow Processing Across a Slow Network Connection   When this option is selected, it does nothing. EFS recovery settings are always downloaded, regardless of whether the computer is connected over a slow network.

Like IP Security, the EFS recovery settings are always downloaded—even over slow networks. Once again, this is the same bug as shown in Figure 3.3 earlier in this chapter. To repeat, EFS recovery policy is always processed, regardless of link speed.

 EFS recovery policies act slightly different from other policy setting categories. EFS recovery policies are not additive; the last applied policy wins.

Do Not Apply During Periodic Background Processing   If this option is selected, the latest EFS recovery settings in Active Directory GPOs are not downloaded or applied during the background refresh.

Process Even If the Group Policy Objects Have Not Changed   If this option is selected, it updates and reapplies the policy settings in this category even if the underlying GPO has not changed. Recall that this type of processing is meant to clean up should a user or an administrator have nefariously gone around our backs and modified a local setting.

Wireless Policy Processing

If this policy setting is enabled, it has three potential options:

Allow Processing Across a Slow Network Connection   Check this option to allow the latest wireless policy settings to download when the user is logging on over slow links. Enabling this could cause your users to experience a longer logon time.

Do Not Apply During Periodic Background Processing   If this option is selected, the latest wireless policy settings will not be downloaded or applied during the background refresh.

Process Even If the Group Policy Objects Have Not Changed   If this option is selected, it updates and reapplies the policy settings in this category even if the underlying GPO has not changed. Recall that this type of processing is meant to clean up should a user or an administrator have nefariously gone around our backs and modified a local setting.

This policy is valid only when applied to Windows XP workstations and Windows 2003 servers.

Disk Quota Policy Processing

If this policy setting is enabled, it has three potential options:

Allow Processing Across a Slow Network Connection   Check this option to allow the latest disk quota policy settings to download and apply when the user logs on over slow links. Enabling this could cause your users to experience a longer logon time.

Do Not Apply During Periodic Background Processing   If this option is selected, the latest disk quota policy settings will not be downloaded or applied during the background refresh.

Process Even If the Group Policy Objects Have Not Changed   If selected, this option updates and reapplies the policy settings in this category even if the underlying GPO has not changed. Recall that this type of processing is meant to clean up should a user or an administrator have nefariously gone around our backs and modified a local setting.

Disk quotas and their corresponding Group Policy settings are discussed in detail in Chapter 9.

Always Use Local ADM Files for Group Policy Object Editor

ADM files are the underlying language that creates policy settings. I'll talk more about ADM files and how to best use them in Chapter 5. However, for reference, if a computer is affected by this policy setting, the Group Policy Object Editor attempts to show the text within the ADM files from your local %windir%\inf directory (usually c:\windows\inf.) If the ADM file is different on the Domain Controller than on your local c:\windows\inf directory, you could end up seeing different settings and helptext than are really inside the Domain Controller.

Indeed, if this policy is enabled, you might now see totally different policy settings than were originally placed in the GPO. However, you might want to enable this policy setting if you know that you will always be using one specific Windows XP management workstation as described in Chapter 5. Stay tuned for Chapter 5 to see how to use this function.

This policy is valid only when applied to Windows XP workstations and Windows 2003 servers.

Group Policy Loopback Processing

As you know, the normal course of Group Policy scope is local computer, site, domain, and then each nested OU. But sometimes it's necessary to deviate from the normal routine. For instance, you might want all users, whoever they are, to be able to walk up and log on to a specific machine and get the same user node settings. For example, this can be handy in public computing environments such as libraries, nurses' stations, kiosks, and manufacturing and production assembly environments. This is also critically necessary for terminal server environments, as discussed in the "Group Policy Loopback—Replace Mode for Terminal Services" section later in this chapter.

Wouldn't it be keen if you could round up all the special computers on which users need the same settings for an OU and force them to use these settings? Whoever logs on to those computers would get the same Internet Explorer settings (such as a special proxy), logon scripts, or certain Control Panel restrictions—just for those workstations.

Reviewing Normal Group Policy Processing

Recall that sometimes computers and users can each be relegated into different OUs. They needn't always be neatly tucked under the same OU heading as we did when we put Frank Rizzo's user account and XPPro1 in the same Human Resources OU.

Indeed, a user from any other portion of the domain, say the Domain Administrator (or anyone else), could log on to XPPro1 located under the **Human Resources Computers** OU. When this happens (for example, the computer and user accounts affected by GPOs are located in different processing locations), the normal behavior is to process the computer GPOs based on the normal hierarchy and then the process the user GPOs based on the normal hierarchy. This is true just by the rules of time: computers start up, their GPOs are processed, users log on, and their GPOs are processed.

 Even with Windows XP's default of Fast Boot disabled, that's generally the way things happen.

So, if the Domain Administrator were to sit down at the XPPro1 machine in the **Human Resources Computers** OU, the normal course of events would apply the policy settings in the Computers node from the Default-First-Site, then the Corp.com domain, and then, finally, the **Human Resources Computers** OU. Next, the policy settings in GPOs linked to the user account would apply; first from the Default-First-Site and then only from the Corp.com domain (as the administrator account is not sitting under any OU in our examples).

With Group Policy Loopback processing, the rules change. There are two Group Policy Loopback modes: Merge and Replace. In both, the computer is tricked into forgetting that it's really a computer. It temporarily puts on a hat that says "I'm a user" and processes the site, domain, and organizational unit GPOs as if it were a user. Kooky, huh? Let's take a look at the Merge and Replace modes.

Group Policy Loopback — Merge Mode

When computers are subject to Group Policy Loopback—Merge Mode, GPOs process in the normal way at startup (and at background refresh time): Computer node for site, for domain, and then for each nested OU. The user then logs on, and policy settings meant for that user are applied in the normal way: all GPOs are processed from the site, the domain, and then each nested OU.

But when computers are affected by Group Policy Loopback—Merge mode, the system determines where the computer account is and applies another round of user node settings—those contained in all GPOs that lead to that computer (yes, user node settings). This means that the logged-on user gets whacked with two different sets of User node policy settings. Here's the timeline:

- The computer starts up and gets the appropriate Computer node policy settings.

- The user logs on and gets the appropriate User node policy settings.

- The computer then puts on a hat that says, "I'm a user." Then all *user* node policy settings apply to the *computer*. Again, this happens because the computer is wearing the "I'm a user" hat.

The net result is that the user settings from the user's account and the user settings from the computer (which temporarily thinks it's a user) are on par and equal to each other; neither is more important than the other, except when they overlap. In that case, the computer settings win, as usual.

The Group Policy Loopback—Merge Mode is rarely used unless you need to modify a property in the user profile, but do it per computer.

Group Policy Loopback — Replace Mode

When computers are subject to Group Policy Loopback—Replace Mode, Group Policy processes in the normal way at startup (and at background refresh time): Computer node for site, domain, and then each nested OU. The user then logs on, and GPOs meant for the user are totally ignored down the food chain for the logged-on user. Instead, the computer puts on an "I'm a user" hat, and the system determines where the computer account is, but applies the User node settings contained in all GPOs that lead to that computer. Therefore, you change the balance of power so all users are forced to heed the User settings based on what is geared for the computer. Confused? Let's generate an example to "unconfuse" you.

By and large, Group Policy Loopback—Replace Mode is more useful than Merge mode and works well in public computing environments such as labs. So let's work though an example to solidify our understanding of Replace mode. In this example, we'll perform a variety of steps:

- Create a new OU called **Public Kiosk**.

- Move a Windows XP machine into the **Public Kiosk** OU.

- Create a new GPO for the **Public Kiosk** OU that performs two functions:

  - Disables the Display Properties dialog box.

  - Performs Group Policy Loopback—Replace Mode processing so that all users logging on to the computers in the **Public Kiosk** OU will be unable to use the Display Properties dialog box.

Setting All Who Log on to a Specific Computer to Use a Specific Printer

You might want to use the Group Policy Loopback—Merge Mode to create a printer and apply it to anyone who uses a particular machine. For instance, you might want anyone who logs on to a machine on the 4th floor to automatically connect to the printer on the 4th floor. One way to do this is to run around to every machine on the 4th floor, log on as the user, and manually connect to the printer on the 4th floor.

If you've ever attempted this feat, you might have also tried to create a Group Policy startup script for a computer to try to connect everyone to a printer on the network; but it won't work. There is no user environment in which to house this newly created printer. So you have a paradox: how do you run a computer startup script for every user who sits down at a machine, but run this startup script after the user is logged on? Group Policy Loopback—Merge Mode comes to the rescue.

In both loopback processing modes, the computer doesn't think it's a computer. It temporarily puts on a user hat and processes the site, domain, and organizational unit GPOs as if it were a user.

With that in mind, you'll need to do several things:

1. Create a VB script that connects you to the printer you want. (Later in this sidebar, you'll see and example, ASSIGNHP4.VBS.)

2. Create an OU, say "4th Floor Computers," and move the computers on the 4th floor into it.

3. Create a new GPO on that OU, and name it, say, "All computers get HPLJ4 Printer."

4. Drill down into the new GPO to Computer Configuration ➢ Administrative Templates ➢ System ➢ Group Policy ➢ User Group Policy Loopback Processing Mode, and specify that it be in Merge mode.

5. Drill down into User Configuration ➢ Windows ➢ Scripts ➢ Logon. Click "Add" to add a new file, click "Browse" to open the File Requester, copy the ASSIGNHP4.VBS script, and add it to the list to run.

Remember, in Loopback Processing mode, the computer thinks it's a user, so use User/Logon scripts, not Computer/Startup script.

Now, whenever you log on as any user to a computer in the 4th Floor Computers OU, the GPOs meant for the user will be evaluated and run. The computer will then put on a user hat and run its own logon script, and you will get the printer assigned for every user on a computer.

Here is the ASSIGNHP4.VBS vbscript you can use for the above example:

```
Set wshNetwork = CreateObject("WScript.Network")


    PrinterPath = "\\server1\HPLJ4"
    PrinterDriver = "HP LaserJet 4"
    WshNetwork.AddwindowsPrinterConnection PrinterPath, PrinterDriver
    WshNetwork.SetDefaultPrinter "\\server1\HPLJ4"
    Wscript.Echo "Default Printer Created"
```

Thanks to Richard Zimmerman of ABC Computers for the inspiration for this Sidebar.

Creating a New OU

To create a new OU called **Public Kiosk,** follow these steps:

1. Log on to the Domain Controller WINDC01 as Domain Administrator.

2. Choose Start ➢ Programs ➢ Administrative Tools and select Active Directory Users And Computers.

3. Right-click the domain name, and choose New ➢ Organizational Unit. Enter **Public Kiosk** as the name in the "New Object - New Organizational Unit" dialog box.

You are creating this new OU on the same level as **Human Resources**. Do not create this new OU underneath Human Resources.

Moving a Client into the Public Kiosk OU

In this case, we'll move a different computer, say XPPro2, into the **Public Kiosk** OU. Follow these steps:

1. In Active Directory Users And Computers, right-click the domain and choose Find to open the "Find Users, Contacts and Groups" dialog box.

2. In the Find drop-down, select Computers. In the Name field, type **XPPro2** (or the name of some other computer) to find the computer account of the same name. Once you've found it, right-click the account, and choose Move. Move the account to the **Public Kiosk** OU.

    Repeat these steps for all other computers you want to move to the **Public Kiosk** OU.

Creating a Group Policy Object with Group Policy Loopback—Replace Mode

We want the Display Properties dialog box disabled for all users who log on to XPPro2. To do this, we need to set two policy settings within a single GPO: **Disable Display in Control Panel** and **User Group Policy Loopback Processing Mode**. Follow these steps using the GPMC:

1. Right-click the **Public Kiosk** OU, and choose "Create and link a GPO here."

2. In the "New GPO" dialog box name the GPO something descriptive, such as "No Display Applet -- Loopback Replace."

3. Highlight the GPO and click Edit to open the Group Policy Object Editor.

4. To hide the Settings tab, drill down to User Configuration ➢ Administrative Templates ➢ Control Panel ➢ Display and double-click the **Remove Display in Control Panel** policy setting. Change the policy setting from "Not Configured" to "Enabled," and click OK.

5. To enable loopback processing, drill down to Computer Configuration ➢ Administrative Templates ➢ System ➢ Group Policy and double-click the **User Group Policy Loopback Processing Mode** policy setting. Change the setting from "Not Configured" to "Enabled," select "Replace" from the drop-down box, as shown in Figure 3.4, and click OK.

6. Close the Group Policy Object Editor.

Verifying That Group Policy Loopback—Replace Mode Is Working

You'll want to log on to XPPro2, but you'll want to restart it because you just moved it from one OU to another. (This will quickly re-jumpstart the policy processing; otherwise you might have to wait 120–150 minutes for it to kick in after a move.) Since we're using Loopback Policy processing in Replace mode, you can choose any user you have defined—a mere mortal or even the administrator of the domain.

FIGURE 3.4 Choose the Loopback Processing mode desired, in this case, "Replace."

Choose Start ➢ Control Panel ➢ Display, and note that no one can access the Display Properties dialog box, as shown in Figure 3.5.

Group Policy Loopback—Replace Mode policy processing is powerful, but really is only useful for specialty machines. Additionally, you'll need to use it sparingly, because loopback processing is a bit more CPU intensive for the client and servers and quite difficult to troubleshoot should things go wrong.

Group Policy Loopback—Replace Mode for Terminal Services

Group Policy Loopback—Replace Mode has one other major use: Terminal Services. If you have lots of servers and lots of users logging on to them, chances are, you want everyone who logs on to your Terminal Services machines to have precisely the same settings, regardless of who they are.

The process of establishing these settings is straightforward:

- Create an OU for your Terminal Services computers and give it an appropriate name, such as **Terminal Services Computers** OU.

- Set Loopback Replace mode to apply to that OU

- Stuff your Terminal Services computer objects into the OU and reboot them

Now any user policy settings within GPOs set upon the Terminal Services computers OU and everyone logging on to the Terminal Services computers will get the exact same settings.

Windows 2000 servers and Windows 2003 Terminal Services respond just fine to Loopback Replace mode. So be sure to stuff your Windows 2000 Terminal Services computer objects into your designated OU too and then manually configure the policy settings on those computers as desired.

F I G U R E 3 . 5   With Group Policy Loopback—Replace Mode processing enabled, all users are affected by a computer's setting.

Yet Another Practical Use for Group Policy Loopback—Replace Mode

I don't know about you, but I just hate it when I walk up to a server and log on. Usually, I have no idea what the server's name, function, IP address, and so on could possibly be. In the NT 4 days, I used the following trick:

1. Fire up Windows Paint.

2. Create a `.bmp` file that detailed the name, function, and IP address and save it as, say, `c:\winnt\background.bmp`.

3. Modify the `.default` user profile so that when no one was logged on at the console, the `.bmp` file was displayed. To do this, open the Registry of the local server and change `HKEY_USERS\.DEFAULT\Control Panel\Desktop\Wallpaper` to path of `c:\winnt\background.bmp`.

But there was one major problem—as soon as I logged on to to the server, the background went away (because my local profile took over), and 20 seconds later, I forgot what the machine's name, function, and IP address were. With Windows 2003 and the Group Policy Loopback—Replace Mode policy, I've discovered a cool trick; you can now force the same background `.bmp` for every user who physically logs on to any given machine.

The idea is simple:

- Create the `.bmp` file as explained earlier, and store it once again, locally, as `c:\windows\background.bmp`.

- Create a new GPO on the Domain Controllers OU or on your own OU for your servers. Call the policy "Forced Background Wallpaper—Loopback Replace."

- Modify the User node of the policy as follows:

1. Drill down through User Configuration ➢ Administrative Templates ➢ Desktop ➢ Active Desktop ➢ **Enable Active Desktop**, and set "Enabled."

2. Drill down through User Configuration ➢ Administrative Templates ➢ Desktop ➢ Active Desktop ➢ **Active Desktop Wallpaper**, and set "Enabled." Set the wallpaper name to c:\windows\background.bmp.

3. Drill down through User Node ➢ Administrative Templates ➢ Desktop ➢ Active Desktop ➢ **Allow Only Bitmapped Wallpaper**, and set "Enabled."

4. To modify the Computer node of the policy, drill down through Computer Configuration ➢ Administrative Templates ➢ System ➢ Group Policy ➢ and enable **User Group Policy Loopback Processing Mode**. Set to Loopback—Replace.

Now, whenever anyone logs on to that server, they will get the exact same background .bmp! This is still true even if they usually get a background dictated via some other Group Policy for their own personal account!

There is one more accompanying tip to seal the deal. If you've enabled Terminal Services Administration mode, you cannot, by default, see the wallpaper when coming in over Terminal Services. Change the default behavior of Terminal Services by using the Terminal Services Configuration application, right-clicking the RDP protocol, and selecting the Environment tab. Choose to view the wallpaper by deselecting the "Disable the Wallpaper" check box.

A similar ability is available from the BGINFO tool, which you can download from www.sysinternals.com. And it's dynamic, so if something changes on the server, the background changes with it. However, this tip is here as a useful example of how to use the Group Policy Loopback—Replace Mode.

As an administrator, you might want to log on to Terminal Services machines, but you don't want the same settings as everyone else. To configure this, simply use the techniques found in Chapter 2, and filter the GPO containing the Loopback policy for, say, Domain Administrators.

As a little side note, additionally, if your Terminal Services are Windows Server 2003, at your disposal is an arsenal of policy settings designed to manage Windows 2003 Terminal Services. You'll find two sets of Terminal Services policy settings for Windows 2003: one for users and one for computers. To manipulate Terminal Services computers, drill down through Computer Configuration ➤ Administrative Templates ➤ Windows Components ➤ Terminal Services. To manipulate Terminal Services clients, drill down through User Configuration ➤ Administrative Templates ➤ Windows Components ➤ Terminal Services.

Including information on how best to use the policy settings that configure Windows 2003 Terminal Services is beyond the scope of this book. To that end, I recommend Christa Anderson's *Windows & .NET Magazine* article "Using GPOs to Configure Terminal Services." You can find it at www.winnetmag.com. InstantDoc ID: 38284.

Group Policy with Cross-Forest Trusts

Windows 2003 brings a new trust type to the table, a forest trust (also known as a cross-forest trust). The idea is that if you have multiple, unrelated forests, you can join their root domains with one single trust; then, any time new domains pop up in either forest, there is an automatically implied trust relationship.

All domains must be in Windows 2003 Functional mode, and all forests must be in Windows 2003 Functional mode. It is then possible to create cross-forest trusts via the Active Directory Domains and Trusts utility. For an example, see Figure 3.6.

In this example, all domains trust all other domains via the cross-forest trust. Indeed, a user with an account housed in bigu.edu, say Sol Rosenberg, could sit down at a computer in either corp.com or widgets.corp.com, and log on to his user account, which is maintained in bigu.edu.

When Sol (srosenberg) from bigu.edu logs on to any computer in domains below corp.com (that is, widgets.corp.com), the logon screen will not present BIGU as an option. To log on, Sol will need to type **srosenberg@bigu.edu** as his logon id along with his password. This is one of the limitations of cross-forest trusts.

FIGURE 3.6   Here's one example of how a cross-forest trust can be used.

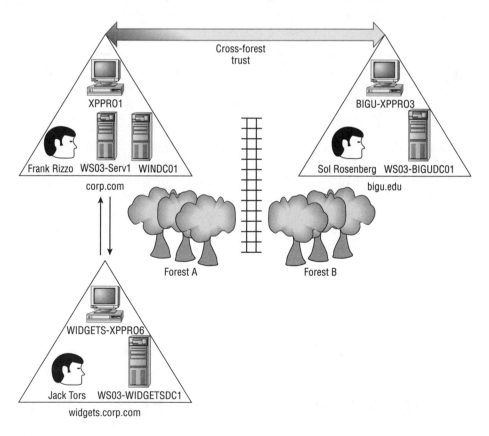

What Happens When Logging on to Different Clients Across a Cross-Forest Trust?

So what happens when Sol from bigu.edu has access to various computer types in the corp.com forest? Let's find out.

Logging on to Windows XP (with no Service Pack or with SP1) Across a Cross-Forest Trust

For users logging on to Windows XP machines in Windows 2003 domains, Group Policy across forests acts as if it were one big forest. For instance, if Sol Rosenberg logs into WIDGETS-XPPRO6 at widgets.corp.com or XPPRO1 at corp.com, Sol would get the GPOs that affect his user account and the user policy settings that affect him. The Windows XP computer Sol uses will get the GPOs meant for it. (The computer would embrace the policy settings based on the site, the domain, and the OU it's in.)

Makes sense. Take a deep breath, and then read the next section.

 Will this change with Windows XP's SP2? Yes. Keep reading.

Logging on to a Windows 2003 Server Across a Cross-Forest Trust

Here's where things get weird, so try to stay with me. Imagine that Sol Rosenberg in bigu.edu is also the SQL database administrator for a server named WS03-Serv1 over in corp.com in the **Human Resources Computers** OU. From time to time, Sol gets in his car and travels from the BigU campus over to the WS03-Serv1 computer sitting at the corp.com headquarters. He sits down, logs on locally to the console (where he's been granted access), and…he doesn't get the GPOs meant for him (and therefore doesn't get his own policy settings).

Instead the server processes GPOs as if it was using Group Policy Loopback Processing Mode—Replace Mode. What does this mean?

- The GPOs that would normally apply to Sol's user account in bigu.edu are ignored by the Windows 2003 server.

- The computer puts on an "I'm a user" hat and says, "Give me the GPOs that would apply to me if I were a user."

So, in our example, we can see that when Sol from bigu.edu logs on to WS03-Serv1, his policy settings are ignored. The computer then looks at the GPOs that would apply to users in the **Human Resources Computers** OU (where the WS03-Serv1 account resides).

Since no GPOs linked to the **Human Resources Computers** OU contain policy settings geared for users, Sol gets no policy settings applied.

After logging on, you can check out the Application Event Log and see Event ID 1109 which states that Sol is "from a different forest logged onto this machine. Cross Forest Group Policy processing is disabled and loopback processing has been enforced in this forest for this user account."

For your own testing and to solidify this concept, you might wish, just for now, to link an existing GPO (which has user policy settings) to the **Human Resources Computers** OU. For instance, link the "Hide Desktop Tab" GPO to the **Human Resources Computers** OU, then log back on as Sol. Sol's user account will be affected by the GPO with the policy setting.

Logging on to Windows 2000 Across a Cross-Forest Trust

Logging on to a Windows 2000 system with SP4 across the trust—either Server or Professional—is just like logging on to Windows 2003 Server. That is, the GPOs that affect the user are ignored, and the computer processes Group Policy Loopback—Replace Mode.

Logging on to a Windows 2000 system that doesn't have SP4 (say, SP3 and earlier) across the trust—either Server or Professional—will not perform loopback. The user will get the expected user settings, and the computer will get the expected computer settings.

The Big Question: Why Loopback Across Cross-Forest Trusts?

At this point, you're likely scratching your head in disbelief. Why would Sol not get the GPOs that should affect him? The answer is simple: if Sol were assigned software (see Chapter 10), logon scripts, or other potentially dangerous settings, our machine's stability could be affected.

This mechanism protects our systems from stuff that we might not want to happen to it. Since we're not administrating Sol, we don't know what potential harm Sol's settings might do. Then, we need to examine what might happen if the folks at Microsoft decided to do things differently, say, have no GPOs affect Sol when he uses our corp.com machines. That might have been really bad too, because then Sol would have free reign to do whatever he wanted.

So what does Loopback buy us? Loopback makes us think about what happens when users from afar use our systems. Even though, as you know, user policy settings don't affect computers, you can start to design your OUs and GPOs for this occasion. That is, if you set up user policy settings in OUs that just contain servers, and someone in a foreign domain logs on, they'll at least get the user policy settings you intend—not what their administrator wanted.

Strange? Yes, but it works, and this becomes strangely more logical the more you think about it.

What about workstation machines? This is a less-critical problem on workstation machines, because, well, it's just a workstation. If someone is assigned an application (see Chapter 10) that maybe does evil stuff, at least it's only affecting a workstation, not a server that a whole team might have access to.

I have more advice on how to manage this in the "Disabling Loopback Processing When Using Cross-Forest Trusts" section later in this chapter.

Microsoft has additional documentation on times when you might not get GPOs applied on Windows 2000 systems. See MSKB 823862 for more information.

Logging on to Windows XP with SP2 Across a Cross-Forest Trust

Logging on to Windows XP with SP2 installed across the trust is just like logging on to Windows 2003 Server (or Windows 2000 Professional with SP4). That is, GPOs that would normally affect users are ignored, and the computer processes Group Policy Loopback—Replace Mode. This might drive system administrators and CIO managers alike nuts.

Imagine that you are halfway through your Windows XP rollout, and then you add Windows XP plus SP2 to the mix. Users will definitely get different settings when logging on to these different machines. So, if things start going haywire, know what the score is by using the chart in the "Cross-Forest Trust Client Matrix" section later in this chapter.

Event ID 1109 will be generated in the Application Event log stating that a user is ..."from a different forest."

Disabling Loopback Processing When Using Cross-Forest Trusts

If you do not want the default behavior, which is that Loopback Replace processing is enabled for the computer, you can set a specific Group Policy to apply to the computers you want to be normal again. Here are my recommendations:

- Keep the default behavior for all servers: Windows 2000 Server + SP4 and Windows 2003 Server. You want them to process in Group Policy Loopback—Replace Mode.

- Return the normal behavior for all workstations: Windows 2000 + SP4 and Windows XP + SP2. Windows 2000 + SP3 (and earlier) and Windows XP + SP1 (and no service pack) are already at the normal behavior. You want them to process GPOs using regular processing rules .

To do this, you need to locate the **Allow Cross-Forest User Policy and Roaming User Profiles** policy setting. Drill down through Computer Configuration ➢ Administrative Templates ➢ System ➢ Group Policy. To set it up, follow these steps:

1. Create a new GPO at the domain level, say, "No Loopback for Cross-Forest". Enable the policy setting named **Allow Cross-Forest User Policy and Roaming User Profiles.** This will initially affect all computers, including servers.

   However, I suggest that you filter out your server machines so that they keep the default loopback behavior. I suggest you do this as follows:

2. Create a security group called "AllMyServers."

3. Add all the Windows 2000 and Windows 2003 servers (regardless of service pack) in the domain to the AllMyServers group.

4. Deny the AllMyServers group the ability to process this new GPO.

In a pure Windows 2003 and Windows XP environment, you can set up a WMI filter to apply the policy just to the servers. See Chapter 10 for information about WMI filters.

This will maintain the loopback behavior for servers, but go back to normal processing for absolutely all workstations in the domain. This way your servers are protected from other users in trusted forests from potentially doing bad stuff to your servers. But those same users are free to have normal processing on all your workstations.

Be careful when using the Deny attribute to deny a group the ability to apply Group Policy. The GPMC will not show you that you are passing over specific users or computers from applying the GPO in the Settings tab. I discussed this earlier in Chapter 2.

Cross-Forest Trust Client Matrix

If your head is spinning about what happens to users when they use a specific client across a cross-forest trust, this table is for you. Additionally, Table 3.1 shows which client systems can be set back to normal processing by enabling the **Allow Cross-Forest User Policy and Roaming User Profiles** policy setting.

TABLE 3.1   Cross-Forest Trust Client Matrix

Client	What Happens When a User Logs on Across the Cross-Forest Trust	Can be Changed by the "Allow Cross-Forest User Policy and Roaming User Profiles" Policy Setting
Windows 2000 Server or Professional, with no service pack, SP1, SP2, or SP3	User gets user settings. Computer gets computer settings.	No
Windows 2000 Server or Professional, with SP4	User settings are ignored. Computer gets settings as if it were a user (that Group Policy Loopback—Replace Mode)	Yes
Windows XP Professional with no service pack or SP1	User gets user settings. Computer gets computer settings.	No

TABLE 3.1 Cross-Forest Trust Client Matrix *(continued)*

Client	What Happens When a User Logs on Across the Cross-Forest Trust	Can be Changed by the "Allow Cross-Forest User Policy and Roaming User Profiles" Policy Setting
Windows XP Professional with the forthcoming SP2	As of this writing, SP2 isn't out yet. However, according to Microsoft, the following will occur: User settings are ignored. Computer gets settings as if it were a user (that is, Group Policy Loopback—Replace Mode)	Yes
Windows 2003 Server with any service pack	User settings are ignored. Computer gets settings as if it were a user (that is, Group Policy Loopback—Replace Mode)	Yes

Understanding Cross-Forest Trust Permissions

Windows 2003 cross-forest trusts have two modes: Forest-wide Authentication and Selective Authentication, as shown in Figure 3.7. To view the screen shown in Figure 3.7, open Active Directory Domains and Trusts, locate the properties of the trust, click the Authentication tab.

In a Windows 2003 Active Directory domain, Full Authentication mode permits Group Policy across forests to act as if it were one big forest. That is, GPOs are processed according to Table 3.1.

FIGURE 3.7 You can set Forest-Wide Authentication or Selective Authentication.

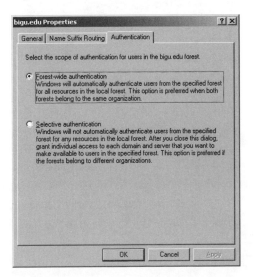

We already know that Sol is the SQL database administrator over at corp.com, and we saw what happened when he logged on to the Windows 2003 member server WS03-Serv1. Twice a week, however, Sol works at widgets.corp.com on the WIDGETS-XPPRO3 for some CAD work. Then, the unthinkable happens.

An attack originating at bigu.edu upon corp.com's computers gets the two domain administrators in a heated battle. The corp.com Domain Administrator decides he wants to prevent attacks from bigu.edu, so he enables "Selective Authentication." Now no one from bigu.edu can log on to any of the machines in corp.com or widgets.corp.com. Ergo, Sol will not be able to log on to either his WS03-Serv1 Windows 2003 member server in corp.com or to his WID-GETS-XPPRO3 machine in widgets.corp.com. Sol needs the "Allowed to Authenticate" right on the computer objects he will use. In this example, you can see what is done for WIDGETS-XPPRO3, as shown in Figure 3.8.

Additional computers in corp.com and widgets.corp.com need these explicit rights if anyone else from bigu.edu is going to use them. Then, Group Policy will process as described earlier and summarized in Table 3.1.

See Chapter 7 for how profiles react in conjunction with cross-forest trusts.

FIGURE 3.8   You need to specifically grant the "Allowed to Authenticate" right in order for Sol to use this machine.

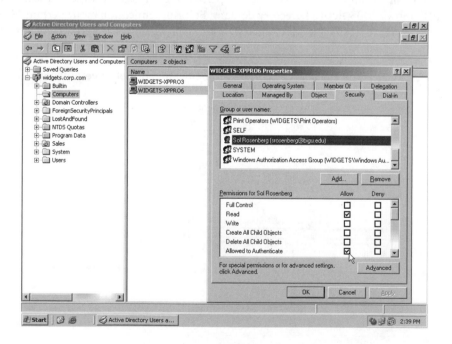

Intermixing Group Policy and NT 4 System Policy

I've already discussed how Group Policy cannot apply to Windows 9X or Windows NT clients. Group Policy applies only to Windows 2000, Windows XP, and Windows 2003 clients. However, the opposite is not true. That is, NT 4 System Policy (whose filename is `NTCONFIG.POL`) is perfectly valid and accepted on Windows 2000, Windows XP, and Windows 2003 Server clients. You might have an occasion to use both at the same time—typically if you're in the middle of an NT 4 to Windows 2000 or Windows 2003 migration. If this happens, it's likely you'll have both Windows 2000 Group Policy and legacy NT 4 System Policy on the same network.

If you're trying to migrate from NT to Active Directory, you basically have four major cases:

1. Both computer and user accounts in a Windows NT domain

2. A computer account in Windows NT and a user account in an Active Directory domain

3. A computer account in an Active Directory domain and a user account in Windows NT

4. Both computer and user accounts in Active Directory

You could, if you wanted, have an NT 4 System Policy (named `NTCONFIG.POL`) file in each and every domain—NT 4 or an Active Directory domain. Hopefully, you won't be taking your `NTCONFIG.POL` files with you when you go to Active Directory, but, if you do, you'll need to know how that calculates into the final RSoP. Additionally, it's important to remember that NT 4 System Policy "tattoos" the machines it touches, meaning that even if you're eventually going to phase out NT 4 System Policy, you'll need a battle plan to specifically reverse the settings in `NTCONFIG.POL` so that your clients can phase out the settings.

Let's briefly examine what will happen in each of these cases, which are illustrated in Figure 3.9.

Case 1: Both computer and user accounts are contained in the Windows NT domain.   When the computer starts up, it first applies any settings in the computer-side of the local GPO. Next, the user logs on to the NT 4 domain and obtains the user-side settings from the `NTCONFIG.POL` file. If present, the user side of the local GPO applies after the `NTCONFIG.POL` settings. These settings are added cumulatively, except if there is a conflict. If there is a conflict, most often the `NTCONFIG.POL` settings win.

Case 2: The computer account is in the Windows NT domain, and the user account is in the Active Directory domain.   When the computer starts up, it logs on to the NT 4 domain. If present, the computer side of the local GPO applies. When the user logs on to Active Directory, two things happen:

- The computer downloads and applies `NTCONFIG.POL` (from the NT 4 domain).

- The user processes GPOs normally. First, user-side local GPO settings apply, followed by the user-side Active Directory GPOs. As expected, these Active Directory GPO settings are added cumulatively to the local GPO settings, except if there is a conflict. If there is a conflict, the last written Group Policy setting wins. If there is any `NTCONFIG.POL` file in the domain where the user's account is located, that old System Policy is ignored for the user.

FIGURE 3.9 There are four main cases when dealing with NT 4 System Policy and Windows 2000 or Windows XP clients.

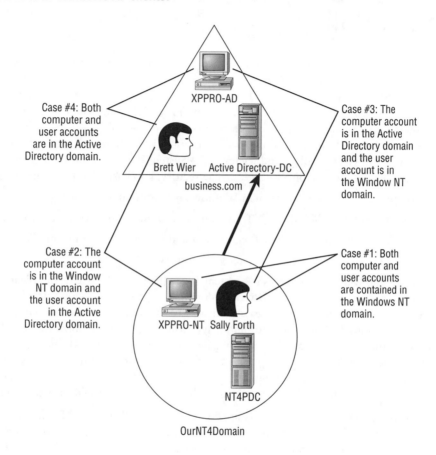

Case #4: Both computer and user accounts are in the Active Directory domain.

Case #3: The computer account is in the Active Directory domain and the user account is in the Window NT domain.

Case #2: The computer account is in the Window NT domain and the user account in the Active Directory domain.

Case #1: Both computer and user accounts are contained in the Windows NT domain.

XPPRO-AD

Brett Wier   Active Directory-DC

business.com

XPPRO-NT   Sally Forth

NT4PDC

OurNT4Domain

WARNING   In some circumstances, it appears that the local Windows 2000 Group Policy wins, such as when you set a background desktop image. As usual, you'll want to test to make sure that what you want is what you get when you intermix NT 4 System Policy and local GPOs.

Case 3: The computer account is in an Active Directory domain, and the user account is in the Windows NT domain.   When the computer starts up, it first applies any settings in the computer side of the local GPO. Then, after the computer logs on to Active Directory, it receives the computer-side GPOs from the site, domain, and OUs. As expected, these Active Directory GPO settings are added cumulatively to the local GPO settings, except if there is a conflict. If there is a conflict, the last-written Group Policy setting wins. If there is an NTCONFIG.POL file in the domain where the computer's account is located, that old System Policy is ignored for the computer.

Upon logon, if present, the user side of the local GPO applies to the user. Then, the user downloads and applies user-side settings from the `NTCONFIG.POL` file on the NT domain. These settings are added cumulatively, except if there is a conflict. If there is a conflict, `NTCONFIG.POL` wins.

Case 4: Both computer and user accounts are in Active Directory.   Most of this book is about this case. Both the computer and user apply local GPO settings first, followed by the GPOs from Active Directory: site, domain, and OUs. These Active Directory GPO settings append the local GPO settings, except if there is a conflict. If there is a conflict, the Active Directory GPO settings win over the local GPO settings. No System Policy (`NTCONFIG.POL`) is downloaded. However, clients that have been tattooed by `NTCONFIG.POL` will stay tattooed, and it's likely that at least some Registry entries will have to be manually scrubbed. Therefore, it's best to reverse the `NTCONFIG.POL` settings while you still can—before both the computer and the user accounts have been migrated. After the migration, neither the user nor the computer will read from the `NTCONFIG.POL` file.

Final Thoughts

Group Policy doesn't just pick and choose when it wants to apply. Rather, a specific set of rules is followed when it comes time to process. Understanding these rules is paramount in helping you pre-troubleshoot Group Policy problems. Many other things can affect the Group Policy engine, including loopback policy processing and how users connect over slow links.

Group Policy processing with a cross-forest trust can be tricky because each operating system and service pack has its own way of doing things; but hopefully the text, examples, and Table 3.1 can help you with any problems.

Last, try to get away from any NT 4 System Policy. Remember that they tattoo and are difficult to fully scrub out of your environment.

Here are a few things to keep in mind:

Remember initial policy processing.   Windows 2000 and Windows 2003 machines process all GPOs when the computer starts up or when the user logs on. Remember, there is no ongoing initial policy processing for Windows XP machines by default.

Remember background refresh policy processing (member servers).   For Windows 2000, Windows 2003, and Windows XP member machines, this happens some time after the user is logged on (usually 90 minutes or so).

Remember background refresh policy for Windows XP.   Windows XP is unique and processes GPOs only in the background (asynchronously). Some features, such as Software Distribution, Folder Redirection, and other functions take two reboots or logons to take effect. Advanced Folder Redirection takes three logons to take effect. This is because these special functions can be processed only in the foreground. You can turn off this feature as described earlier in this chapter.

Remember background refresh policy processing (Domain Controllers).   Windows 2000 and Windows 2003 Domain Controllers receive a background refresh every 5 minutes (after replication has occurred).

Security policy processing occurs every 16 hours   For all operating systems, every 16 hours, only the security settings within all GPOs are reprocessed and applied, regardless of whether security settings have changed. This ensures that all security functions in all GPOs are reprocessed if someone has gone around the security on the system manually.

Leverage "Process Even If the Group Policy Objects Have Not Changed."   You can tell many other Group Policy categories (such as Administrative Templates) to also refresh as the security policy settings do. Note, however, this enforcement takes affect at the background refresh interval.

How Group Policy reacts in cross-domain scenarios depends on the operating system.   See the "Cross-Forest Trust Client Matrix" section earlier in this chapter for information on how specific operating systems react during cross-forest trust scenarios.

Be careful and test when using NT 4 and Active Directory with Group Policy.   If you're still migrating from NT 4 to Windows 2000 or Windows 2003, you'll need to understand the reaction when user and/or computer accounts still have a foot in NT 4. With that in mind, test, test, test before you deploy.

4

Troubleshooting Group Policy

Working with Group Policy isn't always a bed of roses. Sure, it's delightful when you can set up GPOs with their policy settings from upon high and have them reflected on your users' desktops. However, when you make a Group Policy wish, a specific process occurs before that wish comes true. Indeed, the last chapter discussed *when* Group Policy applies. Now you understand the general rules of the game and when they occur.

But what if the unexpected happens? Most specifically, it's difficult to determine *where* a policy setting comes from and *how* it's applied. Or, if Group Policy isn't working, *why* not, and *what* the heck is going on? Additionally, you're usually after *who* to blame (but that's actually something that auditing (discussed in Chapter 6) can help with. For additional information on third-party tools, see the Appendix.

A user might call the Help Desk and loudly declare, "Things have just changed on my desktop! I want them back the way they were!" Okay, sure, you want things better too. But, a lot of variables are involved. First, there are the four levels: Local Group Policy, site, domain, and each nested OU (so perhaps even more levels). Then, to make matters worse, what if multiple administrators are making multiple and simultaneous Group Policy changes across your environment? Who knows who has enabled what Group Policy settings and how some user is getting Group Policy applied?

Additional factors are involved as well. For instance, if you have old-style NT 4 System Policy, things can be particularly complex. Or, perhaps you have a Windows 2003 forest, with cross-forest trusts to another Windows 2003 forest, and users are logging in all over the place. Not to mention a whole litany of things that could possibly go wrong between the time you make your wish and the time the client is expected to honor that wish.

Here's a foretaste of what to expect while troubleshooting GPOs:

Disabled GPOs   If the GPO is disabled or half the GPO is disabled, you need to hunt it down.

Inheritance Troubles   Between site, domain, and multiple nested OUs, it can be a challenge to locate the GPO you need to fix.

GPO Precedence at a Given Level   With multiple GPOs linked to a specific level in Active Directory, you might have some extra hunting to do.

Permissions Problems   Ensuring that users and computers are in the correct site, domain, and OU is one battle; however, ensuring that they have the correct permissions to access GPOs is quite another.

Windows XP Processing   Windows XP changes the way GPOs are processed. And Windows XP with SP2 changes things even more with cross-forest trusts.

Replication Problems   The health of the GPO itself on Domain Controllers is important when hunting down policy settings that aren't applying.

Slow Links   You've rolled out your RAS (Remote Access Service). Now how and when are your clients going to process GPOs?

These are just a few places where you might encounter trouble. Between various client types with different processing behavior, these problems and the occasional solar flare make things crazy. Troubleshooting can get complicated. Fast.

In this chapter, we'll first dive into *where* Group Policy "lives" to give you a better sense of what's going on. We'll then explore some techniques and tools that will enable you to get an even better view of *why* specific policies are being applied.

Under the Hood of Group Policy

As stated in Chapter 1, Group Policy scope really has four levels: Local Group Policy and then the three levels of Active Directory–based Group Policy—site, domain, and OU. When trouble-shooting Group Policy, one approach is to first get a firm understanding of what's going on under the hood. As a kid, I took things apart all the time. My parents went mental when they came home and the dishwasher was in pieces all over the kitchen floor. It wasn't broken; I just wanted to know how it worked. If you're like me, this section is for you.

Inside Local Group Policy

Remember that a GPO is manipulated when someone walks up to the machine, runs the Local Group Policy Object Editor (`Gpedit.msc`), and makes a wish or three. Remember that there is only one local GPO on a machine and that local GPOs affect everyone who logs on to that machine.

Where Local Group Policy Lives

Once wishes are made with Gpedit.msc and a Local Group Policy is modified, the Local Group Policy lives in two places. The first part is file based, and the second part is Registry based:

The File-Based Part of Local Group Policy   The file-based part of the local GPO can be found in c:\windows\system32\grouppolicy. The file structure found here mirrors the way the file-based portion of an Active Directory–based GPO stores its stuff. This is good news, as it makes understanding the two types of GPOs (local vs. domain-based GPOs) nearly equal.

Feel free to inspect the c:\windows\system32\grouppolicy folder, and then jump to the "Group Policy Templates" section later in this chapter to get the gist of the file structure. Note, however, that all the structure may not be present until the local GPO is edited.

The Registry-Based Part of Local Group Policy   Nothing is particularly special about Local Group Policy in regard to the Registry. You'll see later in this chapter in the "Where Are Administrative Templates Registry Settings Stored?" section how to get more information on where the results of Group Policy reaction is seen.

Three Use-at-Your-Own-Risk Local Group Policy Tips

Here are two tips that you are welcome to try—but use at your own risk. I cannot vouch for their validity or soundness, so you're on your own.

Tip #1: Ensure that admins (and other users) avoid Local Group Policy.   Perhaps you've set it up so that your users do not have access to the Start ➤ Run command. However, when you're logged in as the local administrator, you want the Run command. The JSI FAQ site has a tip (`www.jsiinc.com/subl/tip5600/rh5619.htm`) that tells you how admins (and other users) can override Local Group Policy. However, this tip is valid only when the workstation isn't a domain member.

Tip #2: Reset Local Group Policy to the defaults.   If you've set up a Local Group Policy and want to restore it to its default configuration, there's no easy way. However, my good pal Mark Minasi has a newsletter (#32) on the subject. Track it down at `www.minasi.com/archive.htm`. Even Mark admits that this solution might not be totally complete.

Tip #3: Disable a system's Local Group Policy processing.   You can also disable a system's Local Group Policy processing altogether. At your own risk, find out how at `www.winguides.com/registry/display.php/1161/`.

Inside Active Directory Group Policy Objects

Here's the strange part about Group Policy (as if it wasn't already strange enough). Chapter 1 discussed how creating a GPO really involves two steps. First, the GPO is written in the Group Policy Objects container, and then it is *linked* to a level—site, domain, or OU. So, we know that GPOs don't really "live" at the level where they're linked. Specifically, all GPOs live inside the Group Policy Objects container in the domain. That is, they're always kept nestled inside this container yet are logically linked (but not stored) to the other levels to which they point. I referred to the GPOs we created as swimming around in a virtual pool within the domain.

So far in our journey we created four new GPOs:

- "Hide Screen Saver Tab," which we applied to the Default-First-Site-Name site
- "Hide Desktop Tab," which we applied to the Corp.com domain
- "Hide Settings Tab / Restore Screen Saver Tab," which we applied to the **Human Resources Users** OU
- "Prohibit New Tasks in Task Scheduler," which we applied to the **Human Resources Computers** OU

We can check in with our concept of these GPOs as floating in a swimming pool within the Group Policy Objects container as shown here.

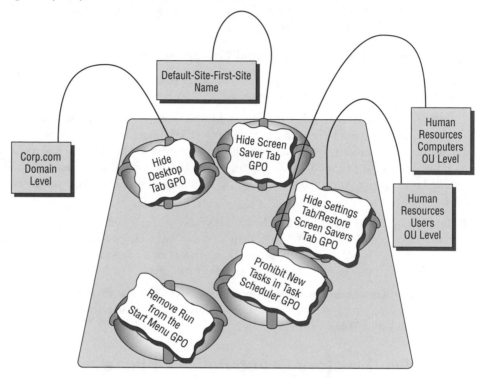

The Corp.com GPO Swimming Pool

As you can see, the GPOs never "live" at any level in Active Directory. They aren't really stored there even though it might seem logical to do so.

To reiterate, if you leverage a GPO that is supposed to affect a site, an OU, or even a domain, the GPO itself is not stored directly at that level. Rather, the GPO is simply linked to the level in Active Directory. When a GPO is called to be used, it has to request a Domain Controller to fetch it from the Group Policy Objects container and pull the information out.

Each time you create a new GPO, it's born and placed into the swimming pool within the domain—ready for action if linked to a level in Active Directory. You can reuse a GPO at multiple levels in Active Directory simply by adding another link to it.

So, when GPOs are created for use at the site, domain, or OU level, they're always created within the domain swimming pool, the Group Policy Objects container, where we just link to the GPOs we need when we need them.

Group Policy Objects from a Site Perspective

Site-level GPOs are a bit unique. If you used (or continue to use) the old-school interface via Active Directory Users And Computers to dictate a site-based GPO, you might be in for a world of pain. By default, all site-level GPOs created using the old-school interface will live in the

Group Policy Objects container of the Domain Controllers of the *root* domain—and only the root domain, that is, the first Active Directory domain brought online. Then, every time a GPO meant for a site is called for use by a client system, a Domain Controller from the root domain must fetch that information. If the closest root Domain Controller is in Singapore, so be it.

If you continue to use the old-school interface, you have two choices if you want to mitigate the pain when using site links:

- Bring a replica Domain Controller from the root domain closer to your users in each site. For instance, if your root domain is in Singapore, but you have placed many site GPOs on the New York site, place a replica Domain Controller from the domain in Singapore into the New York site. That way, when the site GPOs replicate from the Domain Controllers in Singapore to your one root Domain Controller machine in New York, a copy of those site GPOs will be present on a root Domain Controller you placed closer to the user.

- The second option is a bit more roundabout, but helps guarantee speedy delivery of site-based GPOs. Indeed, in Chapter 1 this is *the* way the GPMC forced us to create our "Hide Screen Saver Tab" site-linked GPO. The goal of this option is to plant the GPO in the domain of *your* choosing, not the default location of the root domain. Follow these steps to do so:

  1. Figure out from which domain users should request the GPO. For instance, if you want to create GPOs to be used on your New York site, make sure that the domain that the GPOs "live" in don't contain Domain Controllers across a WAN link. You want to select a domain with Domain Controllers that are available to service your users. You need to consider which exact domain you create a GPO in, making sure that appropriate DCs are near the physical systems and users that will implement the GPO.

  2. In that domain, create a GPO linked to the domain. Call it whatever you want, and modify the GPO as you see fit.

  3. Remove the link from the GPO you just created in the domain. In the old-school interface, you would do this by clicking the Delete button and then selecting "Remove the Link" from two possible options. Remember that by removing the link, you're not deleting the GPO; rather, you're just deleting the link. Once you do, the GPO is just floating freely in the swimming pool of the domain but not being used by anyone.

  4. Use Active Directory Sites And Services, and add a link to a GPO. This will let you add a link to the GPO in the domain you created.

Again, the GPMC forces us to create site-based GPOs this way. As you saw in Chapter 1, first, we create the GPO in the Group Policy Objects container. Then, once we expose the site, we just add a link to our existing GPO.

WARNING   Remember, only members of the Enterprise Administrators group (or members of the Domain Admins group in the root domain) can create new site-level GPOs or link to existing GPOs from the site level.

Group Policy Objects from a Domain Perspective

Since we know that all GPOs are just hanging out in the Group Policy Objects container waiting to be used, we can take this one step further. That is, even those GPOs linked to the domain level aren't exempt from having to be "fetched." When clients use domain-linked GPOs, they have to make the same requests and "ask" the Domain Controller for the GPOs that apply to them.

This is usually not a problem; the Domain Controller doesn't have far to go to get the GPO in the swimming pool to apply it to the domain. But this is precisely why doing *cross-domain* GPO linking is so slow and painful (see the following sidebar). For instance, in an environment with multiple domains, it might appear to be easier to link back to a previously created GPO across a trust relationship. But when it comes time to grab the information inside the GPO, it needs to be brought back all the way from Domain Controllers in the source domain.

Group Policy Objects from an OU Perspective

Since GPOs live in the Group Policy Objects container at the domain level, a distinct advantage is associated with the way Group Policy does its thing: It's tremendously easy to move, link, and unlink GPOs to the domain and/or its OUs. You could, if you desired, simply unlink a GPO in the domain or OU and link it back to some other OU. Or, you could link one GPO to the domain and/or multiple OUs.

It's typical and usual that you'll use OUs to apply most of your GPOs. If GPOs live in the Group Policy Objects container swimming pool, it's easy for multiple, unrelated OUs to reuse the same GPOs and just create new links to existing GPOs.

A Brief Note about Cross-Domain GPO Linking

It is possible to create links to GPOs in other domains. On the surface, this might seem like a real time-saver. Imagine that Harry, in a domain other than yours, created the perfect GPO chock full of precise settings you need. Instead of re-creating the wheel (or, in this case, the GPO), you decide to choose to "Link an Existing Link an Existing GPO…" to the GPO he created.

However, you should not do this. Any time that a GPO needs to be fetched, it's fetched over the wire from the Domain Controllers in the domain that houses the needed GPO. Thus, any time users in your domain need to use that GPO, things could be (and usually are) slow and painful for the logon of your users. Whenever possible, link to only a Group Policy in your own domain.

You need to keep a similar phenomenon in mind regarding using site policies. We'll explore cross-domain and cross-site policies a bit more in the next chapter. Moreover, it's now easier than ever to be able to ask Harry to plunk his perfect GPO on a floppy for you or even e-mail it to you. That way, you can avoid this problem entirely. I'll show you how to do this in the Appendix.

Note, however, that it is not possible to create cross-domain links to domains in other forests—even if the forest has a cross-forest trust.

The Birth, Life, and Death of a GPO

Now that you understand where GPOs actually live, we can take the next step: understanding the "journey" of a GPO. Specifically, a GPO is born and must stay healthy if it's going to stay alive. If its usefulness becomes depleted, you can call in the Sopranos boys to whack it—never to be seen again.

How Group Policy Objects Are "Born"

Before you can give birth to GPOs, you need rights to do so, and you can get these rights in two ways. First, you can be a member of the Group Policy Creator Owners Security group. You can also be granted explicit rights via the Delegation tab in the Group Policy Objects container via the GPMC (as you saw in Chapter 2).

A new Group Policy Object is born when you right-click the Group Policy Objects container and choose "New." Now you're setting into motion a specific chain of events.

First, the PDC Emulator is contacted to see if it's available for writing. If not, the user is prompted about how to proceed, as shown in Figure 4.1.

FIGURE 4.1   If the PDC Emulator is not available for writing, the user is prompted for an alternate location.

GPOs are initially born in the PDC Emulator, and then, a bit later, they are replicated to the other Domain Controllers within the site and then between sites. Assuming the PDC Emulator is available, you can give your GPO a friendly name, say "Hide Settings Tab / Restore Screen Saver Tab," as we did in Chapter 1.

Once that happens, your GPO is officially "born." The PDC Emulator has already performed certain functions on your behalf:

- It created a *Group Policy Container (GPC)* in the "Policies" folder of the Configuration container in the Active Directory database. Think of this as a reference in Active Directory for your new GPO.

- It created a *Group Policy Template (GPT)* in the SYSVOL directory of the PDC Emulator. This is where the real files that make up your GPO live. They're replicated to every Domain Controller for quicker retrieval.

- Additionally, if "Create and link a GPO here…" is used when focused on the domain or OU level (or the old-school interface is used), the new GPO you just created is automatically *linked* to the current level you were focused at—site, domain, or OU.

- The GPO is given a unique ID which takes its form as a globally Unique Identifier (GUID).

When you inspect the properties of any new GPO, you'll see the unique ID it is automatically given, as shown in Figure 4.2.

FIGURE 4.2   Every GPO gets a unique name.

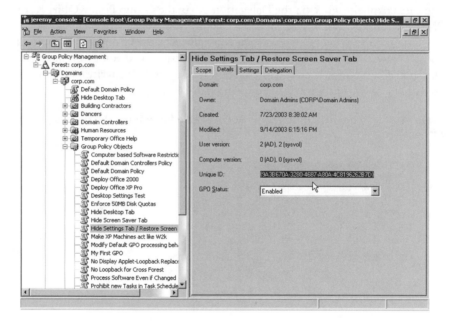

So, every GPO is made up of two components (the GPC and GPT), and those components are split between two places inside that Domain Controller. The good news, though, is it all ties back to the GPO's GUID. We'll explore each of these components in the next two sections.

How a GPO "Lives"

A GPO in Active Directory is made up of two constituent parts. One part isn't enough and without both parts the GPO cannot live. Both parts are required in order to communicate the GPO message.

As we'll see in a bit, and the GPO derives its life from these two parts.

Group Policy Containers (GPCs)

The Active Directory holds GPCs, which hold multiple properties of the Group Policy—for instance, version and status information and some policy settings. A GPC has a name that takes the format of a globally unique identifier (GUID). (Note, however, it's not *actually* a GUID; rather, it just takes the *form* of a GUID. See the sidebar that follows.) In any event, the underlying name is *not* the friendly name we use when administrating the template.

You can see the GPCs for every Group Policy you create by diving into the Active Directory Users And Computers console.

To view the GPCs and their GUIDs, follow these steps:

1. Log on to the server WSDC01 as Administrator of the domain.

2. Choose Start ≻ Programs ≻ Administrative Tools ≻ Active Directory Users And Computers.

3. Choose View ≻ Advanced Features, as shown in Figure 4.3, to display the Policies folder.

GPC Attributes

When a GPC object is created, it is given several attributes:

Common Name (CN)   An LDAP (Lightweight Directory Access Protocol) designation for the name assigned to an object. GPC names use the GUID format to ensure uniqueness throughout a forest. For example, CN=2C53BFD6-A2DB-44AF-9476-130492934271.

Distinguished Name (DN)   The object's common name plus the path to the object from the root of the LDAP tree. For example, CN=2C53BFD6-A2DB-44AF-9476-130492934271, CN=Policies, CN=System, DC=corp, DC=com.

Display Name   The friendly name assigned to the Group Policy in the user interface, for example, the Hide Screen Saver Tab GPO.

Version   A counter that keeps track of updates to a GPC object (more on this topic a little later).

GUID   The GUID assigned to the object itself. Active Directory uses the object's GUID as a reference for handling table moves, building indexes, and doing other database activities.

You might find it a little confusing for the GPC object to have a GUID that refers to the object itself and a name that uses a GUID format. For an important reason, Microsoft needed a way to make the underlying, real name of GPOs unique, independent of their friendly names. Suppose two administrators create two (or more) GPOs with the same friendly name on their own Domain Controllers. When these GPC objects replicate, one of them would have to be discarded, overwritten, or renamed, depending on the exact circumstances of the replication collision. That could be a bad thing. Therefore, Microsoft solves this problem by using underlying unique names formatted with the GUID format. There is a negligible chance of identical GUIDs being created, not only within one Active Directory but across the entire world, should the need arise to coexist with GPOs in other forests (such as with cross-forest trusts).

To see the major attributes for the GPC objects in your domain, take a look at Chapter 7. You'll find a Visual Basic (.vbs) script that lets you see (and document) these objects.

FIGURE 4.3   Turn on the "Advanced Features" setting to see the Policies folder (and a whole lot more).

4. Expand the System folder to display the Policies folder along with the GPCs, as shown in Figure 4.4.

Up until this point, we've been using the GPMC interface to create GPOs. When we use the GPMC to create GPOs, we've made reference to the Group Policy Objects container within the GPMC as representation of the swimming pool. But the GPMC isn't showing you the real swimming pool—it's showing you a *representation* of the swimming pool. Here it is folks, the moment you've been waiting for... Indeed, this is the official swimming pool inside Active Directory that really contains our GPOs.

Again, this Policies folder equates to the Group Policy Objects container when viewing GPOs from the GPMC. You should see one folder for every GPO you have created, plus two more for the two default GPOs (which we'll explore in Chapter 6). In this example, I have lots of GPOs already created; therefore I have lots of folders. You might have fewer.

FIGURE 4.4   Expand the Policies folder to expose the underlying GPC objects.

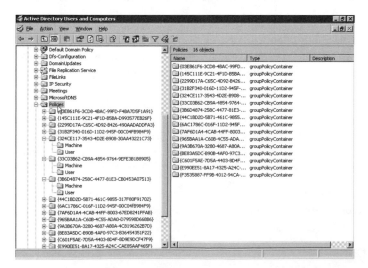

When you try to drill down into the subfolders, some will and some will not expand past the {*GUID*}\Machine and {*GUID*}\Computer levels. Those that do expand do so because you have set up features in that specific GPO that Active Directory needs to maintain information on, such as when you Publish or Assign applications. We'll explore Publishing and Assigning applications in great detail in Chapter 10.

Don't be surprised if, at this stage in working through the book, you do not have any fully expandable subfolders as shown in Figure 4.4. The subfolders that don't expand do not require additional Active Directory references. Everything else the GPO needs to be useful is stored in the GPT, which is explored in the next section.

Who Really Has Permissions to Do What?

In Chapter 2, we applied various permissions on the GPO, including who had "Read" and "Apply Group Policy" permissions, as well as who could see the settings or edit the stuff inside the GPO. The locking mechanism for "Who really has what permissions" on a specific GPO is found right here, at the Policies folder:

- On the one hand, the locking mechanism on the Policies folder itself dictates who can and cannot create GPOs.

- On the other hand, the locking mechanism on the GPC folders underneath the Policies folder (with names of GUIDs) dictates which users have access to "Read" and "Apply Group Policy", or change the GPO itself.

Who Can Create New Group Policy Objects?

Right-click the Policies folder, and select Properties, then click the Security tab to display several names, some of which should be familiar, including the Group Policy Creator Owners and the Domain Administrators group. Additionally present will be anyone you explicitly added via the Delegation tab upon the Group Policy Objects container in GPMC. You saw how to do this in Chapter 2. At that time, we added a user named Joe User from our domain.

If you examine the properties of the Policies folder (as shown in Figure 4.5), you'll see the Group Policy Creator Owners group. Joe is also listed (because he was expressly granted permission via the GPMC). Note also, that the Domain Admins and Enterprise Admins groups are also present, but those names are at the top of the list, so you can't see it in Figure 4.5.

You can click the Advanced button to display Joe's precise "Special Permissions." Indeed, Joe has only one permission, and it's called "`Create groupPolicyContainer Objects`." Once he has this right, the system permits him to create GPC folders and populate them with Group Policy information when he creates a new GPO.

FIGURE 4.5   Expand the Policies folder to expose the underlying GPC objects.

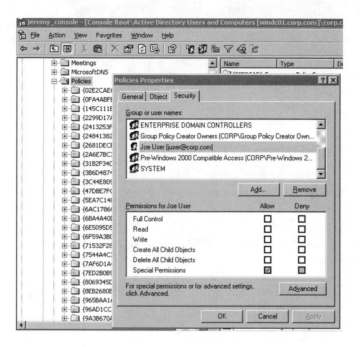

The Group Policy Creator Owners group has many, many more unnecessary permissions on the Policies folder, including "Create all child objects," "Create User Objects," and a whole lot of stuff that, really, doesn't have anything to do with Group Policy. Indeed, if you log on as someone in the Group Policy Creator Owners group and right-click the Policies folder, you can do some things you really shouldn't do, as you can see in Figure 4.6.

FIGURE 4.6   For the love of Pete, please don't do this.

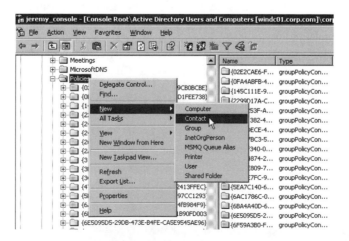

The system (thankfully) won't let you do *all* the functions listed here, but it does let you do *some* of them. And, again, you really shouldn't be poking around like this. However, I show you these things for demonstration purposes so you can get a better feeling for what is different between someone in the Group Policy Creator Owners Group vs. someone who has been explicitly delegated rights via the Delegation tab upon the Group Policy Objects container in GPMC.

The Domain Administrators group and the Enterprise Administrators group also have explicit permissions here. When they create new GPOs, they do so because of their explicit permissions; not because they are members of the Group Policy Creator Owners group.

Who Can Manipulate and Edit Existing Group Policy Objects?

Right-click a GPO folder (with the name of a GUID) under the Policies folder and choose Properties to display the Security tab (see Figure 4.7), which will show the same information when, in Chapter 2, you used the Deny attribute to pass over certain security groups. That is, the same information is shown here as when we clicked the "Advanced" button in the Delegation tab when focused on the GPO (or GPO link, because it's using the same information taken from the actual GPO).

FIGURE 4.7 Each GPC can display the underlying permissions of the GPO.

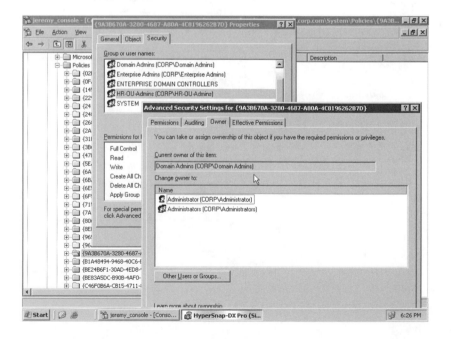

Unless otherwise delegated, the person or group who created the GPO is the only one who can modify or delete the GPO. However, this may be a particularly sensitive issue if you have many Domain Administrators—as they all have "joint ownership" of the GPOs they create. There is a serious potential risk in one administrator taking the reins and modifying another administrator's GPOs.

However, as you saw in Chapter 2, you can also grant someone explicit rights via the Delegation tab upon the GPOs container via the GPMC. In this example, I have done this for Joe. Figure 4.8 shows the security properties upon a GPO that Joe has created.

Since Joe has explicit permissions to create GPOs, he becomes the owner of the GPOs he creates. Hence, Joe doesn't have to worry about other explicitly anointed users or groups changing the GPOs he creates and owns. Note, however, that the Domain Administrators and Enterprise Administrators group will, in fact, be able to change any GPOs that Joe creates.

FIGURE 4.8 If Joe creates a GPO, he owns the GPO. No one else (other than Domain Admins or Enterprise Admins) can edit it.

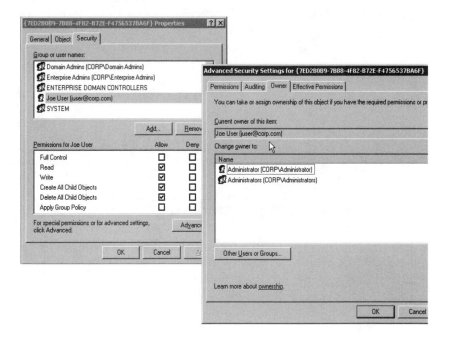

Using LDP to See the Guts of a GPC

The GPC object itself holds even more critical attributes for GPOs:

gPCFileSysPath   The physical path to the associated Policies folder, or GPT, stored in SYS-VOL. The Policies folder has the same name as the GPC, which is another reason that unique-ness is so important. The GPT is discussed in the next section.

gPCMachineExtensionNames   The GUIDs of the DLLs responsible for local processing of the GPO (called *client-side extensions,* or *CSEs*). For instance, if a GPO involves the Administrative Templates node in the Group Policy Object Editor, the gPCMachineExtensionNames list includes the GUID of the Registry processor client-side extension. CSEs are discussed later in this chap-ter in the "How Client Systems Get Group Policy Objects" section.

gPCUserExtensionNames   The GUIDs of the client-side extensions called by a user-related Group Policy. Again, I'll discuss CSEs a bit later in this chapter.

When you try to dive in and view these attributes using Active Directory Users And Computers, you cannot see them. The only way to see them is to use the LDP tool, which is an LDAP browser tool. This tool is found by loading the support tools from the SUPPORT\TOOLS folder on the Windows Server 2003 CD.

LDP lets you perform LDAP queries right into the actual guts of Active Directory. Using LDP, you can see these attributes. Normally, you wouldn't want or need to go poking around in here, but taking the time to learn just where attributes are can help in your understanding of what constitutes a GPO.

To query a specific GPO to see its underlying attributes, follow these steps:

1. After loading the Support tools on the Domain Controller, choose Start ➤ Run to open the Run dialog box, and in the Open field, type **LDP** and press Enter to bind to the domain of your choice.

2. Choose Connection ➤ Bind and in the dialog box type the administrative credentials to the domain. In the Domain field, you'll need to type the DNS name of the domain, for example, corp.com. If you successfully connect, you'll see your first query results in the right pane of the LDP window.

3. Choose View ➤ Tree to open up a dialog that lets you specify the distinguished name of the domain. If your domain is corp.com, enter dc=corp, dc=com. If you do that correctly, your left pane will show the domain name with a plus (+) sign. You should be able to double-click the plus sign and expand the contents within the domain.

4. Find the System container and double-click it to expand it.

5. Find the Policies container and double-click it to expand it.

6. Find the unique name of the GPO you want to inspect and double-click it to expand it. (For information about how to find a specific unique name of a GPO, see the earlier section "How Group Policy Objects Are 'Born'.") In the following illustration, the attributes are highlighted.

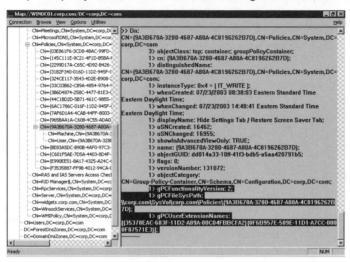

Once you find the unique name, the resultant LDP query will show you the properties on that GPO.

There is one more important attribute to inspect by using LDP: gPLink. Recall that a GPO can be linked by one level, multiple levels, or no levels. If a GPO is to be linked to a site, a domain, or an OU, that level needs to have a *pointer* or *link* to the GPO. When clients log on (computer and user), they use LDAP to query to each level they are a part of (site, domain, OUs) to find out if the level has any gPLink attributes. If so, the client makes an LDAP query to find out what GPOs are meant for it. With the information in hand, it determines what files to download from the SYSVOL share on its logon server. (You can see these queries happening for yourself, when you inspect Userenv.log, explored later in the section "Turning on Verbose Logging.")

To see the gPLink attribute, you can simply click the level you want to inspect. In this case, click the **Human Resources Users** OU you created in Chapter 1.

In the right pane, find LDP's query results. The gPLink attribute has LDAP pointers to the unique names of the GPOs. In this case, the **Human Resources Users** OU has links to both the "Hide Settings Tab/Restore Screen Saver Tab" GPO, in my case, {9A3B670A-3280-4687-A80A-4C8196262B7D}. If you clicked the **Human Resources Computers** OU you should see the "Disable Task Scheduler" GPO, again, in my case {965BAA1A-C60B-4C55-ADA0-D79598D668B6}.

Group Policy Templates

As we just learned, GPCs are stored in the Active Directory database and replicated via normal Active Directory replication. A Group Policy Template (GPT) on the other hand, is stored as a set of files in the SYSVOL share of each Domain Controller. Each GPT is replicated to each Domain Controller through FRS (File Replication Service).

When we used the Properties tab of the GPO, we were able to find its unique name (as we did earlier in Figure 4.2). We can use the same unique name to locate the GPC in Active Directory, and it's the same unique name we can use to locate the GPT in the SYSVOL.

To see the GPTs in SYSVOL, follow these steps:

1. Open Windows Explorer.

2. Change the directory to the SYSVOL container. Its usual location is C:\Windows\SYSVOL\SYSVOL*{domain name}* (in this case, C:\Windows\SYSVOL\SYSVOL\corp.com).

3. Change into the Policies folder. You'll see a list of folders. The folder names match the GPC names stored in Active Directory (seen in the previous exercise). Figure 4.9 shows a Policies folder containing many GPOs.

FIGURE 4.9 The unique names of the GPOs are found as folder names in SYSVOL. This is the unique name for the "Hide Settings Tab/Restore Screen Saver Tab" you saw in Figure 4.2 earlier.

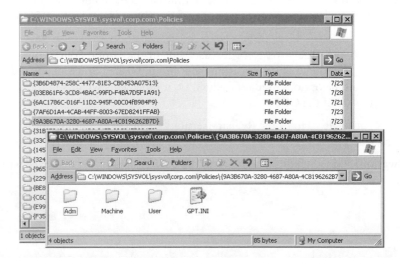

Double-clicking a Policies folder inside SYSVOL displays the contents of the GPT. Inside, you'll see several subfolders and a file:

\Adm   As you'll learn in Chapter 5, the Administrative Templates policy settings are really generated from listings inside plain-old text files with a `.adm` extension. When an Administrative Templates policy is created or modified, the Group Policy Object Editor copies these `.adm` files from the \Windows\INF folder. By default, those `.adm` files are `Conf.adm`, `Inetres.adm`, and `System.adm`. Hang tight. You'll find more info about this as you hit Chapter 5. Double-clicking the \Adm folder displays the templates. Note that the \Adm folder will not exist until the GPO is opened for the first time and you click either the Computer or the User node.

\Machine   This folder contains the settings for the computer side of the GPO, including startup and shutdown scripts, pointers to applications that are assigned, and Registry settings (among other settings). The actual contents of the \Machine folder depend on the computer options specified in the GPO. The potential contents include the following:

> **The Registry.pol File**   Holds the Registry settings set in Computer Configuration ➢ Administrative Templates.

> **The \Applications Folder**   Stores pointer files called Application Assignment Scripts, or AAS files. These files are used in conjunction with deployed with Group Policy Software Deployment. These are the instructions that the client computers use to process Software Installation. Software Installation is further discussed in its own chapter, Chapter 10.

> **The \Microsoft\Windows NT\Secedit Folder**   Stores a file called `Gpttmpl.inf`. This file holds various computer security settings, defined under the Computer Configuration ➢ Windows Settings ➢ Security Settings portion of the GPO. You can also set up these settings in advance and deploy them *en masse* using the techniques described in Chapter 6.

> **The \Scripts\Shutdown Folder**   Contains the actual files used for computer shutdown scripts. Can be of any scripting file type, including `.bat`, `.cmd`, `.vbs`, `.js`, and others. You'll see how to use this in Chapter 6.

> **The \Scripts\Startup Folder**   Contains the actual files used for computer startup scripts. Can be of any scripting file type, including `.bat`, `.cmd`, `.vbs`, `.js`, and others. You'll see how to use this in Chapter 6.

\User   This folder contains the settings for the user side of the Group Policy coin, including logon and logoff scripts, pointers to applications that are published or assigned, and Registry settings. Depending on the options used on each GPO, it represents what is in the \User folder under the computer side of the GPT.

> **The `Registry.pol` File**   Holds the Registry settings set in User Configuration ➢ Administrative Templates.

> **The \Applications Folder**   Stores pointer files called AAS files for files deployed with Group Policy Software Deployment.

The \Documents and Settings Folder   Contains a file called `Fdeploy.iniI`, which stores applicable Folder Redirection settings. Set up Folder Redirection as described in Chapter 10.

The \Microsoft\IEAK Folder   Stores files to represent the changes made in User Configuration ➤ Windows Settings ➤ Internet Explorer Maintenance.

The \Microsoft\RemoteInstall Folder   Stores `Oscfilter.ini`, which specifies Group Policy Remote Installation Services settings. See Chapter 11 for how to set up Remote Installation Services and manage it with Group Policy.

The \Scripts\Logon Folder   Contains the actual files used for user logon scripts. Can be of any acceptable file type, including `.bat`, `.vbs`, `.js`, and others. You'll see how to use this in Chapter 6.

The \Scripts\Logoff Folder   Contains the actual files used for user logoff scripts. Can be of any acceptable file type, including `.bat`, `.vbs`, `.js`, and others. You'll see how to use this in Chapter 6.

GPT.INI   The one file you will always find under the GUID folder. It holds the version number of the GPT. (You'll read about version numbers in the next section.)

Verifying That GPCs and GPTs Are in Sync

The two pieces of information that make up a GPO are GPCs and GPTs:

- GPCs are stored in the Active Directory database and are replicated via normal Active Directory replication.

- GPTs are stored in the SYSVOL folders of every Domain Controller and are replicated using FRS replication.

Here's the trick: in order for Group Policy to be applied on workstations, both the GPC and the corresponding GPT need to be synchronized. *Synchronization* simply means that the Domain Controller in which a user authenticates has a copy of both the GPC object in Active Directory and the GPT files in SYSVOL.

Recall that both the GPC and GPT are originally written to the PDC Emulator by default. Once they're written, the goal is to replicate the GPC and GPT to other Domain Controllers. With just one Domain Controller in a domain, there are no replication issues, because there are no other Domain Controllers to replicate to; it's all happening on one system. But when multiple Domain Controllers in a domain enter the picture, things get a little hairier. This is because normal Active Directory replication and FRS replication are on completely independent schedules (though under normal circumstances, they take the same path).

An administrator can create or modify a GPO, and the GPC might not replicate in lockstep with the files in the GPT. This isn't normally a problem because, over time, all Domain Controllers end up with exactly the same information in their replicas of the Active Directory database and in their SYSVOL folders. But during a given replication cycle, there may be intervals when the GPC and GPT *don't* match on a particular Domain Controller.

Additionally, the GPC and GPT share a *version number* for each half of the GPO—computer and user. The version numbers are incremented each time the GPO is modified and are included in the list of attributes that are replicated to other Domain Controllers. Remember in Chapter 1 I stated that if a specific GPO doesn't change, the default for the client is to not redownload the GPO. After all, if nothing's changed, why should the client bother? The client uses these version numbers to figure out if something has changed. The client keeps a cache of the GPOs it last applied along with the version number. Then, if the GPO has been touched, say, by the modification of a particular policy setting or the addition of a policy setting, the version number of the GPO in Active Directory changes. The next time the client tries to process GPOs, it will see the change, and the client will download the entire GPO again and embrace the revised instruction set! So, version numbers are important for clients to recognize new instructions are waiting for them.

So far, so good. Now, there's a bit more to fully understanding version numbers. According to Microsoft, here's the secret to figuring out whether a GPO is going to process on a workstation:

- Both the GPC and GPT parts of the GPO must be present on the Domain Controller the workstation uses to log on.

- The GPC and GPT must have the same version number.

Microsoft says that if either of these is not true, the workstation cannot process the GPO.

In my testing I have not found the latter statement to be required. That is, even when the version numbers of the GPC and GPT are different, the GPO seems to be processed just fine on the client. However, just because I haven't encountered difficulty with version numbers doesn't mean you won't. Use the following tips to ensure that version numbers are in sync if problems start to occur.

Changing the Default Location for the Initial Write of Group Policy Objects

GPOs are, by default, written to the Domain Controller that houses the PDC Emulator. Sometimes in large Active Directories, this behavior is not desired, as in the following example.

There is one domain but two sites—the United States and China. The U.S. site holds the Domain Controller designated as the PDC Emulator. Therefore, whenever an administrator in China writes a GPO, they must connect across the WAN to write the GPO and then wait for the entire GPO (both the GPC half and the GPT half) to replicate to their local Domain Controllers.

You can, however, specify which Domain Controller to write the GPO to, which is a two-step process:

1. Select a Domain Controller to be *active*. Open the GPMC, right-click the domain name, select "Change Domain Controller," and select the Domain Controller you to which you want the Group Policy to apply.

2. Create your GPO and edit it. At the root node of the Group Policy snap-in, choose View ➢ DC Options. Now you have the following three choices:

   - "The one with the Operations Master token for the PDC Emulator." The default behavior, this option finds the PDC Emulator in the domain and writes the GPO there. Replication then occurs, starting from the PDC Emulator.

- "The one used by the Active Directory snap-ins." Since you just selected the *active* Domain Controller, this is your best bet, as you know exactly which Domain Controller you selected in the first step.

- "Any available Domain Controller." The odds are good that you will get a local Domain Controller to write to (based on Active Directory site information), but not always.

Therefore, the best course of action is to select the Domain Controller you want to initially write to and then select "The one used by the Active Directory snap-in" to guarantee it.

Sound like too much work for each GPO? Alternatively, you can create a GPO that affects those accounts that can create GPOs. Use the policy setting located at User Configuration ➤ Administrative Templates ➤ System ➤ Group Policy named "Group Policy Domain Controller Selection." You'll get the same three choices listed earlier. Set it, and forget it.

Here's one more parting tip for this sidebar. Often, GPOs are created with the additional intent to use Security groups to filter them. After creating a GPO with the GPMC, an administrator will also create some security groups using Active Directory Users And Computers to filter them. However, after creating the GPO and the security groups, many admins are surprised that the security groups they want to add "now" are not immediately available. This is because the GPMC is using one Domain Controller, and the Active Directory Users And Computers is using another Domain Controller. Therefore, replication of the group has not yet reached the Domain Controller the GPMC is using! So the tip is to manually focus both the Active Directory Users And Computers and/or GPMCs explicitly on the same Domain Controller (or just the PDC Emulator) before creating GPOs where you'll also want to filter using groups.

Using *Gpotool.exe*

If you suspect you're having problems with keeping your GPTs and GPCs in sync, you can use Gpotool.exe, a tool included with the Windows 2000 and Windows 2003 Resource Kits. You can run Gpotool.exe on any Domain Controller to verify that both the GPCs and GPTs are in sync and have consistent data among all Domain Controllers in the domain.

Running Gpotool without any parameters verifies that all GPCs and GPTs are synchronized across all Domain Controllers in the domain. If you are having trouble with only one GPO, however, you might not want to go through the intense process required to check every GPO's GPC and GPT on every Domain Controller. Instead, however, you can use the /gpo: switch, which allows you to specify a friendly name or GUID of a GPO you are having problems with. For instance, if you suspect that you are having problems with any of the "Hide Screen Saver Tab," "Hide Appearance Tab," or "Hide Settings Tab / Restore Screen Saver Tab" GPOs we created in Chapter 1, you can run Gpotool /gpo:Hide to search for all GPOs starting with the word *Hide*, as shown in Figure 4.10.

To specifically verify the "Hide Settings Tab / Restore Screen Saver Tab" set-ting, you can also run Gpotool /gpo:"Hide Settings Tab / Restore Screen Saver Tab" as seen in Figure 4.10. Note that the /gpo: switch is case sensitive. For instance, running Gpotool /gpo:Hide is different from running GPOTOOL /gpo:hide.

This example shows when things are going right. This next example (see Figure 4.11) shows when things might be wrong.

FIGURE 4.10 Use Gpotool to see if your GPCs and GPTs are synchronized across your Domain Controllers.

FIGURE 4.11 Gpotool has found trouble in paradise.

In this example, we are verifying the synchronization of the GPO named "Broken2." In this case, the versions between the GPC and GPT do not match. You can see this when comparing what the tool calls the DS version with the SYSVOL version. The DS version represents the GPC, and the SYSVOL version represents the GPT.

Before panicking, recall that this "problem" might not actually be a problem. Remember, the GPC and GPT replicate independently. The DC our clients are currently using might have simply received the SYSVOL (GPT) changes before the Active Directory changes (GPC) or vice versa. Wait a little while, and the two versions might converge. If they do not converge, this problem could indicate either Active Directory or FRS replication issues.

Using *Replmon* to See the Version Numbers

The Replmon (Replication Monitor) tool is available as part of the Support tools on the Windows 2003 (or Windows 2000) Server CD. Replmon is one of the most useful free tools Microsoft has ever created.

For our purposes, we'll use it in a fashion similar to how we used Gpotol; that is, Replmon can tell us if a GPO's GPC and GPT are in agreement with the version numbers.

First, load the Support tools in the \SUPPORT\TOOLS folder. Then, choose Start ➢ Run to open the Run dialog box, and type Replmon in the Open box. Right-click the Monitored Servers icon and choose "Add Monitored Server." For now, just add the PDC Emulator. In my case, I'll add WINDC01. Once the server is being monitored, right-click it and choose "Show Group Policy Object Status" to display a screen like that shown in Figure 4.12.

FIGURE 4.12   Replmon can show you the version numbers of all your GPOs.

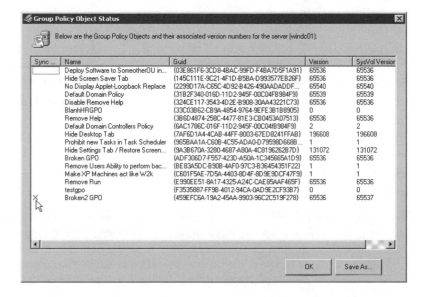

In Figure 4.12, you can see that the GPO named "Broken2" has an X in the Sync Status column. The version numbers are dissimilar in the GPC and GPT. Again, this might not be a real "problem" because the GPC and GPT are being independently replicated. Perhaps this Domain Controller did not yet get the latest updates.

Isolating Replication Problems

You can try to see if Active Directory replication is working (and, hence, if GPC replication is working) by performing several "litmus tests." Here are some examples:

- Create a new GPO in the Group Policy Objects container. Just create it with no policy settings, and don't link it anywhere.

- Create a new OU in Active Directory Users And Computers or the GPMC.

- Add a new user in Active Directory

In each case, you want to see if these objects are replicated to other DCs. After creating your objects on one Domain Controller, use the Active Directory Users And Computers and/or GPMC to check other Domain Controllers. Simply right-click the domain and choose another Domain Controller.

If these litmus tests fail, you can try to force replication using Active Directory Sites And Services. If you need extra-strength replication, `Replmon` can help force replication in multiple ways.

You can try to see if SYSVOL replication is working via FRS (and, hence, if GPT replication is working) by simply throwing any file—say, a `Readme.txt` file—into the SYSVOL share of any Domain Controller, and seeing if it is replicated to the other Domain Controllers' SYSVOL shares. If it is not automatically copied to the other Domain Controllers, test each machine's connectivity using the `ping` command.

Here are some additional tips for troubleshooting FRS replication:

- Microsoft TechNet has an excellent feature-length article, "Troubleshooting FRS" feature-length article. At the TechNet home page (`www.microsoft.com/technet/security/community/default.mspx`), enter "Troubleshooting FRS" in the Search box.

- Microsoft has a new tool, SONAR (part of the Windows 2003 Resource Kit), that can dramatically help with FRS troubleshooting.

- Microsoft has another new tool, ULTRASOUND, that surpasses SONAR's ability to help troubleshoot FRS.

ULTRASOUND and SONAR are available on Microsoft's website at `www.microsoft.com/frs` as of this writing.

The Microsoft Knowledge Base articles Q221112, Q221111, Q272279 and Q229928 are good starting points to learn more about FRS and how to troubleshoot SYSVOL replication problems by debugging FRS. See Q229896 and Q249256 for details on how to debug Active Directory replication.

Death of a GPO

As you saw in Chapter 2, there are two ways to stop using a GPO at a level in Active Directory. One way is to "Delete the link" to the GPO at the level being used in Active Directory. In the swimming pool analogy, we're simply removing the tether to our child in the pool, but we're leaving the object swimming in the pool should other levels want to use it.

The other way to stop using a GPO is to delete it. With the GMPC, you can delete a GPO only by traversing to the Group Policy Objects container, right-clicking it, and choosing Delete, as you saw in Figure 2.7. But, again, be careful; other levels of Active Directory (including those in other domains and forests) might be using this GPO you're about to whack.

How Client Systems Get Group Policy Objects

The items stored on the server make up only half the story. The real magic happens when the GPO is applied at the client, usually a workstation, although certainly servers are not immune. Half of Group Policy's usefulness is in that it can apply equally to servers as well as desktops and laptops. Indeed, with Windows 2003 and the new policy settings it brings to the table, there's more than that you can control and configure. So the details in this section are for all clients—servers and workstations.

When Group Policy is deployed from upon high to client systems, the clients always do the requesting. This is why, when the chips are down and things aren't going right, you'll need to trot out to the system and crack open the Event Log (among other troubleshooting areas) to help uncover why the client isn't picking up your desires.

You can't instantaneously "push" the policy settings inside GPOs to clients, even if you think they should get a new change right now. There's no "push the big red button and force the latest Group Policy to all my clients" command to make sure every client gets your will. This can be a little disappointing, especially if you need a security setting, such as a Software Restriction Policy propagated to all your clients right now.

In Chapter 7, I'll show you a little scripting magic to forcefully push Group Policy out the door. Note, however, that this script needs to be "prepared" on the client machine before you can leverage it.

Unfortunately, Group Policy is only processed when the computer starts up, the user logs on, at periodic intervals in the background, as discussed in Chapter 3. In that chapter, you learned "when" Group Policy is processed; in this section, you'll learn both "how" and "why" Group Policy is processed.

Client-Side Extensions

When a Group Policy "clock" strikes, the Group Policy engine springs into action to start processing your wishes. The GPOs that are meant for the client are downloaded from Active Directory, and then the client pretty much does the rest.

When GPOs are set from upon high, usually not all policy setting categories are used. For instance, you might set up an Administrative Template policy, but not an Internet Explorer Maintenance policy. The client is smart enough to know which policy setting groups affect it. This happens after the client downloads all the GPOs and figures out what it should do with what it just downloaded. To do this, it compares the downloaded instructions with each known client-side extension (CSE).

CSEs are really pointers to DLLs (Dynamically Linked Libraries) that actually perform the Group Policy processing. These DLLs are built into clients capable of processing Group Policy: Windows 2000, Windows XP and Windows 2003. These CSEs are automatically registered in the operating system and are identified in the Registry by their Class IDs (which take the same naming convention as GUIDs).

Today, we know Group Policy by the 13 function groups described in the Introduction. In reality, Group Policy could be an unlimited set of functions, but only 10 are built into Windows 2000 out of the box, and another three are built into Windows XP and Windows 2003.

 The three new Windows XP and Windows 2003 CSEs are Software Restriction policies, 802.11x Wireless policies, and Quality of Service Packet Scheduler policies.

Additional CSEs can be created by third-party programmers who want to control their own aspects of the operating system or their own software.

 Take a look at "Third-Party Group Policy Tools" on this book's website for two products that each have their own CSEs: Policy Maker, by AutoProf, and Special Operations Suite, by Knowledge Factory.

To take a look at the CSEs on a workstation, follow these steps:

1. On Windows XP, log on as Administrator.

2. Choose Start ➢ Run to open the Run dialog box, in the Open box type **Run Regedit**, and press Enter to open the Registry Editor, as shown in Figure 4.13.

FIGURE 4.13   The client-side extension DLLs actually perform the GPO processing.

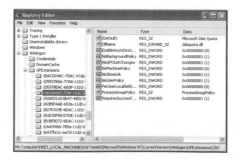

3. Drill down into HKLM ➢ Software ➢ Microsoft ➢ Windows NT ➢ Current Version ➢ Winlogon ➢ GPExtensions. Here you will find a list of Class IDs, each representing a CSE.

Figure 4.13 shows a sample CSE and the settings for disk quotas. See Table 4.1 for the CSEs listed by Class ID, the functions they perform, and the associated DLLs. Note that a particular DLL can be responsible for more than one function.

TABLE 4.1   Table 4.1 Class IDs, Their Functions, and Their Corresponding DLLs

Class ID	Function	DLL
C6DC5466-785A-11D2-84D0-00C04FB169F7	Software deployment	Appmgmts.dll
3610EDA5-77EF-11D2-8DC5-00C04FA31A66	Disk quotas	Dskquota.dll
B1BE8D72-6EAC-11D2-A4EA-00C04F79F83A	EFS recovery	Scecli.dll
25537BA6-77A8-11D2-9B6C-0000F8080861	Folder redirection	Fdeploy.dll
A2E30F80-D7DE-11d2-BBDE-00C04F86AE3B	Internet Explorer settings	Iedkcs32.dll
e437bc1c-aa7d-11d2-a382-00c04f991e27	IP security	Gptext.dll
35378EAC-683F-11D2-A89A-00C04FBBCFA2	Registry settings (Administrative Templates)	Userenv.dll
42B5FAAE-6536-11D2-AE5A-0000F87571E3	Scripts	Gptext.dll
827D319E-6EAC-11D2-A4EA-00C04F79F83A	Security	Scecli.dll
0ACDD40C-75AC-47ab-BAA0-BF6DE7E7FE63	Wireless (802.11x) (Windows XP only)	Gptext.dll
426031c0-0b47-4852-b0ca-ac3d37bfcb39	Quality of Service Packet Scheduler (Windows XP only)	Gptext.dll
None	Software Restriction (Windows XP only)	None
None	Remote Installation Services (RIS)	None

Why Don't All CSEs have DLLs?

Neither Remote Installation Services (RIS) nor Software Restriction polices require CSEs associated with DLLs. RIS is active *before* the operating system is. (For more information on RIS, see Chapter 11.) Software Restriction policies don't require CSEs because Windows XP has a bit of magic that occurs each time a new process starts. That is, each process verifies that it isn't in the "restricted" list. If it's not, it runs! (For more on Software Restriction policies, see Chapter 6.)

 When creating custom ADM templates (see "ADM Template Syntax" on this book's website), the CLIENTEXT keyword specifies which client-side extension is needed to process particular settings on the client computer.

For each CSE, several values can be set or not. Not all CSEs use these values. Indeed, Microsoft does not support modifying them in any way. They are presented in Table 4.2 for your own edification, but in most circumstances, you should not be modify them unless explicitly directed to do so by Microsoft Product Support Services (PSS).

 Remember, the CSE sets these values—you don't, unless you're directed by Microsoft PSS to help make sure the CSE is working the way it's supposed to.

TABLE 4.2 Client-Side Extension Values

Value	Data Type	Function	Data	Default
DLLName	REG_EXPAND_SZ	Contains the DLL name	CSE DLL	Per CSE
ProcessGroupPolicy	REG_SZ	Used to call a subset of the CSE DLL	The function call name	Per CSE
NoMachinePolicy	REG_DWORD	Enable/disable machine processing	0=Process; 1=Don't process	0
NoUserPolicy	REG_DWORD	Enable/disable user processing	0=Process; 1=Don't process	0
NoSlowLink	REG_DWORD	Enable/disable over slow link	0=Process; 1=Don't process	0

TABLE 4.2   Client-Side Extension Values *(continued)*

Value	Data Type	Function	Data	Default
NoBackgroundPolicy	REG_DWORD	Enable/disable background GPO processing	0=Process; 1=Don't process	0
NoGPOListChanges	REG_DWORD	Process if changed or not	0=Always process; 1=Do not process unless changes	0
PerUserLocalSettings	REG_DWORD	Caches policies for user or machine	0=Don't cache; 1=Cache	0
RequiresSuccessful-Registry	REG_DWORD	Forces CSE DLLs to be registered with the operating system	0=Don't care; 1=CSEs must be registered	0
EnableAsynchronous-Processing	REG_DWORD	Enable/disable asynchronous GPO processing	0=Synchronous; 1=Asynchrounous	Depends on the CSE

I hope you won't have to spend too much time in here. But I present this information so that if you need to debug a certain CSE, you can go right to the source and see how a setting might not be what you want.

Remember that most of these settings are established either by the system default or can be changed. You can change the settings yourself—such as the ability to process over slow links, the ability to be disabled, or the ability to be processed in the background—using the techniques described near the end of Chapter 3.

Where Are Administrative Templates Registry Settings Stored?

Because one of the most commonly applied policy settings is the Administrative Templates, let's take a minute to analyze specifically how Administrative Templates are processed when the client processes them.

I've already discussed how Group Policy is more evolved than old NT 4–style policies. Specifically, one of the most compelling features is that most policy settings do not tattoo the Registry anymore. That is, once a setting is applied, it applies only for that computer or user. When the user or computer leaves the scope of the GPO (for example, when you move the user from the **Human Resources Users** OU to the **Accounting Users** OU), the Registry settings that did apply to them are removed, and the new Registry settings now apply.

When an NT 4–style policy was written, the writer could choose to modify any portion of the Registry. Now, as you've seen, when the settings specified in the Administrative Templates section of Group Policy no longer apply (for example, when a new user logs on or the computer is moved to another OU), the settings are removed or applied appropriately for the next user.

Administrative Templates Group Policy settings are usually stored in the following locations:

User Settings   `HKEY_CURRENT_USER\Software\Policies`

Computer Settings   `HKEY_LOCAL_MACHINE\Software\Policies`

Alternatively, some applications may choose the following locations:

User Settings   `HKEY_CURRENT_USER\Software\Microsoft\Windows\ CurrentVersion\Policies`

Computer Settings   `HKEY_LOCAL_MACHINE\Software\Microsoft\Windows\ Currentversion\Policies`

Microsoft is encouraging third-party developers to write their applications so that they look in the first set.

Knowing how this works helps us understand why Windows XP has about 200 more Administrative Templates policy settings that can apply to it. It's quite simple: the specific program that's targeted for the policy setting looks for settings at these two Registry locations. Sometimes that application is one we overlook a lot—`Explorer.Exe`! For Windows XP, `Explorer.Exe` has been "smartened up" and now knows to look in these Registry keys for about 200 new items.

This also answers the question of why Windows 2000 machines "overlook" policy settings that are designed only for Windows XP or Windows 2003. Windows 2000 machines suffer no ill effects; they're just ignored. Since it's just Explorer that needs to know about the changes, the registry is modified, then promptly ignored. Windows 2000 just doesn't know to look for the new Registry changes that new Windows XP or Windows 2003 policy settings change. Occasionally, with the release of a service pack, the application in question might get a new lease on life and understand some new policy settings—because the application has now been updated to look for them in the Registry. This has already happened for Explorer, Software Update Services, Windows Media Player and Office to name a few.

If you have a mixture of Windows 2000 desktops and member servers and Windows XP and Windows 2003 member servers, you might need to keep track of policy settings that affect only XP. It's likely a good idea to create GPOs with names specific to what operating system they apply to: Windows 2000, Windows XP, and/or Windows 2003.

Because the settings inside Administrative Templates are written to only these four locations, we are free from the bonds of having our Registries tattooed. The Administrative Templates CSE and DLL (`Userenv.Dll`) applies the settings placed in any of these four locations to the current mix of user and system. When that mix changes, the settings change. It's as easy as that.

For information on how to use other Administrative Templates, see Chapter 5, and for information on how to create your own Administrative Templates, see "ADM Template Syntax" on this book's website.

Why Isn't Group Policy Applying?

At times you set up Group Policy from upon high, and your users or workstations are not receiving the changes. Why might that be the case?

First, remember how Group Policy is processed:

- The GPO "lives" in the swimming pool in the domain.
- The client requests Group Policy at various times throughout the day; Group Policy is told to apply.
- The client connects to a Domain Controller to get the latest batch of GPOs.
- If nothing has changed on the GPO, the default behavior is to not reprocess the GPOs (though this can be changed as explored in Chapter 3).
- The client-side extensions then process the GPOs that need processing.

That's the long and the short of it.

Now, if you think this is working correctly, try to answer the following questions to find out what could be damming the proper flow of your Group Policy process.

Reviewing the Basics

Sometimes, it's the small, day-to-day things that prevent a GPO from applying. By testing a simple application that has normal features, you can often find problems and eliminate them, which allows Group Policy to behave the way you expect.

Is the Group Policy Object or Link Disabled?

Recall from Chapter 1 that there are two halves of the Group Policy coin: a computer half and a user half. Also recall that either portion or both can be disabled. Indeed, a GPO itself can be fully disabled (see Figure 4.14).

Check the GPO itself or any related GPO links. Click the Details tab and check the GPO Status setting. If it is anything other than "Enabled," you might be in trouble.

If you change the status of the GPO, that status changes on all links that use this GPO.

FIGURE 4.14   You can disable the entire GPO if desired.

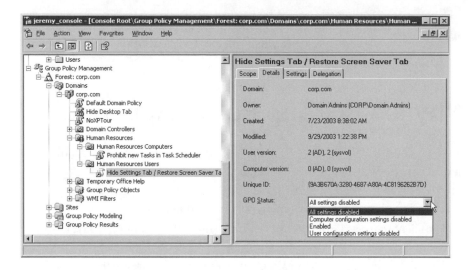

Are You Sure About the Inheritance?

Recall that Group Policy flows downward from each level—site, domain, and each nested OU—and is cumulative. Also recall that there is only one Local Group Policy for a computer, which is applied first.

Multiple Group Policy Objects at a Level

Also recall that there can be many GPOs at any level, which are applied in the reverse order—that is, from bottom to top, as described in Chapter 2. Since any two (or more) GPOs can contain the same or even conflicting settings, the last-applied GPO wins. If you mean for one GPO to have higher precedence, use the Up and Down buttons to manipulate the order.

Examining Your Block Inheritance Usage

The GPMC gives you a quick view of all instances of Block Inheritance with the Blue Exclamation point (!). Remember: once you select to block inheritance, *all GPOs* from higher levels are considered null and void—not just the one policy setting or GPO you had in mind to block. It's as if you were starting from a totally blank slate. Therefore, whenever you block inheritance, you must start from scratch—either creating and linking new GPOs or simply linking to existing GPOs already swimming in the GPOs container. Note, however, that the Default Domain Policy GPO *cannot* be blocked. (This GPO is discussed in Chapter 6.)

Examining Your "Enforced" Usage

Conversely, be aware of all of your "Enforce" directives. The Enforce icon is a little lock next to the GPO link. "Enforce" specifies that the policy settings selected and contained within in a *specific* GPO cannot be avoided at any inherited level from this point forward. When "Block Policy Inheritance" and "Enforce" are seemingly in conflict, "Enforced" always wins. Recall that Enforced was previously known as "No Override" in the old-school parlance.

Are Your Permissions Set Correctly?

Recall from Chapter 2 that two permissions—"Read" and "Apply Group Policy"—must be set so that the affected user processes a specific GPO. By default, Authenticated Users have these two rights, but you can remove this group and set your own filtering via the "Security Filtering" section on the Scope tab of a GPO link.

In Chapter 2, I showed you two ways to filter:

- Round up only the users, computers, or Security groups who *should* get the GPO applied to them.

- Figure out who you *do not* want to get the GPO applied to them, and use the "Deny" attribute over the "Apply Group Policy" right.

When all is said and done, users will need both "Read" and "Apply Group Policy" permissions on the GPO itself to apply GPOs. Having only one of those permissions means that Group Policy will not apply when processing is supposed to occur.

Additionally, make sure to remember that the "Deny" attribute always trumps all other permissions. If an explicit "Deny" attribute is encountered, it is as if it is the only bit in the world that matters. Therefore, if a specific GPO is not being applied to a user or a group, make sure that "Deny" isn't somehow getting into the picture along the way.

Any use of the Deny bit is not displayed in the "Security Filtering" section of the Scope tab; so you really have no notification if it's being used. I predict this will be a common reason for Group Policy not applying; the old-school way to perform Group Policy filtering involved heavy use of the Deny bit, and now the GPMC will not easily display this fact.

Advanced Inspection

If you've gone through the basics, and nothing is overtly wrong, perhaps a more subtle interaction is occurring. See if any of the following questions and solutions fit the bill.

Is Windows XP's Fast Boot On?

The default behavior of Windows XP is different from that of Windows 2000. The default behavior of Windows 2000 is to process GPOs synchronously. That is, for the policy settings that affect a Windows 2000 computer (which will take effect at startup), every GPO is applied—local, site, domain, and each nested OU—even before the user has the ability to press Ctrl+Alt+Delete to log on. Once the user logs on, the policy settings that affect the user side are applied—local, site, domain, and each nested OU—before the user's desktop is finally displayed and they can start working.

But the default behavior of Windows XP is to perform nearly everything asynchronously. Asynchronous Processing means that GPOs can process out of their natural order. The GPOs are simply downloaded in the fastest possible manner at any level in Active Directory and then immediately applied. The Group Policy application happens without regard to the natural order.

This usually isn't too much of a problem for the policy settings within GPOs that affect computers, but it can seriously affect your user's experience if enabled for user policy processing. Even *after* a user is logged on, GPOs can suddenly be downloaded. and policy settings start popping up and change the user's environment.

Moreover, as I stated in Chapter 3, by default, several key items in Windows XP take between two and three reboots to become effective. To that end, I suggest you modify the default behavior. The strongest advice I can give you is to create and link new GPOs at the domain level. Name your new GPO something like "Force Windows XP machines to act like Windows 2000," and enable the **Always wait for the network at computer startup and logon** policy setting. To find this policy setting, drill down through Computer Configuration ➤ Administrative Templates ➤ System ➤ Logon branch of Group Policy. (For more information, see Chapter 3.)

Therefore, if you have erratic Group Policy application (especially for Software Installation, Folder Redirection, or Profile settings), see if the Windows XP default of Fast Boot is still active.

Is Asynchronous Processing Turned On in Windows 2000?

Windows 2000 was born with a way to try to act like Windows XP and process GPOs asynchronously. However, doing so is not recommended as amazingly unpredictable results can occur. Windows XP was built from the ground up to do asynchronous processing; Windows 2000 really wasn't. And to that end, the ability to turn on asynchronous processing has been removed by means of normal policy settings via ADM templates (since Windows 2000 SP3). In other words, if you're managing your Group Policy infrastructure with a machine with Windows 2000 service pack 3, Windows 2003 or XP, you will find no policy setting that can enable Windows 2000 Asynchronous Processing anymore. But if you're still using an older Windows 2000 system to manage Group Policy, you will see a policy setting that *could* enable Asynchronous Processing for Windows 2000 machines. In a nutshell, don't use it. If you are using it, turn it off.

 Asynchronous Processing is independent for both the computer and the user sides.

Are Both the GPC and GPT Replicated Correctly?

As stated in the first part of this chapter, Group Policy is made up of two halves:

- The GPC, which is found in Active Directory and replicated via normal Active Directory replication.

- The GPT, which is found in the SYSVOL share of one Domain Controller and replicated via FRS to other Domain Controllers.

Both the GPC and GPT are replicated independently and can be on different schedules before converging. Only after they converge is the GPO available to be applied to the workstation.

Additionally, according to Microsoft, the GPC and GPT version numbers must match before workstations will apply them, though I haven't found this to be the case.

Use the techniques described earlier in conjunction with `Gpotool` and `Replmon` to diagnose issues with replicating the GPC and GPT.

Did You Check the DNS Configuration of the Server?

In order for the GPC and GPT to actually replicate correctly, the DNS structure must be 100% kosher at all times. If you suspect that the GPC and GPT are not being replicated correctly, you might try to see if the DNS structure is the way you intend. If it is, I don't specifically recommend you rip it all up and reconfigure it if everything else is working.

In some cases, one Domain Controller might not be providing Group Policy to your clients. In the next section, I'll show you how to find out if your clients are really logged on and, if so, what Domain Controller the computer and user are using for logon.

If the Domain Controller they're using does not provide Group Policy, one somewhat radical remedy is to point the DNS client of the "broken" server to the same place where other "working" Domain Controllers are pointing. If this doesn't help, you might consider dropping your Active Directory integrated DNS to a standard primary—I've seen kooky things pop up when running in Active Directory integrated mode.

The purpose of these two radical changes (which you shouldn't do lightly) is to jump-start the broken Domain Controller into working and playing nicely with others. Ordinarily, if a specific Domain Controller isn't giving out the GPOs you expect, the GPC and/or the GPT aren't making it there, and DNS is almost certainly to blame.

Are You Really Logged On?

Windows XP and Windows 2000 perform the logon function differently. Specifically, when a user logs on to a Windows XP machine, Windows XP might or might not have made really made contact with a Domain Controller to validate that user and give them a Kerberos ticket to the network. A Kerberos ticket is the newer authentication mechanism that has supplanted NTLM. Windows XP will try its darndest to speed things up (again) and log on with cached credentials. Windows XP will then try to contact a Domain Controller and get the Kerberos ticket for the user.

In Windows 2000, it is easy to identify the Domain Controller where the local desktop authenticated. You issue a `set` command at a command prompt and look for the contents of the *LOGONSERVER* variable, as shown in Figure 4.15.

In Windows 2000, if you aren't logged on to a Domain Controller, you see the variable set to the local computer name.

WARNING   In Windows XP, you simply cannot trust this *LOGONSERVER* variable to tell you the truth. Additionally, you cannot trust Windows XP's SYSTEMINFO utility either, which claims to provide this data.

FIGURE 4.15   The LOGONSERVER variable shows the Domain Controller where this Windows 2000 client is picking up its Group Policy settings.

Just based on the way Windows XP does its logon thing, you cannot use these aforementioned methods. XP will simply do a bald-faced lie and say that you are logged on (via the *LOGONSERVER* variable, with the information from the last Domain Controller it contacted).

With Windows XP, to ensure your user and computer are really logged on the network, you can count on just one tool—Kerbtray. Kerbtray is found in the Windows 2003 Resource Kit and is small enough to be put on a floppy and run on a suspect machine. When you run it, it puts a little icon in the notification area. If the computer and user have Kerberos tickets, the icon turns green, and you know you're really logged on. However, if the Kerbtray returns a graphic of bunch of loose keys (that, in my opinion, look like question marks), as shown in Figure 4.16, you know you're not actually logged on and, hence, not downloading the most recent GPOs. Again, if you were really logged on, the graphic would be a green ticket.

In Figure 4.16, you can see several things:

- The computer's network card is disabled (as shown in the Network Connections window)

- The *LOGONSERVER* variable is set to a Domain Controller (as shown in the CMD prompt window). Feel free to simply say out loud, "If the network card is off, this is bloody impossible."

- Kerbtray, thankfully, returns that icon of a bunch of loose keys verifying that we're not really logged on.

So, to find out if you're really logged on when using a Windows XP computer, it's "Kerbtray or the highway." Once you've validated with Kerbtray that the computer has really logged on, you can *then* use the *LOGONSERVER* variable to make sure which Domain Controller the Windows XP machine has used. Because, you'll know the truth: whether or not you're really logged on.

FIGURE 4.16 Windows XP's LOGONSERVER variable cannot be trusted. Use Kerbtray instead, which is shown running in the notification area.

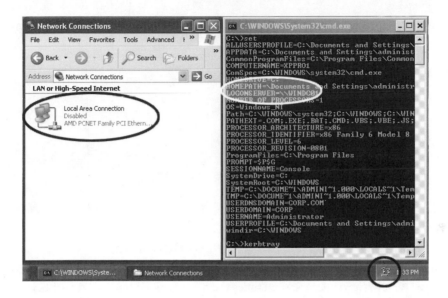

Did Something Recently Move?

If a computer account or a user account is moved from one OU to another, both Windows XP and Windows 2000 can wait as long as 30 minutes to realize this fact. Once they do, they might or might not apply background Group Policy processing for another 90 or more minutes! Running GPUpdate (or SECEDIT for Windows 2000 machines) will not help.

However, if you're expecting a specific setting to take effect on a user or computer that has moved more than 150 minutes ago, you'll then need to figure out if the move has been embraced by the Domain Controller the workstation used to authenticate. (See the previous section for information about how to determine the Domain Controller via the *LOGONSERVER* variable, but make sure you're really logged on!)

You can then fire up Active Directory Users And Computers and connect to the Domain Controller in question, as shown in Figure 4.17.

If the target computer's local Domain Controller does not know about the move, you might want to manually kick off replication using Active Directory Sites And Services. If the target computer's local Domain Controller *does* know about the move, you might want to try logging the user off and back on or restarting the computer. Although using SECEDIT (for Windows 2000 machines) or GPUpdate (for Windows XP and Windows 2003 machines) to refresh the GPO is a good option, it's best to log off and/or reboot the machine to guarantee the computer will perform the initial policy processing as described in Chapter 3.

FIGURE 4.17 You can always manually connect to a Domain Controller to see if Active Directory has performed replication.

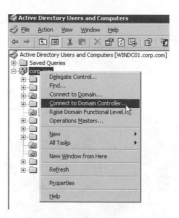

Is the Machine Properly Joined to the Domain?

With Windows 2000, if a device is moved from one OU to another and then the device is rebooted *before* DC replication occurs, sometimes the device can be bumped out of being a domain member because the "computer trust," also known as a "secure channel," is broken. To see if the computer trust (secure channel) to the domain is damaged, you can use NLTEST, which is in the Windows 2000 Support Tools on the Windows 2000 CD. The verification syntax is `nltest /sc_query:domain_name`. If the test passes, then you're kosher. If not, you might need to disjoin and rejoin the device to the domain.

Is Loopback Policy Enabled?

Enabling loopback policy will turn Group Policy on its ear: loopback forces the same user policy settings for everyone who logs on to a specific computer. If you're seeing user policy settings apply but not computer polices or if things are applying without rhyme or reason, chances are, loopback policy is enabled. Review Chapter 3 to see in depth how it works, when you should use it, and how to turn it off.

How Are Slow Links Being Defined, and How are Slow Links Handled?

If you notice that Group Policy is not applied to dial-in users, remember the rules for slow links:

- Registry and security settings are always applied over slow (and fast) links.

- EFS (Encrypting File System) and IPsec (IP Security) policies are *always* applied over slow links. You cannot turn this behavior off, even though settings found under Computer Configuration ➢ Administrative Templates ➢ System ➢ Group Policy branch imply that you can. This is a bug in the interface as described in Chapter 3.

- By default, Disk Quotas, Folder Redirection, Internet Explorer settings, and Software Deployment are not applied over slow links. Updated and new logon scripts are also not downloaded over slow links. You can change this default behavior under Computer Configuration ➢ Administrative Templates ➢ System ➢ Group Policy, as described in Chapter 3.

Additionally, you can change the definition of what equals a slow link. By default, a slow link is 500Kb or less. You can change the definition for the user settings in User Configuration ➤ Administrative Templates ➤ System ➤ Group Policy ➤ **Group Policy Slow Link Detection** and for the computer settings in Computer Configuration ➤ Administrative Templates ➤ System ➤ Group Policy ➤ **Group Policy Slow Link Detection**. Figure 4.18 shows the user settings. If Group Policy is not being applied to your slow-linked clients, be sure to inspect the slow-link definition to make sure they fit.

Last, don't forget about your broadband users on DSL or cable modem. Those speeds are sometimes faster than 500Kb and sometimes slower than 500Kb. This could mean that your broadband users might get GPOs on weekends but not when logged on during peak usage times. Therefore, if this happens, set the definition of slow link up or down as necessary.

Is the date and time correct on the client system?

Times differences greater than 5 minutes between the client system and the validating Domain Controller will cause machines to fail to register in DNS. This could potentially be a Group Policy problem.

Are your Active Directory sites configured correctly?

Sometimes Group Policy won't apply if a Windows XP client isn't in a properly defined Active Directory site (that has IP information associated with it). With that in mind, check the subnet the client is on, and verify that it is correctly associated to an Active Directory site and that the site has Domain Controller coverage.

FIGURE 4.18   Make sure you haven't raised the bar too high for your slower-connected users to receive Group Policy.

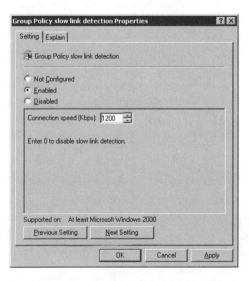

Did You Check the DNS Configuration of the Client?

One of the most frequently encountered problems with Windows 2000 is that things just "stop working" when DNS gets out of whack. Specifically, if you're not seeing Group Policy apply to your client machines, make sure their DNS client is pointing to a Domain Controller or other authoritative source for the domain. If it's pointing to the wrong place or not pointing anywhere, Group Policy will simply not be downloaded. As a colleague of mine likes to say, "Healthy DNS equals a healthy Active Directory."

Moreover, in the age of Windows 2003 with its multiple forests with cross-forest trusts, Group Policy could be applying from just about anywhere and everywhere. It's more important than ever to verify that all DNS server pointers are designed properly and working as they should. For instance, if clients cannot access their "home" Domain Controllers while leveraging a cross-forest trust, they won't get Group Policy.

Are You Trying to Set Password or Account Policy Upon an OU?

As you'll see in Chapter 6, certain Group Policy items, namely password and account policy, cannot be set at the OU level. Rather, these policy settings are only domain wide. The GUI lets you set these policy settings at the OU level, but they don't affect users or machines. Well, that's not really true, as you'll see in Chapter 6, but, for the purposes of troubleshooting, just remember that you can't have, say, six-character passwords in the **Sales** OU and 12-character passwords in the **Engineering** OU. It won't work.

Did Someone Muck with Security Behind the Group Policy Engine's Back?

As you saw in Chapter 3, there are a number of ways to "go around" the back of the Group Policy engine. Remember, though, that these exploits require local administrative access. However, this implies that users with local administrative access can manually hack the Registry and return their systems to just about however they want. Then, as I've described, Group Policy will not reapply upon background refresh, logon, or reboot. It reapplies changes only when the GPO in Active Directory has changed.

Windows 2000 uses the SECEDIT command to refresh Group Policy, but, as I've stated, it still won't forcefully reapply all the settings—even if the /enforce switch is used (which just forcefully reapplies security settings). Windows XP's GPUpdate command will refresh changed Group Policy as well, but its /force switch is quite powerful and will reapply all settings—even those that have not changed.

Is the Target Computer in the Correct OU? Is the Target User in the Correct OU?

This is my personal sore point. This is the one I usually check last, and it's usually what's at fault. That is, I've simply forgotten to place the user object or the computer object into the OU to which I want the GPO to apply. Therefore, the object isn't in the "scope" of where Group Policy will apply.

You can configure all the user or computer policy settings on an OU that you like, but, quite obviously, unless that user or computer object is actually *in* the OU, the target computer will simply not receive the message you're sending. And, no, you cannot just move a security group that contains the user or computer objects and plunk it in the desired OU. Group Policy doesn't work that way. That actual user or computer object needs to be in the site, domain, or OU that the GPO applies! And since no two objects can be in any two OUs at the same time, this can be a challenge.

 Security groups are irrelevant—except for filtering.

Client-Side Troubleshooting

One of the most important skills to master is the ability to determine what's going on at the client. By and large, the Group Policy Results tool, which you run from the GPMC, should give you what you need. However, occasionally, only trotting out to the client can truly determine what is happening on your client systems.

You could be roaming the halls, just trying to get the last Krispy Kreme glazed doughnut from the break room, when someone snags you and plops you in their seat for a little impromptu troubleshooting session. They want you to figure out why Group Policy isn't the same today as it was yesterday or why they're suddenly getting new or different settings.

This section will describe the various means for determining the RSoP (Resultant Set of Policy) while sitting at a client or using some remote-control mechanism such as Microsoft SMS (Systems Management Server), VNC (Virtual Networking Client), or even, in the case of Windows XP, Remote Desktop. As you saw in the last chapter, the GPMC has two tools to help you tap into this data: Group Policy Results and Group Policy Modeling. However, there are other client-side tools at your disposal. Additionally, I'll describe how to leverage a new function in Windows XP and Windows 2003 to determine a target user's and computer's RSoP remotely!

RSoP for Windows 2000

If you're sitting at a Windows 2000 machine, there aren't a lot of options to help you determine the RSoP. However, one particular tool can really bring home the bacon—GPResult.exe. This is one of the most important tools for Group Policy troubleshooting. When the going gets tough and I can't figure out what's going on, I look to GPResult to help tell me the score. You'll find GPResult in the Windows 2000 Server Resource Kit, but it is also built into the Windows 2000 Service Pack 4 and is in c:\Windows\system32.

The main goal of GPResult is to expose which GPOs are applied from where and the settings. The Achilles heel of GPResult on Windows 2000 is that it *must* be run on the client experiencing the problem.

GPResult appears only on Windows 2000 installations on which Service Pack 4 was installed *after* the machine was installed. GPResult will not appear if a slip-streamed Windows 2000 with SP4 was used to create a machine fresh. This is a bug in the definition of the service pack and is subject to change in future service packs. You can just expand GPResult.exe from the service pack files and plunk it in the c:\windows\system32 folder without any penalty.

If you can set up Telnet server on a client system, you can telnet to the client and then run GPResult as if you were at the client. This could save you a hike or two. However, you'll need to log on with the credentials of the user (not of the local administrator) to get the same results.

GPResult has three modes—normal, verbose, and super-verbose—and can expose the user settings, the computer settings, or, by default, both. If you don't have Windows 2000 SP4 loaded, you can copy GPResult onto a floppy (from an SP4 installation or from the resource kit) or run it over the network.

Although GPResult is powerful, it has a limited set of options:

- /v displays verbose output. In the next section, you'll see an example of verbose output.
- /s displays super-verbose output. This equates to the new /z option in GPResult for Windows XP. Again, I'll discuss how you might use this in the next section.
- /c limits the output to the computer-side policy settings.
- /u limits the output to the user-side policy settings.

You can mix and match the options. For instance, to display verbose output for the computer section, you can run GPResult /v /c.

We'll explore GPResult in depth in the next section, but, due to space concerns, I'll describe it from a Windows XP perspective.

The Windows 2000 GPResult isn't nearly as feature rich as its Windows XP or Windows 2003 counterpart, but, as you'll soon see, there is still life in the Windows 2000 version.

RSoP for Windows 2003 and Windows XP

Windows XP and Windows 2003 greatly expand our capacity to determine the RSoP of client machines and users on those machines. In this section, we'll explore several options. The first stop is a grown-up GPResult to help us get to the bottom of what's happening on our client machines.

GPResult for Windows 2003 and Windows XP

GPResult for Windows 2003 and Windows XP is more advanced than its Windows 2000 counterpart. Indeed, you can run GPResult when you're sitting at a user's desktop or at your own desktop, or you can run it remotely and pretend to be that user. If you're running it while sitting at someone's desktop, you'll likely use the following options:

- /v is for verbose mode. It presents the most meaningful information.

- /z is for zuper, er, super-verbose mode. Based on the types of policy settings that affect the user or computer, it displays way more information than you'll likely ever want to see, based on the types of policy settings that affect the user or computer.

- /scope:user limits the output to the user-side policy settings, and /scope:computer limits the output to the computer-side policy settings.

You can mix and match the options. For instance, to display verbose output for the user section, you can run GPResult /v /scope:user.

Here's the result of running GPResult with no arguments while logged on to the XPPro1 workstation (which is in the **Human Resources Computers** OU) as Frank Rizzo (who is in the **Human Resources Users** OU). I have slightly modified the output for formatting purposes. Note that some of the display might be somewhat different from yours.

 You must have Windows XP SP1 in order to properly use GPResult. Without SP1, trying to run GPResult twice will fail to function. For more information, see the Microsoft Knowledge Base article Q322852. Microsoft decided not to honor me by putting my name in this bug I found to enhance their Knowledge Base database. Oh well. <grin>

```
Microsoft(R)WindowsR) XP Operating System Group Policy Result tool v2.0
Copyright(C) Microsoft Corp. 1981-2001


Created On 7/26/2003 at 10:48:23 AM
RSoP results for CORP\frizzo on XPPRO1 : Logging Mode
------------------------------------------------------


OS Type:          Microsoft Windows XP Professional
OS Configuration: Member Workstation
OS Version:       5.1.2600
Domain Name:      CORP
Domain Type:      Windows 2000
Site Name:        Default-First-Site-Name
Roaming Profile:
Local Profile:    C:\Documents and Settings\frizzo
Connected over a slow link?: No
```

```
COMPUTER SETTINGS
------------------
    CN=XPPRO1,OU=Human Resources Computers,DC=corp,DC=com
    Last time Group Policy was applied: 7/26/2003 at 10:45:00 AM
    Group Policy was applied from:      WINDC01.corp.com
    Group Policy slow link threshold:   500 kbps


    Applied Group Policy Objects
    ----------------------------
        Prohibit new Tasks in Task Scheduler
            Filtering:  Denied (Security)



The following GPOs were not applied because they were filtered out
    ------------------------------------------------------
        Hide Desktop Tab
            Filtering:  Not Applied (Empty)
        Hide Screen Saver Tab
            Filtering:  Not Applied (Empty)

        Local Group Policy
            Filtering:  Not Applied (Empty)

        Default Domain Policy
            Filtering:  Not Applied (Unknown Reason)

    The computer is a part of the following security groups:
    ------------------------------------------------------
        BUILTIN\Administrators
        Everyone
        BUILTIN\Users
        XPPRO1$
        HR-Admin-Computers
        Domain Computers
        NT AUTHORITY\NETWORK
        NT AUTHORITY\Authenticated Users



USER SETTINGS
-------------
```

```
CN=Frank Rizzo,OU=Human Resources Users,DC=corp,DC=com
Last time Group Policy was applied: 7/26/2003 at 10:47:55 AM
Group Policy was applied from:      WINDCO1.corp.com
Group Policy slow link threshold:   500 kbps


Applied Group Policy Objects
----------------------------
    Hide Desktop Tab
    Local Group Policy


The following GPOs were not applied because they were filtered out
------------------------------------------------------
    Hide Settings Tab / Restore Screen Saver Tab
        Filtering:  Denied (Security)
    Hide Screen Saver Tab
        Filtering:  Not Applied (Unknown Reason)

    Default Domain Policy
        Filtering:  Not Applied (Unknown Reason)


The user is a part of the following security groups:
------------------------------------------------------
    Domain Users
    Everyone
    Remote Desktop Users
    BUILTIN\Users
    Group Policy Creator Owners
    HR-OU-Admins
    LOCAL
    REMOTE INTERACTIVE LOGON
    NT AUTHORITY\INTERACTIVE
    NT AUTHORITY\Authenticated Users
```

 You can redirect the output to a text file with GPResult > filename.txt.

You can glean all sorts of juicy tidbits from GPResult. Here are the key areas to inspect when troubleshooting client RSoP:

- Find the "Applied Group Policy Objects" entries for both the user and computer. Remember that Group Policy is applied from the local computer first, then the site level, then the domain level, and then each nested OU. If a setting is unexpected on the client, simply use the provided information along with the Group Policy Object Editor to start tracking the errant GPO.

- Use the "Last time Group Policy was applied:" entry to check to see the last time the GPO was applied—via either initial or background refresh processing. Use GPUpdate to refresh this, and then ensure that the value is updated when you re-run GPResult.

- Use the spelled-out distinguished name of the computer and user objects (for example, CN=Frank Rizzo, OU=Human Resources Users, DC=corp, and DC=com) to verify that the user and computer objects are located where you think they should be in Active Directory. If they are not, verify the location of the user and computer accounts using Active Directory Users And Computers. You might need to reboot this client machine if the location in Active Directory doesn't check out.

- Use "The user is a part of the following security groups" and "The computer is a part of the following security groups" sections to verify that the user or computer is in the groups you expect. Perhaps your user or computer object is inside a group that is denied access to either the "Read" or "Apply Group Policy" permissions on the GPO you were expecting.

- Find the "Connected over a slow link?" entry for the log and the "Group Policy slow link threshold" entries for both the user and computer. Remember that the various areas of Group Policy are processed differently when coming over slow links. (See Chapter 3 and 10.)

- Find the "The following GPOs were not applied because they were filtered out" section for both the user and the computer section. If you have GPOs listed here, the user or computer was, in fact, in the site, domain, or OU that the GPO was supposed to apply to. However, the GPOs listed here have not applied this user or computer for a variety of reasons. GPResult can tells you why this has happened. Here are some of the common reasons:

Denied (Security)   The user or computer doesn't have "Read" and "Apply Group Policy" rights to process the GPO. For instance, in the previous example, the "Prohibit new Tasks in Task Scheduler" doesn't apply to XPPro1 because we explicitly denied the XPPro1 computer object the ability to process the "Apply Group Policy" attribute.

Not Applied (Empty)   This GPO doesn't have any policy settings set in the user or computer half. For instance, in the previous example, the "Hide Desktop Tab" GPO doesn't have any computer-side policy settings. Hence, this GPO doesn't apply to Frank's computer object.

Not Applied (Unknown Reason)   Usually Block Inheritance has been used (though other, truly "unknown reasons" could also be valid). In the previous example, the "Hide Screen Saver Tab," which is set at the site level, won't apply to Frank because we've blocked inheritance at the **Human Resources** OU.

 The account policies of the Default Domain GPO cannot be blocked, regardless of the GPResult output.

Three Different *GPResult*s—Three Different Outputs!

If you want to take GPResult to the next level, use it with the /v switch. You can then see which Registry settings are specifically being altered by the GPOs. This could be useful if you want to manually dive into the Registry and perform the same punch the policy setting is doing on a machine that isn't connected to Active Directory and see if you get the same results.

However, running GPResult /v on Windows 2000, Windows XP, and Windows 2003 returns totally different results. For the sake of brevity, here are three comparison snippets to illustrate some additional information possible with GPResult /v. This output has been taken out to show you some specific details and also formatted slightly for readability.

GPResult /v for Windows XP SP1 is the least useful. When you run it, you'll get output similar to the following.

```
Administrative Templates
GPO: Hide Desktop Tab
Setting: Software\Microsoft\Windows\CurrentVersion\Policies\System
State:   Enabled
```

This output merely tells you that the GPO "Hide Desktop Tab" manipulates a Registry key somewhere in the path specified in the Setting field.

When you run the command on a Windows 2003 computer, you get the following:

```
Administrative Templates
-----------------------
GPO: Hide Desktop Tab
KeyName: Software\Microsoft\Windows\CurrentVersion\Policies\
System\NoDispBackgroundPage
Value: 1, 0, 0, 0
State: Enabled
```

This output is even more useful, because it shows you that it's the "NoDispBackroundPage" Registry entry with the value of 1 in the Registry that is performing the function. I'm guessing the difference in output between Windows XP and Windows 2003 is just a GPRESULT bug, but as of Windows XP+SP1 (and the beta of SP2), the output displayed is, in fact, different.

However, the most useful GPResult /v output comes from the GPResult in the Windows 2000 Resource Kit! (Yes! Windows 2000!)

```
The user received "Registry" settings from these GPOs:
    Hide Desktop Tab
        Revision Number:   3
        Unique Name:    {7AF6D1A4-4CAB-44FF-8003-67ED8241FFAB}
```

```
         Domain Name:    corp.com
         Linked to:      Domain (DC=corp,DC=com)
The following settings were applied from: Hide Desktop Tab
         KeyName:    Software\Microsoft\Windows\CurrentVersion\Policies\System
         ValueName:    NoDispBackgroundPage
         ValueType:    REG_DWORD
         Value:    0x00000001
```

The Windows 2000 GPResult /v shows you the ValueName (like the Windows 2003 version), but also shows you the ValueType (REG_DWORD.) Additionally, it can also easily show you the association between the GPO friendly name—say, "Hide Appearance Tab"—and the GUID—in my case, "7AF6D1A4-4CAB-44FF-8003-67ED8241FFAB." You might need this information later with other tools such as the Event Viewer, which may or may not use the friendly name.

So…my advice? The GPResult built into Windows XP and Windows 2003 is much better for basic troubleshooting. Its output describing *why* specific GPOs are not being processed is excellent. However, keep a copy of the Windows 2000 version of GPResult handy. It runs just fine on Windows XP and Windows 2003 machines, and, because of its additional functions in displaying both the Registry and the GPO GUID, you can get a lot closer to knowing *what* has been changed.

Remotely Calculating a Client's RSoP Using Windows XP or Windows 2003 *GPResult*

The Windows 2000 version of GPResult doesn't work the way the Windows XP and Windows 2003 version does. The Windows XP and Windows 2003 version of GPResult has a secret weapon tucked up its sleeve. You can almost hear it say, "Are you talkin' to me?"

Its weapon is that it can tap into the WMI provider built in to both Windows XP and Windows 2003. GPResult is like the GPMC's Group Policy Results Wizard. That is, it can be run from any Windows XP or Windows 2003 machine, and, provided the target machine is turned on, the system can "pretend" to be any particular user who has ever logged on locally. It's then a simple matter of displaying the results. You simply run GPresult, point it to a system, and provide the name of the user to pretend to log on with.

This magic only works on Windows XP and Windows 2003 as both source computers and target computers. Windows 2000 computers don't have a tap into this WMI magic; so they can't play.

WARNING There is one more important caution here (which I talked about in the Group Policy Results section, but bears repeating). That is, this magic only works if the target user has ever logged on to the target machine. They only need to have logged on just once, and they don't even need to be logged on while you run the test. But if the target user has *never* logged on to the target machine, remotely calculating GPResult will fail.

With that in mind, here are your additional Windows XP and Windows 2003 `GPResult` options:

- `/s <target system name or IP address>` points to the target system.
- `/user <optional domain\username>` pretends to log on as the target user.

You can combine any of the aforemented `GPResult` switches as well. If you log on to WINDC01 and want to see only the user-side policy settings when Frank Rizzo logs on to XPPro1, type the following:

```
gpresult /user frizzo /s xppro1 /scope:user
```

Again, this command only succeeds if Frank has ever logged on to XPPro1 (which he has).

`GPResult` is much better at telling you *why* a GPO is applying rather than *what* specific policy settings are contained with a GPO. For instance, notice that at no time did `GPResult` tell us what policy settings were contained in the local GPO. And, even when we performed a `GPResult /v`, we only found out the Registry keys that were modified—not the proper name of the specific policy setting that is doing the work. For these tasks, we'll need to use the GPMC (as seen in Chapter 3) or the Windows XP GUI RSoP (described next).

Windows XP's Group Policy "Help and Support System" RSoP Tool

If wading through a mountain of text-based `GPResult` output isn't your cup of tea, I've got some good news for you: you can view RSoP information graphically in both Windows XP and Windows 2003. If a user has problems, you cannot find a Windows 2003 or Windows XP machine to log on to (to remotely perform the tests), and you still want the user to tell you what their RSoP tool is, this tool is handy. You can get what you need over the phone and have the user just click-click-click to get you the results you want to hear (instead of asking them to dive into the scary world of command-line tools).

To launch the Windows XP or Windows 2003 Group Policy "Help and Support System" RSoP tool, otherwise just known as the "GUI RSoP tool," choose Start ➢ Help and Support to open Help and Support Center. Then click "Get support, or find information in Windows XP newsgroups." Next, click "Advanced System Information." Finally, select "View Group Policy settings applied." Figure 4.19 shows the results.

You'll see the many sections of user and computer Group Policy in the GUI RSoP tool. On Windows XP, this tool is, in some ways, superior to `GPResult` because you can see which Registry keys are being modified by Active Directory GPOs and also what's going on inside the Local GPO. Although this tool does provide the names of the GPOs that apply, it doesn't address "why" GPOs are or are not applying, as `GPResult` does. So, a yin and yang approach with both the `GPResult` and the GUI RSoP tools may be needed to get the whole story.

WARNING   At the bottom of the GUI RSoP, you'll see an option to save the report to an HTML file. The default location is c:\, but nonadministrators cannot save files here. If users save to an HTML file, be sure they have permission for the folder.

FIGURE 4.19   The RSoP tool in the Help and Support Center is useful when you're asking users to help you help them.

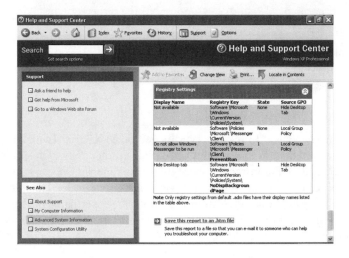

The RSoP MMC Snap-In

Yet another tool can help you determine the RSoP of the client. Technically, this tool is named the RSoP MMC Snap-In, but it comes in a non–snap-in flavor as well. Both tools have, more or less, been rendered obsolete by the GPMC. They do the same things as the GPMC, but you have to use them locally. I'm listing them here only for reference and completeness.

RSoP Generation from Help and Support Center

In Figure 4.19, you can see the "Save this report to an .htm file" option. Just below that (not shown) is the "Run the Resultant Set of Policy tool" option. This option launches this tool (again, technically, the RSoP MMC Snap-In), which will show you only the policy settings that are set and which GPOs they are coming from: local, site, domain, or OU, as shown in Figure 4.20.

FIGURE 4.20   The RSoP MMC Snap-In tool shows you only the policy settings that are configured.

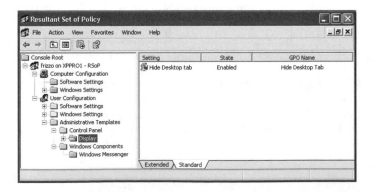

The bad news is that you still need to drill down a bit into each folder to get to the end. The good news is that the list is prefiltered and will only show you the policy setting name, the state, and the GPO from whence it came.

RSoP Generation from the True RSoP MMC Snap-In

Instead of launching the RSoP MMC snap-in tool from within the Help and Support Center, you can do just what its name implies. That is, run it directly as its own MMC snap in. To do so, follow these steps:

1. Choose Start ➢ Run to open the Run dialog box. In the Open box, enter **MMC** and press Enter to open the MMC.

2. Choose File ➢ Add/Remove Snap-in.

3. Click Add to see the list of snap-ins and select "Resultant Set of Policy" to start the Resultant Set of Policy Wizard.

4. Click Next to open the Mode Selection screen. If you're running Windows XP, only Logging is available. If you're running Windows 2003, Planning mode is also listed.

5. You'll then specify to perform the calculation on this computer or another Windows XP or Windows 2003 computer.

6. Next, you'll select the user; you can pretend to log on as any user who has logged on to the machine at least one time before. Note that you won't be able to "pretend" to log on as just anyone unless you're *really* logged in as someone with Administrator rights on the target machine.

7. Once the parameters are plugged in, you can press Next as seen in Figure 4.21 below.

FIGURE 4.21   The RSoP MMC Snap-In tool calculates the reaction between the specified user and computer.

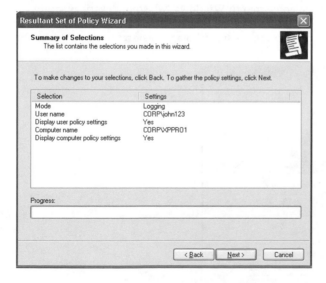

The RSoP MMC Snap-In tool does have one goodie that its bigger brother, the GPMC, does not have. That is, besides showing the "winning" GPO, it also lets you know the "losing" GPOs. After you complete the wizard and close the open screens, the RSoP you just calculated will appear in its own window, similar to what is seen in Figure 4.20.

Advanced Group Policy Troubleshooting with Log Files

We've already explored some of the techniques to troubleshoot Group Policy application. You can enable some underlying operating system troubleshooting tools to help diagnose just what the heck is going on when the unexpected occurs.

Using the Event Viewer

Quite possibly, the most overlooked and underutilized tool in Windows is the Event Viewer. The client's Event Viewer logs both the successful and unsuccessful application of Group Policy (see Figure 4.22).

Before beating your head against the wall, check the client's Event Log for relevant Group Policy records. The Event Log in Windows XP and Windows 2003 spit out much more information and many more warnings than did the Event Log in Windows 2000—so take advantage of it.

In Figure 4.22, the Event Log returned an error code of 1053. Doing a quick search in Microsoft TechNet, you can find a related Windows 2000 article, Q261007, which shows that the client is pointing to an incorrect DNS server. Because Windows XP is still relatively new, not every Windows 2000 article has been converted to Windows XP; so not every event ID is searchable.

FIGURE 4.22   The Event Viewer is a terrific place to start your troubleshooting journey.

In Windows XP+SP1, Event ID 1061 is supposed to help troubleshoot GPOs that are blocked by inheritance. However, a bug inside the event does not show the IDs that are being blocked.

Diagnostic Event Log Registry Hacks

If you really want to go bananas, you can enable *diagnostic logging* to supercharge your Event Log. To do so, a Registry key to the client machine. Traverse to HKEY_Local_Machine\ Software\Microsoft\Windows NT\CurrentVersion. Create a Diagnostics key, but leave the Class entry empty. You can specify logging types by creating one of three REG_DWORD keys.

RunDiagnosticLoggingGroupPolicy   Create this REG_DWORD to log only Group Policy events. To enable logging, set the data value to 1. Log entries appear in the Application Log.

RunDiagnosticLoggingGlobal   This key logs activity as if you added both the RunDiagnosticLoggingGroupPolicy as well as logs entries surrounding software deployment as detailed in Chapter 10. To enable logging, set the data value to 1. Log entries appear in the Application Log.

AppMgmtDebugLevel   Create this REG_DWORD, but do so with a data value of 4b in hexadecimal. At the next targeted software deployment, you'll find a log in the local \windows\debug\ usermode folder named appmgmt.log, which can also aid in troubleshooting why applications fail to load.

Some older Microsoft documentation also shows RunDiagnosticLogging-IntelliMirror and RunDiagnosticLoggingAppDeploy keys as viable options for the "Diagnostics" key. These entries are apparently documentation bugs and do absolutely nothing in Windows 2000.

When you've finished debugging, delete the Diagnostic keys so your Event Logs don't fill up.

Turning On Verbose Logging

Sometimes, all the server pieces are working perfectly, but the end result on the client is cock-eyed. You can examine Group Policy step by step by turning on *verbose logging*, which goes beyond the diagnostic Event Log Registry hacks. When you enable verbose logging by editing the Registry at the client, you are telling the system to generate a file called USERENV.LOG in the \winnt\debug\usermode folder. You can then examine the file to see what the client thinks is really happening.

To enable verbose logging, follow these steps:

1. Log on locally to the client system as the Administrator.
2. Run REGEDIT.

3. In the Registry Editor, traverse to HKEY_Local_Machine\Software\Microsoft\Windows NT\CurrentVersion\Winlogon.

4. In the Edit DWORD Value dialog box, add a REG_DWORD value by entering **UserEnvDebugLevel** in the Value Name box, and Value Data box, enter the hex value of **30002**, as shown in Figure 4.23. Click OK.

5. Close the Registry Editor.

 The value 30002 signifies verbose logging. The value 30001 signifies to log only errors and warnings. The value 30000 doesn't log anything.

After you modify the entry, log off as the local Administrator, and log on as someone with many GPOs that would affect their user object—say, Frank Rizzo in the **Human Resources Users** OU. After logging on as Frank, you can immediately log off and back on as the Administrator for the workstation and then read the log file.

 You can also hack the Registry at a command prompt. You can use the RUNAS command to run the command prompt as the Administrator. For this system, I would type **runas /user:XPPro1\administrator cmd**, and type the password to log on as the Administrator.

FIGURE 4.23 Verbose logging requires a hack to the Registry.

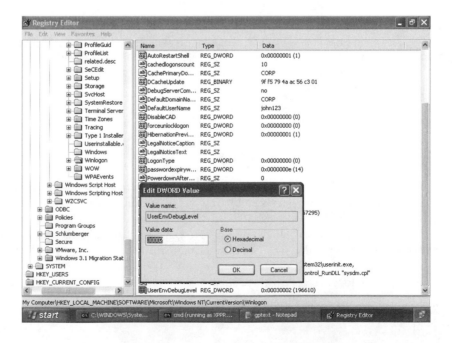

In the Userenv.log file in the \windows\debug\usermode folder, you should come across the following snippet. The output here has been truncated and formatted for better reading and for the sake of example. Additionally, line headers such as ProcessGPOs, AddGPO, and SearchDSObject have all been removed.

```
Starting user Group Policy (Background) processing...
Starting computer Group Policy (Background) processing...
User name is:  CN=Frank Rizzo,OU=Human Resources Users,OU=Human
Resources,DC=corp,DC=com, Domain name is:  CORP
Domain controller is:  \\WINDC01.corp.com  Domain DN is corp.com
network name is 192.168.2.0


User name is:  CN=XPPRO1,OU=Human Resources Computers,OU=Human
Resources,DC=corp,DC=com, Domain name is:  CORP


Domain controller is:  \\WINDC01.corp.com  Domain DN is corp.com
Calling GetGPOInfo for normal policy mode



No site name defined.  Skipping site policy.

Searching <OU=Human Resources Users,OU=Human Resources,DC=corp,DC=com>
Found GPO(s):  <[LDAP://cn={9A3B670A-3280-4687-A80A-
4C8196262B7D},cn=policies,cn=system,DC=corp,DC=com;0]>

Searching <OU=Human Resources,DC=corp,DC=com>
Found GPO(s):  < >
<OU=Human Resources,DC=corp,DC=com> has the Block From Above attribute set
Searching <DC=corp,DC=com>

Found GPO(s):
<[LDAP://cn={7AF6D1A4-4CAB-44FF-8003-
67ED8241FFAB},cn=policies,cn=system,DC=corp,DC=com;0][LDAP://CN={31B2F340-016D-
11D2-945F-00C04FB984F9},CN=Policies,CN=System,DC=corp,DC=com;0]>
GPO will not be added to the list since the Block flag is set and this GPO is
not in enforce mode.



Searching <CN={9A3B670A-3280-4687-A80A-
    4C8196262B7D},CN=Policies,CN=System,DC=corp,DC=com>
User does not have access to the GPO and so will not be applied.
Found functionality version of:  2
```

```
Found file system path of:  <\\corp.com\SysVol\corp.com\Policies\{9A3B670A-
    3280-4687-A80A-4C8196262B7D}>
Sysvol access skipped because GPO is not getting applied.
Found common name of:  <{9A3B670A-3280-4687-A80A-4C8196262B7D}>
Found display name of:  <Hide Settings Tab / Restore Screen Saver Tab>
Found user version of:  GPC is 2, GPT is 65535
Found flags of:  0
Found extensions:  [{35378EAC-683F-11D2-A89A-00C04FBBCFA2}{0F6B957E-509E-11D1-
    A7CC-0000F87571E3}]
```

You can learn a lot quickly by doing a little sleuthing inside the results. First, the computer is processing in Normal mode (as opposed to Loopback mode). And, while you're here, you can sniff out two back-to-back "errors" that I've detailed below.

The first error occurred due to some Active Directory site misconfiguration error. The text is clear: "No site name defined. Skipping site policy."

The second error occurred when the GPO represented by GUID 7AF6D1A4-4CAB-44FF-8003-67ED8241FFAB wasn't applied. This is the "Hide Desktop Tab" GPO we created and linked to the domain. The report states that the "GPO will not be added to the list since the Block flag is set and this GPO is not in enforce mode." This indicates that the GPO isn't being enforced while the OU level (**Human Resources**) is blocking inheritance.

The last error occurred when the GPO with the GUID 9A3B670A-3280-4687-A80A-4C8196262B7D was not applied due to "User does not have access to the GPO." In my case, the GUID matched with the "Hide Settings Tab/Restore Screen Saver Tab" GPO. Back in Chapter 2, one example denied the HR-OU-Admins security group the access to read that GPO, so it would not apply to them. Frank Rizzo is a member of the HR-OU-Admins group and, hence, does not get the GPO.

Final Thoughts

You want to be a better troubleshooter for Group Policy issues? You're well on the way.

In the last chapter, you learned when Group Policy is supposed to apply. It doesn't just happen when it wants to, it happens according to a set of precise timings. In this chapter, you learned two more key items to help on your troubleshooting journey. First, you learned the real story about what's going on under the hood. Then, you learned how to take that knowledge and troubleshoot Group Policy. Hopefully, every page in this chapter will help you further troubleshoot Group Policy should something go awry. However, here are some parting tips when troubleshooting Group Policy:

Check the basics   When troubleshooting, first check the basics. Make sure you're not using "Block Inheritance" or "Enforce" where you shouldn't.

Check Permissions   Users need both "Read" and "Apply Group Policy" permissions to the GPOs. Computers do too. If a user (or group the user is in) is Denied access to either of these permissions, then the GPO will not apply.

Leverage the built-in tools   Use the built-in debugging tools, such as the Event Viewer, super-charged with the Diagnostics key to help troubleshoot even tougher problems.

Leverage additional tools   There are lots of additional troubleshooting tools at your disposal. Be sure to check out "Third Party Group Policy tools" on this book's website, where we introduce WinPolicies, GPMonitor, GPInventory, and more.

Verify Replication is working   If a client isn't getting the GPOs you think they should, it just may be that normal replication hasn't finished yet. GPCs replicate via Active Directory replication. GPTs replicate via FRS replication. They are supposed to take the same path, but sometimes they don't. Use GPOTOOL and REPLMON to troubleshoot.

You'll find a great article on Group Policy troubleshooting at http://go.microsoft.com/fwlink/?LinkId=14949.

5

Windows ADM Templates

Group Policy has lots of nooks and crannies in which many options can be set. It's likely you'll spend most of your time manipulating the Administrative Templates section. Consequently, you need to know where all these settings come from.

In Windows 2000, Windows XP, and Windows 2003, by default the ADM (administrative) templates come in many varieties. Searching through the Administrative Templates section for a policy setting you want to deploy can sometimes be a challenge, however. Occasionally, the policy setting you're hoping to find isn't even a real option. However, the great thing about the Administrative Templates section is that if you can't find a specific policy setting that you need, you can often create your own! Once created, policy settings can be imported into the Group Policy Editor as ADM templates.

These templates hold the key to almost any change on our target systems. They are so important and powerful because they alter the Registry on the target computer. The ADM template holds the Registry settings that can be toggled on or off through the Group Policy Object Editor, where the administrator can modify the settings. Then, when the client system is booted or the user logs on, the Registry is altered based on what was manipulated within the Group Policy Object Editor. The target Windows 2000 client computer simply embraces the settings automatically.

Regardless of whether you want to use the default templates or create your own, you will need to fully understand the syntax in one of these ADM templates. Once you understand the syntax, you can create, modify, and troubleshoot almost any Registry change that is implemented by the Administrative Templates in the Group Policy Object Editor.

 You'll find the complete reference for creating your own ADM templates in "ADM Template Syntax" on this book's website.

Policies versus Preferences

One of the most heralded benefits of moving away from your old Windows NT 4–based System Policy is the nonpersistence of the Registry changes using Group Policy in Windows 2000. Every Windows NT 4 System Policy change was *persistent*. When you Enabled a System Policy, it stayed turned on until you set an explicit policy to turn it off. You couldn't just delete the policy and have the setting go away, as is the case with today's Group Policy engine. If you used Windows NT System Policy, you had to fight the same problem over and over.

With Windows 2000 and newer versions of Windows comes a new model for policies. Microsoft has created special locations in the Registry for Windows 2000, aptly named *Policies*. Microsoft documentation states that four Registry areas are considered the approved places to create policies out of Registry hacks:

- HKLM\Software\Policies (computer settings, the preferred location)

- HKLM\Software\Microsoft\Windows\CurrentVersion\Policies (computer settings, an alternative location)

- HKCU\Software\Policies (user settings, the preferred location)

- HKCU\Software\Microsoft\Windows\CurrentVersion\Policies (user settings, an alternative location)

These locations are preferred because they have security permissions that do not allow a regular user to modify these keys.

When a policy setting is set to "Enabled" and the client embraces the Group Policy directives, a Registry entry is set in one of these keys. When the GPO that applied the keys is removed, the Registry keys associated with it are also removed. Whether an application that is looking for these Registry keys can locate them depends on whether you manipulate the setting.

 A local administrator has security permissions to these keys and can modify the GPO setting for this portion of the Registry.

This is the magic that makes Group Policy shine over old-style NT 4 System Policy; that is, Group Policy won't tattoo because it's being directed to go in a nonsticking place in the Registry. Old-style NT 4 System Policy had no such facility. Today, Microsoft calls these NT-style policies that tattoo, *preferences*.

You might want to control a pet application that you have deployed in-house, say, DogFoodMaker 6.1. Great—you've decided you want more control. Now, you need to determine which Registry values and data DogFoodMaker 6.1 understands. That could take some time; you might be able to ask the manufacturer for the valid registry values or you might have some manual labor in front of you to determine what can be controlled via the Registry. You'll then be able to begin to create your own ADM templates (with the syntax in "ADM Template Syntax" on this book's website.

However, once you've determined how DogFoodMaker 6.1 can be controlled via the Registry, you'll find you have two categories of Registry tweaks:

- Values that fit neatly into the new Policies keys listed earlier

- Values that are anywhere else

You'll have some good news and some bad news. If DogFoodMaker 6.1 can accept control via the Registry, you can still create ADM template files and control the application. The bad news is that if the Registry punches it accepts are not inside the new Policies keys listed earlier, you will not have proper Policies. Rather, they become old-style tattooing preferences.

To reiterate, the target applications must be programmed to look for values in the Policies keys. Some applications, such as Word 2000, check the Policies keys (specifically `HKEY_CURRENT_USER\Software\Policies\Microsoft\Office\9.0\Word\`). Other applications, such as WordPad, do not "understand" the Policies keys. (WordPad looks in `HKEY_CURRENT_USER\Software\Microsoft\Windows\CurrentVersion\Applets\Wordpad`.) Hence, Word-Pad wouldn't be a candidate for which to create official policies; you could still create your own preferences for WordPad that modify and tattoo the Registry. Therefore, you will have to do the legwork to figure out if your applications are compatible with the new Profiles keys.

Because preferences and policies act so differently, you will need to quickly identify them within the Group Policy Object Editor interface. You will want to note whether you're pushing an actual new-style policy to them or a persistent old-style policy. You'll see both cases in this chapter.

New-style policies are designated by blue dots because they modify the Policies Registry keys. Policies that represent Registry punches in places other than the preferred Microsoft policies are designated by red dots. Again, you'll see this distinction a bit later as you work through the examples.

Since this is an important distinction in the rest of this chapter, let's recap:

- New-Style policies are temporary Registry changes that are downloaded at logon and startup. They don't tattoo the Registry (though they are cached should the user log on while offline). These are set to modify the Registry in specific Microsoft-blessed Policies keys. Applications need to be coded to recognize the presence of the keys in order to take advantage of the magic of policies. In the Group Policy interface, these have a blue dot.

- Old-style preferences are persistent Registry changes sent from on high using the Group Policy Object Editor. These typically tattoo the Registry until they're specifically removed. They work like old-style NT System Policy. These are set to modify the Registry anywhere.

Hang tight, dear reader. The differences between preferences and policies will be underscored when you create your own settings to manipulate your clients later in this chapter.

Typical ADM Templates

Before we begin our proper ADM template journey, let's do a brief orientation. ADM templates come in three flavors, and each is used for a different purpose:

Default ADM Templates   These are provided free, right out of the box to help you control your stuff. These templates give you access to the myriad of policy settings inside the Administrative Templates branch when you first open the Group Policy Object Editor.

Vendor-Supplied ADM Templates   Another type of ADM template is provided by a vendor. A good example of vendor-supplied ADM templates are those that come with the Microsoft Office suites. There is a set of ADM templates for almost every one of today's versions of the suite, including Office 2000, Office XP, and Office 2003 as we'll explore later. Vendor-supplied ADM templates let you control aspects of an application. Again, recall that the application needs to be smart enough to be controlled via the Registry and, optimally, controlled via the "proper" `Policies` keys.

Custom Templates   Sometimes you want to do something "outside the box." That is, you want to scratch an itchy problem out there with your own policy settings. Creating these templates is not that difficult if you know the syntax rules. Custom templates are extremely important when you want to take the administration of your network to the next level, and they can truly add to the administrative power of almost any Microsoft network.

As you can see, ADM templates come in many styles and have many options. But keep in mind that all ADM templates, default and custom, do essentially the same thing: they simply spell out how to modify a portion of the Registry on the target computer system.

Default ADM Templates

Many settings are available in both the Computer and the User Administrative Template sections of the Group Policy Object Editor. How these settings are displayed depends on what is inside the default ADM templates. Therefore, when you create any new GPO, you start with baseline policy settings.

The default templates are stored in the %systemroot%\inf folder, which is usually `C:\windows\inf`, and you'll find the following:

- Three ADM templates that are installed by default on Windows 2000 machines:
  - `Conf.adm`
  - `Inetres.adm`
  - `System.adm`
- One additional template, `Wmplayer.adm`, in Windows XP
- One more additional template, `Wuau.adm`, on Windows 2003 and Windows 2000 + SP4 machines

These five ADM templates create both the computer and user portion of a default Group Policy. Table 5.1 provides information about what each default template is and what lives inside it.

TABLE 5.1   Default ADM Templates

ADM Template	Features	Where To Find In Interface
Conf.adm	NetMeeting settings.	Computer Configuration/User Configuration ➢ Administrative Templates ➢ Windows Components ➢ NetMeeting

TABLE 5.1   Default ADM Templates *(continued)*

ADM Template	Features	Where To Find In Interface
Inetres.adm	Internet Explorer settings, including connections, toolbars, and toolbar settings. It is equivalent to the options that are available when using the Internet Options menu inside Internet Explorer.	Computer Configuration/User Configuration ➢ Administrative Templates ➢ Windows Components ➢ Internet Explorer
System.adm	Operating system changes and settings. Most of the Computer and User Administrative Template settings are in this ADM template.	Everything else under Computer Configuration /User Configuration ➢ Administrative Templates
Wmplayer.adm	Windows Media Player 9 settings.	User Configuration ➢ Administrative Templates ➢ Windows Components ➢ Windows Media Player
Wuau.adm	Controls client's access to Software Update Services servers.	Computer Configuration ➢ Administrative Templates ➢ Windows Components ➢ Windows Update

The default templates harness a lot of power, but sometimes you just want more control. Additional ADM templates can quickly give an administrator power over myriad settings on a Windows client system, as you'll see in the next section.

Vendor-Supplied ADM Templates

The templates Microsoft provides with Windows are just the beginning of possibilities when it comes to Administrative Templates. The idea behind ADM templates is that you or third-party software vendors can create them to restrict or enhance features of either the operating system or applications.

Microsoft Office ADM Templates

If you are also interested in deploying Office 2000, Office XP, or Office 2003, you'll be happy to know that they each comes with a slew of customized ADM templates for you to import and use to your advantage.

- For Office 2000, download the Office 2000 Resource Kit tools at: www.microsoft.com/office/ork/2000/appndx/toolbox.htm.

- For Office XP, download the Office XP Resource Kit tools at www.microsoft.com/office/ork/xp/appndx/appa18.htm.

- Office 2003 templates are located in the Office 2003 Resource Kit. Check www.microsoft.com/office.

For information on how to automatically deploy Office 2000, XP, or 2003 (with patches and personalized customizations) to your users, see Chapter 10.

The file you're looking for (with either Office 2000 or XP) is called `Orktools.exe` (for Office 2003, it's `Ork.exe`), and it's about 9MB. Once you install the corresponding Resource Kit on a Domain Controller, the following files are automatically placed in the \windows\inf folder for importation like the other ADM files.

Sometimes this transfer to \windows\inf does not happen automatically. Feel free to copy the files directly to the Domain Controller's \windows\inf folder.

If you're zipping through these exercises in a test lab, feel free to load the Office Resource Kit on your test Domain Controller. Otherwise, don't to this now, and be sure to read the advice later in the "Create a Windows XP Management Workstation" section.

Office 2000, Office XP, and Office 2003 Templates

Here is a list of the ADM templates available for Office 2000, Office XP, and Office 2003.

Office 2000 Templates	Office XP Templates	Office 2003 Templates	Description
Access9.adm	Access10.adm	Access11.adm	Access settings
Clipgal5.adm	Gal10.adm	GAal11.adm	Restrict access to media clips
Excel9.adm	Excel10.adm	Excel11.adm	Excel settings
Frontpg4.adm	Fp10.adm	Fp11.adm	FrontPage settings
Instlr1.adm	Instalr11.adm	Instalr11.adm	Windows Installer settings
Office9.adm	Office10.adm	Office11.adm	Common Office settings
Outlk9.adm	Outlk10.adm	Outlk11.adm	Outlook 2000 settings
Ppoint9.adm	Ppt10.adm	Ppt11.adm	PowerPoint settings
Pub9.adm	Pub10.adm	Pub11.adm	Publisher settings
Word9.adm	Word10.adm	Word11.adm	Word settings

Office 2000 Templates	Office XP Templates	Office 2003 Templates	Description
N/A	N/A	Aer.adm	Corporate Windows Error Reporting (see the "Microsoft Corporate Error Reporting" section later in this chapter)
N/A	N/A	Rm11.adm	Microsoft Relationship Manager File location
N/A	N/A	Scrib11.adm	Microsoft OneNote 2003 settings

Implementing a Customized Office Policy

Once the Office templates are on the server, you can simply load them alongside the currently loaded templates. You can load all, some, or none—it's up to you.

In this example, we'll make believe we need to set up a custom Word 2000 policy for a collection of users. Normally, as in this example, Office template settings are meant for users, not computers. However, Office does include computer-side settings that you can use to override user-side settings if you want.

 If you don't want to use the Office 2000 ADM templates in this example, you can substitute Office XP or Office 2003 templates. Just make sure you also have the corresponding Office suite installed on the target machine!

Here, you'll see how to use an additional template. We'll load the WORD9.ADM template alongside our current default templates. Then, we'll change the default behavior of our Human Resources users for Word 2000 as follows:

- The grammar checker is turned off while we type in Word.
- The spell checker is turned off while we type in Word.
- Word will ignore words in uppercase during spell check.
- Word will ignore words with numbers during spell check.

To change Word's default behavior for the **Human Resources Users** OU, follow these steps:

1. Log on to the server as the Domain Administrator.
2. Download the Office 2000 Resource Kit tools and make sure the ADM templates are properly installed in the \windows\inf folder.
3. Fire up the GPMC.
4. Right-click **Human Resources Users** OU and select "Create and link a GPO here..."
5. Create a new GPO called "Word 2000 Settings."

6.   Edit the "Word 2000 Settings" GPO.

7.   Choose either User Configuration ➢ Administrative Templates or Computer Configuration ➢ Administrative Templates, right-click over either instance of Administrative Templates, and choose Add/Remove Templates (see Figure 5.1) to open the Add/Remove Templates dialog box.

 When adding an administrative template, the interface suggests that you can choose to add it from either the Computer Configuration or the User Configuration node. In actuality, you can add the ADM template from either section, and the appropriate policy settings appear under whichever node the ADM template was designed for.

8.   Click the Add button to open up the file requester, and select to load the Word9.adm template from the \windows\inf folder. Click Close to close the Add/Remove Templates dialog box to return to the Group Policy Object Editor. Policy Object Editor

FIGURE 5.1   Choose Add/Remove Templates from the shortcut menu.

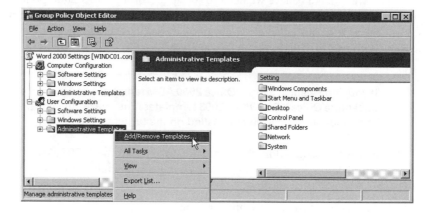

FIGURE 5.2   The Word9 ADM template is now loaded.

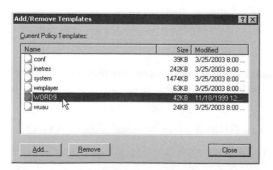

9. To turn off the "Check Grammar As You Type" feature, drill down to User Configuration ➢ Administrative Templates ➢ Microsoft Word 2000 ➢ Tools ➢Options ➢ Spelling & Grammar ➢ Check Grammar As You Type. Then, enable the setting, but do *not* select the check box. This forces the policy on the user, but clearing the check box forces it off.

10. Repeat step 9 for "Check Spelling As You Type," "Ignore Words in Upper case," and "Ignore Words with Numbers."

You can try this exercise with the other Office 2000–supplied templates listed earlier. These will affect Excel, PowerPoint, Access, and the like.

To test your new policy on the **Human Resources Users** OU, simply log on to any Windows 2000 or Windows XP machine loaded with Word 2000 as a user who would be affected by the new policy. For instance, log on to XPPro1 as Frank Rizzo, our old HR pal from Chapter 1 (assuming you have Word 2000 loaded).

Then in Word, choose Tools ➢ Options to open the Options dialog box, as shown in Figure 5.3, and make sure the settings reflect the policy settings you dictated.

FIGURE 5.3 Word obeys your policy commands when you load the corresponding ADM template.

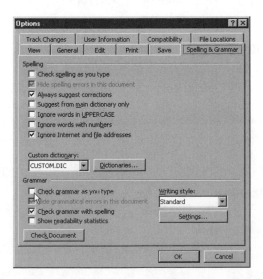

Other Microsoft ADM Templates

Microsoft has two additional applications outside the Office family of products that leverage the Group Policy infrastructure by using ADM templates.

Microsoft Software Update Services

The job of Microsoft's Software Update Services (SUS) job is to ensure that patches are deployed to your Windows 2000, Windows XP, and Windows 2003 client systems. Once a server is set up to deploy the patches, the client systems learns about the server by way of a custom ADM template.

The template is built in to Windows 2003 and Windows 2000 + SP4 as Wuau.adm. However, the template is not built in to Windows 2000 + SP3, and the Wuau.adm template might be upgraded along with the next SUS service pack.

You can learn more about SUS, how to deploy it, and how to use the rather complex ADM templates from two articles I wrote for *MCP Magazine*, which you can find at:

- http://mcpmag.com/Features/article.asp?EditorialsID=336

- http://mcpmag.com/Features/article.asp?EditorialsID=342

These articles form a two-part series about installation and troubleshooting. The latter's main focus is on understanding the ADM template.

Microsoft Corporate Error Reporting

Microsoft has a service that lets corporate IT administrators "trap" error messages to a central server, instead of being sent directly to Microsoft. It's called Corporate Error Reporting (CER). CER can help track systems that frequently crash and can provide an easier way to connect with Microsoft if a system does fail often. It can trap information for a lot of Microsoft's most popular applications including Office XP, Windows XP, Windows 2003, Project 2002, and Sharepoint Portal Server.

Microsoft CER uses the ADM file Cer2.adm. You can get more information on CER at www.microsoft.com/resources/satech/cer/. You'll find the ADM file in the "toolbox" section of the webpage.

Other Vendor ADM Templates

To be honest, finding non-Microsoft applications that have ADM templates that leverage the Group Policy infrastructure can be difficult. The vendors that have stepped up to the 21st century are still few and far between. In my humble opinion, it's a crying shame that everyday applications such as Norton's AntiVirus or Lotus Notes are still controlled from custom über-consoles and custom client-side .exe files instead of via the built-in Group Policy mechanism that's already in place. To that end, here are some third-party vendors that make products that "do it the right way" and that have ADM templates that can be controlled via Group Policy:

Troglodite's Sendto SendTo is a handy little program that lets you move files to your hard drive or use FTP to send files anywhere. You can download the main application at www.trogsoft.com/

products/sendto/, and you can find the ADM file at www.trogsoft.com/downloads/download.php?id=9.

WinAbility's AB Commander   This is a desktop file-copy utility a la the oldie but goodie Amiga file copy DirOpus. The included ADM template lets you manage nearly every menu item if you purchase multiple copies and have multiple installations. Track it down at: www.winability.com/abcommander/.

Raxco's PerfectDisk 6   Raxco is a noted name in the business of disk defragmentation. Its PerfectDisk 6 now supports ADM templates to control much of the application's possibilities. Learn more about PerfectDisk at www.raxco.com.

Okay, these products aren't enterprise-level products like WordPerfect, Lotus Notes, or Norton AntiVirus, but I think with time we'll see ADM files happen. But only if you, the reader, help make it happen. If you're in charge of contracts and negotiations with your larger software vendors, such as Norton or IBM (or even your smaller vendors!), ask them why they haven't made it as easy as possible for you to manage their stuff. Ask for ADM template files from them and see them squirm.

ADM Templates You Shouldn't Use with Windows 2000 or 2003

Both the Office 2000 Resource kit and Windows 2003 Server itself come with additional ADM templates that are not truly meant for the Windows 2000 Group Policy Object Editor. Make a note of them so that you don't use them by mistake.

Office 2000 NT/95 Templates

Additional settings to configure Internet Explorer 5 are included in the Office 2000 Resource Kit, but they are not automatically copied to the \windows\inf folder. These are found, after the Office 2000 Resource Kit is installed, in the \Program Files\IEAK\policies\EN folder. The ADM policies in the ADM templates (located in the table below) are *not* meant for the Windows 2000 Group Policy Object Editor. Rather, these are for the old-style Windows NT/95 Poledit.exe program, which I'll cover in Chapter 9.

Internet Explorer 5 Templates	Description
Aaxa.adm	Data binding settings.
Chat.adm	Microsoft Chat settings.
Conf.adm	NetMeeting settings.
Inetcorp.adm	Dial-up, language, and temporary Internet files settings.
Internet Explorer 5 Templates	**Description**

Inetres.adm	Internet properties, including connections, toolbars, and toolbar settings. Equivalent to the Tools ➤ Internet Options command.
Inetset.adm	Additional Internet properties: AutoComplete, display, and some advanced settings.
Oe.adm	Outlook Express Identity Manager settings. Use this to prevent users from changing or configuring identities.
Sp1shell.adm	Active Desktop settings.
Subs.adm	Offline Pages settings.

Some of these templates *can* be loaded into Windows 2000, but you probably wouldn't want to do so; some settings included in these templates include actual policies (nontattooing), and some include only preferences (only tattoo). To review the difference between policies and preferences, see the opening section of this chapter. You can just use the included Internet Explorer template settings found in Windows 2000's inetres.adm, instead of loading these templates that include both policies and preferences.

Remember, in order to see preferences, you need to perform a step I'll detail in the "Creating Your Own Custom ADM Changes" section, below.

Windows NT Templates

Additionally included with a Windows 2000 computer are even more ADM templates. These are not for use within the Windows 2000 Group Policy Object Editor either; rather, they are for use with the old-style NT Poledit.exe program. This feature set includes the following:

Windows NT Template	Function
Common.adm	User interface options common to Windows NT 4 and Windows 9*x*. For use with System Policy Object Editor (Poledit.exe).
Inetcorp.adm	Dial-up, language, and temporary Internet files settings. For use with System Policy Object Editor (Poledit.exe).
Inetset.adm	Additional Internet properties: AutoComplete, display, and some advanced settings. For use with System Policy Object Editor (Poledit.exe).
Windows.adm	User interface options specific to Windows 95 and Windows 98. For use with System Policy Object Editor (Poledit.exe).
Winnt.adm	User interface options specific to Windows NT 4. For use with System Policy Object Editor (Poledit.exe).

These templates are really not 100% compatible with the Group Policy Administrative Template interface if imported directly. Some will indicate that they are unsupported, as shown here.

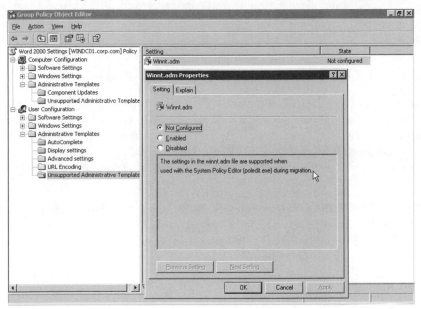

These are to be used with the old System Policy Object Editor (`Poledit.exe`). For instance, if you do end up loading, say, the `Winnt.adm` into the Windows 2003 Group Policy Object Editor, you are informed that it won't work, and the settings will not be displayed.

Creating Your Own Custom ADM Changes

Now that you have seen all the premade ADM templates you have to choose from, it is time to dive in and make some custom changes. You might have many items on your "custom hot-rod" hit list. Maybe you want to change the background color of a target computer, or maybe you want customize Windows Explorer. To make these custom changes, you'll need to create your own custom ADM entry. You can do so in three ways:

- Edit an existing ADM template and add your own custom changes. This can be complicated because you need to add your custom entry in just the right place in the existing ADM template. In other words, if you don't want to dig through someone else's code, try one of these other options.

- Create a new single ADM template to contain all your custom Registry changes.

- Create one ADM template for each unique change.

The best approach is really the second or third. First, you really don't want to pore over the ADM code and inject your own in just the precise location. Next, and more important, the ADM template files can, and often are, updated by service pack releases. If this happens, your custom changes would likely be wiped out.

The ADM templates that come with Windows are chock full of good examples. You can cut the code from the built-in ADM files and copy it to new ADM files.

Creating Your Own Custom ADM Template

For our custom hot-rod example, we'll modify the Windows startup sounds. This customization will work for Windows 2000, Windows XP, and Windows 2003 systems. By default, the startup sound is set to the Windows Logon Sound. By altering this setting through a Group Policy Object, you can make it anything that you like or turn it off.

For this example, we will walk through the steps to add this alteration to an existing ADM template:

1. Using Notepad or some other text editor, create a new file called set_sounds.adm. Don't forget that Notepad likes to append .txt to everything, so be sure you really set the name to set_sounds.adm, not set_sounds.adm.txt.

2. Locate the startup sound in the Registry:

    HKEY_CURRENT_USER\AppEvents\Schemes\Apps\.Default\SystemStart\.Current

Because this Registry key is not one of the two Policies keys we indicated earlier, it will become a tattooing preference.

The next thing to determine is whether this Registry change is for the User or Computer Configuration node. We can clearly see from the Registry path that this is a user setting, because it is located in the HKEY_CURRENT_USER handle key. The opening syntax for all Registry punches that affects HKEY_CURRENT_USER is Class User.

1. You must now put the custom ADM change into the ADM template you just created. The syntax for this is straightforward and detailed in "ADM Template Syntax" on this book's website. For now, don't worry about the syntax; simply insert the following code into your ADM template as shown in Figure 5.4.

```
CLASS USER

CATEGORY Sounds
   POLICY "Sound to hear when starting windows"

      KEYNAME "Appevents\Schemes\Apps\.Default\SystemStart\.Current"
      PART "What sound do you want?" EDITTEXT REQUIRED
      VALUENAME " "
      END PART
   END POLICY
END CATEGORY
```

FIGURE 5.4   Here is your new set_sounds.adm ADM template with the Sound portion of the Registry being manipulated.

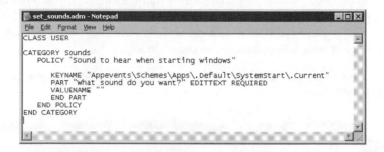

2. Save the file and copy it to c:\windows\inf.

Once you have the new custom ADM file in the \windows\inf folder, add the file as we did in Figure 5.2 earlier in this chapter. Now you can drill down into User Configuration ➢ Administrative Templates ➢ Sounds. However, you'll notice that no policy is shown.

To make it show, continue on to read the next section.

Viewing Old-Style Preferences

If you load additional ADM templates into the Group Policy Object Editor (as shown in Figures 5.1 and 5.2 earlier in this chapter), you won't see the entries for the old-style preferences. In order to see old-style preferences, you need to turn on this ability. In the Group Policy Object Editor, select the Administrative template for either Computer or User (as they work independently for this setting), and then choose View ➢ Filtering to open the Filtering dialog box, as shown in Figure 5.5.

FIGURE 5.5   To see old-style preferences, clear the "Only show policy settings that can be fully managed" check box.

By default the "Only show policy settings that can be fully managed" check box is checked. This is a safety mechanism that prevents old-style tattooing policies from being visible.

After you turn on the ability to see the preferences within the interface, you'll notice that icons for old-style preferences have a red dot on them. This is to indicate that this preference is added to the Group Policy. Once you can see the red-dot old-style preferences, you can see the change you made to your own ADM template, as shown in Figure 5.6.

FIGURE 5.6   The Group Policy Object Editor shows your new custom start sound preference setting for Windows.

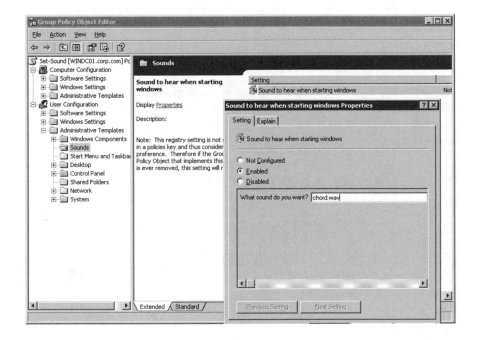

After the new ADM change appears in the Group Policy Object Editor, you need to configure it. For this example, let's change the setting to chord.wav, as shown in Figure 5.6. Enter the new sound file in the "What Sound Do You Want?" field. Remember, you can change this to any .wav file on the client system. Or you could disable it altogether by selecting the Disabled option.

The final step is to have the client log on and confirm that they get the sound that you configured. Figure 5.7 shows the resulting Windows XP Professional computer and the new configuration of chord.wav for the startup sound.

WARNING   Don't forget to move the user into the OU that is affected by a GPO that holds this ADM template.

FIGURE 5.7   Your Windows XP and Windows 2000 clients should embrace this preference.

Managing Windows ADM Templates

You're likely to have a mix of client and server systems. It's likely you'll have Windows 2000 and Windows 2003 Domain Controllers, and Windows 2000 and Windows 2003 Servers and both Windows XP and Windows 2000 Professional clients. As I noted in Chapter 1, Windows XP and Windows 2003 have about 200 more policy settings available to them than their Windows 2000 pals do.

You can see all the new Windows XP and Windows 2003 policy settings in "New Policy Settings for Windows 2003 and Windows XP" on this book's website, or on www.GPOanswers.com.

The good news (as I've previously stated) is that Windows 2000 clients ignore policies meant for Windows XP or Windows 2003. So there's really no reason not to use the latest version of the built-in template files to manage your entire universe: Windows 2000, Windows XP, and Windows 2003. The bad news is that if you're migrating to Windows XP clients but have already done a lot of work by creating GPOs with Windows 2000 Domain Controllers, some potential headaches are just around the corner.

Figure 5.8 shows a typical domain, w2kdomain.com, that has the following:

- Windows 2000 Domain Controllers (various SP levels)

- Windows 2003 Domain Controllers

- Windows XP clients (various SP levels)

- Windows 2000 clients (various SP levels)

The goal is to leverage the latest ADM templates which will allow you to have maximum control over all your client systems.

How Do You Currently Manage Your Group Policy Objects?

Before we proceed, you need to answer this question: How do you currently manage, create, and modify your GPOs? You have three main options:

- Use a Domain Controller (or use Terminal Services to connect directly to a Domain Controller) to create or modify your GPOs.

- Load the administrative tools (specifically Active Directory Users And Computers or the GPMC) on any machine (workstation or server) you want, and then do your management.

- Use a specific machine to manipulate all the GPOs over which you have control. That is, you have a *management workstation* you use when you need to manage your GPOs.

If you use either the first or second option, you're likely going to want to change your habits and start working with a strategy that gets you toward a management workstation. Here's why. Every time a new operating system is released, and again each time a new service pack is released, the base ADM templates will likely change. Over time, Microsoft updates the ADM templates for bug fixes or clarity in the help files. Sometimes Microsoft changes the name of a policy setting for clarity (though its underlying actions are usually the same), and occasionally a new policy setting pops up that a target system might embrace. For instance, about five new policy settings were available in Windows 2000 + SP4, and about two or three were available for Windows XP + SP1.

Microsoft makes updates; you have more power, right? Sure. And this sounds great, until you recognize the behavior of ADM template management.

FIGURE 5.8   A typical Windows 2000 network in transition

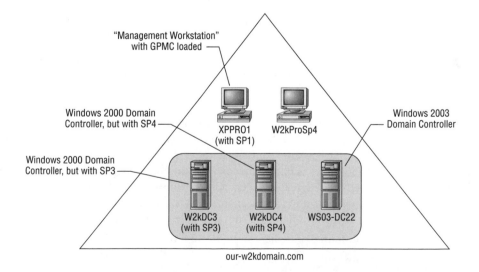

ADM Template Behavior

Recall from Chapter 4 that when you use any ADM templates, including the defaults or any custom or additional ADM templates, these templates are added to the file-based Group Policy Template (found in SYSVOL) of the GPO. Unfortunately, there's no master update location where you can just drop the latest ADM files from Microsoft (or other vendors) and universally update the ADM files of existing GPOs and any future GPO that will be created. Indeed, you'll need to understand where new GPOs get their ADM templates from when you create new GPOs or modify existing GPOs.

Creation Behavior with ADM Templates

If you want to create new GPOs and take advantage of the latest ADM templates, you really have to understand how the ADM update mechanism works. Here's the trick about creating GPOs with regard to ADM template files:

The ADM template files used to make a GPO are always copied from the place where you are running your editor. Not to put too fine a point on it, here's precisely what I mean:

- If you create new GPOs while running Active Directory Users And Computers on a computer running Windows 2000 + SP3, the ADM files are from SP3.

- If you create new GPOs while running Active Directory Users And Computers on a computer running Windows 2000 + SP4, the ADM files are from SP4.

- If you create new GPOs while running Active Directory Users And Computers or the GPMC on a computer running Windows 2003, the ADM files are from Windows 2003.

- If you create new GPOs while running Active Directory Users And Computers or the GPMC on a computer running Windows XP, the ADM files are from Windows XP.

In all cases, the editor you use (either Active Directory Users And Computers or GPMC) really uses the Group Policy Object Editor, which leverages the GPEDIT function when actually poking around or creating new GPOs. GPEDIT pulls the ADM template files from the computer it is running on. And it pulls these ADM template files from \{systemroot}\inf—usually `c:\winnt\inf` or `c:\windows\inf`.

So, if you want the latest ADM templates to be used when creating new GPOs, you need to plop them into the \{systemroot}\inf folder that contains your Group Policy Object Editor. That way, the next time GPEDIT is used to create a new GPO, it pulls the latest ADM files you copied into the \{systemroot}\inf folder.

 Read on to the "ADM Template Management Best Practice" section to learn my take on how to best update your GPOs.

Modification and Update Behavior with ADM Templates

Now, let's imagine that you created 200 GPOs in this way. That is, you created 200 GPOs by using the machine named W2kDC3 (which has the SP3 version of the ADM files.) Now, you learn of a policy in Windows 2000 SP4 that requires the corresponding Windows 2000 SP4 template.

ADM File Fine Print for Windows 2000 SP4 and Windows XP SP1

As I just stated, ADM templates are automatically updated if your editor has access to newer ADM files than those stored on the server. However, things aren't always as they seem. You might be thinking to yourself: "This is great! I'll run out and update all my current GPOs that have Windows 2000 ADM templates so now they have the Windows XP or Windows 2003 templates." That way, all GPOs—old and new—can be used to manage Windows 2000, Windows XP, and Windows 2003.

The plan is good; just make sure you don't fall into the following trap. That is, the time/date stamp on Windows 2000 SP4 ADM files is more recent than even the time/date stamp on Windows XP + SP1 ADM files. Here's what this means:

- You upgrade all your Windows 2000 Domain Controllers to SP4.

- You create a Windows XP machine with SP1 and load the GPMC on it.

- You attempt to modify an existing GPO that you created with Windows 2000 + SP4 to update it with the Windows XP ADM templates.

When you launch the GPMC on the Windows XP machine with SP1, you would expect that the ADM files from Windows XP's SP1 would overwrite the Windows 2000 ADM files. But the Windows 2000 + SP4 ADM files in the GPT won't be updated. Windows XP's + SP1's ADM templates are dated 9/3/2002. Windows 2000 + SP4's ADM templates are dated 6/19/2003. Who's newer? Windows 2000 + SP4, actually, so the ADM templates won't automatically update.

The solution is simple: change the date/time stamp on the Windows XP + SP1 ADM templates to today's date. It's easy: just open each of them (Conf.adm, Cntetres.adm, and System.adm) in Notepad, and then resave them. The next time your Windows XP machine with the GPMC opens the GPOs created with Windows 2000 + SP4's ADM templates, the timestamp on the ADM templates will be newer and will, in fact, be updated.

You want to update your GPOs with the SP3 version of the ADM files to the Windows 2000 SP4 version of the ADM files. Here's the trick about modifying GPOs with regard to ADM template files: the ADM template files used to modify and update a GPO are always copied from the place where your editor is running.

ADM templates are automatically updated when you re-edit a GPO on a machine where the editor (Active Directory Users And Computer or GPMC) has newer ADM templates than are already in the GPT. Recall that the GPT is the Group Policy Template—the files-based portion of Group Policy.

For instance, if you walk up to the machine named W2kDC4 (running SP4) and manipulate any old SP3-level GPO by editing it and merely look at the policy settings in the Administrative Templates section, the editor will say: "Ah-ha! I've got SP4 ADM templates available to me! This specific GPO's ADM templates are only SP3! I'll update the underlying ADM templates automatically—without even saying a word."

And it then proceeds. And it proceeds because the time/date stamp for SP4 ADM templates your editor has access to is more recent than the time/date stamp for SP3 ADM templates. It's doing you a favor behind your back. You must repeat for every old GPO you want to update. That is, you must open each old GPO and look at the policy settings in the Administrative Templates section. Then they'll be updated. Again, there's no universal master update location.

ADM Template Management Best Practice

It's highly likely that you'll have to maintain various levels of service packs throughout the rest of your Group Policy career. To that end, here are several suggestions for the best practice of managing ADM template files.

Create a Windows XP Management Workstation

As I suggested in the previous section, I believe you'll want to create a management workstation to control precisely where the ADM files are coming from. First, create a Windows XP machine with the latest service pack. Whenever Microsoft releases a service pack for Windows XP, immediately load it on that management workstation. If Microsoft releases a service pack for Windows 2003, pluck out the ADM files from the service pack and plunk them into the Windows XP's \windows\inf folder.

Additionally, if you use any ADM templates for Office or other applications, plunk those into the \windows\inf folder of your management workstation as well. This has a multilayered benefit:

- Whenever you create new GPOs from this management workstation, the latest ADM files are used.

- Whenever you modify old GPOs from this management workstation, the latest ADM files are used for updates.

- Whenever you run reports using the GPMC, the GPMC will have the latest version of the ADM template files, and reports will show properly.

- Whenever you want a nondefault template (such as Word9.adm from Office 2000 or the set_sounds.adm file you created), you'll always have it at your fingertips.

We've already looked at the first two bulleted items; now let's examine the last two.

Ensuring GPMC Reports Come Out Right

Figure 5.9 displays an ad hoc report from the Settings tab of a GPO where the management workstation does not have the latest copy of the ADM templates.

In Figure 5.9, you can see that the GPMC cannot determine the names of the actual policy settings; therefore, doing the best it can, it displays the Registry path that the policy setting is supposed to set. Clearly, this is not ideal. Again, the best thing to do is to drop the latest ADM templates into the \windows\inf folder on the management workstation—and you'll be golden.

FIGURE 5.9 Without the latest ADM templates, your GPMC reports could come up short.

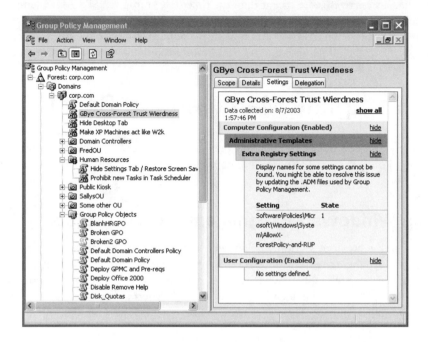

 You'll have to rerun some reports to see the updated settings, or you might have to close the GPMC and reopen it.

Using Add-In ADM Templates on Your Management Workstation

As you saw earlier, you can use Microsoft or third-party ADM templates to get a broader reach on your applications, such as Microsoft Office. The same advice applies here: place the latest ADM files for your applications on your management workstation. That way, whenever you create a new GPO or modify an existing GPO, you'll never have to worry about not having the ADM template you need. When you right-click Administrative Templates, you'll be able to select any template you placed on your management workstation's \{systemroot}\inf folder.

Throttling an Automatic ADM Template Upgrade

You can specify two policy settings that affect how your Group Policy Object Editor deals with ADM templates:

- **Always use local ADM files for the Group Policy Object Editor** (located in Computer Configuration ➢ Administrative Templates ➢ System ➢ Group Policy).

- **Turn off automatic update of ADM files** (located in User Configuration ➢ Administrative Templates ➢ System ➢ Group Policy).

GPMC Reporting Options

The GPMC has some options for specifying where to look for ADM files when running reports. If you choose View ➤ Options ➤ Reporting, you open the Options dialog box at the Reporting tab (see Figure 5.10), in which you'll see the options for hunting down the ADM templates used in reports.

You can point the reporting mechanism toward a centralized path if you want to maintain a repository for the latest ADM templates; but this is only for reporting purposes.

Be careful regarding the Default option, as shown in the above figure. It implies that if the latest version is in the SYSVOL (and not on the local {systemroot}\inf folder), the report will function. This does not appear to be the case. The latest ADM templates must be loaded in the local {systemroot}\inf folder for reports to work. Otherwise, you get the message shown in Figure 5.9 earlier in this chapter.

The first policy setting describes what should happen when you're using the Group Policy Object Editor. Enabling this policy setting uses the {systemroot}\inf version of the ADM files while you view and edit the GPOs—regardless of what version is really inside the GPO. You might want to do this, as the policy setting suggests, if you have administrators modifying the same GPOs with different languages. You can see the policy settings in English, and the other administrator can see the policy settings in their language. That is, if you've set this policy to force their Group Policy Object Editor to look in their local {systemroot}\inf folder while editing.

Enabling the second policy setting prevents the local {systemroot}\inf versions of the ADM template from being copied into your GPO. In other words, whatever is on the server is used. If you disable the second policy setting, the default behavior is used; that is, the local {systemroot}\inf versions of the ADM template are always copied to the GPO. This might be useful if you're concerned about your SYSVOL getting too large and you want to micromanage which ADM templates are to be updated. Personally, I don't think you should use this setting.

You can learn more about the interaction between the two policy settings in the Microsoft Knowledge Base article 316977: "Group Policy Template Behavior in Windows Server 2003."

Cracking the ADM Files

Chapter 4 discusses many ways to troubleshoot if Group Policy doesn't seem to be applying. However, if you've verified that you're getting the policy setting via GPRESULT or the Group Policy Results Wizard and you're certain you should be getting a specific policy you set, perhaps the problem is elsewhere.

Occasionally, there are bugs in the help text definitions of some policy settings in the ADM templates. Sometimes the policy setting states that Enable does one thing and Disable does another—and, really, it doesn't work that way at all. Other times, the actual underlying definition of the policy setting is incorrect, and the Registry location it's set to modify doesn't really do anything. In all honesty, these problems are few and far between, but it is precisely what service pack updates to existing ADM files try to correct.

So, if you're 1000% convinced you're getting the GPO laid down on the client system, yet you're still not seeing the result of a specific policy setting, take it to the next step. That is, crack open the ADM template that has the policy setting you're trying to deliver, locate the policy definition, find the portion of the Registry that the policy will be setting, and manually enter that hack into your client system. Once you do, verify it against what the policy setting says it's supposed to do.

FIGURE 5.10 Open the ADM template to locate the policy and the corresponding Registry hack.

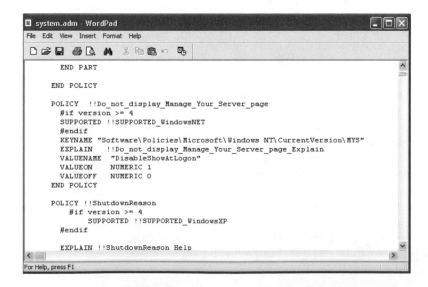

Is it actually doing what it says it's supposed to do? For instance, if you suspected that the **Manage Your Server Page** policy setting wasn't doing what it says it was going to do, simply crack open System.adm, and locate the **Do not display Manage Your Server Page** policy setting (as shown in Figure 5.10).

As you can see, the policy setting modifies `HKEY_Local_machine\Software\Policies\ Microsoft\Windows NT\CurrentVersion\MYS`. It adds a value of `DisableShowAtLogon` and sets it to 1 to force the page to go away. You can plunk this into the Registry yourself and see this actually happen; you don't need to set a GPO to try it. Once you verify the results, you're closer to knowing precisely what's going on.

Final Thoughts

It's easy to use Microsoft and third-party, vendor-supplied ADM templates to control your applications or to make your own ADM modifications. But remember—only applications coded to read Registry settings from the Policy keys will be true Policies. These will be applied and removed when different users log on or off. They will not tattoo. They will appear with a blue dot in the Group Policy Object Editor.

Most applications are not yet Policy key–aware, which means if you want to create your own modifications, you'll likely need to make them preferences. Preferences do not modify the Policy keys. They tattoo the Registry. They will appear with a red dot in the Group Policy Object Editor.

Be wary of download ADM templates you find online. They'll usually work as advertised, but the problem, again, is that they're likely chock full of preferences, not policies. One site that's full of such ADM templates is `http://worldofasp.com/ts/download.cfm`.

Creating an ADM template can sometimes be difficult. The hardest part can be figuring out which Registry setting you need to modify on the client system. You can use several tools to help you. One such tool is called Regmon from Sysinternals, at `www.sysinternals.com/ntw2k/ source/regmon.shtml`. Regmon can help point out what's changing on the client. Then, armed with that information, you can triumphantly create your own custom ADM template and try it.

You can find the syntax you use to create your own custom ADM templates in "ADM Template Syntax" on this book's website..

You'll find a good article to supplement your reading on creating a management workstation in the Microsoft Knowledge Base: see "Administering Windows Server-Based Computers Using Windows XP Professional–Based Clients" (304718).

6

Implementing Security with Group Policy

Security is hot. Hot, hot, hot. Microsoft has a big security push underway, with lots of proposed changes to their product lines to make them all more secure—right out of the box. Windows 2003 is the start of that trend, and it's inarguably more secure out of the box than its predecessors. With that in mind, we'll pay special attention to several areas of security that can be designed and maintained with the power that Group Policy offers.

First, we'll look at the two default GPOs: the "Default Domain Policy" GPO and the "Default Domain Controllers Policy" GPO and how they help tighten security. Then, we'll take a walk through the park and see all that can be set via security-related policies:

- Local vs. effective permissions: why do settings show up on our clients?

- Auditing: who is using our clients and servers?

- User and computer scripts: logon scripts were never like this.

- Internet Explorer maintenance settings: allow you to set IE settings centrally.

- Restricted Groups: force group membership and nested group membership.

- Software restriction policies: allow/disallow specific applications to run.

Last, but certainly not least, we'll harness and focus our Group Policy power.

Often, you'll want to find a way to tie down a specific machine so it will be nigh invulnerable to outside forces. You might want to do this in public computing environments, such as libraries or nursing stations, or if you have machines in open areas that you feel are specifically vulnerable to physical attack or theft. You'll learn all about that in the final section in this chapter, "Securing Workstations with Templates."

The Two Default Group Policy Objects

Whenever you create a new domain, three things automatically happen:

- The initial (and only) OU, named **Domain Controllers,** is created automatically by the DCPROMO process.

- A default GPO is created and linked to the domain level, called "Default Domain Policy."
- A default GPO is created for the **Domain Controllers** OU, called "Default Domain Controllers Policy."

This section helps answer, "Why are these GPOs different from all other GPOs?"

These two GPOs are special. First, you cannot easily delete them (though you can rename them). Next, it's a best practice to only modify these GPOs for the security settings that we'll describe in this section. Too often, people will modify the "Default Domain Controller Policy" GPO or "Default Domain Policy" GPO—only to mess it up beyond recognition. So, these special default GPOs system shouldn't be modified with the "normal stuff" you do, day to day. In general, stay clear of them, and modify them only when a setting prescribed for them is actually required.

Instead of modifying the "Default Domain Controller Policy" GPO or "Default Domain Policy" GPO for normal stuff, instead you should create a new GPO and link it at the level you want, then implement your policy settings inside that new GPO.

> The "Default Domain Policy" GPO and "Default Domain Controllers Policy" GPO can actually be deleted, but I strongly recommend that you don't. If you truly want to delete either of the default policies, you'll need to add back in the "Delete" Access Control entry to a group you belong to, Domain Administrators, for instance. Even then, I can't see why you would want to delete them. If you want to unlink them for some reason (again, I can't imagine why), do that, but leave the actual GPOs in place.

It's not that the GPOs themselves are really all that different, but rather that the location of these GPOs is special, as you'll see later in this chapter. The locations in question are the domain level and the **Domain Controllers** OU.

GPOs Linked at the Domain Level

If you take a look inside the domain level, you'll see one GPO that was created by default, the "Default Domain Policy". The purpose of this GPO is to set the default configurations for the "Account Policies" branch in the Group Policy Object Editor. These Account Policies encompass three important domain-wide security settings:

- Password policy
- Account Lockout policy
- Kerberos policy

Again, the default policy settings are set inside the "Default Domain Policy" GPO and linked to the domain level. However, you can change the defaults of the Account Policies in one of several ways:

- By modifying the "Default Domain Policy" GPO directly
- By creating your own GPO linked to the domain level and changing the precedence order within the domain level

You'll see how shortly.

Again, the special part about the domain level of Group Policy is that this is the only place these three policy settings can be set for the domain. And the default settings for the domain are prespecified in the "Default Domain Policy" GPO.

If you try to set Password policy, Account Lockout policy, or Kerberos policy anywhere else in the domain, (say, at any OU or on any site), the settings are ignored when users log on to the domain; they don't matter, and only those linked to the domain level take effect.

Microsoft has taken a lot of heat for the fact that Account Policies must agree for all the accounts in the domain. This means that if two administrators of two OUs can't agree on Account Policies (usually things like password length), they'll need to split into two domains—a major administrative overhead and nightmare.

Special Policy Settings for the Domain Level

In addition to Password policy, Account Lockout policy, and Kerberos policy, three additional policy settings take effect only when a GPO is linked to the domain level. They are located under Computer ➢ Windows Settings ➢ Security Settings ➢ Local Policies ➢ Security Options:

Automatically Log Off Users When Logon Time Expires   You can set up accounts so that users logged on to Active Directory must log off when they exceed the hours available to them.

Rename Administrator Account   You can use this policy setting to forcefully rename the Administrator account. This works only for the Domain Administrator account when set at the domain level. This is useful as a level of "extra protection" so that no matter what the Administrator account is renamed to in Active Directory Users And Computers, it will "snap back" to this name after Group Policy refreshes. The "display name" in Active Directory Users And Computers won't actually change, but the underlying "real" name of the account will be changed.

Rename Guest Account   You can rename the domain Guest account using this policy setting. This works only for the Guest account when set at the domain level.

Setting these special security settings at any other level has no effect on member computers in Active Directory.

Modifying the "Default Domain Policy" GPO Directly

You can dive into the "Default Domain Policy" GPO in two ways. Use the Group Policy Management Console (GPMC), and click the domain name. You'll see the "Default Domain Policy" GPO linked to the domain level. If you try to edit the GPO at this level, you'll see the standard set of policy settings you've come to know and love while inside the Group Policy Object Editor. (Though again, as I've stated, you won't want to add "normal stuff" to this GPO.)

However, since the "Default Domain Policy" GPO is "special," Microsoft provides an alternate way to get right into the Security settings of the "Default Domain Policy". Follow these steps:

1. Log on to the Domain Controller WINDC01 as a Domain Administrator.

2. Choose Start ➢ Programs ➢ Administrative Tools ➢ Domain Security Policy.

You will be immediately placed into the "Default Domain Policy" GPO focused on the Security settings, as seen in Figure 6.1. These two methods are identical and modify the exact same location; however, the second method is a special "limited view" and shows *only* the security settings within the GPO.

FIGURE 6.1 The "Default Domain Policy" GPO (linked to the domain level) sets the domain's default Account Policies, Kerberos policy, and Password policy. If you link GPOs containing these policy settings anywhere else, they are essentially ignored when Active Directory is being used.

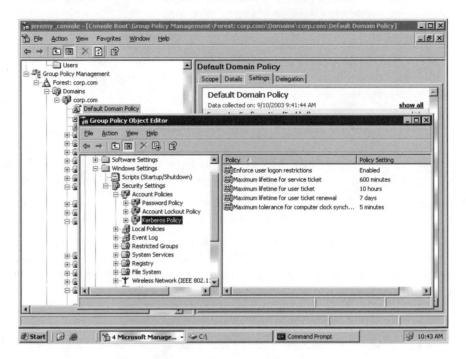

For instance, you can specify (among other settings) that the password length is 10 characters, the user is locked out after the third password attempt, and Kerberos ticket expiration time is 600 minutes. But these values are only valid for the entire domain.

WARNING Again, if you want to add more policy settings at the domain level (which would affect all users or computers in the domain)—great! But try to leave the "Default Domain Policy" GPO alone, except when you need to change the "special" policy settings as described in this section.

Creating Your Own Group Policy Object Linked to the Domain Level and Changing the Precedence

Recall that at any level (site, domain, or OU), all the policy settings within all the GPOs linked to a level are merged unless there is a conflict. Then, the GPO with the highest precedence "wins" at a level. I talked about this in Chapter 2. The same is true regarding the settings special to the domain level: Password policy, Account Lockout policy, and Kerberos policy.

The defaults for these three policies are set within the "Default Domain Policy" GPO, but you could certainly create and link more GPOs to the domain level that would override the defaults. Though that doesn't necessarily mean that you should. Take a look at the example in Figure 6.2.

FIGURE 6.2   If you have a GPO with a higher precedence than the "Default Domain Policy" GPO, it will "win" if there's a conflict.

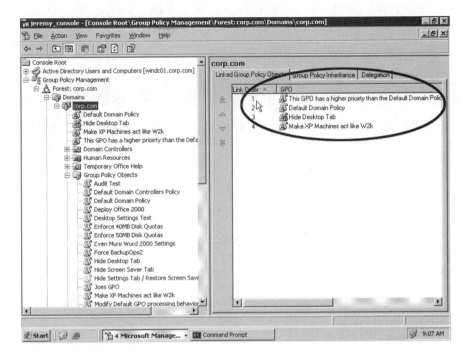

Here, a GPO is higher in priority than the "Default Domain Policy". If you do this, you better know precisely what you are doing! Again, this is because any policy setting within any GPO with a higher priority than the "Default Domain Policy" GPO will "win."

Which Approach Do You Take?

As you've seen, you can either modify the "Default Domain Policy" GPO or create your own GPO and ensure that the precedence is higher than the "Default Domain Policy" GPO. If you need to modify a special domain-wide account policy setting, which approach do you take? Here are the two schools of thought:

School of Thought #1   Modify only the Account Policies settings in the "Default Domain Policy" GPO. Then, ensure that it has the highest precedence at the domain level. This guarantees that if anyone does link other GPOs to the domain level, this one always wins.

School of Thought #2   Leave the defaults in the "Default Domain Policy" GPO. Never modify the "Default Domain Policy" GPO—ever. Create a new GPO for any special settings you want to override in the "Default Domain Policy" GPO. Then, link the GPO to the domain level, and ensure that it has higher precedence than the "Default Domain Policy" GPO (as seen in Figure 6.2).

Various Microsoft insiders have given me different (sometimes conflicting) advice about which to use. So what do I think?

If you want to modify any special domain-wide security settings, use School of Thought #1. This is the simplest and cleanest way. If you do it this way, you'll always treat the "Default Domain Policy" GPO with kid gloves and know it has a special use. And you can check in on it from time to time to make sure no one has lowered the precedence on it.

School of Thought #2 has its merits. Leave the "Default Domain Policy" GPO "clean as a whistle," and then create your own GPOs with higher precedence settings. However, I don't think this is a great idea, because you might forget that you set something important inside this new GPO.

Either way works, but my preference is for School of Thought #1.

Group Policy Objects Linked to the Domain Controllers OU

How is the **Domain Controllers** OU different? You can see there is also a default GPO linked, named the "Default Domain Controllers Policy" GPO. But, before we dive into it, let's take a step back. First, it's important to think of all the Domain Controllers as essentially equal. If one Domain Controller gets a policy setting (Security setting or otherwise), they should all really be getting the exact same policy settings. On logon, users choose a Domain Controller for validation at random; however, you want the experience they receive to be consistent, not random. Moreover, when you, as the Domain Administrator, log on to a Domain Controller at the console, you also want your experience to be consistent.

Oh, and did I mention that when servers are finished being promoted into Domain Controllers via DCPROMO, they automatically end up in the **Domain Controllers** OU? So, that's where the "Default Domain Controllers Policy" GPO comes in to play. Again, it's easy to find the "Default Domain Controllers Policy" GPO. It's linked to the **Domain Controllers** OU.

You can also get right into the Security settings of the "Default Domain Controllers Policy" GPO by following these steps:

1. Log on to the Domain Controller WINDC01 as a Domain Administrator.

2. Choose Start ➢ Programs ➢ Administrative Tools ➢ Domain Controller Security Policy.

You will be immediately placed into the "Default Domain Controllers Policy" GPO focused solely on the Security settings.

These two methods are essentially identical and modify the exact same location; however, the second method shows only the available *security* settings within the GPO. Since all Domain Controllers are, by default, nestled within the **Domain Controllers** OU, all Domain Controllers are affected by all the aspects inside the "Default Domain Controllers Policy" GPO. Of specific note are the Security settings, as shown in Figure 6.3.

For instance, you'll want the same Event Log settings for all Domain Controllers. You'll want to set it once, inside a GPO linked to the **Domain Controllers** OU, and have it affect all Domain Controllers. By default, the "Default Domain Controllers Policy" GPO has the following set to specific defaults, which should remain consistent among all Domain Controllers.

Right-click any node and choose "Export List..." from the shortcut menu to export to a text file for an easy way to document complex settings, such as User Rights Assignments.

FIGURE 6.3   The "Default Domain Controllers Policy" GPO affects every Domain Controller in the domain.

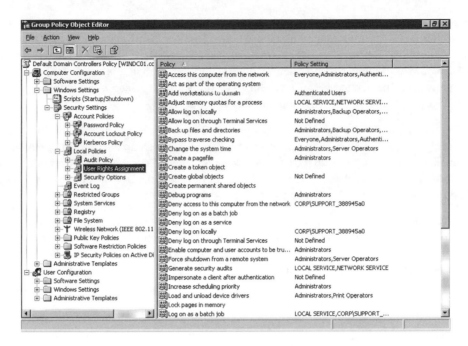

Audit Policies   Located in Computer Configuration ➤ Security Settings ➤ Audit Policy. It's here you can change the default auditing policies of Windows 2000 or Windows 2003. Windows 2000 is a little light for my taste, and Windows 2003 is a little strong. We talk about auditing later in this chapter in the "Auditing with Group Policy section.

User Rights Assignment   Located in Computer Configuration ➤ Security Settings ➤ User Rights Assignment. It's here you can configure which accounts you will "Allow log on locally" or "Log on as a service" among other specific rights.

Domain Controller Event Log Settings   Located in Computer Configuration ➤ Security Settings ➤ Event Log. Set them here, and all Domain Controllers will obey. Settings such as the maximum size of logs are contained here. Note, however, that decreasing the size of an Event Log will not take effect on the DCs; you can enforce a log size increase, but not a decrease.

Various Security Options   Located in Computer Configuration ➤ Security Settings ➤ Local Policies ➤ Security Options. It's here you'll find settings such as "Interactive logon: Do not display last user name," which will affect the behavior of clients, servers, and/or Domain Controllers. Windows 2000 domains have different names for these settings. In "Security Options Comparison" on this book's website. You can download a chart that shows how to convert between Windows 2000 domains and Windows 2003 domains.

Mea Culpa

In the last edition of this text, I made a mistake. It was a whopper. And I'm sorry if my mistake caused you any harm. I claimed that the "Default Domain Controllers Policy" GPO itself had one additional "superpower." That is, I claimed that the "Default Domain Controllers Policy" GPO would hunt down and affect any Domain Controller no matter which OU the Domain Controller was in. That isn't true. Not at all. But, upon reflection, I can see where I made my mistake, and I can explain, at least, *why* I thought this was the case.

If you modify the "Default Domain Controllers" GPO after a Domain Controller has been moved to another OU and then forcefully perform a background refresh on the Domain Controller, that Domain Controller will pick up the changes. However, once the Domain Controller realizes that it has been moved to another OU (between 30 and 120 minutes), the Domain Controller will stop honoring the policies in the **Domain Controllers** OU.

I performed a bad test and didn't wait 120 minutes (or reboot the machine). I got bad data and reported it. So, again, I apologize. In short: don't move your Domain Controllers out of the **Domain Controllers** OU. You'll get erratic behavior, your Domain Controllers won't all be alike in the settings they receive, and they'll receive error messages in the Event Log. All in all—not good.

The same rules apply to the **Domain Controllers** OU as they do for the domain level. That is, you can put a GPO in at a higher precedence than the "Default Domain Controllers Policy" GPO. However, my recommendation is to use the "Default Domain Controllers Policy" GPO for the "special" things that you set at this level, and ensure that it's got the highest precedence when being processed within the OU.

Oops, the "Default Domain Policy" GPO and/or "Default Domain Controllers Policy" GPO Got Screwed Up!

If you modify the "Default Domain Policy" GPO or "Default Domain Controllers Policy" GPO such that you want to return it back to the defaults, you might just have a shot. The procedure is different for Windows 2000 domains or those with Windows 2003 Domain Controllers. First, you'll need to determine which default GPO got screwed up; then you need to take the appropriate steps. These procedures are among the most popular request for Microsoft Product Support Services.

Repairing the Defaults for Windows 2000 Domains

If the "Default Domain Policy" GPO got screwed up, you should check out Microsoft's Knowledge Base article "How to Reset User Rights in the Default Domain Group Policy" (KB 226243). The steps are simply too in-depth to repeat here. Note, however, that this procedure doesn't truly return all the defaults—rather it just resets the Password policies, Account policies, and Kerberos policies. If you do change other sundry entries in the GPO, they will not be reverted.

If you modify the "Default Domain Controllers Policy" GPO beyond repair, see Microsoft's Knowledge article "How to Reset User Rights in the "Default Domain Controllers Group Policy Object" (KB 267553). Following the steps recommended in this article should restore the audit settings, Event Log settings, and User Rights Assignment. Note, however, that the Security Options do not appear to be restored.

You can also get back the default GPOs by performing a backup, migration, and restore of known good defaults from a fresh, test Windows 2000 domain. We'll explore how to do a backup and migration in a manner such as this in the Appendix.

Repairing the Defaults for Windows 2003 Domains

As long as you have even one Windows 2003 Domain Controller, you have it made in the shade. Well, not too made, as you might already be in the doghouse if the default GPOs are screwed up. However, Windows 2003 domains with their Windows 2003 Domain Controllers come with a new command-line tool, DCGPOFIX, to make it easy to restore back to the defaults. You can tell DCGPOFIX to restore the "Default Domain Policy" GPO (with the /Target:Domain switch) or the "Default Domain Controllers Policy" GPO (with the /Target:Domain Controller switch.) Or both with the /Target:BOTH switch, as in Figure 6.4.

FIGURE 6.4   Use DCGPOFIX with Windows 2003 Domain Controllers to restore the defaults if necessary.

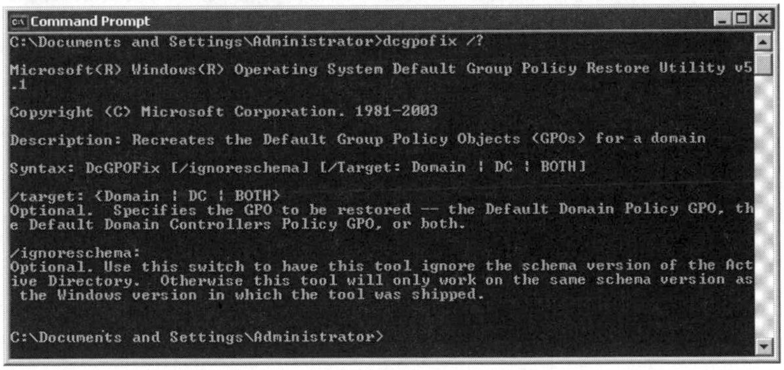

Optionally, you can simply reset the User Rights Assignment for Windows 2003 instead of plowing back the entire "Default Domain Controllers" GPO. To do so, see the Knowledge Base article "HOW TO: Reset User Rights in the Default Domain Group Policy in Windows Server 2003" (KB 324800).

Understanding Local and Effective Security Permissions

The whole point of Group Policy is that when you make a wish from upon high, your client machines will embrace your wish. I've already discussed that Group Policy can be set, if you like, on the local machine. However, GPOs from Active Directory that contain policy settings that conflict with those on the local machine will "win" and override those set at the local machine.

If a local security policy is set on a machine and then a GPO in the domain "wins" you'll want to know at a glance which changes are coming from upon high within Active Directory Group Policy. This is the difference between "local" policies and "effective" policies.

With Windows 2000 clients it was sometimes difficult to tell that your security wishes were being embraced. Windows 2000 local policy has a Local Setting and Effective Setting column to assist; but it wasn't always accurate. See Q257922 titled "Local Security Policy May Not Accurately Reflect Actual System Settings" for more details.

The user interface in Windows XP and Windows 2003 member servers has changed a bit since Windows 2000. Specifically, it now clearly distinguishes between security policies that can be changed locally versus security policies that are coming from upon high.

Figure 6.5 shows the local machine policy via GPEDIT.MSC. Many Security Option settings are not being enforced from an Active Directory GPO (say, at the domain level or in an OU that contains the client machine). However, in Figure 6.5, I've set up one one policy setting, the **Devices: Restrict CD-ROM access to locally logged in user,** is set to **Enabled** within a GPO linked to the OU that contains the computer. Since Active Directory GPOs trump local computer policy, this security policy setting therefore cannot be adjusted locally.

FIGURE 6.5 Active Directory GPOs restrict the modification of local computer policy. The icon within the local computer policy has changed from "1/0" icons to a scroll and computer icon.

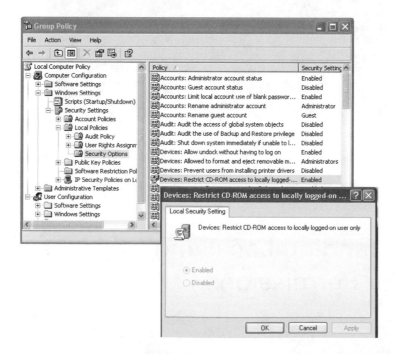

Attempting to try to set this security policy setting locally (once it's set from a GPO linked to the OU) is not permitted. Indeed, the icon changes within GPEDIT.MSC to show you that the security policy is set within Active Directory:

- The security policies that are being dictated from a GPO in Active Directory have a little scroll icon flanked with two computers.

- The security policies that can still be set locally have "1/0" icons.

This same "effective setting" icon theme is valid throughout other security settings categories: Account Policy (including Password policy), Audit Policy, User Rights Assignment, and Security options.

The Strange Life of Password Policy

If you create a new GPO, link it to any OU, and then edit your new GPO, it certainly appears as if you *could* set the Password policy and Account Lockout policy.

For example, I have a **Sales** OU in which I recently placed XPPRO2. As you can see in Figure 6.6, I created and linked a GPO, called "Sales Password policy," to the **Sales** OU. I am setting the Password policy such that the minimum password length is 10 characters.

FIGURE 6.6   It might seem counterproductive to set the Password policy at any level but the domain.

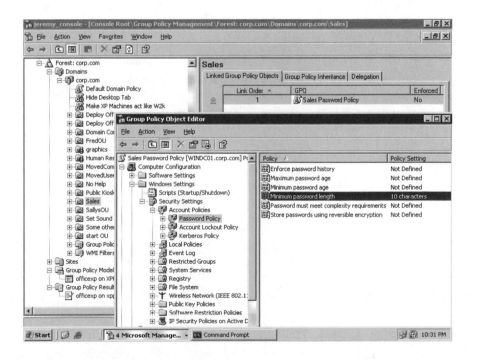

At first glance this would seem to be counterproductive, because, as already stated, these policy settings only take hold of the accounts in the domain via the "Default Domain Policy" GPO. But administrators might actually want to perform this seemingly contradictory action. That is, when the user logs on locally to the Windows 2000 or Windows XP workstation, the account policy settings contained in the GPO linked to the OU will have been magically planted on their machine to take effect for *local* accounts. In Figure 6.7, I have logged in as the local administrator account on the workstation.

FIGURE 6.7   Setting a Password policy in the domain (other than at the domain level) will affect passwords used for local accounts upon member machines.

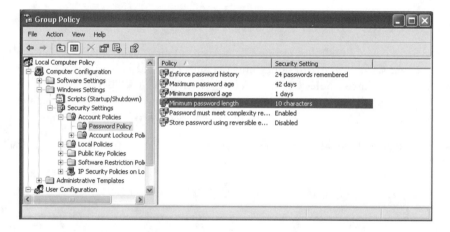

Again, this won't affect users' accounts when users are logging on to the domain; rather, it affects only the local accounts on the targeted computers. This could be helpful if you grant local administrator rights to users upon their workstations or laptops and want to set a baseline.

If you are still using Windows 2000 machines, the contents in Figure 6.7 would should show both "Local" and "Effective" settings for Windows 2000 Professional machines. However, because of the behavior described here, the effective settings might not be accurate. Again, be sure to check out the Knowledge Base article "Local Security Policy May Not Accurately Reflect Actual System Settings" (KB 257922) for more information.

Auditing with Group Policy

Auditing is a powerful tool. It can help you determine when people are doing things they shouldn't, as well as help you determine when people are doing things they should. Either way, you'll use Group Policy to turn on your auditable events. Certain aspects of auditing you'll turn on at the **Domain Controller** OU level, inside the "Default Domain Controllers Policy" GPO. Other aspects of auditing you'll typically turn on at other OU levels (via a GPO linked to the OU containing the systems you want to audit).

In Figure 6.8, you can see the default auditing settings contained within the "Default Domain Controllers Policy" GPO.

FIGURE 6.8 Windows 2003 enables lots of auditable events by default.

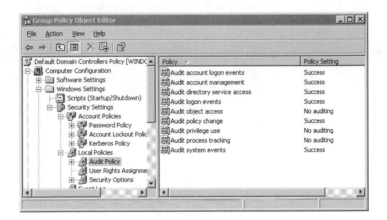

The list of possibilities for auditing are numerous and confusing. Table 6.1 shows what can be audited, along with where you should perform the audit.

No matter how much you audit, it does you no good unless you're actually reviewing the logs! There is no way out of the box to centralize the collection of logs from your Domain Controllers, servers, or workstations. Consider a third-party tool, such as Microsoft MOM or Event Log Sentry from www.engagent.com. By the time you read this, Microsoft should have its own free, basic audit-log centralization tool called MACS.

TABLE 6.1 Auditable Events

Auditing Right	What It Does	Where You Should Set It	Is It On by Default in Windows 2003 Active Directory?	Notes
Audit account logon events	Enters events when someone attempts to log on to Active Directory.	In the "Default Domain Controllers Policy" GPO to monitor when anyone tries to log on to Active Directory.	Yes.	By default, only successes generate events. Settings can be changed to record logon failures as well.

TABLE 6.1 Auditable Events *(continued)*

Auditing Right	What It Does	Where You Should Set It	Is It On by Default in Windows 2003 Active Directory?	Notes
Audit account management	Enters events when someone attempts to create, delete, rename, enable, or disable users, computers, groups, and so on.	In the "Default Domain Controllers Policy" GPO to generate events for when users, computers, and so on are created in Active Directory. Set at the OU level to generate events on file servers for when users and groups are created on member machines.	Yes. Enabled on Domain Controllers, which log Active Directory events only. Not enabled on member servers.	By default, only successful object manipulations generate events. Settings can be changed to record failures as well.
Audit directory service access	Enters events when Active Directory objects are specified to be audited.	In the "Default Domain Controllers Policy" GPO.	Yes. In "Default Domain Controllers Policy" GPO, which will log Active Directory logons and GPO creation, deletion, and modification. See Auditing Group Policy Object changes" section. Not enabled on member servers.	Works in conjunction with the actual attribute in Active Directory that has auditing for users or computers enabled. Can be used to audit other aspects of Active Directory. See "Auditing Group Policy Changes" below.
Audit logon events	Enters events for interactive logon (Local logon) and network logon (Kerberos).	Set at OU level to generate events on servers you want to track access for. Tracks access to files, registry and other generic objects in the system.	Yes — in "Default Domain Controller Policy" GPO which affects only Active Directory logons.	Set this setting to determine if UserA touches a shared folder on ServerA. This will constitute an auditable event for "Audit logon Events."

TABLE 6.1 Auditable Events *(continued)*

Auditing Right	What It Does	Where You Should Set It	Is It On by Default in Windows 2003 Active Directory?	Notes
Audit object access	Enters events when file objects are specified to be audited.	If you store files on your Domain Controllers, you can set this at the "Default Domain Controllers Policy" GPO. Else, set at the OU level to monitor specific files within member machines.	No.	Works in conjunction with actual file on file server having auditing enabled. See the "Auditing File Access" section.
Audit policy change	Enters events when changes are made to user rights, auditing policies, or trust relationships.	In the "Default Domain Controllers" GPO to monitor when changes are made within Active Directory. Set at OU level to monitor when changes are made on member machines.	Yes. In "Default Domain Controllers Policy" GPO, which affects only Active Directory events.	
Audit privilege use	Enters events when any user right is used, such as backup and restore.	In the "Default Domain Controllers Policy" GPO to generate events for when accounts in Active Directory are used. Set at the OU level to generate events on file servers when accounts on member machines are used.	No.	

TABLE 6.1   Auditable Events *(continued)*

Auditing Right	What It Does	Where You Should Set It	Is It On by Default in Windows 2003 Active Directory?	Notes
Audit process tracking	Enters events when specific programs or processes are running.	In the "Default Domain Controllers Policy" GPO to affect Domain Controllers. Set at the OU level to monitor processes on specific servers within the OU.	No.	This is an advanced auditing feature that can generate a lot of events once turned on. Only turn this on at the behest of Microsoft PSS or other trouble-shooting authority.
Audit system events	Enters events when the system starts up, shuts down, or any time the security or system logs have been modified.	In the "Default Domain Controllers Policy" GPO to determine when Domain Controllers are rebooted or logs have been modified. Set at an OU level to monitor when member machines are rebooted or logs have been modified.	Yes. In "Default Domain Controllers Policy" GPO, which affects only Domain Controllers.	

Auditing Group Policy Object Changes

You might be asked to determine who created a specific Group Policy and when it was created. To that end, you can leverage Active Directory's auditing capability and use Group Policy to audit Group Policy! Whenever a new Group Policy is born, deleted, or modified, various events such as the event in Figure 6.9 are generated.

These events are generated in Windows 2003 because two things are automatically set up by default in Windows 2003 Active Directory:

- **Audit Directory Service access** is enabled in the "Default Domain Controllers Policy" GPO. You can see this in Figure 6.8, earlier in this chapter.

- Auditing is turned on for the "Policies" object container within Active Directory. The Policies folder is where the GPC (Group Policy Container) is stored in Active Directory. Auditing is turned on so that events are generated when anyone creates, destroys, or modifies any objects inside the folder.

FIGURE 6.9 This type of event is generated when GPOs are modified.

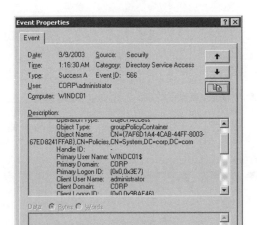

To view the Policies container, follow these steps:

1. Launch Active Directory Users And Computers.

2. Choose View ➤ Advanced Features. This enables you to see some normally hidden folders and security rights within Active Directory Users And Computers.

3. Drill down into Domain ➤ System ➤ Policies.

4. Right-click the Policies folder, and choose the Properties from the shortcut menu to open the Properties dialog box.

5. Click the Security tab.

6. Click the Advanced button to open the "Advanced Security Settings for Policies" window.

7. Click the Auditing tab, which is shown in Figure 6.10.

If you drill down even deeper, you'll discover that the "Everyone" group will trigger events when new GPOs are modified or created. It is this interaction that generates events, such as what is seen in Figure 6.9.

 If you wanted to hone in on who triggered events (as opposed to the Everyone group) you could remove the Everyone group from being audited (seen in Figure 6.10) and plunk in just the users or groups you wanted to monitor.

Clearly, you can do a lot when creating or modifying a GPO. As you saw in Figure 6.9, the Event ID for GPO Auditing is Event ID number 566. However, there are numerous instances of Event 566, each with information that depends on precisely what you do to the GPO. The bad news is that the audit doesn't show you the GPO's "friendly name"; rather, it shows only the GUID, which is a little disappointing and makes things difficult to track down.

FIGURE 6.10   Auditing for GPO changes is set on the Policies folder within Active Directory Users And Computers.

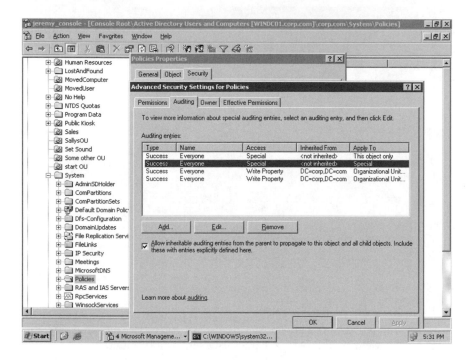

Table 6.2 shows what to expect when looking within Event 566.

TABLE 6.2   The Contents of Event 566

Action that Occurred	Field to Look For	What It Shows in the Field
Create a new GPO	Accesses	Create Child groupPolicyContainer
Modify a GPO	Properties	Write Property—Default property set versionNumber gPCMachineExtensionNames groupPolicyContainer
Remove a GPO	Access	WRITE_DAC
	Properties	WRITE_DAC groupPolicyContainer
Change GPO status	Properties	Write Property—Default property set flags
Remove the "Link Enabled" status or remove the link from an OU	Properties	Write Property—Default property set gPLink

TABLE 6.2   The Contents of Event 566 *(continued)*

Action that Occurred	Field to Look For	What It Shows in the Field
Enforce/unenforce a GPO link	Properties	Write Property—Default property set gPLink
Block/unblock inheritance on an OU	Object Type	domainDNS
	Properties	Default property set gPOptions organizationalUnit
Change permissions	Properties	WRITE_DAC groupPolicyContainer

Windows 2000 shows these as Event 565, whereas Windows 2003 shows these as Event 566. The "Field to Look For" column and the "What It Shows" column may not be precisely the same for Windows 2000 domains.

Windows 2000 will also pop up Event 643 whenever the "Default Domain Policy" GPO is processed (whether changed or unchanged). You might see a lot of these, and you can safely ignore them.

Auditing File Access

If you want to enable auditing when users attempt to access files on file servers, you need to do the following within Active Directory:

- Create an OU.
- Move the accounts of those file servers in the OU.
- Create a GPO linked to the OU.
- Enable the **Audit object access** policy setting inside the GPO linked to the OU.

Once you do this, you then specify which files or folders on the target file server you wish to audit. To do so, follow these steps:

1. At the target file server itself, use Explorer to drill down into the drive letter and directory that you want to audit. Right-click the folder (or just one specific file), and choose Properties from the shortcut menu to open the Properties dialog box.

2. Click the Security tab, and then click the Advanced button to open the "Advanced Security Settings" for the share.

3. Click the Auditing tab.

4. Click Add, to pop up the "Auditing Entry" dialog as seen in Figure 6.11. This dialog will allow you to add users to the Auditing entries.

The simplest and most effective entry you can add is the "Everyone" group, as shown in Figure 6.11. When anyone tries to touch the file, you can audit for certain triggers, such as the "Read " permission.

FIGURE 6.11   Set auditing for files on the file or folder on the target system.

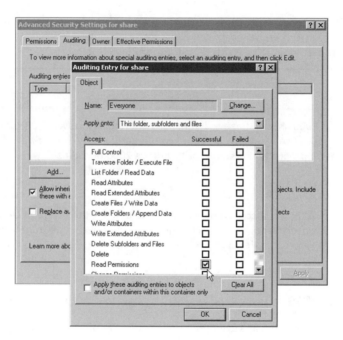

Logon, Logoff, Startup, and Shutdown Scripts

Users have always been able to get logon scripts. NT 4 used User Manager For Domains to assign logon scripts, and Windows 2000 and 2003 domains may use Active Directory Users And Computers to assign logon scripts. However, you can step up to the next level using Group Policy and get more than just logon scripts:

▪ Users can get logon and logoff scripts.

▪ Computers can get startup and/or shutdown scripts.

And, the best part is, you're not limited to old DOS-style batch files. Scripts deployed via Group Policy can use DOS-style `.bat` or `.cmd` scripts, VBScript (`.vbs` files), or JavaScript (`.js` files).

Although logon and startup scripts might be useful to map to network drives and automatically fire up Excel, the scripts can be equally useful when logging off or shutting down. Imagine automatically scripting the clean up of the Temp folder or the ability to kick off a full-drive sweep of your virus scanner.

To use scripts with Group Policy, users must be in the site, domain, or OU linked to a GPO that contains a logon or logoff script. As the name of the script implies, users execute the script only at logon or logoff. Computers must also be in the site, domain, or OU linked to a GPO that contains a startup or shutdown script, which they run only at startup or shutdown.

User and computer scripts delivered via Group Policy do not run "visible" to the user, which prevents users from canceling the script. To that end, scripts run silently in the background unless there is a problem. At that point, you have to wait until the script times out (5 minutes by default.) I'll show you a bit later how to expose the scripts to run visible.

In these examples, I'll use basic DOS-style `.bat` commands to explain the concept. Here is an example of a script that displays "Hello World" and then pauses for a key press, before removing the files from the %temp% folder. In Notepad, create the following file:

```
Echo "Hello World."
Pause
Del /Q /S %temp%
Pause
```

Only your Windows XP, Windows 2000, and Windows 2003 clients receive scripts from GPOs. If you have downlevel clients (such as Windows NT), they can run only old-style logon scripts. The old-style logon scripts is located as a "Logon Script" field in the user's Profile tab inside "Active Directory Users And Computers."

Startup and Shutdown Scripts

The Startup and Shutdown script settings are found under the Computer node in the Windows Settings ➤ Scripts branch. You can get your proposed script into the proper GPO in many ways; however, I think I have found the ideal way as follows:

1. Once you're in the Group Policy Object Editor, drill down to Computer Node ➤ Startup Scripts and double-click it. The Startup Properties dialog box will appear.

2. Click the Add button to open the Add a Script dialog box.

3. In the Script Name field, you can enter a filename or click Browse to open the Browse dialog box, as shown in Figure 6.12.

FIGURE 6.12 You can create .bat or .vbs files on the fly with this little trick.

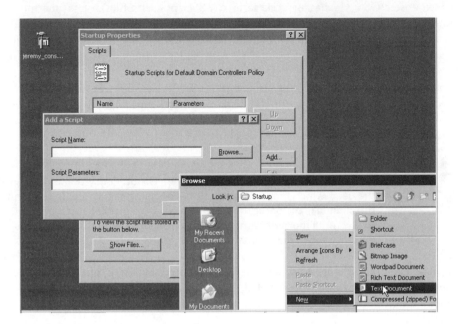

4. To create a new file, right-click in the Browse dialog box, and choose New ➤ Text Document, for example.

5. Enter a name for the file, for example, myscript.bat.

6. When asked if you want to change the file extension, click Yes, right-click the file, and choose Edit from the shortcut menu to open Notepad.

7. Type your script, and save the file.

8. Select the new file as the proposed script.

Again, the computer account must be in an OU with a linked GPO that contains a script. However, don't reboot yet. By default, you won't see the script run. And, since our script contains a Pause statement, your users will wait a really long time before the script times out. To allow the script to be visible (and enable you to press any key at the pause), enable a policy setting that also affects the machine. Traverse to Computer Settings ➤ Administrative Templates ➤ System ➤ Scripts, and select either **Run startup scripts visible** or **Run shutdown scripts visible,** or select both options.

Last, it's important to understand the context in which Startup and Shutdown scripts run. Specifically, they run in the system context. If you want to connect to resources across the network, you'll need to ensure that those resources allow for computer access across the network (not just user access).

Logon and Logoff Scripts

The Logon and Logoff script settings are under the User node in the Windows Settings ➤ Scripts tree. If you're implementing new logon scripts, I suggest you follow the steps in the previous section.

Again, the user must be in an OU with a linked GPO with a script. However, don't log off and log back on yet. By default, you won't see the script run. To allow the script to be visible (and enable you to press any key at the pause), you need to enable a Group Policy. Traverse to User Settings ➢ Administrative Templates ➢ System ➢ Scripts, and select either **Run logon scripts visible** or **Run logoff scripts visible,** or select both options.

Startup and shutdown scripts run in the user's context. Remember that a user is just a mere mortal and might not be able to manipulate Registry keys that you might want to run in a logon or logoff script.

Even though it looks as if you can add additional logon scripts for a user, you cannot. You can have only one logon script in a GPO for a user.

Internet Explorer Maintenance Policies

You spend Friday night at the office putting together a new Internet proxy server. You have 10,000 clients, and you could walk around to each of them to tell Internet Explorer the name of the new proxy server. However, if you use Group Policy with Internet Explorer Maintenance policies, you simply set the name of the new proxy server from upon high and go home for the night.

You set Internet Explorer Maintenance settings for users by traversing down to User Configuration ➢ Windows Settings ➢ **Internet Explorer Maintenance.** You'll find all sorts of gizmos to play with that control Internet Explorer: home page settings, proxy settings, security zone settings, favorites, and so on. A complete rundown of all the Internet Explorer Maintenance Mode settings is beyond the scope of this book; however, there is one "not so obvious" element to this branch of Group Policy: the two modes you can use to deploy Internet Explorer Maintenance settings.

Mandatory Mode   Acts like other Group Policy settings; that is, your desires are forced upon your client machines. If users change them, the settings are restored. Using this mode is helpful when you want to guarantee important options such as security settings and proxy settings. Additionally, you'll need to set the **Internet Explorer Maintenance Policy Processing** policy setting (located in Computer Configuration ➢ Administrative Templates ➢ Group Policy). You also need to ensure that the **Process even if Group Policy Objects have not changed** setting is selected. Again, you must specify both settings for this to work properly.

Preference Mode   Sends down the settings only once and then allows users to change them if they desire. This mode is good for users whom you want to give some degree of liberty (for example, developers) but want to encourage to use your preferred settings.

The Internet Explorer Maintenance interface is a little goofy. For some items (such as customized program settings), you'll literally import the settings from the machine on which the Group Policy Object Editor is actually running. Additionally goofy is that once you make a change to Preference mode, you cannot return to Mandatory mode without wiping out all your settings (via the Reset Browser Settings option).

Windows 2003 and Windows XP allow for what is known as "Internet Explorer Hardening," which is meant to prevent rogue Active X controls and the like from applying. Active X controls are little pieces of code that enhance the Internet Explorer experience, but could be used maliciously. Microsoft has two great references on the subject: `www.microsoft.com/downloads/details.aspx?FamilyID=d41b036c-e2e1-4960-99bb-9757f7e9e31b&DisplayLang=en` and `www.microsoft.com/technet/treeview/default.asp?url=/technet/prodtechnol/windowsserver2003/proddocs/entserver/iesechelp.asp`. You can also search Microsoft's website for "Internet Explorer Enhanced Security Configuration."

If you set up Internet Explorer Maintenance policies at multiple levels in Active Directory, you'll want to test to see the "merging" of your policy settings. Some Internet Explorer Maintenance policy settings "merge," and others do not—it depends on what you are setting up. Proxy settings, for instance, do not merge; the last applied policy "wins." However, this is not true for the "Trusted Sites" configuration settings. These policy settings *will* merge. Again, be sure to test your GPOs with Internet Explorer Maintenance policies to verify whether your specific policy settings merge or not.

Wireless Network (802.11) Policies

Built-in support for wireless networks is new for Windows XP and Windows 2003, and each operating system has a Client Side Extension (CSE) to support Group Policy. You'll find Wireless Network policies in Computer Configuration ➢ Windows ➢ Security Settings ➢ **Wireless Network (IEEE 802.11) Policies.** This category has the most honorable distinction for including the absolute shortest wizard in the history of Microsoft products. Simply right-click "**Wireless Network (IEEE 802.11) Policies,**" and choose "Create Wireless Network Policy..." from the shortcut menu to start the wizard. After the introduction screen, you give the policy a name, click Next, then click Finish! After that, you're ready to edit the policy.

You can set all sorts of wireless parameters for your Windows XP or Windows 2003 computers (though it's unlikely you'll have many Windows 2003 computers with wireless cards.) The policy settings themselves are beyond the scope of this book and include options such as WEP, EAP/Smartcard usage, and other scary-sounding wireless settings. However, you can learn about the controllable settings in Chapter 6 of the "Windows Server 2003 Planning Guide." Just search TechNet for "Planning Guide 6 - Designing Wireless LAN Security Using 802.1X."

Restricted Groups

In Windows 2000 and Windows 2003, you can use Restricted Groups to strictly control the following tasks:

- The membership of security groups that you create in Active Directory
- The security group membership on groups created on member machines (workstations or servers)
- The security groups that are nested within each other

You might want to strictly control these security groups or nestings to make sure that users in other areas of Active Directory, say, other domain administrators, don't inadvertently add someone to a group that shouldn't be there. Here are some practical uses of this technology:

- Ensure that the domain's Backup Operators group contains only Sally and Joe.
- Ensure that the local Administrators group on all desktops contains the user accounts of the help desk and support personnel.
- Ensure that the domain's Sales global group contain the domain's East Sales, West Sales, North Sales, and South Sales local groups.

You set up these Restricted Groups' wishes via a GPO. You might be thinking to yourself that if the domain administrator creates the GPO, can't any domain administrator just delete the GPO and work around the point of the Restricted Groups settings? Yes, but the point of Restricted Groups is additional protection, not ultimate protection.

Strictly Controlling Active Directory Groups

The ideal way to strictly control Active Directory groups with specific Active Directory users is to create a new GPO and link it to the **Domain Controllers** OU.

You *could* modify the "Default Domain Controllers Policy" GPO directly, but, as stated earlier, it's better to create a new GPO when dealing with "normal" settings such as this one. This keeps the "Default Domain Controllers Policy" GPO as clean as possible. Likewise, you *could* modify the "Default Domain Policy" GPO. But, again, keeping away from the defaults for other than their special uses (as previously discussed) is preferred.

 If you set up Restricted Groups policies at multiple levels in Active Directory, there is no "merging" between Restricted Groups policy settings. The "last applied" policy wins. For example, if you set up a Restricted Groups policy, link it to the domain, create another Restricted Groups policy, and link it to the **Domain Controllers** OU, the one linked to the **Domain Controllers** OU "wins."

1. Open the GPO and traverse to Computer Configuration ≻ Windows Settings ≻ Security Settings ≻ **Restricted Groups.**

2. Right-click Restricted Groups, and choose Add Group from the shortcut menu, which opens the "Add Group" dialog box.

3. Click Browse to open the Browse dialog box, and browse for a group, say, the domain's Backup Operators, then press OK.

4. When you do, the Backup Operator Properties dialog box, as shown in Figure 6.13, appears.

You can now choose domain members to place in the "Members of this group" list. In Figure 6.13, I have already added Sally User's account, which is in the domain, and I'm about to add Joe User's domain account.

FIGURE 6.13   You can specify which users you want to ensure are in specific groups.

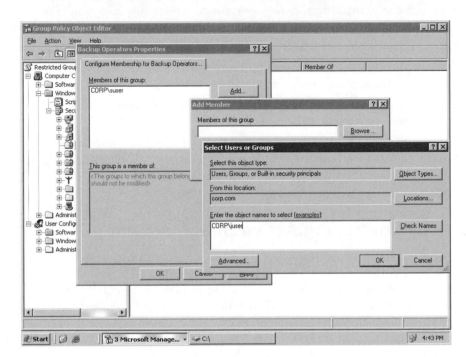

 WARNING   Be careful about just typing in the user account names without either browsing the domain or manually entering the domain with the DOMAIN\user syntax. Restricted Groups in Active Directory will not apply correctly unless you do this.

When Restricted Groups Settings Take Effect

After you enter the users in the "Members of this group" and click OK, you can sit back and wait for all Domain Controllers to get the change and process Group Policy. However, if you have only one Domain Controller in your test lab, this change should occur quickly. You can run GPUpdate to make it occur even faster in this case. This happens because any new GPO you create and link to the **Domain Controllers** OU should get picked up and applied right away—about 5 minutes after replication occurs.

Now, take a look inside the Backup Operators group using Active Directory Users And Computers. Sally's and Joe's accounts should be forced inside Backup Operators.

When Restricted Groups Settings Get Refreshed

If someone were to *remove* Sally and Joe from Backup Operators in Active Directory Users And Computers, their accounts would be repopulated during the Background Security Refresh, which is every 16 hours.

As described in Chapter 3, you have two choices if you don't want to wait 16 hours for the Background Security Refresh:

- Link a GPO to the **Domain Controllers** OU level, with the **Security policy processing** policy setting with the "Process even if the Group Policy objects have not changed" flag set. Then, the Background Security Refresh will process with the normal background refresh (every 5 minutes).

- Force a manual refresh with by running `GPUpdate /FORCE` on your Domain Controller. Recall that `GPUpdate /FORCE` may be used when the underlying GPO hasn't changed and you want your changes reflected immediately.

The users removed from Backup Operators will pop right back in!

There is one caveat with the "Members of this group" section of Restricted Groups. That is, this is an explicit list. If you then add more users using Active Directory Users And Computers, they will also be removed when the Restricted Groups policy is refreshed! Only the users listed in the "Members of this group" section will return.

Strictly Controlling Local Group Membership

You can ensure that specific users are members of specific groups on local machines—workstations or servers. For instance, you can guarantee that Joe and Sally are members of the local Administrators group on all the machines in the **Nurses** OU.

To do this, follow these steps:

1. Create a new GPO, and link it to the **Nurses** OU. Make sure the Nurses computer accounts are in the **Nurses** OU.

2. Dive in to Computer Configuration ➢ Windows Settings ➢ Security Settings ➢ **Restricted Groups.**

3. Right-click **Restricted Groups,** and select the "Add Group" option from the shortcut menu to open the "Add Group" dialog.

4. These initial steps are nearly identical to the previous exercise where we wanted to restrict an Active Directory group. In the last exercise, we clicked the "Browse" button to locate a security group in Active Directory. However, to signify a local group, we'll just type in the word **Administrators**; *don't click Browse.*

5. You'll then see a similar Properties dialog box as seen in Figure 6.13.

6. At this point, you can populate the "Members of this group" in the same way you did before. Simply click "Add", and choose the domain members of Sally and Joe, similar to what is seen in Figure 6.13.

When the machine is rebooted or the background is refreshed, the local Administrators group is populated with Sally and Joe.

The caveat of the "Members of this group" still applies. That is, this is an explicit list. By default, all workstations have the "DOMAIN\Domain Admins" listed as members within their local Administrators group. If you don't add "DOMAIN\ Domain Admins" while creating a Restricted Group, they won't be there on the next background refresh.

Strictly Applying Group Nesting

The last trick Restricted Groups can perform is that it can ensure that one domain group is nested inside another. Like the "Strictly Controlling Active Directory Groups" trick, you need a GPO linked to the **Domain Controllers** OU.

The interface is a bit counterintuitive; the idea is that you name a group (say, HR-OU-Admins) and then specify the group of which it will be a member.

To nest one group within another:

1. Open the GPO and traverse to Computer Configuration ➢ Windows Settings ➢ Security Settings ➢ **Restricted Groups.**

2. Right-click Restricted Groups, and choose "Add Group" from the shortcut menu, which opens the "Add Group" dialog box.

3. Click Browse to open the Browse dialog box, and locate the first group.

4. When you do, the Properties dialog box appears, as shown earlier in Figure 6.13.

5. Then, you'll click the "Add" button in the "This group is a member of" section of the Properties dialog box. You'll then be able to specify the second group name.

When you're finished, and the Group Policy applies, the result will be that the first group will be forcefully nested within the second group. In order for this to really work well, it helps to remember that different domain modes allow for different levels of group nesting. Here's the Cliffs Notes version:

- Windows 2000 mixed mode domains and Windows 2003 interim mode domains can nest global groups only into domain local groups.

- Windows 2000 and Windows 2003 native mode domains can nest global groups into domain local groups. Additionally, global groups can be nested into global groups.

Here's a final thought: You can take advantage of an undocumented feature with the "This group is a member of…" section. Stay with me here: you don't actually have to tell this section about a *group*. You can lie to it, and tell it about a *user*. Strange, but true. When you do this, that user is ensured to be in the group—sort of like what we saw earlier with "Members of this group…" Doing so might cause problems (see the Warning).

WARNING   While you are creating a Restricted Groups policy, take care. Results can be unpredictable when you mix the "This group is a member of…" and "Members of this group…" sections. If you have ensured a group's membership using the "Members of this group…" setting, don't attempt to further modify that group's membership by feeding the "This group is a member of… " users (by lying to it) to extend the original group's membership! On occasion, the "This group is a member of…" and "Members of this group…" will conflict if you try to add users to both headings.

Which Groups Can Go into Which Other Groups Via Restricted Groups?

The processing of Restricted Groups can sometimes be picky depending on the scenario. (This is officially documented in the Knowledge Base article KB 810076.) And the "out of the box" processing changes a little bit and becomes more standardized for the most up-to-date clients: Windows 2003, Windows 2000 with SP4, and Windows XP with SP2. To that end, four tables in "Restricted Groups Tables" on this book's website spell out specifically when you can use "Members of this group…" and "This group is a member of…" in Windows 2000 and Windows 2003 domains. Again, to ensure that the tables work for you, you need Windows 2003, Windows 2000 with SP4, or Windows XP with SP2, or you need the hot fix in the Knowledge Base article KB 810076 applied to machines that will receive the forced users or groups.

Software Restriction Policy

Windows XP and Windows 2003 servers have a CSE (Client Side Extension) that Windows 2000 doesn't have: Software Restriction Policies. Software Restriction Policies enable you, the administrator, to precisely dictate what software will and will not run on your Windows XP desktops.

Many viruses show up in your users' inboxes as either executables or .vbs scripting files. Just one launch within your confines, and you're cleaning up for a week. Additionally, users will bring in unknown software from home or download junk off the Internet, and then, when the computer blows up, they turn around and blame you. What an injustice!

To that end, Microsoft developed Software Restriction Policies, which can put the kibosh on software that shouldn't be there in the first place. You can restrict software for specific users or for all users on a specific machine. You'll find Software Restriction Policies in Computer Configuration ➢ Windows Settings ➢ Security Settings ➢ **Software Restriction Policies.** Just right-click over the Software Restriction Policies node, and select "New Software Restriction Policies" as shown in 6.14 to get started.

Software Restriction Policies is also available as a node under User Configuration ➢ Windows Settings ➢ Security Settings ➢ **Software Restriction Policies,** which can also be seen in Figure 6.14.

Like other policies that affect users or computers, you'll need an OU containing the user or computer accounts you want to restrict, and you'll need a GPO linked to that OU. Or you can set a GPO linked to the domain level, which affects all Windows XP and Windows 2003 machines (or, alternatively, users). Typically, you'll use the Computer side branch of Software Restriction Policies. That way, all users on a specific machine are restricted from using specific "known bad" applications.

Software Restriction Policies are also valid when set upon a local computer within a local policy (via GPEdit.msc). This can be particularly useful for a Windows 2003 acting as a Terminal Server. Software Restriction Policies are meant to replace the APPSec.exe tool.

FIGURE 6.14   Software Restriction Policies are available in both the Computer and User nodes.

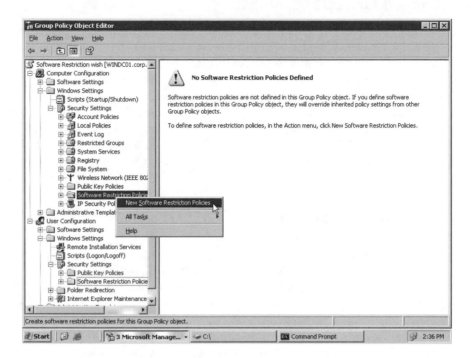

GPOs containing Software Restriction Policies might be common in environments that include Windows XP, Windows 2003, and Windows 2000 machines. However, Windows 2000 machines that are affected by GPOs containing Software Restriction Policies will simply ignore the settings and restrictions contained within.

Software Restriction Policies' "Philosophies"

Using Software Restriction Policies with your Windows XP users involves three primary philosophies. You can choose your philosophy by selecting the "Security Levels" branch of Software Restriction Policies as shown in Figure 6.15.

Philosophy #1   *Allow everything to run except specifically named items.* I nickname this one "Nearly open door." The "Unrestricted" option is selected. Windows XP allows all programs to run, like normal. However, if the administrator names certain applications, such as a virus or a game, it will be prevented from running.

Philosophy #2   *Don't allow programs of a certain type to run.* Allow only specifically named items of that type to pass. I nickname this one "Doggie Door." The "Unrestricted" option is selected. You can choose to squelch all files of a certain type, say, all .vbs files. However, you can instruct Windows XP to allow .vbs files that are digitally signed from your IT department to run.

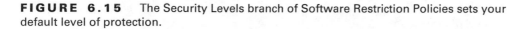

FIGURE 6.15 The Security Levels branch of Software Restriction Policies sets your default level of protection.

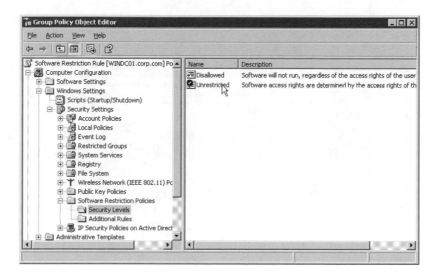

Philosophy #3 *Nothing is allowed to run but the operating system and explicitly named items.* This is the "Full Lockdown" approach. The "Disallowed" option is selected. This is the most heavy-handed approach, but the safest. Only operating system components will run, unless you specifically open up ways for programs to be run. Be careful when using this method; it can get you into a lot of trouble quickly.

Software Restriction Policies' Rules

Once you've chosen your philosophy, you can choose how wide the door is for other stuff. There are four rules to either allow or deny specific software:

- Hash

- Path

- Certificate

- Internet Explorer zone

To create a new rule, select the "Additional Rules" folder, and right-click in the right pane to see your choices, as shown in Figure 6.16.

 By default four Path rules are set that enable access to critical portions of the Registry. These are enabled so that the operating system can write to the Registry even if the "Disallowed" option is set in the "Security Levels" branch.

FIGURE 6.16 The Security Levels branch of Software Restriction Policies sets your default level of protection.

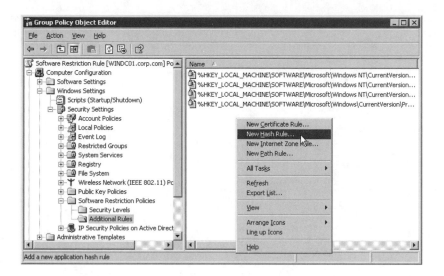

Hash Rule In computer science terms, a "hash value" is a numeric representation, or fingerprint, that can uniquely identify a file should it be renamed. For instance, if I rename Doom.exe to Gloom.exe, the actual bits, the 1s and 0s, contained within the .exe file are the same. Therefore, the hash value is the same. However, if any changes are made to the file (even one bit is changed), the hash value is different. Hash rules are quite useful in containing any application that's a .exe or a .dll.

Sure, it's true that a user could use a hex editor (such as FRHED from www.geocities.com/thestarman3/tool/frhed/FRHED.htm) and change just one bit in a .exe or .dll file to get a new hash value, but it's bloody unlikely. And that's reasonably good protection for most of us.

Path Rule You can specify to open (or restrict) certain applications based on where they reside on the hard drive. You can set up a Path rule to specify a specific folder or full path to a program. Most environment variables are valid such as %HOMEDRIVE%, %HOMEPATH%, %USERPROFILE%, %WINDIR%, %APPDATA%, %PROGRAMFILES%, and %TEMP%. Additionally, Path rules can stomp out the running of any file type you desire, say, Visual Basic files. For example, if you set up a Path rule to disallow files named *.vb*, all Visual Basic file variants will be unable to execute.

Certificate Rule Certificate rules use digitally signed certificates. You can use certificate rules to sign your own applications or scripts and then use a certificate rule to specify your IT department as a "Trusted Publisher." Users, admins, or Enterprise Admins can be specified as trusted publishers.

Zone Rule Users will download crap off the Internet. This is a fact of life. However, you can specify which Internet Explorer zones are allowed for download. You can specify Internet, Intranet, Restricted Sites, Trusted Sites, and My Computer. The bad news about Zone rules, however, is that they simply aren't all that useful. They prevent downloads of applications with the MSI format, but nothing else. So, in my opinion, they're not quite ready for primetime use. (Note that we talk more about MSI files in Chapter 10.)

Setting Up a Software Restriction Policy with a Rule

As stated, you can craft your Software Restriction Policies in myriad ways. Space doesn't permit explaining all of them, so I'll just give you one example. We'll test our Software Restriction Policies by locking down a nefarious application that has caused countless distress to innumerable, hapless people: Solitaire for Windows XP!

To restrict Solitaire from your environment, follow these steps:

1. Create a new hash rule as seen in Figure 6.16 earlier in this chapter.

2. Click Browse, and locate Sol.exe.

You might have to type **\\XPPRO1\c$\windows\system32\sol.exe** to point to a copy of Solitaire on one of your Windows XP machines if you're logged on at a domain controller (because Solitaire isn't present on Windows 2003 servers).

The "File hash" entry is filled in with the file hash value of Sol.exe from the machine, as shown in Figure 6.17.

FIGURE 6.17   Once you specify the file, the hash value is filled in.

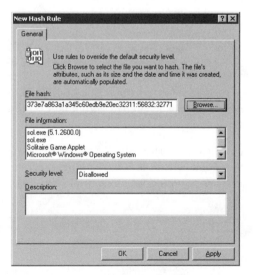

Testing Your Software Restriction Policies on Windows XP

In the previous example, you could create a Software Restriction Policy that affects users or computers. If your policy is for users, for this very first test, log off. If your policy is for computers, reboot the machine. Follow these steps to immediately demonstrate the desired behavior of Software Restriction Policies.

1. Log on the machine that should get the Software Restriction Policies.

2. Choose Start ➢ Run to open the Run dialog box.

3. In the Open box, type **Sol.exe.** You'll see the message shown in Figure 6.18.

FIGURE 6.18 On Windows XP machines, Solitaire is prevented from running.

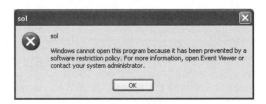

If you were to open a command prompt and then type **Sol.exe,** you would also be restricted. You'll see the message "The system cannot execute the specified program." This is what you expect. Software Restriction Policies are enforced. However, Software Restriction Policies has some strange behavior when the policy is removed (or reenabled), and this behavior is vitally important for you to understand in order to make the most out of Software Restriction Policies.

Using Group Policy to Manipulate Software Restriction Policies

Note that there is a security policy setting named **System settings: Use Certificate Rules on Windows Executables for Software Restriction Policies** located in Computer Configuration ➢ Windows Settings ➢ Security Settings ➢ Local Policies ➢ Security Options.

You'll need to enable this policy setting if you create a Hash rule or Certificate rule on a *digitally signed* .EXE. You can tell if a file is digitally signed by checking out its properties and looking for a Digital Signatures tab, as seen here in the file's properties. Winword.exe has a Digital Signatures tab, while Calc.exe has none.

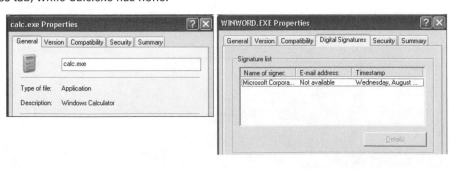

In the earlier example, when we set a Hash rule upon Calc, enabling this policy setting was unnecessary because calc.exe *isn't* digitally signed. However, if you were to restrict a digitally signed .EXE, such as WINWORD.EXE, this policy setting would be necessary for the Hash rule to be embraced by your client systems.

As stated, this policy setting is only necessary for digitally signed .EXEs. However, if you only deal with digitally signed VBS or MSI files, you don't have to worry about this setting at all.

Understanding When Software Restriction Policies Apply

As you just saw, Software Restriction Policies appear to apply at the initial policy processing time, that is, when the user logs on to the machine. However, Group Policy's "Initial policy processing" isn't the mechanism that enforces the Software Restriction Policies. This is a little confusing, so stay with me.

When you log on to a machine, you're running a shell program that launches other programs. This is sometimes called a "launching process." That shell program (or launching process) is familiar—`Explorer.exe`. Whenever `Explorer.exe` (or other launching processes) launch restricted software, they check a portion of the Registry for any restrictions. How does this help determine when Software Restriction Policies apply?

Software Restriction Policies are housed in KEY_LOCAL_MACHINE\SOFTWARE\ Policies\Microsoft\Windows\Safer\CodeIdentifiers.

When Windows XP Applies Software Restriction Policies

Let's imagine that we haven't deployed any Software Restriction Policies to our computers or users and walk through a basic scenario:

Sally the nurse is already logged on to XPPRO2 (her workstation) in the **Nurses** OU. She likes to play Solitaire—a lot. We want to prevent the computers in the **Nurses** OU from running Solitaire (`Sol.exe`). We create a new GPO called "Computer Side Software Restriction" and link it to the **Nurses** OU. We drill down into Computer Configuration ➢ Windows Settings ➢ Security Settings ➢ **Software Restriction Policies.** Our new Software Restriction Policy contains a Hash rule to restrict Solitaire. Group Policy applies in the background (maximally 120 minutes later), or you ask Sally to run `GPUpdate /FORCE`. This guarantees that the GPO containing the Software Restriction Policy is received.

Now, you want to see how Sally (who is already logged on) will embrace the Software Restriction Policy.

If Sally is running `Sol.exe`; it will continue to run until she closes it. You can understand how this makes sense. However, after she closes it, things get strange.

- If Sally then choose Start ➢ Run to open the Run dialog box, then enters **CMD** in the Open box (to spawn a new shell), types **Sol.exe**, and then presses Enter, Solitaire will be restricted.

FIGURE 6.19 On Windows XP, a logoff and logon will be required for all "Launching Programs" to get the signal to restrict software.

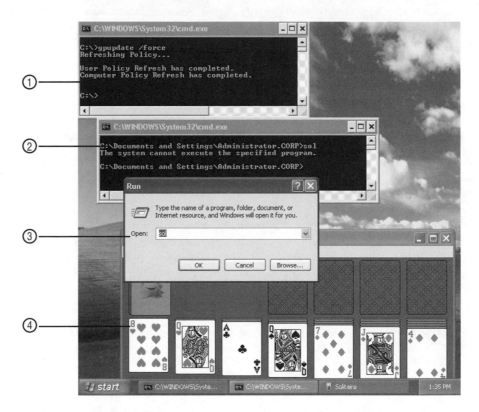

- If Sally chooses Start ≻ All Programs ≻ Games ≻ Solitaire (or chooses Start ≻ Run to open the Run dialog box, types **Sol.exe** in the Open box, and then presses Enter, Solitaire will run!

You can see this interaction in Figure 6.19.

Looking at Figure 6.19, we see in number 1 that the topmost command prompt was opened first. In this command prompt, GPUpdate /FORCE was run to make sure the computer received the GPO containing the Software Restriction Policy. In number 2, Sally then opened a new command prompt and tried to run Sol.exe. It is restricted. You can see the command prompt respond with "The system cannot execute the specified program." Yet, when Sally then ran Sol.exe via Explorer (that is, from the Start menu), in number 3, Solitaire ran, as seen in number 4.

Why does this happen?

Because the "Launching programs" (either CMD or Explorer) control which software is restricted. And it's the launching program that needs to get the "signal" from the Software Restriction Policies—not the actual application! And the launching program only checks Software Restriction Policies when it's first initialized. For Explorer, that's when the user logs on.

So, when Sally logs off and logs back on—she again uses the Start menu and locates and starts Solitaire (or uses the Run dialog box)—Solitaire is restricted. This is because Explorer (the launching program) has been refreshed and checks the Software Restriction Policies entries in the Registry.

What about Windows XP with Service Pack 2?

As of this writing, Windows XP with SP2 beta acts just like Windows XP. That is, there is no change. However, by the time you read this, the real SP2 will be out. Microsoft is working hard to change the behavior of Windows XP once Service Pack 2 is installed. The desired behavior is much like Windows 2003, as described below. Be sure to follow up on www.GPOanswers.com for an update to see if Service Pack 2 for XP will indeed change the behavior of Software Restriction Policies.

When Windows 2003 Applies Software Restriction Policies

If you place Software Restriction Policies on Windows 2003 or users working on Windows 2003, Software Restriction Policies apply a bit more rationally. That is, as soon as the Software Restriction Policies are downloaded via Active Directory Group Policy, no new instances of that application are possible.

It doesn't matter if the launching program has already been started; it doesn't need a refresh. It just restricts the software as specified in the Software Restriction Policies as soon as the Group Policy containing the Software Restriction Policies is applied. This is good. Very good.

I just wish Windows XP Software Restriction Policies worked like Windows 2003 right out of the box.

One Windows 2003 Software Restriction Policy anomaly should be noted. Specifically, if you log on locally to a stand-alone or member server and create a Software Restriction Policy, the Software Restriction Policy acts like Windows XP. That is, the "launching program" must be reset in order for the Software Restriction Policy to take effect. Again, this is only when local GPOs are set upon Windows 2003 stand-alone or member machines.

Troubleshooting Software Restriction Policies

You can troubleshoot Software Restriction Policies in two primary ways:

- Inspect the Registry to see if the Software Restriction Policies are embraced.

- Enable advanced logging.

Inspecting the Software Restriction Policies Location in the Registry

If Software Restriction Policies aren't being applied, and you logged off and back on, log on again as the administrator at the target machine and check KEY_LOCAL_MACHINE\SOFTWARE\Policies\Microsoft\Windows\Safer\CodeIdentifiers. Inside, you'll see numbered branches containing the rules. In Figure 6.20, you can see Sol.exe being restricted by a hash rule.

Do note that operating system files change with service packs—sometimes, even innocuous things like Sol.exe! If, after a service pack, your client isn't restricting applications as you expect, make sure the version number of the restricted application matches the version actually located on the client. More specifically, make sure the hash values match.

FIGURE 6.20   The Registry lays out what will be restricted.

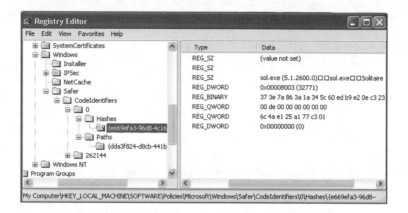

Software Restriction Policies Advanced Logging

You can troubleshoot Software Restriction Policies via a log file. To do so, follow these steps:

1.   In the Registry, traverse to KEY_LOCAL_MACHINE\SOFTWARE\Policies\Microsoft\ Windows\Safer\CodeIdentifiers.

2.   Create a new string value named LogFileName.

3.   In the Data field of the new Registry key, enter the full path and name of a log file, for example, **c:\srplog.txt.**

Now, whenever an application runs, a line is written to the log file explaining why it can or cannot run. Here are two lines from that log file: the first when I run Notepad (which is free to run), and the second when I run the Sol.exe (which is restricted).

```
cmd.exe (PID = 1576) identified C:\WINDOWS\system32\notepad.exe as Unrestricted

    using path rule, Guid = {191cd7fa-f240-4a17-8986-94d480a6c8ca}

cmd.exe (PID = 1576) identified C:\WINDOWS\system32\sol.exe as Disallowed using
    hash rule, Guid = {e669efa3-96d8-4c16-b506-2fec88fbee33}
```

You'll find a great article on Software Restriction Policies in TechNet. Just search on "Using Software Restriction Policies to Protect Against Unauthorized Software."

Oops, I Locked Myself Out of My Machine with Software Restriction Policies

If you make a Software Restriction Policy too tight, you can lock yourself right out of the system! Don't panic. If the policy is a GPO in Active Directory, remove the policy setting or disable the GPO. After Group Policy processes on the client, log on again as the user, and you should be cleared up.

However, if you make a Software Restriction Policy using the local policy editor (`GPEdit.msc`) and you lock yourself out, you have a slightly longer road to recovery. Follow these steps:

1. Reboot the machine, and press F8 upon startup to open the Advanced Options Menu at boot time.

2. Select SAFE MODE and allow the computer to continue to finish booting.

3. Log on as the machine's local administrator.

4. Dive in to `HKLM\Software\Policies\Microsoft\Windows\Safer\CodeIdentifiers`. Delete everything below the "CodeIdentifiers" key.

5. Reboot the machine.

You should be out of the woods now.

Securing Workstations with Templates

Additionally, it's necessary in many environments to ensure that workstations have the same level of security. What good is it if one machine is locked down tight when the bad guys can simply move along to another machine to get on to your network? The "out of the box" security on Windows 2000 and Windows XP machines may or may not be adequate for your environment.

You'll need tools to ensure environment-wide security. The Security Templates MMC snap-in and the Security Configuration and Analysis tool are your partners for generating a baseline of security. You can use these tools to "tattoo" the Registry of the computer to make it more difficult to attack—both on and off your network. After you define your security goals with these tools, you can use Group Policy to easily ensure that all affected machines embrace the same baseline for security.

To get started, we'll load the appropriate snap-ins. In this exercise, we'll use one MMC and load the two snap-ins on a Windows XP Professional machine while logged on as a local administrator. After we load the MMC snap-ins, we'll use the tools to become familiar with the predefined templates and start locking down some of our machines.

 This exercise assumes you're loading the snap-ins at a Windows XP Professional machine, though you can certainly perform a similar exercise at a Windows 2000 machine.

1. Choose Start ➤ Run to open the Run dialog box, and in the Open box, enter **MMC** and press Enter to fire up a "naked" MMC.

2. Choose Console ➤ Add/Remove Snap-in to open the Add/Remove Snap-in dialog box.

3. Click Add to open the Add Standalone Snap-in dialog box.

4. Locate and add the Security Configuration and Analysis and Security Templates snap-ins by scrolling through the list and clicking "Add." Add each snap-in individually, so they'll both be on your MMC palette.

5. Click Close to close the "Add Standalone Snap-in" dialog box.

6. Click OK to close the "Add/Remove Snap-In" dialog box

    When finished, your MMC should look like that in Figure 6.21.

FIGURE 6.21   The Security Configuration And Analysis and Security Templates nodes are loaded in the MMC. The available security templates are listed here.

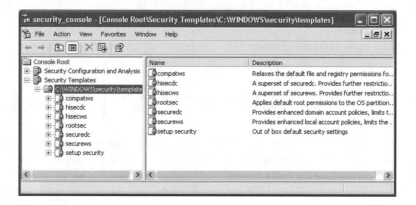

Security Templates

To get multiple machines to embrace a collection of security settings, you'll roll your proposed settings into what is called a security template. A security template is nothing more than a collection of security settings wrapped up in an easy-to-deploy, text-based .inf file. Once you have the .inf file locked and loaded the way you want, you can leverage Group Policy to assert your will across your enterprise.

You leverage security templates that come from many sources:

▪   Some templates are built into Windows. These predefined templates exist for workstations, servers, and domain controllers, and they range in intensity from "default security" to "highly secure."

▪   You can create your own security templates from scratch or use the predefined templates as a jumping-off point to create your own.

▪   Microsoft and other noted third parties have their own collection of security templates for your use. More on third-party templates in a bit.

In these next sections, we'll take a look at the predefined templates and see what they can offer us. We'll then plan a lockdown of our own machines by customizing a template (leveraging one of the predefined templates). Once we actually lock down our machines by applying our templates, we'll see if our lockdown was successful—using both the graphically provided MMC snap-in tools and the command-line interface.

Finally, in the last section, we'll use the template we customized to lock down multiple machines at once using the broad stroke of Group Policy.

Security templates are supposed to help you set a baseline of security upon a gaggle of systems. Let's take a quick look at the available templates within Windows.

 I would encourage you to not actually do anything with these templates until you read all the way through this section.

Default Security for Windows 2003 and Windows XP

If a machine is a "fresh install." three templates define the default "out of the box" security for a Windows XP or Windows 2003 Domain Controller or a Windows 2003 member server. On Windows XP, you'll find `delftwk.inf` in the c:\windows\inf folder. The system used this file when it was being born to set the out-of-the-box settings.

On Windows 2003, you'll find `defltdc.inf` and `defltsv.inf` in c:\windows\inf folder. These templates define the baseline security for Windows 2003 Domain Controllers and Windows 2000 servers. The `DCFirst.inf` template is used to populate the first Windows 2003 Domain Controller with the default Account Policies (Password policy, Account Lockout policy, and Kerberos policy.)

Additionally, if a Domain Controller is upgraded from NT 4 or Windows 2000, a different set of security is placed on that machine. The templates used by an NT 4 system are called `DCup.inf`, and the templates used by Windows 2000 are called `DCup5.inf`. An NT 4 Terminal Server Edition or Windows 2000 machine with Terminal Services/Application mode will run `Dsupt.inf` to write its default configuration settings. The system automatically uses these files, which are discussed here only for reference. You shouldn't need to touch them again after the system uses them.

Incremental Security Templates

You can use several predefined security `.inf` template files as a jumping-off point. Rather than use them as is, you can modify them to suit your specific requirements. Indeed, you'll see how to leverage an existing template a bit later in this chapter.

The supplied templates tighten or loosen a workstation, server, or DC (whichever the specific case may be), using the Security Configuration and Analysis MMC snap-in or the `secedit` command-line tool. (Both are described in detail later in this chapter.) You can see the provided incremental security templates listed in the Security Templates node as seen in Figure 6.21 earlier in this chapter.

Before we look at how to apply these `.inf` files to workstations, let's briefly examine each template (based on machine type) and see what it's supposed to do.

This information in this section is specific to Windows 2003 and Windows XP and is not compatible with Windows 2000. When upgraded from NT 4, Windows 2000 machines need to be enhanced with "Basic" templates that are not listed here. For more information on Windows 2000 and security templates, see the previous edition of this book. Other helpful resources are on TechNet at http://support.microsoft.com/?kbid=234926. An additional reference to Windows 2000 templates is at the end of this chapter in the "Final Thoughts" section.

Domain Controller *.inf* Template Files

These .inf settings apply to Windows 2003 Domain Controllers.

securedc Increases the security required in the Password policy and Account Policy, bumps up the amount of auditing that occurs on the Domain Controller, and increases some Event Log settings, such as the size. This template doesn't modify any file or Registry ACLs (Access Control Lists).

hisecdc Chokes off all communications with downlevel machines by turning off NTLM communication. Only those machines that use NTLM v2 or Kerberos will be able to communicate with any machines to which this template is applied.

You can find certification guidelines for applications at www.microsoft.com/windowsserver2003/partners/isvs/cfw.mspx.

Applying the Hisecdc.inf template to Domain Controllers is dangerous and can prevent clients from authenticating to your Domain Controllers.

XP Professional *.inf* Template Files

These settings apply to Windows XP Professional machines.

compatws Applications must pass certification guidelines to be considered "Windows Logo"–compliant. Sometimes, an older application does not follow the new rules once it's up and running. Use this template to allow some older applications (such as Office 97), which are not Windows Logo certified, to run properly when mere mortals in the Users group run them.

This template elevates the permissions of the Users group by modifying common Registry keys, files, and folders. Often, administrators will give in and grant users who complain about incompatible applications admission into the Power Users group. Applying this template should satisfy their needs without putting them in the Power Users group. Because of this, this template removes all users and groups from the Power Users group.

You can see this behavior for yourself. As an administrator, load Word 97 with the Office 97 spelling check feature onto an NTFS volume on a Windows 2000 or Windows XP machine.

Then, log back on as a regular user and, using that Word 97 installation, try to run the spelling utility. As a regular user, you cannot because certain files must be read/writeable to the installation point of Office 97 (usually under Program Files). Apply this template, and your woes disappear. The compatws.inf template modifies NTFS permissions on the Program Files folder so that mere mortals can modify the settings.

securews These settings increase the security required in the Password policy and the Account Policy, bump up the amount of auditing that occurs on the workstation, and increase some Event Log settings such as the size. This template doesn't modify any file or Registry ACLs.

hisecws This template turns off NTLM communication and allows only communication with other machines that are running NTLM v2 or Kerberos. NTLM v2 is available on Windows 2000, Windows 2003, and Windows XP machines and on Windows 9*x* machines and Windows NT 4 machines that have the Directory Services client installed. Kerberos is available only on Widows 2000 machines (and higher). Like the compatsw template, all users and groups are flushed from the Power Users group. A note of caution here: The hisecws.inf template turns off NTLM authentication and allows communication only with other machines that are running NTLM v2 or Kerberos.

Special Microsoft Templates

Depending on how a machine was born or upgraded, two templates will be different from machine to machine: DC security.inf and setup security.inf. The contents of DC security.inf are created "on the fly" when you upgrade or create a Domain Controller from scratch. During DCPROMO, a combination of defltdc.inf, dcfirst.inf, and defdcgpo.inf are used to configure the system; then DC security.inf is generated. The setup security.inf template is created on the fly when you upgrade or create a member machine from scratch.

These templates contain a snapshot of some of the security that was configured on the system just prior to performing an upgrade or running DCPROMO. (They'll contain default settings if you performed a fresh install.) This can be particularly helpful if something fails to work after an upgrade or DCPROMO. You can look inside these files to determine what the previously set security was on that system and try to adjust it on the new system.

The templates listed in the previous section won't affect User Rights Assignments that were specifically added to your machine. However, applying the setup security.inf and DC security.inf templates resets the changed User Rights Assignments to the defaults (or your previous configuration.). If you want to do this, my advice is to restore only the specific area you want; don't apply the whole template lock, stock, and barrel. You can see how to do this via the secedit command's /areas switch (described in Table 6.3). Usually, you don't want to roll back your entire security to the defaults. Rather, you can pick and choose which sections you want to restore.

Microsoft gives you a nitty-gritty look at the provided templates at www
.microsoft.com/technet/treeview/default.asp?url=/technet/prodtechnol/
windowsserver2003/proddocs/standard/sag_SCEdefaultpols.asp.

Other Security Template Sources

There are several places that you locate additional templates to use on your systems.

Security Templates from Uncle Bill   On Microsoft's website, you'll find two publications that work in tandem to help administrators secure both Windows 2003 and Windows XP: "Windows Server 2003 Security Guide" and "Threats and Countermeasures: Security Settings in Windows Server 2003 and Windows XP." You can find a more helpful chapter-by-chapter breakout of them at www.jsiinc.com/SUBN/tip6800/rh6858.htm. In both cases, the downloads include several ready-to-use security templates that will go a long way to help you secure your environment. You'll find new templates for Domain Controllers, IIS, IAS, member server, print servers, client systems, and more! Just three words say it all: Great job, Microsoft.

An older work from Microsoft, the "Windows 2000 Hardening Guide," contains tips as well as security templates. You can find it at www.microsoft.com/technet/treeview/default.asp?url=/technet/security/prodtech/windows/win2khg/default.asp.

Security Templates from Uncle Sam   Two U.S. governmental agencies have each provided their take on some proper security templates.

- The National Security Agency has free advice and templates for securing Windows XP and Windows 2000 and even some NT, Cisco, and e-mail server advice at www.nsa.gov/snac/index.html.

- The National Institute of Standards and Technology (NIST) has some templates to help secure Windows 2000 at http://csrc.nist.gov/itsec/guidance_W2Kpro.html.

Security Templates from Elsewhere   The Center for Internet Security (www.cisecurity.org/bench_win2000.html) has its own security templates. Use them in conjunction with their own tool to help determine if your system is vulnerable. As of this writing, the tool and templates are available only for Windows 2000.

Your Own Security Templates

Now that you know which built-in templates perform which functions, you have three options:
- Apply a built-in template as is to a workstation.
- Create your own template from scratch, and apply it to a workstation.
- Modify a built-in template that is already close to what you want to suit your needs, and then apply it to a workstation.

In this section, we'll primarily explore the third option, which essentially covers the skills required to utilize the other two options as well.

You might want to copy the default templates for safekeeping. You can copy them from the \%windir%\securityemplates folder to a floppy, another folder, a partition, or a computer. However, other Windows XP machines in your environment probably hold the default versions of these files as well, so it is relatively easy to get them back.

Creating a Fresh Template from Scratch

To create your own template, in the Console Root folder just right-click the default folder under Security Templates and choose "New Template" from the shortcut menu, as shown in Figure 6.22. You would then give your new template a name.

FIGURE 6.22 You can create your own security templates if desired.

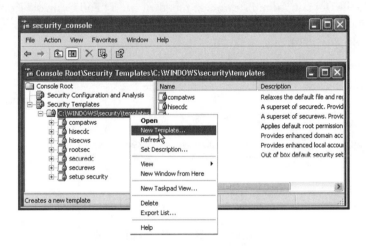

When you do this, no security features are defined. This could mean a lot of manual labor handcrafting the template to your heart's desire. The rewards are great, however, as you'll know exactly what is and what is not defined. When you define your own templates, you can either specify a setting on the target or keep the default setting on the target.

Reusing an Existing Template

Instead of going through the laborious task of handcrafting every Account Policy, Event Log setting, and Registry setting (to name a few), you can use one of the existing templates and modify it to suit your needs.

For instance, you might want to increase the security above and beyond what the hisecws.inf provides as follows:

- Turn off the Indexing Service. (Only administrators can turn it on.)
- Place the Repair folder (where the Registry backup lives) under stronger lock and key.

In this example, we'll modify the hisecws.inf template. To use that template as a jumping-off point, right-click it and save it under a different name, for example, hisecws_plus.inf. Your hisecws_plus.inf template should show up as an additional entry in the list next to the other templates seen in Figure 6.22.

Modification 1: Stop the Indexing Service

First, we'll disable the Indexing Service at startup. When disabled, this process won't kick off unless an administrator manually turns it on or a process running in the system context turns it on. Follow these steps (which you can also use to disable other services):

1. Drill down into hisecws_plus ➢ System Services ➢ Indexing Service.

2. Double-click Indexing Service to open the "Indexing Service Properties."

3. Click the "Define this Policy Setting in the Template" check box.

4. You can optionally select the "Edit Security" button to modify the security settings. You don't really have to change anything to enforce this policy. Though, for completeness, you could add the Domain Administrators group to ensure that they always have Full Control. If you want, add the Domain Administrators group, then select "Full Control" from the list of properties, and click OK.

5. Click the "Disabled" radio button if it is not already selected.

6. Click OK to close the Template Security Policy Setting dialog box.

   The Indexing Service is now disabled, as shown in Figure 6.23.

FIGURE 6.23   The Indexing Service has been set to be disabled.

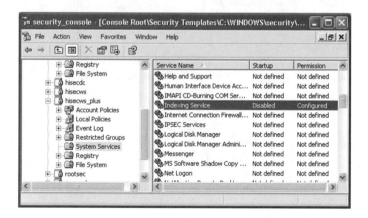

Modification 2: Tweak the Repair Folder

The Repair folder within Windows contains a backup of your Registry data. The files in this folder need to be well protected to ensure that password-cracking programs and the like are not run against the files, exposing the sensitive passwords.

   To protect the Repair folder from prying eyes, follow these steps:

1. Drill down into hisecws_plus ➢ File System. Right-click File System and choose Add File from the shortcut menu to open the Security dialog box.

2. Locate the %systemroot%\Repair folder (usually c:\windows\repair).

3. You'll be prompted to edit security for this folder.

4. You can deny local users and add the HR-OU-ADMINS group, as shown in Figure 6.24.

FIGURE 6.24   Use the Security dialog box to allow or deny access to specific folders.

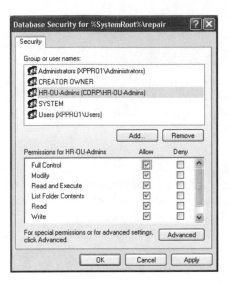

For this example, we want to ensure that the members of our own HR-OU-ADMINS group can access the files at any time. When you click OK in the Security dialog box, you are presented with several choices.

- If you choose "Propagate Inheritable Permissions to all Subfolders and Files," any files or subfolders will receive these NTFS permissions by inheritance only. If there are explicit ACLs on the files or folder, they will not be overwritten.

- If you choose "Replace Existing Permission on All Subfolders and Files with Inheritable Permissions," all current permissions on all affected files and folders are wiped out and replaced with what you have here. This is the default setting.

- If you choose "Do Not Allow Permissions on this File or Folder to Be Replaced," you're asking the operating system not to allow normal inheritance to flow from upper-level folders down to this folder. This option is not valid if an upper-level folder has the "Replace Existing Permission on All Subfolders and Files with Inheritable Permissions" setting.

In this instance, we'll choose the defaults, and click OK to exit the Template Security Policy Setting dialog box.

Now that you've created your templates, you can leverage them to create a safer, tighter, more secure computing environment. The next section will show you how to apply your template to a workstation.

WARNING   Be sure, at this point, to right-click the `hisecws_plus.inf` template and select Save. If you don't, your settings could be lost.

The Security Configuration and Analysis Snap-In

The Security Configuration and Analysis snap-in has one purpose: to compare a template with the currently defined settings on a target machine. If the security doesn't match, the Security Configuration and Analysis snap-in can force the settings defined inside the template to be thrust upon the target computer.

The Security Configuration and Analysis snap-in performs an apples-to-apples comparison between the guidelines you set up in the template and what's currently running on the target machine. If there are holes in the target machine, you have two choices: live with the holes, or plug up those holes with the template.

Creating a Baseline

The first step in creating a baseline is to create a database to hold the results of your comparison. You've already loaded the Security Configuration snap-in alongside the Security Templates snap-in on a sample workstation in your domain at the beginning of this chapter, so we're ready to proceed. If you didn't load the two snap-ins on a sample workstation in your domain, do so now.

To create our database, follow these steps:

1. Right-click Security Configuration And Analysis snap-in, and choose Open Database from the shortcut menu to open the "Open Database" dialog box.

2. Since we're using the `hisecws_plus.inf` template, you might want to be consistent and enter **hisecws_plus.sdb** in the "File Name" field, though you're certainly not obligated to. Additionally, it's usually best to house the `.sdb` file in the same location as the `.inf` file so you can find it easier later. Press "Open" when you've entered in a name.

3. The "Import Template" dialog box appears. Select your `hisecws_plus.inf` template file.

 WARNING   You will get inconsistent baseline results if you try to run the templates meant for workstations against a server or domain controller. Remember, the templates are geared toward specific types of machines.

Once the database is generated, the right pane changes to show you the path of the database, as shown in Figure 6.25.

You are now ready to analyze the current computer.

Run the Analysis on the Current Machine

Once you've got your database that houses the sum of the security settings set up, you are ready to analyze the machine against a template. Follow these steps:

1. Right-click the Security And Configuration Analysis snap-in, and choose "Analyze Computer Now" from the shortcut menu to open the "Perform Analysis" dialog box.

2. A default temporary log location is specified in the "Perform Analysis" dialog box. It really doesn't matter what the name is. Click OK to run the analysis, which is shown in Figure 6.26.

When the analysis is complete, the right pane in the Security Configuration And Analysis snap-in changes to a style similar to that of the Security Templates snap-in.

FIGURE 6.25 The security analysis checks out the seven categories of security.

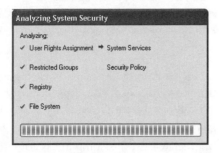

FIGURE 6.26 The right pane changes to reflect your database path.

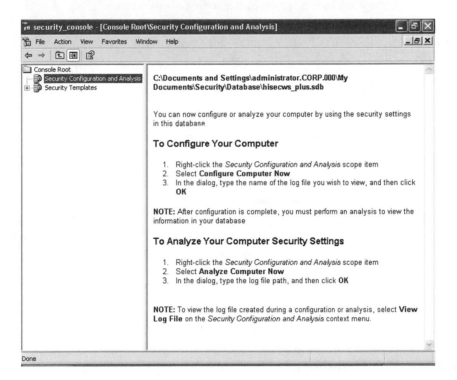

Analyzing the Results

You can analyze the results in two ways.

- You can use the graphic user interface of the Security Configuration and Analysis tool to drill down and double-check that the settings you specified in the template are, indeed, being applied or not being applied to the current workstation.

- You can paw through the log file by hand and see what it came up with.

The former is much less painful, but there are reasons, described in the "Using the Log File to Find Differences" section, that you might want to paw through the log files.

You can check for the changes that were present in the original hisecws.inf template or the modifications you made, such as the NTFS restrictions in the %systemroot%\repair folder.

Graphically Displaying Differences

A lot of settings are configured within the hisecws_plus.inf template. For example, in the Security Configuration and Analysis snap-in, drill down to Local Policies ➢ Security Options. You'll see the following possibilities when graphically analyzing the results:

- If the setting has a green checkmark, the template you used has a definition, and the computer has a setting that already matches. In other words, this computer is compliant with your guidelines for this setting.

- If the results have a big red X, the template has a definition, but the computer you're analyzing either doesn't have a setting or the setting doesn't match.

- If the results don't have either a green checkmark or a big red X (only the little 1s and 0s icon), the computer has a setting, but nothing is defined in the template—so there's technically no "problem."

- If the results have a big red exclamation mark, the setting wasn't analyzed. This can happen for one of two reasons:

  - The item was not originally defined in the baseline policy.

  - An error (for example, Access Denied) occurred when querying the item.

As Figure 6.27 shows, many Security Options have a big red X, meaning that they were defined in the template but the test machine is not compliant.

Using the Log File to Find Differences

You might want to rerun the analysis, but save the log file in an easy-to-get-to location, such as the c:emp folder. You can then open and read the log in any text editor, such as Notepad or WordPad. You can, if you're feeling adventurous, paw through the file and manually locate the changes—though this is messy and cumbersome. If you want to go the nongraphical route, you can sometimes speed things up by using your text editor's search feature to find all instances of "Mismatch."

If you're particularly command-line savvy, use the FINDSTR.EXE command to sift through the hisecws_plus.log and output just those lines that contain the word "Mismatch."

Applying the Template

Now that you know which attributes your target machine does and does not subscribe to, you're ready to apply the template. You can do so in two ways: graphically, via the Security Configuration and Analysis snap-in tool, or via the command-line tool, secedit.

 If you want to heavily armor your test machine, go ahead and apply the template. Else, cancel out now.

FIGURE 6.27   A big red X indicates that the machine is not complying with specific settings in the template.

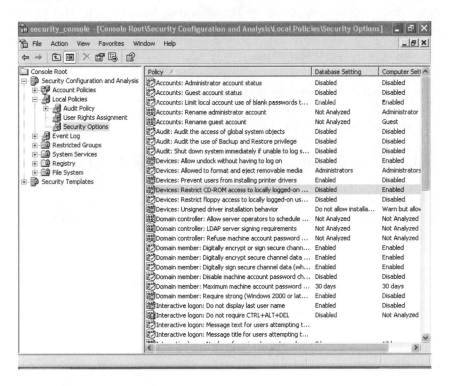

Graphically Applying the Template

After you perform the baseline analysis using the Security Configuration and Analysis snap-in tool, you can apply the settings to your test machine. To do so, right-click the Security Configuration and Analysis snap-in tool and choose "Configure Computer Now…" from the shortcut menu. An analysis is not technically required before applying the template, but it's highly recommended so that you know where you currently stand. You'll be prompted for a location to save the log file.

At this point, the computer is configured to the settings you specified in the template. You could, if desired, rerun the analysis phase to see if the application took place. When you see the red Xs change to green checkmarks, you'll know the application was successful.

Using *secedit* to Analyze and Apply the Template

You can use `secedit` in Windows 2003, Windows XP, and Windows 2000 if you want to write batch files that analyze or apply the policy as we did with the graphical Security Configuration and Analysis tool.

USING *SECEDIT* TO ANALYZE

You can use secedit to analyze the template against the computer's database at any time. To start secedit in analyze mode, you'll need to know the parameters it takes. The following is a sample command line (to be typed alll on one line):

```
secedit /analyze /db c:\temp\hisecws_plus.sdb
        /cfg
   c:\windows\securityemplates\hisecws_plus.inf
        /log
   c:\temp\hisecws_plus.log
        /verbose
```

Let's break this command into bite-sized chunks.

The secedit /analyze chunk requires a /DB parameter, which you must point toward an existing .sdb database. If no database exists, secedit creates a new one on the fly. In this case, we're specifying /DB to use the file and path of c:\temp\hisecws_plus.sdb. This assumes that c:\temp exists. (It may not.)

If you want to generate a new database on the fly, you'll need to specify the /CFG parameter to point toward your .inf template file, say c:\windows\security\templates\hisecws_plus.inf. Use the /log flag to specify a location and name for your log, for instance, c:\temp\hisecws_plus.log.

Optional parameters are /verbose, which spells out in detail the status, or /quiet, which spits out nothing. The verbose parameter can be useful in debugging situations, and quiet can be useful in batch files when you don't want anyone to know anything is happening.

Now that you understand the command and its parameters, open a command shell and type the secedit command, as shown in Figure 6.28.

You can analyze the data in two ways, as discussed earlier. You can do so graphically, using the Security Configuration and Analysis tool, or you can use the log at c:\temp\hisecws_plus.log. To analyze the data graphically, right-click the Security Configuration and Analysis tool, and choose Open Database from the shortcut menu. To analyze the data using Notepad or another text editor, open c:\temp\hisecws_plus.log.

FIGURE 6.28   Use the secedit command to perform batch analysis.

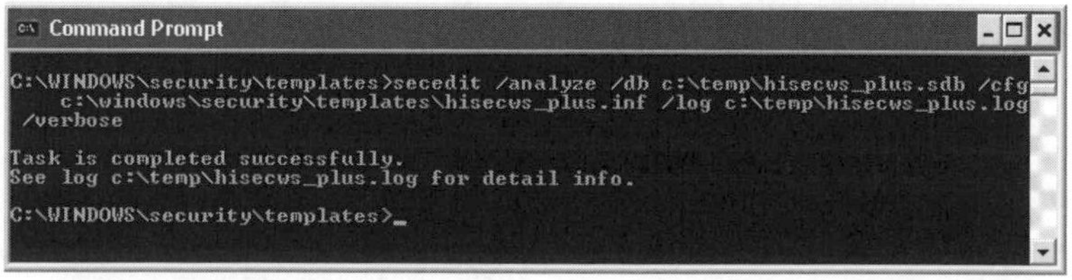

USING SECEDIT TO GENERATE A ROLLBACK TEMPLATE

The Windows 2003 version of the `secedit` command can do something that Windows XP's and Windows 2000's secedit command cannot. It can be used to create a new template which can be used if you want to rollback after a botched template application. Here's the trick though: you must do this *before* you actually apply the template (next step).

To run `secedit` in this mode, you'll need to know the appropriate parameters. A sample command line using `secedit` to generate a rollback template on a Domain Controller might be:

```
secedit /generaterollback /db c:\temp\anyname.sdb
        /cfg
    c:\windows\security\templates\securedc.inf
        /rbk
    c:\save_my_bacon
```

In this example, we use the /cfg command that we're about to apply the securedc.inf template. And, should we need to rollback, it will create the file rollback_before_securedc.inf to rollback to the state before we applied the securedc.inf template (again, you'll see how to apply templates in the next step.)

Here's the big warning though (first of two): if you later decide to apply *another* security template, you'll need to run this command *again*. If you need to perform a rollback, simply apply the security templates back in order such that the most recently created is applied first, and so on back to the first one that was created.

The second big warning is that the resulting template will not have data sufficient to rollback file or registry ACLs. These templates will rollback everything else though.

Again, note, however, that Windows XP doesn't have the /generaterollback switch, so, unfortunately, you can't use it here, before the next step.

USING *SECEDIT* TO CONFIGURE

You can use `secedit` to configure the machine using the template you defined. To run `secedit` in configure mode, you'll need to know the appropriate parameters. The following is a sample command line:

```
secedit /configure /db c:\temp\hisecws_plus.sdb
        /cfg
    c:\windows\security\templates\hisecws_plus.inf
        /log
    c:\temp\hisecws_plus.log
        /verbose
```

Again, let's break the command into bite-sized chunks. The `secedit /configure` chunk requires a /DB parameter, which you must point toward an existing `.sdb` database, say, `c:\templatecopy\hisecws_plus.sdb`.

Use the /CFG parameter to point to your `.inf` template file, `c:\templatecopy\hisecws_plus.inf`. If you don't specify a /CFG entry, `secedit` applies the currently stored template in the database specified in the /DB parameter.

Use the /log flag to specify a location and name for your log, for example, c:\temp\ hisecws_plus.log.

Use the /overwrite switch to overwrite the current information in the database with the information in the security template.

The secedit can also surgically replace a specific area in the template to the target machine. Use the /areas switch to isolate and specify one or several areas, as shown in Table 6.3.

TABLE 6.3   Valid keywords for Secedit's /AREAS switch

Area	Where to Find
SECURITYPOLICY	Sets all security settings inside the template, except for the Restricted Groups, User Rights Assignment, Registry Keys, File Services, or System Services
GROUP_MGMT	The Restricted Groups branch in the template
USER_RIGHTS	The Local Policy ➢ User Rights Assignment in the template
REGKEYS	The Registry branch in the template
FILESTORE	The File System branch in the template
SERVICES	The System Services branch in the template

To specify multiple areas, you can simply string them together (with a single space between each one), such as /areas REGKEYS SERVICES. To apply all areas, don't specify the /areas switch, since they'll all apply by default. Optional parameters are /verbose, which spells out in detail the status, or /quiet, which spits out nothing at all.

The use of the parameter /cfg c:\temp\hisecws_plus.inf is optional because we already used that .inf file to create our .sdb database in the last step.

If you get an "Access is Denied" error, try closing the MMC snap-in in order to close the file lock on the .sdb database.

Once this process is complete, your system is as secure as the template file dictates.

You can learn more about the secedit command by opening a command shell and typing **secedit /?**.

Applying Security Templates with Group Policy

You could schlep around to each workstation or server and run secedit with the /configure switch. This works reasonably well in stand-alone environments, if you only need to tie down a handful of machines, or if you're still in an NT 4 domain or a Novell environment and haven't yet upgraded to Active Directory. But a much more common scenario occurs when you want to enforce the same required security setting on multiple machines simultaneously. This requirement is typical at call centers, nursing stations, and public kiosks.

Group Policy's mission is to make broad-stroke enforcement a piece of cake, and this instance certainly qualifies.

Let's say you want to deploy the hisecws_plus.inf template on all the computers in the **Nurses** OU. Follow these steps:

1. Ensure that the **Nurses** OU exists.

2. Move all machines to be affected by this security edict into the **Nurses** OU.

3. Copy the hisecws_plus.inf template from the workstation to a location accessible to the server. You can do this in several ways. The goal is to get the hisecws_plus.inf template that you generated on the workstation over to the server. You can use a network share, e-mail, or even a floppy! When you transfer the file, simply place it into any folder on the server you desire. The best location is the Domain Controller's c:\windows\security\templates folder.

4. Create a new GPO and link it to the **Nurses** OU. This GPO will be used to import the settings inside the hisecws_plus.inf template you created. Give the GPO a descriptive name, such as "Force hisecws_plus.inf."

Once you're editing the GPO, drill down to Computer Configuration ➢ Windows Settings ➢ Security Settings. To utilize any security .inf template, simply right-click Security Settings (as shown in Figure 6.29) and choose "Import Policy…" from the shortcut menu.

1. Select the policy you want to use by pointing the file requester toward the hisecws_plus.inf file and selecting it. You'll also notice a "Clear this Database Before Importing" check box:

   - When this check box is checked, the current Security settings are replaced with those that you defined in the custom .inf template.

   - When this check box is unchecked, only the attributes you specifically modified are changed. In other words, the state is maintained in those attributes that have no definition.

2. You can ensure that the template was imported correctly by verifying that the changes you modified in the hisecws_plus.inf template are reflected. For instance, when modifying the hisecws_plus.inf template, make sure the %systemroot%\repair folder is listed. You can even dive in and inspect the settings.

3. When ready, close the Group Policy Object Editor.

Now, you are ready to reboot the machines affected by the **Nurses** OU, or you can wait (maximally) 16 hours until the machines embrace the new security settings you specified in the GPO. Afterward, you can verify that the settings you specified in the hisecws_plus.inf template are indeed being reflected and locked down across all machines in the OU.

FIGURE 6.29   Drill down into the Security Settings, right-click, and then import a template.

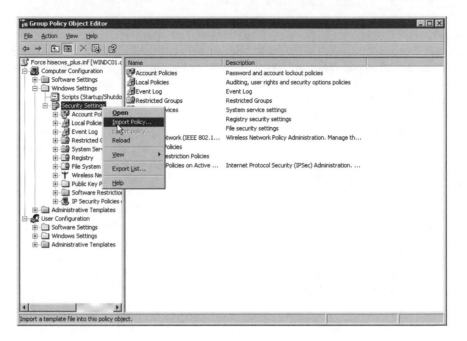

Final Thoughts

To know security, you need to know Group Policy. To that end, we've toured the major sights along the Group Policy security highway. From the "Default Domain Controllers Policy" and "Default Domain Policy" GPOs, to Windows XP and Windows 2003 Software Restriction Policies, to Security Templates—a lot that can be accomplished in there.

Walking up to a specific machine and applying local security sounds like a great, straightforward idea—until you have so many machine you couldn't possibly walk up to them all. This chapter covered some alternate methods for asserting your will across the network.

Remember that items in the security branch will take affect, maximally, every 16 hours—even if the Group Policy doesn't change in Active Directory. This ensures that if a nefarious local administrator changed the policies on his workstation, they'll eventually be refreshed. However, recall that this "Security Background Refresh" will not affect other areas of Group Policy by default. If you want similar behavior, be sure to read Chapter 3 where we discuss the implications of the setting named "Process even if the Group Policy objects have not changed." You can enable different sections of Group Policy to do this by drilling down in the Group Policy Object Editor within Computer Configuration ➢ Administrative Templates ➢ System ➢ Group Policy. Again, this was covered in Chapter 3. So, for fullest security and protection, re-read that chapter to understand why and how to enable those settings.

What I Didn't Cover

Unfortunately, space limitations restrict me from delving into *all* security functions of Group Policy. Of note, three categories are missing from this Group Policy security roundup:

- IP Security
- Certificate Services and Public Key Infrastructure (PKI)
- EFS and the EFS Recovery Policy

For more on IP Security   For getting a grip on IP Security, check out "The Technical Overview of Network and Communications for Windows Server 2003" at `www.microsoft.com/ windowsserver2003/techinfo/overview/netcomm.mspx`.

For more on Certificate Services and PKI   For getting a grip on Certificate Services and PKI, check out "Best Practices for Implementing a Microsoft Windows Server2003 Public Key Infrastructure" at `www.microsoft.com/technet/prodtechnol/windowsserver2003/maintain/ operate/ws3pkibp.asp`.

For more on EFS and the EFS Recovery Policy   You'll find information on the Encrypting File System in Windows XP and Windows Server 2003 at `www.microsoft.com/WINDOWSXP/pro/ techinfo/administration/recovery/default.asp`.

For some EFS Recovery tips, see "Encrypting File System for Windows 2000" at `www.microsoft.com/windows2000/techinfo/howitworks/security/encrypt.asp`.

Additionally, see the Knowledge Base articles "HOW TO: Configure a Domain EFS Recovery Policy in Windows 2000" (KB313376) and "Best Practices for the Encrypting File System" (KB 223316).

Even More Resources

If you get really gung-ho and want to hack the security templates yourself to add your own security settings, it's difficult and ornery, but possible. You'll find an excellent reference, "How to Customize Security Settings within Templates," at `www.shavlik.com/Whitepapers/ Customizing%20Microsoft%20Security%20Templates.pdf`.

Another third-party treatise on the older Windows 2000 templates, their names, and functions can be found in the white paper "Comprehensive Review of Windows 2000 Security Policy Templates and Security Configuration Tool" at `www.ists.dartmouth.edu/IRIA/ knowledge_base/sectemplates/sectemplates_full.htm`.

Designing versus Implementing

This chapter is titled "Implementing Security with Group Policy" because that's what we did. However, an equally challenging project is the *design* of your security policy battle plans *before* you march headlong into implementation. One excellent Microsoft resource, made specifically for the task of working through some examples to design security with GPOs, is the "Common Scenarios" white paper at `www.microsoft.com/downloads/details.aspx?FamilyId=354B9F45-8AA6- 4775-9208-C681A7043292&displaylang=en`. You can also just search for "Group Policy Common Scenarios Using GPMC" on Microsoft's website.

The "Common Scenarios" white paper includes several "canned" GPOs that help you learn how to design a security policy, and includes situations where computers should be Lightly Managed, Mobile, and Kiosk. Once you play with each scenario, you can decide which features you want to keep in your own environment. These GPOs aren't really meant to be deployed as-is (you should modify them to suit your own business), but you'll get a better handle on some security design options. A white paper is included to help you work though the scenarios. In all, I think it's an excellent follow-up once you've been through the exercises in this chapter.

7

Scripting GPMC Operations

The GPMC makes it simple to manage individual GPOs, but if you routinely handle large numbers of GPOs or if you want a convenient way to protect your investment in Group Policy by backing up GPOs and GPO link information on a regular schedule, you might want to automate Group Policy operations with scripts. Using GPMC scripts, you can perform just about any task you can do in the GPMC interface, including the following:

- Creating and deleting GPOs
- Linking and unlinking GPOs with containers
- Reporting on the status of GPOs and GPO links
- Searching for GPOs
- Modifying GPO permissions
- Generating Resultant Set of Policy (RSoP) reports
- Backing up and restoring GPOs
- Importing and exporting GPOs

And we're going to perform these scripting magic tricks right in this chapter.

To get the most out of this chapter, you'll need to be fairly well versed in VBScript, as all the scripts use VBScript.

 I've included only minimal error checking so as to keep the scripts as uncluttered as possible for instruction purposes. For the same reason, I don't declare variables before using them; but best practice for scripting dictates that you do this.

 Don't run the scripts in a production environment without first testing them to your satisfaction in a lab. These scripts are for example only, and neither Sybex, nor Jeremy Moskowitz, nor Bill Boswell will be held liable for any damage used when running scripts. Not that they are expected to run amok or harm your Active Directory, but please—use at your own risk.

This chapter was written by Bill Boswell.

Getting Started with GPMC Scripting

Before we dive in to the actual architecture of the GPMC scripting interface, let's briefly look at what you can and cannot do with scripting, as well as refer you to some additional scripting references and, give you some tips about what to do before writing your first line of code.

You can download the full source code for the scripts in this chapter from the Sybex website at www.sybex.com.

GPMC Scripting Caveats

You can run GPMC scripts only on a machine that has GPMC installed, which, as I described in Chapter 1, means you must either run the scripts on a Windows Server 2003 member server or Domain Controller, Windows XP/SP1 (on which the GPMC will automatically load QFE326469), or Windows XP/SP2 or higher.

GPMC scripts, like the GPMC itself, can manage GPOs in Windows 2000 domains and Windows 2003 domains. You just need the GPMC loaded on the workstation on which you want to perform the scripting. Although you can use GPMC scripts to manage GPOs themselves, you cannot use scripts to manipulate the policy settings inside a GPO. In other words, you can use a script to create a GPO called **"Desktop Lockdown"** but you can't use a script to enable the policy setting that would **Remove Run menu from Start menu.** As you'll see a little later in the chapter, you can work around this limitation somewhat by importing the contents of an existing GPO into a new GPO.

Scripting References

If you're new to scripting, you may find that GPMC scripting is a tough place to start. The Microsoft documentation for GPMC scripts assumes a fairly detailed knowledge of Windows Script Host (WSH) operation and coding experience with one of the two WSH script engines: either VBScript or JavaScript. If words such as *loops*, *variables*, *functions*, and *methods* don't conjure fairly clear images in your head, work your way into scripting more gradually.

Jerry Lee Ford's book *Microsoft WSH and VBScript Programming for the Absolute Beginner* (Premier Press, 2003) is a good place to start.

The foremost reference for Windows scripting comes from Microsoft Press, *Microsoft Windows 2000 Scripting Guide* (2002), written by "The Microsoft Scripting Guys." If you've never written a line of code in your life, you may find this book a little toward the deep end of the pool, but it's certainly a good investment that you'll use more and more as you get sophisticated with your scripts.

The best reference for writing and using GPMC scripts is the Platform Software Developer's Kit, or SDK. You can download the most current version from the MSDN website at www.microsoft.com/msdownload/platformsdk/sdkupdate. Don't be intimidated by the size of the download or the extent of the documentation in other areas. You only need the GPMC and VBScript documentation. The search and locator tools in the SDK make it simple to avoid the other reference material.

If downloading many megabytes of files just to get a bit of documentation doesn't appeal to you, the MSDN website has all the documentation online. The search engine in the Platform SDK is more flexible, but the Microsoft area of Google is almost as good. See www.google.com/microsoft.html.

Also, a version of the GPMC SDK documentation is included with the GPMC installation. See the file %programfiles%\gpmc\scripts\gpmc.chm. You can also gain quite a bit of insight into GPMC scripting by studying the scripts in this folder. More on this topic at the end of this chapter.

References regarding Scripting Group Policy operations on the Internet are tough to come by, at least until the technology really starts to catch on. Check out the Win32Scripting site, http://cwashington.netreach.net, and the MSDN scripting resources at http://msdn.microsoft.com/scripting. Microsoft hosts a series of scripting newsgroups under microsoft.public.scripting that get lots of traffic and are kind to beginners.

Scripting Tools

The simplest way to build a script is to open Notepad and start typing. But if you want the convenience of an integrated development environment (IDE) consider investing in an application intended primarily for developing scripts.

The best-of-breed application for building scripts, in my opinion, is PrimalScript from Sapien Technologies (www.sapien.com). PrimalScript simplifies writing scripts by coloring entries based on their use (variables, methods, functions, comments, and so forth), automatically displaying the properties and methods of registered classes and allowing you to test your scripts without leaving the application. You'll also find a WMI (Windows Management Instrumentation) automation tool that lists all registered WMI classes and builds a script to enumerate all properties of a selected class.

> This functionality is also available in the free Scriptomatic utility from Microsoft. We'll explore Scriptomatic in Chapter 9.

Another excellent scripting application is VbsEdit from Adersoft (www.adersoft.com). Also check out Web-Ed from Joe's Software (www.jsware.com), which costs less than the other two alternatives.

Setting the Stage for Your GPMC Scripts

Before getting too involved with GPMC scripting, let's take a minute or two and review some terms commonly used in Windows scripting documentation.

Scripts cannot communicate directly with the computer in the way that compiled languages such as C++ can. Instead, scripts rely on interfaces created by the developers of a Windows executable. The developer packages information about the executable (*properties*) and ways to control the executable (*methods*) into a tidy bundle called an *object*. Microsoft defines the structure of a Windows object in a set of requirements called the Component Object Model, and an object that meets these requirements is called a *COM object*.

Scripts communicate with a special type of COM object called an *automation object*. An automation object exposes an interface called IDispatch that is used by languages such as VBScript, JavaScript, Visual Basic, and so forth.

When you install the GPMC, the setup program registers a set of automation objects for managing GPOs. Collectively, these are called the GPMC scripting objects. Figure 7.1 shows the hierarchy of these objects.

FIGURE 7.1 The GPMC object model

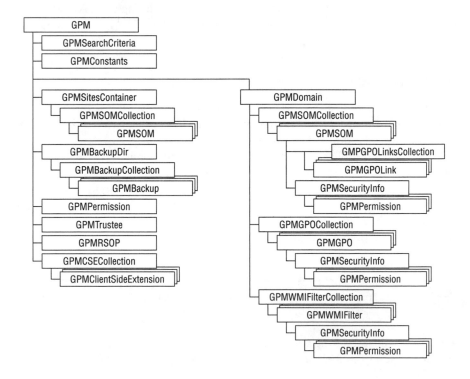

The principal object in the hierarchy, the GPM (Group Policy Management) object, has a set of methods for creating the other objects. For example, the GPM object has a `GetDomain` method that returns a GPMDomain object that you can use to create and query GPOs in an Active Directory domain.

The object model contains the acronym SOM, which stands for Scope of Management, a GPMC term indicating a container that can have a link to one or more GPOs. A SOM is any container that can be linked to a GPO. This includes domain objects, site objects, and OUs.

 You were briefly introduced to the concept of SOM in Chapter 2.

Several objects in the GPMC object model are identified as *collections*. A collection is a special automation object that contains a set of objects indexed by a sequence number. A typical collection has a method for counting the items in the collection and a method for enumerating items by index number and not much else.

VBScript has a `For Each … In … Next` function designed to handle constructs such as objects and collections. You can use `For Each … In … Next` to walk through the properties of an object or a collection one item at a time, displaying the properties of each item or using method calls to perform operations on the items as you enumerate them.

The GPMConstants object contains a variety of constants used by other objects in the GPMC model. For example, if you use a script to generate a report containing the settings inside a GPO, you must set a flag specifying whether you want an HTML report or an XML report. Rather than memorizing the integers representing the options for this flag, you can use the ReportHTML or ReportXML properties of the GPMConstants object.

Initial GMPC Script Requirements

Each GPMC script you write should start with at least two initial method calls, one to create a GPM object and one to create a GPMConstants object. Use the VBScript `CreateObject` method to create the GPM object. Use the `GetConstants` method of GPM to create the GPMConstants object. Here's the example syntax. You can use any name you like for the variable names:

```
Set gpm = CreateObject("gpmgmt.gpm")
Set gpmConstants = gpm.GetConstants
```

Many code samples from Microsoft use Hungarian notation, in which a prefix letter describes the variable type. For example, in Hungarian notation, the GPM object created by CreateObject would have a name such as oGPM. This book does not use Hungarian notation so that the variable names are easier to read.

Once you have a GPM object and a GPMConstants object, you can begin crafting scripts to query and manage GPOs. Let's look at a short example that uses the `GetDomain` method of GPM to create a domain object and then prints the properties of this object. The `GetDomain` method call requires three parameters:

A DNS Domain Name   For now, let's hard-code a domain name by instantiating a variable called dnsDomain. In the examples, I'll use company.com, but you can certainly change the name to suit your tests, such as corp.com or corp.com.local.

The Dns Name of a Domain Controller from Which to Obtain GPO Information   Leave this as an empty string (`""`) if you simply want to use the PDC Emulator.

A Flag That Controls Which Domain Controller to Use for Lookups   The GPMConstant object defines three properties for this flag: `UsePDC` specifies to use the PDC Emulator, `UseAnyDC` uses any Domain Controller, and `DoNotUseW2KDC` uses any DC as long as it runs Windows Server 2003.

Here's the GetDomain syntax for using the PDC Emulator:

```
dnsDomain = "company.com "
set gpmDomain = gpm.GetDomain(dnsDomain,"",gpmConstants.UsePDC)
```

Once you have a GPMDomain object, you can print its Domain and DomainController properties using the `WScript.Echo` method as follows:

```
WScript.Echo "This script uses " & gpmDomain.DomainController & _
             " in the & " gpmDomain.Domain & _
             " domain to obtain its GPO settings."
```

An underscore at the end of a line tells the VBScript interpreter to include the code on the next line in the method call. You do not need to enter the underscores if you type all code on a single line in your script editor.

To get an object representing a site rather than a domain, use the `GetSitesContainer` method of GPM. This method requires four parameters:

The DNS Name of the Forest Root Domain   The forest root domain is the first Active Directory domain in the forest. If you don't know the name of the root domain, launch Active Directory Sites And Services, open the Properties dialog box for any object, and click the Object tab. The DNS name at the left of the Canonical Name field is the name of the forest root domain. For now, let's hard-code the forest root DNS name as follows: `dnsForestRoot = "Company.com"`.

The DNS Name of a Domain   This is used in conjunction with the Domain Controller name in the next parameter. If you leave these two parameter null (`" "`), the method uses the PDC Emulator in the forest root domain.

The DNS Name of a Domain Controller   From this, you obtain GPO information.

A Flag   This controls which Domain Controller to use for lookups.

The GetSitesContainer syntax that uses the PDC Emulator in the forest root domain looks like this:

```
Set gpmSitesContainer =_
gpm.GetSitesContainer(dnsForestRoot,"","",gpmConstants.UsePDC)
```

Now use `WScript.Echo` to list the properties of the GPMSitesContainer object. The following code snippet uses the `With...End With` function in VBScript to avoid typing the same object name over and over again.

```
WScript.Echo "Here's a little information about the Sites container:"
With gpmSitesContainer
  WScript.Echo "The forest root domain is " & .forest & "."
  WScript.Echo "This script obtains site settings from " & ._
    DomainController & " in the " & .Domain & " domain."
End With
```

With these preliminary objects populated, it's time to write some scripts. But first let's see how to make those scripts a little more portable.

Obtaining Domain DNS Names Automatically

Every Active Directory Domain Controller exposes a special LDAP (Lightweight Directory Access Protocol) object called RootDSE that contains information about the directory service hosted by the server. You can use Active Directory Services Interface (ADSI) code in a script to query RootDSE for the name of the Domain Controller's domain, the name of the forest root domain, and other useful information. Using this technique, you don't need to hard-code domain and forest names into your scripts.

You'll need to do a bit of string manipulation because RootDSE stores names in LDAP Distinguished Name format, whereas GPMC uses Fully Qualified DNS Names (FQDNs). VBScript has a `Replace` function that's useful in these situations, as the following code snippet shows:

```
Set RootDSE = GetObject("LDAP://RootDSE")
adsiDomain = RootDSE.Get("DefaultNamingContext")
dnsDomain = ConvertToDNS(adsiDomain)

adsiForestRoot = RootDSE.Get("RootDomainNamingContext")
dnsForestRoot = ConvertToDNS(adsiForestRoot)

Function ConvertToDNS(distinguishedName)
'Skip past the first "DC=" in the DN
initialStrip = Mid(distinguishedName,4)

'Replace the remaining typeful prefixes with periods
rs = Replace(initialSTrip,",dc=",".",1,-1,1)
```

```
'Return the FQDN to the calling program
ConvertToDNS = rs

End Function
```

The ConvertToDNS function starts at the leftmost element of the domain's distinguished name, skips the first typeful prefix, and then converts the remaining typeful prefixes to periods, which is the format used by DNS names.

Obtaining Basic Domain and Site Information

Let's put together everything we've seen so far into a script that lists GPMC domain and site information. This script is available on the Sybex website for this book.

 The script is called List_GPMC_Information.vbs.

```
Set gpm = CreateObject("gpmgmt.gpm")
Set gpmConstants = gpm.GetConstants

Set RootDSE = GetObject("LDAP://RootDSE")
adsiDomain = RootDSE.Get("DefaultNamingContext")
dnsDomain = ConvertToDNS(adsiDomain)
adsiForestRoot = RootDSE.Get("RootDomainNamingContext")
dnsForestRoot = ConvertToDNS(adsiForestRoot)

set gpmDomain = gpm.GetDomain(dnsDomain,"",gpmConstants.UsePDC)
Set gpmSitesContainer =_
gpm.GetSitesContainer(dnsForestRoot,"","",gpmConstants.UsePDC)

WScript.Echo "Here's a little information from the GPMDomain object:"
With gpmDomain
  WScript.Echo "This script uses domain controller " & .DomainController &_
    "in the " &   .Domain & " domain to obtain its GPO settings."
End With

'The vbNL constant adds a blank line to the listing
WScript.Echo vbNL

WScript.Echo "Here's a little information from the GPMSitesContainer object:"
With gpmSitesContainer
  WScript.Echo "The forest root domain is " & .forest & "."
```

```
    WScript.Echo "This script obtains settings from " & .DomainController & _
                 " in the " & .Domain & " domain."
End With



'=====Functions and Subroutines===============

'This function converts a DN to a FQDN
Function ConvertToDNS(distinguishedName)

'Skip past the first "DC=" in the DN
initialStrip = Mid(distinguishedName,4)

'Replace the remaining typeful prefixes with periods
rs = Replace(initialSTrip,",dc=",".",1,-1,1)

'Return the FQDN
ConvertToDNS = rs

End Function
```

Here's a sample of the output from this script:

```
Here's a little information from the GPMDomain object:
This script uses W2K3-S3.company.com in the company.com domain to obtain its
    GPO settings.

Here's a little information from the GPMSitesContainer object:
The forest root domain is company.com.
This script obtains site settings from W2K3-S3.company.com in the
    company.com domain.
```

Creating Simple GPMC Scripts

Now that we've created GPMC objects that represent domains and sites, it's time to ask those objects to do something useful, such as listing GPOs and their properties, such as their display names, creation times, version numbers, and so forth.

 The script in this section is called List_GPO_Properties.

The GPMDomain object has a `SearchGPOs` method designed to return a collection of GPOs (GPMGPOCollection object) in a domain that meets given search criteria. This collection object has a Count property that tells you the number of GPOs in the collection and an Item property that returns a handle to a selected GPO in the collection based on its index number.

The simplest way to see how this works is to create a GPMGPOCollection object and walk through its contents. Create a collection of all GPOs in a given domain by using a null set of search criteria. The following code listing creates a GPMDomain object, searches it for all GPOs to create a GPMGPOCollection, and walks through the collection to display information about the GPOs.

Like all GPMC scripts, start by creating an initial set of GPM objects. The `ConvertToDNS` function is documented earlier in this chapter.

```
Set gpm = CreateObject("gpmgmt.gpm")
Set gpmConstants = gpm.GetConstants
Set RootDSE = GetObject("LDAP://RootDSE")
adsiDomain = RootDSE.Get("DefaultNamingContext")
dnsDomain = ConvertToDNS(adsiDomain)
adsiForestRoot = RootDSE.Get("RootDomainNamingContext")
dnsForestRoot = ConvertToDNS(adsiForestRoot)
set gpmDomain = gpm.GetDomain(dnsDomain,"",gpmConstants.UsePDC)
Set gpmSitesContainer =_
    gpm.GetSitesContainer(dnsForestRoot,"","",gpmConstants.UsePDC)
```

Now create a GPMSearchCriteria object to hold the criteria for the GPO search. You'll provide this object to the `SearchGPOs` method as a parameter. Providing one object as a parameter to another object's method call is not an unusual thing to see in scripts, but it can be a bit confusing the first time you encounter it. Leaving the GPMSearchCriteria object empty tells `SearchGPOs` to return all GPOs in the domain.

```
set gpmSearchCriteria = gpm.CreateSearchCriteria()
set GPO_Domain_List = gpmDomain.SearchGPOs(gpmSearchCriteria)
```

The script now walks through the collection using `For Each … In … Next` and displays the properties of each GPMGPO object in the collection. The variable you use as the argument in the `For Each` expression becomes the handle to the object within the loop.

```
For Each GPO In GPO_Domain_List
WScript.Echo String(20,"=")
With GPO
    WScript.Echo "GPO Friendly Name: " & .DisplayName
    WScript.Echo "GPO GUID:" & .ID
    WScript.Echo "GPC Object Active Directory Path: " & .Path
    WScript.Echo "GPO Domain Name: " & .DomainName
```

```
    WScript.Echo "GPO Created: " & .CreationTime
    WScript.Echo "GPO Last Modified: " & .ModificationTime
    WScript.Echo "Computer GPC Object Version: " & .ComputerDSVersionNumber
    WScript.Echo "Computer GPT File Version: " & .ComputerSysvolVersionNumber
    WScript.Echo "User GPC Object Version: " & .UserDSVersionNumber
    WScript.Echo "User GPT File Version: " & .UserSysvolVersionNumber
    WScript.Echo vbNL
End With
Next
```

If you want more information about the individual properties enumerated in this loop, see the GPMGPO documentation in the Platform SDK. Here's a sample output of the script:

```
====================
GPO Friendly Name: Default Domain Controllers Policy
GPO GUID:{6AC1786C-016F-11D2-945F-00C04fB984F9}
GPC Object Active Directory Path: cn={6AC1786C-016F-11D2-945F-
    00C04fB984F9},cn=policies,cn=system,DC=company,DC=com
GPO Domain Name: company.com
GPO Created: 12/4/2003 11:45:32 AM
GPO Last Modified: 12/28/2003 1:52:24 PM
Computer GPC Object Version: 13
Computer GPT File Version: 13
User GPC Object Version: 2
User GPT File Version: 2
```

You don't have to content yourself with simply listing parameters. You can perform useful calculations, as well. For example, you can emulate the information provided by the GpoTool utility (as seen in Chapter 3) to show the status of the user and computer sides of a GPO and compare the version numbers of the Active Directory GPC (Group Policy Container) object that represents the GPO and the version numbers of the GPT.ini file in SYSVOL to see if you have a replication problem. Do this in the same script with another For Each ... In ... Next loop as follows:

```
For Each GPO In GPO_Domain_List
WScript.Echo String(20,"=")

With GPO
  WScript.Echo "GPO Friendly Name: " & .DisplayName
  If .isuserenabled Then
    WScript.Echo "The User settings in this GPO are enabled."
  Else
    WScript.Echo "The User settings in this GPO are disabled."
```

```
   End If

   If .iscomputerenabled Then
     WScript.Echo "The Computer settings in this GPO are enabled."
   Else
     WScript.Echo "The Computer settings in this GPO are disabled."
   End If


   If .ComputerDSVersionNumber = .ComputerSysvolVersionNumber Then
     WScript.Echo "The versions assigned to Computer settings in this GPO " &_
                 "are consistent between Active Directory and Sysvol."
   Else
     WScript.Echo "WARNING! The Computer settings in this GPO show a " &_
                 "version mismatch between Active Directory and Sysvol."
   End If

   If .UserDSVersionNumber = .UserSysvolVersionNumber Then
     WScript.Echo "The versions assigned to User settings in this GPO " &_
                 "are consistent between Active Directory and Sysvol."
   Else
     WScript.Echo "WARNING! The User settings in this GPO show a " &_
                 "version mismatch between Active Directory and Sysvol."
     End If
     WScript.Echo vbNL

End With
Next
```

Here is sample output from the script:

```
====================
GPO Friendly Name: Default Domain Controllers Policy
The User settings in this GPO are enabled.
The Computer settings in this GPO are enabled.
The versions assigned to Computer settings in this GPO are consistent between
    Active Directory and Sysvol.
The versions assigned to User settings in this GPO are consistent between
    Active Directory and Sysvol.
```

Automating Routine Group Policy Operations

Now that you've seen how GPMC scripting works, in general, and gone through a couple of simple examples, it's time to start automating some common Group Policy tasks. These examples show you how to use each of the major objects in the GPMC object model to perform the following operations:

- Link document GPOs
- Generate GPO reports
- Create new GPOs and link them to new or existing containers
- Back up all GPOs
- Restore a specific GPO
- Migrate a GPO from one domain to another
- Change permissions assigned to a GPO

Documenting GPO Links and WMI Filter Links

As you know from the preceding chapters, a GPO does not take effect until it is linked to a site, a domain, or an OU. The GPMC and the GPMC scripting objects permit you to back up and restore GPOs, but they do not back up and restore the GPO links from containers.

WMI filters are discussed in Chapter 9. Once you understand what they are and how to use them, come back here to be sure they're documented for easy restoration. Also, return to Chapter 2 to see how to set permissions on their use.

As I suggested in Chapter 2, it is best then to run a script that documents your GPO links regularly so you can refer to the list if you need to recover a GPO.

The script in this section is called List_GPOs_and_Links.vbs.

As discussed previously, GPMC represents a site, a domain, or an OU container with a Scope of Management (SOM) object. Links to GPOs are properties of the SOM object, not of a GPO. This is an important concept so it's worth repeating in a different way. If you want to know where a particular GPO is linked, you can't query the GPO itself; you must query a SOM to determine if it has a link to the specific GPO. The GPMDomain object uses a SearchSOMs method to do this work.

On the other hand, links to WMI filters are most definitely properties of the GPO objects themselves. Therefore, documenting WMI filter links requires obtaining a collection of the WMI filters and then searching for any GPOs linked to them.

When searching for SOM links, the SearchSOMs method requires to you supply a GPMGPO object representing a specific GPO. The following script first searches all GPOs using the same code as the previous section, and then it uses each GPO as a selection criterion for the SearchSOMs method call. This creates a collection of SOMs that contain a link to the specified GPO. The script then walks through the collection and prints the SOM name, its type (domain, OU, or site), and whether the SOM has inheritance blocked.

The script starts by creating the initial GPMC objects.

```
Set gpm = CreateObject("gpmgmt.gpm")
Set gpmConstants = gpm.GetConstants
Set RootDSE = GetObject("LDAP://RootDSE")
adsiDomain = RootDSE.Get("DefaultNamingContext")
adsiForestRoot = RootDSE.Get("RootDomainNamingContext")
dnsDomain = ConvertToDNS(adsiDomain)
dnsForestRoot = ConvertToDNS(adsiForestRoot)
set gpmDomain = gpm.GetDomain(dnsDomain,"",gpmConstants.UsePDC)
Set gpmSitesContainer =_
    gpm.GetSitesContainer(dnsForestRoot,"","",gpmConstants.UsePDC)
```

The script now creates two search criteria objects, one to use when searching for GPOs and one to use when searching for SOMs linked to a particular GPO. It then obtains a collection of GPOs in a domain by feeding the SearchGPOs method an empty search criteria object.

```
set gpmSearchCriteria = gpm.CreateSearchCriteria()
set somSearchCriteria = gpm.CreateSearchCriteria()
set GPO_List = gpmDomain.SearchGPOs(gpmSearchCriteria)
```

The script now walks through the GPO collection and uses each GPO object in the collection as a search criterion for finding any linked SOMs. The String(Len(gpo.displayname),"-") function prints an underline the same length as the GPO friendly name.

```
WScript.Echo "The following list contains GPOs in the " & gpmDomain.Domain &_
    "domain, the containers linked to them, and their inheritance settings:" &_
    vbCrLf

For Each GPO In GPO_List
 WScript.Echo GPO.DisplayName
 WScript.Echo String(Len(gpo.displayname),"-")
 somSearchCriteria.Add gpmConstants.SearchPropertySOMLinks,_
    gpmConstants.SearchOpContains, GPO
 Set SOM_List = gpmDomain.SearchSOMs(somSearchCriteria)
```

Now that the script has a SOM collection, it walks through the collection to print properties for each SOM. The script uses a common VBScript technique to build a long string with various elements and then prints the string contents with a single `WScript.Echo` command. The `ConvertSOMType` function takes a numeric value representing the SOM type and returns a friendly name. The code is listed at the end of this section.

```
For Each SOM In SOM_List
  rs = SOM.Name
  rs = rs & " (Type - " & ConvertSOMType(SOM.Type) & ")"
  rs = rs & " (Inheritance Blocked? " & SOM.GPOInheritanceBlocked & ")"
  WScript.Echo rs
Next
```

At this point, the script has listed links to domain and OU SOMs. The GPO might also be linked to site SOMs, so the script now obtains a collection of site SOMs using the `SearchSites` method and then walks through the resultant SOM collection looking for any links to the specified GPO.

```
Set siteSOM_List = gpmSitesContainer.SearchSites(somSearchCriteria)
For Each SOM In siteSOM_List
  rs = SOM.Name
  rs = rs & " (Type = " & ConvertSOMType(SOM.Type) & ")"
  rs = rs & " (Inheritance Blocked = " & SOM.GPOInheritanceBlocked & ")"
  WScript.Echo rs
Next
WScript.Echo vbCr
Next
```

Here is the code for the `ConvertSOMType` function that returns a friendly name for the SOM type.

```
Function ConvertSOMType(SOMType)
Select Case SOMType
 Case gpmConstants.SOMDomain
    rs = "Domain"
 Case gpmConstants.SOMOU
    rs = "OU"
 Case gpmConstants.SOMSite
    rs = "Site"
End Select
ConvertSOMType = rs
End Function
```

Documenting WMI Filter Links

> **NOTE** The script in this section is a continuation of the List_GPOs_and_Links.vbs script.

It's time to document the WMI filter links. Because WMI filters are used rather infrequently, it makes sense to list them in a separate portion of the script rather than complicate the main body of the code. The WMI filter link list in this script has two parts. First, the script uses the SearchWMIFilters method of the GPMDomain object to get a collection of all WMI filters, and then it searches for GPOs that are linked to each filter.

```
'Search for any WMI Filters in the domain
Set wmiSearchCriteria = gpm.CreateSearchCriteria()
Set wmi_Filter_List = gpmDomain.SearchWMIFilters(wmiSearchCriteria)

'Prepare the correct prefix and display the count
If wmi_Filter_List.Count <> 1 Then
  plural = "s"
Else
  plural = ""
End If
WScript.Echo "The " & gpmDomain.Domain & _
                " domain has " & wmi_Filter_List.Count &_
                " WMI filter" & plural & "."
WScript.Echo vbNL

For Each WMI_Filter In wmi_Filter_List
  With WMI_Filter
    WScript.Echo .Name & " (" & .Description & ")"
    WScript.Echo String(Len(.Name)+ Len(.Description)_
                + 3,"-")
  End With

Set gpoSearchCriteria = gpm.CreateSearchCriteria()
gpoSearchCriteria.Add gpmConstants.SearchPropertyGPOWMIFilter,_
    gpmConstants.SearchOPEquals, WMI_Filter

Set Linked_GPO_List = gpmDomain.SearchGPOs(gpoSearchCriteria)
If Linked_GPO_List.Count = 0 Then
  WScript.Echo "No GPOs are linked to this WMI Filter."
```

```
Else
  For Each GPO In Linked_GPO_List
    WScript.Echo "Linked to: " & GPO.DisplayName
  Next
End If
WScript.Echo vbNL
Next
```

Output of List_GPOs_and_Links.vbs

Here is a sample output from the script showing information about a single GPO linked to a variety of SOMs:

```
The following list contains GPOs in the company.com domain, the containers
    linked to them, and their inheritance settings:

High_Speed_Desktops
-------------------
Phoenix (Type - OU) (Inheritance Blocked? False)
Sydney (Type - OU) (Inheritance Blocked? True)
company.com (Type - Domain) (Inheritance Blocked? False)
Phoenix (Type = Site) (Inheritance Blocked? False)
Melbourne (Type = Site) (Inheritance Blocked? False)


High_Memory_Desktop
-------------------
No links to this GPO.


Completed GPO link search. Starting WMI Filter link search...
The company.com domain has 2 WMI filters.

High_Speed_Desktops (Filters for processor speeds faster that 3GHz)
----------------------------------------Linked to: Analytical Processing
    Deployment

High_Memory_Desktops (Filters for RAM greater than or equal to 256MB)
----------------------------------------
Linked to: Adobe Illustrator Deployment
```

 The output here has been modified slightly for better reading.

Documenting GPO Settings

You can't use a GPMC script to modify the settings in a GPO directly, but you can use it to create reports that document the settings. You can generate these settings reports using a script, as well. By running the script every evening using Task Scheduler, you can have an up-to-date reference of settings in case you think a Group Policy has been changed. This complements auditing of Group Policy changes in the Security log, which does not have the granularity that a report would provide.

 The script in this section is `Generate_HTML_Settings_Report.vbs`.

Start with the object initialization code. The `ConvertToDNS` function is documented earlier in the chapter.

```
Set gpm = CreateObject("gpmgmt.gpm")
Set gpmConstants = gpm.GetConstants
Set RootDSE = GetObject("LDAP://RootDSE")
adsiDomain = RootDSE.Get("DefaultNamingContext")
dnsDomain = ConvertToDNS(adsiDomain)
set gpmDomain = gpm.GetDomain(dnsDomain,"",gpmConstants.UsePDC)
```

The next few lines use methods of the Shell object in the WSH to obtain the full path to the user's Desktop folder. If you prefer to save the reports to some other location, the `SpecialFolders` method accepts a variety of system folders. See the Platform SDK for details.

```
Set shell = CreateObject("WScript.Shell")
userDesktop = shell.SpecialFolders("Desktop")
WScript.Echo "This script creates an HTML report on your Desktop using the" &_
    "path" & userDesktop
```

The next few lines use the now familiar technique of generating a full GPO collection by feeding a null value to SearchGPOs.

```
set gpmSearchCriteria = gpm.CreateSearchCriteria()
set GPO_List = gpmDomain.SearchGPOs(gpmSearchCriteria)
```

The script now loops through the collection and uses the `GenerateReportToFile` method to create a GPO settings report. Each GPO gets a separate file. The `GenerateReportToFile` method can create XML or HTML reports (specified in the final parameter of the method call.) The HTML report is friendlier to use.

```
For Each GPO In GPO_List
WScript.Echo "Generating HTML report for " & gpo.DisplayName & "..."
Set gpmReport = gpo.GenerateReporttoFile(gpmConstants.reportHTML,userDesktop &_
              "\GPO_Report_" & StripInvalidChars(gpo.DisplayName) & ".html")
```

It's possible that a GPO can have a display name that does not conform to the requirements for a filename because the GPO name contains the characters ∧ | > < : ? " * . This would cause the GenerateReportToFile method call to fail. To avoid this problem, the `StripInvalidChars` function replaces any invalid filename characters with a dash (-). This VBScript function is derived from a Jscript function called GetValidFileName in Microsoft's library of GPMC functions called Lib_CommonGPMCFunction.js.

```
Function StripInvalidChars(gpoName)
    rs = gpoName
    rs = replace(rs,"/","-")
    rs = replace(rs,"\","-")
    rs = replace(rs,"|","-")
    rs = replace(rs,">","-")
    rs = replace(rs,"<","-")
    rs = replace(rs,":","-")
    rs = replace(rs,"?","-")
    rs = replace(rs,Chr(34),"-")
    rs = replace(rs,"*","-")


    StripInvalidChars = rs
End Function
```

GPMC methods such as GenerateReportToFile include error checking in the form of the GPMResult object, which contains a collection of status messages returned by the calling method. The method call only returns status messages if something went wrong, so you only need to enumerate the GPMReport object if the Count property is not equal to 0. It's possible for a method call to fail in a way that prevents it from populating the GPMReport object with status messages. Use the OverallStatus method of GPMReport to generate an error message and cause the script to exit. Here's the sample error-checking code:

```
Set gpmResult_Status = gpmResult.Status
If gpmResult_Status.count <> 0 Then
  For i=1 to gpmResult_Status.Count
    WScript.Echo gpmResult_Status.Item(i).Message
  Next
  gpmResult.OverallStatus()
  Else
    WScript.Echo vbTab & "Report generated."
End If
Next


WScript.Echo "Completed report generation. Read the reports by double-clicking
    the icons on your Desktop."
```

WARNING
After you run this script, you'll find a set of HTML files on your Desktop. If you don't want your Desktop filled with HTML files for each GPO in your domain, be sure to change the storage location for the reports!

Double-click one of the files to see the contents. This is the same as launching the GMPC, drilling down to a particular GPO, and selecting the Settings tab. In production, you might want to add a timestamp to the filename to save historical copies of the files or to create a new folder for each set of files.

Creating and Linking New GPOs

As I said earlier, you cannot write a script that enables or disables actual policy settings in the GPO. So, for new GPOs that you create while scripting, you usually just use the GPMC and select "Edit" to add policy settings as you see fit. However, as you'll see a bit later, you can create a new GPO and then import the settings from the backup of an existing GPO. This makes it simple to dump the contents of a GPO from a test domain and create a corresponding GPO in a production domain. Let's start by seeing how to use a script to create and link a new GPO.

NOTE
The script in this section is called `Create_and_Link_New_GPO.vbs`.

The following script uses ADSI to create an OU called TestOU, then uses GPMC to create a GPO called General Desktop Settings, and links the new GPO to TestOU. And the script creates TestOU on the fly—it doesn't need to be created in advance.

WARNING
This script changes Active Directory, so you should only run it in a test environment.

The script starts with standard GPMC housekeeping:

```
Set gpm = CreateObject("gpmgmt.gpm")
Set gpmConstants = gpm.GetConstants
Set RootDSE = GetObject("LDAP://RootDSE")
adsiDomain_DN = RootDSE.Get("DefaultNamingContext")
dnsDomain = ConvertToDNS(adsiDomain_DN)
set gpmDomain = gpm.GetDomain(dnsDomain,"",gpmConstants.UsePDC)
```

The following lines create an ADSI domain object and use it to create an OU called TestOU.

```
ouName = "TestOU"
Set adsiDomain = GetObject("LDAP://" & adsiDomain_DN)
```

```
Set TestOU = adsiDomain.Create("OrganizationalUnit", "ou=" & ouName)
TestOU.Setinfo
WScript.Echo "An OU named " & ouName & " has been created."
```

The next lines create a GPO called General Desktop Settings and display its friendly name and Globally Unique Identifier (GUID), just to show how the properties look. In production, you would not need to know GUIDs or Active Directory path information because GPMC keeps track of all that low-level information in the background.

```
Set TestGPO = gpmDomain.CreateGPO()
TestGPO.DisplayName = "General Desktop Settings"
WScript.Echo "A GPO with the friendly name '" & TestGPO.DisplayName &_
    "' has been created. Here are the details: "
With TestGPO
    WScript.Echo vbTab & "The GPO GUID is " & .ID
    WScript.Echo vbTab & "The ADSI path to the GPC object in"
    " Active Directory is " & .Path
End With
WScript.Echo vbNL
```

To link a GPO to an OU, you first need a SOM object for the OU. The GetSOM method of the GPMDomain object does this chore. Armed with a GPMSOM object that represents TestOU, the script uses the CreateGPOLink method of the GPMSOM object to link the OU to the GPO.

CreateGPOLink accepts a parameter that specifies the precedence of the GPO within the SOM. A 0 (zero) puts the GPO at the top of the precedence list. A –1 (negative one) puts it at the bottom of the list. If you know the number of existing GPO links, you can place the GPO at a specific location in the precedence list. The following code listing uses the ConvertSOMType function, which is documented earlier in this chapter.

```
set gpmSOM = gpmDomain.GetSOM(TestOU.distinguishedName)
WScript.Echo "Linking the GPO " & TestGPO.DisplayName & " to an " &_
    ConvertSOMType(gpmSOM.Type) & " container called " & gpmSOM.Name & "...."
Set gpmSOM_Link = gpmSOM.CreateGPOLink(-1, TestGPO)
WScript.Echo "Successfully linked " & TestGPO.DisplayName & " to " &_
    gpmSOM.Name & "."
```

That's all it takes. Here is a sample listing of the script output:

```
An OU with the name TestOU has been created.
A GPO with the friendly name 'General Desktop Settings' has been created. Here
    are the details:
    The GPO GUID is {390C2741-ABCD-43BB-8EDA-88CED9371EA4}
    The ADSI path to the GPC object in Active Directory is cn={390C2741-ABCD-
    43BB-8EDA-88CED9371EA4},cn=policies,cn=system,DC=company,DC=com
```

Linking the GPO General Desktop Settings to an Organizational Unit container
     called TestOU....
Successfully linked General Desktop Settings to TestOU.

After running this script, you can use the GPMC to verify that the new OU exists, that the new GPO exists, and that the OU has a link to the GPO. Let's see how to get backups of existing GPOs, and then we'll import the contents of a GPO backup into the GPO we've created.

Backing Up GPOs

A natural use for scripts is to create backups of your GPOs on a regular basis by scheduling the script to run each evening with Task Scheduler. The next section has a script that lists the backups by name and allows you to restore a selected backup.

   The script in this section is called Backup_All_GPOs.vbs.

For convenience, this script creates a Backup folder in your My Documents folder. In production, you'd probably want the backup script on a support server, and you'll want to save the backups to a more convenient location. You can provide a UNC (Universal Naming Convention) path to the backup folder. You can save multiple backups in the same folder. Each backup gets a GUID as a unique name, so no files are overwritten. Older backups act as historical copies that can be restored should the need arise.

As always, the script starts with initial object creation. The **ConvertToDNS** function is documented earlier in the chapter.

```
Set gpm = CreateObject("gpmgmt.gpm")
Set gpmConstants = gpm.GetConstants
Set RootDSE = GetObject("LDAP://RootDSE")
adsiDomain = RootDSE.Get("DefaultNamingContext")
dnsDomain = ConvertToDNS(adsiDomain)
```

The next few lines use **WSHShell** methods and properties to get the path to the user's My Documents folder.

```
gpoBackupFolder = "GPO_Backups"
Set shell = CreateObject("WScript.Shell")
userMyDocuments = shell.SpecialFolders("MyDocuments")
userName = shell.ExpandEnvironmentStrings("%username%")
gpoBackupFolderFullPath = userMyDocuments & "\" & gpoBackupFolder

WScript.Echo "This script backs up all GPOs in the domain " & dnsDomain & _
             " into a folder called " & gpoBackupFolder & " under MyDocuments."
```

The next lines use `FileSystemObject` methods to either create the backup folder or get a handle to the folder should it already exist. The Platform SDK has extensive documentation for `FileSystemObject`.

```
Set fso = CreateObject("Scripting.FileSystemObject")
If fso.FolderExists(gpoBackupFolderFullPath) Then
    WScript.Echo "Using the existing " & gpoBackupFolder & " folder."
    Set fsoBackupFolder = fso.GetFolder(gpoBackupFolderFullPath)
Else
    WScript.Echo "Creating the " & gpoBackupFolder & " folder."
    Set fsoBackupFolder = fso.CreateFolder(gpoBackupFolderFullPath)
End If
```

The next lines create a collection of all GPOs in the domain using the technique used in previous scripts.

```
set gpmDomain = gpm.GetDomain(dnsDomain,"",gpmConstants.UsePDC)
set gpmSearchCriteria = gpm.CreateSearchCriteria()
set GPO_List = gpmDomain.SearchGPOs(gpmSearchCriteria)
```

We're now at the business end of the script. The next lines walk through the GPO collection and back up each GPO to the target folder. The script announces success as it performs each GPO backup and when it completes all backups. The `GPMResult` object provides error checking in case something goes wrong.

```
For Each GPO In GPO_List
  WScript.Echo "Backing up the " & gpo.DisplayName & " GPO...."
  Set gpmResult = gpo.backup(fsoBackupFolder.path,"Backup performed by " & _
                    userName)
  Set gpmResult_Status = gpmResult.Status
  If gpmResult_Status.count <> 0 Then
    For i=1 to gpmResult_Status.Count
    WScript.Echo gpmResult_Status.Item(i).Message
    Next
    gpmResult.OverallStatus()
  Else
    WScript.Echo vbTab & "GPO Backup successful."
  End If
Next

WScript.Echo "Completed GPO backups."
```

Verify the completion of the backups using the GPMC.

Restoring GPOs

Backups aren't much good without a way to restore them, and as you might expect, GPMC provides a fully scriptable way to perform this process.

> The script in this section is called `Restore_GPO.vbs`.

The following script restores a selected GPO from the set of most current backups. The script assumes that the backup files are in the folder used by the previous script. Be sure to change the path and name of the backup folder if you want to use an alternate location.

> This script requires that you either run the script from a command prompt using a script or set the default script engine to `cscript`. Do this as follows: `cscript //h:cscript //s`.

The script starts with initial housekeeping chores.

```
Set gpm = CreateObject("gpmgmt.gpm")
Set gpmConstants = gpm.GetConstants
Set RootDSE = GetObject("LDAP://RootDSE")
adsiDomain = RootDSE.Get("DefaultNamingContext")
dnsDomain = ConvertToDNS(adsiDomain)
set gpmDomain = gpm.GetDomain(dnsDomain,"",gpmConstants.UsePDC)
```

The next lines get the path to the Backup folder in My Documents.

```
gpoBackupFolder = "GPO_Backups"
Set shell = CreateObject("WScript.Shell")
userMyDocuments = shell.SpecialFolders("MyDocuments")
gpoBackupFolderFullPath = userMyDocuments & "\" & gpoBackupFolder
```

At this point, the script needs a list of the backed-up GPOs. It uses the `GetBackupDir` method of the GPM object to obtain a collection of backup GPOs. This method requires the full path to the backup folder.

Armed with the backup GPO collection, the script uses the `SearchBackups` method to enumerate the list of GPOs and provide the user with an option of which GPO to restore. The `SearchBackups` method requires a search criteria object. If you leave the search criteria object empty, `SearchBackups` returns all backups in the Backup folder. You can use the `SearchPropertyBackupMostRecent` constant to filter out all but the most recent backups for each GPO.

```
set gpmSearchCriteria = gpm.CreateSearchCriteria()
gpmSearchCriteria.Add gpmConstants.SearchPropertyBackupMostRecent, _
```

```
                          gpmConstants.SearchOPEquals, True
Set gpmBackupDir = gpm.GetBackupDir(gpoBackupFolderFullPath)
Set gpmBackup_List = gpmBackupDir.SearchBackups(gpmSearchCriteria)

WScript.Echo "Here is a list of the most current GPO backups:"

For i=1 To gpmBackup_List.Count
  With gpmBackup_List.Item(i)
    rs = i & ") "
    rs = rs & .GPODisplayName & ": "
    rs = rs & "Backed up on " & .Timestamp
    rs = rs & " (" & .Comment & ")"
  End With
  WScript.Echo rs
Next
```

The script outputs a numbered list of GPO backup items. Each number corresponds to the ID number of the GPO backup. The script now asks the user to enter the number of the GPO they want to restore and then uses the ID number to obtain an instance of a GPMBackup object. There is minimal error checking, just a verification that the user entered a number on the list. In a production script, you'd also verify that the entry was an integer to prevent a type mismatch error.

```
WScript.Stdout.write vbCrLf & "Enter the number of the GPO you want to " &_
    " restore: "
rs = int(WScript.StdIn.ReadLine)

If rs >= 1 AND rs <= gpmBackup_List.Count Then
    restoreGPO_ID = gpmBackup_List.item(rs).ID
    set gpmRestoreGPO = gpmBackupDir.GetBackup(restoreGPO_ID)
Else
    WScript.Echo vbCrLf & "Please run the script again and select a number " &_
    " in the displayed range."

    WScript.Quit()
End If
```

The script now enumerates the properties of the selected GPMBackup object to let the user verify that the proper GPO was selected.

```
WScript.Echo vbCrLf & "Here's information about the GPO backup you selected:"
    With gpmRestoreGPO
    WScript.Echo "GPO Friendly Name: " & .GPODisplayName
    WScript.Echo "Domain: " & .GPODomain
    WScript.Echo "Comment: " & .Comment
```

```
    WScript.Echo "GPO GUID: " & .GPOID
    WScript.Echo "GPO Backup GUID: " & .ID
    WScript.Echo "Backup Timestamp: " & .Timestamp
    WScript.Echo vbNL
End With
```

The next line uses the `Stdout.Write` method of `WScript` rather than the `Echo` method to avoid the Carriage Return/Line Feed inserted by `Echo`. The `ReadLine` method plucks the entry made by the user and instantiates a response variable.

```
WScript.StdOut.Write "Are you sure you want to restore this GPO? (y or n) "
rs = WScript.StdIn.ReadLine
WScript.Echo vbCrLf
```

The next line uses the `StrComp` function in VBScript to see if the user entered Y. `StrComp` has an advantage over a simple comparison operator because it succeeds if the user enters lowercase y or capital Y thanks to the **vbTextCompare** parameter. For all other entries, the script prints a short exit message.

```
If StrComp(rs,"y",vbTextCompare) = 0 Then
    WScript.Echo "Restoring selected GPO..."
    Set gpmResult = gpmDomain.RestoreGPO(gpmRestoreGPO,0)
    WScript.Echo "Completed restoring GPO. This did not restore links from " &_
    " containers."
Else
    WScript.Echo "Restore aborted. No GPOs restored."
End If
```

Here is a sample printout of the script:

```
Here is a list of the most current GPO backups:
1) SUS-Mode4: Backed up on 12/12/2003 9:34:58 AM (Performed by administrator)
2) SUS-Mode3: Backed up on 12/12/2003 9:34:50 AM (Performed by administrator)
3) General Desktop Settings: Backed up on 12/12/2003 9:34:56 AM (Performed by
   administrator)
4) Default Domain Controllers Policy: Backed up on 12/12/2003 9:34:52 AM
   (Performed by administrator)
5) Default Domain Policy: Backed up on 12/12/2003 9:34:46 AM (Performed by
   administrator)

Enter the number of the GPO you want to restore: 1

Here's information about the GPO backup you selected:
```

```
GPO Friendly Name: SUS-Mode4
Domain: company.com
Comment: Performed by administrator
GPO GUID: {F714858E-A060-424D-BD18-9F5BD68EE2EF}
GPO Backup GUID: {E79AE647-18E7-41A1-A5EB-DD7BFECA8D58}
Backup Timestamp: 12/12/2003 9:34:58 AM


Are you sure you want to restore this GPO? (y or n) y


Restoring selected GPO...
Completed restoring GPO. This did not restore links from containers.
```

Here's a simple test of the error-checking code included in the previous listing. First, use the script to list the friendly name and ID of a test GPO. Then open the folder containing the backup GPO files and drill down to the folder that matches the test GPO ID. Rename the Backup.XML file by adding the .TEST extension. Then run the restore script again and select the modified GPO for restoration. The error-checking code identifies the error, and then the OverallStatus() method spits out a final error message and exits the program. Here's a sample:

```
Are you sure you want to restore this GPO? (y or n) y


Restoring selected GPO...
The file [C:\Documents and Settings\administrator.COMPANY\My
    Documents\GPO_Backups\{04D31DB6-947C-4B6C-8BE8-89CA204F7338}\Backup.xml]
      cannot be opened. The task will not continue.
The following error occurred:
At Line : 0, Description : System error: -2146697210.


An error occurred during the restore task, and the GPO [cn={F714858E-A060-424D-
    BD18-9F5BD68EE2EF},cn=policies,cn=system,DC=company,DC=com] could not be
    rolled back to its original state. You should reattempt the restore.
The following error occurred:
```
Not enough storage is available to complete this operation.

```
C:\scripts\Restore_GPO.vbs(71, 2) (null): The data is invalid.
```

As you can see by the error message shown in bold, GPMResult status messages aren't always correct, but at least they give you a place to start. The final line, with the error message "The data is invalid," comes from the OverallStatus() method. Microsoft recommends you perform both sets of error checking; therefore, you'll want to call OverallStatus() last so you can get the GPMResult status messages before the script stops running.

Importing GPOs

If you maintain a development domain for use in testing GPOs prior to using them in production, you probably have the task of transferring GPOs from development domains into production domains. You can use the Copy feature in GPMC, but backing up and importing GPOs provides a more controlled evolution that retains the current permissions and links on the existing GPOs.

You can see how to do these functions via the GPMC and migration tables in the Appendix.

The script for this section is called Import_GPO.vbs.

Automatically updating production GPOs from a development domain requires careful coordination with the development team. When you import the settings from a backed-up GPO, you overwrite all the settings in the target GPO. Needless to say, this can cause users some consternation if the development GPO is filled with test settings that have not been approved for production deployment.

To accomplish the import, the script should do the following at a minimum:

- Back up the production GPOs (just in case something goes wrong)

- Back up the development GPOs (to use for importing)

- Select a backup GPO for importing

- Verify that a production GPO exists with a name that matches the selected backup GPO or create the GPO in production

- Verify that the SOM links in the production domain match the SOM links in the development domain, or create the SOM links

- Import the backup GPO file into the production GPO

The only new item on this list is the importing of the GPO backup file. The GPMGPO object has a method called Import that handles this operation. The Import method accepts three parameters:

- A flag indicating whether to use a migration table for mapping security principals and UNC paths between the source domain and the target domain.

- A GPMBackup object representing the backup GPO you've selected to import.

- The full path to the migration table, if used. If you do not use a migration table, leave this option blank, and use a 0 for the migration table flag in the first parameter.

See the Appendix for a description of migration table structure and how to use migration tables.

The following code snippet assumes you have selected a backup GPO, created a GPMBackup object for it, selected a production GPO, and created a GPMGPO object for it. The script on this book's website contains the code for performing the other operations.

```
importGPOName = gpmImportGPO.DisplayName
productionGPOName = gpmProductionGPO.DisplayName

WScript.StdOut.Write "Are you sure you want to import the settings in " &_
    importGPOName & " into " & productionGPOName & "? (y or n) "
rs = WScript.StdIn.ReadLine
WScript.Echo vbCrLf

If StrComp(rs,"y",vbTextCompare) = 0 Then
  WScript.Echo "Importing selected GPO..."
  Set gpmResult = gpmProductionGPO.Import(0,gpmImportGPO)
  Set gpmResult_Status = gpmResult.Status
  If gpmResult_Status.count <> 0 Then
    For i=1 to gpmResult_Status.Count
    WScript.Echo gpmResult_Status.Item(i).Message
    Next
    gpmResult.OverallStatus()
    Else
    WScript.Echo "The GPO was successfully imported."
  End If
Else
  WScript.Echo "Operation aborted. No GPOs imported."
End If
```

You can use the GPMC to verify that the production GPO has new settings from the backed-up GPO.

Changing GPO Permissions

One of the more troublesome chores in Windows scripting involves changing the security permissions assigned to protected objects such as a files, Registry keys, Active Directory objects, GPOs, and so forth. Changing permissions with a script typically involves many lines of code to dissect the current permissions, add new ones, reassemble the permission list, and apply the new permissions to the object. The GPMC developers did a great service to administrators by simplifying the chore of assigning permissions to GPOs. I won't say that GPMC makes scripting permissions fun … no, I won't ever say that … but GPMC does make it possible to script changes to GPO permissions without wanting to gnaw your arm off just to escape from the computer terminal.

   The script in this section is called List_GPO_Permissions.vbs.

Before diving into an example script, here's a quick review of the cast of characters that control access to GPOs (and any other security object in Windows).

First, each GPO has a *security descriptor*, a data structure that holds the permission information. Security descriptors are like onions. You peel back one data structure only to find another lurking inside. This can make them an ogre to work with. The security descriptor contains a *Discretionary Access Control List* (DACL). A DACL contains a set of *Access Control Entries* (ACEs), each of which contains the *Security ID* (SID) of a trustee (user, group, or computer) and an *access mask* that defines what the trustee can do.

With all this in mind, writing a GPO permission script involves creating an object that gives you access to the DACL in the security descriptor, creating a collection of objects that represent ACEs in the DACL, creating an object that represents the trustee in each ACE, and then enumerating the properties of all those objects.

First, as always, start the script with object initialization chores.

```
Set gpm = CreateObject("gpmgmt.gpm")
Set gpmConstants = gpm.GetConstants
Set RootDSE = GetObject("LDAP://RootDSE")
adsiDomain = RootDSE.Get("DefaultNamingContext")
dnsDomain = ConvertToDNS(adsiDomain)
set gpmDomain = gpm.GetDomain(dnsDomain,"",gpmConstants.UsePDC)
```

Now use the `SearchGPOs` method to find the GPO whose security you want to change. The script uses a GPO called "General Desktop Settings." If you want to make the script more flexible, create a collection of all GPOs and select from the collection. Use caution when hardcoding display names. If you type the name wrong, you'll get an "Invalid Procedure Call or Argument" error.

```
set gpmSearchCriteria = gpm.CreateSearchCriteria()
gpmSearchCriteria.Add gpmConstants.SearchPropertyGPODisplayName,
    gpmConstants.SearchOPcontains, "General Desktop Settings"
Set gpmGPO_List = gpmDomain.SearchGPOs(gpmSearchCriteria)
set gpmGPO = gpmDomain.GetGPO(gpmGPO_List.item(1).ID)
WScript.Echo "Here's information about the selected GPO:"
WScript.Echo String(30,"=")
WScript.Echo "GPO Friendly Name: " & gpmGPO.DisplayName
WScript.Echo "Domain: " & gpmGPO.DomainName
WScript.Echo "GPO GUID: " & gpmGPO.ID
WScript.Echo "Modification Timestamp: " & gpmGPO.ModificationTime
WScript.Echo vbNL
```

The script now creates a GPMSecurityInfo collection that contains the ACEs from the DACL of the GPO security descriptor. GPMC represents an ACE with an object called GPMPermission, which bundles the normally abstruse contents of an ACE into an easy-to-use package. The Count method of GPMSecurityInfo lists the number of GPMPermission objects in the collection.

```
Set gpmSecurityInfo = gpmGPO.GetSecurityInfo()
WScript.Echo "The GPO has " & gpmSecurityInfo.Count & _
                " entries in the DACL of its security descriptor."
```

The next line tells the script to proceed even if a particular line fails to execute correctly.

```
On Error Resume Next
```

This entry is necessary because some of the trustees on the permission list do not have domain-based SIDs and therefore do not have a TrusteeDSPath attribute. Use caution with On Error Resume Next. It can mask other problems in your code.

The script now walks through the collection listing the trustee information. GPMC represents a trustee with an object called GPMTrustee. The script uses a function called ConvertTrusteeType to convert a bare integer into a friendly name that describes the trustee type (such as User, Group, Domain Local Group, and so forth.) The conversion information comes from the Platform SDK. The code for the function is listed at the end this section.

```
For i=1 To gpmSecurityInfo.Count
WScript.Echo vbCrLf & String(40,"=")
set gpmPermission = gpmSecurityInfo.item(i)

'Show the trustee information in the GPMPermission object
With gpmPermission.trustee
    WScript.Echo "Trustee Name: " & .trusteeName
    WScript.Echo "Trustee Type: " & ConvertTrusteeType(.trusteeType)
    WScript.Echo "Trustee Domain: " & .trusteeDomain
    WScript.Echo "Trustee DS Path: " & .trusteeDSPath
    WScript.Echo "Trustee SID: " & .trusteeSid
End With
```

The script now displays the remaining permission information such as the access type granted by the access mask, a flag indicating whether the permission denies rather than grants access, whether the permission has been inherited, and whether the permission can itself be inherited. The ConvertAccessSetting function takes the integer stored in the GPMPermission object and converts it to a friendly name that describes the access permission. The code for this function is listed at the end of this section.

```
With gpmPermission
  WScript.Echo "Access Setting: " & ConvertAccessSetting(.permission)
  WScript.Echo "Denied? " & .denied
  WScript.Echo "Inheritable? " & .inheritable
  WScript.Echo "Inherited? " & .inherited
```

```
End With

Next

WScript.Echo vbCrLf & "Completed processing the security entries for " &_
    gpmGPO.DisplayName & "."
```

Here's the code for the ConvertTrusteeType and ConvertAccessSetting functions. Fortunately (and thankfully), the GPMC developers rolled up the various bits in a standard ACE mask into logical settings that are much easier to visualize and apply. Without these logical settings, the script would need to check each bit in the 32-bit access mask and convert the bit to a corresponding access type, a much more daunting task.

```
Function ConvertTrusteeType(trusteeValue)
Select Case trusteeValue
    Case 1
        rs = "User"
    Case 2
        rs = "Group"
    Case 3
        rs = "Domain"
    Case 4
        rs = "Domain Local Group"
    Case 5
        rs = "Well Known Group"
    Case 6
        rs = "Deleted Account"
    Case 7
        rs = "Invalid"
    Case 8
        rs = "Unknown"
    Case 9
        rs = "Computer"
End Select
ConvertTrusteeType = rs
End Function

Function ConvertAccessSetting(PermValue)
Select Case PermValue
    Case gpmConstants.PermGPOApply
        rs = "Apply"
```

```
    Case gpmConstants.PermGPOCustom
        rs = "Custom"
    Case gpmConstants.PermGPOEdit
        rs = "Edit"
    Case gpmConstants.PermGPOEditSecurityandDelete
        rs = "Edit and Delete"
    Case gpmConstants.PermGPORead
        rs = "Read"
End Select
ConvertAccessSetting = rs
End Function
```

Here's a sample listing for one permission entry in a selected GPO:

```
==============================
GPO Friendly Name: General Desktop Settings
Domain: company.com
GPO GUID: {390C2741-ABCD-43BB-8EDA-88CED9371EA4}
Modification Timestamp: 12/12/2003 8:39:34 AM


The GPO has 5 security entries on the ACL.


===========================================
Trustee Name: Authenticated Users
Trustee Type: Well Known Group
Trustee Domain: NT AUTHORITY
Trustee SID: S-1-5-11
ACE Mask: Apply
Denied? False
Inheritable? True
Inherited? False
```

Once you get the hang of viewing the permissions assigned to a GPO, you can create a script to change those permissions. In the GPMC, this is called Delegation. In Chapter 2, you saw how to remove the Authenticated Users group from the permission list of a GPO and then add just selected groups to which you want the GPO to apply.

The example script takes a group called Sales in a domain called Company.com and puts it on the permission list for a GPO called General Desktop Settings with the Read and Apply permissions set. The end result? Only users in an OU linked to General Desktop Settings who are also members of the Sales group get the settings in a GPO (assuming that you have already removed the Authenticated Users group from the permission list).

To use this script in your test environment, be sure to replace the *newGroup* variable with the name of your domain and a group from that domain.

```
'Identify the group to add - use domain syntax
newGroup = "company\Sales"

'Do initial housekeeping chores
Set gpm = CreateObject("gpmgmt.gpm")
Set gpmConstants = gpm.GetConstants
Set RootDSE = GetObject("LDAP://RootDSE")
adsiDomain = RootDSE.Get("DefaultNamingContext")
dnsDomain = ConvertToDNS(adsiDomain)
set gpmDomain = gpm.GetDomain(dnsDomain,"",gpmConstants.UsePDC)

'Select a GPO by name
set gpmSearchCriteria = gpm.CreateSearchCriteria()
gpmSearchCriteria.Add gpmConstants.SearchPropertyGPODisplayName, _
                      gpmConstants.SearchOPcontains, "General Desktop Settings"
Set gpmGPO_List = gpmDomain.SearchGPOs(gpmSearchCriteria)
set gpmGPO = gpmDomain.GetGPO(gpmGPO_List.item(1).ID)
```

The next lines obtain a copy of the GPO's permission list using the same technique used previously.

```
Set gpmSecurityInfo = gpmGPO.GetSecurityInfo()
WScript.Echo "You've selected the " & gpmGPO.DisplayName & " GPO for " & _
             "security permission modification. This GPO currently has " & _
             gpmSecurityInfo.Count & " security entries in its DACL."
```

It's now time to create a new GPMPermission object that specifies the Sales group as a trustee. To do this, use the `CreatePermission` method of the GPM object, which takes the domain name of an Active Directory user of group as a parameter, along with a constant indicating the type of permission to assign as a TRUE parameter to flag the permission as inheritable.

You can assign a variety of permissions. The example shows the Apply GPO permission. Additional options include Read, Edit, Create, and so on. The inheritance flag is only a formality because GPO permissions do not have child objects. The `ConvertTrusteeType` function is documented in the previous section.

```
Set gpmNewPermission = gpm.CreatePermission(newGroup,_
    gpmConstants.PermGPOApply, TRUE )

WScript.echo "Here is general information about the new permission entry:"
```

```
With gpmNewPermission.trustee
    WScript.Echo vbTab & "Trustee Name: " & .trusteeName
    WScript.Echo vbTab & "Trustee Type: " & ConvertTrusteeType(.trusteeType)
    WScript.Echo vbTab & "Trustee Domain: " & .trusteeDomain
    WScript.Echo vbTab & "Trustee DS Path: " & .trusteeDSPath
    WScript.Echo vbTab & "Trustee SID: " & .trusteeSid
End With
```

The next lines add the new permission to the set of existing GPO permissions and overwrite the current security descriptor with the result.

```
gpmSecurityInfo.Add(gpmNewPermission)
gpmGPO.SetSecurityInfo(gpmSecurityInfo)


WScript.Echo vbCrLf & "Completed processing. The GPO now has " & _
            gpmSecurityInfo.Count & " security entries in its DACL."
```

Here's a copy of a sample script output:

```
Here's general information about the selected GPO:
==============================
GPO Friendly Name: General Desktop Settings
Domain: company.com
GPO GUID: {390C2741-ABCD-43BB-8EDA-88CED9371EA4}
Modification Timestamp: 12/12/2003 8:39:34 AM


The GPO currently has 5 security entries in the ACL.


Adding a group called company\Sales to the permission list with Read and Apply
    settings...
Here is general information about the new permission entry:
    Trustee Name: Sales
    Trustee Type: Group
    Trustee Domain: COMPANY
    Trustee DS Path: CN=Sales,OU=Groups,OU=Phoenix,DC=company,DC=com
  Trustee SID: S-1-5-21-2705897113-3534554689-3977090560-2139


Completed processing. The GPO now has 6 security entries on the ACL.
```

You can use the GPMC to verify that the group now appears in the Delegation list for the GPO with the correct permissions.

Forcing a Group Policy Object Refresh

In some situations, you might want change a GPO and apply it immediately to a group of users and machines rather than waiting for background refresh to kick in and request the latest updates. Group Policy does not have a "push" feature because, as you learned in Chapter 3, the client systems are responsible for requesting and then downloading new updates from Active Directory. If you want a client to refresh Group Policy right away, you ordinarily need to trot out to a client computer and run GPUpdate (Windows XP or Windows Server 2003) or Secedit /refreshpolicy (Windows 2000). Using remote scripting, you can instruct a member computer to forcefully perform both user and computer background refresh of GPOs using GPUpdate or SECEDIT—without visiting the machine.

Remote scripting uses two scripts. One script runs on a management workstation and acts to send a second script out to a target machine for execution. You'll need WSH 5.6 or later on both the remote machine and the machine where you run the script.

Windows XP and Server 2003 come with WSH 5.6. For Windows 2000, download WSH 5.6 from www.microsoft.com/scripting.

Mark Russinovich and Bryce Cogswell have a tool on their www.sysinternals.com website called Psexec that can also execute a command on a remote machine. This utility exposes your password in clear text on the wire, though, whereas remote scripting uses NTLMv2 authentication.

Enabling Remote Scripting

Remote scripting is disabled by default. Enabling it involves performing two operations at both the management workstation where you launch the script and at each target machine where you want the remote script to execute. The best news is that this procedure is fairly safe because only users with administrator rights are allowed to execute scripts remotely.

You need to tell the script engine that it can use remote scripting. Do this by running the following command:

```
wscript -regserver
```

You also need to make the following Registry entry:

```
Key: HKLM | Software | Microsoft | Windows Script Host | Settings
Value: Remote
Data: 1 (Reg_SZ)
```

The Reg_SZ in the last line is not a typo. The value really is Reg_SZ, not Reg_DWORD.

If the thought of visiting the consoles of thousands of machines to do these two chores doesn't appeal to you, you can automate the process. You can include the wscript -regserver command in a logon script. Registration does not require admin permissions.

You can distribute the Registry update in the same logon script, or you can use the REG command to make the change from a central location. The syntax is as follows:

```
reg add "\\<computer_name>\HKLM\Software\Microsoft\Windows Script➡
   Host\Settings" /v Remote /t REG_SZ /d 1
```

Scripting the Forced Background Refresh

To test to see if you can forcefully refresh a client, either create a new GPO or put a new setting in an existing GPO. Then build two scripts, one to run at a remote desktop and one that sends the script to the remote desktop. The script that runs on the remote desktop needs to run only GPUpdateor SECEDIT, depending on the operating system. You can use WMI to target the script delivery, but since the machine will ignore a command that it doesn't support, you can put both versions into the same script.

```
'script name: refresh_group_policies.vbs
Set shell = CreateObject("WScript.Shell")
cmdline = "gpupdate /force"
shell.Run(cmdline)
cmdline = "secedit /refreshpolicy /machine_policy /enforce"
shell.Run(cmdline)
cmdline = "secedit /refreshpolicy /user_policy /enforce"
shell.Run(cmdline)
```

Save this script to a folder on your management workstation. In the example, I'll use a folder called C:\RemoteScripts.

The next script is a bit more complicated. It first creates an instance of the WSHController object, the object that manages remote scripting. The script then uses the CreateScript method of WSHController to package the client script and executes the script at the remote client using the Execute method. The script then checks the status of the remote script every 100 ticks until the script finishes running. In the sample listing, the target machine is a desktop named XPPro1.

```
'script name: force_gp_refresh.vbs
Set controllerobj = CreateObject("WSHController")
Set processobj = controllerobj.createScript(c:\remotescripts" &_
   "\refresh_group_policies.vbs" , "\\xppro1") processobj.Execute
Do While processobj.Status <> 2
   WScript.Sleep 100
Loop
WScript.Echo "The remote script process has finished."
```

You can verify that the script ran by checking GPResult on the target machine to verify it downloaded the new settings in the test GPO.

Using the Included GPMC Scripts from Microsoft

If you like the functionality and flexibility provided by GPMC scripting but you can't dedicate the time to writing scripts—or you just want more examples to follow when creating your scripts—take a look at the scripts that Microsoft includes when the GPMC is loaded on a client. They're located in `\Program Files\GPMC\Scripts`.

Even if you prefer a roll-your-own approach to building scripts, the Microsoft scripts deserve your study because they demonstrate how to use the many GPMC methods. The Platform SDK does not contain example code on the assumption that you can look at the GPMC scripts for guidance.

With a couple of exceptions, these GPMC scripts have a `.wsf` extension. This indicates that the scripts use the Windows Script File structure, with XML tags that define various features not available in ordinary `.vbs` scripts. For example, the `<script>` tag allows you to define multiple languages in a script, a feature that Microsoft uses to blend external JavaScript functions into a main script that uses VBScript. These JavaScript functions are stored in a library called `Lib_CommonGPMCFunctions.js`. Microsoft's GPMC End User License Agreement (EULA) permits you to freely use the extensive set of functions in `Lib_CommonGPMCFunctions.js` in your own scripts. The library file must be located in the same folder as the `.wsf` file that calls it.

The XML formatting in `.wsf` files makes scripts look complex, but their operation is relatively straightforward. The `<job>` tag defines a discrete section of a script that can be called by the name you define a name in the tag. The GPMC scripts from Microsoft each contain a single job, so they do not need to define a name.

The `<script>` tag declares a language you'll use in the file. You can define multiple languages using multiple `<script>` tags. For example:

```
<job>
<script language="JScript" src="Lib_CommonGPMCFunctions.js"/>
<script language="VBScript">
WScript.Echo "Hello, World, from inside a scripting framework file."
localPath = "c:\documents and settings"
WScript.Echo "Using a function from the Lib_CommonGPMCFunctions library " & _
             "to validate '" & localPath & "'."
If ValidatePath(localPath) Then
    WScript.Echo "The path is valid."
Else
    WScript.Echo "The path is invalid."
End If
</script>
</job>
```

The `<runtime>` tag provides a convenient way to communicate proper command-line arguments and syntax to the user. This is invaluable if you want your colleagues to use your scripts correctly, especially if you use named arguments, a feature of WSH 5.6. The Platform SDK shows how to format text inside a set of `<runtime> </runtime>` tags to describe script usage, or you can copy from the canned GPMC scripts. For example, here's a snippet from the `BackupGPO.wsf` script:

```
<runtime>

<description>
Takes a GPO name or ID and backs up that GPO to the specified file system
    location.
</description>

<unnamed name="GPOName" helpstring="GPO name or ID" type="string"
    required="true" />
<unnamed name="BackupLocation" helpstring="File system location to back up to"
    type="string" required="true" />
<named name="Comment" helpstring="Optional comment for the backup"
    type="string" required="false" />
<named name="Domain" helpstring="DNS name of domain" type="string"
    required="false" />

<example>
Example: BackupGPO.wsf TestGPO c:\GPO-Backups /comment:"Weekly backup"
</example>

</runtime>
```

If you decide to use a blend of code from the canned scripts and your own scripts, strive to maintain a consistent syntax for your variable names. Thankfully, the GPMC scripts do not use Hungarian notation extensively.

Final Thoughts

Even if you are fairly new to scripting, try your hand at building a few simple Group Policy scripts. It won't take long before you start looking for new, more efficient ways to use your skills. Before you know it, you'll have all your Group Policy management chores rolled up into a few custom command-line tools, leaving you time to handle all the rest of your work, like answering user complaints when they don't like the policy settings within the GPOs you've deployed.

When you've written and tested your own script, and it works, be sure to e-mail: jeremym@moskowitz-inc.com. If you like, Jeremy will post your examples on www.gpoanswers.com.

8

Profiles: Local, Roaming, and Mandatory

When a user logs on to any Windows NT, Windows 2000, Windows XP, or Windows 2003 machine, a profile is automatically generated. A *profile* is a collection of settings, specific to a user, that stick with that user throughout the working experience. In this chapter, I'll talk about three types of profiles.

First is the *Local Profile*, which is created whenever a user logs on. Next is the *Roaming Profile*, which enables users to hop from machine to machine—maintaining the same configuration settings at each machine. Along our journey, I'll also discuss some configuration tweaks that you can set using specific policy settings—specifically for Roaming Profiles.

The third type of profile is the *Mandatory Profile*. Like Roaming Profiles, Mandatory Profiles allow the user to jump from machine to machine. But Mandatory Profiles force a user's Desktop and settings to remain exactly the same as they were when the administrator assigned the profile; the user cannot permanently change the settings.

 In general, your users will use Windows 2000 Professional and Windows XP machines in their daily lives. However, the information in this entire chapter is equally valid should you have a user, such as a SQL Server admin, use a Windows 2000 Server or Windows Server 2003 machine as well. However, for the majority of this chapter, we'll assume (and therefore usually only address) when users use Windows 2000 Professional or Windows XP machines for ease of reading.

What Is a User Profile?

As we stated, as soon as a user logs on to a machine, a Local Profile is generated. This profile is two things: a personal slice of the Registry (contained in a file), and a set of folders stored on a hard drive. Together, these components form what we might call the *user experience*—that is, what the Desktop looks like, what style and shape the icons are, what the background wallpaper looks like, and so on.

The *NTUSER.DAT* File

The Registry stores user and computer settings in a file called NTUSER.DAT, which can be loaded and unloaded into the current computer's Registry—taking over the HKEY_CURRENT_USER portion of the Registry when the user logs on.

In Figure 8.1, you can see a portion of HKEY_CURRENT_USER, specifically, the Control Panel ➢ Desktop ➢ Wallpaper setting, which shows c:\WINDOWS\web\wallpaper\Bliss.bmp in the Data column.

FIGURE 8.1 A simple Registry setting shows the entry for the wallpaper.

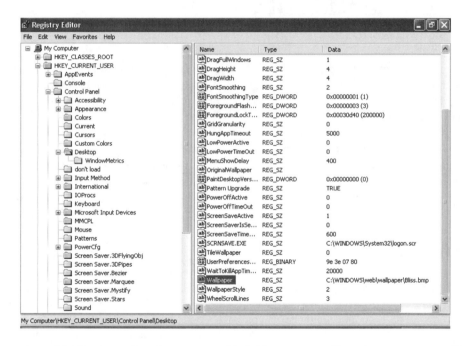

This portion of the Registry directly maps to a file in the user's profile—the NTUSER.DAT file. You'll find that many of a user's individual settings are stored in this file. Here are detailed descriptions for some of the settings inside NTUSER.DAT.

Accessories   Look-and-feel settings for applications such as Calculator, Clock, HyperTerminal, Notepad, and Paint.

Application   Settings for Office applications and most newer applications, such as toolbars.

Control Panel   The bulk of the settings in NTUSER.DAT. Settings found here include those for screen savers, display, sounds, and mouse.

Explorer   Remembers how specific files and folders are to be displayed.

Printer   Network printer and local printer definitions.

Taskbar   Designates the look and feel of the taskbar.

Profile Folders

By default, Windows 2000, Windows 2003, and Windows XP profiles are stored in a folder underneath the C:\Documents and Settings folder. The name is unique for each user name.

Items in the profile folders can be stored in lots of nooks and crannies. As you can see in Figure 8.2, both visible and hidden folders store User Profile settings.

To show hidden files in an Explorer window, choose Tools ➢ Folder Options to open the Folder Options dialog box, and click the View tab. Click the Show Hidden Files and Folders radio button, and then click OK.

Here are the folders and a general description of what each contains:

Application Data   Used by many applications to store specific settings, such as the Office 2000 toolbar settings. Additionally, items such as Word's Custom Dictionary are stored here. MST (Microsoft Transform Files) are stored here by default. MST files modify Windows Installer applications by providing customized application installation and runtime settings. (See Chapter 10 for more information on MST files.)

Cookies   Houses Internet Explorer cookies so that pages on the Internet can remember specific user settings.

Favorites   Houses Internet Explorer Favorites—the list of saved web page links.

Desktop   Contains only files that users store directly on the Desktop. Special icons such as My Network Places, My Computer, and the Recycle Bin are not part of the Desktop profile.

FIGURE 8.2   A look inside Frank Rizzo's profile reveals both visible and hidden folders.

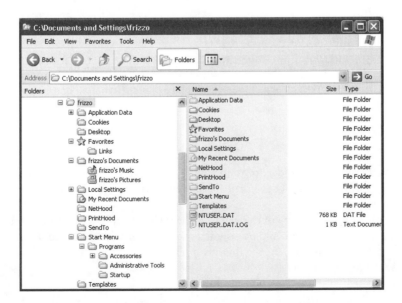

Local Settings Contains application data specific to the user's machine, such as Internet Explorer History, temporary file storage, and other application data. This folder does not roam when Roaming Profiles are set up (see the "Roaming Profiles" section later in this chapter). Like the Application Data folder, this folder is to be used at an application vendor's discretion.

My Documents Now, users of all sophistication levels can leverage this centralized repository for their data files. The My Documents folder has the advantage that it's easily understood by end users, instead of wondering about which file goes in which drive letter path. In fact, the default Office 2000, Office XP, and Office 2003 "Save as" path is to My Documents. This will come in handy, as you'll see in the next chapter. My Documents contains My Pictures, and Windows XP Profiles also contains My Music.

NetHood Contains shortcuts to network drives. Even though the NT 4 Network Neighborhood has been renamed to My Network Places, the NetHood folder is still around and still performs the same functions.

PrintHood Contains shortcuts to network printers; similar to NetHood.

Recent Contains a list of the most recently used application files.

SendTo Contains icons that applications can use to tie in to Explorer to allow file routing between applications.

Start Menu Contains the shortcuts and information that users see when they choose Start ➢ Programs. Each user's Start Menu folder is different. For example, if Joe installs DogFoodMaker 4 and Sally installs CatFoodMaker 8.1, neither will see the other's icons. To see each other's icons, the icons need to live in the All Users ➢ Start Menu folder.

Templates Contains the templates that some applications, such as Excel and Word, use to perform conversions. Like the Application Data folder, this folder is to be used at an application vendor's discretion.

The All Users profile found at the variable location %ALLUSERSPROFILE% typically maps to C:\Documents and Settings\All Users. Applications often add icons to the %ALLUSERSPROFILE%\Start Menu to ensure that all users can run them.

The Default Local User Profile

The Default Local User Profile folder, contains many of the same folders as any user's own Local Profile. Indeed, the Default User Profile is the template that generates all new local User Profiles when a new user logs on.

When a new user logs on, a copy of the Default Local User Profile is copied for that user. As will often happen, the user changes and personalizes settings through the normal course of business. Then, once the user logs off, the settings are preserved in a personal local folder in the C:\Documents and Settings folder.

Changing the Profiles Folder

Older applications sometimes balk at the new Local Profiles location, because they had occasionally hard-coded information to the NT 4 style profile paths. This is probably why Microsoft chose to maintain the original profile location (C:\WINNT\PROFILES) when an NT 4 machine is upgraded to Windows 2000 or Windows XP.

If you come across any applications in your testing that prohibit you from using the new path, you can change the storage point for the Profiles folder. Although the storage point for the Profiles folder cannot be changed once a Windows 2000 (or Windows XP) machine is loaded, you can change it during an unattended setup. For instance, if you want to store the profiles under the old path of C:\WINNT\PROFILES or, say, under the Profiles folder on a large D: partition or hard drive, you can set up your answer file to contain the following:

```
[GUIUnattended]
Profilesdir="D:\PROFILES"
```

This technique works only for freshly installed systems, not for machines being upgraded from NT 4. Additionally, use this procedure when preparing servers for Terminal Services. This keeps users' profiles from choking the system partition with thousands of profile files and folders.

     This Default Local User Profile is different from the Default Domain User Profile described later.

As an administrator, you can create your own ready-made standard shortcuts or stuff the folders with your own files. You can also introduce your own NTUSER.DAT Registry settings, such as a standard Desktop for all users who log on to a specific machine. In the following example, you can set up a background picture in the Default Local User Profile. Then, whenever a new user logs on locally to this machine, the background picture is displayed.

To set up your own Registry settings in NTUSER.DAT, follow these steps:

1. Choose Start ➢ Run to open the Run dialog box. In the Open box, type **regedt32.exe** and press Enter to open the Registry Editor.

2. Select HKEY_USERS, as shown in Figure 8.3.

3. Choose File ➢ Load Hive.

4. Browse to the **C:\Documents and Settings\Default User** folder, shown in Figure 8.3.

5. Select NTUSER.DAT.

FIGURE 8.3 Load the NTUSER.DAT file into the Registry.

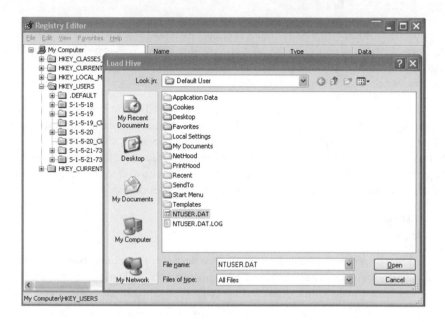

6. When prompted to enter a key name, anything will work, but for our example let's use **this is a dummy key name**, and click OK. Figure 8.4 shows an example. The key name is only temporary, so its name doesn't particularly matter.

FIGURE 8.4 It doesn't matter what the temporary dummy key is called.

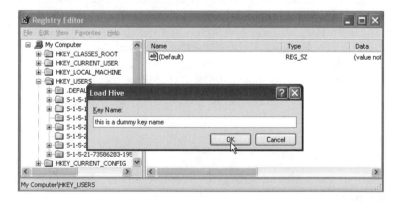

FIGURE 8.5   Enter the full path where the desired wallpaper is stored.

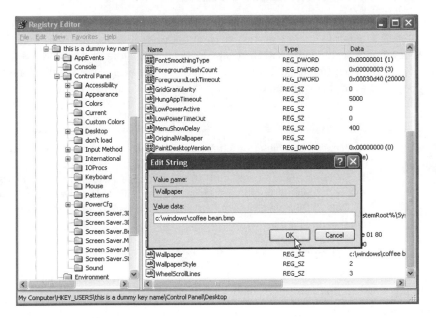

7. Traverse to any Registry key and value. In this case, we'll change all future wallpaper to Coffee Bean.bmp. To do that, traverse to Dummy Key Name ➤ Control Panel ➤ Desktop and double-click "Wallpaper". Enter the value in this example, **C:\windows\coffee bean.jpg**, as shown in Figure 8.5.

If the wallpaper file does not reside on the local system, you must alter the path to point to a server share. If the wallpaper is not present in the folder specified, no wallpaper will show up.

8. After you complete your changes, select your dummy key name, and then unload it by choosing File ➤ Unload Hive, and click OK to save the changes. Again, you must be highlighting your dummy key name to unload the hive.

Every time a new user generates a Local Profile, it pulls the settings from the Default Local Profile, which now has the coffee bean background picture. (Current users do not see the change because they've already generated Local Profiles before the coffee bean picture was set in the default local profile.)

Test your changes by creating a new local user and logging on. Since this user has never logged on before, this should create a new user profile from the default profile. See if the new user gets the coffee bean background.

The Default Domain User Profile

The Default Domain User Profile is similar to the Default Local User Profile, except that it's centralized. Once a Default Domain User Profile is set up, users logging on to workstations in the domain will automatically download the centralized Default Domain User Profile instead of using the any individual Default Local User Profile. This can be a way to make default centralized settings, such as the background or Desktop shortcuts, available for anyone whenever they first log on to a machine.

WARNING   Don't create a Default Domain User Profile using Windows 2000, Windows XP or Windows 2003 and expect your Windows NT clients to understand it. The two profile types are not compatible in this instance. Actually, the Windows NT clients will receive it, but the results can be unpredictable. However, you can create the Default Domain User Profile using Windows 2000 and/or Windows XP and use it upon those systems interchangeably.

It's easy to create a Default Domain User Profile. Follow these steps:

1. Create a new, mere mortal user in the domain. In this example, we'll create Brett Wier. From any workstation in your domain, log on as Brett.

2. Modify the Desktop as you wish. In this example, we'll use the Appearance tab in the Display Properties dialog box to change the color scheme to olive green. All you need to do is right-click upon the desktop and select Properties. Then, select the Appearance tab. Once done, and you're back at the desktop, create a text file, FILE1.txt.

FIGURE 8.6   Select Brett's entry in the User Profiles dialog box.

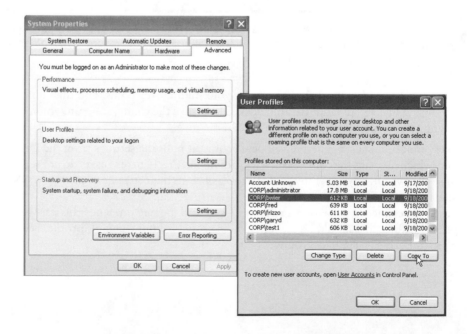

FIGURE 8.7   Copy the profile you just created to the NETLOGON share of a Domain Controller. Then, click Change to allow Everyone to use the profile.

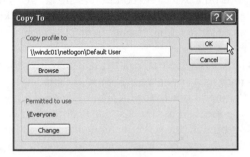

3. Log off as Brett Wier.

4. Log back on to the workstation as the domain Administrator.

5. Click Start, and then right-click My Computer and choose Properties from the shortcut menu to open the System Properties dialog box.

6. Click the Advanced tab, and then click the Settings button in the User Profiles section to open the User Profiles dialog box.

7. Select bwier, as shown in Figure 8.6.

8. Click the Copy To button to open the Copy To dialog box, and in the "Copy profile to" field, enter the full path plus the default user of the NETLOGON share of a Windows 2000 or Windows 2003 Domain Controller, as shown in Figure 8.7. In this example, it's \\windc01\netlogon\Default User. The Default User folder is automatically created.

9. Click the Change button in the Permitted to Use section, and change the default from the original user to Everyone, as shown in Figure 8.7. This lets everyone use the profile in the domain.

10. Click OK to actually copy the profile to the new folder and to close the Copy To dialog box.

11. Click OK to close the System Properties dialog box.

You can test your Default Domain Profile by creating a new user in the domain and logging on to any Windows XP or Windows 2000 machine. Verify that the Default Domain Profile is working by seeing if the olive green color scheme appears and that FILE1.TXT is present on the Desktop. Remember, you'll only see the magic for users who have no Local Profiles already on target machines.

Roaming Profiles

Now that you're familiar with the files and folders that make up Local Profiles, you're ready to implement Roaming Profiles. Roaming Profiles are a logical extension to the Local Profiles concept.

Basically, when users hop from machine to machine, the customized settings they created on one machine are automatically placed on and displayed at any machine they log on to.

For instance, you might have an organization in which 30 computers are at each site for general use by the sales team. If any member of the sales team comes into any office, they know they can log on to any machine and be confident that the settings from their last session are patiently waiting on the server.

Setting up Roaming Profiles for users in Active Directory is a straightforward process: share a folder to house the profiles, and then point each user's profile toward the single shared folder. By default, Roaming Profiles save a copy of the profile to the local hard drive. That way, if the network or server becomes unavailable, the user can use the last-used profile as a cached version. Additionally, if the user's Roaming Profile on the server is unavailable (and there is no locally cached copy of the Roaming Profile), the system downloads and uses the Default User Profile as an emergency measure to get the user logged on with some profile.

As you'll see in the next chapter, another advantage associated with Roaming Profiles is that if a machine crashes, the most recent "set" of the user environment is on the server for quick restoration.

For those of you threw up your hands and gave up using Roaming Profiles in Windows NT, I encourage you to try again with Windows 2000 and Windows XP. The Roaming Profile algorithm is much improved since the NT 4 days. Specifically, most people had problems when a single user logged on to multiple machines at the same time. In NT 4, the profile was preserved only from the last computer the user logged off from—potentially losing important files in the profile. Windows 2000 and Windows XP don't work that way. They do a file-by-file comparison of files *before* they get sent back to the server—sending only the latest time-stamped file to help quell this problem. So, give it another go if you despaired in the past.

However, one warning should be noted. All the user's settings are represented as one single file—NTUSER.DAT. Since the last writer wins, the NTUSER.DAT with the latest time stamp overwrites all others. If you make two independent changes to a setting on two different machines, you can lose one because only the NTUSER.DAT with the latest time stamp "wins."

Setting Up Roaming Profiles

The first thing we need to do on our server, WinDC01, is to create and share a folder in which to store our profiles. In this example, we'll choose a novel name—Profiles. To create and share a folder in which to store Roaming Profiles, follow these steps:

1. Log on to WinDC01 as Administrator.

2. From the Desktop, click My Computer to open the My Computer folder.

3. Find a place to create a users folder. In this example, we'll use D:\PROFILES. After entering the D: drive, right-click and select New ➢ Folder. Name your new folder **Profiles**.

You can substitute any name for Profiles. Additionally, you can hide the share name by placing a $ after the name, such as Profiles$.

4. Right-click the newly created Profiles folder, and choose "Sharing and Security" from the shortcut menu to open Profiles Properties dialog box at the Sharing tab.

5. Click "Share this folder." Windows 2000 and Windows XP client computers require that the permissions on the share are set to "Full Control." The defaults on Windows 2003 servers are for Everyone to have Read rights, which isn't sufficient. Use the Permissions button to change the rights so that Authenticated Users have at least Change rights as shown in Figure 8.8.

FIGURE 8.8   Change the permissions on the Profiles share so that Authenticated Users have Change control.

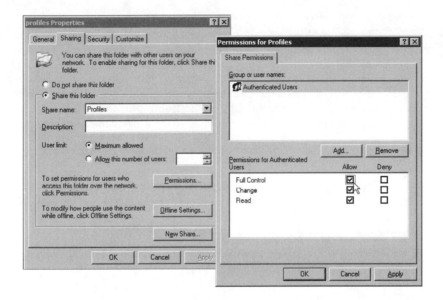

 WARNING   Do not attempt to use the Offline Settings button (shown in Figure 8.8) in conjunction with Roaming Profiles. In Windows 2000 servers, the Offline Settings button is seen as "Caching." Roaming Profiles are automatically cached with their own independent algorithm. Therefore, leave the default settings as they are. Although the Offline Settings button is, in fact, useful, it's largely incompatible with Roaming Profiles. For more information on this phenomenon, see the Knowledge Base article "Offline File Caching Option Must Be Disabled on Roaming Profile" (Q287566). (For more on the Caching button, see Chapter 9.) Additionally, do not use the Encrypting File System (EFS) on shares containing Roaming Profiles. If you do so, roaming will not work.

Now you need to specify which network user accounts can use Roaming Profiles. In this example, you'll specify Brett Wier. Brett will now be able to hop from workstation to workstation. When he logs off one workstation, the changes in the profile will be preserved on the server. He can then log on to any other workstation in the domain and maintain the same user experience.

To modify accounts to use Roaming Profiles, you'll leverage Active Directory Users and Computers as follows:

1. Choose Start ➢ Programs ➢ Administrative Tools ➢ Active Directory Users and Computers.

2. Expand Corp.com in the tree pane, and double-click Brett Wier's account to open the Brett Wier Properties dialog box; click his Profile tab.

3. In the Profile Path field, specify the server, the share name, and folder you want to use, such as **\\WinDC01\profiles\%username%**, as shown in Figure 8.9. For our purposes, you can leave all other fields blank.

> The syntax of *%username%* is the secret sauce that allows the system to automatically create a Roaming Profiles folder underneath the share. The *%username%* variable is evaluated at first use, and Windows springs into action and creates the profile. Windows is smart too—it sets up the permissions on the folder with only the required NTFS permissions, such that only the user has access to read and modify the contents of the profile. If you want administrators to have access along with the user, see the information in the "Add the Administrators Security Group to Roaming User Profiles" section later in this chapter.

4. Click OK.

FIGURE 8.9   Point the user's profile path settings at the server and share name.

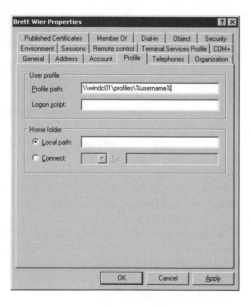

Modifying Multiple Users' Profile Paths

After you set up Roaming Profiles and get comfortable with their use, you'll likely want the rest of your users to start using Roaming Profiles as well. The Windows 2003 Active Directory Users and Computers tool allows you to modify the profile paths of multiple users simultaneously. To do so, follow these steps:

1. Select the users (hold down Ctrl to select discontiguous users).

2. Right-click the selection, and choose Properties from the shortcut menu to open the "Properties on Multiple Objects" dialog box:

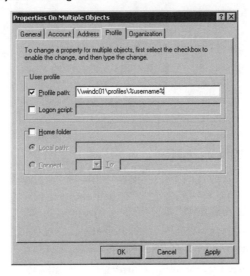

3. Click the Profile tab, if necessary.

4. Click the Profile Path check box, and enter the path.

5. Click OK to give all the selected users the same path.

If you're running Windows 2000 (or just want to put on your coding hat), you can use the following sample VBScript code to run though all the users in the domain Corp.com in the Phoenix OU and change their profile path so that they have access only to their own profile folder. Upon first use by the user, the folder is automatically created, and the user is granted exclusive access to that folder.

```
Set UserContainer = getobject("LDAP://ou=Phoenix,dc=Corp,dc=com")
UserContainer.filter = array("User")

for each User in UserContainer
```

```
    Username = User.SamAccountName
    Userprofilepath = "\\Profile_server\Profiles\" & Username


    Wscript.Echo User.ProfilePath


    If User.ProfilePath = "" Then
          User.Put "ProfilePath" , UserProfilePath
          User.Setinfo
          Wscript.Echo "Profile for user " & Username & " has been set to " &
UserProfilePath & "."
     Else
          Wscript.Echo "Profile for user " & Username & " was already set to " &
UserProfilePath & "."
     End if

next
```

Testing Roaming Profiles

You can easily test Roaming Profiles if you have multiple workstation machines. Make sure Roaming Profiles are working by logging on to the domain as Brett Wier from a workstation that's a member in your domain.

Make two simple changes to the profile for testing:

1. In the My Documents folder, create FILE1.TXT, and save some dummy data inside.

2. Change the color scheme to something different—like silver.

3. Log off as Brett Wier.

4. Log on to another workstation as Brett Wier, and make sure that FILE1.TXT was properly sent to the second machine and that the background has changed.

Right-click the FILE1.TXT, and choose Properties from the shortcut menu to see the file's properties. Take note of the path where the file is actually residing. You can compare that file's location now (the local hard drive) with the file's location after the next chapter is completed. Hopefully, by the time the next chapter is completed, the file will be magically transported to the server, and the display will demonstrate this.

Back on the server, log on as Administrator and take a look inside Brett's folder. If you try, however, you'll be denied as witnessed in Figure 8.10.

FIGURE 8.10   Administrators cannot poke around user profiles (by default).

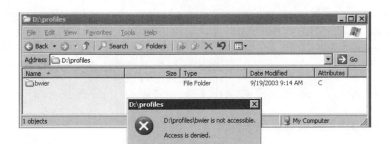

Even if you're an administrator, you cannot dive in to Brett's folder. This is a safety mechanism that gives Brett exclusive permissions over his own sensitive stuff. If you want administrators to have access along with the user, see the information in the "Add the Administrators Security Group to Roaming User Profiles" later in this chapter.

The Impact of Users Latching On to My Documents

Because My Documents is part of the profile, there is the extra burden of lugging all the files in My Documents back and forth across the network each time a user logs on. This can have serious ramifications. Once users start using the My Documents folder, they generally don't want to stop. They place 10MB worth of PowerPoint files, 30MB of Word documents, and 20MB of Visio files in My Documents, and then roam to another workstation, and they've just moved 60MB of data across the network at logon time! Ouch!

Fortunately, this pain can is mitigated in two ways. Windows 2000, Windows XP, and Windows 2003 handle roaming profiles differently than their Windows NT cousin does.

Let's imagine that we have two users: one on Windows NT and another on Windows 2000, Windows XP, or Windows 2003. Each user puts 300MB of files into the Roaming Profile. When a user on Windows NT does this, all files in the profile are copied up to the server—lock, stock, and barrel—up to the server and then back over to the target workstation every time a user logs on or off. Can you say "Painful?"

Windows 2000, Windows XP, and Windows 2003 transfer *only* changed files up and back between the client and server. Thus, if a user transfers 60MB of data and then changes one file, only that file is sent back to be saved in the Roaming Profile. This feature is great news if a user uses the same machine day in and day out; only the changes are pushed up and back. But the usefulness of this feature breaks down any time a user roams to a computer they have never used before. In this case, the entire contents of the Roaming Profile (including My Documents) is brought down from the server.

That's why the real power comes with an IntelliMirror feature, Redirected Folders, which we'll explore in the next chapter.

Migrating Local Profiles to Roaming Profiles

In some situations, you might already have lots of machines with Local Profiles. That is, you didn't start off your network using Roaming Profiles, and now you have either many machines with Local Profiles or just pockets of machines with a combination of Roaming Profiles and Local Profiles. You can, if you want, maintain the user's Local Profile settings and transfer them to the spot on the server you set up earlier. You can convert a Local Profile to a Roaming Profile in two ways. Whichever option you choose, you first need to set up a share on a server.

Automatic Upload of Existing Local Profiles

In general, this step couldn't be easier. As we did earlier, on each user's Profile tab, point the profile path to \\servername\share\%username% as seen in Figure 8.9. The next time the user logs on to a machine with a Local Profile (and then logs off), the Local Profile is automatically uploaded to the server to become their future Roaming Profile. For most users, this is the way to go.

Manual Upload of Existing Local Profiles

If the user has logged on to multiple workstations and therefore has multiple Local Profiles, you might want to guarantee that one specific Local Profile becomes the Roaming Profile for that user. The procedure is nearly identical to the one you used to create the Default Domain User Profile. To preserve a specific Local Profile and convert it to a Roaming Profile, follow these steps:

1. Log on as the Administrator to the workstation where the desired Local Profile resides.

2. Choose Start, right-click My Computer, and choose Properties from the shortcut menu to open the System Properties dialog box. Click the Advanced tab, and then in the User Profiles section, click Settings to open the "User Profiles" dialog box.

3. Select the Local Profile you want to convert to a Roaming Profile, and then click the Copy To button to open the Copy To dialog box, as shown in Figure 8.11.

4. Enter the server name, shared folder name, and folder name of the profile storage path, as shown in Figure 8.11.

5. Also, be sure to change the profile so that at least the user has access. It's generally okay to modify the profile permissions to Everyone. Click OK. The jkissel folder is automatically created in the shared folder.

FIGURE 8.11 To move a specific profile to the server, use the Copy To dialog box.

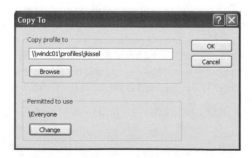

Changing the Profile Type from Roaming to Local

Mere mortal users (those without administrative privileges) can go to the User Profiles dialog (as seen on Figure 8.6), choose their own profile, then change the profile type with the "Change Type" button. This will change their profile from Roaming to Local or back again and thus specify which copy of the profile (local or Roaming) is to be used when they log on.

If a user selects Local Profile, a Roaming Profile revert to a Local Profile. The Roaming Profile on the server stays there, but the user doesn't use it when working at this local machine. The next time the user works at this specific workstation, the changes are only saved to the local profile.

If the user selects Roaming Profile, and the Roaming Profile is on the server, the system determines which copy is newer. If the local copy is newer, the user is asked whether to keep or ditch the profile on the server.

Also, don't forget that for each specific user Local Profile that you manually convert to a Roaming Profile, you'll need to modify the profile path (similar that seen in Figure 8.9 earlier). Once you've done this, this user, Jimmy Kissel can now log on to any Windows 2000 or Windows XP machine as jkissel, and this specific profile (that you just pushed up) will follow him as a Roaming Profile.

Roaming and Nonroaming Folders

Now that you have a grip on which folders constitute the profile and how to set up a Roaming Profile, it might be helpful to know a bit about what's going on behind the scenes. Remember that several folders make up our profile.

Local settings, including local machine-specific application folders and information, do not roam when Roaming Profiles are enabled. This is true for the following elements:

- Local computer Application Data. Some applications write information specific to the local computer here. This folder is located in `\Documents and Settings\{Username}\Local Settings\Application Data`. Any subfolder below this folder also do not roam, including:
  - History
  - Temp
  - Temporary Internet Files

All others do roam with the user:

- Application Data. This folder is located in `Documents and Settings\{Username}\Application Data`. This is typically a per-user store for application data, such as Office 2000/Windows XP/2003 Custom Dictionary.
- Cookies
- Desktop

- Favorites
- My Documents
- My Pictures
- NetHood
- PrintHood
- Recent
- Send To
- Start Menu
- Templates

Indeed, My Documents, My Pictures, Desktop, Start Menu, and Application Data have an additional property; they can each be redirected to a specific point on the server, as you'll see in the next chapter.

Windows XP and Windows 2003 Profile Changes

Everything stated until this point is valid for Windows 2000, Windows XP, and Windows 2003. However, both Windows XP and Windows 2003 contain additional stuff that their Windows 2000 cousins do not. Let's examine that stuff below.

Additional System Profiles

Windows XP and Windows 2003 contain two new profiles that are meant to be used by newly installed services: Local Service and Network Service.

Local Service   Meant to be used by services that are local to the computer but do not need intricate local privileges or network access. This is in contrast to the "System" account, which pretty much has total authority over the system. If a service runs as Local Service, it appears to be a member in the local users group. When a service runs as Local Service across the network, the service appears as an anonymous user.

Network Service   Similar to Local Service, but has elevated network access rights—similar to the System account. When a process runs under Network Service rights, it does so as the SID (Security ID) assigned to the computer.

Windows XP and Windows 2003 automatically create these profiles, which are basically normal but still a little special. For instance, you will not see the Local Service or Network Service in the listing of Profiles in the System Properties dialog box. You can see them in the Documents and Settings folder; however, they're "super-hidden" so that mere mortals cannot see them by default. You can see them in the top window in Figure 8.12.

Windows can also load software, services, and its own profile when the computer starts up. Indeed, you see this profile in the "Log on to Windows" dialog box, in which you are prompted to press Ctl+Alt+Del. Basically, this is the profile for when no one is logged on.

When this happens, Windows loads what is called the .DEFAULT (pronounced "dot default") profile. In Windows 2000, the .DEFAULT profile was in `c:\winnt\%computername%`, in which

%computername% is the name of the computer. But applications sometimes flipped out if services tried to load portions of this part of the profile's Registry. To adjust for this, Windows XP and Windows 2003 plunked the .DEFAULT profile in c:\windows\system32\config\SystemProfile. Applications that leverage the .DEFAULT profile always use this Registry part, and troublesome application problems related to .DEFAULT should be quelled. You can see the SystemProfile in the command prompt window in Figure 8.12.

FIGURE 8.12 You can see the two new "service profiles" in the upper window. You can see the system's own profile in the lower window.

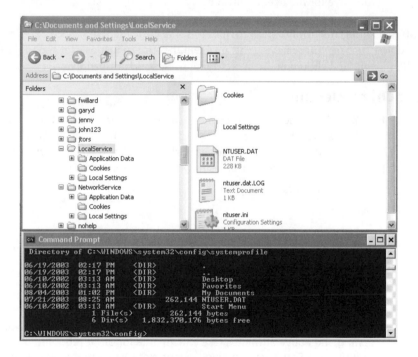

Better Terminal Services Support for Roaming Profiles

When the user logs off a session, the system tries 60 times—about once a second by default—to tidy up the NTUSER.DAT file and send it back to the server to be housed in the Roaming Profile. Usually, it only needs one try (and about one second) to do this task. It might need more tries (and more time) if a process has the Registry locked when a user is trying to log off (and Windows is frantically trying to close every process). However, if you're using Terminal Services, it's quite possible that the Registry is being hammered by multiple users when you're logging off. If this is the case, you might need more than one shot to lock the Registry and tidy up after yourself.

Windows XP and Windows 2003 save the Registry at the end of 60 seconds, correctly tidy up the Roaming Profile, and release any in-use memory the profile has used. Windows 2000 doesn't quite work as well. To that end, if you're using Windows 2000 Terminal Services can increase the number of tries to release the Registry. Use the "Maximum Retries to Unload and Update User Profile" policy setting in the "Affecting Roaming Profiles with Computer Group Policy Settings" section to increase the number of tries.

> The hive for the user does not unload until all the handles to the Registry are closed (or until a reboot). If the user logs on to the machine again, any newer NTUSER.DAT settings from the server don't roam to that machine (since the current hive for the user is still in use.

Microsoft has an internal tool that it provides to some customers that need extra assistance in this area. If you suspect you're having this problem, be sure to just ask for the tool by name. It's called UPHClean, and should assist in rectifying these kinds of problems.

Fast Boot On by Default

I talked about "Fast Boot" and the pitfalls therein in Chapter 3. But, as a brief refresher, out of the box, Windows XP tries to make startup and logon times as fast as possible. Indeed, it doesn't even wait for the users to really be logged on the network before letting them start to use the system! The upshot is that certain profile attributes may take two logons to process:

- Roaming Profile path changes
- The home folder
- Old-style logon scripts

Again, if any of these properties is changed in Active Directory, users of Windows XP machines might have to log on twice for these changes to take effect. For information about how to revert Windows XP Professional to the Windows 2000 "synchronous" behavior, see Chapter 3.

> As I stated in Chapter 3, I have not been able to observe this behavior. In my testing, the above attributes take exactly one logoff or reboot to process—regardless if Fast Boot is enabled or not. Yet Microsoft maintains that under certain circumstances (with Fast Boot enabled), the above will hold true. So, if the user is using Windows XP, and any of these properties is changed in Active Directory, it *could* take two logons for these changes to actually take affect.

Merging Local Profile and Roaming Profile

Once a Roaming Profile is established, users can hop from machine to machine confident that they'll get the same settings. However, if a user with a Roaming Profile hops to a Windows XP machine on which they once had a Local Profile, something special happens: the previous Local Profile and the existing Roaming Profile are merged (except for the NTUSER.DAT settings.) This data is then saved to the Roaming Profile folder on the server at logoff time.

This is helpful should a user have just the one copy of a critical document stored in the My Documents folder of XPPRO2. The next time he logs on to XPPRO2, that missing document will now appear in his My Documents in his Roaming Profile. Oh, and you don't have to worry about overwriting existing files in the profile either; the latest time-stamped file is preserved.

You can prevent this behavior on Windows XP machines. For information on how to do this, see the "Prevent Roaming Profile Changes from Propagating to the Server" section later in this chapter.

Guest Account Profile

Who uses the Guest account anymore? Apparently someone, because Microsoft has slightly changed the behavior of the Guest account in Windows XP and Windows Server 2003, which act like Windows 2000 and Windows NT and delete the profile of guest users—but only when the computer is joined to a domain. If the Windows XP or Windows 2003 machine is in a workgroup, all guest profiles (of users in the Guests group) are not deleted at logoff.

If the Windows XP or Windows 2003 computer is in a domain, and a user is a member of both the Guests and the Local Administrators group, the profile is not deleted—quite an unlikely scenario.

Cross-Forest Trusts

Roaming Profiles, like GPOs, are affected by Cross-Forest Trusts. Whether a user gets a Roaming Profile depends on the client operating system they're logged on to. (This operating-specific variance is documented in Chapter 3.) When clients log on to computers that enforce the rule, you'll get the message shown in Figure 8.13.

FIGURE 8.13   Users roaming within Cross-Forest scenarios receive this message.

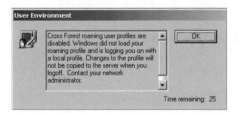

You can use a policy setting to prevent this from affecting your client computers. To do this, locate the **Allow Cross-Forest User Policy and Roaming User Profiles** policy setting by drilling down in Computer ➢ Administrative Templates ➢ System ➢ Group Policy.

Affecting Roaming Profiles with Computer Group Policy Settings

Roaming Profiles are simple to set up and maintain, but sometimes you'll want to use certain policy settings to affect their behavior. The policies you'll be setting appear in the Computer

Configuration section of Group Policy. Drill down into Administrative Templates ➢ System ➢ User Profiles, as shown in Figure 8.14. In Windows 2000, these User Profiles policies were not located under their own branch but in Administrative Templates ➢ System ➢ Logon.

Recall from Chapter 1 that computers must be in the OU that the GPO affects (or in a child OU that inherits the setting).

> You might also need to reboot the machine once you move the computer into an affected OU for your wishes to take immediate effect.

Before implementing any policy setting that affects Roaming Profiles, read through this section and determine if it adds value to your environment. Then, create a test OU and ensure that the behavior is as expected.

Do Not Check for User Ownership of Roaming Profile Folders

Windows XP without a service pack and Windows 2000 with SP3 and earlier may have a potential security hole. If someone, such as a person in the Server Operators group, can pre-create the user's target profile subfolder on the server, that creator is also the owner of the subfolder. When the user then pushes up their profile to the subfolder, the user isn't the only one with access to the profile; the creator/owner also has access. This could mean that the creator/owner can peer inside and get stuff they really shouldn't have.

FIGURE 8.14   There are many policy settings that affect profiles.

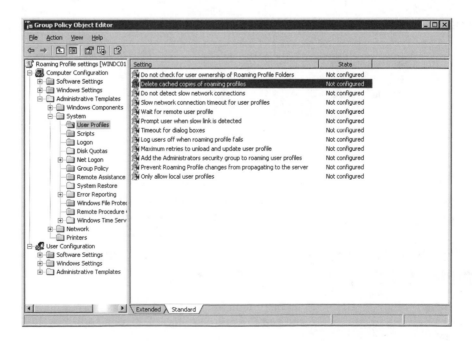

If a client logs on to a Windows 2003, Windows XP/SP1, or Windows 2000/SP4 computer, the machine is smart enough to first check to see if the user is the only one with permissions on the folder (as seen earlier in Figure 8.10) before moving sensitive profile data up. If you enable this policy setting, you're telling newer machines to act like older machines and allow sensitive profile information to move up to the server, even if the user doesn't have exclusive access and ownership to the subfolder. Personally, I would leave this unconfigured. (You can read more about this in the Knowledge Base article KB 327259.)

This policy setting applies only to Windows 2003 computers, Windows XP/SP1 computers, and Windows 2000/SP4 computers.

Delete Cached Copies of Roaming Profiles

This is a space-saving and security mechanism that automatically deletes the user's locally cached profile when the user logs off. The default behavior is to allow these to be copied and pile up on each hard drive to which the user roams. You can enable this policy setting to do as the forest rangers say: "Leave only footprints and only take away memories at your campsite." Heck, you won't even be leaving any footprints.

This policy setting has one downside, however; let's walk though a scenario to examine this potential problem. This policy setting is set to delete cached copies of Roaming Profiles. The user logs on, makes some changes, and logs off. The profile is automatically sent back to the server, and the footprints are washed away on the local machine.

Now, let's say that the server that houses the Roaming Profiles goes down. By default, if the user tries to log on and the server is unavailable to deliver the Roaming Profile, the locally cached copy of the profile is summoned to take its place. Once you enable this policy setting, you're severing a potential lifeline to the user if the server that houses the Roaming Profile become unavailable. Enabling this policy setting sweeps up after the user on the local machine at logoff. If the server goes down, the user will not get their locally cached version of the Roaming Profile because there is no locally cached version of the profile. Rather, the only profile the user will get is a temporary Local Profile that is not saved anywhere when the user logs off.

Conversely, if for some reason the server becomes unavailable to receive the Roaming Profile at logoff time, the default behavior (without the policy setting Enabled) is to maintain a locally cached copy for the user at logoff time. When the server recovers, and the user next logs on to that machine, they will pick up their locally cached version of the profile. At next logoff time, the changes are sent back to the server, and the locally cached version is deleted. If you enable this policy setting, there is no way for the system to maintain the locally cached copy for the user when the server recovers.

Once this policy setting is Enabled, the profile is erased only on logoff. And then it erases only profiles from machines on which users don't already have an existing cached copy! If you need to maintain a high-security environment, be sure to enable this policy setting early so that users don't have time to roam from machine to machine sprinkling copies of their profiles around (which won't get erased later by use of this policy setting).

This policy setting is, however, useful in high-security environments where you need to make sure that no trace of potentially sensitive data in the profile is left behind. Be careful in using it with laptops, however, because frequently users need to use their copy of the locally cached version of the profile to get their work done. Additionally, enabling this policy setting does prevent third-party tools from "resurrecting" deleted files inside the profile. This deletes the files but doesn't obliterate them to prevent industrious hackers from any possible recovery.

> To use this policy setting, you'll need to disable (or not configure) the **Do Not Detect Slow Network Connection** policy setting, as described shortly. If a network connection is determined to be slow, it automatically tries to grab the locally cached copy of the profile—which doesn't exist if you've enabled this **Delete Cached Copies of Roaming Profiles** policy setting.

Slow Network Connection Timeout for User Profiles

Enabling this entry performs a quick ping test to the profiles server. If the speed is greater than the minimum value, the Roaming Profile is downloaded. If, however, the speed is not fast enough, the locally cached profile is used unless you've enabled the previous entry (**Delete Cached Copy of Local Profiles**). In that case, the user ends up with a temporary profile as described earlier.

> Setting the **Do Not Detect Slow Network Connection** policy setting, as described in the next section, forces anything set in this policy setting to be ignored.

This policy setting has two modes, which it uses automatically: IP and non-IP. If the computer housing the profiles is connected to a network using IP, the speed is measured in kilobits (Kb) per second. If the computer housing the profiles is not connected using IP, the speed is measured in milliseconds (ms).

This policy setting is a bit strange: even if it's not configured, it has a default. That default speed threshold for IP mode is 500KB; that is, if the ping test determines that the bandwidth to the machine that houses the profiles is greater than 500KB, the profile is downloaded. If the ping returns a bandwidth of less than 500KB, the Roaming Profile is skipped, and the locally cached profile is used.

That default speed threshold for non-IP mode is 120ms; that is, if a machine that houses the profiles responds in less than 120ms, the profile is downloaded. If the machine that houses the profiles does not respond to the test in 120ms, the profile is skipped, and the locally cached profile is used.

You might want to enable this policy setting and increase the value thresholds if you want to increase the chances of a dial-up connection receiving the Roaming Profile instead of the locally cached profile. If you enable this policy setting, you'll need to manually specify both an IP ping time test and a non-IP ping millisecond test.

Unrelated speed tests can verify the ability to apply GPOs for both the user and computer. They are in the Group Policy Editor under Computer or User Configuration ➢ Administrative Templates ➢ System ➢ Group Policy ➢ **Group Policy Slow Link Detection**.

Do Not Detect Slow Network Connection

Like the previous policy setting, this one is a little strange. If it's not configured, it still has a default; that is, the users affected by this policy setting check the **Slow Network Connection Timeout for User Profiles** setting to see what a "slow network" actually means. If you enable this policy setting, you're disabling slow network detection, and the values you place in the **Slow Network Connection Timeout for User Profiles** policy setting don't mean diddly, nor do the default values of 500KB or 120ms.

Wait for Remote User Profile

Again, even if this policy setting is not defined or disabled, there is still a default; if the speed is too slow, it will load the locally cached profile. If you enable this policy setting, the system waits until the Roaming Profile is downloaded—no matter how long it takes. You might turn this on if your users hop around a lot and the connection to the computer housing the Roaming Profiles is slow but not intolerable. That way, you'll still use the Roaming Profile stored on the server as opposed to the locally cached profile.

Prompt User When Slow Link Is Detected

When the ping test determines that the link speed is too slow, the user can be asked if they want to use the locally cached profile or grab the one from the server. If this policy setting is not configured or it's disabled, the user isn't even asked the question. If the **Wait for Remote User Profile** policy setting is enabled, the profile is downloaded from the server—however slowly. If this policy setting is enabled, the user can determine whether they want to accept the profile from the server or utilize the locally cached profile.

If you've enabled the **Delete Cached Copies of Roaming Profiles** policy setting, there won't be a local copy of the Roaming Profile, so the user will be forced to accept the Default User Profile. If the **Do Not Detect Slow Network Connection Properties** policy setting is enabled, this GPO is ignored.

Timeout for Dialog Boxes

If the **Prompt User When Slow Link Is Detected** policy setting is enabled, the user has a 30-second countdown to respond. Once this policy setting is enabled, the default value of 30 seconds can be changed. This dialog box timeout is also presented when the server that houses the Roaming Profile is unavailable, when the user logs off, or when the locally cached profile is newer than the Roaming Profile stored on the server. In all cases, the user can be prompted to determine what do to. The value you specify here is how many seconds to wait for an answer before the other policy settings make the decision for the user.

Log Users Off When Roaming Profile Fails

This is the harshest sentence you can offer the user if things go wrong. By default, if the server is down (or the profile is corrupted), the user first tries to load a locally cached profile. If there is no locally cached profile, the system creates a TEMP profile from the Default User Profile.

However, if you choose to enable the setting, the behavior changes. If no Roaming Profile or locally cached profile is available (presumably because you've enabled the **Delete Cached Copies of Roaming Profile** policy setting), the user is not permitted to log on.

Maximum Retries to Unload and Update User Profile

As previously discussed, this policy setting is meant to assist Windows 2000 Terminal Services when trying to log users off and release their Roaming Profiles. Increase this value to increase the number of attempts made at unloading the pertinent Registry information and update the profile when users start to complain that things aren't the same when the last logged off (especially on Terminal Services). Setting this upon Windows XP or Windows 2003 machines should not be necessary, as the underlying algorithm is changed on those systems to automatically adjust when necessary.

Add the Administrators Security Group to Roaming User Profiles

As you saw in Figure 8.10 earlier in this chapter, only the user can dive in and poke around their own user profile. However, you can specify that the administrator and the user have joint access to the folder.

Oddly, this policy setting is found under the computer side of the house—not the user. Therefore, it's somewhat difficult to implement this policy setting on a small scale, because it's sometimes a mystery which client machine users will log on to. If you want to use this policy setting, I recommend creating a GPO with this policy setting at the domain level, to guarantee that any client computers that users log on to will be affected. Setting this policy setting such that it affects the file server housing the profiles doesn't do anything for you. It's the target client computers that need to get this policy setting.

This policy setting *only* takes effect when new users first log on to effected client computers. Once they're on, they'll make some changes that affect the profile, and then log off. When they log off, a signal is sent back to the directory housing the profile, which then finalizes the security on the directory so that both the user and the administrator can both plunk around in there.

To be especially clear, as I implied, this policy setting works only for new users—that, is those users who don't already have a Roaming Profile. Users who *already* have established Roaming Profiles are essentially left in the dark with regard to using this; but there is a ray of light. If you want the same effect, you can take ownership of a profile and manually establish administrative access for the administrator and the user, as described in the upcoming section "Mandatory Profiles from an Established Roaming Profile."

This policy setting works with Windows 2000's Service Pack 2 and later, although the policy setting's ExplainText states that it's only applicable to Windows XP and Windows 2003.

Prevent Roaming Profile Changes from Propagating to the Server

As previously discussed, when a user jumps from machine to machine and lands on one with an existing Local Profile, the system merges the Local Profile as a favor to the user. The idea is that if this Local Profile has a data file, say, RESUME.DOC, that's missing in the user's Roaming Profile, this is a perfect time to scoop it up and keep it in the Roaming Profile. You can dictate specific machines for which you don't want this to happen.

In general, you set this policy setting only on computers that you are sure you don't want the merge between Local Profiles and Roaming Profiles—perhaps because the Local Profiles contained many unneeded files.

This policy setting affects only Windows XP and Windows 2003 machines; though the "merge" algorithm is the same for Windows XP, Windows 2003, and Windows 2000 machines. Even so, Windows 2000 machines can not be affected by this policy setting (and hence, will always merge regardless if this policy setting is Enabled or not).

Only Allow Local User Profiles

This policy setting is useful when you have set up specialty machines, such as lab machines, library machines, kiosk machines, and so on. By setting this policy setting on the machines, you can ensure that a user's Roaming Profile doesn't "get in the mix" for what you designed this machine to be.

If trying to figure out all the ins and outs of Roaming Profile policies is giving you a headache, use the handy flowchart in Figure 8.15 to help figure out what each policy setting does and how it will affect your users.

Affecting Roaming Profiles with User Group Policy Settings

As you have just seen, most policy settings regarding Roaming Profiles are associated with the computer itself. Two policy settings, however, affect Roaming Profiles but are located on the user side of the fence: **Limit Profile Size** and **Excluding Directories in Roaming Profile**. These policy settings are found under User Settings ➤ Administrative Templates ➤ System ➤ User Profiles, as shown in Figure 8.16.

Limit Profile Size

This setting limits how big the profile can grow. Remember, now the My Documents folder is part of the profile. If you limit the profile size, the profile can hit that limit awfully quickly.

It is recommended that you avoid using this setting unless you use the techniques described in the next chapter for redirecting folders for the My Documents folder. When that technique is applied, the redirected My Documents folder is no longer part of the profile, and the size can come back down to earth.

FIGURE 8.15   Roaming Profile policy settings flowchart

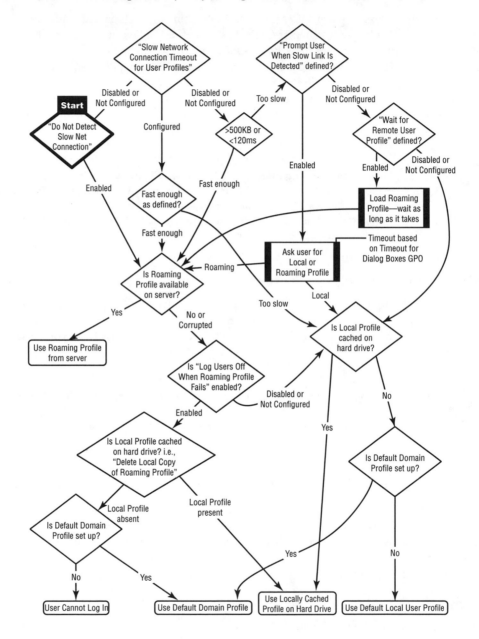

FIGURE 8.16   Some entries for profiles are found under the User Node in Group Policy.

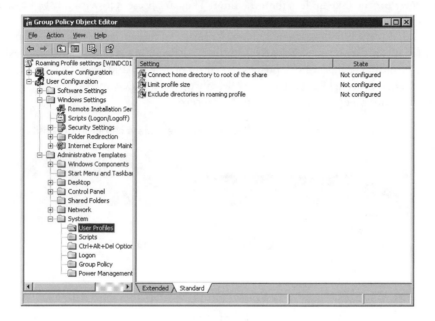

This setting allows the administrator to include or exclude the NTUSER.DAT file in the total calculations on space in the Roaming Profile. Additionally, you can notify the user about size infractions by checking the "Notify user when profile storage space is exceeded" box (shown in Figure 8.17) and setting it so that the user is annoyed every so often (as determined in the "Remind user every X minutes" spinner control). By default, this setting is not configured.

FIGURE 8.17   You can limit the Roaming Profile size, if desired.

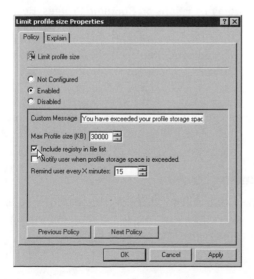

Once this policy setting is configured, the affected users cannot log off until the files that compose their profile take up less than the limit. They are presented with a list of files in their profile, as shown in Figure 8.18, from which they must choose some to delete.

In general, this is a blunt instrument. The original use of this entry was for situations in which users stuffed lots of documents into their Windows NT Roaming Profile—onto the Desktop, for instance. Recall that Windows NT pushes the entire profile up and back causing major bandwidth headaches. Indeed, because users rely heavily on the My Documents folder (which is part of the profile), there's even more reason to be concerned.

FIGURE 8.18 Once the Roaming Profile size is set, users can't log off until they delete some files.

 Don't try to place disk quota restrictions on Roaming Profiles. Because applications sometimes put their own data inside the profile, users have a hard time tracking down files to delete if the quota prevented them from writing. Instead, use disk quotas on redirected folders, such as the My Documents folder. This is explored in the next chapter.

But instead of being forced to use this policy setting as your only weapon to fight disk space usage, you have an ace in the hole; in the next chapter, you'll learn how to use Folder Redirection to redirect My Documents. You can then place a disk quota on the redirected My Documents folder.

Excluding Directories in Roaming Profile

As previously stated, several folders in the profile will not roam. Again, these are the `Documents and Settings\Username\Local Settings\Application Data` (and everything below it, including Local Settings, History, Temp, and Temporary Internet Files).

You can add additional folders to the list of those that do not roam, if desired. You might do this if you want to fix a specific file to a Desktop (if you maintain locally cached profiles). For instance, you can exclude Desktop\LargeZipDownloads if you want to make sure those types of files do not roam with the profile (see Figure 8.19).

 In Windows 2000, some, but not all, of the automatically excluded folders are presented in the Group Policy Editor. As far as I can tell, they're only there for show; deleting them produces no appreciable gain. (For example, you can't make the Temp, History, or other folders roam in the profile.) You can only add your own entries in addition to or in lieu of the presented entries. These are not listed for Windows XP/Windows 2003.

FIGURE 8.19 Prevent specific folders, such as the Desktop, from roaming.

 Enter additional entries relative to the root of the profiles. For instance, if you want to add the Desktop, simply add **Desktop** (not **c:\Documents and Settings\ Desktop** or anything similar), because the Desktop folder is found directly off the root of each profile.

Connect Home Directory to Root of the Share

I'm pretty sure by the time you get to the end of this book, you won't want to use old-style "Home Drives" anymore. That's because the changes in Roaming Profile behavior and redirected folders (next chapter) present a better way for users to store their files. However, if you do end up using Home Drives for each user (located in the Account tab of each user's account's Properties), you can specify a location for users to store their stuff. Specific environment variables typically used when setting up home directories are defined differently in NT 4 and Windows 2000 (and later).

Those two environment variables *%HOMEDRIVE%* and *%HOMEPATH%* are automatically set when you set up, share, and assign a home directory for a user. NT 4 client computers aren't as smart as Windows 2000 computers, and they understand the "meaning" of the *%HOMEDRIVE%* and *%HOMEPATH%* shares a bit differently. To make a long story short, the fully qualified name path to the share isn't represented when those variables are evaluated on NT 4 clients; but it is for Windows 2000 and later clients. You can "dumb down" Windows 2000 and newer clients by applying this policy setting, and making new clients act like old NT 4 clients.

Mandatory Profiles

Mandatory Profiles enable the administrator to assign a single user or multiple users the same, unchanging user experience regardless of where they log on and no matter what they do. In non–mumbo-jumbo terms, Mandatory Profiles ensure that users can't screw things up. When you use Mandatory Profiles to lock down your users, you guarantee that the Desktop, the files in the profile, and the Registry continue to look exactly as they did when they were set up.

Mandatory Profiles are great when you have a pesky user who keeps messing with the Desktop or when you have general populations of users—such as call centers, nurse's stations, or library kiosks—on whom you want to maintain security.

Once the Mandatory Profile is set for these people, you know you won't be running out there every 11 minutes trying to fix someone's machine when they've put the black text on the black background and clicked Apply. Actually, they can still put the black text on the black background and click Apply, and it does take effect. But when they log off or reboot (if they can figure out how to do that in the "dark"), the values aren't preserved. So, voilà! Back to work!

You can create a Mandatory Profile in two ways—either from a Local Profile (or locally cached profile) or from an existing Roaming Profile. I recommend creating your Mandatory Profile from a local (or locally cached) profile. By default, if you try to dive into an existing Roaming Profile folder on the server, you are denied access, as shown in Figure 8.10 earlier in this chapter. The system utilizes the *%username%* variable and automatically sets up permissions such that only the user specified can access that folder. To dive in, you have to take ownership of the entire subfolder structure first and then give yourself permission to access the folder.

In the next sections, you'll find the steps for both methods.

If you previously set up the **Add the Administrators Security Group to Roaming User Profiles** policy setting, you won't need to worry about not being able to dive into the profile. Note, however, that the policy setting must be placed before the Roaming Profile is placed.

Establishing Mandatory Profiles from a Local Profile

The first thing to do when trying to establish the Mandatory Profile is to log on locally to any Windows 2000 or Windows XP machine as a mere mortal user (without an existing Roaming Profile), make the modifications you want, and log off as that user.

Now that you have a local (or locally cached) profile that you want to use as your Mandatory Profile, follow these steps:

1. Log on as Administrator to the machine that houses the local (or locally cached) profile.

2. Click Start, and then right-click My Computer and choose Properties from the shortcut menu to open the System Properties dialog box.

3. Click the Advanced tab, and then click the Settings button in the User Profiles section to open the User Profiles dialog box (as seen previously in Figure 8.6).

4. Click the "Copy To" button to open the "Copy To" dialog box, and then enter the full path plus a folder for the common users, as shown in Figure 8.20. This example has `\\WinDC01\profiles\allnurses`. The Allnurses folder is automatically created under the Profiles share.

FIGURE 8.20   Use the Copy To dialog box to copy one profile for many users.

5. Click the Change button in the "Permitted to Use" section, to open the "Select User or Group" dialog box and change the default from the original user to Everyone, as shown in Figure 8.20. This lets everyone use the profile in the domain.

6. Click OK to actually copy the profile and to close the "Copy To" dialog box.

7. Click OK to close the System Properties dialog box.

Next, use Explorer to locate the share we created earlier, named Profiles. Inside the Profiles directory, you should now see the Allnurses folder. Locate the NTUSER.DAT and rename it to NTUSER.MAN, as shown in Figure 8.21.

> Because NTUSER.DAT is hidden by default, you might have to change the default view options. In Explorer, choose Tools ➤ Folder Options to open the Folder Options dialog box. Click the View tab, click the "Show Hidden Files and Folders" button, clear the "Hide File Extensions for Known File Types" check box, and click OK.

FIGURE 8.21   Change a Roaming Profile to a Mandatory Profile by renaming NTUSER.DAT to NTUSER.MAN.

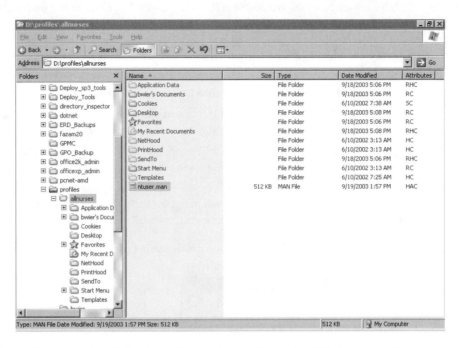

Finally, in the Properties dialog box, change the profile path of all the users who are to use the profile to `\\WinDC01\profiles\allnurses`, as shown in Figure 8.22.

FIGURE 8.22   Point all similar users to the new Mandatory Profile.

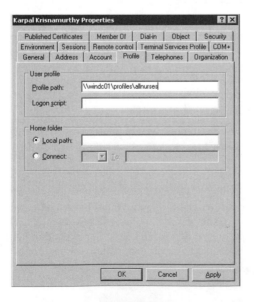

Since you copied the profile to the server with permissions for Everyone to use, you'll also want to modify the NTFS permissions of the Allnurses folder under the Profiles share to make sure it's protected. You might choose to protect the Allnurses folder by setting the Permissions as shown in Figure 8.23.

FIGURE 8.23   You can prevent people from inadvertently modifying the newly established profile.

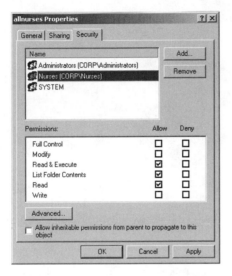

Mandatory Profiles from an Established Roaming Profile

You might not be able to use a local (or locally cached) profile to generate the Mandatory Profile. This might be because you enabled the **Delete Cached Copies of Roaming Profiles** policy setting, and there are no locally cached profiles for you to use. In this case, you'll need to log in as Administrator on the server that houses the Roaming Profile, locate the profile folder, and take ownership of it. You can then copy the profile to another folder and have the user take back ownership of the folder. In this case, we'll take ownership of a profile for a user named garyd. To take ownership of a user's Roaming Profile, follow these steps:

1. Log on at the server as Administrator.

2. Locate the user's profile folder, right-click it, and choose Properties from the shortcut menu to open the User Properties dialog box.

3. Click the Security tab. You should get a message stating that the user is the only one with access to their own folder.

4. Click the Advanced button on the Security tab to get the "Advanced Security Settings" dialog box. Next, click the Owner tab.

5. Select Administrator (or Administrators) from the list, click the "Replace Owner on Subcontainers and Objects" check box (as shown in Figure 8.24), and then click OK.

FIGURE 8.24 Take ownership of the folder.

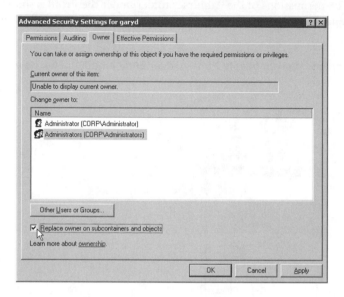

6. You will be prompted to confirm that you want to take ownership. Select Yes and wait until you have ownership.

You can now rename the folder to a sensible name and then rename the NTUSER.DAT file to NTUSER.MAN. Last, point each user account to use this new profile, specifically pointing each account to the profile as shown in Figure 8.22 earlier in this chapter.

Since everyone now has Full Control (inherited from the parent), you might want to restrict access to the profile, similarly to that seen in Figure 8.23 earlier in this chapter.

 You might need to add the Administrator account or the Administrators group to the ACL of the folder and let the permissions flow downward in order to be able to see the contents. In some extreme cases, you might also need to log off and back on as Administrator to get another access token.

Forced Mandatory Profiles (Super-Mandatory)

Mandatory Profiles might not always be so; if the server is down or a user unplugs their network cable, the Mandatory Profile does not load. Indeed, the user will get the Local Default User Profile. This could be a potential security problem and possibly a violation of your corporate policy.

In instances like this, you need to determine if it's more important that a user logs on (and gets the Default Local User Profile) or that, if they don't get the Mandatory Profile, they don't get to log on at all. Microsoft calls this type of profile "Super-Mandatory." In Figure 8.21 earlier in this chapter, we used a folder named Allnurses as our Mandatory Profile folder. We can take this to the next step and ensure that all users using the Allnurses folder cannot log on unless they can connect to the share on the server.

To force users to use the Mandatory Profile, or lose logon capability, simply follow these steps:

1. Create a Mandatory Profile as described earlier, including renaming the `NTUSER.DAT` to `NTUSER.MAN`.

2. Rename the entire folder from Allnurses to Allnurses.man.

3. Change the affected users' Profile tabs to point to the new location, such as `\\WinDC01\profiles\allnurses.man`, as shown in Figure 8.25.

FIGURE 8.25   You can force a Mandatory Profile if absolutely necessary.

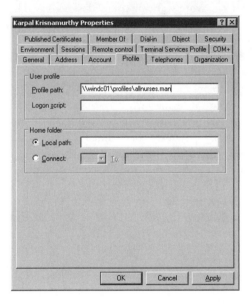

Once the forced Mandatory Profile is introduced onto a system, the system always checks to see if the Profile is available. If the forced Mandatory Profile is unavailable, the user is not permitted to log on.

Technically, you can couple a Mandatory Profile with the **Log Users Off When Roaming Profile Fails** policy setting to create the same effect. However, the method detailed here is preferred.

Final Thoughts

In this chapter you learned about the three profile types: Local, Roaming, and Mandatory.

Local Profiles alone are great—for only the smallest of environments. However, remember that there's a lot you can do to get a similar look and feel for when new users show up on the job. You can craft a Default Local User Profile, or, even better, a Default Domain User Profile.

Step up to Roaming Profiles when you have even a handful of users and you want to allow them to bounce from machine to machine and keep their look and feel. Roaming Profiles have really grown up since the days of Windows NT. The algorithm to move the profiles up and back is much improved, and you should really give it another try if you once gave up in frustration.

Roaming Profiles are especially useful if you want to bring users' desktops and laptops back from the dead, as we'll explore in the next two chapters. Indeed, you can use Roaming Profiles as a handy way to upgrade users' machines while preserving their Desktops.

Remember that the Windows 2003 version of the Active Directory Users And Computers tool allows you to select multiple users at once and set their roaming profile path to a server. And, as stated earlier, there's no need to precreate the folder underneath the shared directory— the system will automatically do that once the %username% variable is encountered.

As stated earlier, there are a lot of policy settings you can utilize to hone how profiles work. You can set up your environment to be moderately secure when using the **Delete Cached Copies of Roaming Profiles** policy setting. And you can also allow joint ownership of the user's roaming profile directory on the server by utilizing the **Add the Administrators Security Group to Roaming User Profiles** policy setting.

Use Mandatory Profiles sparingly. With Group Policy settings available to tie down all sorts of settings, Mandatory Profiles are really only a last resort. And Forced Mandatory Profiles are a really, really last resort (if that's such a thing).

9

IntelliMirror, Part 1: Redirected Folders, Offline Files, Synchronization Manager, and Disk Quotas

You get Active Directory, you get Group Policy. That's the good news. The better news is how you can put your knowledge of Group Policy to use to keep your users happy. Here's the idea: easily create a consistent environment for your users no matter where they roam.

In the previous chapter, you used Roaming Profiles to kick off your journey to a consistent environment. Now, let's explore IntelliMirror. In this chapter, I'll give you an overview of what IntelliMirror is and is not and show you how to implement a slew of its features: Redirected Folders, Offline Folders, Synchronization Manager, and Disk Quotas.

In the next chapter, I'll wrap up IntelliMirror with a discussion of software deployment via Group Policy. Finally, in Chapter 11, you'll see how the "circle of life" for a computer, so to speak, comes together with Shadow Copies and Remote Installation Services.

Overview of Change and Configuration Management and IntelliMirror

Believe it or not, you're expensive. Your salary, the percentage of rent your office takes up, the software you use that helps the business run—it all costs money. Making those costs tangible is a difficult proposition. Some costs are hard to put into concrete numbers. How do you quantify the cost of sending a technician to a user's desktop when they've inadvertently set the background color, the foreground color, and the font color to black and hit the Apply button?

Accounting for these costs is a constant challenge, and bringing these costs under control is even more difficult. The Gartner Group, in the early 1990s, generated a new strategy to help with this predicament and proposed a new *TCO (Total Cost of Ownership)* model. This philosophical model essentially attempted to take the voodoo out of accounting for computing services. Simply account for every nickel and dime spent around computing, and voilà! Instant accounting!

You can find more info on Garner Group's TCO model at www.gartnerweb.com/ 4_decision_tools/measurement/decision_tools/tco/tco.html.

Microsoft's first foray into aligning with the TCO philosophy was back in the NT 4 timeframe with their Zero Administration for Windows (ZAW) initiative. The first major technology set based on ZAW was called the Zero Administration for Windows Kit (ZAK).

Most organizations have two types of users: those who work on one application and one application only, and those who use a few apps (but seem to never stop playing with their Desktops). With those two types of users in mind, ZAK could be run in two modes: Taskstation, in which users were locked down to one (and only one) application, and Appstation, in which users could move between several strategically selected applications. ZAK's goal was noble—reduce the user's exposure to the Desktop and the operating system. Once that was reduced, less administration would be required to control the environment.

Although ZAK was a respectable first attempt, only a few organizations really used ZAK in the way it was intended. The adoption of ZAK never quite caught on due to the intricacy of implementation and lack of flexibility. Surprisingly, Microsoft still supports ZAK (under NT 4), and it is still available for free download at www.microsoft.com/windows/zak/.

With Active Directory as the backdrop to a new stage, a new paradigm of how administrators manage users and their Desktops could be created. Enter the Active Directory version of Zero Administration for Windows—now known as Change and Configuration Management (CCM) and IntelliMirror. Again, recall that the Zero Administration for Windows program was an "initiative," not a specific technology. With Windows 2000, Microsoft renamed the ZAW initiative to Change and Configuration Management and introduced several new technologies—the greatest being IntelliMirror—in order to move closer to the TCO philosophy.

You can't run down to CompUSA and buy a shrink-wrapped copy of Microsoft IntelliMirror for Active Directory, nor is there an IntelliMirror administration MMC snap-in. It's a collection of different technologies, implemented via Group Policy, that are designed to reduce overall administration.

In accordance with the TCO philosophy, each IntelliMirror feature tries to chip away at each of the sore points of administrating your network by implementing specific technologies. Figure 9.1 shows how Microsoft envisions the Change and Configuration Management initiative, the IntelliMirror features, and the specific technologies therein. IntelliMirror implementation isn't an all-or-nothing proposition as ZAK had been. Administrators can pick and choose the features and functionality they want to deploy and when they want to deploy it.

Although some IntelliMirror features that I'll describe in detail here are available when using Windows 2000 Professional or Windows XP workstation by itself (such as Offline Folders), most are actuated only when you have the marriage between Active Directory and Windows 2000, Windows XP, or Windows 2003 as clients (such as Redirected Folders).

FIGURE 9.1 This is Microsoft's picture of the relationship between CCM and IntelliMirror.

		Features	Benefits	Technologies
Change and Configuration Management	IntelliMirror	User Data Management	Increased protection and availability of people's data "My documents follow me!"	Active Directory Group Policy Offline Folders Synchronization Manager Disk Quotas Redirected Folders
		User Settings Management	Centrally defined environment "My settings follow me!"	Active Directory Group Policy Offline Folders Roaming Profiles
		Software Installation and Maintenance	Centrally managed software "My software follows me!"	Active Directory Group Policy Windows Installer Service
		Remote OS Installation	Fast system configuration "Get Windows 2000 working on this machine"	Active Directory DNS DHCP Remote Installer Services

Again, you built a bit of a foundation for your IntelliMirror journey in the last chapter when you implemented Roaming Profiles. This enabled the basics of the "My documents follow me" and the "My settings follow me" philosophies. In this chapter, we'll explore the implementation of some of the other IntelliMirror features: Redirected Folders, Offline Folders, the Synchronization Manager, and Disk Quotas.

Redirected Folders

Redirected Folders allows the administrator to provide a centralized repository for certain noteworthy folders from client systems and have the data contained in them actually reside on shared folders on servers. It's a beautiful thing. The administrator gets centralized control; users get the same experience they always did. It's the best of both worlds.

You can set Redirected Folders for the following:

- My Documents
- My Pictures
- The Start Menu
- The Desktop
- Application Data

For each of these settings, there is a Basic and an Advanced configuration.

The idea is to set up a GPO that contains a policy setting to redirect one or more of these folders for clients and "stick them" on a server. Usually the GPO is set at the OU level, and all users inside the OU are affected; however, there might occasionally be a reason to link the GPO with the policy setting to the domain or site level.

In the **Basic** configuration, every user that is affected by the policy setting is redirected to the same shared folder. Then, inside the shared folder, the system can automatically create individual, secure folders for each user to store their stuff.

In the **Advanced** configuration, Active Directory security group membership determines which users' folders get redirected to which shared folder. For instance, you could say, "All members of the **Graphic_Artists** Global security group will get their desktops redirected to the 'ga_Desktops' shared folder on 'Server-6'" or "All members of the Sales Universal security group will get their Application Data redirected to the 'appdata' share on Server 'Pineapple.'"

For our journey through Redirected Folders, we'll work primarily inside **My Documents**. All the principles that work on the special **My Documents** folder work equally well for the other special "redirectable" folders, unless otherwise noted. At the end of the "Redirected My Documents" section, I'll briefly discuss why you might want to redirect some other folders as well.

Redirected My Documents

In the last chapter, we explored how to leverage Roaming Profiles to maintain a consistent state for users if they hop from machine to machine. Roaming profiles are terrific, but one significant drawback is associated with using Roaming Profiles. Recall that My Documents is part of the profile. On the one hand, this frees you from the bondage of drive letters and home drives. No more, "Ursula, put it in your U: drive" or "Harry, save it to the H: drive."

On the other hand, once the user data is in My Documents, your network will be swamped with all the up-and-back movement of data within My Documents when users hop from machine to machine—20MB of Word docs here, 30MB of Excel docs there. Multiply this by the number of users, and it'll add up fast!

But, with Redirected Folders, you can have the best of both worlds. Users can save their files to the place they know and love, My Documents, and anchor the data to a fixed location, so it *appears* as if the data is roaming with the users. But it really isn't; it's safe and secure on a file share of your choice.

 There are two added bonuses to this scheme. Since all the My Documents files are being redirected to specific fixed-shared folders, you can easily back up all the user data in one fell swoop. Perhaps you can even make a separate backup job specifically for the user data that needs to be more closely monitored. Additionally, you can set up Shadow Copies on the specific shares that house redirected My Documents files so users can restore their own files if necessary. Shadow Copies are explored in Chapter 11.

Basic Redirected Folders

Basic Redirected Folders works best in two situations:

- Smaller environments—such as a doctor's office or storefront—where all employees sit under one roof

- In an organization's OU structure that was designed such that similar people are not only in the same OU but are also in the same physical location

The reason these simple scenarios make a good fit with the basic option is that such situations let you redirect the users affected by the policy setting to a server that's close to them. That way, if they do roam within their location, the wait time is minimal to download and upload the data back and forth to the server and their workstation.

In the following example, I've created an OU called **LikeUsers** who are all using the same local server—WinDC01. Setting up a basic Redirected Folders for My Documents is a snap. It's a three-step process:

- Create a shared folder to store the data.

- Set the security on the shared folder.

- Create a new GPO and edit it to contain a policy setting to redirect the My Documents folder.

To create and share a folder to store redirected My Documents data, follow these steps:

1. Log on to WinDC01 as Administrator.

2. From the Desktop, double-click My Computer to open the My Computer folder.

3. Find a place to create a users folder. In this example, we'll use D:\DATA. Once you're inside the D: drive, right-click D:\ and select the Folder command from the New menu, then type in **Data** for the name.

You can substitute any name for Data. Some use MYDOCS or REDIRDOCS. Some administrators like to use hidden shares, such as Data$, MYDOCS$, or MYDOCUMENTS$.

4. Right-click the newly created Data folder, and choose "Sharing and Security," which opens the Properties of the folder, but focused on the Sharing tab. Note that Windows Server 2003 will default such that the share is Everyone:Read. Click "Share This Folder," and ensure the share is set so that Authenticated Users have Full Control, as seen in Figure 9.2. Keep the rest of the defaults, and click OK.

Be sure that the NTFS permissions allow write access for the users you want as well. In other words, both the Share level and NTFS permissions must allow the user to write in order for success.

FIGURE 9.2 Share the Data folder such that Authenticated Users have Change permissions.

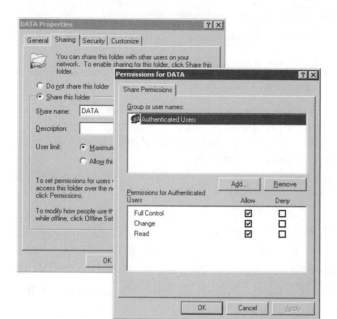

Share Permissions: Full Control versus Change

In the last chapter, we set up a shared folder for our Roaming Profiles. We put Change control on the permissions, and this was enough. Interestingly, here, on the share that will house our redirected folders, we need Full Control permissions, or the Folder Redirection will fail.

So, is there a problem using Full Control? Is there a way to exploit an attack on a share with Full Control? Not really, unless the underlying NTFS permissions are open for an attack. Basically, as long as the root folder of the share is an NTFS folder with appropriate permissions, there is no reason to use anything other than Everyone:Full Control on the share; though there's certainly nothing wrong with Authenticated Users: Full Control either.

Some people had insisted on using share permissions, but it was often because they instituted the practice in the dark days of OS/2 and Microsoft LanManager and got used to it. The share permission is simply a security descriptor stored in the Registry entry for the share in the LanManServer entries on the server. Giving Everyone:Full Control doesn't change the permissions on the Registry entry itself, so it cannot be used as an exploit for getting a toehold on the server.

The moral of the story: have the correct NTFS permissions underneath the folder that contains the share. Indeed, share permissions aren't sufficient if someone gets physical access, or near-physical access, to the box; for example, via Terminal Services access.

Now that the share is created, we're ready to create a new GPO to do the magic. To set up Redirected Folders for My Documents, follow these steps:

1. In the GPMC, right-click the OU on which you want to apply Folder Redirection (in my case, the **LikeUsers** OU), and choose "Create and link a new GPO here..."

2. Name the GPO, say, "My Docs Folder Redirection," as shown in Figure 9.3.

3. Right-click the new GPO, and choose Edit from the shortcut menu to open the Group Policy Object Editor.

4. Drill down to Folder Redirection by choosing User Configuration ➤ Windows Settings ➤ Folder Redirection. Right-click the My Documents entry in the Group Policy Object Editor, and choose Properties to open the My Document Properties dialog box, as shown in Figure 9.4.

5. In the Setting drop-down list box, select "Basic—Redirect everyone's Folder to the same location."

FIGURE 9.3   The LikeUsers OU has a GPO named "My Docs Folder Redirection." After drilling down into the folder you want to redirect, right-click and choose Properties.

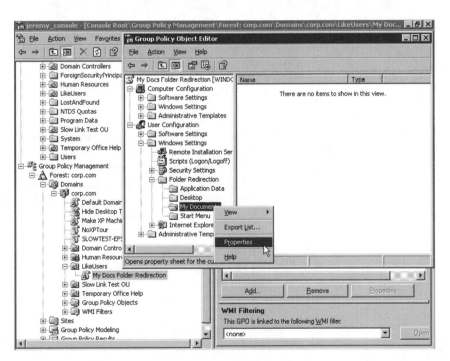

FIGURE 9.4   The Basic settings redirect all users in the OU to the same location.

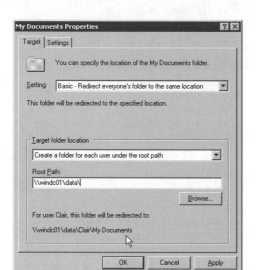

The Target Tab

The "Target folder location" drop-down list box has the following four options:

Redirect to the user's home directory.   Many companies use home drives for each user and have the users store all their stuff there. To set a home drive for each user, in Active Directory Users And Computers click the "Profile" tab for the user and enter a path in the "Home folder" section. The idea behind this setting is that it's an easy way to help users continue to use a drive letter they already know and love, say, H: (for Home directory) in addition to the My Documents redirection. If you choose this setting, both H: and My Documents point to the exact same place—the path you set in the Home folder section in Active Directory Users And Computers. In this book, we didn't set up home drives because My Documents redirection frees us from the need to do so. This setting is provided here only as a convenience for organizations that want to continue to use home folders. If you plan to eventually getting rid of home drives in your company in lieu of just a redirected My Documents folder, my advice is not to use this setting; instead use the **Redirect to the following location** setting (explored shortly).

    If the user has no home folder, this option is ignored, and the folder stays in its current location.

Create a folder for each user under the root path.   If you plan to redirect more than just the My Documents folder (say, the Application Data or Desktop), you might want to select this option. This creates secure subfolders underneath the point you specify. As you can see in Figure 9.4 earlier in this chapter, entering **\\windc01\data** in the Root Path box shows an example of how all users affected by this policy setting are redirected.

This choice might be good if you don't want to have to remember what the specific environment variables point to.

In the example, you can see that My Documents for a user Clair will be redirected to her own folder in the Data share. Go ahead and perform this now.

In our example, we're using WinDC01, a Domain Controller. You usually wouldn't do this; rather, you'd use a regular run-of-the mill file server (as a member, not a Domain Controller). We're doing that here simply for the sake of example.

Since we used the rather generic name "Data" for our share, it makes sense that user's have their own folders containing their own data.

Redirect to the following location.   This option makes sense if you plan to redirect only My Documents or just one other redirectable folder. This selection allows you to specifically dictate where you want the folder placed. This was the only option available in previous versions. To use this setting, type **\\WinDC01\data\%username%** in the Target Folder Location text box. Then, a subfolder for the user is created directly under the Data shared folder. This is the selection to choose when none of the others is to your liking; that is, you have the most flexibility with this option.

Redirect to the local userprofile location.   With this option, you redirect the folder for the user back to their Local Profile. It's useful when you want to remove redirection for a particular folder without affecting the rest of the other redirected folders.

The Settings Tab

When you click the Settings tab, you have access to additional options for Folder Redirection. The Settings tab is the hidden gem of Folder Redirection; it activates a bit of magic. There is a Settings tab for each redirected folder: My Documents (and the corresponding My Pictures), the Desktop, the Start Menu, and Application Data. Figure 9.5 shows the Settings tab for My Documents.

By default, users have exclusive NTFS permissions to their directories, and the contents of their My Documents folders are automatically moved to the new directory. You can change this behavior, if desired, by making the appropriate choices on the Settings tab.

Since we're discussing My Documents at this point, we'll dive into the Settings tab specifically for My Documents. However, each setting discussed here affects each redirected folder in exactly the same way. Let's take a look at some of the options available on this tab.

Grant the User Exclusive Rights to My Documents   By default, this check box is checked. You're instructing the system to create a secure directory underneath the redirection. This check box sets NTFS permissions on that directory such that only that user can enter the directory.

This keeps prying eyes, even those of nosy administrators, out of people's personal business. If you want to change this setting, uncheck the box.

Unchecking the "Grant the user exclusive rights to My Documents" check box sets no additional permissions, nor does it modify the target directory permissions in any way. Any permissions on the folder are left as they were by default. The NTFS permissions are not modified. Because Windows 2000 and Windows 2003 use NTFS inheritance, newly created folders receive the same permissions as the parent folder.

If this box is checked, and you do need to dig into someone's personal directory, you'll have to take ownership of the directory, as described in the previous chapter. Or, if you set it up in advance (using the information in the following sidebar), you'll be able to get in whenever you want! (Again, though, you need to set it up in advance.)

Move the Contents of My Documents to the New Location   By default, this check box is checked. When you start out on your IntelliMirror journey, Microsoft is betting that the first thing you do is to set up Roaming Profiles and then move on to setting up Redirected Folders. In between those two periods of time, however, users have surely created their own documents and started putting them in their My Documents folder in their Local or Roaming Profile. This check box magically moves (not copies) their documents from their profile (Roaming or Local) to the appointed place on the server the next time they log on.

If users have bounced from machine to machine and sprinkled data in the local My Documents folder, the files in My Documents will move them to the redirected location the next time the user logs on to that machine.

FIGURE 9.5   The Settings tab in Folder Redirection holds all sorts of magical powers!

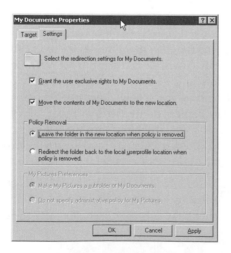

Policy Removal   You must select one of the two settings under the Policy Removal heading. The point of having OUs is that you can move users easily in and out of them. If the user is moved out of an OU to which this policy applies, the following options help you determine what happens to their redirected folder contents.

Leave the Folder in the New Location When a Policy Is Removed.   If this option is selected, and the user is moved out of the OU to which this policy applies, the data stays in the shared folder and directory you specified. This is the default. The user will continue to access the contents of the redirected folder.

Redirect the Folder Back to the Local User Profile Location When the Policy Is Removed. If this check box is selected, and the user moves (or the policy no longer applies), a copy of the data is sent to the profile.

If Roaming Profiles is not set up, a copy of the data is sent to every workstation the user logs on to. If you've set up Roaming Profiles, the data will get pushed back up to the server and shared folder that house the user's Roaming Profile when the user logs off.

This setting is useful if a user under your jurisdiction moves to another territory. Once this happens, you can eliminate their junk cluttering your servers (as long as you're not the administrator of the target OU). Use this option with care, though; since the users' data isn't anchored to a shared folder, the network traffic will increase when this data roams around the network.

It is recommended that you check with the target OU administrator to ensure that some Folder Redirection policy will apply to the user. This eliminates all the "up and back" problems associated with maintaining user data inside regular Roaming Profiles.

My Pictures Preferences   The Settings tab in the My Documents dialog box has an additional setting regarding the My Pictures folder. Usually, My Pictures is located underneath My Documents in normal Local and Roaming Profiles. With Redirected Folders, though, one server and shared folder can hold My Documents, and another server and shared folder can hold My Pictures. This option is grayed out when using a Basic folder redirection policy for My Documents and is available only when using an Advanced folder redirection policy (as explored later in this chapter).

Make My Pictures a Subfolder of My Documents   This is the default. It keeps the hierarchical structure of My Documents\My Pictures as it is normally found in the profile.

Do Not Specify Administrative Policy for My Pictures   If this is selected, the My Pictures settings (the folder under My Documents in the policy) determines what happens to this folder first.

If the My Pictures policy is left blank, My Pictures is located within the profile (Local or Roaming). Interestingly, the default setting in the My Pictures policy is 100 percent dependent on what is configured in the My Documents Settings tab for My Pictures.

The My Pictures portion of the My Documents Settings tab is only configurable at the initial setup of policy for redirection. After finalizing the setting, you can change the My Pictures setting only from the My Pictures policy. The My Documents setting for My Pictures is then unavailable.

How to Grant Administrators Access to My Documents (or Other Redirected Folders)

As you learned in the last chapter, it's possible to grant administrators access to the folders where users store their Roaming Profiles. In that chapter, you set up a policy setting that affects the client computers, and the first time the user jumps on the computer, the file permissions are set such that both the user and the administrator have joint access. However, that's not the case with redirected folders.

If you want both the user and the administrator to have joint access to a redirected folder such as My Documents, you need to perform two major steps.

1. Clear the "Grant the user exclusive rights to My Documents" setting (as seen in Figure 9.5).

2. Set security on the subfolder you are sharing that will contain the redirected folders.

In the Security Properties dialog box of the folder you shared, select Advanced. Uncheck the "Allow inheritable permissions from parent to propagate to this object" check box. Now, remove the permissions, and then add four groups, assign them permissions, and dictate where those permissions will flow. Here's the breakdown:

Administrators Full Control, which applies to "This folder, subfolders and files"

System Full Control, which applies to "This folder, subfolders and files"

Creator Owner Full Control, which applies to "This folder, subfolders and files"

Authenticated Users Create Folders / Append Data, Read Permissions, Read Extended Attributes, which apply to "This folder only" (as seen here)

This information is valid for both Windows 2003 and Windows 2000 servers, and you can find more details in the Knowledge Base article Q288991. Adding these groups and assigning these permissions appears to remove the automatic synchronization of redirected folders, as you'll see a bit later. However, you can restore this functionality with the **Administratively Assigned Offline Files** policy setting—again, explored later.

In some circumstances when redirecting to Windows 2000 servers, I needed to grant the Authenticated Users the **List Folder / Read Data** access for this process to work fully.

But we have a problem. What if you've already set up Redirected Folders and suers already have their own protected subfolders? How do you "go back in time" and fix the ones that already were created? In our example, our redirected folders are in D:\data. Follow these steps:

1. Start cmd.exe, and type **AT nn:nn /interactive cmd.exe** (nn:nn is a couple of minutes in the future).

2. Wait until the new command window opens.

3. Run cacls "d:\data" /T /E /G DOMAIN\Administrator:F.

This command edits the ACL (/E) rather than replacing it. It grants the user DOMAIN\Administrator Full Control (/G DOMAIN\Administrator:F) and sets the permissions on all subfolders (/T). This should allow you to set all previously created folders to nearly the same standard.

Advanced Redirected Folders

You select Advanced Redirected Folders from the Setting drop-down list box, as shown in Figure 9.4 earlier in this chapter. Advanced Redirected Folders works best in two situations, both larger environments, for example:

- A campus with many buildings. You'll want to specify different Redirected Folders locations that are closest to the biggest groups of users.

- More likely, a specific department that is charged with purchasing its own server and storage. In this scenario, there's usually a battle over who can store what data on whose server. With this mechanism, everyone can have their own sandbox.

In either case, you can still have an OU that affects many similar users, but that breaks up where folders are redirected, depending on the users' respective security groups. For example, we have an OU called **Sales** that contains two global security sales groups: East_Sales and West_Sales. Each Sales group needs their folders redirected to the server closest to them, either East_Server or West_Server. First, you'll want to create the shares on both the East_Server and West_Server as directed earlier. For this example, they're each shared out as Data. To perform an Advanced Folder Redirection, follow these steps:

1. If you're not already logged on to WinDC01 as Administrator of the domain, do so now.

2. Start the GPMC.

3. Right-click the OU on which we want to apply folder redirection, in this case **Sales** OU, and select "Create and link a GPO here..."

4. Enter a descriptive name, such as "Advanced Folder Redirection for the **Sales** OU," for the GPO. Select it, and click Edit to open the Group Policy Object Editor.

5. The GPO for the OU appears. Drill down to Folder Redirection by choosing User Configuration ➢ Windows Settings ➢ Folder Redirection.

6. Right-click the My Documents folder in the Group Policy Object Editor, and choose Properties from the shortcut menu to open the My Documents Properties dialog box. In the Setting drop-down list box, select "Advanced—Specify Locations for Various User Groups." The dialog box changes so that you can now use the AddÖ button to add security settings, as shown in Figure 9.6. Click OK.

7. Click the "Add..." button in the My Documents Properties to open up the "Specify Group and Location" dialog box. Click Browse under Security Group Membership, and locate the **East_Sales** global security group.

8. In the Target Folder location, enter the UNC path of the redirected folder. In this case, it's `\\east_server\data\%username%`. Click OK to close the Specify Group and Location dialog box.

9. Repeat steps 8 and 9 for the **West_Sales** global security group.

FIGURE 9.6 Use the Advanced redirection function to choose different locations to move users' data.

When finished, you should have both **East_Sales** and **West_Sales** listed.

The next time the user logs on, the settings specified in the Settings tab take effect; that is, by default, a new folder is generated specifically for each user, and the current documents in the user's My Documents folder are transported to the newly redirected folder location.

Testing Folder Redirection of My Documents

In the last chapter, you used Brett Wier's account to verify that Roaming Profiles were working properly. You did this by creating a test file, FILE1.TXT, in the My Documents folder and noting that the file properly roamed with the user when they hopped from machine to machine. Additionally, you noted that the file location was on the local hard drive—in his locally cached copy of his Roaming User Profile. To see whether My Documents is being redirected, move Brett's user account into an OU that has the My Documents folder redirected as specified in either the Basic or Advanced Folder Redirection settings.

You will need to log off and back on as Brett to see the changes take affect. Group Policy background refresh (as detailed in Chapter 3) does not affect Redirected Folders.

Log on to a Windows 2000 machine as Brett Wier, and open My Documents. Right-click FILE1.TXT and note its location, as shown in Figure 9.7.

The file was automatically transported from the Roaming Profile and anchored to the fixed point on the server, in this case \\WinDC01\data\bwier\My Documents.

FIGURE 9.7   Windows 2000 Folder Redirection in action

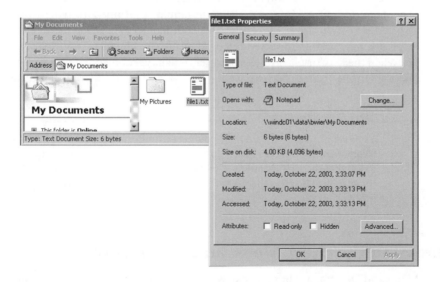

FIGURE 9.8 Windows XP Folder Redirection in action

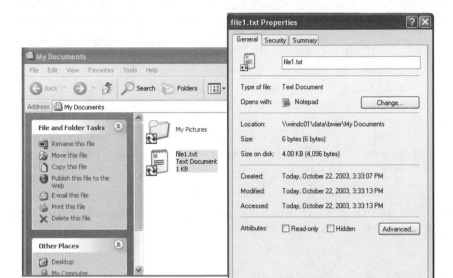

If you perform the same experiment on a Windows XP machine, you'll see the same results, but notice the curious arrows on the files and folders (see Figure 9.8).

The arrows signify that another IntelliMirror feature is in force—Offline Files, which I'll talk about in the next major section. However, one point should be gleamed from these previous two figures. The behavior of Windows XP is different from that of Windows 2000. That is, when a Windows XP machine uses a redirected folder, the entire contents are automatically cached offline. Thus, when the network is offline, your users still have total access to the files they need.

Stay tuned for Offline Folders…where we'll discuss how to actually put this knowledge to good use.

You will not see the arrows if you performed the procedure in the "How to Grant Administrators Access to My Documents (or Other Redirected Folders)" sidebar earlier in this chapter. However, you will see these arrows if you follow these instructions in the "Administratively Assigned Offline Files" section later in this chapter.

Redirecting the Start Menu and the Desktop

The Start Menu and Desktop might seem like weird items to redirect. Indeed, the only use I can imagine is in a common computing environment—such as a nurse's station, library computer, or kiosk—where you want to make sure the same Start Menu and/or Desktop are always presented. Then, you can lock down the target location of the redirected items to ensure that they cannot be changed.

In cases like these, you specify a shared folder with Read-only access for the Security group who will use it and Full Control for just one person who could change the Start Menu or Desktop (such as a fake account that no one uses within that Security group.) That way, no one in the affected group could normally change the common Start Menu or Desktop, except for the administrative user of the bogus account you created, who has Full Control permissions over the share.

Instead of using the *%username%* variable, you fix the redirection to a specific shared folder and directory, as shown in Figure 9.9. Since all users are to use the same settings, there's no need to use *%username%*. Indeed, since you're locking the shared folder down as Read-only for the Security group, the username is moot.

FIGURE 9.9   Use one static path to ensure that all desktops receive the same setting.

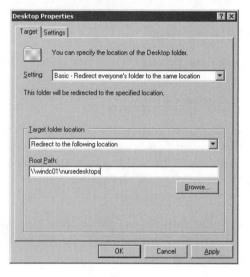

 You'll find additional Group Policy settings regarding the configuration of the Start Menu in User Configuration ➢ Administrative Templates ➢ Start Menu & Taskbar.

Redirecting the Application Data

Because application designers can decide what to put in the Application Data folder in the profile, an administrator never knows what size this folder could grow to. By redirecting the Application Data, files—such as custom dictionaries or databases—can be firmly planted on the server instead of having to go up and back with each logon with the Roaming Profile.

One potential downside is that this folder contains the user's private PKI (Public Key Infrastructure) keys. If you redirect this folder to a server, the keys are available to anyone with access to those files on the server. This isn't necessarily a security breach, because the keys are encrypted with a hash of the user's password and other elements, but take special precautions just in case.

The real danger in redirecting Application Data shows up when users need to decrypt EFS (Encrypting File System) files. To do so, they need access to their private PKI keys. If you've redirected Application Data to the server, and the server goes down or offline, how will users get their keys to decrypt their EFS files? Answer—they don't.

If the connection to the PKI keys is lost, one of two things happens.

- If the client is a Windows 2000 Professional machine, the keys are cached in memory until they are cleared out by reboot.

- If the client is a Windows XP Professional machine, the EFS files are simply unable to be accessed because the PKI keys are not cached in memory. A network or local connection to the PKI keys must be established for Windows XP Professional machines.

Troubleshooting Redirected Folders

Occasionally, Folder Redirection doesn't work as it should. Or, maybe it does. We'll check out some cases in which it appears not to be working but really is.

Windows XP Fast Boot and Folder Redirection

If you see the message in Figure 9.10, you might initially think that Folder Redirection isn't working as it should. This event tells us that because Fast Boot is enable in Windows XP (the default), Folder Redirection will not take affect until the next logon. With Fast Boot enabled, Basic Folder Redirection needs two logons to take effect. With Fast Boot enabled, Advanced Folder Redirection needs three logons to take effect. (See Chapter 3 for more information.)

FIGURE 9.10   Fast Boot in Windows XP can delay Folder Redirection until multiple reboots

Permissions Problems

Be sure that the user has access to the folder; specifically, make sure that the share you use for Folder Redirection is set for Authenticated Users:Full Control. Without it, you might encounter EventID: 101s, as shown in Figure 9.11.

FIGURE 9.11 Be sure the user has permissions to write to the share you set up.

Another common event for security problems is Event 112: "The security descriptor structure is invalid."

Use *GPResult* for Verification

First, make sure the user is actually being affected by the GPO you set up that contains your Folder Redirection policy. Use the GPResult tool we explored in Chapter 3. Figure 9.12 shows a snippet from the output of GPResult /v on Windows XP when Folder Redirection is working.

FIGURE 9.12 GPResult can help you determine if Folder Redirection is working.

```
Folder Redirection
-------------------
    GPO: My Docs Folder Redirection
        Setting:   InstallationType:  basic
            Grant Type:         Not Exclusive Rights
            Move Type:          Contents of Local Directory moved
            Policy Removal:     Leave folder in existing location
            Redirecting Group:  Everyone
            Redirected Path:    \\windc01\data\bwier\my documents\My Pictures

    GPO: My Docs Folder Redirection
        Setting:   InstallationType:  basic
            Grant Type:         Not Exclusive Rights
            Move Type:          Contents of Local Directory moved
            Policy Removal:     Leave folder in existing location
            Redirecting Group:  Everyone
            Redirected Path:    \\windc01\data\bwier\my documents
```

If no Folder Redirection policy displayed in the output when you run `GPResult /v`, chances are the user is not being affected by the policy. Check to see if the user has permissions on the GPO for both "Read" and "Apply Group Policy." If they are getting the GPO as indicated via `GPResult /v`, also make sure that the target server is still available, that the share is still shared, and that the users have rights to write to that share and folder. Last, make sure the user isn't hitting a disk quota on the volume on which the shared folder resides, as this can generate mixed results.

Enabling Advanced Folder Redirection Logging

Folder Redirection can provide a detailed log should the event log and `GPResult` not turn up what you're looking for. To create a log file for the Folder Redirection process, you need to modify the Registry as follows:

```
HKLM\Software\Microsoft\Windows NT\CurrentVersion\Diagnostics
```

If the `Diagnostics` key doesn't exist at the end of this Registry path, you'll need to create it. Then, you'll add a new Reg_DWORD of `FdeployDebugLevel` and set it to `0f` in hex or 15 in decimal.

Once you do this, you can find the log file at:

```
%windir%\debug\usermode\fdeploy.log.
```

Only the administrator can read the log file, so you have only two options. First, you can log out as the user, and log back in as the local administrator to read the log file. in action. Alternatively, you can use the `runas` command to view the log as an administrator while you're still logged in as the user.

Offline Files and the Synchronization Manager

We've mitigated the amount of traffic our network will have to bear from Roaming Profiles by implementing Redirected Folders—especially for My Documents. But we still have another hurdle. Now that we're anchoring our users' data to the server, what's to happen if the server goes down? What happens if our network cable is unplugged? What if our top executive is flying at 30,000 feet? How will any of our users get to their data? The answer, in fact, comes from another IntelliMirror feature—Offline Files—and its cousin, the Synchronization Manager.

Offline Files Basics

Offline Files seeks to make files within shares that are normally accessed online available offline! You can be sitting under a tree, on an airplane, in a submarine—anywhere—and still have your files with you.

Here's a brief overview of the magic: Once you enable a particular share to support the function, the client's Offline Files cache (called auto-cache) maintains files as they're used on the network. When users are online and connected to the network, nothing really magical happens. Users continue to write files upon the server as normal. However, in addition to the file writes at the server, the file writes additionally get reflected in the local cache too, as a protection to maintain the files in cache.

You can use Offline Files for any share you like and practically guarantee that the data users need is with them. The following examples use Offline Files to guarantee users access to their private data in their My Documents folders. However, it's certainly possible to use Offline Files for public "common" shares. For example, an administrator can set up shares for customer data, and a server can have a "general repository" from which multiple users can access files.

WARNING Note, however, that there are two shares that you should place Offline Files upon. Don't use Offline Files with the SYSVOL share. Nor should you use Offline Files with the Profiles share you created in the last chapter (more on this later).

Synchronization Manager Basics

But a potential problem lies in these public "common" shares: what if someone on the road and someone in the office change the same document? In that event, the Synchronization Manager handles conflict resolution on behalf of the Offline Files component.

In specific terms, the Synchronization Manager is a framework for "handlers" (also known as "plug-ins") such as the Offline Files mechanism to use. This is a bit confusing, because when conflicts occur, it certainly looks as if the Synchronization Manager is doing all the work, as you can see in Figure 9.13. When a conflict arises, The "Resolve File Conflicts" dialog box opens, with a rudimentary conflict-resolution engine.

FIGURE 9.13   The conflict-resolution engine helps users decide which version of a file they want to keep.

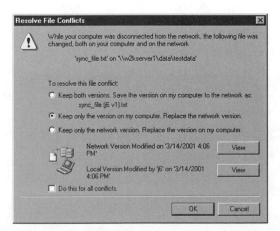

Turns out, the credit doesn't go the Synchronization Manager; rather, it goes to the Offline Files handler! You can also plug in other handlers to the Synchronization Manager, such as the built-in Offline Web Pages snap-in and a SQL plug-in.

When conflicts occur, the Offline Files handler asks the user whether they want to keep the copy on the server, keep the copy on the workstation, or preserve both by renaming the local version. Additionally, the user can inspect the contents of each version of the file, although that's usually not much help because there's no "compare changes" component to this resolution engine, and there's no way to "merge" the documents. But you can paw through the file yourself if you can remember where the last change was. It's not much, but it's a start.

In general, the Offline Files handler is fairly smart. If a file is renamed on either side (network or local cache), the engine wipes out the other instance of the file (because it thinks it's been deleted) and creates a copy of the new one. Hence, it appears a rename has occurred.

Be sure to continue reading to understand the relationship between Offline Files and the Synchronization Manager. In this section, we'll explore how Offline Files works—out of the box for both Windows 2000 and Windows XP—and you'll see how to configure the Synchronization Manager. You'll also see how to configure both the Offline Files mechanism and the Synchronization Manager with policy settings.

All in all, Offline Folders with the Synchronization Manager is kind of like the Windows 95 Briefcase, except that it works!

Making Offline Files Available

When you set up any shared folder on Windows 2000 or Windows 2003, you'll notice a new "Offline Settings…" button, as highlighted in Figure 9.14 (seen as the Caching button on Windows 2000). The Offline Settings dialog box is slightly different in Windows 2000 and Windows 2003. Figure 9.14 shows the Windows 2003 version, and the default in 2000 is "Manual Caching for Documents." The default named "Only the files and programs that users specify will be available online" setting may not really be the most efficient setting for this feature. The four settings are described in the following sections.

FIGURE 9.14   Four Offline Settings for caching behavior are available in Windows 2003.

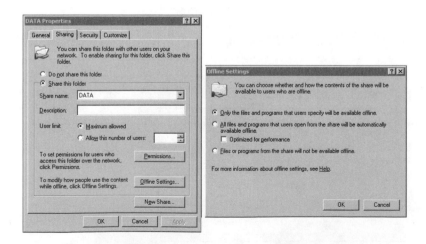

Only the files and programs that users specify will be available offline (or Windows 2000's "Manual Caching for Documents")

With this setting, users must specify which files they want to keep with them offline. They can do this in the My Documents folder by right-clicking a file and choosing "Make Available Offline" from the shortcut menu, as shown in Figure 9.15 for a Windows 2000 machine. The unofficial term for this is *pinning* a file, but you won't see that term in any Microsoft documentation. Users can pin as many files as they like, the number of files limited only by the size of their hard drive.

If a Windows 2000 or Windows XP user chooses to pin individual files manually (again, by right-clicking over a document and selecting "Make Available Offline" as seen in Figure 9.15, the Offline Files Wizard asks them some simple questions. This wizard runs only the first time a user pins one or more files, and each user on a computer who pins files from that computer walks through the wizard once. Figures 9.16 and 9.17 show two screens from the wizard.

FIGURE 9.15   Users can "pin" files by right-clicking them and making them available offline.

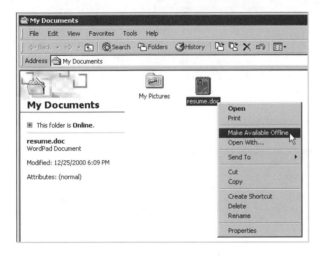

FIGURE 9.16   The Offline Files Wizard asks if the user wants to synchronize upon logon and logoff—usually a pretty good idea.

FIGURE 9.17 If the Enable Reminders check box is checked, your users will know if something happens to the network; the only problem is that your users then know that something has happened to the network!

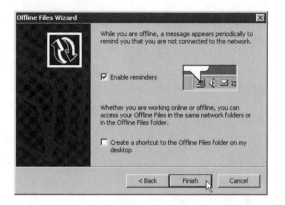

A balloon announces changes in Offline Files cache state, although a user who does not enable reminder balloons will still see the initial state change balloon tips. Once the wizard is finished (as shown in Figure 9.18), the pinned files are automatically brought down into the local cache.

FIGURE 9.18 When synchronization is complete, this dialog box automatically closes.

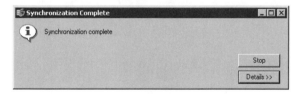

Users get a little graphical reminder attached to the pinned file's icon, as shown in Figure 9.19.

FIGURE 9.19 Pinned files can easily be recognized by their "roundtrip" yin-yang icon.

The reminder is an unobtrusive yin-yang icon symbolizing the harmony users will feel knowing their files are safe on the server and cached locally. Or maybe it's just two arrows showing the file can be "round-tripped." You can be the judge.

If you want, you can disconnect the network cable to your test client and still access any file that's now available offline.

As you saw in Figure 9.8 earlier in this chapter, users logging on to Windows XP machines with the redirected My Documents folder already have these yin-yang icons on their files and folders. Windows XP does a little extra magic and guarantees that all files in important redirected folders (such as the redirected My Documents) are available wherever the user roams.

All files and programs that users open from the share will be automatically available offline (or "Automatic Caching for Documents" for Windows 2000)

If you plan to use Offline Folders for more than just the user's private data, typically you select this option. When users access any files in a share with this setting, the files are copied and stored in a local cache on the workstation, where, by default, 10 percent of the C: hard drive space is used to maintain files in a first in/first out fashion.

For example, let's say you have a 1GB C: partition. In this case, 100MB of data flows in and out of your cache. Let's also say that you have 11 files, each 10MB in size, named FILE1.DOC through FILE11.DOC. You consecutively click each of them to open them and bring each into the cache. FILE1.DOC through FILE10.DOC are maintained in the cache until such time as FILE11.DOC is read. At that time, since FILE1.DOC was first in the cache, it is also the first to be flushed from the cache to make way for FILE11.DOC.

> The files are ejected in a background thread called the "CSC Agent." The agent periodically makes a pass over the cache removing auto-cached files as necessary. If a WRITE operation grows the cache size beyond the established limit, it doesn't immediately evict the least recently used auto-cached file. The CSC Agent is only periodically brought into memory for execution.

Additionally, files can be pinned, as they were in the "Only the files and programs that users specify will be available online" (or Windows 2000's "Manual Caching for Documents") option. Pinned files don't count toward the cache percentage. In other words, pinned files are exempt from being flushed from the cache and are always available to your users.

> While it's tempting, do not use Automatic Caching for Documents for the share that houses the Roaming Profiles you set up in Chapter 6. See the section "'Files or programs from the share will not be available offline' (or 'Disallow Caching for Files of Any Type' on Windows 2000)" later in this chapter for the reasons.

Files or programs from the share will not be available offline (or "Disallow Caching for Files of Any Type" for Windows 2000)

If you choose this option, no files are cached for offline use, nor can they be pinned. This doesn't prevent users from copying the files to any other place they might have access to locally or to another network share they have access to that does have caching enabled.

Another Option: "Optimized for Performance" (or "Automatic Caching for Programs" for Windows 2000)

This option's name is highly misleading. The idea is to use this setting for Read-only files that you want available offline and in the cache, such as executables. According to Microsoft, this setting does a "version check" instead of creating a handle on the server if the access is Read-only. Since there is no server handle, the system tries to use the local version first to save bandwidth when it can use either the locally cached version or the network version.

Upon performing a network trace of the interaction of "Optimized for Performance" (for Windows 2003) and "Automatic Caching for Programs" (in Windows 2000), there seems to be no discernible difference between it and Windows 2003's "All files and programs that users open from the share will be automatically available offline" (or "Automatic Caching for Documents" for Windows 2000). Therefore, use "All files and programs that users open from the share will be automatically available offline" (or "Automatic Caching for Documents") whenever possible.

Client Configuration of Offline Folders

Most of the time, you'll configure your servers to specify "All files and programs that users open from the share will be automatically available offline" (or "Automatic Caching for Documents" for Windows 2000). With that in mind, let's pay some special attention to this area. You can configure clients to use Offline Folders with the aforementioned setting in three ways:

- Take the "do nothing" approach.
- Run around to each client and manually specify settings.
- Use Group Policy. (Insert fanfare music here.)

This section explores the options a client can set on their own computer (or with your assistance.) Then, in two sections, "Using Group Policy to Configure Offline Files (User and Computer Node)" and "Using Group Policy to Configure Offline Files (Exclusive to the Computer Node" we'll explore the broader stroke pen of GPOs to see what sort of configuration we can do.

The "Do Nothing" Approach

If you do absolutely nothing at all, your clients will start to cache the files for offline use the first time they touch files in a share. This is called auto caching. The underlying Offline Files behavior is the same for Windows 2000 and for Windows XP. However, Windows XP has a trick up its sleeve, depending on how Explorer is configured.

 Note that Windows 2003 client computers do not ever cache files; this feature is specifically disabled in the operating system.

This difference will be important and should be noted if you plan to enable caching for your shares to use Offline Folders. In the examples in this section, we have a share called SALES, which contains some important files for our sales users. For this example, again, ensure that the

> ### Roaming Profile Shares and Offline Cache Settings
>
> You should not use any caching with shares for Roaming Profiles. If any caching is enabled for profiles, Roaming Profiles can fail to act normally. Roaming Profiles has its own "internal" caching that is incompatible with Offline Files caching.
>
> The correct choice for Roaming Profile shares is to select "Files or programs from the share will not be available offline" for shares on Windows 2003 or "Disallow Caching for Files of Any Type" for shares on Windows 2000.
>
> The Windows 2003 caching default is to select "Only the files and programs that users specify will be available online," and the Windows 2000 default is to select "Manual Caching for Documents." These settings are not ideal, as there might be a way for a user to get into the contents of their profile and make portions available offline.
>
> If you did set up a profile share in the last chapter, go back to that share and ensure that the share is set to disallow all caching.

"All files and programs that users open from the share will be automatically available offline" caching option is set on the share on our server.

Windows 2000 Reaction to Enabling Caching on Shares

Wanda is using her Windows 2000 laptop. She maps a drive to the sales share (which maps as E:, as shown in Figure 9.20). When she uses Explorer to view the files on E:, she sees one she needs (`Customer1.doc`) and double-clicks it to open it (as you can see in the bottom rightmost window in Figure 9.20). The file is now placed inside the Offline Files cache.

To see which files are within the file cache, Wanda chooses Tools ➢ Folder Options ➢ Offline Files ➢ View Files to open the topmost window in Figure 9.20. I'll discuss selecting View Files later in the "Windows XP Reaction to Enabling Caching on Shares" section.

Wanda continues, using several documents in her redirected My Documents folder. Only the files she specifically opens will automatically be placed in the cache. She logs off and goes home.

Windows XP Reaction to Enabling Caching on Shares

Wanda's co-worker, Xena, is using a Windows XP laptop to do similar work. She maps a drive to the sales share (which maps as Y:, as shown in Figure 9.21). When she uses Explorer to view the files on Y:, she sees one she needs (`Customer1.doc`) and double-clicks it to open it (as shown in the bottom rightmost window in Figure 9.21). That file is immediately placed inside the Offline Files cache.

To see which files are win the file cache, Xena choose Tools ➢ Folder Options ➢ Offline Files ➢ View Files to open the topmost window (in Figure 9.21).

Additionally, as shown in Figure 9.8 earlier in this chapter, any files in redirected My Documents have the yin-yang roundtrip icons. As I alluded to, this icon means that any file in a redirected folder is automatically always available offline. What's interesting is that you can see the same icon demonstrating the file is roundtripped in two places. You can see the same icon in a document in My Documents (`file1.txt`) and also in the "Offline Files Folder" window. The file will be listed as "Always available offline." The other files within the redirected My Documents are present within the Offline Files Folder window, but are simply not displayed in Figure 9.21 due to space constraints.

When Xena then uses Explorer to open Y: to see the Sales files, she sets into motion a flurry of events that are particular to Windows XP. That is, as soon as Explorer touches the rest of the files in the Sales share, they begin to download and are automatically in the offline cache. Again, Xena didn't click each of the `.doc` files in the Sales share; rather, she only opened an Explorer window. This behavior is specific to Windows XP (and not to Windows 2000). The Explorer in Windows XP is different from that in Windows 2000. Specifically, Windows XP Explorer performs an actual "file touch" to retrieve additional information, such as the file's Summary information or, for instance, when it tries to create a mini-view of a graphic. This "file touch" occurs only in Explorer's Thumbnails view in Windows XP, not in List or Details view.

In Figure 9.21, the "Synchronization" field for the other files in the Sales share is listed as "Local copy is incomplete." This signals that the files are currently being downloaded into the cache. Once the files are fully downloaded and the window refreshed, the field changes to "File is synchronized" as seen next to the file Customer1.doc in Figure 9.21.

FIGURE 9.20   The files in the Offline Files folder cache are only those that Wanda (on her Windows 2000 laptop) has actually used.

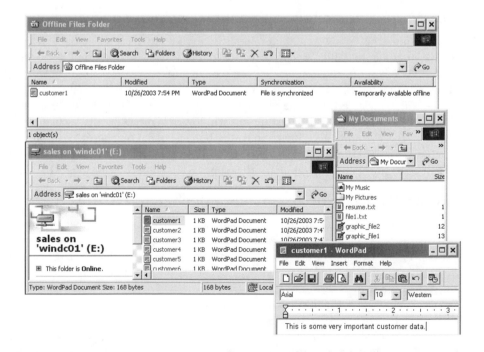

FIGURE 9.21   An Offline Files folder in Windows XP shows much more activity than an Offline Files folder on a Windows 2000 machine.

It's Not Offline Files... It's Explorer!

As you saw, Windows 2000 and Windows XP cache files in different ways. Windows 2000 caches only files that are specifically pinned or files that are specifically used in shares that have caching enabled. Windows XP caches files that are specifically pinned, files that are in redirected folders, and any file in a share that has caching enabled (once Explorer is used to touch the file).

But it's not really the offline cache that changes at all... it's Explorer! Because Explorer's Thumbnails view in Windows XP is more rigorous than Windows 2000's counterpart, you're simply "more likely" to download stuff into the cache. Indeed, Explorer isn't the only possible program that works like this; any application that requires anything more than a basic touch to the file triggers a download of the file into the offline cache—regardless of whether the client is Windows 2000 or Windows XP! For instance, searching for files in network shares also plunks data into the cache. Basically, any time a file is opened for read, it's put in the cache.

On the surface, you might think this behavior Windows XP's Explorer's Thumbnails view is a good thing. Sure, it's silently downloading files! Indeed, how could this be a bad thing? Because if Wanda puts a 100MB file in the Sales share, Xena will be forced to download it. Take it to a high pitch, and this could be a potential exploit to a denial of service attack.

Table 9.1 shows specifically what happens with Windows XP and Windows 2000 Explorer.

TABLE 9.1 How Windows Explorer Reacts to Caching with Offline Files

Explorer View	Action for Windows XP	Action for Windows 2000
Thumbnails	As soon as you open a window in Thumbnails view, all files begin downloading into the cache.	Files are not downloaded into the cache when users open a window and are simply look at the files. However, as soon as the file is clicked, it is downloaded into the cache.
Tiles	Files are not downloaded into the cache when a window is open and users are simply looking at the files. However, as soon as the file is clicked, the file is downloaded into the cache.	Not an option.
List	Files are not downloaded into the cache when a window is open and users are simply looking at the files. However, as soon as the file is clicked, the file is downloaded into the cache.	Files are not downloaded into the cache when a window is open and users are simply looking at the files. However, as soon as the file is clicked, the file is downloaded into the cache.
Details	Files are not downloaded into the cache when a window is open and users are simply looking at the files. However, as soon as the file is clicked, the file is downloaded into the cache.	Files are not downloaded into the cache when a window is open and users are simply looking at the files. However, as soon as the file is clicked, the file is downloaded into the cache.
Large Icons	Not an option.	Files are not downloaded into the cache when a window is open and users are simply looking at the files. However, as soon as the file is clicked, the file is downloaded into the cache.
Small Icons	Not an option.	Files are not downloaded into the cache when a window is open and users are simply looking at the files. However, as soon as the file is clicked, the file is downloaded into the cache.

Running Around to Each Client to Tweak Offline Files and the Synchronization Manager

As you saw, Windows 2000 and Windows XP have a baseline interaction with the synchronization of files. Optionally, you can manually configure your clients for some additional features of Offline Files and the Synchronization Manager. Earlier I described the synchronization mechanism of Offline Files as a "plug-in" for the Synchronization Manager. When you want to change the client-side behavior of how Offline Files works, you need to fundamentally understand this concept.

Since Offline Files is one entity and the Synchronization Manager another, they have two separate interfaces. Since they're independent entities, some pieces work independently; however, since Offline Files has a plug-in to the Synchronization Manager, they are also interdependent. To get a unified idea of how these two components work separately and together, you first need to locate their interfaces and see what goodies each has. You then need to know how they interact.

The Offline Files Interface

To manually tweak the Offline Files behavior, you'll need to get to the Offline Files interface. To do so, open the My Documents folder, and choose Tools ➢ Folder Options, as shown in Figure 9.22, to open the "Folder Options" dialog box, as shown in Figure 9.23. In this case, we're using the My Documents folder, though any Explorer window returns the same results. The default folder options are shown in Figure 9.23. As stated, 10 percent of the C: drive is configured to hold the cache.

The defaults are different for Windows 2000 Professional and Windows XP versus Windows 2000 and 2003 Server. In Windows XP and Windows 2000 Professional, the "Enable Offline Files" check box is checked, but it is unchecked for Windows 2000 Server and Windows Server 2003.

FIGURE 9.22   The Folder Options item on the Tools menu is the first place to start your Offline Folders configurations.

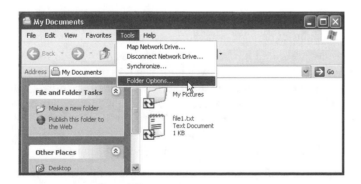

FIGURE 9.23 The default options for Offline Files on a Windows XP Professional machine. Only administrators can change all the options.

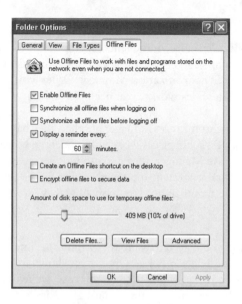

On the Offline Files tab, click the "Enable Offline Files" check box to display the other options (as follows), which user can configure.

Synchronize All Offline Files When Logging On   This setting is available only for Windows XP, and the user can change it. This entry co-interacts with the Synchronization Manager's similar entries entitled "When I log on to my computer" and "When I log off my computer." I'll talk more about this in the section "Offline Files and Synchronization Manager Interaction."

Synchronize All Offline Files Before Logging Off   The user can change this option. This entry co-interacts with the Synchronization Manager's similar entries entitled "When I log on to my computer" and "When I log off my computer." I'll talk more about this in the section "Offline Files and Synchronization Manager Interaction."

Display a Reminder Every… (or Enable Reminders for Windows 2000)   When this box is selected (and a number is entered), users get a little pop-up balloon explaining that the connection to the machine where the files are stored has been severed. This is another win-lose area. On the one hand, if this option is selected, your users are well informed that the network has gone down. On the other hand, your users are well informed that the network has gone down, and they will probably call you, complaining. (This is because every new dialog box a user encounters automatically means that you need to be called, but I digress.) You can leave this option on or off here or use Group Policy to turn it off (as you'll see a bit later.) Figure 9.24 shows a special case for balloon reminders that cannot be turned off. This occurs when the state changes.

Create an Offline Files Shortcut on the Desktop (or Place Shortcut to Offline Files Folder on the Desktop for Windows 2000)   Enabling this option displays a shortcut on the Desktop, the same as if you were to click the "View Files" button in the Folder Options dialog box. I'll discuss "View Files" in a moment.

FIGURE 9.24   Pop-up balloons inform your users that they have lost connectivity to the network.

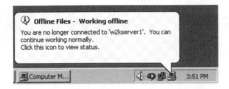

Encrypt Offline Files to Secure Data   Only administrators can choose this setting, which is available only for Windows XP and Windows 2003. Administrators everywhere should be running to enable this setting. This is one of the major benefits for putting Windows XP on desktops and especially on laptops. That is, if the user uses EFS (Encrypting File System), the files stored in the offline cache are also encrypted. In Windows 2000, this was a major security hole. Specifically, if the laptop was stolen, the bad guy wouldn't be able to get to the encrypted data files on the hard drive, except for those still preserved in the offline files cache! With just a little know-how, this was a major exploit. Did I mention how major this is? Be sure to select this check box (or use a GPO to ensure the policy setting gets delivered to all your Windows XP and Windows 2003 machines). The bad news is that even with this nice plug, an attack is still possible on EFS. See `www.sans.org/newsletters/hacking_efs1.htm` for more information.

Amount of Disk Space to Use for Temporary Offline Files   This slider goes from 0 percent to 100 percent of your C: drive. The default is 10 percent. Again, only files set up to use "All files and programs that users open from the share will be automatically available offline" (or "Automatic Caching for Documents" for Windows 2000) use this setting. Files that are manually pinned are not counted toward the percentage specified here; they are always available. You can change this percentage using Group Policy, as you'll see a bit later. Due to a limitation in the way Windows 2000 and Windows XP were written, only 2GB of disk space can maximally be used.

The following three additional option buttons are certain to scare away even the most fearless of end users. You just click on each of the following three buttons which gives you more stuff to play with:

Delete Files...   This opens up the "Confirm File Delete" dialog box. Users run in terror when they see the word "Delete." Because of this, there's a good chance that they won't go poking around here. Indeed, nothing actually gets deleted other than the files in the local cache. Files on the server stay on the server.

View Files   This opens up the "Offline Files Folder" window. This button lets you peek into the local cache, as shown in Figures 9.20 and 9.21 earlier in this chapter. Files that are pinned are represented as "Always Available Offline." Those that are just in the cache for now are listed as "Temporarily Available Offline." This interface is similar to Explorer; it's really Explorer with rose-colored glasses on to make sure that the under-the-hood manipulations of the local cache are properly handled. The local cache is actually stored in the hidden directory `C:\windows\CSC`. Do not use Explorer or a command prompt to poke around there. The best way to manipulate locally cached files is through the View Files GUI.

Offline Files and Windows 2000 Server and Windows 2003 Server

By default, Offline Files is enabled only on the workstation versions of the operating system, such as Windows XP and Windows 2000. On Windows 2000 servers and Windows 2003 servers, you specifically enable it (either via Group Policy or manually, as seen in the section "Offline Files Interface" and in Figure 9.23). The idea is that this function is largely used when mere-mortal users log on to their desktop systems—not when administrators log on to servers. However, it can be manually enabled.

If you intend to use Offline Files when logged on to Windows 2003, you must disable Remote Desktops. To do so, right-click My Computer and choose Properties from the shortcut menu to open the System Properties dialog box. In the Remote tab, ensure that "Allow users to connect remotely to this computer" is cleared. Of course, this will disable Remote Desktop connections, but, indeed, will allow you to utilize Offline Files while logged on at Windows 2003 systems.

Advanced   This opens up the "Offline Files—Advanced Settings" dialog box. In this scary dialog box, you can specify what happens if a computer becomes unavailable. You can prevent the user of this workstation from accessing files in the local cache should the corresponding server go down. To be honest, I don't know why on earth you would ever do this, except for some wacky security concern. This is on a per-server, not per-share basis, so be especially careful if this user has many shares on one particular server.

The Synchronization Manager Interface

The Synchronization Manager is a framework for plug-ins such as Offline Files to use. You can open the Synchronization Manager (the Items to Synchronize dialog box, which is shown in Figure 9.25) in two ways.

- From the Desktop, choose Start ➢ Programs ➢ Accessories ➢ Synchronize.
- In Explorer, choose Tools ➢ Synchronize.

Users can specifically choose which plug-ins they want to use, such as "Offline Files" or "Offline Web Pages" as shown in Figure 9.25. For each plug-in, they can select which data (such as shares) they want the Synchronization Manager to handle. Additionally, the buttons in this dialog box perform the following functions:

Synchronize   Forces the Synchronization Manager to pop into the foreground and start the synchronization process.

Properties   Allows the user to open the Offline Files folder to view the files in the local cache. Same as the "View Files" button shown earlier in Figure 9.23.

Setup...   Allows you to refine how synchronization is controlled. You can see the result in Figure 9.26.

FIGURE 9.25   Users can select specific shares on which to synchronize items.

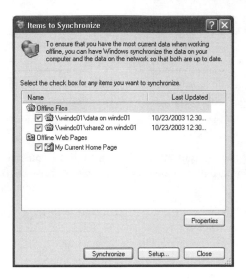

FIGURE 9.26   The Synchronization Manager is a framework for snap-ins such as "Offline Files" and "Offline Web Pages."

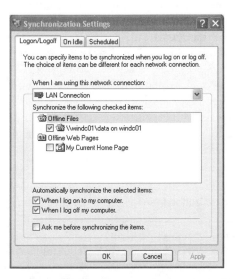

Here a user can specify which Synchronization Manager snap-ins to use. In this case, the "Offline Files" snap-in is selected (with one entry), and the "Offline Web Files" is not selected. The other entries on the Logon/Logoff tab that need specific attention are the "When I log on to my computer" and "When I log off my computer." These entries co-interact with the Offline Files "Synchronize All Offline Files before Logging off" and "Synchronize All Offline Files when logging on," as in Figure 9.23 earlier in this chapter. Now, we'll take some time to explore that interaction.

Offline Files and Synchronization Manager Interaction

As I've alluded to several times, Offline Files and Synchronization Manager are both independent and co-interdependent processes. In other words, when the Offline Files handler is used as a snap-in for the Synchronization Manager, they become co-interdependent.

Offline Files has two possible synchronization modes: Quick Sync and Full Sync. Here's how each works:

Quick Sync At logon, the files that were modified in the local client cache are pushed up to the server. At logoff, only the files that the user actually opened on the server are brought down into the local cache.

Full Sync At logon, *all* the files the user has in cache are synchronized with the copies on the server. Updated files on the server also come down into the cache. Also, if the user is caching an entire folder, those files come down into the cache. At logoff, the same occurs. That is, all the files the user has in cache and any new files on the server are synchronized in the cache.

For Full Sync, we're mainly concerned with the two options: "Synchronize All Offline Files before Logging off" and "Synchronize All Offline Files when logging on." The key word to focus on in these options is *all*. You can see these settings in Figure 9.23 earlier in this chapter. Checking either of these options (or both) directs the Offline Files handler to utilize the Synchronization Manager to synchronize *all* content.

The Synchronization Manager settings (seen in Figure 9.26 earlier in this chapter) control how the Synchronization Manager responds to the "logon" and "logoff" conditions on the computer. If these check boxes are *not* checked, *no* Synchronization Manager activity occurs at the corresponding time. These settings apply equally to all handlers registered with Synchronization Manager—not just the Offline Files handler.

So that's how they work together: the two dialog boxes' settings are interdependent for how Offline Files will synchronize. Indeed, if the corresponding Synchronization Manager setting is *not* enabled, the Offline Files setting has no effect.

Table 9.2 describes the behavior at logon.

TABLE 9.2 Logon behavior with Synchronization Manager settings and Offline Files settings

Synchronization Manager Setting "When I Log on to My Computer"	Offline Files "Synchronize All Offline Files When Logging On"	Resulting Behavior
Off	Off	No sync activity at logon
Off	On	No sync activity at logon
On	Off	Quick Sync at logon
On	On	Full Sync at logon

Table 9.3 describes the behavior at logoff.

TABLE 9.3   Logoff behavior with Synchronization Manager settings and Offline Files settings

Synchronization Manager Setting "When I Log off My Computer"	Offline Files "Synchronize All Offline Files before Logging Off"	Resulting Behavior
Off	Off	No sync activity at logoff
Off	On	No sync activity at logoff
On	Off	Quick Sync at logoff
On	On	Full Sync at logoff

Unfortunately, there is little coordination between the Synchronization Manager and Offline Files user interfaces. However, there is one small interaction: If you enable Offline Files' "Synchronize All Offline Files when logging on" or "Synchronize All Offline Files before Logging off," Windows automatically enables the corresponding Synchronization Manager setting. The opposite is not true.

People often think there is more coordination between Offline Files and Synchronization Manager than there really is. It's not uncommon for people to think that Synchronization Manager *is* Offline Files. Synchronization Manager is simply a place to host various synchronization plug-ins (such as Offline Files), a place where those plug-ins can display their items, and a place for users to select specific items for synchronization at specific times (and in response to specific events).

Using Folder Redirection and Offline Files over Slow Links

In Windows 2000 and Windows XP, Offline Files thinks a slow link is 64Kbps. Since no analog modem is going to achieve that speed, every normal dial-up user will be, theoretically, coming in over a slow link. When a user comes in over a slow link (less than 64Kbps), the system automatically uses their locally cached version of network files. Additionally, the foreground Synchronization Manager will not run.

When using Offline Files over a slow link, you need to consider both private stuff and public stuff and then how Windows 2000 and Windows XP will react to that stuff.

Synchronizing over Slow Links with Redirected My Documents

The first place you can run into trouble is if the user has never synchronized on a particular machine. For example, Charlie is a member of the Marketing group. He's given a generic "workgroup" laptop to take to an emergency meeting in China. But Charlie doesn't synchronize with the fast LAN network before he runs out the door to catch his plane. Of course, he won't have any files while he's on the long flight to China; but worse, when he gets to China and dials in, he won't see any files in his My Documents folder either, although we know they're still safe and sound on the redirected network share set up for him.

Why does this happen for Charles in China? Because the default behavior for Charles's computer is that it won't process Folder Redirection over slow links. If you're planning to make redirected My Documents a reality over slow links (for users who haven't ever synchronized with the LAN), you'll need to set up a GPO that affects target computers; and, ideally, these target computers will receive this GPO before they leave for their trip. You'll need to set up a GPO that enables the **Folder Redirection policy processing** policy setting and inside set it to "Allow processing across a slow network connection." Again, if you don't do this, users won't see their files in My Documents when they dial up unless they've already performed a synchronization with the Synchronization Manager before they left for the trip.

Now, you have to consider what operating system Charles is using. If you gave Charles a Windows 2000 laptop, the logon time won't be too long. However, if you gave Charles a Windows XP laptop, the logon time might be tremendously long. Why? Remember that Windows XP in conjunction with any redirected folder, such as My Documents, attempts to "Make available offline" every file. If Charles has 300MB of files in his redirected My Documents folder, the system tries to automatically pin all 300MB of those files by copying the data from the server to the local system.

I hear you yelling at me now. "Jeremy, why on earth would I enable **Allow processing across a slow network connection** if I'm setting my Windows XP users up for torture?" My answer? See the new Windows XP policy setting entitled **Do not automatically make redirected folders available offline**, which will return Windows XP to the behavior of Windows 2000 and not pin all redirected files. That way, the bandwidth your Windows XP users utilize when dialing up won't get crushed when using slow connections with redirected folders.

Remember though that unless the user copies the files he needs locally or manually pins them, the files in My Documents will not be available offline. This philosophy is a yin-yang thing… just like the icon.

Synchronizing over Slow Links with Public Shares

Let's look at another example. Harold, Walter, and Xavier are members of the Sales group. Harold stays put in the home office and works on a desktop machine. Walter has a Windows 2000 Professional laptop, and Xavier has a Windows XP laptop. Walter and Xavier are sometimes in the office and sometimes on the road. When in the home office, all employees plunk files into the share \\east_server\salesfigures, which is configured to use "All files and programs that users open from the share will be available offline." They all use the Frankfurt.doc file. Both Walter and Xavier normally synchronize their computers every time they log off, grabbing the latest version of Frankfurt.doc.

Both Walter and Xavier leave for Frankfurt, Germany, to woo a prospective account. During the time that Walter and Xavier are on the plane, Harold (who's back in the office) modifies the `Frankfurt.doc` file with up-to-the-minute information on their prospective customer. Walter and Xavier get drunk on the plane ride over and sleep the entire way. They don't even crack open their laptops to look at the `Frankfurt.doc` file on each of their laptops. In short, they don't modify their copies on the laptops; only Harold modifies a copy at the home office.

Walter and Xavier check in to the same hotel (different rooms) and dial the home office. They both want to ensure that the latest copy of `Frankfurt.doc` on the server is downloaded to their laptops to present to their client in the morning.

Windows 2000 Offline Files over Slow Links

When Walter connects, he's coming in over a slow link. Room service arrives just as he connects, and he forgets that he's logged on. An hour passes, and Walter remembers that he's dialed in! Frantically, Walter disconnects. Even with that hour-long connection, Walter does not receive any updated files via Quick Synchronization. Unfortunately, he will end up looking like a jerk in tomorrow's meeting.

Walter has four choices if he wants to get the latest copy of the file from the server:

- Manually copy the file from the share to a place on his local computer. (How quaint.)

- Right-click the file in the share and pin it with "Make available Offline." The file is now permanently available offline.

- Double-click the file to open it. Then, the synchronization field changes to "Temporarily available offline" (though it should be already), and the "Modified" field is updated to the current time stamp from the server. The file is then updated in the cache.

- Manually force a synchronization over the slow connection to synchronize any pinned file or file already in the cache, including `Frankfurt.doc`.

Windows XP Synchronization Manager over Slow Links

Xavier dials the office as well. Room service arrives just as he connects, and, like Walter, he forgets that he's logged on. If Explorer in Windows XP is set up to display files in Thumbnails mode, Explorer is actually opening the files. Because `Frankfurt.doc` is actually opened, it naturally makes its way into the cache. You can see this by peering into the Offline Files folder. You can see its status is changed to "Local copy is incomplete."

FIGURE 9.27   In Windows XP, Explorer is more vigorous in actually touching and opening files; hence, they are downloaded into the cache.

Some time later, the Synchronization column for `Frankfurt.doc` will change to "File is synchronized." Here's the upshot:

- Files aren't just automatically downloaded because it's Windows XP. They're downloaded because of Explorer's Thumbnails view touches the files.

- All other files in the share that Xavier has used will try to update via Quick Synchronization (if Xavier hasn't updated the files himself on his laptop).

- As soon as Xavier uses Explorer to examine the files in the share with Windows XP's Thumbnails view, all the files in the share will try to be downloaded over the slow link. This could be painful.

Synchronization Manager State Transitions

Mobile users access their locally cached versions of files. They then return to the office and dock their systems—without a new logon or logoff. This is called a *state transition.* When a state transition occurs, the system evaluates several criteria to decide if it should keep working offline (using the files in the local cache) or start working online (using the files on the network).

A successful transition to an online state requires the following:

- All offline files in the local cache must be closed.

- The connection must be greater than 64Kbps (by default).

If either of these requirements is not met, the user will still be using the locally cached version of the file—even if the network share is theoretically usable across the network.

Again, if this user wants to use a fast connection instead of the locally cached files, they can choose Start ➤ Programs ➤ Accessories ➤ Synchronize to kick-start the connection, or they can click on the little computer icon in the notification area.

To get the latest files in the share, the user needs to synchronize again by choosing Start ➤ Programs ➤ Accessories ➤ Synchronize. If the connection is determined to be a fast connection, changed files are automatically added to the cache for recurring synchronization.

Sometimes an automatic state transition does not function as it should. In this case, users are advised to log off before docking. Once they are docked and network connectivity is established, logging on causes a normal synchronization cycle. Sometimes automatic state transition functions as it should, but a little slower than expected. Don't forget that Microsoft Office isn't the only application that can keep files open. Other day-to-day productivity applications you deploy for users can keep files open, and, hence, a state transition does not occur.

Xavier's computer is connected over a slow, expensive connection. And now he's downloading the `Frankfurt.doc` file (small) and any other (potentially very very large) file that is now on the share. This could be a major problem if Xavier just wants that one file fast. Poor Xavier is after just the `Frankfurt.doc` file that Harold modified. Xavier has some options while using the slow connection:

- Wait long enough, and `Frankfurt.doc` will automatically download in the background. Again, this happens because in Windows XP Explorer opens the file in Thumbnails view.

- Wait long enough, and all files on the share will synchronize automatically. Windows 2000 will not do this. Again, this happens because in Windows XP Explorer opens the file in Tiles or Thumbnails view. However, files Xavier might not care about are also being synchronized.

- Double-click the file to open it. The Synchronization column then immediately changes from "Local copy is incomplete" to "File is synchronized."

- Manually copy the file from the share to a place on his local computer.

- Right-click the file in the share and pin it with "Make available Offline."

- Manually synchronize `Frankfurt.doc` and all other files in the share. This spawns the Synchronization Manager to help ensure that Xavier has the latest file and also helps if any conflicts arise.

Using *Cachemov.exe* to Move the Client Side Cache

You might find a reason to change the original placement of the CSC folder. For instance, you might have some PCs with two (or more) physical hard drives. Perhaps you're running out of space on the C drive, or maybe you just want to tune a machine's performance by splitting the duties over two hard drives.

You can use the `Cachemov.exe` utility in the Windows 2000 Server Resource Kit. Simply run `Cachemov.exe` on the workstation that has multiple hard drives. When you are done, you have a choice as to where to move the C:\%windir%\CSC, as shown here:

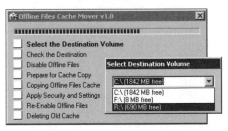

You can also use `Cachemov.exe` to execute batch-style in a logon script. If you want to affect multiple computers, you can run `Cachemov.exe -unattend d:\`, in which d is the drive to which the new CSC folder will move. `Cchmvmsg.dll` needs to be in the path when running `cachemov.exe` in unattended mode. This tool is not available in the Windows 2003 Server Resource Kit, but seems to work fine with Windows XP. Use at your own risk.

Using Group Policy to Configure Offline Files (User and Computer Node)

In both Offline Files and the Synchronization Manager, a user can be thoroughly confused. The good news is that most Offline Files settings can be delivered from upon high. The bad news is that there are no policy settings for the Synchronization Manager. This is kind of a bummer.

The policy settings for the Offline Files are found in two places in the Group Policy Object Editor. Some settings affect users specifically. To get to those settings, fire up the Group Policy Object Editor, and traverse to User Configuration ➢ Administrative Templates ➢ Network ➢ Offline Files, as shown in Figure 9.28.

Nearly all the same settings are also found in the Computer side of the house, at Computer Configuration ➢ Administrative Templates ➢ Network ➢ Offline Files, as shown in Figure 9.29.

This gives you flexibility in how to configure Offline Files. You can mix and match—within the same GPO or from multiple GPOs. The general rule is that if both computer and user settings are specified on the target—the computer wins.

In this section, I'll briefly detail what each Offline Files policy setting does. Since most of the policies overlap in both User and Computer configuration nodes, I'll discuss all the User and Computer configuration settings and then discuss those that apply only to the Computer configuration settings.

FIGURE 9.28   You'll find a slew of Offline Files options under the User node.

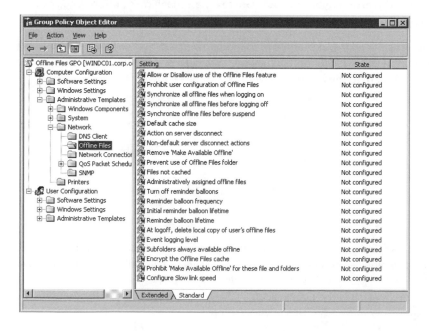

FIGURE 9.29   Many Offline Files options can also be found under the Computer node.

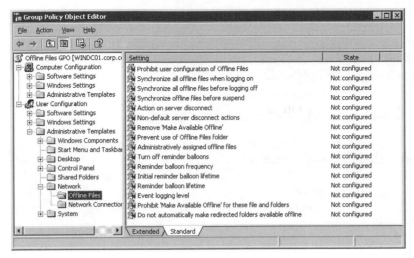

Prohibit User Configuration of Offline Files

If this policy setting is enabled, users on the target client computer embrace the default Offline Files settings and won't be able to change them. Indeed, this happens by the forceful removal of the Offline Files tab normally found in the Folder Options dialog box, as you saw in Figure 9.23 earlier in this chapter.

Synchronize All Offline Files When Logging On

Enabling this setting grays out the "Synchronize all offline when logging on" check box in the "Offline Files" tab in the Folder Options dialog box (as seen in Figure 9.23) on the target machine, so the user can't change it. Be sure to read the section "Offline Files and Synchronization Manager Interaction" earlier in this chapter to understand how this setting works.

Synchronize All Offline Files When Logging Off

Enabling this setting grays out the "Synchronize All Offline Files before Logging Off" check box in the "Offline Files" tab in the Folder Options dialog box (as seen in Figure 9.23) on the target machine, so the user can't change it. Be sure to read the section "Offline Files and Synchronization Manager Interaction" earlier in this chapter to understand how this setting works.

Synchronize All Offline Files Before Suspend

Enabling this setting ensures that a full synchronization occurs before the user suspends or hibernates the machine (which usually means they will undock it or otherwise take it offline). The operating system must know about the change, and this will not work if you just close the lid on a laptop.

Action on Server Disconnect

If this policy setting is enabled, you can select one of two options from the "Action" drop-down list box. This is analogous to the Advanced dialog box mentioned in the section, "The Offline Files Interface" In a nutshell, you can allow normal operation of Offline Folders, or cease the use of Offline Folders if the server goes offline. Again, avoid using this function, as it essentially defeats the whole purpose of Offline Folders.

Nondefault Server Disconnect Actions

This is similar to the previous policy setting. It corresponds to the "Exception List" which is revealed after pressing the Advanced button—again, found in the Folder Options Offline Files tab Whereas the previous policy setting specified the defaults for all servers, this policy setting specifies settings for specific servers.

Settings enabled here override those in the **Action on Server Disconnect** policy setting as well as any other policy settings set for the target systems. When this policy setting is enabled, the Exception list is removed to prevent users from making changes.

When you configure the Computer or User option of this policy setting, the box's radio buttons above the Exception list are gray, but the Exception list itself is not. You can add any computers you desire, but they will not take effect with the policy setting in place.

This policy setting is a bit wacky. That is, the policy setting will take effect on refresh, but the radio buttons don't show the actual setting until you reboot. My testing proved that a reboot was necessary for both Computer and User option settings to show in the interface. Also, when the User and Computer configurations conflict, the least restrictive setting takes precedence. If the Computer policy says you can't see the server when offline, but the User configuration says you can, you will be able to see the Offline Files when offline.

To configure this policy setting, choose Enable ➢ Show ➢ Add to open the Add Item dialog box. In the "Enter the Name of the Item to Be Added" field, type the name of the server that you want to have an explicit setting, such as **MysteryServer**. In the "Enter the Value of the Item to Be Added" field, enter either a **1** to keep the users offline or a **0** to keep them online, as shown in Figure 9.30. Click OK to add the server as an exception, click OK to close the Show Contents dialog box, and close the **Nondefault Server Disconnect Actions** policy setting.

Remove "Make Available Offline"

Enabling this policy setting prevents users from pinning files by right-clicking them and selecting "Make Available Offline." Files are still cached normally as dictated though other policies or by the defaults. Additionally, enabling this policy setting will not unpin already pinned files. Therefore, if you think you might not want users pinning files, you'll need to turn this setting on early in the game, or you'll be forced to run around from machine to machine to unpin users' pinned files.

Enabling this setting does not interfere with either the "Automatic Caching for Documents" or the "Automatic Caching for Programs" setting on shared folders (as described earlier). Those files are not permanently cached (pinned).

FIGURE 9.30   Use this feature to prevent users from using a specific server's files when offline.

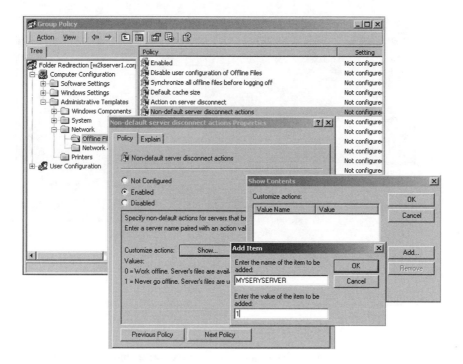

Prevent Use of Offline Files Folder

This setting prevents users from clicking the View Files button inside the Folder Options dialog box. Once this option is set, users may not know which files are currently available in the cache or always available in the cache.

Administratively Assigned Offline Files

This is arguably the most useful setting in the bunch. Recall that Windows XP automatically pins all files in redirected folders such as My Documents, which Windows 2000 will not do. However, with this policy setting, you can guarantee that your Windows 2000 users (especially laptop users) have all the files in their My Documents folder both on the local hard drive and safely synchronized to the server—not just redirected there. This ensures that the copy is both synchronized at the server and pinned to the local hard drive.

Remember, though, that since these files are pinned; they are exempt from the percentage cache used (10 percent by default.) This means that the cache can be used for other network files as your users use them. Follow these steps:

1. Enable the setting.

2. Click the Show button next to Files and Folders.

FIGURE 9.31 Use the Administratively Assigned Offline Files policy setting to force specific files or folders to be pinned—like the My Documents folder!

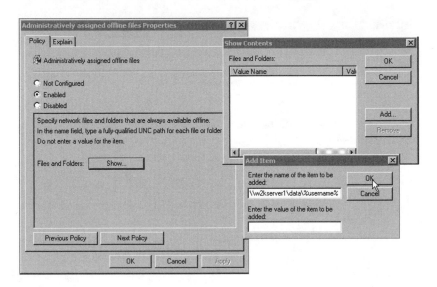

3. In the Show Contents dialog box, click Add to open the Add Item dialog box.

4. Enter the server and share name. If you want to guarantee the redirection of My Documents (only necessary for Windows 2000), enter the server, share and folder for the user, or leverage the *%username%* variable, as shown in Figure 9.31.

5. Leave the "Enter the Value for the Item to Be Added" field blank.

6. Click OK to render the share Assigned Offline.

7. Click OK to close the Show Contents dialog box and the Administratively Assigned Offline Files policy setting.

The next time your users get this policy setting assigned, all the files affected will be pinned. Every newly created file will be pinned as well, as shown in Figure 9.32.

Additionally, by enabling this setting, you can force a file or folder to be pinned for a user in any other share you like. For instance, you can force the vice president of sales to always have their sales figures available. This might be useful if they're on an airplane without a 30,000-foot network cable plugged back into the network on the ground. You can forcefully command that they receive certain files—even if they didn't pin them.

Turn off Reminder Balloons

This corresponds to "Enable Reminders" in the Folders Options dialog box. Again, you might want to disable the balloons, because they may only serve to spook the herd. See Figure 9.20 earlier in this chapter for an example of a reminder balloon (though that particular balloon cannot be removed). Enabling this policy setting disables the balloons. Disabling this policy setting prevents users from disabling the balloons.

FIGURE 9.32   All files inside the My Documents folder on this Windows 2000 system are now pinned.

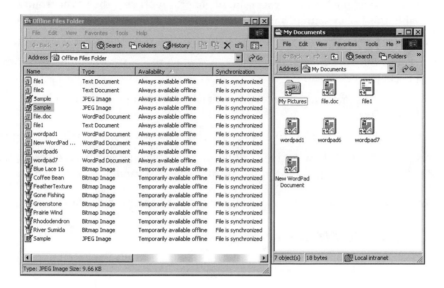

Reminder Balloon Frequency

By default, balloons pop up every 60 minutes to remind the user that they are working offline. Enabling this policy setting and setting a time in the spin box sets that frequency and prevents the user from changing it. Disabling the policy setting keeps the default (60 minutes) and prevents users from changing the defaults.

Initial Reminder Balloon Lifetime

The first balloon that pops up lasts 30 seconds. Use this setting to specify how long the first balloon stays up. Enabling this policy setting and entering a time in the spin box sets that duration and prevents the user from changing it. Disabling the policy setting keeps the default (30 seconds) and prevents users from changing the defaults.

Reminder Balloon Lifetime

After the first balloon pops up, consecutive balloons pop up every 60 minutes by default (or for whatever value is configured in the **Reminder Balloon Frequency** policy setting) for a total of 15 seconds each, as defined by this policy setting. Enabling this policy setting and entering a time in the spin box sets that duration and prevents the user from changing it. Disabling the policy setting keeps the default (15 seconds) and prevents users from changing the defaults.

Event Logging Level

This is a good debugging feature if users complain, er, report that their synchronizations are failing. Enable this policy setting, and enter a value of 0, 1, 2, or 3:

- Level 0 records an error to the Application Log when the local cache is corrupted.

- Level 1 logs the same as level 0, plus an event when the server that houses the offline file disconnects or goes down.

- Level 2 logs the same as level 1, plus an event when the computer affected by this policy setting disconnects.

- Level 3 logs the same as level 2, plus an event when the corresponding server gets back online.

Figures 9.33 and 9.34 show examples of notifications when a server becomes available again. Remember, these logs appear in the log at the workstation, not at the server.

FIGURE 9.33   The workstation log shows that the server is available.

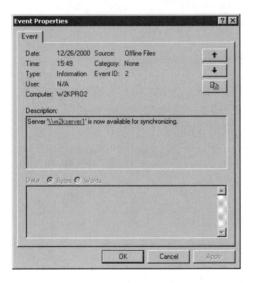

Prohibit "Make Available Offline" for These File and Folders

Okay, so there's a grammar problem in the name of this policy setting, but it's still useful. If you want to allow most users to pin files in a share, but ensure that certain users can't pin files in a share, this is the policy setting for you. After you enable this setting, just add the full UNC (Universal Naming Convention) path to the share or share and file you want to block from being pinned. For instance, if you want to block \\windc01\sales from being pinned, enter it in this policy setting and then ensure that it applies to the appropriate users.

 This policy setting only applies to Windows XP and Windows 2003 computers.

FIGURE 9.34   The workstation log shows state transitions in relation to the server.

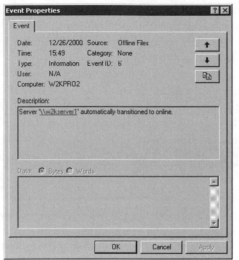

Do Not Automatically Make Redirected Folders Available Offline

I get several e-mails a month asking me how to prevent Windows XP from pinning all files in redirected folders such as My Documents. Here it is. Ensure that it affects all the users you want.

 This policy setting only applies to Windows XP and Windows 2003 computers.

Using Group Policy to Configure Offline Files (Exclusive to the Computer Node)

As we just explored, most policy setting settings for Offline Files are duplicated in both the User and Computer halves of Group Policy. But several settings appear only on and apply only to the Computer half.

Allow or Disallow Use of the Offline Files Feature

Previously, in Windows 2000, this policy setting was called **Enabled**, a really horrible name; so I'm glad they renamed it for Windows 2003. This policy setting is similar to the **Prohibit**

user configuration of Offline Files setting discussed in the previous section. Once that policy setting is enabled, the Offline Files feature is active, and users cannot turn it off. If this policy setting is enabled, Offline Files is enabled, but users can change the settings. If no additional GPOs are defined, the defaults are used. Once this policy setting is disabled, the target machine's Offline Files tab in the "Folder Options" dialog box (seen in Figure 9.23) has grayed-out check boxes, and Offline Files is disabled.

Recall that Offline Files is enabled only for Windows 2000 Professional and Windows XP. It's disabled for servers by default. You can use the **Allow or Disallow use of the offline files feature** policy setting to your advantage to turn on Offline Files on all your Windows 2000 Servers or Windows Server 2003 computers easily—not that you would need to, as it's highly unlikely your servers will often be offline. Note that Windows Server 2003 requires that Remote Desktop Connections be disabled in order for Offline Files to function. See the sidebar entitled "Offline Files and Windows 2000 Server and Windows Server 2003" earlier.

If you enable this feature, it should kick in right away (when the background refresh interval hits). However, disabling this feature is another story. If one or more files are open in the cache when you try to disable the feature, that disable operation will fail; a reboot is required. You can experience the same behavior when trying to disable the feature through the user interface.

Default Cache Size

This corresponds to the "Amount of disk space to use for temporary online files" slider in the Offline Files tab in the Folder Options dialog box, as shown in Figure 9.23 earlier in this chapter. You can control what percentage of the C: partition is available for automatic caching.

If you enable this policy setting, you must enter a whole number that represents what percentage of the partition you will be using. If you want to use 31 percent, enter 3100. (The total range begins at 0 percent, then can be set to 100 or 1 percent, and ends at 10,000 or 100 percent.) This setting is then locked in, and users can't change it. If you disable this policy setting, the default of 10 percent is locked in, and users can't change it. Remember that this has a maximum size of only 2GB. Since this policy setting works with a percentage value, it can be difficult to know if that percentage exceeds 2GB on any target volume.

You might need to reboot the target machine for this policy setting to take effect. It does not always work when a background refresh is kicked off.

Files Not Cached

By default, several file extensions cannot be cached, due to their sensitive nature. Microsoft is concerned that especially large files will be shuttled up and back with just 1 byte changed. Therefore, the synchronization is hard-coded not to cache certain file extensions, most notably databases. That is, for extra protection, Microsoft prevents databases from being cached. The following file types cannot be cached:

- `.pst` (Outlook personal folder)
- `.slm` (Source Library Management file)
- `.mdb` (Access database)
- `.ldb` (Access security)
- `.mdw` (Access workgroup)
- `.mde` (Access compiled module)
- `.db?` (Everything that has the extension `.db` plus anything else in the third character, such as `.dbf`, is never included in the cache.)

If you enable this policy setting, you can add to this list. For instance, you can add your own file types in the form of `*.doc`, `*.exe`, and `*.jam` to also eliminate the caching of only `.doc`, `.exe`, and `.jam` files. In my testing, there appears to be no way to allow the caching of the hard-coded database files listed earlier. If users try to synchronize any of these file types, the Synchronization Manager balks with a "Files of This Type Cannot Be Made Available Offline" message.

At Logoff, Delete Local Copy of User's Offline Files

This policy setting sort of defeats the purpose of using Offline Files in the first place. Its main purpose is for logon use at a kiosk-style machine. That is, a user logs on for a bit and then logs off. You'll want to ensure their Offline Files are cleaned up behind them. Another reason I can see using this policy setting is to prevent files from being lifted off a user's hard drive. Theoretically, you can do this by digging around in the c:\windows\CSC folder. Even if the files are deleted at logoff, a good hacker could theoretically get the files back via an "undelete" program of some type.

Moreover, this policy setting doesn't guarantee a synchronization before it wipes the local cache clean upon logoff. Therefore, it is highly recommended that if you use this policy setting, you pair it with the "Synchronize All Offline Files before Logging Off" option (seen in Figure 9.23), which will save your users' bacon. Avoid using this option unless you have some workstation that needs extra security and is infrequently used, and you don't mind if the occasional file gets lost when using it.

If protection is what you're after, and you use EFS setup for your laptops users, a better option (for Windows XP machines only) is to use the "Encrypt the Offline Files cache" policy setting, discussed shortly.

Subfolders Always Available Offline

This policy setting is useful if you want to ensure that all subfolders are also available offline. Essentially, it prevents users from excluding the ability to cache subfolders and makes subfolders available offline whenever their parent folder is made available offline. Any new folder a user creates under cached subfolders is automatically cached and synchronized when the parent folder is scheduled for synchronization.

Encrypt the Offline Files Cache

If you have EFS set up for your laptop users, enabling this policy setting is a good idea. By default, even files stored in an encrypted format on shares are not protected in the Windows 2000 file cache. With Windows XP, they can and should be.

 This policy setting only applies to Windows XP and Windows 2003 computers.

Synchronization Manager Limitations

You might see some weird behavior if a single computer is shared among multiple people. You can see this behavior in the following example:

Configure two GPOs that redirect My Documents to two different locations, \\WS03ServerA\ UserDocs and \\WS03ServerB\UserDocs. Link the first GPO to OU-A and the second GPO to OU-B. OU-A contains Fred, and OU-B contains Robin.

Fred logs on and verifies that the My Documents redirection has taken effect by looking at the path in the Properties dialog box. If Fred opens the Synchronization Manager after creating or modifying a file in \\WS03ServerA\Data, he sees the \\WS03\UserDocs UNC in the synchronization list. When he logs off, he sees the synchronization happen for this UNC.

Now Robin logs on to the same Windows XP workstation and verifies that My Document redirection has taken effect. When Robin opens Synchronization Manager, she sees the \\WS03ServerB\UserDocs UNC and the \\WS03ServerB\UserDocs UNC in the synchronization list. When she logs off, she sees both paths attempting to perform a synchronization.

You can take this to extremes too. Try to configure five users in five different OUs with five different GPOs, each redirecting My Documents to one of five different servers. As each user logs on to a single Windows XP desktop (or a Windows 2000 desktop and chooses to manually cache the share), the UNC path for that user is added to the UNC paths for the other users in Synchronization Manager.

So what should you do? Allow only your laptop users to use offline caching. You can configure a GPO to stop block offline caching for desktops and leave it enabled for laptops. Since laptop users don't tend to share their machines often, they don't build up many synchronization links. The workaround for those users is to open Synchronization Manager and uncheck all UNC paths except their own. But no user is going to do this. The answer here is not ideal, but it should help a bit.

Thanks to Bill Boswell for inspiration on this tip.

Configure Slow Link Speed

Recall that the Synchronization Manager in Windows 2000 and XP thinks a slow link is 64Kbps. When a user comes in over a slow link (less than 64Kbps), the system automatically uses their locally cached version of network files. Additionally, the foreground Synchronization Manager does not run. You can change the definition of the speed of a slow link, but only for Windows XP and Windows 2003 clients.

 This policy setting only applies to Windows XP and Windows 2003 computers.

Disk Quotas

Disk quotas restrict users' disk space—either on their local workstations or on your servers. Disk quotas are necessary because, without them, one user can monopolize an entire volume on a server by taking up all its disk space.

The underlying code for Windows NT disk quotas has been around since the Stone Age of the computer world—Windows NT 3.1 to be exact—but the interface never made its way out of Redmond. Until now.

 Don't take my word for it—check out the Knowledge Base article Q103657.

Microsoft's scheme for disk quotas in Windows 2003 is Per User/Per Volume—the same as it was for Windows 2000. Since a disk volume appears in Windows Explorer as a drive letter, you can just as easily think of it as Per User/Per Drive Letter. Quick Quotas in Windows 2003 entail but one improvement over Windows 2000. That is, Quick Quotas can charge disk quotas to users on files that are open as well as files that are closed. In Windows 2000, the files were only charged to the user when the files were closed.

This has several ramifications and limitations. First, there is no centralized "Quota Administrator" in Active Directory. You can't set up quotas centrally to say "On every server in the Corp.com domain, Johnny Badguy gets 20MB." Nor can you say "In total, on every server in the Corp.com domain, Johnny Badguy's total used disk space shall never be more than 200MB." Maybe some day, but not today. Some third-party independent software vendor is going to make a killing figuring out how to restrict a user's quota per domain or per forest. However, I made the challenge in the initial writing of this chapter some years ago, and today it's still not done.

Understanding File Ownership

The quota system figures out who is over quota based on the File Ownership attribute, which is only available under NTFS. Thus, only NTFS drives can be monitored for quotas.

At this point, you might be scratching your head and thinking this is a good time to, perhaps, run the convert utility on any partitions housing user data. But beware: converted FAT to NTFS partitions do not automatically assign ownership to the user who seemingly owns the folder. Rather, the administrator becomes the owner of all files on the converted partition. In this case, the user who owns the file can actually take ownership of the file in two ways:

- Standard taking ownership

- Taking ownership the easy way

You can give the user's folder the Take Ownership right in the Permission Entry for Converted dialog box as shown here:

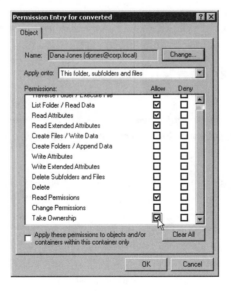

When a user logs on, they can then do the following:

1. Open Windows Explorer.

2. Right-click the folder, and choose Properties from the shortcut menu to open the Properties dialog box.

3. Click the Security tab, and then click the Advanced button to open the Access Control Settings dialog box.

4. Click the Owner tab, select their username, click the "Replace Owner on Subcontainer and Objects" check box, as shown here, and click OK.

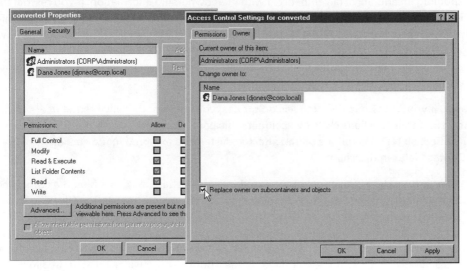

Between you and me, I bet there's a greater chance of the New York Mets winning the Super Bowl than any of your users figuring out that sequence!

A much better way to dictate ownership is through one of the following third-party tools.

Chown.exe   You can get this tool, which is distributed by MKS Sortware, in three ways:

- By accessing the APPS/POSIX subfolder on the Windows 2000 Resource Kit CD

- By downloading the evaluation version at www.datafocus.com/eval/

- By copying it from the Microsoft Services for Unix CD

The command syntax is as follows:

```
Chown.exe -R Djones d:\data\converted_directory
```

Here, –R signifies you are working on a directory, Djones is the username to be assigned ownership, and d:\data\converted_directory is a directory that is now on an NTFS drive.

Subinacl.exe   You'll find Subinacl.exe on the Windows 2000 Server Resource Kit CD. This is the Swiss Army Knife of permissions altering. If you want to change the ownership of the d:\data\converted_directory directory, as we just did, the syntax is:

```
subinacl /file d:\data\converted_directory\*.* /setowner=CORP\Djones
```

You must specify the domain name in the short NetBIOS form of CORP, not the FQDN Windows 2000 DNS style name of, say, corp.com.

Ownership also plays another role when users print to the printing subsystem; they are essentially spooling an additional file embedded with their ownership information. If you restrict the partition that houses the print spooler too tightly with disk quotas, users might hit their limit and hence not be able to print. Usually, this isn't a problem because most configurations have the spooler on the C: drive and a user's data volume on the D: drive. Since Windows 2000 uses Per User/Per Volume criteria, affecting the D: drive with quotas, yet performing the print spooling from the C: drive, leaves printing functions unaffected.

However, if you use Group Policy to assign quotas, you could potentially restrict users from printing and other functions quite by accident. This could happen because the Group Policy actions affect all NTFS partitions on the affected system, as explored in the section "Enable Disk Quotas" later in this chapter.

Ownership information is also important if multiple users share the same file on a common share. For example, Frank and Harry, both have Read and Write access to the SalesFigures share on the D: volume. Frank's quota on the D: volume is 10MB, and Harry's quota is 30MB. Frank creates a new Excel worksheet, puts in three figures, and closes the file. The file size is 200Kb. Harry then opens the Excel worksheet, adds 5 million new figures, and closes it. Now the file is 9.98MB. That 9.98MB is charged to Frank's quota—because he created the file and is the owner.

Quotas and Groups

As previously stated, the quota scheme is Per User/Per Volume. There is no way to leverage Active Directory security groups to deny the writing disk data. In other words, you cannot say, "The engineers' share, which is on the D: volume, can only grow to 300MB." Frustratingly, it's only Per User/Per Volume.

To add insult to injury, the underlying code is there to verify against group quota checking. For instance, the Administrators group is exempt from quotas by default. You can change this default behavior (for administrators only), as in the example in the later section "Apply or Exempt Quotas for a Specific User."

It's sad that quotas are only Per User/Per Volume, and but you can change this using third-party tools.

Designing and Implementing a Quota Strategy

Setting up quotas on a volume is easy. First, you must decide on your strategy. You have three:

- Apply a default quota to anyone who owns any files on the volume.
- Apply specific quotas to specific users who own files on the volume.
- Apply a default quota to anyone who owns any files on the volume and apply or exempt a specific user to a quota on the volume.

To set up quotas on a volume, follow these steps:

1. Open Windows Explorer on a server.

2. Right-click the drive letter, and choose Properties from the shortcut menu to open the Properties dialog box.

3. Click the Quota tab, as shown in Figure 9.35.

4. Click the Enable Quota Management check box to display the other options.

Warn or Restrict?

There are two schools of thought regarding quotas. One school says that, once warned, users will actually remove some unwanted files once a line in the sand has been drawn with regard to space. The other school says that users never delete anything from the time they're born until the time they're dead, and no wimpy warning message is going to stop them from writing more data. With that in mind, you need to choose your school of thought.

The options on the Quota tab are a little confusing. Let's take a look at them.

Do Not Limit Disk Usage   This disables a general warning level and hard limit for users on the server. You can still set limits for specific users on the server via the "Quota Entries..." button (explored in the "Apply or Exempt Quotas for a Specific User" section).

Limit Disk Space To   Enabling this setting restricts the user to a certain amount of disk space.

Set Warning Level To   Instead of restricting the user right away, you can specify a warning limit. When the user hits the warning limit, they get a message. Usually, it's a good idea to set the warning at 80% of the actual hard quota.

FIGURE 9.35   You modify the options on the Quota tab for each drive letter.

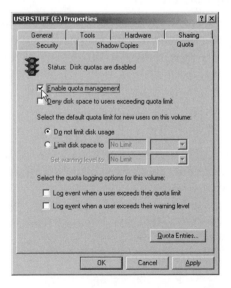

The final two check box options are found under the "Select the Quota Logging Options for This Volume section. They are "Log event when a user exceeds their warning level" and "Log event when a user exceeds their quota limit." Instead of enforcing a quota limit right away, you might want to monitor usage for a period of time, gathering a baseline of disk usage. It's true, however, that you'll have to spend some quality time with the server's log files to determine which users have gone over the set threshold.

Remember that, by default, the numbers you specify in the "Limit Disk Space to" and the "Set Warning Level to" entries affect all users who write any files to the volume. Once you've set up your defaults, click Apply to open the Disk Quota dialog box, as shown in Figure 9.36.

FIGURE 9.36   Once you apply Quota Defaults, the system looks for all users on that volume who own files.

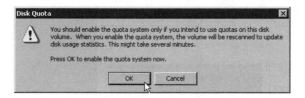

When you click OK, the quota system runs through the initial calculation of which users own which files on the volume and how much they own. The little traffic light symbol in the Quota Properties dialog box changes from red to yellow when performing this scan. When it's finished, it will change to green, and quotas will be activated.

Apply or Exempt Quotas for a Specific User

Usually, the needs of the many outweigh the needs of the few. But occasionally someone makes a legitimate request for exemption, such as your friend in the Accounting Department who promised you he'd burn more CDs of MP3 junk he downloaded from Kazaa for you on his lunch hour.

If you want to bump up or drop down a quota for a specific user or exempt them from quota analysis completely, start by clicking the "Quota Entries..." button in the Quota tab of the Properties dialog box to open the "Quota Entries for Local Disk" dialog box. Now follow these steps:

1.   To enter a specific quota for a user or group of users, choose Quota ➢ New Quota Entry. You'll then be prompted to enter the name of the user. Once you do, you'll see the "Add New Quota Entry" dialog box, as shown in Figure 9.37.

2.   You can now set a specific quota or no quota for that user, as shown in Figure 9.37. To exempt the user from the quota, click the "Do Not Limit Disk Usage" button.

FIGURE 9.37 In the Add New Quota Entry dialog box, set a specific user's quota differently from the defaults.

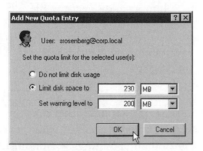

Once all users are entered, you can see which user is using how much disk space, as shown in Figure 9.38.

FIGURE 9.38 You can get a bird's-eye view of who's using how much disk space.

Status	Name	Logon Name	Amount Used	Quota Limit	Warning Level	Percent Used
OK	Sol Rosenberg	srosenberg@corp.local	277.87 KB	230 MB	200 MB	0
OK	Like User	luser1@corp.local	13.87 KB	20 MB	15 MB	0
OK	Jimmy Kissel	jkissel@corp.local	194.43 KB	25 MB	20 MB	0
OK	Dana Jones	djones@corp.local	257.9 KB	No Limit	No Limit	N/A
OK	Brett Wier	bwier@corp.local	730.31 KB	20 MB	15 MB	3
OK		NT AUTHORITY\SYSTEM	267.62 KB	20 MB	15 MB	1
OK		CORP\Administrator	381.6 KB	20 MB	15 MB	1
OK		CORP\Domain Admins	0 bytes	20 MB	15 MB	0
OK		BUILTIN\Administrators	2.82 GB	No Limit	No Limit	N/A

Quota Entries for Local Disk (D:)

Quota   Edit   View   Help

9 total item(s), 0 selected.

Import and Export Quota Entries

Although it's true that there's no way to set quotas so they apply over multiple servers, you can do the next best thing. You can export the list of users and quotas that you set up in the previous section to a file. You can then take that file to another server and import it. Voilà! Instant disk quotas. There's no way to keep the two lists in sync. If you change one entry, the other server doesn't know about it. But this is a good way to move the exemptions list from one server to another quickly.

To export the list of quota entries, follow these steps:

1. In the Quota Entries dialog box, select the quota entries you want to export. (Click and entry, hold down the Control key, and select additional entries.)

2. Choose Quota ➢ Export.

3. In the "Export Quota Settings" dialog box, provide any filename you want (with or without an extension) and select Save.

4. On the server to receive the list, choose Quota ➢ Import and select the file.

That's it.

Using Group Policy to Affect Quotas

Certain aspects of the quota system can be embraced from edicts from upon high. However, I think it's better to use the fine-stroke quill of individual server settings rather than these settings, which are more like a two-inch-thick Magic Marker. You may, however, find them useful.

You'll find the policy settings for Disk Quotas in Computer Settings ➢ Administrative Templates ➢ System ➢ Disk Quotas, as shown in Figure 9.39.

FIGURE 9.39   You can use policy settings to dictate quotas on specific machines.

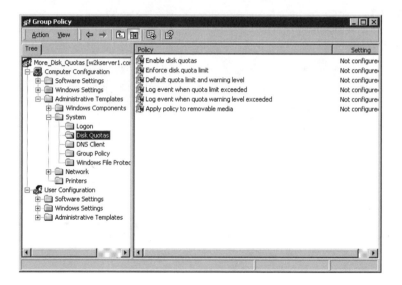

Enable Disk Quotas

This entry is analogous to "Enable Quota Management," as shown in Figure 9.35. Once this policy setting is enabled, all NTFS volumes on those computers that this policy setting affects will be part of the quota management system. Even administrators sitting at the local server will not be able to turn off the management once this policy setting is set. If this setting is disabled, disk quotas cannot be turned on, and even administrators sitting at the local server will not be able turn them on. By default, this setting is not configured, meaning that administrators can set up the quota system (or not) as they please.

Enforce Disk Quota Limit

This setting corresponds to the "Deny Disk Space To Users Exceeding Quota Limit" check box in the Quota tab in the Properties dialog box, as shown in Figure 9.35 earlier in this chapter. If this policy setting is enabled, users are denied space if the quota is reached. Administrators cannot clear the "Deny Disk Space To Users Exceeding Quota Limit" check box once this is set. If this policy setting is disabled, users can cross the "line in the sand" at will.

By default, this setting is not configured, meaning that administrators can choose to deny or not deny as they please.

Pair this policy setting with the next, **Default Quota Limit and Warning Level,** to set realistic warnings. Otherwise, the only limit is the physical space on the volume.

Default Quota Limit and Warning Level

This entry, as shown in Figure 9.40, corresponds to the "Limit Disk Space to" and "Set Warning Level to" entries as shown in Figure 9.35, earlier in this chapter.

FIGURE 9.40 You can set the default disk warning and disk limit of the affected computers.

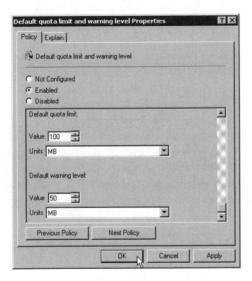

Simply enter the desired values in the "Default Quota Limit" and "Default warning level" fields. These entries apply for every NTFS volume on the affected computer.

In the event that this policy setting is applied after disk quotas are manually set up on a system, this policy setting overlooks current users (users who already own files on the volume) as well as users who explicitly have applied quotas or are exempt from them, as defined in the Quota Entries dialog box.

If this policy setting is not configured or is disabled, it is assumed that there is no limit to a user's space. Therefore, the warning and limit are ostensibly set to the maximum space available on the volume.

Log Event When Quota Limit Exceeded and Log Event When Quota Warning Level Exceeded

You might not be quite ready to put up the electric fence that prevents users from writing more files should their quotas be exceeded. You might want to simply log the actions for trend analysis. Enable this policy setting to generate the log entry; afterward, administrators cannot clear the corresponding check box. Disable the policy setting to guarantee no log entries.

Apply Policy to Removable Media

By default, JAZ, ZIP, and CD drives are exempt from quotas. Enable this policy setting to force the same compliance for removable media. Only NTFS formatted media can be affected by this policy setting.

Final Thoughts

IntelliMirror is a multiple-pronged approach to desktop management. In the previous chapter, you set up Roaming Profiles, which enable users' desktops to follow them on whatever workstation they use.

In this chapter, you set up Redirected Folders, which anchored the My Documents folder (among others) to the server. This gave you several key features: a centralized backup place for critical files, the ability for users' My Documents contents to be available on any workstation, and the ability to mitigate the generated traffic caused by My Documents being located within the profile. By default, the My Documents folder is located within the profile.

You also set up Offline Folders and the Synchronization Manager so that files work offline as though they were online. You used Group Policy to specify how your users and computers would use this function. Don't forget to use the **Administratively Assigned Offline Files** policy setting when necessary to force the My Documents folder of your Windows 2000 clients to be pinned—especially for your laptop users. Recall that My Documents are already automatically pinned if you use Windows XP.

Last, you used quotas to mitigate how much disk space your users can eat on any given volume.

In the next chapter, we'll continue our IntelliMirror journey. We'll learn how to distribute software to our users and computers. So, turn the page and get started!

IntelliMirror, Part 2: Software Deployment via Group Policy

Two chapters ago, I discussed and implemented the first big feature of IntelliMirror—Roaming Profiles. Once Roaming Profiles are enabled, the user can roam from machine to machine, comfortable that their working environment will follow wherever they go.

In the last chapter, I discussed and implemented more IntelliMirror features. First, we tackled Redirected Folders, which took Roaming Profiles one step further and anchored the user's My Documents folder to a share on a server. We then used the Group Policy settings on Offline Folders and the Synchronization Manager to ensure that certain files are always available in the cache if our connection to the server goes offline or if the server itself goes offline.

We're well on our way to getting the full point of IntelliMirror. That is, we want our users to roam freely across our entire environment and take all their stuff with them. But we're missing a fundamental piece of the equation: how can we guarantee that a specific application is ready and waiting for them on that machine? What good is having your user data follow you if an application needed to access the data isn't available? That's what we're going to handle in this chapter.

GPSI Overview

Without any third-party software distribution mechanism (such as Microsoft's Systems Management Server (SMS) or MobileAutomation's Mobile System Manager), most environments require that you spend most of your time running from desktop to desktop. In a typical scenario, a user is hired and fills out the human resources paperwork, and a computer with the standard suite of software is dropped on their desk. Usually this machine comes from some sort of "deployment farm" in the backoffice, where scads of machines are imaged (a la *Ghost*) by the scores.

The user then starts to surf the Internet—er, I mean—gets to work. Soon enough, it's discovered that the user needs a specific or special application, and a desktop technician is dispatched to fulfill the user's request for new software. When the desktop technician arrives, they either load the user's special software via the CD drive or connect to a network share to pull down the software.

Group Policy Software Installation, or GPSI for short, is the next IntelliMirror feature we'll set up. It's with this feature that users can automatically pull applications through the network, without needing anyone to be dispatched. This feature further chips away at the total cost of ownership (TCO) regarding workstation maintenance.

There are essentially four steps to going from zero to 60 when it comes to deploying software with IntelliMirror's GPSI features:

- Acquire software with a `.msi` extension

- Share and secure a software distribution shared folder

- Set up a GPO to deliver the software

- Assign or Publish the software

We will approach each of these steps in our software configuration journey in the next few pages.

The good news is that Group Policy GPSI can solve many of your software deployment woes. The bad news is that, like all other Group Policy features, the magic only happens with the marriage between Active Directory on the back end and Windows 2000 Professional, Windows XP, or Windows 2003 on the client.

Before we get too far along, I want to clear up a terminology misnomer. Specifically, many people incorrectly refer to the Group Policy Software Installation mechanism as the lone word "IntelliMirror." But as you can see, the Group Policy Software Installation mechanism is but one part of the unified IntelliMirror plan. So, to that end, we'll keep on truckin' with the proper terminology of Group Policy Software Installation or simply GPSI.

 Although it's true that Microsoft provides an "Active Directory Client" for Windows 9x and for Windows NT Workstation to be used with Active Directory, that "Active Directory Client" does not enable any Group Policy functionality. That client, by the way, is available on the Windows 2000 Server CD under the clients\win9x directory and provides additional features such as NTLMv2 authentication and some Active Directory searching. But it doesn't allow old clients to take advantage of Group Policy or GPSI.

The Windows Installer Service

A background service called the *Windows Installer Service* must be running on the client for the software deployment magic to happen. Although the actual service is the same, I like to think about there being almost two versions of this service—the "full" and the "lite" versions. The full version is built into Windows 2000, Windows XP, and Windows 2003 on the client. The full version can understand when Group Policy is being used to install or retract an application and react accordingly. The full version is also extra smart; it can run under "elevated" privileges. In other words, the user does not need to be a local administrator of the workstation to get software deployed via Group Policy. The Windows Installer Service installs the software with administrative privileges. Once installed, however, the program is run under the user's context.

The full version can also be initiated using *document invocation*; that is, it is automatically started when you choose a specific extension or extensions. For instance, if you select a file with a `.pdf` extension, the Windows Installer Service can be automatically invoked to bring down Adobe Acrobat Reader from one of your servers. This is also called *auto-install* and is described in more detail in the "Advanced Published or Assigned" section, later in this chapter. Additionally, the full version can determine when an application is damaged and repair it automatically by downloading the required files from the source to fix the problem.

The lite version of the Windows Installer Service, however, can only perform that last function: that is, it can determine when an application is damaged and repair it automatically by downloading the required files from the source to fix the problem. But it has no way to understand Group Policy, so it only gets us half of the equation. Installing Office 2000, for instance, on a Windows NT machine installs the lite version of the Windows Installer Service. And, if Office 2000 becomes damaged (for instance, `Winword.exe` is suddenly deleted), the user is prompted for the location of the source distribution: CD, network, or otherwise.

Again, there really isn't a full or lite version of the service; they are really the same animal. However, the number of features you can leverage depends on the underlying operating system.

Since Windows 2000 was released, there has been an update to the Windows Installer Service. It is integrated into Windows 2000 Service Pack 3 and higher. However, if you don't yet have Windows 2000 Service Pack 3 (and I can't imagine why you wouldn't), you can install the Windows Installer 2.0 Redistributable, which, at last check is, located at `go.microsoft.com/fwlink/?LinkId=7613`

Understanding *.msi* Packages

About 99% of the magic in software deployment with Group Policy is wrapped in a file format called `.msi`. The new `.msi` standard file has two goals: increase the flexibility of software distribution and reduce the effort required to make new packages. Files in the `.msi` format are becoming more and more "standard issue" when a software application is rolled out the door (though sometimes they are not.) For instance, every edition of Office since Office 2000 has shipped as a `.msi` distribution.

On the surface, `.msi` files appear to act as self-expanding distribution files, like familiar, self-executing ZIP files. But really, under the surface, `.msi` files contain a database of "what goes where" and can contain either pointers to additional source files or all the files rolled up inside the `.msi` itself. Additionally, `.msi` files can "tier" the installation; for instance, you can specify "Don't bother loading the spell checker in Word, if I only want Excel." Sounds simple, but it's revolutionary.

Moreover, because `.msi` files are themselves a database, an added feature is realized. The creator of the `.msi` package (or sometimes the user) can designate which features are loaded to the hard drive upon initial installation, which features are loaded to the hard drive the first time they are used, which features are run from the CD or distribution point, and which features are never loaded. This lets administrators pare down installations to make efficient use of both disk space and network bandwidth.

With `.msi` files, the bar is also raised when it comes to the overall management of applications. Indeed, two discreet `.msi` operations really come in handy: Rollback and Uninstall. When

.msi files are being installed, the entire installation can be cancelled and simply rolled back. Or, after a .msi application is fully installed, it can be fully uninstalled. You are not, however, guaranteed the exact same machine state from Uninstall as you are with Rollback. The GPSI features in Active Directory are designed mainly to integrate with the new .msi file format. There is other legacy support, as you'll see later.

Utilizing an Existing *.msi* Package

As stated, lots of applications come as .msi files. Some are full-blown applications, such as Office 2000 and later. Others are smaller programs that you might use a lot, such as the GPMC (Group Policy Management Console) or the .NET Framework. All these aforementioned applications come as a .msi. Be forewarned: just because an application comes as a .msi doesn't necessarily mean it can always be deployed via GPSI; however, that's a pretty good indication. Yet there are posts all over the Internet about how the Norton AntiVirus client now ships as a .msi but doesn't install via GPSI. Ditto for the full version of Adobe Acrobat; no dice via GPSI.

Additionally, some .msi applications (such as Office 2000 and later) can be deployed to either users or computers. However, some applications, such as the GPMC.msi and the .NET Framework's .msi can only be deployed successfully to computers.

You'll want to check with the manufacturer of the .msi file to understand specifically how it needs to be installed. The .msi files that can be deployed via GPSI usually come in two flavors:

- Some .msi packages are just one solitary file, and they come ready to be deployed. The GPMC, the .NET Framework, and the Windows Administration tools (Adminpak.msi) are examples in this category.

- Other .msi files need to be "prepared" for installation. Usually, these applications are more complex. Office 2000 (and later) as well as the service packs for Windows 2000 (and later) are examples in this category.

 The last edition of this text used an Adminpak.msi as its demonstration package for GPSI. The goal of Adminpak.msi is to plunk down all the administrative tools on your client systems for when you're performing system administration. If you don't have Adminpak.msi handy, you can read the previous edition to see how to distribute Adminpak.msi. Adminpak.msi is a bit special; however, there are versions specific for Windows 2000, Windows 2003, and Windows XP. See the Knowledge Base article Q304718 for more details.

Many people want to deploy big applications, such as the Office suite. In the following example, I'll assume you have a copy of Office XP and that you're licensed to distribute it to all your targeted clients. This same procedure will work for the enterprise editions of Office 2000 and Office 2003 if you are licensed for those instead.

Setting Up the Software Distribution Share

The first step is to set up the software distribution shared folder on a server. In this example, we'll use WinDC01 and create a shared folder with the name of Apps. We want all our users to be able to read the files inside this software distribution share because later we might choose to create multiple folders to house additional applications' source. Later, we'll create our first application subfolder and feed Office XP into its own subfolder.

To set up the software distribution shared folder, follow these steps:

1. Log on to WinDC01 as Administrator.

2. From the Desktop, click My Computer to open the My Computer folder.

3. Find a place to create a Users folder. In this example, we'll use D:\APPS. Once you've opened the D: drive, right-click D: and select the Folder command from the New menu; then type in **Apps** as the name.

 You can substitute any name for Apps.

4. Right-click the newly created Apps folder, and choose Sharing from the shortcut menu to open the Properties of the Apps folder, but focused on the Sharing tab. Click "Share this Folder." Windows 2003 servers should automatically have the Everyone group set to Read. While you're in the Permissions for the Apps dialog, additionally click the Add button and add the Administrators group to have Full Control permissions upon the share. Click OK to return back to the Apps properties, then click OK at the properties of the folder to share the folder.

You can use Share permissions, NTFS permissions, or both to restrict who can see which applications. The most restrictive permissions between Share level and NTFS level permissions are used. Here, at the Apps share, you want everyone to have access to the share. You'll then create subfolders to house each application and use NTFS permissions to specify, at each subfolder level, which groups or users can see which applications' subfolders.

Setting Up the *.msi* Package with an Administrative Installation

For our examples, we'll deploy Office XP. As stated, not all .msi files are "ready to go"; some need to be prepared. To prepare Office XP (or other Office installations later than Office 2000), you must perform an *Administrative Installation* of its .msi file. In this procedure, you rebuild and copy the .msi package to your source folder for download by your clients. While the package is being rebuilt, it injects the serial number for your users and other customized data. Again, to be clear, not all .msi packages must be prepared in this manner. Be sure to check your documentation.

To perform an Administrative Installation of Office 2000 or later, you'll use the msiexec command built in to Windows 2000 and Windows 2003. The generic command is msiexec /a whatever.msi. For Office XP, the command is msiexec /a PROPLUS.MSI.

When you run this command, Office XP is not installed on your server (or wherever you're performing these commands). This can be confusing, as the Office Installation Wizard is kicked off, and it will write a bunch of data to your disk. Again, to be clear, an Administrative Installation simply prepares a source installation folder for future software deployment.

The Office Installation Wizard will show that it's getting ready for an Administrative Installation, as shown in Figure 10.1.

Normal Shares versus Dfs

The GPSI features are like the postal service; they're a delivery mechanism. Their duty is to deliver the package and walk away. But it's something of a production before that package is delivered into your hands, and that's what we'll tackle in the next section.

Before we get there, however, you need to prepare for software distribution by setting up a *distribution point* to store the software. You can choose to create a shared folder on any server— hopefully one that's close to the users who will be pulling the software. The closer to the user you can get the server, the faster the download of the software and the less saturated your network in the long run.

In a nutshell, IntelliMirror's GPSI routines deliver a message to the client about the shared folder from which the software is available. However, if you are concerned that your users will often roam your distributed enterprise, you can additionally set up Dfs. *Dfs* is the *Distributed File System* that, when used in addition to Active Directory Site Topology definitions, can automatically direct users toward the share containing the software closest to them. The essence of Dfs is to set up a front end for shared folders and then act as the traffic cop, directing users to the closest replica. To explore Dfs, visit `www.microsoft.com/windows2000/techinfo/planning/fileandprint/dfssteps.asp` and `www.microsoft.com/windowsserver2003/techinfo/overview/dfs.mspx` Or, if you want an explanation in plain English, read *Mastering Windows Server 2003* by Mark Minasi (Sybex, 2003).

When you set up shared folders, also lock them down with NTFS permissions to prevent unauthorized users from accessing the installations. Even though GPSI can *target* specific users, it makes no provisions for security. Rather, if your users discover the distribution shared folder, they'll have the keys to the candy store unless you put security upon the shared folder or, even better, utilize NTFS permissions as a deadbolt on the lock.

You can expose or hide your shared folders; to hide them, add a $ (dollar sign) to the end of the share name. You can have one shared folder for each package or one shared folder for all your software with subfolders underneath, each with the appropriate NTFS permissions.

It is not recommended (or really possible) to dump all the installations in one shared folder without using subfolders. Using subfolders lets you differentiate between two applications that have the same name (for example, `Setup.msi`) or two versions of the same application (Office 2000 and Office XP).

Your next steps in the installation wizard are to specify the organization and the installation location and to enter the product key. For the installation location, choose a folder in the share you already created, say, `d:\apps\officexpdistro`. Be sure to enter a valid product key, or you cannot continue. The next screen asks you to confirm the End User License Agreement. Finally, the administrative installation is kicked off, and files are copied to the share and the folder.

FIGURE 10.1   You need to perform an Administrative Installation to prepare a source installation folder for Office.

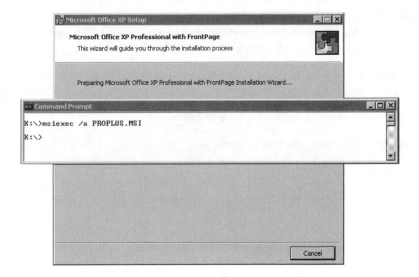

FIGURE 10.2   The files are simply copied to the share; Office isn't being installed (despite the notification that it is).

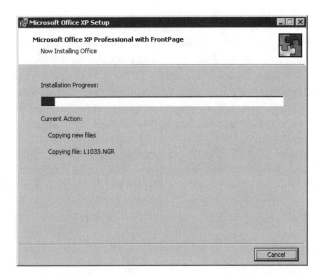

Creating Your Own *.msi* Package

It's great when applications such as Office XP come with their own .msi packages, but not every vendor supplies .msi packages. You can, however create your own .msi packages to wrap up and deploy the software you've already bought but that doesn't come with a .msi package.

WinINSTALL LE (for Light Edition) is included with the Windows 2000 Server CD. And an updated version is available for free download at www.ondemandsoftware.com/FREELE2003/.

The general steps for using WinINSTALL LE are as follows:

1. Take a snapshot of a clean source machine.

2. Run the current setup program of whatever you want to wrap up.

3. Fully install and configure the application as desired.

4. Reboot the machine to ensure that changes are settled in.

5. Take a snapshot again, and scour the hard drive for changes.

Once the changes are discovered, they're wrapped up into a .msi file of your choice, which you can then Assign or Publish!

Due to page count, I can't go in to the ins and outs of creating your own .msi files. However, I have two options for you. First, you can take a look at the previous edition of this book (ISBN 0-7821-2881-5), which includes the step-by-step process. Or you can check out another resource that demonstrates this process with free and "pay" tools. *The Definitive Guide to Windows Installer Technology for System Administrators* (which is free and which I wrote) is available at www.wise.com/ebook. The free WinINSTALL LE is good for light use, but if you want to deploy many applications across your enterprise, you'll start bumping heads with DLL conflicts and other nasties. To that end, you might have to check out some of the bigger, badder, third-party tools. Some of the more popular are InstallShield for Windows Installer (www.installshield.com) and Wise for Windows Installer (www.wisesolutions.com).

The third-party tools have some fairly robust features to assist you in your .msi package creation. As I stated, the .msi format lets you detect a damaged component within a running application. This feature is called *keying* files for proper operation. For example, if your Ruff.dll gets deleted when you run DogFoodMaker 7, the Windows Installer springs into action and pulls the broken, but keyed, component back from the distribution point—all without user interaction.

Assigning and Publishing Applications

Once you have a `.msi` package on a share, you can offer it to your client systems via Group Policy. GPSI is located under both Computer and User directories and then Software Settings ➤ GPSI. Before we set up our first package, it's important to understand the options and the rules for deployment. You, the administrator, can offer applications to clients in two ways: *Assigning* or *Publishing*.

Assigning Applications

The icons of Assigned applications appear in the user's Start menu. More specifically, they appear when the user selects Start ➤ All Programs. However, colloquially, we just say that they appear on the Start menu. You can Assign applications to users or computers.

What Happens When You Assign Applications to Users   If you Assign an application to users, the application itself isn't downloaded and installed from the source until its initial use. When the user first clicks the application's icon, the Windows Installer (which runs as a background process on the client machine) kicks into high gear, looks at the database of the `.msi` package, locates the installation point, and determines which components are required.

Assigning an application saves on initial disk space requirements since only an application's entry points are actually installed on the client. Those entry points are shortcuts, CLSIDs (Class Identifiers), file extensions, and sometimes other application attributes that are considered `.msi` entry points.

Once the icons are displayed, the rest of the application is pulled down only when necessary. Indeed, many applications are coded so that only portions of the application are brought down in chunks when needed, such as a help file that is only grabbed from the source when it's required the first time.

When portions of an application are installed, the necessary disk space is claimed. The point is that if users roam from machine to machine, they might *not* choose to install the Assigned application, and, hence, it would not use any disk space. If users are Assigned an application but never get around to using it, they won't use any extra disk space. Once the files are grabbed from the source, the application is installed onto the machine, and the application starts. If additional subcomponents within the application are required later (such as the Help files in Office XP's Word 2002, for example), those components are loaded on demand in a *just-in-time* fashion as the user attempts to use them.

What Happens When You Assign Applications to Computers   If the application is Assigned to computers, the application is *entirely* installed and available for all users who use the machine the next time the computer is rebooted. This won't save disk space, but will save time because the users won't have to go back to the source for installation.

Publishing Applications

The icons of Published applications are placed in the Add or Remove Programs folder in Control Panel. You can Publish to Users (but not computers.) When you Publish applications to users, the application list is dynamically generated, depending on which applications are currently being Published. Users get no signals whatsoever that any applications are waiting for them in the Add or Remove Programs folder.

Once the application is selected, all the components required to run that application are pulled from the distribution source and installed on the machine. The user can then close the Add or Remove Programs folder and use the Start menu to launch the newly installed application.

By default, the icons of Assigned applications are also placed in the Add or Remove Programs folder for download. In other words, by default, all Assigned applications are also Published. The "Do Not Display this Package in the Add/Remove Programs Control Panel" option is unchecked by default; therefore, the application appear in both places by default upon Assignment. (I'll discuss this option in the "Advanced Published or Assigned" section.)

Rules of Deployment

Some rules constrain our use of GPSI, regardless of whether applications are Assigned through the Computer or User node of Group Policy. As just stated, the icons of Assigned applications appear on the Start menu, whereas the icons of Published applications appear in the Add or Remove Programs folder. With that in mind, here are the deployment rules:

RULE #1 Assigning to computers means that anyone who can log on to machines affected by the GPO sees the Assigned application on the Start menu. This is useful for situations such as nurses' stations. You can also Assign applications to users in the GPO, which means that whenever users roam, their applications follow them—no matter which machine they reside at physically.

RULE #2 You can't Publish to computers; You can only Assign to computers within a GPO.

Why the funky rules? Although I have no specific confirmation from Microsoft, I'll make an observation that might help you remember these rules: Most users can use the Start menu to launch applications. Therefore, Assigning applications to users makes sense.

Additionally, since applications Assigned to computers apply to *every* user who logs on to a targeted machine, the users in question can also surely use the Start menu to launch the Assigned applications. But using Published applications takes a little more computer savvy. Users first need to know that applications are Published at all and then check the Add or Remove Programs folder to see if any applications are targeted for them. A specific user might know that applications are waiting for them, but it's unlikely that all users using a computer would know that. Since this level of sophistication isn't really the norm, I bet Microsoft avoided providing Publishing capabilities for computers because there is no guaranteed level of sophistication for a specific user of a specific computer.

In any event, just remember the following rules:

- You can Assign to users.
- You can Assign to computers.
- You can Publish to users.
- You cannot Publish to computers.

Package-Targeting Strategy

So far, we've set up our software distribution shared folder, prepared the package to the point of distribution, and (optionally) tied it down with NTFS permissions. Now we need to target a group of users or computers for the software package. Here are some possible options:

- Leverage an OU for the users you want to get the package, move the accounts into this OU, and then Assign or Publish the application to that OU. Whenever members of the OU log on, the application are available for download. Each user can connect to the distribution source and acquire a copy of the installation.

- Leverage an OU for the computers that you want to get the package, and then Assign the application to the computers in that OU. Whenever any user logs on to the targeted machines, the application is fully downloaded and ready to go.

- Assign or Publish the application at the domain or OU level, and then use GPO Filtering with Security Groups (see Chapter 2).

- Assign or Publish the application at the domain or OU level, and then use WMI (Windows Management Instrumentation) Filtering based on specific information within machines. (See the section "GPO Targeting with WMI Filters" later in this chapter.)

We could use any of these methods to target our users. The first two options are the most straightforward and most common practice. In our first example, we'll leverage an OU and Assign the application to our computers. We'll use the **Human Resources Computers** OU and Assign them Office XP.

Creating and Editing the GPO to Deploy Office

We are now ready to create our GPO and Assign our application to our users. Open the GPMC, and then follow these steps:

1. To create a GPO that deploys Office XP to the **Human Resources Computers** OU, right-click the OU and choose "Create and link a GPO here" from the shortcut menu to open the "New GPO" dialog box. Enter a descriptive name, in the New GPO dialog box such as **Deploy Office XP (to computers)**. The GPO should now be linked to the **Human Resources Computers** OU.

2. Right-click the link to the GPO (or the GPO itself), and choose Edit from the shortcut menu to open the Group Policy Object Editor.

The software distribution settings are found in both Computer Configuration and Users Configuration, as shown in Figure 10.3.

For this first package, we will Assign the application to the computers in the **Human Resources Computers** OU.

1. Choose Computer Configuration ➢ Software Settings.

2. Right-click Software Installation and choose New ➢ Package, as shown in Figure 10.3 to open the Open dialog box, which lets you specify the MSI file.

Before You Ramp Up... Let's Talk about Licensing

A FAQ I often get when I teach GPO essentials is this: "If I use GPSI to deploy applications to my users, how does this affect my licensing agreements with Microsoft or other software vendors?" The next most frequently asked question about GPSI is this: "If I use GPSI to do mass rollouts, how can I keep track of licensing for reporting during audits?" Bad news on both fronts, friends.

Occasionally, the Microsoft technology doesn't work in lockstep with usable licensing agreements. Specifically, if you use GPSI as your mechanism to get software to the masses, you need to be especially careful with your Microsoft licensing agreements or any other licensing agreements. When you deploy any software via GPSI, you have the potential to load the software on a machine and make it available to any number of users who can log on to that machine. As I discussed, using GPSI to deploy to computers gives everyone who logs on to the machine (via the domain) access to the icons on the Start menu. And, if you target users, whether the application is available only for that user depends on the application. For instance, a well-written .msi, say Office XP, prevents users who aren't assigned the application from using it; but other .msi applications (especially those you create with third-party tools) may not. And when you use GPSI to deploy an application to, say, users in an OU, you won't know how many users accept the offer and how many users don't end up using the application.

With that in mind, GPSI is a wonderful mechanism for deploying software. But in terms of licensing and auditing, you're on your own. My advice is that if you're planning to use GPSI for your installations, check with each vendor to find out their licensing requirements when you Assign to Users and Assign to Computers.

Remember: you have a large potential for exposure by doing a GPSI to users and/or computers; protect yourself by checking with your vendor before you do a mass deployment of any application in this fashion. Additionally, it's important to remember that there is no facility for counting or metering the number of accepted offers of software for auditing purposes.

You'll find an excellent article on the subject from TechRepublic at http://techrepublic.com.com/5100-6296-5088829.html.

That's where Microsoft's SMS is supposed to come into play...to help you determine "who's using what." But stay tuned—more on that later.

You will need to specify the full UNC path on the shared folder for the application. Back at Figure 10.1, we put our Office XP Administrative Installation inside the APPS share on the WinDC01 server inside the OFFICEXPDISTRO directory. Therefore, the full UNC path to the application is \\windc01\apps\officexpdistro\PROPLUS.msi, as shown in Figure 10.4.

FIGURE 10.3   Right-click the GPSI settings to deploy a new package.

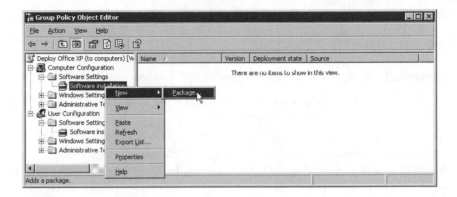

FIGURE 10.4   Always use the full UNC and never the local path when this dialog box requests the file.

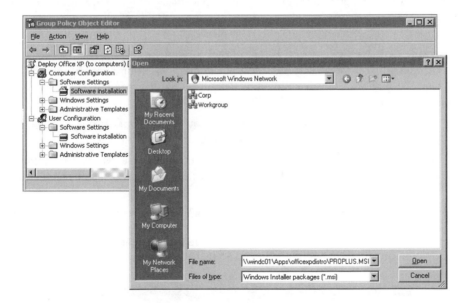

Do not—I repeat—do not use the Open dialog box's interface to click and browse for the file locally. Equally evil is specifying a local file path, such as d:\apps\ officexpdistro\proplus.msi. Why is this? Because the location needs to be from a consistently available point, such as a UNC path. Entering a local file path prevents the Windows Installer at the client from finding the package on the server. Merely clicking the file doesn't guarantee that the package will be delivered to the client. Again—entering the full UNC path as shown in Figure 10.4 is the *only* guaranteed method to deliver the application to the client.

Once the full UNC path is entered, a dialog box will appear, asking which type of distribution method we'll be using: "Assigned", or "Advanced." "Published" will be grayed out because you cannot Publish to computers.

For now, choose "Assigned" And press OK. When you do, you'll see the application listed as shown in Figure 10.5.

Understanding When Applications Will Be Installed

Once you've Assigned or Published an application, you'll need to test it to see if it's working properly. Here's how users and computers should react:

- Applications Published to users on any operating system should show up right away in the Add or Remove Programs folder in Control Panel. No reboot or log out (and log back in) should be required, but you might have to refresh the Add or Remove Programs folder. An application isn't installed until a user specifically selects it (or the application is launched via Document Invocation (also called *Auto-Install*). Recall that Document Invocation allows the application to be installed as soon as a file associated with the application is opened.

- Applications Assigned to users on Windows 2000 or Windows 2003 computers should show up on next logon on the Start menu. Applications Assigned to Windows 2000 or Windows 2003 computers should show install upon next reboot. All users logging on to those computers will see the icons on the Start menu.

- If you're deploying to users on Windows XP computers or directly to Windows XP computers themselves, you need to know whether Fast-Boot is turned on t. Recall from Chapter 3 that Fast Boot is enabled by default for Windows XP machines, and you will need to explicitly turn it off. To review:

  - If Windows XP Fast-Boot is enabled, and you Assign applications to users, it will take two logoffs and logons for the icons to appear on the Start menu

  - If Windows XP Fast-Boot is enabled, and you Assign applications to computers, it will take two reboots before the Assignment is installed. Afterward, icons appear for all users on the Start menu.

- If you want to turn off this behavior for Windows XP, you can do so. Just check out Chapter 3.

FIGURE 10.5 The applications you assign are listed under the node you chose to use (Computer ➤ Software Installation or User ➤ Software Installation).

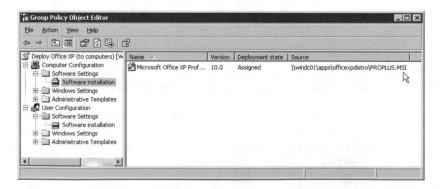

WARNING You'll need to adjust the deployment properties before certain applications will deploy properly to users. (More on this in the "Advanced Published or Assigned" section later in this chapter.)

Testing Assigned Applications

Before you go headlong and try to verify your deployment of Office XP, first verify that a Windows 2000 or Windows XP machine is in the **Human Resources Computers** OU, and then reboot the first test machine in the OU. Office XP should load on the machine, as shown in Figure 10.6.

FIGURE 10.6   Applications Assigned to computers install completely upon reboot.

Go ahead and get a cup of coffee while this is installing. It takes a while. Really. Go ahead. I'll wait.

Once the application is fully installed, you can log on as any user in the domain (or the local computer) and see the application's icons on the Start menu, as shown in Figure 10.7.

FIGURE 10.7   The Office XP icons and program names will appear on the Start menu (more specifically on the Start ➢ All Programs menu).

at Windows XP and Windows 2003 feature is that they highlight icons and program
r newly installed items on the Start ➢ All Programs menu. If you try this experiment with
ndows 2000 client, you'll notice that the new icons and program titles are not highlighted.
Any user can select any Office application, and the application is briefly prepared and then
displayed for the user.

Stay tuned for more information on Assigning and Publishing .msi applications (particularly to users.) For now, however, let's switch gears and look at another deployment option.

Understanding *.zap* Files

Using .msi files is one way to distribute software to your computers and users, but one disadvantage is associated with this process: you must actually have a .msi package that you deploy. Indeed, some applications don't come with .msi packages, and repackaging them with a third-party tool doesn't always work as expected. If you already have your own **Setup.exe** (or similar program), you can leverage a different type of installation—.zap files, which invoke your currently working **Setup.exe** program.

Sounds great—but there is a downside: .zap files are not as robust as .msi files. This "unrobustness" comes in several forms:

- They do not take advantage of the Windows Installer, and therefore they are not self-repairing should something go awry on the client.

- You can Publish but not Assign .zap files. Their icons are available only in the Add or Remove Programs applet in Control Panel, and the application is installed all at once. And since .zap files are always Published, they can only be Published to users, not computers.

- The user is in full control of the install, unless you've magically scripted **Setup.exe**. This can create trouble for end users.

- The .zap files run with the user's privileges. They cannot run with elevated privileges. Again, only .msi applications (not .zap files) automatically run elevated even for nonprivileged users once deployed via GPSI.

Like .msi files, .zap files (and their corresponding setup executables) can also be automatically invoked when a specific extension (or set of extensions) is chosen via *document invocation* (also called *Auto-Install*). Auto-Install is described in more detail in the "Advanced Published or Assigned" section, later in this chapter.

Creating Your Own *.zap* file

A .zap file resembles a .ini file. That is, it is a simple file created with a text editor such as Notepad, and it has headings and values. Instead of repackaging WinZip 8 with WinINSTALL LE (or any of the third-party applications), you can simply create a .zap file for a WinZip 8 setup executable, WinZip80.exe.

A sample WinZip 8 .zap file might look like this:

```
[Application]
FriendlyName = "Winzip 8.0 ZAP Package"
SetupCommand = "WINZIP80.exe"
```

```
DisplayVersion = 8.0
Publisher = WinZip Computing

[EXT]
.ZIP=
.ARC=
```

Let's briefly break down each entry. The [Application] heading is required, and the only other required elements are the FriendlyName and the SetupCommand, which are self-explanatory.

The entry pointed to in the SetupCommand should be in the same folder as the .zap file itself. If it isn't, you can use UNC paths to specify, such as:

```
SetupCommand = "\\WinDC01\winzipsource\winzip8.exe"
```

Everything else is completely optional, but might help you and your users sort things out. The [EXT] heading can list the file extensions that can fire off this particular .zap installation and the corresponding WINZIP80.exe setup executable. Listed in this sample file are .zip and .arc, but you can also add file types such as .tar and .z. The [EXT] heading is not required and may not even be desired, depending on the application and its setup routine.

Publishing Your Own ZAP File

If you want to Publish your own ZAP file, you'll need to bring all the steps you've learned together.

1. Place the setup executable (in this case, WINZIP80.exe) in a subfolder (say, WINZIPSOURCE) underneath a shared folder (in this case APPS).
2. Lock down the WINZIPSOUR CE subfolder with NTFS permissions.
3. Create the WINZIP8.zap file as directed earlier using Notepad.
4. Copy the .zap file to the distribution subfolder (WINZIPSOURCE).
5. Finally distribute (Publish) the .zap package to your users.

Testing Your ZAP File

Test your ZAP file and distribution point by logging on to a workstation to which the GPSI policy applies. Open the Add or Remove Programs folder in Control Panel, and click Add New Programs in the column on the left. The application should appear in the list of programs available to add, named according to the entry in the FriendlyName field that you specified in the .zap file, as shown in Figure 10.8.

Once you've selected it and clicked Add, the WinZip setup program will launch and can be set up in any desired fashion.

 Alternatively, you can double-click either a .zip or .arc file to automatically launch the .zap file setup application via Document Invocation (also known as Auto-Install.)

FIGURE 10.8   You always Publish .zap files in Add/Remove Programs.

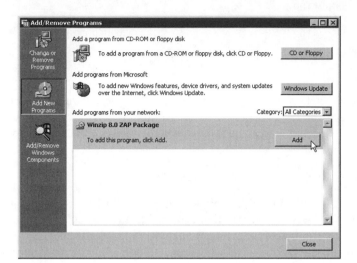

Testing Publishing Applications to Users

You can also test Publishing applications before continuing. Recall that the icons of Published applications appear in the Add or Remove Programs folder in Control Panel. However, the usefulness of Published applications is minimal, which is why it's relegated to such a small section for discussion. Users must be specifically told there's something waiting for them, hunt it down themselves, and install it. To test this for yourself, simply select "Publish" when adding a new application, or right-click an existing package Assigned to users and choose "Publish" from the shortcut menu.

To see a Published application in action, follow these steps from a client who is receiving a Published application:

1. Choose Start ➤ Control Panel ➤ Add or Remove Programs to open the Add or Remove Programs applet in Control Panel.

2. Click the "Add New Programs" button to display those applications that have been Published for the user as seen above in Figure 10.8.

3. Ask the user to click the Add button next to the application, and it will be fully loaded upon the machine.

The applications will then appear on the Start ➤ All Programs menu as seen previously in Figure 10.7, ready to be utilized.

A Published application needn't be fully relegated to lying dormant until a user selects it. Indeed, the default is to specify that the application automatically launch via Document Invocation (also known as Auto-Install) as soon as an associated file type is opened. In this way, you can have the application available for use, but just not have the application's icons appear on the Start menu as you do when you Assign it. However, you can turn off Document Invocation by clearing the "Auto install this application by file extension activation" check box as specified in the Deployment Options section a bit later.

You'll need to adjust the deployment properties before certain applications will deploy properly to users. (More on this in the "Advanced Published or Assigned" section later in this chapter.)

Application Isolation

In many circumstances, applications are *isolated* for their intended use. Here are some examples:

- Users do not share Assigned or Published applications that an administrator has set up. For instance, User A is Assigned an application and installs it. User B can use User A's machine, but is not Assigned the application via Group Policy. Therefore, when User B logs on to that machine, they do not see the Assigned icons for User A.

- Users require their own "instance" of the application. If User A and User B are Assigned the same application, each user must contact the source and download their own copy of the application. In most circumstances, this will not double the used disk space, and the time for installation for the second user would not be very long because portions of the application are already installed for User A.

- If two users are assigned different applications that register the same file types, the correct application is always used. For instance, Joe and Dave share the same machine. Joe is assigned Word 2000, and Dave is Assigned Office XP. When Joe opens a .doc file, Office 2000's Word 2000 launches. When Dave opens a .doc file, Office XP's Word 2002 launches.

- Depending on the .msi application, users might not be able to go "under the hood" and select the .exes of installed programs. For instance, if User A is Assigned an application, User B (who is not Assigned the application) cannot just use Explorer, locate the application on the hard drive, and double-click the application to install it. This is not a hard-and-fast rule and is based on how the .msi application itself is coded. In Figure 10.9, you can see what happens when a user who is not specifically Assigned Office 2000 tries to run Winword.exe from Program Files.

- Users can uninstall applications that they have access to in the Add or Remove Programs folder. This has a two-part implication. First, by default, all Assigned applications are also Published, and thus users can remove them using the Add or Remove Programs folder. The icons for the applications will still be on the Start ➤ All Programs menu the next time the user logs on. The first time the user attempts to run one of these applications by choosing Start ➤ All Programs ➤ *application*, the application reinstalls itself from the distribution point. The second implication deals with who, precisely, can remove Assigned (or Published) applications. First, users cannot delete applications that are directly Assigned to computers. Next, users cannot delete applications that aren't directly Assigned to their user account.

FIGURE 10.9 Office installations prevent users from just clicking the actual .exe of the installed file. Again, this behavior is entirely application specific.

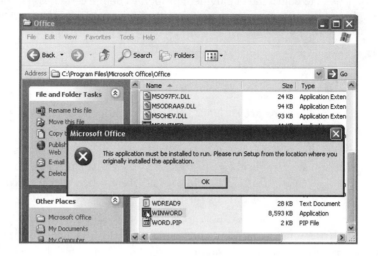

 Office 2000 and later can prevent users from just clicking their installed `.exes`. These applications use `.msi` APIs to verify the application state. For more information about how an application can become "installer-aware," see www.microsoft.com/msj/0998/windowsinstaller.aspx.

Advanced Published or Assigned

When you attempt to Publish or Assign an application to your users or computers, you are given an additional selection of "Advanced". If you didn't choose "Advanced" when you initially deployed the application, that's not a problem. You can simply right-click the package, and choose Properties from the shortcut menu to open the Properties dialog box. The only option that is not available in this "after the fact" method is the ability to add *Microsoft Transform Files*, which I'll describe in the "Modifications Tab" section later in this chapter.

The Properties dialog box has six tabs: General, Deployment, Upgrades, Categories, Modifications, and Security. In Figure 10.10, the Properties dialog box is focused on the Deployment tab, which is discussed in detail, in this section.

The General Tab

This tab contains the basic information about the package: the name that is to be displayed in the Add or Remove Programs folder, the publisher, and some language and support information. All this is extrapolated from the `.msi` package.

FIGURE 10.10   These are the options on the Deployment tab when Assigning to computers.

If you're using the Windows 2003 administrative tools to deploy your package, you'll get another little goodie: you can specify the URL of a web page that contains support information for the application. For instance, if you have specific setup instructions for the user, you can place the instructions on a page on one of your intranet servers and include the URL with the package. The client's Add or Remove Programs folder displays a hyperlink to the URL next to the package. Although `.zap` files also display this information, you can't configure these files once they are Published.

The Deployment Tab

This tab, as shown in Figure 10.10, has three sections: Deployment Type, Deployment Options, and Installation User Interface Options. There is also an Advanced button at the bottom of the tab. Depending on how you wish to deploy, The options on the Deployment tab depend on how you want to deploy the application and whether you are Assigning to computer or Assigning or Publishing to users. In our first example, Figure 10.10 shows the options when Assigning to computers.

Figure 10.11 shows the options on the Deployment tab when Assigning an application to users. You'll notice that many more options are available than when Assigning to computers. The options in the "Installation user interface options" section are critical, and you will likely need to change them before applications are correctly Assigned or Published to users.

The Deployment Type Section

The options in this section let you instantly change the deployment type from Published to Assigned and vice-versa, and it is available only when you are deploying applications to computers. When you are deploying applications to computers, Assigning is the only option. If you're deploying to user accounts, you can also change the deployment type by right-clicking the package definition (as seen in the Group Policy Object Editor dialog box in Figure 10.5) and selecting the deployment type, Assign or Publish, from the shortcut menu.

FIGURE 10.11 These are the options on the Deployment tab when Assigning or Publishing to users.

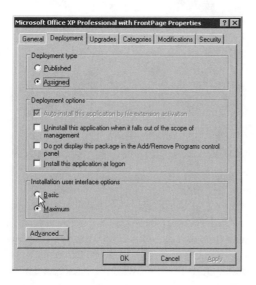

The Deployment Options Section

This section has four check boxes:

Auto-Install This Application by File Extension Activation When .msi applications are Published or Assigned (or .zap packages are Published), each of their definitions contains a list of supported file types. Those file types are actually loaded inside Active Directory. When a GPO applies to a user or a computer and this check box is selected, the application is automatically installed based on the extension. This is, essentially, application execution via Document Invocation. Note, this option is always automatically selected (and cannot be un-selected) if you Assign the application. That is, document invocation is only optional when Publishing.

Document Invocation is most handy when new readers and file types are released, such as Adobe Acrobat Reader and its corresponding .pdf file type. Simply Assign or Publish an application with this check box enabled, and Acrobat Reader is automatically shot down to anyone who opens a .pdf file for the first time. This check box is selected by default when you are Assigning applications to users or computers.

Uninstall This Application When It Falls out of the Scope of Management GPOs can be applied to sites, domains, or OUs. If a user is moved out of the scope to which this GPO applies, what happens to the currently deployed software? For instance, if a user or computer is moved from one OU to another, what do you want to happen with this specific software package? If you don't want the software to remain on the workstation, click this check box. Remember—the applications aren't removed immediately if a user or computer leaves the scope of the GPO. As you'll see shortly, computers receive a *signal* to remove the software. (This is described in the "Removing Applications" section later in this chapter.)

Do Not Display This Package in the Add/Remove Programs Control Panel   As mentioned, icons and program names for Assigned applications appear in the Start ➢ All Programs menu, but, by default, they also appear as Published icons in the Add or Remove Programs applet in Control Panel. Thus, users may choose to install the application all at once or perform an en masse repair. However, the dark side of this check box is that users can remove any application they want. To prevent the application from appearing in the Add or Remove Programs folder, check this check box. When the application is then earmarked for being Published, the application is available only for loading through document invocation.

Install This Application at Logon   This option is new and applies only to Windows XP and Windows 2003 Server clients. See the section "Assigning Applications to Users over Slow Links Using Windows XP and Windows 2003" later in this chapter for a detailed explanation.

The Installation User Interface Options Section

Believe it or not, the two little innocuous buttons in this section make a world of difference for many applications when Assigning or Publishing applications to users. Some .msi packages can recognize when Basic or Maximum is set and change their installation behavior accordingly. Others don't. Consult your .msi package documentation to see if the package uses this option and what it does.

For Office XP, Assigning applications to users can be disastrous if you retain the default of Maximum. Instead of the application automatically and nearly silently loading from the source upon first use, the user is prompted to step through the Office XP installation wizard (the first screen of which is shown in Figure 10.12).

FIGURE 10.12   The default of "Maximum" results in many applications no longer being a silent install.

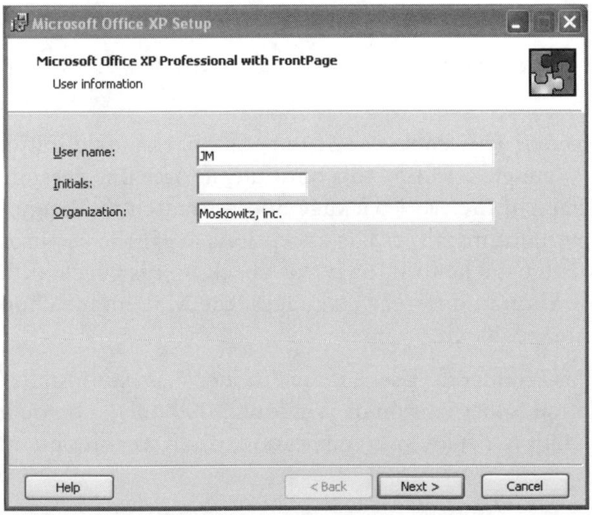

Simply choosing Basic remedies this problem. That is, Office XP is magically downloaded and installed for every user targeted in the OU. Why is this the default? I do not know. It wasn't the default in Windows 2000. For now, if you're Assigning applications to users, be sure the Basic check box is checked. For information about how to change the defaults, see the "Default Group Policy Software Installation Properties" section later in this chapter.

The Advanced Button

Clicking the Advanced button opens the Advanced Deployment Options dialog box, as shown in Figure 10.13. This dialog box has two sections: "Advanced deployment options" and "Advanced diagnostic information."

FIGURE 10.13 The options in the Advanced Deployment Options dialog box in Windows 2003 Server

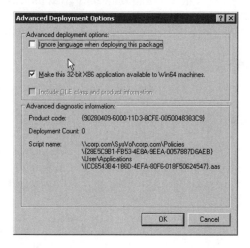

The Advanced Deployment Options Section

In Windows 2003 Server, this section has three options, and in Windows 2000 Server, it has four options:

Ignore Language When Deploying This Package If the .msi package definition is coded to branch depending on the language, selecting this option can force one version of the language. Normally, if the language of the .msi package doesn't match the language of the operating system, Windows will not install it. The exceptions are if the application is in English, if the application is language neutral, or if this check box is checked. If there are multiple versions of the application in different languages, the MSI engine chooses the application with the best language match.

Remove Previous Installs of This Product for Users, If the Product Was Not Installed by Group Policy-Based Software Installation (older version of Windows 2000 only) If you use older Windows 2000 administrative tools to deploy your application, you'll see this option. However, in Figure 10.13, there is just an empty hole (where the mouse pointer is). For each `.msi` application, a unique product code (which is shown in Figure 10.13) is generated at initial compilation time. If your users somehow get their own copy of the `.msi` source and the product code matches the `.msi` application, they can forcibly uninstall their copy before loading the copy you specified.

This can come in handy if the folks in your organization run out to CompUSA and buy a version of a program you weren't ready to deploy using Group Policy—say Office XP. If users acquire and install their own copy of Office XP before you're really ready to officially deploy it using Group Policy, you can forcibly remove the copy they install. Once you are ready to deploy Office XP using Group Policy, be sure to check this check box to remove all copies of Office XP that you did not deploy using Group Policy. The copy you're shooting down from on high will then be installed. In this way, you can ensure that all copies you deploy using Group Policy are consistent, even if your users try to sneak around the system.

This works because the unique product code you're sending via Group Policy matches the product code of the `.msi` package the user loaded on the machine. The Office XP you deploy is essentially the same as the Office XP they deploy. The product codes match, and the application you deliver "wins" if you select this check box.

Why is this option absent from the later versions of the Windows 2000 tools or the Windows 2003 Server version of the Adminpak tools? Because this feature is built in to the latest Windows 2000 Service Pack (SP4) and standard issue for Windows 2003 Server. This procedure is performed automatically and is no longer required as an option.

> Even if you repackage your own applications (such as WinZip, Adobe Acrobat Reader, and so on) using a third-party tool (such as WinINSTALL LE), a product code is automatically generated at compile time. However, if you deploy those repackaged applications with Group Policy (in conjunction with this check box in Windows 2000), this procedure does not remove copies of applications that users installed with "Setup.exe" style programs. It removes only applications on the target machine that have a `.msi` product code.

Make This 32-Bit X86 Application Available to Win64 Machines   Software distribution with Windows 2003 Server gets a little more complex because of the support for IA-64 computers. The IA-64 version of Windows XP supports 32-bit applications by running them in a special Win32-on-Win64 emulator. This is similar to the way NT and Windows 2000 support 16-bit Windows applications. In general, 32-bit applications should run fine on IA-64 platforms, but you can encounter an ill-behaved application that does not function correctly in the emulator. Additionally, Service Pack 1 for Windows 2003 Server and Windows XP Service Pack 2 should make 32-bit applications run even more stably on IA-64 computers.

Include OLE class and product information   This feature allows applications that contain COM services to be deployed such that COM clients can find their deployed applications. Basically, check with your application vendor to see if you need this switch; generally you don't. Enabling the switch increases the likelihood that the application will fail to deploy unless the application specifically requires this setting.

The Advanced Diagnostic Information Section

You can't modify anything in this section, but it does have some handy information.

Product Code As mentioned, if the unique product code of the application you are deploying matches an existing installed product, the application will be removed from the client. Some diagnostic information in the Event Log may refer only to Product Code (also known as Product ID).

Deployment Count A bit later in this chapter, you'll learn why you might need to redeploy an application to a population of users or computers. When you do, this count is increased. See the section "Using MSIEXEC to Patch a Distribution Point" a bit later in this chapter for more information.

Script Name Whenever an application is Published or Assigned, a pointer to the application, also known as a .aas file, is placed in the SYSVOL in the Policies container within the GPT (Group Policy Template). This entry shows the name of the .aas file, which can be useful information if you're chasing down a GPO replication problem between Domain Controllers.

The Upgrades Tab

You can deploy a package that upgrades an existing package. For instance, if you want to upgrade from Office XP to Office 2003, you can prepare the Office 2003 installation (as we did earlier with Office XP) and then specify that you want an upgrade, which can be either mandatory or optional.

 There is no Upgrades tab for .zap package definitions.

Moreover, you can "upgrade" to totally different programs. For instance, if your corporate application for ZIP files is WinZip but changes to UltraZip, follow these steps to upgrade:

1. Create the UltraZip .msi package, Assign or Publish the application, open the Properties dialog box, and click the Upgrades tab.

2. Click the Add button to open the Add Upgrade Package dialog box, as shown in Figure 10.14.

3. In the Package Upgrade section, select the package definition (in this case WINZIP 8.0).

 Although you can click the Browse button to open the Browse dialog box and select another GPO for this to apply to, it's easier to keep the original package and upgrade in the same GPO scope.

4. Use the options at the bottom of the "Add Upgrade Package" window, to choose either to uninstall the application first or to plow on top of the current installation, and then click OK.

5. Back in the Upgrades tab, check the "Required Upgrade for Existing Packages" check box and click OK to force the upgrade.

FIGURE 10.14   Use the Upgrades tab to migrate from one application to another.

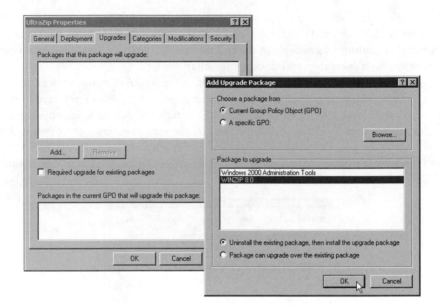

If the "Required Upgrade for Existing Packages" check box is cleared, users can optionally add the program using the Add or Remove Programs applet in Control Panel. This can cause grief for some applications, such as Office 97 and Office 2000 together on the same machine. Moreover, if the check box is not checked, the old application is started whenever an associated file extension (such as .doc) is invoked.

 When Assigning to computers, the "Required Upgrade for Existing Package" check box is always checked and not available for selection.

The Categories Tab

The Categories tab allows administrators to give headings to groups of software, which are then displayed in the Add or Remove Programs applet in Control Panel. Users can select the category of software they want to display and then select a program within the category to install. (See earlier Figure 10.8 above the mouse cursor, which shows the Category drop-down box.)

For example, you might want to create the category "Archive Programs" for WinZip and UltraZip and the category "Doc Readers" for Adobe Acrobat Reader and GhostScript. If you want, you can list a package in multiple categories. You can also create categories. For information on how to do so, see the "Default Group Policy Software Installation Properties" section later in this chapter.

The Modifications Tab

The Modifications tab is used to support *MST* files, or *Microsoft Transform* files, or just "Transform Files" for short. Transform files are applied upon current .msi packages either to filter the number of options available to the end user or to specify certain answers to questions usually brought up during the .msi package installation.

Each vendor's .mst transform-creation program is unique. Ask your application vendor if they have a transform-generation utility for your package. If not, you might have to step up to a third-party .msi/.mst tool, such as Wise Package Studio or AdminStudio by InstallShield. Some applications, such as Office 2000 and later, come with their own .mst generation tool.

In this screenshot, you can see I've loaded an MST file named NOMSACCESS.MST. This MST will prohibit the use of Microsoft Access 2003 from Office XP, but allow all other functions of Office XP to run.

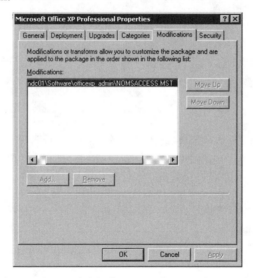

The Modifications tab is only available for use when "Advanced Published or Assigned" is selected when a new package is deployed. If a package is already Published or Assigned, the Modifications tab is not usable. As you can see in the screenshot above, all of the buttons on the Modifications tab are grayed out. Again, this is because the MST file was loaded at package deployment time, and afterward there is no way to Add or Remove MST files after deployment. We'll reiterate and reexamine this issue a bit later.

There is no Modifications tab for .zap package definitions because transform files apply only to .msi files.

You might be wondering how you can create your own MST files for Office—and that's what the next section is about. After you're done, you'll have the chance to load your MST file as well to test it out.

Using the Office *.mst* Generation Tool

You can deploy Office 2000, Office XP, and Office 2003, for instance, whole hog by using their included .msi package. Indeed, you saw this earlier. All versions of Office were available when our users chose to use Office. But what if we didn't want, say, Access available to our users? Or what if we want to adjust an Office property at a global level?

Using the Custom Installation Wizards from the Office Resource Kit, you can create a .mst transform file that can limit which options can be installed, as well as specify all sorts of custom options, including the default installation path, the organization name, the custom Outlook behavior, and more! The tool has the same name in all three versions of Office (but the application is unique to each). Table 10.1 shows you where to find the downloads.

TABLE 10.1   Location of Office Resource Kit downloads

Office Version	Where to Find the Resource Kit
Office 2000	www.microsoft.com/office/ork/2000/default.htm in the Toolbox folder
Office XP	www.microsoft.com/office/ork/xp/default.htm in the Toolbox folder
Office 2003	www.microsoft.com/office/ork/2003/default.htm in the Toolbox folder

The procedure to create an MST is straightforward, but quite long, and I simply don't have room available to dedicate to each and every step. In this example, I'll assume you're using the Office XP Custom Installation Wizard (CIW). Here is the basic overview:

1. Choose Start ➢ All Programs ➢ Microsoft Office Tools ➢ [*the version of the tool you loaded*] ➢ Custom Installation Wizard to start the CIW.

2. Tell the CIW where your administrative installation of that version of Office is. Remember, you created an administrative installation of Office XP in the section "Setting Up the .msi Package with an Administrative Installation" earlier in this chapter.

3. Give your .mst file a creative name, for example, nomsaccess.mst.

4. Continue to follow the wizard's instruction, choosing your specific installation options. In this example, on screen 7 (of 22), as shown in Figure 10.15, we'll tell Office XP that we don't want Access available to users.

5. At the final screen, click Finish and save the .mst file to a handy location.

As the CIW presents the final Wizard screen, it will give you information about how to run the .msi file along with the .mst file manually. But you can ignore this because you're about to use the .mst file in a Group Policy Software Installation GPO.

FIGURE 10.15   Use the CIW to choose the options you want and create the .mst file.

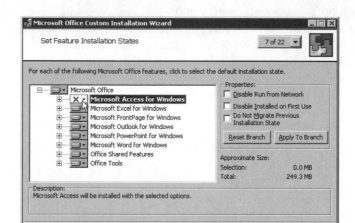

Applying Your *.mst* File to the Installation

As previously stated, you can add .mst files only when you're initially Assigning or Publishing a package. You previously performed these steps in the "Creating and Editing the GPO to Deploy Office" section at Figure 10.3. When you do, the "Select deployment method" dialog box will appear. Afterward, follow these steps:

1.   In the "Select deployment method" dialog box, click "Advanced" to open the Properties dialog box.

2.   Click the Modifications tab, and click Add to open the "Open" dialog box.

3.   In the File name field, enter the full UNC path of the .mst file, for instance, \\WinDC01\apps\officexp\nomsaccess.mst.

 The .mst file needn't be in the same location as the .msi distribution, as long as the path is available via the UNC name.

4.   Click OK.

Your screenshot should be similar to what is seen in the graphic at the beginning of the "The Modification Tab" section.

Once you press OK, the .mst file will be locked in and cannot be changed. You have only two options if you are unhappy with the .mst file:

▪   Remove the package and deploy it again.

▪   Create an upgrade package as described earlier.

What's with the Up and Down buttons in the Modifications tab?

If you wanted to, you could add multiple MST files before pressing the OK button to lock in your selection. But why would you do this?

Multiple, autonomous administrators can individually create .mst files and layer them such that each transform file contains some of the configuration options. These files are then ordered so that the options are applied from the top down. If configured options overlap, the last-configured option wins.

However, in my travels I really haven't seen administrators choose to add multiple MST files for the same MSI. Typically, only one MST file is used as we did in this previous example.

Removing the entire Office suite and reinstalling it can be a pain for your users, so, if you want to deploy Office with (or without) .mst files, be sure to test in the lab before you really get started in your actual deployment.

The Security Tab

Individual applications can be filtered based on user or security group membership. For instance, if you Assign Office XP to all members of the **Human Resources Users** OU, you set it up normally, as described earlier.

 If a user who happens to administer the application in the GPO is not given Read access, they will no longer be able to administer the application. Therefore, don't use filtering based on user or security group membership on the administrators of the application.

If, however, you want to exclude a specific member, say, Frank Rizzo, you can deny Frank Rizzo's account permissions to "Read" the package. A better strategy is to create a security group—say, DenyOfficeXP—and put those people not allowed to receive the application inside that group. You can then set the permissions to "Deny" the entire security group the ability to read the package as shown in Figure 10.16.

Default Group Policy Software Installation Properties

Each GPSI node (one for users and one for computers) has some default installation properties that you can modify. In the Group Policy Object Editor, simply right-click the GPSI node and choose Properties from the shortcut menu, as shown in Figure 10.17, to open the Software Installation Properties dialog box (also shown on Figure 10.17), which has three tabs: General, File Extensions, and Categories.

FIGURE 10.16   Use the Security tab to specify who can and cannot run applications.

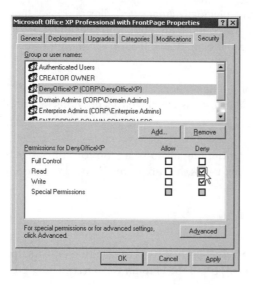

FIGURE 10.17   Use the GPSI Properties dialog box to set up general deployment settings.

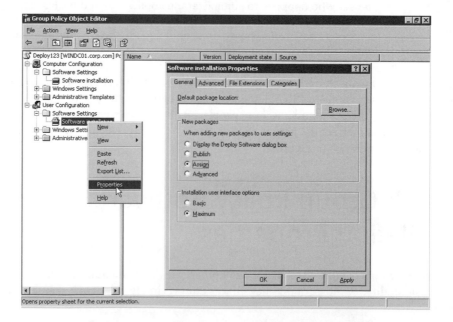

The General Tab

Most settings on the General tab are self-explanatory. Do note that you can specify a default package location, such as \\WinDC01\apps, so that you can then use the GUI when adding packages. Avoid using direct paths such as C:\apps\, as C:\apps probably won't exist on the client at runtime.

Also, you can specify a default setting if the user or computer is moved out of the scope for the package. By default, applications are not uninstalled, though you can change this behavior.

Last, you can establish the critical setting of Basic vs. Maximum here (when Assigning applications to users). The bummer is that these default setting changes are local only for this specific GPO. That is, the next GPO you create that uses GPSI will not adhere to the defaults you set in this GPO.

The Advanced Tab (Windows 2003 Server Tools Only)

The Advanced tab, as shown in Figure 10.18, allows you to set some default settings for all the packages you want to deploy in this GPO. You saw some of these settings with similar names before in the Advanced Deployment Options (Figure 10.13).

FIGURE 10.18   You can set up some default settings for new packages in this GPO.

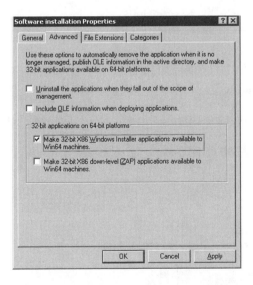

Uninstall the Applications When They Fall out of the Scope of Management   I'll discuss this setting in the "Removing Applications" section later in this chapter.

Include OLE Information When Deploying Applications   As stated earlier, this feature allows applications that contain COM services to be deployed such that COM clients can find their deployed applications. Again, check with your application vendor to see if you need this switch; generally you don't.

The 32-Bit Applications on 64-Bit Platforms Section   As stated, it's possible to run IA-64 versions of Windows 32-bit applications on Windows XP 64-bit edition. You can set the defaults to block IA-64 machines from downloading 32-bit software packages. If you want to find out more about Windows XP 64-Bit Edition just check out `http://www.microsoft.com/WindowsXP/64bit/default.asp`

The File Extensions Tab

As stated earlier, you can install and start applications by double-clicking or by invoking their document type. For instance, double-clicking a `.zip` file can automatically deploy a Published or Assigned WinZip application. The correspondence of a file type to a package is found in either the `.zap` file definition or the `.msi` file database. Once the application is set to be deployed, the file types are automatically entered into Active Directory.

Occasionally, two Published or Assigned applications are called by the same file extension. This can occur if you're upgrading a package from, say, WinZip to UltraZip, and both are using the `.zip` extension or if you're upgrading from Office XP to Office 2003 and both Word applications use the `.doc` extension.

In those cases, you need to specify which extension fires off which application. To do so, follow these steps:

1. In the Software Installation Properties dialog box, click the File Extensions tab, as shown in Figure 10.19.

2. Click the Select File Extension drop-down list box, and select the extension to display all the applicable Assigned or Published applications in the Application Preference list.

3. Select an application, and then click the Up or Down button to change the order.

FIGURE 10.19   Use the File Extensions tab to set the priority for conflicting file extensions.

The Categories Tab

Categories is a domain-wide property that puts Published or Assigned software into bite-sized chunks instead of one giant-sized alphabetized list in the Add or Remove Programs folder. As noted earlier, you might want to group WinZip and UltraZip in the "Archive Programs" category or put Adobe Acrobat Reader and GhostScript in the "Doc Readers" category. On this tab, simply click the Add button to enter the names of the categories in the "Enter new category" dialog box.

This whole business of Categories is a bit strange, as it lets any OU administrator add categories into Active Directory. Oddly, there appears to be no way to centrally manage this property.

Therefore, if possible, select one administrator to control this property, set it up to be centrally managed, and then use the Properties dialog box to associate a package with a category or categories.

Removing Applications

You can remove applications from users or computers in several ways. First, under some circumstances, users can manually remove applications, but, as an administrator, you hold the reigns. Therefore, you can set applications to automatically or forcefully be removed.

Users Can Manually Change or Remove Applications

If an application is Assigned or Published to a user, they can use the Add or Remove Programs folder to change the installed options or remove the bits to save space. There seems to be no way to prevent this. However, Microsoft's position is that it provides the best of both worlds: the user can remove the binaries, but if the application is Assigned, the icons and program names are forced to appear on the Start ➢ All Programs menu.

But, in practice, I've found that this is a bad thing. Users remove their applications and then go on the road with their laptops. Well, on the other hand, if they do this, they deserve what's coming to them. Note, however, that applications Assigned to the computer cannot be changed or uninstalled by anyone but local computer administrators. This is a good thing.

Automatically Removing Assigned or Published *.msi* Applications

Applications can be automatically uninstalled when they no longer apply to the user. Earlier in the "Advanced Published or Assigned" section, you saw that in the Deployment tab of the Software Installation Properties dialog box you can check the "Uninstall This Application When It Falls out of the Scope of Management" check box. This was back in Figure 10.11. You can specify that the application is to be uninstalled if either of the following occurs:

- The user or computer is moved out of the OU to which this software applies.
- The GPO containing the package definition is deleted.

The software is never actually forcibly removed while the user is logged on to the current session but is removed a bit later in the following manner:

- Applications Published to users are removed upon next logon.

- Applications Assigned to users are removed upon next logon.

- Applications Assigned to computers are removed upon next reboot.

- Applications Assigned to computers that are currently not attached to the network are removed the next time the computer is plugged in to the network, rebooted, and the computer account "logs on" to Active Directory.

- Applications Assigned or Published to users on computers that are currently not attached to the network are removed the next time they log on and are validated to Active Directory.

 These rules assume that the target system is Windows 2000, Windows 2003, or Windows XP and Fast Boot is not enabled. If Fast Boot is enabled, these rules don't apply; expect two logons or two reboots for the change to take effect.

In these cases, the software is automatically removed upon next logon (for users) or upon next reboot (for computers). For example, Figure 10.20 shows what happens when a computer is moved out of an OU and then rebooted. Moving users and computers in and out of OUs might not be such a hot idea if lots of applications are being Assigned.

FIGURE 10.20 When applications fall out of the scope of management, they uninstall.

One final warning about the automatic removal of applications. GPSI cannot remove the icons and programs names for the application if the GPO has been deleted and the user has a Roaming Profile and has roamed to a machine after the application was uninstalled. In this case, there is not enough uninstall information on the machine, and, hence, the icons and program names will continue to exist, though they will be nonfunctional.

Forcefully Removing Assigned or Published *.msi* Applications

You have seen how applications can be automatically removed from users or computers when the user or computer object moves out the scope of management. But what if you want to keep the user or computer in the scope of management and still remove an application? You can manually remove Published or Assigned applications. To do so, simply right-click the package definition, and choose All Tasks ➢ Remove, as seen in the following graphic. This will open the "Remove Software" dialog box. The options presented in this dialog box depend on whether you deployed .msi or .zap applications.

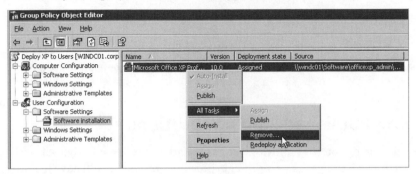

If you are removing a .msi file, you have two options, as discussed in the next sections.

Immediately Uninstall the Software from Users and Computers

If you choose this option, all connected computers receive a signal to uninstall the software, and they follow the rules for uninstalling as in the previous section.

The signal to remove an application (such as Office XP) lives in the actual GPO definition. Therefore, if you're looking for success in the forceful removal of applications, don't delete the GPO right after selecting this option. If you do, the signal to remove the application won't be available to the workstations. Rather, remove the application, and leave the GPO definition around for a while to ensure that the computers get the signal to remove the software. If you remove the GPO before the target user receives the signal (upon next logon) or the computer receives the signal (upon next reboot), the application is orphaned on the Desktop and must be manually unloaded via the Add or Remove Programs applet in Control Panel or by some other means (for instance, MSIEXEC as described later in this chapter).

This is a second warning in case you overlooked the ominous message in the previous paragraph: if you remove the GPO definition before a target user or computer receives the signal, the application is orphaned on the Desktop. You can, however, likely get out of this trap if the application was specified with the "Uninstall This Application When It Falls out of the Scope of Management" check box. You can move the user or computer out of the scope of management to remove the application and then bring it back in when the application removal is completed. It's a bit rough, but should work.

Allow Users to Continue to Use the Software, but Prevent New Installations

When you remove applications using this option, current installations of the software remain intact. Users to which this edict applies, however, will no longer be able to install new copies of the software. Therefore, those who do not have the software will not be able to install it. Those who do have it installed will be able to continue to use it.

The self-repair features of the Windows Installer will still function (for example, if Winword.exe gets deleted, it will come back from the dead), but the application cannot be fully reinstalled via the Add or Remove Programs applet in Control Panel for fixing an application en masse.

 WARNING   Once you use this option, you will no longer be able to manage the application and force it to uninstall from the machines on which it is installed.

Removing Published *.zap* Applications

You have only one option for removing .zap applications. When you right-click the package definition and select Remove (as seen earlier in previous graphic), you'll have to answer but one question: "Remove the Package but Leave the Application Installed Everywhere It Is Already Installed."

Remember that since the .zap file really calls only the original Setup.exe program, ultimately, that Setup.exe is in charge of how the application is uninstalled. Therefore, once applications are deployed using .zap files, the power to forcibly uninstall them is out of your hands.

Troubleshooting the Removal of Applications

Sometimes, applications refuse to leave the target system gracefully. Usually, this is because an application has been Published or Assigned, and the user has "double-dipped" by throwing in the CD and installing a program on top of itself. Sometimes, the Windows Installer becomes confused. When you then try to remove the application from being Published or Assigned, the application doesn't know what to do.

If an application refuses to go away (or you're left with entries in the Add or Remove Programs applet in Control Panel), you have two tools at your disposal: The Windows Installer Clean Up Utility (also known as MSICUU) and MSIZAP. Both were originally in the Windows 2000 Support Tools located in the \SUPPORT folder of the Windows 2000 Server CD. Updates are now available at Microsoft's download site. Both do essentially the same thing: they manually hunt down all Registry settings for an application and delete them. This should remove all vestigial entries in the Add or Remove Programs applet in Control Panel.

Windows Installer Clean Up Utility (also known as MSICUU)   This tool has a GUI, Programs displayed in the Installed Products list, as shown in Figure 10.21, are the same as those in the Add or Remove Programs applet in Control Panel. At last check, the download was available at http://download.microsoft.com/download/office2000pro/util20/1/NT4/EN-US/msicuu.exe.

MSIZAP   MSIZAP is a command-line tool with a similar function. You must specify a specific .msi product code (GUID) to hunt down and destroy. At last check, additional reference and download for MSIZAP is at http://msdn.microsoft.com/library/default.asp?url=/library/en-us/msi/setup/msizap_exe.asp. However, you'll have to download and install the monstrous Windows Installer SDK just to get it.

FIGURE 10.21   The MSICUU program in the Windows 2000 Support Tools can whack entire programs off your system.

Using Group Policy Software Installation over Slow Links

First things first: applications Assigned to computers cannot ever be installed over a slow dial-up link or a VPN (virtual private network) connection. Why? Because the computer must see the network, log on to it, and then start to actually download the program. If you're using a dial-in or other slow connection, manual intervention to connect to the network must be involved. Hence, no applications Assigned to computers will ever install unless the computer is connected to the LAN.

However, when applications are Assigned or Published to users (not computers), it's a different story. When a user connects via a slow link, they will not see new Assignment offers. By default, only users connected at faster than 500Kbps or greater will see new Assignments on the Start ➢ All Programs menu. This is a good thing too, as you wouldn't want someone dialing in over a 56Kbps modem to try to accept the offer of Office XP.

You can change this behavior by modifying the GPO at Computer Configuration ➢ Administrative Templates ➢ System ➢ Group Policy ➢ **Software Installation Policy Processing**, as shown in Figure 10.22.

Checking the "Allow processing across a slow network connection" check box forces all clients, regardless of their connection speed, to adhere to the policy setting. If you want to be a bit less harsh, you can change the definition of a "slow link" and modify the **Group Policy Slow Link Detection** policy setting. After you Enable the policy setting, set a value in the "Connection speed (Kbps)" spin box.

FIGURE 10.22 Use Group Policy to change the default slow-link behavior.

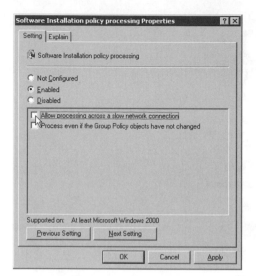

One word of warning with regard to slow links: users who are Assigned or Published applications can find other ways to install applications over slow links. First, they can trot out to the Add or Remove Programs folder and select the application. Sure, the offer isn't displayed on the Start ➤ All Programs menu, but it's still going to be available in the Add or Remove Programs applet in Control Panel. To prevent this, select the "Do Not Display this Package in the Add/Remove Programs Control Panel" check box, which is found on the Deployment tab of the application's Properties (see Figure 10.11).

Last, if dialed-up users receive a Word document in e-mail, and Word isn't already installed, look out! Because .doc is a registered file type for Office XP, Word will attempt to install over a slow link. To prevent this, simply clear the "Auto-install this Application by File Extension Activation" option in the Deployment tab in the Properties dialog box of the application (again, seen in Figure 10.11).

Assigning Applications to Users Over Slow Links Using Windows 2000

If you are planning on utilizing GPSI with Windows 2000 laptops, there are two things to keep in mind. Here they are.

Dealing with Already-Assigned Applications

Here's a scenario that illustrates the problem with Assigning an application, such as Office, to users. While at headquarters in Washington, D.C., Wally, on his Windows 2000 Professional laptop, sees and accepts your offer for Office. Specifically, Wally clicks Word on the Start ➤ All Programs menu. Because Wally is connected over a fast link, the download is quick and painless. Wally is shipped off from Washington DC to Walla Walla, WA.

Oh, by the way, to learn more about the fine city of Walla Walla, WA, be sure to visit www.ci.walla-walla.wa.us/.

While on the airplane from Washington, DC to Walla Walla, WA, Wally decides to accept the offer for Excel and clicks that item on the Start ➢ All Programs menu. He gets the message shown in Figure 10.23.

FIGURE 10.23   This is what happens when a user tries to use a program that isn't fully installed.

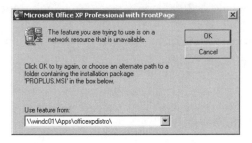

This is a major problem for Wally because the source files are only available on the server from which he originally receive the installation (or from a Dfs share, if that's available). Long story short, Wally is woeful. Wally calls the help desk, and the help desk calls you. Worst part of the story—there's not a whole lot you can do to help him now.

You can ask Wally to dial in, but that's likely going to be fruitless. Trying to install Excel over a dial-up connection won't be painless. Can Wally with his Windows 2000 laptop be helped? Not easily now that he's on the road. He really needs to connect using a fast link to download the rest of Excel.

However, Wally could have been helped *before* he set out on the road in two ways:

- The application could have been Assigned to his computer (instead of to his user account), which would have ensured that the entire application was available and ready to go when he hit the road. You saw this earlier when we installed Office XP. The entirety of Office XP was installed on the next reboot. Sure, it took a long time, but when it was done, it was done.

- Even though the application was Assigned to Wally's user account, the application could have been fully installed via a little scripting magic. We'll explore that option right now.

"Fully Installing" New Applications to Users on Windows 2000 When Using Assign

As I stated earlier, users dialed up over a slow link will not see *new* Assignment offers. The key word here is *new*.

However, this wasn't Wally's problem. He wasn't accepting a new offer over a slow link, rather, Wally had already accepted an offer before he left. Therefore, his problem could have been prevented if the application were already fully installed. But I already said that when you Assign applications to users, the .msi file is downloaded in chunks—not all at once—which is precisely why Wally had problems when he tried to download Excel. He had the "chunk" for Word, but not for Excel. Hence, he needed to reach the original source for a download.

To that end, you can install a special logon script for users on Windows 2000 laptops. Here's the gist. When users connect at a high speed, the computer sees the new offer. This special logon script downloads and installs each "chunk" of the .msi—all at once to ensure that the application is fully installed. Hence, even though the application is Assigned to Wally's user account, the entirety of the application is available.

Sure, the application takes a while to download the first time the offer is available, and, of course, all the disk space the application will ever use is used right away. But it's a darn good idea to set up this logon script for your Windows 2000 laptop users. You don't want them to get the message seen in Figure 10.23.

Space doesn't permit me to print the script right here, but you can download it from my website, www.GPOanswers.com. One warning about this script: if the user has already accepted any part of the offer (that is, already downloaded Word, but not Excel), this script won't work for them. You need to set up the script *before* you start Assigning applications to users, that is, before they start accepting your offers. If you've already deployed applications in this way, you'll need to remove them (see the section "Removing Applications" earlier in this chapter) and then Assign the applications again after the special logon script is in place.

Assigning Applications to Users over Slow Links Using Windows XP and Windows 2003

Microsoft has fixed the problem that plagued Wally. However, the solution is only available when the client system is Windows XP or Windows 2003. However, it's doubtful you'll have many Windows 2003 systems for use "on the road." When a Windows XP or Windows 2003 machine sees an offer for a newly Assigned application for a user (which it will only see when connected over a fast link), the entirety of the application can be installed—instead of waiting for it to come down in chunks.

Ideally you'll set this up for packages you want to Assign to users using Windows XP laptops. When you Assign this application to users, in the Deployment tab of the Properties dialog box, click the "Install This Application at Logon" check box (as seen in Figure 10.11). This setting is only valid for Windows XP or Windows 2003 clients when applications are Assigned to users. Windows 2000 machines simply ignore it.

WARNING   If the user opens the Add or Remove Programs folder and manually uninstalls the application, neither the logon script nor the "Install this application at logon" setting will kick back into high gear and install the application. This might be a big deal if your users dink around in the Add or Remove Programs folder. You might also want to select the "Do not display this package in the Add/Remove Programs control panel" check box also located on the Deployment tab in the Properties dialog box.

Managing *.msi* Packages and the Windows Installer

Users might occasionally want to install their own .msi packages, which can be on CDs from vendors, such as Office XP and GPMC.msi (from Microsoft), other vendors, or applications that you create using WinINSTALL LE, for example. To manually install a .msi application on a workstation, you can either double-click the application from the CD or shared folder or use a command-line tool called MSIEXEC to kick off (or repair) the installation.

This section explores the options when manually installing existing .msi packages that you've deployed via Group Policy. As we've explored in the previous section, most of the things we need to do can be performed using the GUI. However, some functions are available only in the command-line tool.

Inside the *MSIEXEC* Tool

MSIEXEC is a tough little nut of a tool to crack. Simply typing **MSIEXEC /?** on the command line is no help either. To get the full syntax of MSIEXEC, you'll need to use the Windows help file and search for MSIEXEC.

You can use MSIEXEC in several ways, but here we're going to look at how to use it to manage existing .msi packages. Indeed, you can use MSIEXEC to script an installation of a .msi package at a workstation, but why bother? You're already using the power of Group Policy. However, you might need to check out how an installation works by hand or enable additional logging for deeper troubleshooting. Or you could trigger a preemptive repair of an application at specific times. You can even use MSIEXEC to remove a specific application.

You can also use MSIEXEC as a maintenance tool for existing packages on distribution points. We'll explore a bit of both uses.

Instead of diving into every MSIEXEC command here, I'll simply highlight some of the most frequently used. Indeed, you may never find yourself using MSIEXEC unless specifically directed to do so by an application vendor's Install program.

Using *MSIEXEC* to Install an Application

The first function of MSIEXEC is to initiate an installation from a source point. This is essentially the same as double-clicking the .msi file, using the /I switch (for Install). The syntax for your application might be as follows:

```
Msiexec /I \\WinDC01\apps\yourapp.msi
```

Using *MSIEXEC* to Repair an Application

You can script the repair of applications by using MSIEXEC with the /f switch and an additional helper-switch, as indicated in the Windows help file. For instance, you might want to ensure that ProPlus.msi (Office XP) is not corrupted on the client. You can do so by forcing all files from inside the Office XP .msi to be reinstalled on the client. Use the following command (which overwrites older or equally versioned files):

Msiexec /fe \\WinDC01\apps\officexpdistro\proplus.msi

If you simply want to ensure that no older version is installed, you can execute the following command:

Msiexec /fo \\WinDC01\apps\officexpdistro\proplus.msi

Again, be sure to consult the Windows help file for the complete syntax of MSIEXEC in conjunction with adhering to your specific application vendor's directions

Using *MSIEXEC* to Patch a Distribution Point

You can also use MSIEXEC to *patch*, that is to incorporate vendor-supplied bug fixes and the like to the code base of an existing package. The vendor supplies the patches by using a .msp, or *Microsoft Patch* file. Office XP's service packs, for instance, come with several .msp files that update the original .msi files.

Office XP has two service packs. You can download the first one from www.microsoft.com/office/ork/xp/journ/Oxpsp1.htm. It contains MAINSP1_Admin.msp and OWC10SP1_Admin.msp. And you can download the second from www.microsoft.com/office/ork/xp/journ/Oxpsp2a.htm. It contains Mainsp2ff.msp and Owc10sp2ff.msp. You must update the source individually with each and every .msp file provided among all service packs.

Throughout this chapter, we've leveraged our Office XP administration point. We'll continue with that trend. In the following example, the Office XP distribution, located at \\WinDC01\apps\officexpdistro, is to be patched with the MAINSP1_Admin.msp patch that comes with Office XP Service Pack 1. The resulting log file will be called logfile.txt.

Since each vendor may have a different way of patching, be sure to check out the Readme file that comes with the patch files.

The following command line is written as directed from the Office XP Service Pack SR-1 Readme file:

msiexec /p MAINSP1_Admin.msp /a \\WinDC01\apps\officexpdistro\proplus.msi
SHORTFILENAMES=TRUE /qb /L* logfile.txt

Again, you'll have to run the command for each and every patch file in all the service packs. This means you'll have to run the command four times to update an Office XP distribution point to SR-2. You'll only be able to use Office SR-2 updates if you've applied the SR-1 .msp patches to the distribution point.

This next step is a point of order that I left out of the last edition of this book. That is, once the .msi is patched, all your users (or computers) need to reinstall the application. The underlying application has changed, and the client system doesn't know about the change until you tell it.

Users also need to do this because of what is termed the "client-source-out-of-sync" problem. Until the client reaches and reinstalls from the updated administrative image, it won't be able to use the administrative image for repairs or on-demand installations. This is because a source location is validated by the Windows Installer before use. The criteria for validation are the name of the package file and the package code (seen as a GUID) of the package. When you patch the administrative image, you change the underlying package code GUID. Thus, the client needs the recache and reinstall in order to pick up the updated package code information.

So, specifically, after you patch a distribution point (or otherwise change the underlying .msi package in a distribution point), you need to right-click the offer and choose All Tasks ➢ Redeploy Application, as shown in Figure 10.24.

FIGURE 10.24   Once you patch a .msi source, be sure to select "Redeploy Application."

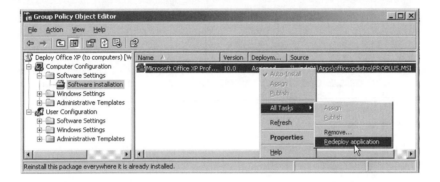

Affecting Windows Installer with Group Policy

You can use several policy settings to tweak the behavior of the Windows Installer. Most tweaks do not involve how software is managed or deployed via GPSI because there's not much to it. You deploy the application, and users (or computers) do your bidding. Rather, these settings tweak the access the user has when software is not being Assigned or Published.

There are two collections of policy settings for the Windows Installer; one is under Computer Configuration, and the other is under User Configuration. As usual, to utilize these policy settings, just create a new GPO, Enable the policy settings you like, then ensure that the corresponding user or computer account is in the scope of management of the GPO.

Computer Side Policy Settings for Windows Installer

To display the settings in Computer Configuration, as shown in Figure 10.25, choose Computer Configuration ➢ Administrative Templates ➢ Windows Components ➢ Windows Installer.

FIGURE 10.25   Use Group Policy to affect the Windows Installer settings.

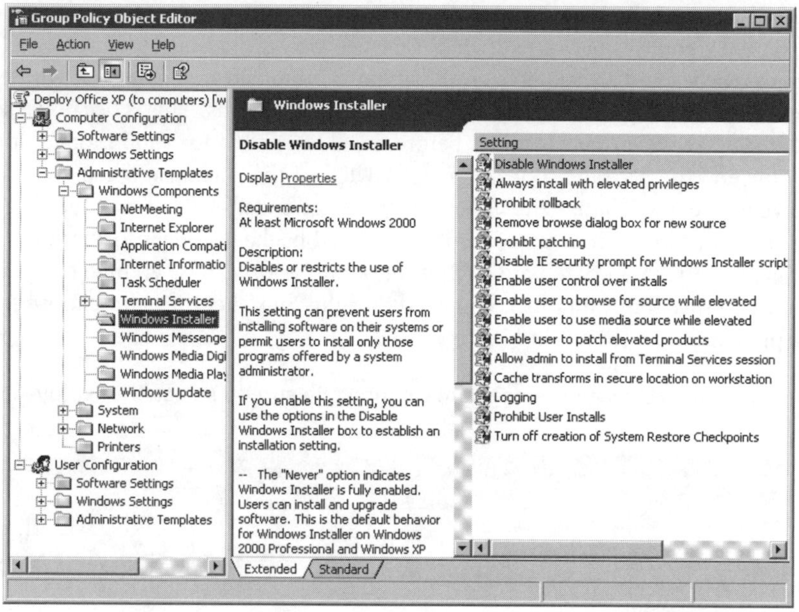

Disable Windows Installer

Once enabled, this setting lets you specify one of four options:

Not Configured   Uses the settings at a higher level.

Enabled/Never   Always keeps the Windows Installer active.

Enabled/For Non-Managed Apps Only   Turns off the Windows Installer when users try to manually install their own applications. This is useful if you want to guarantee no foreign .msi packages are making it through the doors. This option permits users to install only those programs that a system administrator Assigns or Publishes.

Enabled/Always   Essentially turns off all methods (managed and unmanaged) for loading .msi packages.

These settings specify only settings for .msi packages—not other programs that users can install, such as those from SETUP.EXEs and the like.

Always Install with Elevated Privileges

Deploying applications with GPSI is awesome: we do all the work with .msi files, and we don't have to worry about users having administrative privileges. As we've already seen, we can deploy applications to users, and have the system take care of the installation in the system context (not the user context.)

And, what's more, mere mortals cannot just download an MSI application and necessarily expect it to install correctly. Many .msi applications will fail installation if attempted in the user context. You can, however, bypass the normal security mechanism so that users can install .msi files by Enabling this policy setting. You'll need to do the same with the corresponding policy setting in the User Configuration, as discussed in the "User Side Policy Settings for Windows Installer" section.

If you are deploying .msi applications with Group Policy, you need not use and enable this setting.

Prohibit Rollback

As stated, .msi files can be "rolled back"— during the actual installation of the application, after the fact in the Add or Remove Programs applet in Control Panel. If you enable this policy setting, you're effectively telling the system not to maintain "backup files" in the case of an on-the-fly rollback. Since a rollback can be initiated during the actual installation, a "fractured" and, hence, nonworking program could remain on the system.

Personally, I would never use this policy setting.

Remove Browse Dialog Box for New Source

Recall that, at any given point, only the components required to run a .msi application are actually downloaded. For instance, the help files in Word are downloaded the first time it is used from the installation source (usually the server), not necessarily the first time Word runs. But what happens if you move the source?

When you move an application from one shared folder to another, the application can become confused, and users need to specify a different installation point to get to the source. By default, users cannot choose another source; thus they are left in limbo. Enable this setting to allow users to choose another source if the original source becomes unavailable.

Prohibit Patching

If users can install some .msi applications under their own security context, by default, they can also patch their own .msi files with .msp (Microsoft Patch) files by using the MSIEXEC command-line application. Enabling this setting prevents users from patching even their own installed .msi applications.

Disable IE Security Prompt for Windows Installer Scripts

Recall that users can manually install .msi applications from a CD, or a shared folder, or a web page. The default behavior before executing any downloaded application via Internet Explorer is to warn the user about potentially damaging content. Enabling this setting squelches this warning.

This scenario should be rare, because normally you Publish or Assign applications in order to install them to your users' desktops. At times, however, some applications may be best suited for downloading via Internet Explorer, and, hence, a warning message could appear and frighten your users.

Enable User Control over Installs

When an administrator Publishes or Assigns applications, all the settings specified in the .msi application are forced upon the user. Sometimes this behavior is undesirable. For example, you might want to let the user specify the destination folder or decide which features to download. If you enable this setting, you grant users the ability to change the default .msi application settings.

 This policy setting affects all applications installed on the client system. However, if you want to let the user set up a specific product in their own way, you can use a transform that sets a special properties inside the .msi. You can use the .mst tool to set the EnableUserControl property to 1 or add specific properties to the SecureCustomProperties list (using a customization transform). If your application doesn't have a way to create .mst files, you can create them with third-party .msi creation tools.

Enable User to Browse for Source While Elevated

When an administrator Publishes or Assigns applications, all the settings specified in the .msi application are forced upon the user from the installation point the administrator specifies. Sometimes this behavior is undesirable because the user knows of a closer source to the application in their branch office. In cases like this, you might want to let the user specify the source to locate a closer source point. If you enable this setting, you grant users the ability to change the default .msi source location.

 Once users are affected by this policy setting, they can basically browse anywhere they like, including the local system. If you have locked down the Desktop to prevent such behavior, enabling this setting could be a potential security hole during .msi application install times.

Enable User to Use Media Source While Elevated

When users install .msi packages under their own security context, they can choose whatever source they desire for the software. But when you, the administrator, Assign or Publish an application, you are essentially dictating the source of the .msi file. If you enable this setting, you permit the user to choose a nonnetworked source, such as a CD or floppy drive, from which to install a program you specify. Enable this setting only if the **Enable the User to Browse for Source While Elevated** is enabled.

Enable User to Patch Elevated Products

By default, only the administrator who Assigns or Publishes the application can use a .msp file (in conjunction with MSIEXEC) to patch a program. If you enable this setting, users can use MSIEXEC to patch their local versions of Published or Assigned applications.

Allow Admin to Install from Terminal Services Session

By default, administrators using the Terminal Services "Remote Administration Mode" on Windows 2000 or Windows 2003 Server are prevented from installing additional Published or Assigned applications.

If you want Administrators to be able to install MSI applications while logged in via Terminal Services session, just Enable this setting so that servers and Domain Controllers download the setting and, hence, reverse this default.

Cache Transforms in Secure Location on Workstation

Recall that you can specifically customize a `.mst` file to hone a `.msi` application. Transform files are applied on `.msi` packages either to filter the number of options available to the end user or to specify certain answers to questions usually raised during the `.msi` package installation.

Once a user starts using a `.msi` application applied with a `.mst` file, that `.mst` file follows them in the Roaming Profile—specifically, in the Application Data folder, as described in Chapter 8. You can change this default behavior by enabling this setting, which takes the `.mst` file out of the Roaming Profile and puts it in a secure place on the workstation. On the one hand, this closes a small security hole that sophisticated users might hack into their own `.mst` files in their profiles. On the other hand, users are forced to return to the machine that has their `.mst` files in order to additionally modify their application.

Avoid using this setting unless specifically directed to do so by your application vendor, a security bulletin, or Microsoft.

Logging

Applications Assigned or Published using Windows Installer do not provide much information to the administrator about the success of their installation. By default, several key tidbits of information are logged about managed applications that fail. The log files are named `.msi*.LOG`; the * represents additional characters that make the log file unique for each application downloaded.

Logs for Assigned applications are on the client machine in the system's Temp folder (typically c:\windows\temp). Installs for Published applications (as well as install transactions from shortcut and Document invocations) are in the user's Temp folder (%temp%). Thus, centralized logging and reporting is an arduous, if not impossible, task for anything more than a handful of users who are using Windows Installer. For additional logging and reporting, Microsoft recommends their Systems Management Server, as described in the section titled "Fitting Microsoft SMS into Your Environment," later in the chapter.

To add logging entries, modify the Logging setting. Some settings that might come in handy are Out of Memory and Out of Disk—two common reasons for Windows Installer applications failing to load.

You can also turn on Application Management debugging logs by manually editing the Registry of the client machine. Simply run `regedit` or `regedt32` and edit the following key: HKEY_LOCAL_MACHINE\Software\Microsoft\Windows NT\CurrentVersion. Create a "Diagnostics" key, and add Reg_DWORD called AppMgmtDebugLevel of 4b in hexadecimal. You'll then find a log in the local %windir%debug\usermode folder named `appmgmt.log`, which can also aid in finding out why applications fail to load.

Prohibit User Installs

On occasion an administrator might dictate that a user is Assigned Office XP, and another administrator dictates that a computer gets Office XP (but perhaps without Access). What if the user who is Assigned Office XP sits down at a computer that is Assigned Office XP without Access? Which one "wins"? The application (and settings therein) Assigned to the user takes precedence.

This policy setting has three options (once enabled): Allow User Installs, Hide User Installs, or Prohibit User Installs. Computers that are affected by "Hide User Installs" display only the applications Assigned to the computer. However, the user can still install the applications assigned to them using the Add or Remove Programs applet in Control Panel (hence, overriding the applications assigned to the computer).

If you set **Prohibit User Installs,** the user won't get the applications Assigned to them on the machines to which this policy setting applies. And the user cannot load Assigned applications to their user account via the Add or Remove Programs folder. If they do so, they'll get an error message. If this policy setting is set somewhere else, you can also return the default behavior by setting "Allow User Installs."

This policy setting can be especially handy in Terminal Services sessions or Kiosk settings (for example, lab machines) where you want all users of the machine to get the applications Assigned only to computers (not to users).

 This setting is valid for Windows XP and Windows 2000 machines (with Windows Installer 2 or later loaded.) See the section "The Windows Installer" earlier in this chapter.

Turn off Creation of System Restore Checkpoints

On a Windows XP machine, a System Restore Checkpoint is created when users load their own .msi files unless there is no user interface. The .msi system creates System Restore Checkpoints on first installation and uninstall. System Restore Checkpoints are not created when deploying (or repairing) applications via GPSI.

Enable this setting if you want to ensure that no System Restore Checkpoints are created when .msi files are loaded.

 This setting is only valid on Windows XP machines.

User Side Policy Settings for Windows Installer

To display the Group Policy settings that affect the Windows Installer, as shown in Figure 10.26, choose User Configuration ➢ Administrative Templates ➢ Windows Components ➢ Windows Installer. These settings affect the behavior of the users in the scope.

FIGURE 10.26   The Windows Installer user settings

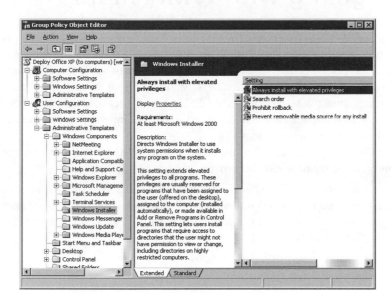

Always Install with Elevated Privileges

Enabling this policy setting allows users to manually install their own .msi files and bypass their own insufficient and lowly user rights in order to correctly install applications. Some applications install correctly in the users' context, but many don't.

After you enable this setting, you'll also need to set the corresponding setting in the Computer half, as noted in the previous section.

Search Order

By default, applications that are Published or Assigned using the Windows Installer search their original location for updates or repairs. If that original location is not available, the application tries other locations.

This policy setting allows you to specify any or all of the following locations: Network, removable media, or URL (Web site).

Prohibit Rollback

See the **Prohibit Rollback** policy setting in the "Computer side policy settings for Windows Installer" section.

This setting is found in both User Configuration and Computer Configuration. Recall that computer settings have precedence over user settings.

Prevent Removable Media Source for Any Install

If you enable this setting, which works only for .msi application, users cannot install applications under their own context. Rather, only administrators can install applications, or applications must be Published or Assigned for users to use them. This prevents users from running down to the computer store, obtaining the latest version of a program, and installing it via CD.

GPO Targeting with WMI Filters

In Chapter 2, I alluded to a new power called WMI Filters. I like to think of WMI Filters as adding laser-sighting to the gun of Group Policy. With WMI Filters, you can dive into and inspect the soul of your client machines, and if certain criteria are met, you can then apply the GPO to them.

You might be asking yourself why I waited so long to talk about WMI Filters and, why, of all places, am I talking about WMI Filters in the GPSI chapter? Because, although WMI Filters can be used on any GPOs in your Active Directory, I'm predicting you'll usually use them for targeting GPSI when you use Group Policy.

Before we jump headlong into ferreting out the power of WMI Filters, let's make sure we have the machinery necessary to wield this power:

- The domain is a Windows 2003 domain or a Windows 2000 domain with an updated Windows 2003 schema. You update a Windows 2000 Active Directory domain's schema to the Windows 2003 domain schema via the command prompt. This is performed via the command `ADPREP /Domainprep`.

- Your target clients are Windows XP or Windows 2003 clients.

 Windows 2000 clients ignore WMI Filters; for Windows 2000 clients, the GPO is always applied—regardless of the evaluation of the WMI filter.

WMI is a huge animal, and you can choose to filter on thousands of items. Hot items to filter on typically include the following:

- The amount of memory
- The available hard-drive space
- CPU speed
- A hotfix

But you don't have to stop there. You can get creative and filter GPOs on obscure items (if they exist and are supported by the hardware) such as the following:

- BIOS revision
- Manufacturer of the CD drive
- Whether a UPS is connected
- The rotational speed of the fan

The potential esoteric criteria you can query for, and then filter on, goes on and on. If this example, I'll limit our Office XP distribution to client machines that have at least 128MB or more memory. To do this, we'll first need some tools to help us figure out which pieces of WMI to query. We'll then take what we've learned and use the GPMC to create a WMI filter to specifically target the systems we want.

Unfortunately, I don't have room to dive into how or why WMI works on a molecular level. If you're unfamiliar with WMI, take a peek at www.2000trainers.com/printarticle. aspx?articleID=286 and other documentation at www.dtmf.org.

Tools (and references) of the WMI Trade

To master WMI, you have to do a lot of work. You'll have to read up on and master four crucial key pieces of WMI documentation, which are found at the following websites:

- http://msdn.microsoft.com/library/en-us/dnclinic/html/ scripting06112002.asp

- http://msdn.microsoft.com/library/en-us/dnclinic/html/ scripting08132002.asp

- http://msdn.microsoft.com/library/en-us/dnclinic/html/ scripting01142003.asp

And you'll have to get the accompanying "Windows 2000 Scripting Guide" from Microsoft—the de facto (and very large-o) book on scripting—and work through all the hundreds of examples.

What? You don't have time for that? No problem! You can do the next best thing and "wing it." We'll use two tools to create WMI queries, and then we'll manually bend them into WMI Filters.

- WMI CIM Studio is available on Microsoft's website. At last check it was at www.microsoft.com/downloads/release.asp?releaseid=40804.

- The WMI Scriptomatic tool is also available from Microsoft. At last check it was at www.microsoft.com/technet/treeview/default.asp?url=/technet/scriptcenter/ tools/wmimatic.asp.

My favorite is the WMI Scriptomatic tool, made by my pals the "Microsoft Scripting Guys." This cool tool zips through all the available WMI classes and then makes them available for an easy-breezy query. In Figure 10.27, the WMI class Win32_LocalMemoryConfiguration is selected. Then, scriptomagically, all the WMI attributes in that class are exposed in a ready-to-run VBscript application. You can see them in Figure 10.27, including AvailableVirtualMemory, TotalPageFileSpace, and the one we're after, TotalPhysicalMemory. Just click the Run button and you can see the output with the values on *this* machine.

Don't ask me why TotalPhysicalMemory is an attribute of the Win32_LogicalMemory-Configuration—it just is. Actually, it turns out that you can query another variable to gather the physical memory. It's under win32_ComputerSystem, and the variable name is also Total-PhysicalMemory. Oddly, it returns a slightly different value on the same machine. Again, don't ask me why.

This tool was released before Windows 2003 Server, so the title says "Windows .NET Server Resource Kit." By the time you read this, Scriptomatic 2.0 should be out and even better!

FIGURE 10.27   The Scriptomatic tool from the "Microsoft Scripting Guys"

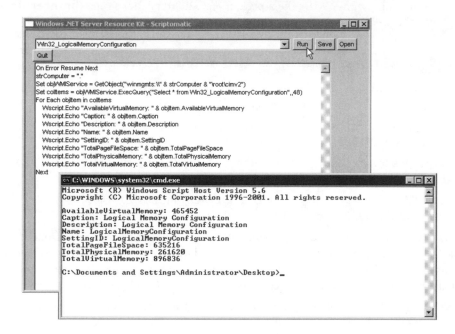

When you click Run, the script runs in a little prompt window. You can see that the TotalPhysicalMemory of this box is 261620, which is 256MB. The point here, however, is that the unit measurement and expected output of this field is expressed in thousands of bytes. We'll leverage this information when we bend this WMI query into a WMI filter.

WMI Filter Syntax

You can start nearly all the WMI Filters you'll create using Scriptomatic. All that's left is to wrap a little logic around the output. All the WMI Filters we'll create have the following syntax:

```
SELECT * from Win32_{something} WHERE {variable} [=,>,<,is, etc] {desired result}
```

Now, all we have to do is plug in the stuff we already know, and we're off and running. In this example, we're using Win32_LogicalMemoryConfiguration. We know the variable we want is *TotalPhysicalMemory*, and we know that we want it to be greater than 128MB, which we can represent as > 128000. Yes, I know 128000 isn't exactly 128MB of memory, but it's close enough. Anyway, when you put it all together, you get:

```
SELECT * from Win32_LogicalMemoryConfiguration WHERE TotalPhyisicalMemory > 128000
```

Easy as pie. However, not all WMI Filters are this easy. Some WMI variable entries have text, and you must use quotes to specifically match what's inside the string to what's inside the WMI variable.

Creating and Using a WMI Filter

Once your WMI filter is in the correct syntax, you're ready to inject it into an existing GPO for filtering. Again, this can be any GPO you want—not just GPOs that control GPSI. Again, we're using GPSI as an example because I think you'll get the most use of it this way. Creating and using a WMI filter is a two-step process: creating and then using. (I guess that makes sense.)

WMI Filter Creation

Before you can filter a specific GPO, you need to define the filter in Active Directory. Follow these steps:

1. Fire up the GPMC, then drill down to Forest ➢ Domain ➢ WMI Filters node.

2. Right-click over the WMI Filters node and select New as seen in Figure 10.28.

3. When you do, you'll be presented with the New WMI Filter dialog box as seen in Figure 10.29. You'll be able to type in a name and description of your new filter, as seen below. Then, click the Add button, and in the Query field, just enter in the full SELECT statement from before.

4. When done, click Save. Your query is now saved into Active Directory and can be leveraged for any GPO you want. We'll explore how to do that next.

FIGURE 10.28   Right-click over the WMI Filters node to create a WMI filter

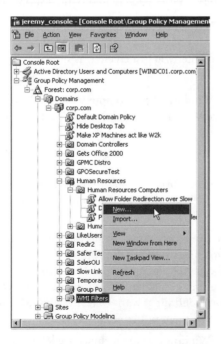

FIGURE 10.29 Enter in a name and description, then click the Add button to enter in your WMI filter.

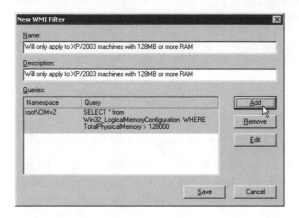

WMI Filter Usage

Using the GPMC, it's easy to find the GPO you want and then leverage the WMI filter you just made. Follow these steps:

1. Locate the "Deploy Office XP (to computers)" GPO you created (which should be within the **Human Resources Computers** OU).

2. Click the Scope tab of the GPO.

3. In the WMI Filtering section, select the WMI Filter you just created, as shown in Figure 10.30.

4. At the prompt, confirm your selection.

Now this GPO applies to Windows XP and Windows 2003 computers with 128MB of RAM or more. Windows 2000 machines simply ignore WMI Filters, and this GPO still applies to them.

Final WMI Filter Thoughts

WMI Filters can be a bit tough to create, but they're worth it. You can filter target machines that meet specific criteria—for GPOs that leverage GPSI or any other Group Policy function. But keep two things in mind.

WMI Performance Impact WMI Filters take some percentage of performance away from logon (or startup) when evaluated. Indeed, if you link a GPO to the domain that leveraged WMI Filters, every single Windows XP and Windows 2003 machine works hard to evaluate that WMI query. The upshot: be careful where you link GPOs with WMI queries. You could seriously affect GPO processing performance. You'll definitely want to test your WMI Filters first in the lab for performance metrics before you roll them out companywide.

WMI Filters Don't Apply to Windows 2000 Windows 2000 machines are left out of the mix. They simply ignore the WMI Filters placed on GPOs. When a Windows 2000 machine processes a GPO that leverages a WMI filter, it's as if the query always evaluates to "True." However, with a little downloadable magic, you can hack Windows 2000 machines to play in the WMI Filter game. A free, quasi-supported download, called "WMI Filtering for Windows 2000," is available at www.mml.ru/WMIF2K/, and it can inject the necessary code to support WMI Filters. It's a little unwieldy to set up, but afterward you should be able to have a unified WMI scheme across your environment.

FIGURE 10.30   Choose the GPO (or GPO link) and select a WMI Filter.

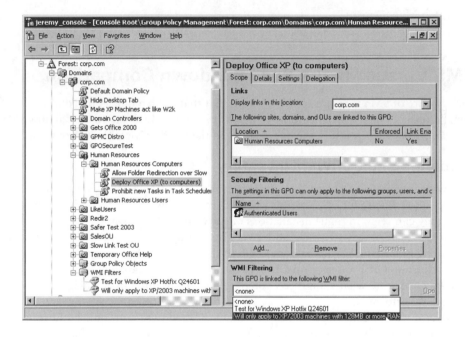

Return to Chapter 2 some time when you can review how to back up and restore WMI Filters as well as how to delegate their creation and use. Also, don't forget about Chapter 7, which also discusses how to script the backup and restore of WMI Filters.

Fitting Microsoft SMS into Your Environment

Microsoft's *SMS*, or *Systems Management Server*, is a component in the Windows Server System. Recently, SMS 2003 was released to manufacturing, and it is somewhat more robust under the hood than its older SMS 2 cousin. It costs an arm and a leg, has a thoroughly esoteric licensing scheme, and requires a client component on every Windows PC and server on your network. But, if you can get over these drawbacks, it houses a pretty amazing collection of core features:

- Software and Hardware Inventory
- Remote Control
- Software Metering
- Software Deployment
- Patch Management

Most of these features would be a welcome addition to any managed environment.

SMS Versus "In the Box" Rundown Comparison

Each feature of SMS is meant to chip away at that that golden nugget of Total Cost of Ownership. I often get asked which has more power, SMS or GPSI. Let's take a look at how SMS stacks up against the stuff we get in the box, that is, all the stuff we've looked at thus far.

Hardware and Software Inventory

Hardware inventory and software inventory are two critical elements that administrators need to keep in touch with what's currently out there in their environment. With this information in hand, they can reign in rogue installations of software and hardware.

Without SMS, once software is added via GPSI (or by hand or otherwise), there is no native way, using just Active Directory with GPSI, to really know who has installed what software. Although using GPSI to set up an OU, a package, and an Assignment is a "pretty good" yardstick for measuring what's out there, you're never certain until an actual inventory of the machine is performed.

No hardware or software inventory is built in to Windows. You could build your own WMI scripts to pull out the hardware and software inventory data you want, but, in doing so you'd go insane. So SMS wins in this category.

Remote Control

The Remote Control feature is Microsoft's version of Symantec's pcAnywhere, but it is extremely lightweight and takes up nearly no disk space. However, it could be argued that having a program such as SMS that specifically contains Remote Control is becoming less important. You can implement remote control "on the cheap" with various other options. In Windows 2000, you can use Netmeeting, which is workable, if not optimal. Or you can use the 100% free multiplatform VNC from `www.realvnc.com`.

Additionally, Windows XP has quite decent remote control built in via its Remote Assistance facilities. Oh, and Terminal Services has its own version of Remote Control called "shadowing."

So, although Remote Control is a great feature, it isn't as important as it used to be.

So, who wins in this category? SMS or "In the Box"? It's a tie.

Software Metering

The Software Metering component has two methods of operation: Lock Out and Log Only.

Lock Out   This method (only available in SMS 2 and dropped from SMS 2003) is for strict license compliance. With this option, you can lock out users from applications if the number of licenses dries up across the environment. For example, if you purchased only 25 copies of Dog-Food Maker 4.5, the 26th person cannot run it.

Log Only   This version doesn't lock users out of applications; rather, it simply logs the amount of copies in use. This is useful for gauging licensing compliance, but not quite as intensive as the Lock Out method.

Without SMS, there is no way to gauge who's using what or to force users into compliance. Winner: SMS.

Software Deployment

This feature does overlap with the Windows 2000 IntelliMirror feature of GPSI. As we explored in this chapter, Group Policy has a decent set of features when it comes to deploying software to clients.

In the previous edition of this book, I said that "SMS's Software Deployment features trounce the built-in features of Active Directory." I don't know if I would still agree with that. SMS does have quite a robust deployment mechanism, and one reason is that it can leverage the WMI query data to target to machines' CPU speeds, amount of RAM, BIOS revision, and so on. But we just did the same thing several pages ago with our Windows XP clients, so GPSI is certainly catching up!

Several facets of SMS software deployment are better than the GPSI. Specifically, SMS can do the following that GPSI cannot:

- Deploy software to users or computers any time of the day or night—not just on logon or reboot.

- Compress the application and send it to a distribution point close to the user. Even if we set up GPSI with Dfs, we cannot do this.

- Target software to all Windows 32-bit platforms, including Windows 9x, Windows NT, and Windows 2000 clients and servers. GPSI works only with Active Directory and Windows 2000, Windows XP, and Windows 2003 clients.

- Once a machine is targeted for a delivery and the package is received, the machine can send back detailed status messages describing success or failure of the transaction.

- Dribble the applications to clients over slow links without slowing down the connection. Only when the software is fully downloaded is the install initiated.

So, SMS wins in this category by some margin if you have Windows XP clients and, by a larger degree, if you have anything else. However, with a little elbow grease you can really get an amazing amount of mileage out of GPSI—even in really big environments.

Patch Management

SMS also has decent patch management support, which is really just a customized extension of its Software Deployment feature. It's really, really good. You can target specific machines with specific patches. Once the patches are received, you can dictate how to react: wait for reboot, reboot now, and so on.

Today's Microsoft solution for those customers without SMS is Software Update Services, or SUS (`www.microsoft.com/windowsserversystem/sus/default.mspx`). However, SUS can't target specific machines with specific patches; rather, all machines that use the SUS server get the same packages. However, if rumors come to fruition, Microsoft may release some patches as `.msi` packages. If that's the case, you might be able to deploy those patches via GPSI Group Policy. You would certainly be able to target specific patches to specific machines. This area is growing within Microsoft, with rumors of a "unified" patch management from SUS 2 on the horizon.

Winner? SMS today, but who knows tomorrow.

GPSI and SMS Coexistence

Okay, I'm forced to admit it—SMS does have more raw power. However, I would argue that with a little finesse, you can squeeze quite a lot out of the IntelliMirror tools you have come to learn about with Group Policy. Some organizations use either GPSI or SMS, and some shops use both. Although no two organizations ever do anything exactly the same way, there does seem to be a general trend in those places where SMS and GPSI coexist.

First, SMS is generally used in heterogeneous environments—that is, where there's a mix of Windows 2000 and non–Windows 2000 workstations and servers. Because GPSI works only with Active Directory and Windows 2000, Windows XP, and Windows 2003 clients, SMS makes sense in these cases.

If whether to use GPSI or SMS is a toss-up, GPSI is generally used to deploy smaller applications that need to be rapidly fired off due to document invocation. For example, if a user is sent an Adobe Acrobat PDF file via e-mail but doesn't have the reader, double-clicking the document automatically installs the application on the machine.

SMS, on the other hand, is typically used to deploy larger applications, such as the Office suite, when you need definitive feedback about what went wrong (if anything). This philosophy provides a good balance between the "on demand" feel of GPSI and the "strategic targeted deployment" feel of SMS.

As you've seen, most of the features do not overlap, making SMS a terrific addition to any medium or large environment.

Final Thoughts

In this chapter we inspected Software Installation using Group Policy, or just GPSI for short. GPSI works with Active Directory and Windows 2000, Windows XP, and Windows 2003 clients. Use Microsoft SMS (or other tool) for non–Windows 2000, Windows 2003, and Windows XP clients.

In order to make the most of GPSI, you really need to leverage MSI applications. You can either get MSI applications from your software vendor, or wrap up your own with 3rd party tools (listed in this chapter and also in the Appendix and "Third-Party Group Policy Tools" on this book's website.)

Share a folder on a server you want to send the package from. Plop the application in its own subfolder, and use both share and NTFS permissions to crank down who is able to read the executables and install files. Remember, though that not all MSI applications are ready to be deployed. Some are, indeed, ready-to-go (like the .NET Framework), others require an Administrative Installation (like Office XP), and still others ship as MSI files but cannot be deployed via GPSI (such as Adobe Acrobat Writer).

Once you have your package, you can Assign or Publish your applications.

Assign applications when you want application icons to appear on the Start ➤ All Programs menu; Publish applications when you want users to dive into the Add or Remove Programs folder to get the application. You can leverage Microsoft Transform Files (MST files) to hone an MSI and customize it. You can patch existing MSI applications with Microsoft Patch Files (MSP files) but afterward, you need to redeploy the application.

Try not to orphan applications by removing the GPO before the target computer gets the "signal" upon the next reboot (for computer) or logon (for user). If you think you might end up doing this, it's best to ensure that the "Uninstall This Application When It Falls out of the Scope of Management" checkbox is checked, as seen in Figure 10.11.

WMI Filters are used to change the scope of management for when a GPO will apply. You can use WMI Filters for any GPO you create—not just ones that leverage GPSI. However, I predict that the most common use for WMI Filters will indeed be for GPOs that leverage GPSI. Don't forget that WMI Filters don't apply at all to Windows 2000 clients. Additionally, Windows XP and Windows 2003 clients set to evaluate a WMI filter will take some extra processing time for each filter they need to work through. Be sure to test all your WMI Filters in the test lab first.

Beyond IntelliMirror: Shadow Copies and Remote Installation Services

Technically, this book is over. You could put it down right now and feel that you've explored and conquered every major Group Policy and IntelliMirror function. At this point in our journey, we've tackled all the true IntelliMirror components. We started with Roaming Profiles and then moved on to Redirected Folders, Offline Folders, the Synchronization Manager, and Disk Quotas. We technically wrapped up IntelliMirror with Software Distribution in the previous chapter. If you take a look back at Chapter 9, Figure 9.1, you'll see just how far we've come in our journey.

All these IntelliMirror technologies are terrific, and they chip away at the TCO (Total Cost of Ownership) by preventing administrators from having to run out to a workstation to make a specific tweak or configuration changes or to fix something when users hop from machine to machine. IntelliMirror can help when it comes to a user needing to be sure their user data and applications stay with them, but it misses the mark in two key areas.

- What happens if a user overwrites a key file (or deletes it)?

- What happens if the machine (usually a laptop) goes belly up, catches fire, or is stolen?

We spent the last several chapters ensuring that our critical data is safely stored on the server. But how can we further protect our users from disaster? Actually, more realistically, how can we protect our users from themselves?

To answer these questions, we'll investigate two more features: Shadow Copies and Remote Installation Services. Shadow Copies help users restore data by themselves, without requiring us to grab the restore tapes. This feature isn't part of the marketing that is IntelliMirror, but boy howdy—it should be. I mean, IntelliMirror is all about data protection, and this fits that description perfectly.

The last major feature, as seen in Figure 9.1, is under the broader heading of Change and Configuration Management. That feature is Remote Installation Services (RIS). After a crash, or other loss, you can get the PC back up and running with RIS. Then, all the IntelliMirror features spring into action and return the user's configuration to exactly where they left off.

So, why are we dedicating a full chapter to non-IntelliMirror technologies? Because, in order to get a holistic picture of how to care for and feed your network, you really, really need these two features implemented to have the full safety net in place.

Shadow Copies

The idea behind Shadow Copies is awesome: preserve some number of copies of the user's precious files on the server. When the user performs a CLM (Career-Limiting Move) by deleting a file or overwriting a file with data that cannot be undone, they can simply get that file back from a point in time. Microsoft's code name for this feature was "Time Warp," and I think that pretty much says it all.

Technically, the system doesn't precisely store "copies" of a file. Really, this current magic preserves a "point-in-time" copy of a file—not a copy of all the bytes that compose the entire file. Sometimes, this magic is referred to as "Snapshots," though, technically again, it's not a direct bitwise snapshot of the file.

This feature only works when the files are stored on a Windows 2003 server. However, the clients can be either Windows 2000 or Windows XP. You must take care of two tasks before the user can use Shadow Copies:

- Set up the Windows 2003 server to start creating these snapshots.
- Deliver the Shadow Copies client piece to the desktops.

So, let's do that now.

 You might not want to deliver the client piece now, but wait until a user needs it—particularly if you have tens of thousands of desktops and are concerned about the extra overhead required to deliver the client (though it isn't much). When the user calls for help, you can deliver the client piece, and the files can be recovered.

Setting Up Shadow Copies on the Server

Shadow Copies works because you're making a *point-in-time* copy of the users' data files, which preserves them in case of a future calamity. The best place to do this is on the volume to which you've redirected My Documents. However, first you need to ask yourself several questions:

- How much junk, I mean, data, are my users taking up on each drive on the server?
- How much more space on this drive am I willing to cordon off to preserve previous versions of files?
- How often do I want to take a snapshot to preserve user data?

Once you answer these questions, follow these steps:

1. Right-click a drive letter on a server and choose Properties from the shortcut menu to open the Properties dialog box, as shown in Figure 11.1.

2. Click the Shadow Copies tab, select a drive letter, and click the Settings button to open the Settings dialog box, as shown in Figure 11.2.

FIGURE 11.1   You set the Shadow Copies characteristics on a per-volume basis.

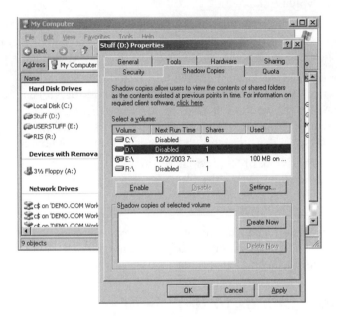

FIGURE 11.2   You can specify how much space to dedicate when files change, set a schedule to make Shadow Copies, and specify where to locate the storage area.

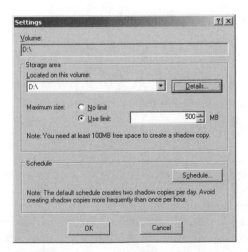

Here you can specify how much space you want to set aside for this particular volume. My recommendation is to set aside about 20%–30%. The point of Shadow Copies isn't to keep backup copies of all user files forever; rather, similar to the Offline Caching mechanism, user files that get old will be flushed out of this space to make room for new files. Although Shadow Copies is a great preventive measure, it's not a substitute or replacement for general backups should the file turn out not to be available for restore.

1. In the Use Limit spin box, specify the size, and then click the Schedule button to open up the Schedule tab for the volume.

2. The schedule tab is pretty self explanatory. You might just wish to leave the defaults for now. When ready, press OK to confirm a changed schedule, or press Cancel to return back to the Settings tab. Click OK or Cancel again to return to the Properties tab.

The default schedule for any enabled volume is at 7:00 A.M. and 12:00 P.M. workdays (Monday through Friday). The idea is that you'll snag points in time of the data before the workday begins and also again at the halfway point in the workday. If a user screws up and deletes a file, you've got at least two potentially restorable files from just today! If you have even more space available, you can store days or weeks of restorable data! Set the schedule however you want, but note two things.

•   Shadow Copies keeps a maximum of 64 previous versions of a file. Every time you take a snapshot, you're *potentially* dumping older files. The default schedule is usually pretty good for most organizations; it's estimated that it should provide about a month's worth of previous versions.

•   The server will be hammered for a bit while the Shadow Copy snapshot is being made. Consequently, taking multiple snapshots during the day might not be such a hot idea. Therefore, you might want to perform fewer snapshots, say, once a day.

Delivering Shadow Copies to the Client

Once you set up the server, you're ready to deploy the client piece. The good news is that the Shadow Copy client is valid for Windows XP and Windows 2000. Although a version of the Shadow Copies client is on the Windows 2003 Server CD, it's better to download the update, which you'll find at www.microsoft.com/windowsserver2003/downloads/shadowcopyclient.mspx.

To do the deployment, simply take what you learned in the previous chapter and use it to your advantage:

•   Share the file out on a shared folder or Dfs.

•   Round up the computers you want to get the Shadow Copy client into an OU.

•   Create a GPO, link it to the OU, and then use GPSI to deploy the .msi file

Figure 11.3 demonstrates how to assign the application to your Windows 2000 and Windows XP computers.

Restoring Files with the Shadow Copies Client

Before you can restore a file, the data must be shadow copied at least once, changed, and then shadow copied again. This process maintains a point in time of the volume—in its changed state and ready to be reverted to a previous version or restored if it was deleted altogether.

FIGURE 11.3 You can simply use GPSI to deploy the Shadow Copy client to your Windows 2000 and Windows XP machines.

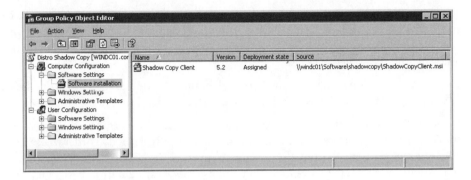

Reverting to a Previous Version of a File

Oftentimes, users inadvertently overwrite their documents with data. To that end, you have now given them the ability to revert to a previous version of the file. To do so, users follow these steps:

1. Users can now open up their My Documents folder, and right-click any file and choose Properties from the shortcut menu to open the Properties dialog box, as shown in Figure 11.4.

FIGURE 11.4 Once at least one change is preserved, users can revert to a point-in-time file.

2. Click the Previous Versions tab.

3. Select the version you want, and can then click View, Copy, or Restore:

View   Clicking View launches the program associated with the file type, and you can view the file. You might be able to make temporary changes in the document, but you cannot save them back to the same place on the server as the original document. You can do a Save As and save the file somewhere else.

Copy   You can copy the file to an alternate location. A popular location is the desktop, but any locations that users have access to are equally valid.

Restore   The title of this button is sort of a misnomer. When I think of the word *Restore*, I think of restoring a deleted file, but the file needn't be fully deleted in order to use this option. Clicking this button will cause the selected to revert to the previous version. Note, however, that it will overwrite the current version. So, use this Restore button with caution, because any changes in the document since a Shadow Copy was performed are deleted.

Restoring a Previous Version of a File

If a user actually deletes a copy of a preserved file you or they can restore it. Since we're using Shadow Copies on the volume that houses our redirected My Documents, we can leverage this magic. Simply right-click the user's My Documents folder, choose Properties from the shortcut menu to open the Properties dialog box, and click the Previous Versions tab, as shown in Figure 11.5.

FIGURE 11.5   You can restore the entire contents of the folder, or just use View to drag and drop the file to be restored to an alternate location.

You'll have the same three options as before: View, Copy, or Restore. My suggestion is to select View and then drag the file you need to the intended location. Restore is quite dangerous, actually, and will restore the entire contents of the folder upon the live copy. This is not a good idea. Clicking Copy copies the entirety of the folder to a specific location; this is not all that useful either, as the user might not want to restore the entirety of the point in time of the folder.

Shadow Copies completes the circle of user data protection. Without it, the only data protection (other than normal, regularly scheduled backups) is Offline Files. Offline Files is a good piece of technology, but ultimately not enough if the data on the server is deleted or inadvertently overwritten.

Inside Remote Installation Services

In the previous section, you set out to protect user's files if they are deleted or overwritten. But what if a user leaves their laptop at the airport? Or the desktop malfunctions due to a lightning strike? You can leverage Active Directory to help roll out new machines or replacements for old machines using *Remote Installation Services*, or *RIS*. Its goal is to provide the administrator with the ability to roll out any number of Windows 2000, Windows XP, and Windows 2003 configurations in a short amount of time. In a nutshell, you simply prepare your server for RIS, boot the target client from a specially prepared floppy (or special onboard boot-ROM), answer a few questions, and away the installation goes.

After you create your first RIS-based client machine, you can customize it with commercial or homegrown apps and save that configuration to the server as well, making that machine appear as another downloadable "image."

Server Components

Before you can use RIS, you need to make sure several components are present on your network.

DHCP Server   The DHCP server is the first place the client machines look to get a temporary TCP/IP address while the system is being installed.

DNS Server   DNS server is also required, because not only is it the key ingredient for Active Directory, but, more specifically, it points the clients to servers running RIS.

RIS Server   At least one server in your environment needs to be running RIS. We'll set up this service later in the chapter.

Although you can run all these services on just one server, in practice you probably wouldn't want to due to the potential heavy processor and disk load the RIS server will have to shoulder. Most real-world configurations run the DHCP and DNS servers on the same box, but configure one or more specific servers solely for the purpose of running RIS server and dishing out RIS images. You must also authorize your DHCP server to participate in Active Directory if you want it to dish out any TCP/IP addresses.

For the sake of this learning example, however, you can use one server to run it all: DNS, DHCP, and RIS. In this case, we'll use WinDC01.

What's New in Windows 2003 RIS

If you're already familiar with RIS, you might just want to locate what's new and changed. Really only two big things have changed since Windows 2000 RIS was released. First, Windows 2003 can deploy the following Windows system via RIS: Windows 2003 RIS can deploy Windows 2000 Professional (with any service pack level), Windows XP (with any service pack level), and Windows Server 2003 (and any future service packs.) Actually, Windows 2000 Server's original ability was just to deploy Windows 2000 Professional machines. A hotfix allowed Windows XP to be deployed, and, finally, with the advent of Windows 2000 Service Pack 3, all the aforementioned operating systems were then officially supported. And, indeed, that same list is supported with Windows Server 2003.

The other major new capability of Windows 2003 is something that's tucked away inside the bowels of RIS's underlying "Blue Screens of Life." Specifically, those pages are really HTML pages, masquerading as .osc files that live on the server. HTML, as you might know, is made up of tags such a <//BEGIN> and </END>. A new tag for Windows 2003 RIS inside the .osc files is called Autoenter feature. This allows for an unattended RIS installation. Unfortunately, I don't have space to go on about it at length. However, in my classes, I do teach how to customize RIS with this new function.

Additional security has also been added to RIS servers running on Windows 2003. Specifically, the local machine's passwords are encrypted in the answer files, and NTLM v2 is tried first when logging on with credentials in order to start RIS.

 If you want to run DHCP on one server and RIS on another server, you'll need to additionally authorize your RIS server itself. See the section "Authorizing Your RIS Server" later in this chapter.

Client Components

The downside to using RIS for rolling out your workstations is that you must pay a small price; the workstations' network cards need to be PXE Boot ROM–capable. *PXE (Pre-boot eXecution Environment)* is a new architecture type for network cards that lets them pre-execute and talk to the network before the system itself or the hard drive becomes active.

A client can connect to RIS servers in only two ways:

PXE Boot ROM   If your network card actually has the PXE Boot ROM code embedded, you can boot directly to the network. You might need to turn this feature on in the network card's BIOS or in the PC's BIOS—or both.

PXE Boot ROM Floppy   Remember that the specifications state that the network card must be PXE-capable. Some cards, which are technically non–PXE compliant, are still capable but just don't have the boot ROM code itself. Other network cards (such as the older Compaq Net-Flex 3 cards) have the PXE boot ROM code, but it's older code so it's incompatible with RIS. Windows 2000 Server or Windows 2003 Server can create a PXE Boot ROM emulator floppy that can kickstart your network card into thinking it actually has a PXE Boot ROM that's up to snuff.

Not all network cards are PXE-capable. Indeed, only a handful are. First, if the card doesn't fit into a PCI slot, it's not PXE-capable—period. Therefore, by definition no ISA (Integrated Systems Architecture) cards are PXE-capable. Next, you can check with the manufacturer to see if the card is indeed PXE-capable. Some cards that are not on the list might also work, but there's certainly no guarantee.

If your card isn't specifically listed as PXE-compliant, you might still be able to use the boot floppy generator program Just click the Adapter List button in the RBFG.EXE application (see the section "Creating a Remote Boot Disk," later in this chapter.)

The good news is that more and more laptops are RIS capable. Generally, laptop network cards come in two flavors:

- Built in
- Credit-card style PC Card (or PCMCIA, Personal Computer Memory Card International Association) adaptors

In general, those with the PC Card network adaptors cannot leverage RIS (though I have seen exceptions). However, most laptops that have built-in on-board network cards generally are compatible with RIS. These on-board NICs (network interface cards) are considered "mini-PCI" network cards, and I've seen many of them that are indeed capable of running RIS.

If your laptop is not PXE-capable, you might be able to use a docking station that has a PXE-capable network card. However, don't try to deploy all your laptops with one PXE-capable docking station. RIS machines are registered in Active Directory based on a *globally unique identifier*, or *GUID*. The GUID is either hardcoded or based on the MAC address. If you deploy all your machines with a single docking station, you risk multiple machines appearing to have the same GUID. Active Directory requires that machines have a GUID to function properly.

If you're shopping around for new laptops, I recommend that you get only those that have mini-PCI cards that are PXE-capable, and verify that they work with RIS before buying a slew of them.

Setting Up RIS Server

You can easily add the RIS to any Windows 2000 Server or Windows Server 2003 installation. (RIS is not available in Windows 2003 Server, Web Edition.). In the following examples, I'll add a Windows XP image to a Windows 2003 Server for distribution. Note that the installation is quite similar should you want to utilize Windows 2000 on the server or other operating systems as clients.

Before you set it up, you'll need a decently sized NTFS partition that is *not* the system or boot partition for the RIS components and the RIS images. I'll use drive letter R: for my RIS server components and images, but you can use any drive letter.

> Although you can use a second partition on the same hard disk as your system or boot partition, this results in poor performance of both RIS and the system as a whole. The recommendation is to place the RIS partition on a separate physical disk from that on which Windows resides.

RIS servers use a special background service called the Single Instance Storage Groveler, which performs some special magic; it figures out when multiple RIS images use the same exact versions of a file and keeps only one copy in a separate location, putting in a pointer to it from each copy of the file it finds. This can save a significant amount of disk space compared with using cloned images a la Ghost or Drive Image Pro images that store the entire hard drive from multiple clients on the server. RIS depends on the Single Instance Storage Groveler, but the Single Instance Storage Groveler does not work on either the system or boot partitions. Therefore, you'll need another NTFS partition for RIS, and it's recommended that this partition's only function is housing RIS images.

Loading RIS

If you did not select RIS as an optional component when you created the server, you can load it now. Follow these steps:

1. Choose Start ➢ Control Panel to open Control Panel

2. Click Add or Remove Programs to open the Add or Remove Programs window.

3. Click Add/Remove Windows Components to start the Windows Components Wizard, as shown in Figure 11.6.

4. In the Components list, scroll down, click the Remote Installation Services check box, click Next, and then click OK. You'll then be asked to reboot your server.

Installing the Base Image

Once RIS is installed and the server is rebooted, you're ready to fire up RIS and load the first image. The first image is generated by pointing RIS server toward a Windows distribution folder (typically just called i386). This can be on a CD or a slipstreamed service pack located on a hard drive. In this example, I'll use Windows XP, which is already slipstreamed with SP1. The previous edition of this book used Windows 2000, though the steps are nearly identical.

FIGURE 11.6 Adding the RIS components is easy—even after Windows 2000 Server or Windows 2003 Server is fully installed.

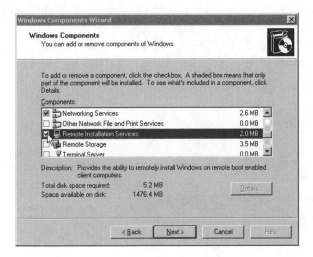

 To read more about slipstreaming service packs, check out the README.TXT files in the service pack.

1. Choose Start ➢ Run to open the Run dialog box, in the open box type **RISETUP,** and press Enter to open the Remote Installation Services Setup Wizard.

2. Click Next, to open the Remote Installation Folder Location screen.

3. Choose a folder on an NTFS volume that is not the system drive. In this example, I'm choosing R:\RemoteInstall. Click Next to open the Initial Settings screen.

4. The RIS server must be turned on to accept client connections. Click the "Respond to Client Computers Requesting Service" check box. For this example, do not choose "Do Not Respond to Unknown Client Computers." Click Next to open the Initial Source Files Location screen.

 Clicking the "Do Not Respond to Unknown Client Computers Requesting Service" check box lets you lock down a computer's GUID to a specific RIS server. Make this connection when manually adding a computer to Active Directory Users and Computers by selecting "This Is a Managed Computer" and then entering the computer's GUID. You can find the computer's GUID either in the computer's BIOS or in the MAC address of the network card—it's the 12 zeros padded with 20, for example, 00000000000000000000A309CDE24601.

5. In the Path field, type the path of the Windows XP Professional CD's \i386 folder, such as F:\I386, and then click Next to open the Windows Installation Image Folder Name screen.

6. Enter the name of the folder to create on the server. I suggest something like "WindowsXP-SP1." Click Next to open the Friendly Description and Help Text screen.

7. Change the Friendly Description and Help Text if you want to give special instructions to the people installing the workstations. Click Next to open the Review Settings screen.

8. Make sure the values are what you want and click Finish.

9. The Remote Installation Services Setup Wizard continues, as shown in Figure 11.7. It will take awhile to copy all the files and create the initial folder. When the installation is finished, the Cancel button turns into Done. Click Done.

FIGURE 11.7   Windows XP is copied from the installation source to be your first image.

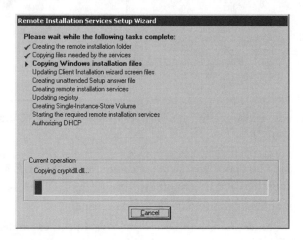

Authorizing Your RIS Server

You must authorize each Windows 2000 and Windows 2003 DHCP and RIS server to feed your clients. This procedure is necessary if the RIS server is not the same as the DHCP server (which needs to be authorized anyway). In other words, if the RIS server and the DHCP server are on the same box, you need perform this procedure only once. If the services are on two different boxes, you'll need to perform this procedure twice. To authorize your RIS server, follow these steps:

1. Fire up the DHCP manager on any server. (Yes, the DHCP manager.) Do this by selecting Start ➢ Programs ➢ Administrative Tools ➢ DHCP.

2. Right-click the word DHCP above the server name, and choose Manage Authorized Servers from the shortcut menu to open the Manage Authorized Servers dialog box.

3. Click the Authorize button to open the Authorize DHCP Server dialog box.

4. In the Name or IP Address field, enter the name or IP address of the RIS server.

5. Click OK to authorize the RIS server.

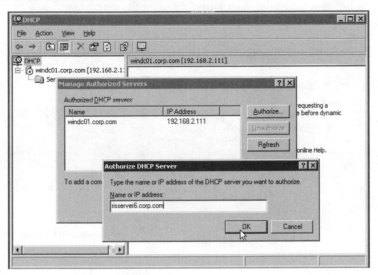

Managing the RIS Server

Before you roll out your first client, you might want to tweak RIS. You actually manage RIS inside Active Directory Users and Computers. Follow these steps:

1. Open Active Directory Users and Computers, locate the server on which you loaded RIS, and double-click it to open the server's Properties dialog box.

2. Click the Remote Install tab.

3. Click the Advanced Settings button to open the Remote Installation Services Properties dialog box, as shown in Figure 11.8.

    Three tabs contain options that you can configure: New Clients, Images, and Tools.

The New Clients Tab

When using RIS, the computer name is automatically generated. You can specify the behavior of this name by selecting from the "Generate Client Computer Names Using:" drop-down menu. In the "Client Account Location" section, specify the OU the computer will automatically fall under upon generation. The default location is the "unmanageable" Computers folder inside Active Directory; so, in general, it's a good idea to change this to an OU (even if it's a temporary "holding pen" for the computers).

The Images Tab

The Images tab contains two options: "Load a New Installation Image" and "Associate a New Answer File to an Existing Image." Select "Load a New Installation Image" if you want to deploy another operating system via RIS or to deploy an existing operating system with a new service pack. Selecting this option is basically the same as performing the procedure for loading your first image.

We'll talk about "Associate a New Answer File to an Existing Image" in a bit in the "How to Create Your Own Automated RIS Answer Files" section below.

FIGURE 11.8   You can customize some RIS defaults, such as the client's computer name.

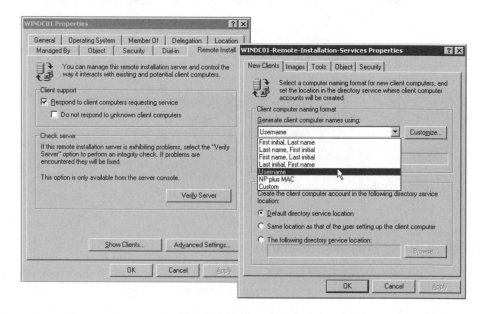

The Tools Tab

You use the options on the Tools tab to select third-party tools to snap in to RIS. I know only two vendors that make RIS–snap-in tools: Argon Technology (`www.ArgonTechnology.com/risme`) and EmBoot (`www.emboot.com/RISME.htm`). Both tools do exactly the same thing: enable RIS to create a staging area to load other operating systems such as Windows 9X, Windows NT, and even Linux (if you try hard enough).

Installing Your First Client

You're almost ready to start rolling out your clients. Remember that your clients need network cards that are PXE Boot ROM–capable. To use the NICs that have the ROM code built right onto the card, watch the PC to flash "Hit F12 for Network Boot" upon reboot. If your computer doesn't flash that message (or something similar), you'll need to check the network card's BIOS, the PC's BIOS, or both to see if the PXE feature is disabled, or you can create the PXE Boot ROM emulator disk as described in the next section.

RIS versus PXE

Many other vendors use PXE technology, but their tools might not hook into RIS. Indeed, if RIS is installed alongside some third-party tools, clients can get confused about what server is going to serve them, and you might get unpredictable results.

Some tools that use PXE technology (but aren't related to RIS) include On Technology's CCM (recently bought by Symantec), PowerQuest's v2i builder (also recently bought by Symantec), and Norton Ghost (also by Symantec). It seems like a little monopoly is happening over at Symantec with regard to these tools.

Creating a Remote Boot Disk

The code to write an RIS boot disk is less than 1Kb. Therefore, creating a remote boot disk takes only a moment. Moreover, the PXE boot disk supports a slew of network cards. If you have multiple cards that you need to boot from, it doesn't matter what brand the NIC is, since all are supported by the same floppy. To create your PXE Remote Boot Disk, follow these steps:

1. Run the RBFG.EXE program from the \Admin\i386 directory where you installed RIS. Click Start ➤ Run, and type **R:\RemoteInstall\Admin\i386\rbfg.exe** in the Open dialog box.

2. Put a blank floppy in the floppy drive and click the Create Disk button to start the boot disk generation.

3. When prompted to create another disk, click No, and click Close to close the "Microsoft Windows Remote Boot Disk Generator."

If your card isn't listed, you still have a ray of hope. Check out Argon Technologies at www.argontechnology.com/mbadisk/index.shtml and www.pxeondisk.com. They make special PXE boot floppies that could support your hardware!

Installing Your First Client

With boot disk in hand, you're ready to install your first client.

Running RIS on your workstations completely formats the first hard drive.

To use RIS to install a client, follow these steps:

1. Insert the floppy disk you just made in the previous exercise into the client computer and turn on the machine.

2. The boot floppy will query for the nearest DHCP server and get an address. When prompted, immediately press F12 to start the DOS-based Client Setup Wizard.

3. When the first information screen appears, press Enter to open the Client Installation Wizard Logon screen.

4. Enter a valid username, password, and domain. In this case, you can enter the username and password of the administrator of the domain. Press Enter to open the Client Installation Wizard Caution screen.

Anyone who has the "Create Computer Object" for "This object and all child objects" of an OU right can use RIS to deploy machines.

5. Read the text explaining that all data on the hard drive will be deleted. Agree by pressing Enter, which opens the Client Installation Wizard Information screen.

6. Verify that the information is correct and press Enter. This is your last chance to reset the machine to abort the installation.

If you ever need to know the GUID of a machine but can't find it anywhere else, you can use this screen to get the information and then cancel at this point.

7. The "Blue Screens of Life" will appear, load some necessary files into RAM, automatically format the hard drive, and start the installation.

8. Remove the floppy from the drive and take a coffee break. It will be a while before you can get to the next step. If the floppy is out of the drive, the machine will automatically reboot and then start and finish the graphical part of the installation.

If all goes well, the computer will be left at a logon prompt, waiting for the user to log on for the first time.

Mere Mortals Can Add Only 10 Workstations

In Windows NT, only administrators can add computer accounts to the domain. Now, under Active Directory, the Authenticated Users group can add computer accounts to the domain via the Add Workstation to Domain user right. But there's a catch. Each authenticated user can add only 10 new computer accounts. On the next try, the user is presented with the error message: "The machine account for this computer either does not exist or is unavailable."

This is a little-known problem that has three little-known solutions.

Administrators can pre-create the computer accounts.

Administrators can create as many accounts as they like. They are exempt from the "10 strikes and you're out" rule.

You can grant the "Create Computer Objects" (and if desired) the "Delete Computer Objects" rights to the Computers folder in Active Directory.

These rights are different from the Add Workstation to Domain user right that all Authenticated Users are given. To make this change, follow these steps:

1. Choose Start ➢ Programs ➢ AdministrativeTools ➢ Active Directory Users and Computers.

2. Choose View ➢ Advanced to enable the Advanced view.

3. Right-click the Computers folder, and choose Properties from the shortcut menu to open the Properties dialog box.

4. Click the Security tab, and then click the Advanced button to open the Advanced Settings for Computers properties.

5. On the Permissions tab, click Authenticated Users, and then click the Edit button to open the Permissions Entry for Authenticated Users.

6. Before proceeding, make sure the "This Object and All Child Objects" option is displayed in the "Apply Onto" box.

7. In the Permissions list, click the Allow check box for "Create Computer Objects" and, optionally, "Delete Computer Objects" as seen here.

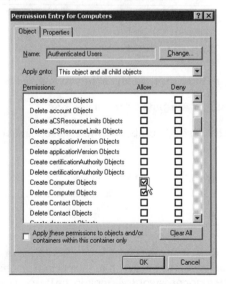

Use ADSI edit to manipulate the ms-DS-MachineAccountQuota to increase (or decrease) the value to the desired number of times a user can create a computer account.

1. Load an MMC console with the "ADSI Edit" snap-in.

2. Expand the Domain NC partition to expose the first level, which is the domain. Right-click the domain and choose Properties to open the Properties dialog box.

3. Ensure that you have the Attribute Editor tab selected.

4. In the Select a Property to View drop-down list box, select ms-DS-Machine-AccountQuota.

5. Click Edit to open the Integer Attribute Editor dialog box.

6. In the Value field enter the desired number of times a user can create computer accounts, and then click OK.

7. Click OK to close the Domain Properties dialog box.

By default, new client machines born via RIS will have no Administrator password. You can gain finite control over many aspects of an unattended installation, including Administrator password, via tools in the Resource Kit. See the section on "How to Create Your Own Automated RIS Answer files" later in this chapter as well as the Resource Kit documentation, specifically the UNATTEND.DOC for more information. On Windows XP machines, the local Administrator account is disabled. If you want to change this, remove the line that says "DisableAdminOnDomainJoin= YES" from your answer file.

The Remote Installation Prep Tool (RIPrep)

Well, you've blasted down your first base image using RIS. But RIS images can, if you want, additionally contain all your base applications, including commercial and homegrown applications, provided the application(s) are supported for imaging. Most client applications and some server applications are. Check with your vendor to be sure imaging is supported.

At this point, you need to choose one of the following

- Put your applications inside your RIS image.

- Use the techniques described in the previous chapter and have clients pull down the software to your users and/or computers.

- Use a combination of the previous two techniques such that a bunch of general applications are in the image and the remainder of the applications are deployed via Group Policy Software Installation (GPSI).

On the one hand, it's certainly faster to load an application, such as Office XP inside the RIS image, and then deploy the image all at once, rather than deploying a base RIS image and then using GPSI to shoot down Office XP. But, remember, our GPSI features have the added ability to upgrade packages and perform magic such as applying transform files to packages; these abilities are lost if the applications are embedded inside the RIS image.

Therefore, you'll need to analyze each application to determine if it's better to embed it inside the RIS image or deploy the package after the fact using GPSI. In my experience, in almost all cases, it's better to use GPSI to deploy your applications. Later, if you want to do some of the stuff we explored in Chapter 10, such as upgrading an existing package or revoking existing applications, you can only do so if you've originally deployed the applications via GPSI—and not by installing the applications in an imbedded fashion via RIS. So, for the record, if you do choose to imbed applications in your RIS images, I'm presenting that information here. Again, however, *I encourage you not to do this*. After you install the applications on your target machine, you can simply run RIPREP from the client PC, which creates another RIS image on the server.

In this example, you'll create a special image for the Nurses group, which automatically has any application or applications loaded.

1. Create your first RIS workstation as described in the preceding exercise.

2. Log on to the workstation with the local Administrator account (there should be no password), and load the desired software.

3. Since you're logged in as the local Administrator, the configuration changes—such as icons—affect only the Administrator account. In order for the changes to take effect for every user, you'll need to copy the Administrator's profile to the Default User's profile. Right-click My Computer and choose Properties from the shortcut menu to open the System Properties dialog box. Click the User Profiles tab, select the Administrator profile, and then click the Copy To button to open the Copy To dialog box.

4. In the "Copy profile to" field enter the path for the Default User folder, usually C:\Documents and Settings\Default User. Click the Change button to open the "Select User or Group" dialog and designate the Everyone group to be able to use the profile. Click OK to close the Copy To dialog box, and click OK again to close the System Properties dialog box.

5. Do this at the workstation by clicking Start ➢ Run, and then typing **\\windc01\reminst\ admin\i386\riprep** in the shared RIS directory. The RIPREP Wizard starts. Click Next.

6. After the RIPREP Wizard starts, click Next to open the Server Name screen.

7. By default, the server you used to create this image appears in the Server Name box. Leave the defaults and click Next to open the Folder Name screen.

8. You can give a somewhat descriptive name for how this image will be used. Click Next to open the Friendly Description and Help Text screen.

9. The text you enter here is displayed when administrators load RIS images. An example is shown in Figure 11.9.

10. If you don't use a freshly installed machine, you might get a warning message stating "Multiple Profiles Detected." This warning alerts you that other users' sensitive data can be available whenever this machine is used as an image. The best advice is to use a freshly installed machine that has only been logged on with the local Administrator account. Click Next.

11. The "Stop Services" screen may appear next. You'll see a list of the running services that will automatically be stopped. Click Next.

12. The "Programs or Services Are Running" screen may appear next. Close all running programs, and stop any remaining running services to get the cleanest image possible. Click Next to open the Review Settings screen.

13. Verify that the information is correct, and click Next. One additional information screen appears, stating that this process can be repeated if desired. Click Next to continue.

The RIPREP image will then be uploaded to the server and can be seen as an additional image. The next time you initiate RIS with the PXE boot disk or ROM, a new menu selection will be available, asking which image to load.

FIGURE 11.9 When running RIPREP, give the image a descriptive name.

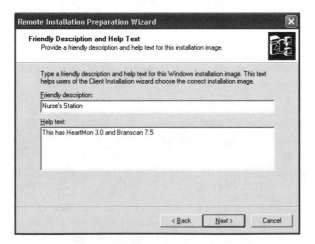

How to Create Your Own Automated RIS Answer Files

The process of bringing back a machine from the dead takes a little while. The average range to fully install an RIS image onto a machine is anywhere from 12 to 40 minutes, depending on how fast the machine is and how many applications are embedded in the image. However, the biggest chunk of time is usually spent answering the questions presented to the installer about the upcoming configuration. You can, instead, take care of network settings, screen resolution, time zone, area code, and the like via an unattended answer file.

Here's the idea. You've already got your own CD- based RIS image on the server. Perhaps you've used RIPREP and added another image chock full of software (though, again, I advise against this.) You can create your unattended answer files in two ways:

- Create the file from scratch.
- Get a helping hand from the Windows 2000 or Windows XP Setup Manager Wizard.

In the following examples, I'll use the Windows XP Setup Manager Wizard.

The Windows XP Setup Manager builds the unattended answer file with all the proper syntax by walking you through an easy-to-digest wizard-style interface. The output of the Setup Manager is a text file that you can edit. For example, you might want to add your own changes—perhaps something that the Setup Manager doesn't provide as an option.

Even though the Windows XP Setup Manager appears on the CD, you'll want to download the latest Windows XP Setup Manager. As of this writing, you can find it at `www.microsoft.com/WindowsXP/pro/downloads/servicepacks/sp1/deploytools.asp`, or search for "Windows XP Service Pack 1 Deployment Tools."

To use the setup manager, just drag at least the `SETUPMGR.EXE` to a usable place, and double-click the icon to start the wizard.

 Once the Setup Manager is installed, you can learn about all the customized changes by reading the `REF.CHM` file in the download. This file also contains parameters for other cloning methods, such as SYSPREP and unattended network installations.

Creating a Sample Fully Automated Answer File

In this example, we'll create a fully automated answer file, which will, as its name suggests, blast through the entire installation, providing all the answers as it goes.

1. At the first screen of the wizard, click Next to bypass the splash screen and open the New or Existing Answer File screen.

2. Choose to create a new answer file and click Next to open the Type of Setup screen.

3. Choose to create a new RIS answer file and click Next to open the Product screen.

4. Choose Windows XP Professional, and click Next to open the User Interaction Level screen.

5. Choose "Fully Automated." There are other choices, but none is quite as useful as this one.

Finally, you'll be presented with all the possible options to make a fully automated system, as shown in Figure 11.10.

FIGURE 11.10   If you answer all the questions, your RIS installations will blast on through.

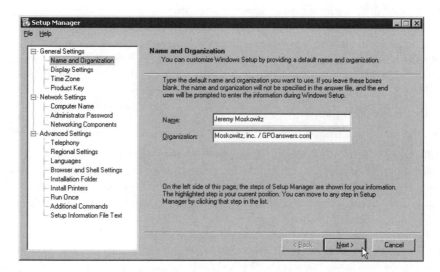

At this point, the questions are on the left, and you can bounce all around and answer them in any order you like, or you can keep clicking Next to walk through them step by step. The only required field is Product Key.

When you're finished and ready to save your answer file, place it where you'll be able to get to it quickly. You can name the answer file anything you like (such as XPfully_auto.sif), but the .sif extension is required.

Associating an Answer File with an Image

You created your image when you provided the Windows XP installation files (and/or when you used RIPREP). You just created your answer file when you ran the Windows XP Setup Manager. Now you need to marry the two so that you have an image that can be downloaded and installed in a fully unattended fashion.

To associate an answer file with an image, follow these steps:

1. Log on to the RIS server as the Domain Administrator.

2. Choose Start ➢ Programs ➢ Administrative Tools ➢ Active Directory Users and Computers.

3. Find the server running RIS (WinDC01), right-click it, and choose Properties from the shortcut menu to open the Properties dialog box.

4. Click the Remote Install tab, and then click the Advanced Settings button to open the Remote Installation Services Properties dialog box.

5. Click the Images tab to see a list of RIS images you have created.

6. Click the Add button to open the Add dialog box, as shown in Figure 11.11.

FIGURE 11.11 In this screen, tell the RIS server you want to associate an answer file with an image.

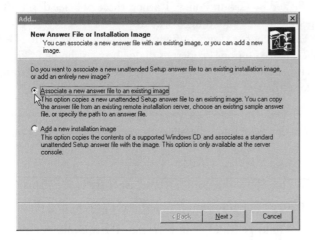

7. Choose "Associate a New Answer File to an Existing Image" and click Next to open the "Unattended Setup Answer File Source" page.

8. Here, you can specify from where you want to grab the answer file. Select "An Alternate Location" and click Next.

9. You'll then see the "Select an Installation Image" page where you specify one of your images, such as the image you created earlier. Then click Next.

10. At the "Location of Answer File" page, you can select Browse, and locate the answer file you created earlier (XPfully_auto.sif), select it, and click Next.

11. At the "Friendly Description and Help Text" page, you can enter in an alternate Friendly Description or Help Text.

You cannot marry a Setup Manager answer file to a RIPREP image. You can only marry a Setup Manager answer file to a CD-based image file.

12. The "Review Settings" page is the last screen in the wizard reviews and reviews what you're about to do. Click Finish to associate the answer file with the image.

Now, whenever you press F12 to boot the system, you'll see a new downloadable choice—with the description you put into the answer file. When used, it will be (almost magically) fully unattended!

Using Group Policy to Manipulate Remote Installation Services

RIS installations can also be affected by Group Policy. Rather, these policies don't affect the installations; they affect the people actually loading workstations via RIS.

In the Group Policy Object Editor, choose User Configuration ➤ Windows Settings ➤ Remote Installation Services to open the Choice Options Properties dialog box, as shown in Figure 11.12.

This dialog box has four sections: Automatic Setup, Custom Setup, Restart Setup, and Tools. Each section has three possible settings:

    RIS policies are enforced immediately with nearly no waiting period.

Enabled (Allow in Windows 2000)   Show the option to the users affected by this GPO.

Disabled (Deny in Windows 2000)   Hide this option to the users affected by this GPO.

Not Configured (Don't Care in Windows 2000)   Show or hide the option if a GPO linked at a higher level (i.e., OU, domain, site) has something set (for instance, Enabled or Disabled is set higher in the food chain).

The default option for GPOs you create is "Not Configured." If you leave this default, Group Policy continues up the food chain or until an Allow or Deny is encountered for each or any of the four sections. Higher up in the food chain, in the Default Domain Policy, lie the final answers. Everything is set to "Disabled," except Automatic Setup, which is set to "Not Configured." Therefore, if you never touch this setting, the default behavior is to use the Automatic Setup setting, which forces installers to use the settings defined within the RIS administration console at the server level.

The Automatic Setup Section

By default, this section displays the settings you selected in the Remote Installation Services Properties dialog box. Specifying "Allow" forces users inside the OUs and below you to obey the settings you specified in the Remote Installation Services Properties dialog box. Specifying "Disabled" forces users to enter Custom Setup options, as described in the next section.

FIGURE 11.12 Use the RIS Group Policy objects to affect the users working with RIS.

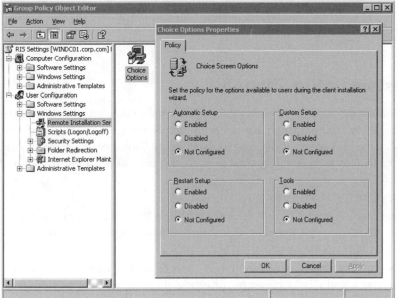

  If the Custom Setup option is also set to "Deny" at this level, or if Custom Setup is set to "Don't Care" at this level and "Deny" at a higher level (the default is Deny at the Default Domain Policy), no one affected by this policy can use RIS to set up machines.

Choosing "Not Configured" permits upper-level policies to dictate the setting.

  If you dictate no settings, the highest level, the Default Domain Policy, also has a Don't Care option, which is similar to an implicit "Allow." Therefore, Automatic Setup is permitted throughout the domain by default.

The Custom Setup Section

This setting allows the person configuring the RIS workstation to override the defaults set previously in the Remote Installation Services Properties dialog box. Specifically, the installer can enter a computer name—as well as a folder service path, such as `corp.com/Sales`—to put the computer in the **Sales** OU under the Corp.com domain. This option is not enabled by default on any level.

Specifying Allow enables a Custom Setup selection while creating a workstation via RIS. If "Disabled" is selected, no one who can create RIS workstations at this level will see the Custom Setup option even if it is set to "Enabled" at a higher level. Choosing "Not Configured" permits upper-level policies to dictate the setting.

If you dictate no settings, the highest level, the Default Domain Policy, has a "Deny." Therefore, Custom Setup is not permitted throughout the domain by default.

The Restart Setup Section

This setting allows the person configuring the RIS workstation to restart the options of the machine fails in the middle of the installation. Restart Setup simply looks up the GUID of the machine and matches it with the corresponding machine GUID in Active Directory and an existing answer file on the RIS server, thereby eliminating the need to retype the name of the computer or OU that's going to house the computer account.

This is useful in two situations.

- If a power failure occurs during the installation, at least you don't need to remember the machine name already entered or its location. This helps prevent unused computer accounts from showing up in Active Directory.

- If the machine ever needs to be rebuilt (for instance, in the event of a hard-drive failure), its previous name and OU location are automatically preserved.

This is one of the reasons you must have a unique GUID for each workstation or laptop. Using a single docking station means all machines have the same GUID, and, hence, this functionality is lost.

The Restart Setup option is not enabled by default on any level. Specifying "Enabled" enables a "Restart a Previous Setup Attempt" selection when you create a workstation via RIS. If you select "Disabled," no one who can create RIS workstations at this level will see the Restart Setup option even if it is set to "Allow" at a higher level. Choosing "Not Configured" permits upper-level policies to dictate the setting.

If you dictate no settings, the highest level, the Default Domain Policy, has a "Deny." Therefore, Restart Setup is not permitted throughout the domain by default.

The Tools Section

Unless you select the "Enable" option in this section or at a higher level, third-party tools are not available by default to those creating RIS workstation. This option is not enabled by default on any level. Specifying "Enabled" displays a "Maintenance and Troubleshooting" selection while creating a workstation via RIS. If you choose "Disabled," no one who can create RIS workstations at this level will see the Maintenance and Troubleshooting option, even if it's set to "Enabled" at a higher level. Choosing "Not Configured" permits upper-level policies to dictate the setting.

If you specify no settings, the highest level, the Default Domain Policy, has a Deny. Therefore, the Tools option is not permitted throughout the domain by default.

Final Thoughts

In the beginning, Microsoft created Group Policy, and it was good. Now, you can take this goodness and leverage it to protect and serve your subjects.

At the beginning of this book, you learned the ins and outs of Group Policy. You learned how to get around in the GPMC and how to script Group Policy operations. You went on and leveraged your Group Policy knowledge to implement a secure environment with Group Policy and a robust IntelliMirror environment to allow your users to roam freely—*online and offline*—and maintain the same user experience.

This, the final chapter, talked about what happens *beyond* IntelliMirror. Here, you used Shadow Copies to further ensure that users' data is protected should they inadvertently delete or overwrite it. You used Remote Installation Services to bring back a Windows machine from the dead.

I hope you can fully appreciate the beauty in this holistic approach to user settings and data management. No longer are users tied to a specific desktop or laptop as a single point of failure. If a machine gets lost or dies, the user environment (Profile), the data (My Documents with Redirected Folders), and the applications (via GPSI) are always preserved on the server for when that new machine arrives.

Dropping a new machine on the desk (perhaps with RIS) is like magic: Roaming Profiles, Redirected Folders, Offline Folders, Disk Quotas, and Group Policy Software Installation perform exactly as they did before the machine blew up. You'll bring it all back for the user with one floppy. Maybe even no floppies. You'll be a hero.

Thank you for reading this book and using it to its fullest! Let's keep the information flowing! Come join your peers at www.GPOanswers.com for ongoing support of the material in this book. You'll find free downloads and a community discussion forum regarding all Group Policy, Profiles, IntelliMirror, Shadow Copies, and RIS topics!

Appendix

Group Policy Tools

Obviously, the power of Group Policy is awesome, but some aspects of Group Policy and Intelli-Mirror management are better suited to additional tools. In this appendix, we're going to leverage a variety of tools to perform several key duties. We'll also finish the functionality of what the GPMC has to offer, specifically, migrating existing GPOs between domains. We'll then dive into the other free Group Policy and IntelliMirror management tools from Microsoft. Last, we'll round up third-party Group Policy tools, third-party Profiles tools, third-party ADM editing tools, and third-party MSI repackaging tools.

Migrating Group Policy Objects between Domains

For years I've stood in front of large audiences and recommended testing the power of GPOs in a test forest. In return, I'd get blank stares because this advice was inherently impractical. Sure, it was safe—safer than testing GPOs in production—but ultimately my advice was doomed. How can you do the hard work in a test domain, test it, debug it, get it all right, and then lift it out of its home domain and put it in production? Answer? You couldn't. Until now.

These examples will continue with our fictional multidomain environment. You can flip back to Figure 3.6 to see the relationship between our three domains: corp.com, widgets.corp.com, and the Cross-Forest Trust between bigu.edu and corp.com.

Basic Interdomain Copy and Import

Now using the GPMC, you can take existing GPOs from any domain and copy them to another domain. The target domain can be a parent domain, a child domain, a cross-forest domain, or a completely foreign domain that has no trusts! Both the Copy and the Import operations transfer only the policy settings; these operations do not modify either the source or the destination links of the GPOs.

The Copy Operation

The interdomain Copy operation is meant to be used when you want to copy live GPOs from one domain to another. That is, you have two domains, connectivity between them, and appropriate rights to the GPOs. To copy the GPO, you need "Read" rights on the source GPO you want to copy and "Write" rights in the target domain.

First, you want to tweak your GPMC console so that you can see the two domains you want.

Recall that to add new domains to the GPMC, you simply right-click "Domains" and choose "Show Domains" from the shortcut menu to open up the Show Domains dialog box. Then simply select the domains you want to see. To add other forests, right-click "Group Policy Management" and choose "Add Forest" from the shortcut menu to open the "Add Forest" dialog box. You can then enter the name of the forest in the field labeled "Domain" (yes, domain!).

In this first example, we'll copy a GPO from corp.com to widgets.corp.com. An enterprise administrator will have rights in all domains. Since we're logged in as an enterprise administrator, we have rights in both corp.com (to read) and widgets.corp.com (to write.) Follow these steps:

1. In the Group Policy Objects container, right-click the GPO you want to copy, as shown in Figure A.1 For this example, I've chosen the "Hide Settings Tab/Restore Screen Saver Tab" GPO.

FIGURE A.1 You can copy a GPO from the Group Policy Objects container.

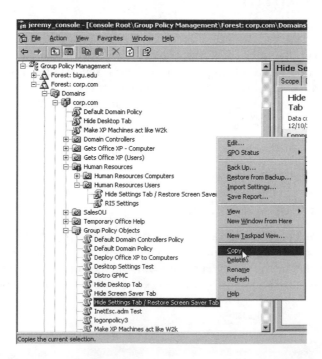

2. Adjust your view of the GPMC so that you can see the target domain. In Figure A.2, I've minimized the view of corp.com and expanded widgets.corp.com—especially the Group Policy Objects container.

3. Right-click the target domain's Group Policy Objects container, and choose "Paste" to start the "Cross-Domain Copying Wizard."

4. Click Next to bypass the initial splash screen and open the Specifying Permissions screen as shown in Figure A.2.

FIGURE A.2 When you paste a GPO, you can choose how to handle permissions.

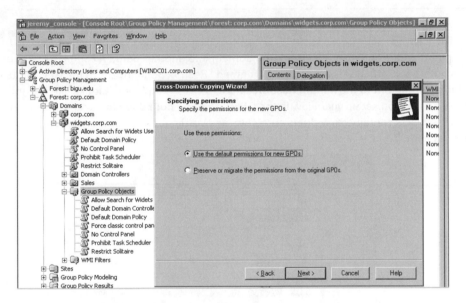

You can now choose to create a GPO with the default permissions or copy the original permissions to the new GPO. The latter might be useful if you've delegated some special permissions to that GPO and don't want to go through the hassle of redoing your efforts. Most of the time, however, the first option is fine. You can now zip through the rest of the wizard.

You might see a message about Migration tables. Don't fret; they're right around the corner. For this specific GPO, you won't need Migration tables, so it won't be an issue.

If you copy a GPO between domains, the WMI filtering is lost because the WMI filter won't necessarily exist in the target domain.

The Import Operation

In the previous scenario, we copied a GPO from corp.com to widgets.corp.com. We did this when both domains were online and accessible. But if you are working on an isolated testing network, this won't be possible. How then do you take a GPO you created in the isolated test lab and bring it into production? First, create a backup as described in Chapter 2. You'll then have a collection of files that you can put on a floppy, a CD, and so on and take out the door of your test lab into the real world. You can then create a brand new GPO (or overwrite an existing GPO) and perform the import! Follow these steps:

A Word about Drag and Drop

Dragging and dropping a GPO from one domain into another domain can be hazardous! For example, your intention is to copy a GPO named "Restrict Solitaire" from the GPO container in widgets.corp.com to the **Human Resources Users** OU in corp.com. It looks like it's going to make sense: you set up your view in the GPMC to show both domains, you can see the Group Policy Objects container in widgets.corp.com, and you can see the **Human Resources Users** OU in corp.com. Then, you drag and drop, and you're asked the following question:

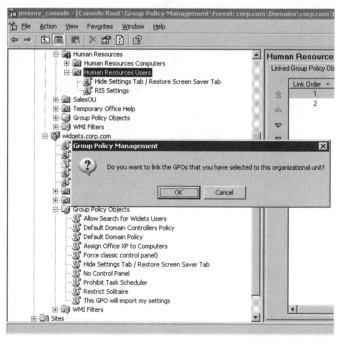

If you click OK, you're not actually copying! Indeed, you're performing a no-no! You are creating a cross-domain link to the GPO, as you can see when you click the Details tab of the GPO:

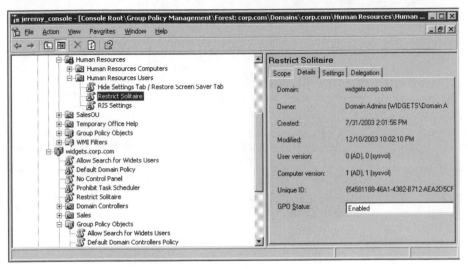

In this example, the "Domain" field shows that it "lives" in widgets.corp.com, even though the GPO is linked to an OU in corp.com.

Whenever a GPO is linked from across a domain, the GPO must be pulled from a Domain Controller that actually houses it. If it's across the WAN, so be it. And that could mean major slowdowns.

The moral of the story is to be sure you're copying (as described earlier) and not just linking.

1. Right-click the Group Policy Objects container, choose New from the shortcut menu to open the "New GPO" dialog box, and in the Name Field enter the name of a new GPO.

2. Right-click that GPO and choose Import Settings from the shortcut menu, as shown in Figure A.3. This then starts the Import Settings Wizard.

 Anyone with "Edit" rights on the GPO can perform an Import.

 You can choose to overwrite an existing GPO, but that's just it. It's an overwrite, not a merge. So, be careful!

FIGURE A.3   You can import the settings and overwrite an existing GPO.

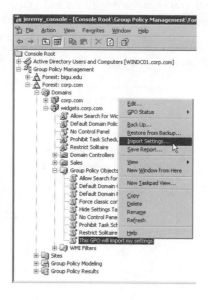

3. The wizard then presents the "Backup GPO" screen, which allows you to back up the newly created GPO; however, this is unnecessary. This is a safety measure should you decide to overwrite an existing GPO. You can then click Next to see the "Backup Location" screen.

4. In the "Backup Location" screen, use the Backup folder field to input the path to where your backup set is and select Next. The "Source GPO" screen will appear as seen in Figure A.4.

5. At the "Source GPO" screen, select the GPO from which you want to import settings, as shown in Figure A.4 and click Next.

You should now be able to zip through the rest of the wizard. Ignore any references to Migration tables; they're coming up next.

FIGURE A.4   Select a GPO from which you want to import settings.

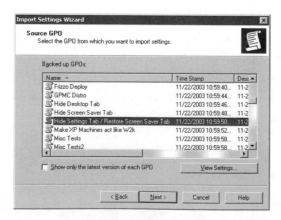

Copy and Import with Migration tables

In the previous examples, we migrated the very simple GPO named "Hide Settings Tab/Restore Screen Saver Tab." That particular GPO contained only Administrative Template settings that affected the desktop. Nothing fancy, for sure.

However, certain policy settings do perform some fancy footwork. Some GPOs can include references to security groups, such as "Allow Log on Locally." Other GPOs can include references to UNC paths, such as Folder Redirection. Indeed, an Advanced Folder Redirection policy setting contains both security group references and UNC path references! Other possibilities include Restricted Groups, Group Policy Software Installation policy settings, and pointers to scripts.

When you migrate GPOs across domains, you need to take care of these references. Copying a GPO in one domain that redirects folders to the \\WinDC01\Data folder will not likely make much sense when used in another domain.

With that in mind, both the Copy and Import functions can leverage *Migration tables*. Migration tables let you rectify both security group and UNC references that exist in a GPO when you transfer the GPO to another domain. You'll be given the opportunity to use the Migration tables automatically if your Copy or Import operation detects that a policy setting needs it! After the GPO is ready to be copied or imported, you'll be notified that some adjustments are needed. It's that easy!

In the Migrating References screen of the wizard (as shown in Figure A.5), you can choose two paths here:

- Selecting "Copying them identically from the source" can be risky. Again, you won't know what the source is using for security groups or UNC paths. The existing security groups and UNC paths may be valid, but they may not be.

- Selecting "Using this migration table to map them in the destination GPO" gives you the opportunity to choose an existing Migration table (if you have one), or you can click the New button to open the Migration Table Editor and create on the fly.

FIGURE A.5   A migration table can smooth the bumps between domains.

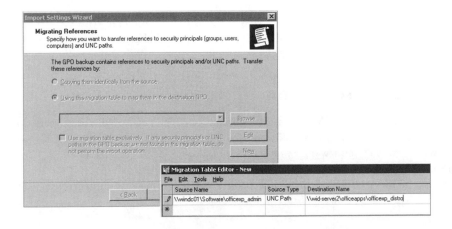

To start out with, use a new, blank migration table (after pressing the New button), follow these steps:

1. If you're performing a Copy, choose Tools ➤ Populate from GPO to open the Select GPO screen, then simply select the live GPO. If you're performing an Import, choose Tools ➤ Populate from Backup to open the "Select Backup" dialog, which allows you to select a GPO from backup.

2. Choose the GPO you're copying or importing to display a list of all the references that need to be corrected.

3. In Figure A.5, you can see both the Source Name and Destination Name fields. The Source name field will automatically be filled in. All that's left is to enter in the Destination Name UNC path for the new environment and you're done!

4. Save the file (with a `.migtable` extension), and close the "Migration Table Editor—New" screen.

5. Back at the Migrating References page, simply click Browse and choose the Migration table you just made.

Before clicking the Next button, you can optionally choose the check box that begins with "Use migration table exclusively." In this example, we have but one UNC reference that needs to be rectified. You might have a meaty GPO with 30 UNC paths and another 50 security principles that need to be cleared up. Perhaps you can't locate all the destination names. If you select this check box, the wizard will not proceed unless all the paths in the destination name are valid. Use this setting if you really need to be sure all settings will be verified successfully.

When ready, click Next, click Next again past the summary screen, and you're finished.

Microsoft has a detailed white paper you'll want to check out if you're planning to do a lot of this. You'll find it at `www.microsoft.com/windowsserver2003/gpmc/migrgpo.mspx`.

Microsoft Tools Roundup

As might be expected, Microsoft has a slew of tools to help manage your Group Policy infrastructure as well as your user profiles. In this section, we'll check out the Microsoft tools and where to find them.

Group Policy Tools from Microsoft

Except for Active Directory Monitor and GPInventory, you can download the remainder of the Microsoft tools for free from the Windows 2003 Resource Kit. As of this writing you can find it at `www.microsoft.com/windowsserver2003/downloads/tools/default.mspx` under the heading "Windows Server 2003 Resource Kit Tools." After you install the Resource Kit, you'll find the tools in the \Program Files\Windows Resource Kits\Tools folder. Some of these tools are ready to use; others require additional installation.

Active Directory Monitor and GPOTOOL

These tools help to troubleshoot GPOs if the GPC and GPT get out of sync. See Chapter 4 for information.

admX (within *ADMX.MSI*) — ADM Template Comparison Utility

This tool prints (or redirects) an ADM template into a nice readable format for documentation. It will parse an ADM file and list: Registry path, Symbolic Policy Name, Full Policy Name, Registry Settings, and the `Supported on` keyword. You can also use it to show the differences between two similar ADM files.

This tool requires additional installation. Be sure the latest .Net Framework is installed (the one built in to Windows 2003 is not sufficient). Next, run the ADMX.MSI to install and follow the wizard. After installation, the default location for admX is `c:\Program Files\Microsoft\admx`. You'll need to execute admX.exe from there.

GPMonitor — Group Policy Monitor Tool

The purpose of GPMonitor, which is shown in Figure A.6, is to perform historical analysis of what has changed between different Group Policy refresh intervals on your clients and servers. This tool requires an armload of additional installation; it unpacks to a set of files that need to stay together. You deploy the MSI (Microsoft Installer) to two locations: the clients you want to monitor and a management station that you'll use to see your results. After you unpack the MSI, you deploy the MSI file via GPSI (Group Policy Software Installation) to the clients. Additionally, this package comes with an ADM template, which you need to import into the Group Policy Object Editor. The point of the ADM file is to push the data about the client's Group Policy application to a central shared folder location.

FIGURE A.6   GPMonitor

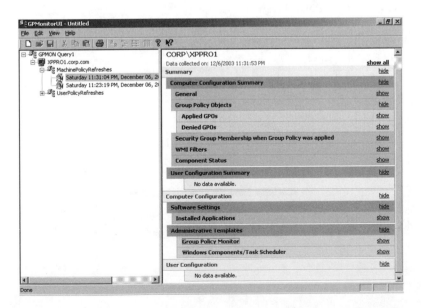

Once your clients start pushing up the data, you can run the GPMonitorUI at your management station to see what's going on. The clients will upload their historical data every N Group Policy refreshes. (The default is every 8.) From your management station, you can then see which GPOs have or have not applied yesterday, but are applying today—among other possibilities.

Your management station needs the GPMC loaded in order to display the data as seen in Figure A.6, but the clients you want to monitor do not.

GPInventory—Group Policy Inventory Tool

GPInventory is a late addition to the Windows 2003 Server Resource Kit. You must download and install it separately. To find it, search for "Group Policy Inventory" on Microsoft's website.

GPInventory can reach out across the network and query your clients and servers for a list of attributes you want to document in Excel or a text file. Simply point GPInventory toward a list of clients, select the attributes you want to gather, and then let it do its thing. Afterward, just save the resulting file.

In Figure A.7, I can easily find out how much memory my Windows XP clients have by selecting the "WMI: Computer Memory" field and documenting the RSoP (Resultant Set of Policy) status of all my clients with some of the other attributes.

InetESC.adm

InetESC.adm is a Group Policy template that enhances the security configuration of Internet Explorer for Windows 2003 Server. Be sure to read the Resource Kit notes for specifically how to use it.

FIGURE A.7   Group Policy Inventory

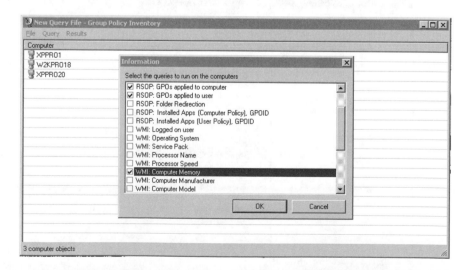

The WinPolicies Tool

WinPolicies, which is shown in Figure A.8, is also known as the "Policy Spy" (which happens to be what my next costume for Halloween will be, coincidentally). Anyway, WinPolicies can perform lots of the ultra-propeller head client-side troubleshooting stuff you saw in Chapter 4, without having to get your fingers too dirty.

FIGURE A.8   WinPolicies

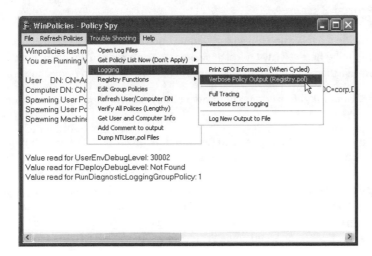

Specifically, you can enable verbose logging, perform tracing, refresh policies (enforced, or not enforced), and get additional troubleshooting information. Typically, you run this tool on the client system experiencing the problem. You can run it as a mere-mortal user or as an administrator. Several features let you enter alternative credentials so you can use it, mostly, as a mere mortal, but still see log files that are for admins only. That's a nice touch.

WinPolicies doesn't really add any new features to the Group Policy troubleshooting arsenal, but it does consolidate them. And you still need to understand what you're looking at in order to make heads or tails of the output. Hopefully, the information in Chapter 4 gets you off to the right start.

Profile Tools from Microsoft

Microsoft also has two tools to help manipulate Profiles if they need a kick in the pants. Here they are.

The Delprof Tool

You use this utility to bulk-delete profiles—either locally or remotely. An update is available at `www.microsoft.com/windowsserver2003/techinfo/reskit/tools/default.mspx`. This is a command-line tool, so be careful, you can get in a lot of trouble in a hurry. Microsoft has a nice Knowledge Base article on this tool, MSKB 315411, that discusses how to eliminate profiles if they are not used in, say, 30 days.

The Proquota Tool

You can use this tool to limit the size that the roaming user profile can become. This isn't a tool you can run, per se. It's part of the operating system. It is invoked whenever the **Limit profile size** policy setting in User Configuration ➢ Administrative Templates ➢ System ➢ User Profiles is set to Enabled.

Documenting Policy Settings

I get tons of e-mails asking the following question: "Jeremy, do you know if there's a policy setting that does <insert crazy thing here>"? My typical answer is, "I don't know. I'll have to look it up." Then I do. That's because there are more than 800 policy settings, each with nooks and crannies.

To that end, you can (hopefully) hunt down your own policy setting that does what you want in several ways.

GP.CHM   GP.CHM is part of the Windows 2000 Resource Kit. It's a .CHM file, which means it's a compiled HTML file, and that basically means it's a help file like other help files. The good news is that it mirrors the hierarchy of the Windows 2000 Group Policy Object Editor. That is, it has both user and computer nodes and then all the levels of Group Policy nooks and crannies underneath in a beautiful hierarchical manner. Best of all, you can search within the text file for the policy setting's help text and get what you want. The bad news is that it's getting kind of old. Many policy settings have been renamed since Windows 2000, but GP.CHM is still useful.

SPOLSCONCEPTS.CHM   This .CHM file is built in to Windows XP and Windows 2003 Server. To open it, choose Start ➢ Run to open the Run dialog box and then enter **hh spolsconcepts.chm** in the Open box. You'll then see another help file that discusses only the security-related settings, such as the meaning of each of the User Rights Assignments, what each of the Audit Policies is, and all the Security Options. This is truly a nice built-in resource.

PolicySettings.XLS   If you want a definitive list of all policy settings that can affect both Windows 2000 and Windows 2003 Server machines, you can download a spreadsheet from Microsoft at http://download.microsoft.com/download/a/a/3/aa32239c-3a23-46ef-ba8b-da786e167e5e/ PolicySettings.xls or bounce off this more typeable link: www.jsiinc.com/SUBN/tip6600/ rh6622.htm. Note, however, that Microsoft's spreadsheet doesn't go into much detail beyond the "Explain Text" setting for each policy setting. But they're all there and searchable, and you can sort by which operating systems will embrace which policy settings. It's quite good.

Third-Party Group Tools   I also encourage you to check out this web resource, which highlights all the new Windows XP and Windows 2003 Server policy settings. You can download it for free at this book's website and also at www.GPOanswers.com.

Third-Party Tools

When I wrote the previous version of this book, only one or two vendors were really doing interesting stuff with Group Policy. Now, many vendors are recognizing the power that Group Policy provides. Some vendors are adding to the management capabilities of GPOs, still others help in GPO troubleshooting, and others take the next logical step and extend Group Policy to harness even more power!

Tables A.1, A.2, and A.3 list some tools that can help you in your Group Policy journey. In these tables I provide an incredibly short description of the product. On the book's website and `www.GPOanswers.com`, you'll find "Third-Party Group Policy Tools," a reference that provides the vendors an opportunity in their own words to have more than just a sentence fragment to explain their product. Additionally, the web download has more contact information as well as screenshots of the products. Check it out!

TABLE A.1   Group Policy Management Tools

Vendor	Product	Website	Brief Description
Aelita	Enterprise Directory Manager (EDM)	www.aelita.com/ products/EDM4.htm	A secure "Rules & Roles" management platform that facilitates secure administration of Active Directory and Exchange
AutoProf	Policy Maker Professional	www.autoprof.com	A set of Group Policy extensions that perform common administration tasks
AutoProf	Policy Maker Software Update	www.autoprof.com	A Group Policy extension that manages and applies software updates and patches to computers
AutoProf	Policy Maker Framework Security	www.autoprof.com	A Group Policy extension that allows an administrator to perform granular configuration changes to the XML files that control .Net Framework security
AutoProf	Profile Maker	www.autoprof.com	A comprehensive stand-alone computer configuration system that also eases the task of transitioning to Group Policy management

TABLE A.1 Group Policy Management Tools *(continued)*

Vendor	Product	Website	Brief Description
Configuresoft	Enterprise Configuration Manager	www.configuresoft.com	Centralizes and automates the labor-intensive task of planning, auditing, and monitoring changes in Group Policy objects on Windows systems deployed in large enterprise networks or Web server farms
FullArmor	Group Policy Anywhere	www.fullarmor.com	Separates Group Policy from Active Directory, allowing you to start using Group Policy today, even if you are still planning for Active Directory or Group Policy
FullArmor	GPx	www.fullarmor.com	Enhances native Group Policy software distribution with robust features such as success/failure status reporting, installation ordering and dependencies, and the ability to distribute patch files
Knowledge-Factory	Special Operations Suite 2	www.specialoperationssuite.com	A broad and deeply Active Directory integrated Desktop Management suite for all sizes of organizations
NetPro	DirectoryAnalyzer	www.netpro.com/products/directoryanalyzer	The most comprehensive monitoring solution available for Active Directory
NetPro	DirectoryTroubleshooter	www.netpro.com/products/directorytroubleshooter	The most comprehensive Active Directory troubleshooting and diagnostic solution available

TABLE A.1   Group Policy Management Tools *(continued)*

Vendor	Product	Website	Brief Description
NetIQ	Group Policy Administrator (Created by FullArmor)	www.netiq.com/products/ gpa/default.asp	The industry's leading solution for planning, managing, troubleshooting, and reporting on Group Policy
NetIQ	Group Policy Guardian (Created by FullArmor)	www.netiq.com/products/ gpg/default.asp	Minimizes the risks associated with Group Policy Object (GPO) change management
Quest	Quest / Fastlane ActiveRoles	www.quest.com/fastlane/ ActiveRoles/index.asp	Centralizes the management of native security, Group Policy, Windows resources, and helpdesk tasks across Active Directory
Quest	Quest / Fastlane Spotlight on Active Directory	www.quest.com/ spotlight_ad/index.asp	A real-time diagnostic tool for troubleshooting Active Directory Replication, performance, and Availability within Windows 2000/ Server 2003 Environments
Small Wonders Software	Active Administrator	www.smallwonders.com/ activeadmin.htm	A full-featured Active Directory security and Group Policy management package
SYSPro	Polman	www.SysProSoft.com	A Policy Management tool for more easily interpreting Policy settings

TABLE A.2   Third-Party ADM Management Tools

Vendor	Product Name	Website	Brief Description
Advanced Toolware	Policy Template Editor 2	www.advtoolware.com/ t4e/pte/pte_ default.htm	A tool to ease the creation of ADM templates.
SYSPRO	ADM Template Editor	www.SysProSoft.com	A tool to ease the creation of ADM templates.

TABLE A.3 Third-Party MSI Repackaging Tools

Vendor	Product Name	Website	Brief Description
Installshield	AdminStudio	www.installshield.com/products/adminstudio/	Gives systems administrators a complete suite of software packaging, customization, conflict resolution, and testing tools that makes it easy to quickly prepare reliable, manageable applications and patches for enterprise use
New Boundary	PrisimPack	www.newboundary.com/products/prismpack/prismpack_info.htm	Packages any software for deployment to any PC or laptop anywhere in the world
OnDemand Software	WinInstall LE	www.ondemandsoftware.com/FREELE2003/	The latest edition of the FREE MSI packager, built for the new Windows 2003 Server operating system
OnDemand Software	WinInstall MSI Packager Professional	www.ondemandsoftware.com/Winstall/msi-pak.asp	The enhanced version of the standard edition packager, WinINSTALL LE 2003
OnDemand Software	WinInstall 8	www.ondemandsoftware.com/Winstall/default.asp	Takes major strides in helping administrators know more about the relationship between what is running on the desktop and the contents of packages
Wise Solutions / Altiris	Wise Package Studio	www.wise.com/wps.asp	The premier application lifecycle management solution used by deployment and desktop management teams to prepare applications for the enterprise

Index

Note to the Reader: Page numbers in **bold** indicate the principle discussion of a topic or the definition of a term. Page numbers in *italic* indicate illustrations.

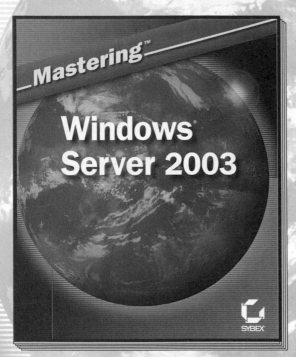

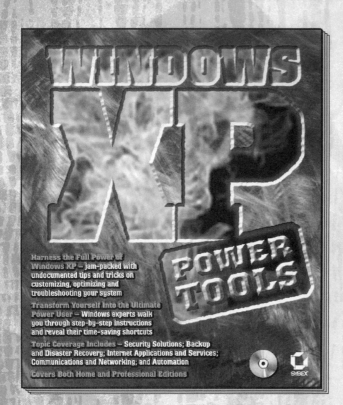

TELL US WHAT YOU THINK!

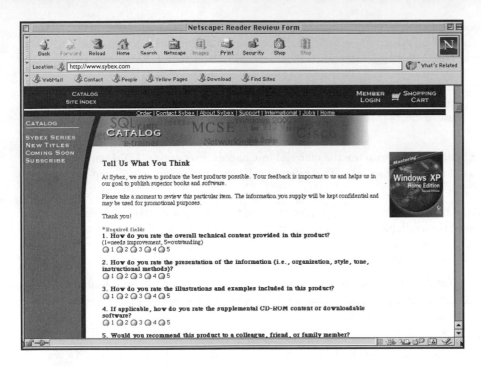

Your feedback is critical to our efforts to provide you with the best books and software on the market. Tell us what you think about the products you've purchased. It's simple:

1. Go to the Sybex website.
2. Find your book by typing the ISBN or title into the Search field.
3. Click on the book title when it appears.
4. Click **Submit a Review.**
5. Fill out the questionnaire and comments.
6. Click **Submit.**

With your feedback, we can continue to publish the highest quality computer books and software products that today's busy IT professionals deserve.

www.sybex.com

SYBEX Inc. • 1151 Marina Village Parkway, Alameda, CA 94501 • 510-523-8233

Using the Downloadable Web References

Since I simply don't have room here in this printed book to discuss every policy setting or even every policy category, I've placed some additional information on both www.sybex.com and www.GPOanswers.com. You can download all these resources, which include the following:

> **NOTE** You'll need passwords to open the downloadable PDF files. Instructions on how to locate the password should be alongside the download.

ADM Template Syntax After you use the material in Chapter 5 regarding ADM templates, you might be jazzed to create your own. This reference shows you the ropes with step-by-step examples.

Third-Party Group Policy Tools The Appendix at the end of the book contains a table which gives an overview of the available third-party tools that can enhance Group Policy, create ADM templates, and repackage MSI files. More company and product information and screenshots are available in this downloadable reference.

Restricted Groups Tables This reference is a companion to some of the material found in Chapter 6 regarding restricted groups. Specifically, these tables show when specific Restricted Groups features are available and how they react.

New Policy Settings for Windows 2003 and Windows XP This reference has an at-a-glance list of some of what's completely new and configurable in Windows 2003 and Windows XP via Group Policy and that doesn't have anything to do with IntelliMirror. This reference describes more than 200 policy settings that deal with Windows XP and Windows 2003 specific features: System Restore, DNS, Terminal Services, Remote Access, VPNs, and other stuff that I won't generally discuss in other areas of the book. Again, if you're already somewhat familiar with Group Policy, you may find a ripe peach in this reference you'll want to pluck and start using right away.

Security Options Comparison In Windows 2003, all the security policy settings have been renamed for clarity. However, you might have a mixed environment in which you're manipulating Group Policy on both Windows 2003 and Windows 2000 systems. This reference contains two tables that deal with the Group Policy security policy settings: Windows 2000 to Windows 2003 and Windows 2003 to Windows 2000. That way, you can see which policy settings have the same function—just different names.